W9-BCI-739

*The Social Psychology
of Psychological Research*

Editor
ARTHUR G. MILLER
Miami University (Ohio)

THE

Social Psychology of Psychological Research

THE FREE PRESS, *New York*
COLLIER-MACMILLAN LIMITED
London

The Free Press
A DIVISION OF THE MACMILLAN COMPANY
866 Third Avenue, New York, New York
10022

Collier-Macmillan Canada Ltd.
Toronto, Ontario

Library of Congress
Catalog Card Number: 76-143522

printing number
1 2 3 4 5 6 7 8 9 10

Contents

v

Preface

There has been, in recent years, a substantial and increasing interest in viewing the psychological experiment as a social-psychological problem. In an influential and prognostic paper, Riecken characterized the "process of data collection . . . as a particular type of interaction in a particular social situation."[1] Although the original impetus for this interest was to call attention to neglected methodological weaknesses and artifacts in the experimental method, the social psychology of the experiment presently constitutes a province of its own in social psychology. The experimental setting is investigated, not for self-corrective purposes alone, but for the insights concerning human social behavior which can be gained from such inquiry. In addition to substantive and methodological concerns, a close examination of the experimental context allows us to consider certain ethical or philosophical aspects of the human relationships that characterize the research enterprise. All of these considerations reflect the simple but profound truism that the psychological experiment involves man's obtaining scientific knowledge from man himself. Indeed, all of the selections in this book are variations on this theme.

The book is organized into five sections. Part One presents general critiques of contemporary research with human subjects. A major concern is with certain stylistic features of psychological research—the manipulative aspects of the role of experimenter and the ramifications of viewing the human being as an object of scientific analysis. In addition, the significance of what is being investigated in social psychology is questioned. All of these issues appear to have serious implications for the ultimate viability of human experimentation.

Part Two presents Milgram's research on obedience and a number of probing reactions to his work. Although a major emphasis in this section is on the negative emotional reactions of subjects to experimental conditions, what results is a rather good illustration of how a single research effort can stimulate substantive, methodological, and ethical discussion. A general theme here is the recurrent conflict between vigorous scientific inquiry and human values seemingly opposed to such activity.

1. Riecken, H. W. A program for research on experiments in social psychology. In N. F. Washburne (Ed.), *Decisions, values, and groups*. Vol. 2. New York: Pergamon Press, 1962, p. 26.

Part Three is devoted to the problem of deception in psychological research. This issue has received exceptionally thoughtful and provocative analysis, as well as the beginning of needed empirical attention. Deception involves ethical and methodological considerations but, in addition, presents critical problems for the public image of psychological research.

Part Four focuses upon the perspective of the human being as he assumes the role of an experimental subject. The emphasis here is methodological. The basic proposition is that subjects may construe the psychological experiment in ways systematically different from that of the experimenter. Interest in this problem was stimulated by Orne's incisive paper, which opens the section.

Part Five attends to the other participant in the research process, the experimenter. The work of Robert Rosenthal and his colleagues—and critics—constitutes the papers in this section. At issue is the proposition that the experimenter himself unwittingly biases his conduct of the experiment. His vested interests work against the goals of detached objectivity. Although Rosenthal's work is heartily endorsed by several authors in this volume, the paper by Barber and Silver suggests that his may not be the final word on the subject.

Psychology is in the midst of a self-appraisal without precedent in its history. Major shifts in values and procedure are being advanced. Critics of the contemporary scene may, however, expect well-informed resistance. Fortunately it was possible to include in each section of this book a measure of pro and con or rebuttal. The reader will, it is hoped, experience the intrinsic excitement of such debate in several selections of the volume.

Each section opens with an introduction, the purpose of which is to give the reader a brief perspective of the area and to make salient certain issues in each of the papers. The attempt has been neither to abstract nor to criticize each selection, although occasionally a conclusion or tentative disposition is made which seems to follow from the issues in question. It is hoped that the reader will also be stimulated to note similarities, disagreement, and perhaps inconsistencies throughout the various selections. The papers in each section are representative of contemporary thought and research but should not be construed as the totality of published material relevant to the various concerns of this book. The annotated bibliographies at the close of each section introduction may assist the reader interested in pursuing the various problems in greater depth.

The book is intended for all students interested in the application of the experimental method to human behavior. Most of the selections should be appropriate to students comfortable in advanced undergraduate courses in psychology. The book may serve as a supplement to texts in social psychology, personality, clinical research, and general experimental psychology. Graduate students may find the book useful in topical seminars, for it was in that context that the present collection of papers was developed.

ARTHUR G. MILLER

PART ONE

Dissenting Views on Research with Human Subjects

A number of psychologists have recently voiced discontent with certain features of psychological research involving human subjects. Their focal concern is the style or manner in which research is conducted, although there is also disenchantment with more substantive matters. The human being, it is said, is debased in his role as a research subject and the experimenter is unethical in his manipulation and treatment of the subject. Four of the papers in this section are representative of this kind of reasoning. McGuire might justifiably be cast as the voice of the establishment, but he, too, is somewhat critical. Fortunately each author presents what he considers to be constructive alternatives to current deficiencies.

A long-honored proposition in scientific psychology is that the experimenter must establish an objective relationship with his subject, that he detach himself psychologically, and perhaps physically, so that his judgments reflect scientific rather than personal interests. In short, the experimenter-subject relationship should be, to the extent possible, a constant in the experimental design. This has been viewed as a fundamental and rather unique contribution of the scientific analysis of behavior, in contrast to a religious or literary description of the human condition. Two kinds of criticism have been addressed to this matter. One is methodological and is reviewed in the final section of this book. It asks, essentially, for empirical verification for the alleged objectivity of the experimenter. The second criticism holds that the traditional experimenter-subject encounter is a deficient interpersonal relationship from an ethical point of view.

In the first two selections of this section, Jourard confronts traditional psychological approaches to the study of man with a humanistic conception, and he opts for the latter as a more viable philosophical base for psychological research. Central to the humanistic position are the values of regarding man as a choosing agent and focusing upon the ultimate or optimal status of man. Rather than viewing man in terms of unconscious conflicts or as the end result of the social roles into which he has been cast, humanistic psychology explains behavior in terms of personal growth and self-actualization—and the conditions which inhibit or facilitate this process. A central point in the first paper is when Jourard asks "What are the outer limits of human potential for *transcending* biological pressures, social pressures, and the impact on a person of his past conditioning?" (p. 9). Unlike the traditional philosophy of science which treats theories of behavior as man-made, *scientist*-oriented constructions of reality, the humanistic position holds that what we know of man is, in large measure, a function of what *he* will show to us. The methodological implications of this kind of reasoning make obvious a concern with the experimenter-subject relationship.

Jourard poignantly describes his perception of what the traditional scientific conception has made of the interaction between the experimenter and his subject. It is not a flattering portrait for either participant. Central to his suggestions for revamping the research process is the establishment of dialogue between experimenter and subject, an atmosphere in which openness and trust replace manipulation and control. Rather than striving for machinelike constancy, the experimenter acknowledges his own humanity and reaps considerable benefits from doing so. Jourard is iconoclastic and extreme, but his views are in harmony with a number of influential thinkers in psychology—figures such as Allport (1962), Brown (1965), Kelman (1968), and M. Brewster Smith (1969). There can be little doubt that future theory and research will be influenced by these ideas. For the present, one questions the applicability of Jourard's innovations to the vast scope of problems investigated by psychologists. Might not his views best be regarded as sources of testable hypotheses about behavior, e.g., that experimenter disclosure produces disclosure in subjects (Jourard & Friedman, 1970), and as correctives regarding the treatment of subjects, rather than as a format for a totally new conception of a scientific approach to man? Is there room for both traditional scientific procedure and humanistic values, or must there be an inevitable distancing between the investigator and his subject in the process of psychological inquiry? These vital questions are reconsidered in Part Three.

Schultz presents a scholarly and definitive historical review of the human subject's participation in psychological experimentation. He offers an overview of a number of issues with which this book is concerned, thereby enabling the reader to gain a sense of perspective. As he surveys the panorama of ethical and methodological crises in contemporary research, a pessimistic tone emerges in Schultz' writing, and he appears to endorse with enthusiasm the humanistic position advanced by Jourard. It is somewhat paradoxical that Schultz, and Jourard as well, buttress their arguments by citing the research of Orne and Rosenthal—work which is in the established tradition of experimental social psychology, which features the use of deception, and which is, itself, complex and not without its critics (cf., Parts Four and Five). It is almost as if research which exposes defects in existing methodology becomes, for that very reason, exempt from criticism. One does not observe in the writings of Orne and Rosenthal, themselves, any clear implications for the humanistic revolution that their work appears to have for Schultz and Jourard. Schultz views role playing as a promising alternative to deception, although the reader may wish to reconsider the enthusiasm for this technique after reading the third section of this book. That Schultz' paper appears in a journal of wide circulation to psychologists of varied persuasions is, itself, significant in documenting the timeliness and centrality of these issues.

Kenneth Ring opens by deploring the increasing departure from Kurt Lewin's idealized fusion of scientific and action-oriented research in social psychology. What prevails today, Ring asserts, is neither of these but rather a "fun and games" attitude in which research assumes a kind of Pollyanna atmosphere. Experimenters seem to be manipulating their subjects for the sheer joy of it. More emphasis is placed on how to study a phenomenon than on what phenomenon to study. His remarks bring to mind the conclusion to Aronson and Carlsmith's comprehensive chapter on methodology in the *Handbook of Social Psychology*:

Although it is generally considered unbecoming for scientists to talk this way, we feel that we must close this chapter with a statement regarding what to us is one of the most important aspects of experimentation in social psychology: It's fun [1968, p. 75].

Ring is particularly disturbed over the consequences of these trends for the teaching and ultimate development of social psychology. The antidote? Ring argues that more effort be directed at systematic inquiry into significant problems—without the automatic use of ethically questionable manipulations. Ring's plea for significant research seems admirable in the abstract. However, the term *significant*, as in its statistical usage, may be more applicable after research is completed than when it is being contemplated. The reader might consider whether Ring is directing his attack more at the motives of the researcher than at the nature of his product.

McGuire's response is moderate as rebuttals typically go. His argument for research in natural settings is timely, as an examination of several contemporary journals in social psychology will document. Whether such inquiry will necessarily prove more relevant to conditions in the nonexperimental world than does laboratory research, as McGuire suggests, seems debatable (e.g., Freedman, Part Three, p. 206), but it is a provocative point. McGuire scans a variety of problems in human experimentation, noting that a departure to the natural habitat will lessen, although not totally alleviate, these difficulties. He makes the engaging observation that social psychologists should be concerned about the moral implications of *not* doing research, lest they become overburdened with the deficiencies in existing procedure. McGuire is uncertain as to the target of Ring's "fun and games" attribution, but he acknowledges the propriety of the label, nevertheless. He is clearly less concerned with the motives of researchers than with the quality of their efforts, and he suggests that there are sufficient monitoring influences within the scientific community to realign errant values or priorities.

FURTHER READING

ALLPORT, G. W. The general and the unique in psychological science. *Journal of Personality*, 1962, **30**: 405–422. A leading personality theorist advocates recognition of the unique features that distinguish each man from his fellows and challenges the prevailing trend of studying groups of subjects, with the inherent loss of the individual. Although the distinction between idiographic and nomothetic research is a complex one, Allport's thesis has sensitized the psychological community to the need for understanding the behavior of individual persons.

ARGYRIS, C. Some unintended consequences of rigorous research. *Psychological Bulletin*, 1968, **70**: 185–197. An analogy is drawn between psychological research and organizational theory, particularly concerning strains in the experimenter–subject relationship that have parallels to those between management and employee. Argyris would predict that the experimenter may face an increase in absenteeism, psychological withdrawal, overt hostility, covert hostility, and an emphasis upon monetary reward—conditions that have been the unintended consequences of the relationship between top management and workers in formal organizations.

ARONSON, E., & Carlsmith, J. M. Experimentation in social psychology. In G. Lindzey & E. Aronson (Eds.), *Handbook of Social Psychology.* Vol. 2. Reading, Mass.: Addison-Wesley, 1968. Pp. 1–79. The most thorough and sensitive general discussion of social psychological research available. Their recognition of the subtle interpersonal aspects of research and their awareness of the many conflicts facing the researcher make this chapter a rewarding experience for the reader—a work of considerable perspective.

BROWN, R. *Social psychology.* New York: The Free Press, 1965. P. 580. An influential social psychologist expresses skepticism regarding deception and advocates role playing as a promising research strategy.

JOURARD, S. M., & Friedman, R. Experimenter-subject "distance" and self-disclosure. *Journal of Personality and Social Psychology*, 1970, **15**: 278–282. A recent experiment from Jourard's research program on self-disclosure at the University of Florida. Under specified conditions, a decrease in the physical distance between experimenter and subject, and more self-disclosure on the part of the experimenter, result in increased self-disclosure in subjects.

KELMAN, H. *A time to speak: On human values and social research.* San Francisco: Jossey-Bass, 1968. A set of essays on a variety of themes in a humanistic conception of social research. Kelman argues that the role of the social psychologist is that of a systematic thinker—that experimentation is but one vehicle for the systematic analysis of social phenomena. He appears doubtful about the generality of experimental data to social problems in any immediate sense, but is nevertheless an extreme proponent of a relevant and action-oriented social psychology.

RIECKEN, H. W. A program for research on experiments in social psychology. In N. F. Washburne (Ed.), *Decisions, values and groups.* Vol. 2. Pp. 25–41. This paper derives from a conference in the behavioral sciences held at the University of New Mexico in 1958. It essentially forecasts most of the developments that have taken place in the social psychology of research. Particularly striking is the fact that Riecken was able to construe the social psychological aspects of research both in terms of improving experiments and in terms of understanding certain fundamental aspects of human interaction—long before any major lines of empirical inquiry had been initiated on these issues.

SMITH, M. B. *Social psychology and human values.* Chicago: Aldine, 1969. A work parallel to that of Kelman. It is humanistic in orientation, is devoted to research having significance for the problems of our times, and views experimental procedures as but one of the many faces of scientific inquiry. Of particular interest is Smith's essay on ethical considerations in psychological research with children.

Sidney M. Jourard

A Humanistic Revolution
in Psychology

> *If I complain I have no will of my own, that people are influencing me in subtle and mysterious ways, you'll accuse me of being paranoid, and direct me to a psychotherapist.*
>
> *If I put on a white laboratory coat, and assert that* you *have no will of your own, that your action and experience can be manipulated, predicted, and controlled, then I am recognized as a scientific psychologist, and honored.*
>
> *This is most peculiar.*

A revolution is going on in psychology. A different image of man is being tried as a guide to research, theory, and application. Over the years, theorists have conceptualized man as a machine; as an organism comparable to rats, pigeons, and monkeys; as a communication system; as an hydraulic system; as a servomechanism; as a computer—in short, he has been viewed by psychologists as an analogue of *everything but what he is*: a person. Man is, indeed, like all those things; but first of all he is a free, intentional subject. The closest analogue we psychologists can find as a model for man is *ourselves*. The other man is more like me than he is like any machine, rat, or pigeon. We have found that the earlier models of man produced unintended consequences at the hands of those who apply psychology. The consumers of psychological writing tended to take our models too seriously and actually started to treat people as if they *were* the models that theorists used only as tentative guides to inquiry.

The disciplines of existentialism, phenomenology, humanism, and personalism are gradually being absorbed by workers in the field; and psychology is in process of being reworked, rewritten, and reapplied. Psychologists are using their experience of themselves as persons as a guide to exploring and understanding the experience of others. This is

From *Disclosing Man to Himself* by Sidney M. Jourard. Copyright © 1968, by Litton Educational Publishing, Inc., by permission of Van Nostrand Reinhold Company.

not the death of "objective," scientific psychology. Rather, it may prove to be the birth of a scientifically informed psychology of human persons—a *humanistic* psychology.

Humanistic psychology is a goal, not a doctrine. It owes its renaissance to the growing conviction that current and past approaches to the study of man have reached their limits in elucidating man's behavior and his "essence." It is a growing corpus of knowledge relating to the questions, "What is a human being, and what might man become?" Thus, humanistic psychology can be regarded in analogy with industrial psychology or the psychology of mental health or of advertising. These specialities are systems of knowledge bearing on particular families of questions; e.g., what variables affect morale, or the output of workers, or the maintenance of wellness, or the purchasing behavior of potential customers. Humanistic psychology asks, "What are the possibilities of man? And from among these possibilities, what is *optimum man*, and what conditions most probably account for his attainment and maintenance of these optima?"

The aim of science is to know, to gain understanding of some phenomenon which is in question. Sciences addressed to nature, the "natural sciences," seek understanding of natural phenomena in order to tame them, to bring them under control of human beings, for human purposes. Understanding of the processes and phenomena in nature enables man to predict, alter, and control them.

Psychology, the science addressed to man's being, likewise seeks to know and understand. But a sharp distinction must be drawn here between the science of psychology and the natural sciences. While psychologists and physicists seek to understand the phenomena they study, it is appropriate only for the physicists to aim at increased control of these phenomena. If psychologists aim to predict and control human behavior and experience, as in their textbooks they claim, they are assigning man to the same ontological status as weather, stars, minerals, or lower forms of animal life. We do not question anyone's right to seek understanding in order the better to control his physical environment and adapt it to his purposes. We properly challenge any man's right to control the behavior and experience of his fellows. To the extent that psychologists illumine human existence to bring it under the deliberate control of someone other than the person himself, to that extent they are helping to undermine some person's freedom in order to enlarge the freedom of someone else. If psychologists reveal knowledge of "determiners" of human conduct to people other than the ones from whom they obtained this understanding, and if they conceal this knowledge from its source, the volunteer subjects (who have offered themselves up to the scientist's "Look"), they put the recipients of the knowledge in a privileged position. They grant them an opportunity to manipulate men without their knowledge or consent. Thus, advertisers, businessmen, military leaders, politicians, and salesmen all seek to learn more about the determiners of human conduct, in order to gain power and advantage. If they can sway human behavior by manipulating the conditions which mediate it, they can get large numbers of people to forfeit their own interests and serve the interests of the manipulator. Such secret manipulation of the masses or of an individual by some other person is possible only if the ones being manipulated are kept mystified as to what is going on, and if their experience of their own freedom is blunted.

Psychologists face a choice. We may elect to continue to treat our *S*s as objects of study for the benefit of some elite; or we may choose to learn about determiners of the human condition in order to discover ways to overcome or subvert them, so as to enlarge the *S*s'—that is Everyman's—freedom. If we opt for the latter, our path is clear. Our ways of conducting psychological research will have to be altered. Our definition of the purpose of psychology will have to change. And our ways of reporting our findings, as well as the audiences to whom the reports are directed, will have to change. We shall have to state openly whether we are psychologists-for-institutions or psychologists-for-persons.

The trouble with scientific psychologists—among whom I number myself—is that we have, in a sense, been "bought." We have in our hands the incredible power to discover conditions for behavior or for ways of being in the world. We have catalogued many of the factors which have a determining effect on human behavior and on our condition. We know that, in every experiment that we analyze, there is always an error term, "residual variance"; and we seek to exhaust this residual variance to the best of our ability. We get better at it as we learn how to identify and measure more and more relevant variables. The trouble is, as I see it, that if we exhaust all the variance, the subject of our study will be not a man, a human person, but rather a robot.

Scientific psychology has actually sought means of artificially reducing variance—humanness—among men, so that they will be more manipulable. Our commendable efforts (from a technical viewpoint) in the fields of human engineering, teaching methods, motivation research (in advertising), and salesmanship have permitted practitioners in those realms to develop stereotyped methods that work at controlling outcomes—outcomes that are good for the businessman or politician, but not necessarily good for the victim. We have taught people how to shape man into a way of being that makes him useful. We have forgotten that an image of man as useful grows out of a more fundamental image of man as the being who can assume *many* modes of being, when it is of importance to him to do so.

I think that a scientific psychologist committed to the aims of humanistic psychology would utilize his talents for a different purpose. For example, if individuality and full flowering growth as a person were values, he would seek means of maximizing or increasing the odds for maximization of these ways of being. An example of the biased use of scientific know-how is brainwashing. The brainwasher, through scientific means, seeks to insure that the prisoner will behave and believe as his captors wish. The same psychologists who invented the means of brainwashing know how to prevent it from happening. The latter class of knowledge is more in keeping with the aims of humanistic psychology and should be more avidly sought and then applied in more realms than presently is the case, if humanistic psychology is to be furthered.

How odd it seems that psychology has learned more about man at his worst than at his best. How sad it seems that psychology has employed its powers of truth-finding to serve ignoble masters. I would like to propose that we don't wait until the scarcity of "full-functioning men" becomes a national emergency. Rather, I would propose that we psychologists reconcile our aims and commitment to truth and our adherence to the canons of scientific inquiry with our human concerns that man be free, that he grow. I propose that we commence an all-out program of investigation on many fronts to seek answers to the questions humanistic psychology is posing. For example, we need psychologists with the most informed imaginations and talent for ingenious experimentation to wrestle with such questions as, "What are the outer limits of human potential for *transcending* biological pressures, social pressures, and the impact on a person of his past conditioning?" "What developmental and interpersonal and situational conditions conduce to courage, creativity, transcendent behavior, love, laughter, commitment to truth, beauty, justice, and virtue?" These questions themselves, and even my proposal that we address them, once struck me as less than manly, as tenderhearted and sentimental. I would never have dared pose them to most of my mentors during my undergraduate and graduate-student days. We were supposed to be tough and disciplined, which meant that we were only to study questions about some very limited class of behavior, not questions about larger human concerns. "Leave those to the philosophers, ministers, and politicians," we were told. Questions about the image of man smacked too much of philosophy and were not our proper concern. Actually, our teachers intended only that we learn the tools of our trade, not that we stifle our humanistic concerns; but they produced that outcome.

Wilse B. Webb has pointed out, in his paper "The Choice of the Problem," that there are many reasons entering into the selection of an area for scientific investigation. I am proposing that the quest for a more adequate image of man, for specification of peculiarly human optima, and the quest for the conditions which maximize or actualize these optima are worthwhile and important areas for study. I guess that, from another point of view altogether, I am inviting more of us to become educated men as we become trained psychologists. I suspect that psychologists who are educated men cannot help but be active humanistic psychologists. One measure of a man is the questions he raises, and another is the goals for which he uses his powers and talents. I am not making a plea for less rigorous inquiry. I am making a plea for the powers of rigorous inquiry to be devoted to questions, answers to which will inform a growing, more viable image of man as a human being with potentiality, not solely a biological or socially determined being.

When researchers are transparently pledged to further the freedom and self-actualizing of their subjects, rather than be unwitting servants of the leaders of institutions, then they will deserve to *be* and *to be seen* as recipients of the secrets of human being and possibility. I envision a time when the psychologist will be the guardian of the most intimate secrets of human possibilities and experience, and the possessor of knowledge as to how man can create his destiny because man has shown him; and I hope that if we "sell" these secrets to advertisers, businessmen, politicians, mass educators, and the military, we shall not do so until *after* we have informed our subjects, after we have tried to "turn them on," to enlarge their awareness of being misled and manipulated. I hope, in short, that we turn out to be servants and guardians of individual freedom, growth, and fulfillment, and not spies for the institutions that pay our salaries and research costs in order to get a privileged peep at human grist. Indeed, we may have to function for a time as counterspies, or double spies—giving reports about our subjects to our colleagues and to institutions, and giving reports back to our subjects as to the ways in which institutions seek to control and predict their behavior for their (the institutions') ends.

A LETTER FROM *S* TO *E*

For some time now I have been talking to people who have served as subjects (Ss) in psychologists' experiments. They have told me of their experience, and it has troubled me. I want to share my concern with my colleagues. The letter that follows is my effort to consolidate the attitudes and feelings of the people to whom I talked.

Dear *E* (Experimenter):

My name is *S*. You don't know me. I have another name my friends call me by, but I drop it, and become *S* No. 27 as soon as I take part in your research. I serve in your surveys and experiments. I answer your questions, fill out questionnaires, let you wire me up to various machines that record my physiological reactions. I pull levers, flip switches, track moving targets, trace mazes, learn nonsense syllables, tell you what I see in inkblots—do the whole barrage of things you ask me to do. I have started to wonder why I do these things for you. What's in it for me? Sometimes you pay me to serve. More often I have to serve, because I'm a student in a beginning psychology course, and I'm told that I won't receive a grade unless I take part in at least two studies; and if I take part in more, I'll get extra points on the final exam. I am part of the Department's "subject-pool."

When I've asked you what I'll get out of your studies, you tell me that, "It's for Science." When you are running some one particular study, you often lie to me about your purpose. You mislead me. It's getting so I find it difficult to trust you. I'm beginning to see you as a trickster, a manipulator. I don't like it.

In fact, I lie to you a lot of the time, even on anonymous questionnaires. When I don't lie, I will sometimes just answer at random, anything to get through with the hour, and back to my own affairs. Then, too, I can often figure out just what it is you are trying to do, what you'd like me to say or do; at those times, I decide to go along with your wishes if I like you, or foul you up if I don't. You don't actually say what your hopes or hypotheses are; but the very setup in your laboratory, the alternatives you give me, the instructions you offer, all work together to pressure me to say or do something in particular. It's as if you are whispering in my ear, "when the light comes on, pull the *left* switch," and then you forget or deny that you have whispered. But I get the message. And I pull the right or the left one, depending on how I feel toward you.

You know, even when you are not in the room—when you are just the printed instructions on the questionnaire or the voice on the tape recorder that tells me what I am supposed to do —I wonder about you. I wonder who you are, what you are *really* up to. I wonder what you are going to do with the "behavior" I give you. Who are you going to show my answers to? Who is going to see the marks I leave on your response-recorders? Do you have any interest at all in what I think, feel, and imagine as I make the marks you are so eager to study and analyze? Certainly, you never ask me what I mean by them. If you asked, I'd be glad to tell you. As a matter of fact, I do tell my roommate or my girl friend what I thought your experiment was about and what I meant when I did what I did. If my roommate could trust you, he could probably give you a better idea of what your data (my answers and responses) mean than the idea you presently have. God knows how much good psychology has gone down the drain, when my roommate and I discuss your experiment and my part in it, at the beer-joint.

As a matter of fact, I'm getting pretty tired of being S. It's too much like being a punched IBM card in the University registrar's office. I feel myself being pressured, bulldozed, tricked, manipulated everywhere I turn. Advertisements in magazines and commercials on TV, political speeches, salesmen, and con men of all kinds put pressure on me to get me to buy, say, or do things that I suspect are not for my good at all. Just for their good, the good of their pocketbooks. Do you sell your "expert knowledge" about me to these people? If that's true, then you're really not in good faith with me. You have told me that when I show myself to you and let you study me, that in the long run it will be for my good. I'm not convinced. You really seem to be studying me in order to learn how to influence my attitudes and my actions without my realizing it. I resent this more than *you* realize. It's not fair for you to get me to show how I can be influenced and then for you to pass this information along to the people who pay your salary, or who give you the money to equip your laboratory. I feel used, and I don't like it. But I protect myself by not showing you my whole self, or by lying. Did you ever stop to think that your articles, and the textbooks you write, the theories you spin—all based on your data (my disclosures to you)—may actually be a tissue of lies and half-truths (my lies and half-truths) or a joke I've played on you because I don't like you or trust you? That should give you cause for some concern.

Now look, Mr. E, I'm not "paranoid," as you might say. Nor am I stupid. And I do believe some good can come out of my serving in your research. Even some good for me. I'm not entirely selfish, and I would be glad to offer myself up for study, to help others. But some things have to change first. Will you listen to me? Here is what I would like from you researchers:

I'd like you to help me gain a better understanding of what has made me the way I am today. I'd like to know this because I want to be more free than I feel. I would like to discover more of my own potentialities. I'd like to be more whole, more courageous, more enlightened. I'd like to be able to experience more, learn better, remember better, and express myself more fully. I'd like to learn how to recognize and overcome the pressures of other people's influence, of my background, that interfere with my going in the paths I choose. Now, if you would promise to help me in these ways, I would gladly come into your lab and virtually strip my body and soul naked. I would be there *meaning* to show you everything I could that was relevant to your particular interest of the moment. And I can assure you, that is different from what I have been showing you thus far, which is as little as I can. In fact, I cross my fingers when I'm in your lab, and say to myself, "What I've just said or done here *is not me.*" Wouldn't you like that to change?

If you'll trust me, I'll trust you, if you're trustworthy. I'd like you to take the time and trouble to get acquainted with me as a person, before we go through your experimental procedures. And I'd like to get to know you and what you are up to, to see if I would like to expose myself to you. Sometimes, you remind me of physicians. They look at me as the unimportant envelope that conceals the disease they are really interested in. You have looked at me as the unimportant package that contains "responses," and this is all I am for you. Let me tell you that when I feel this, I get back at you. I give you responses, all right; but you will never know what I meant by them. You know, I can speak, not just in words, but with my action. And when you have thought I was responding to a "stimulus" in your lab, my response was really directed at *you*; and what I meant by it was, "Take this, you unpleasant so-and-so." Does that surprise you? It shouldn't.

Another thing. Those tests of yours that have built-in gimmicks to see if I'm being consistent, or deliberately lying, or just answering at random—they don't fool me. Actually, they wouldn't be necessary if you would get on the level with me. There are enough con men in the world, without your joining their number. I would hope that psychologists would be more trustworthy than politicians or salesmen.

I'll make a bargain with you. You show me that you are doing your researches *for me*—to help me become freer, more self-understanding, better able to control *myself*—and I'll make myself available to you in any way you ask. And I won't play jokes and tricks on you. I don't want to *be controlled*, not by you or anyone else. And I don't want to control other people. I don't want you to help other people to understand how I am or can be "controlled," so that they can then control me. Show me that you are for me, and I will show *myself* to you.

You work for me, Mr. *E*, and I'll truly work for you. Between us, we may produce a psychology that is more authentic and more liberating.

Yours sincerely, *S*

Sidney M. Jourard

Experimenter–Subject Dialogue:
A Paradigm for a Humanistic Science of Psychology

The image of man that emerges from traditional experimental psychology is of a "determined" being, subject to the controlling influences of assorted variables. This is not at all an image of man with which we can gladly identify. Indeed, one of the aims of a humanistic science of psychology is to liberate man from the constraining or inciting pressures of "determiners." A humanistic psychologist, like his less humanistic colleague, is concerned to identify factors that affect man's experience and action, but his aim is not to render man predictable to, and controllable by, somebody else. Rather, his aim is to understand how determining variables function, in order that man might be liberated from their impact as he pursues his own free projects.

In pursuing the project of developing a humanistic research methodology for psychology, the hypothesis occurred to me that the aspect which human subjects show to psychological experimenters may be an artifact of the typical relationship established by the researchers with their subjects. If people show only certain of their possibilities to investigators who relate to human subjects in a prescribed, impersonal way, it is possible that if a different and mutually revealing kind of relationship between experimenters and subjects were established, different facets of the latters' beings would be disclosed. Perhaps a more valid image of man might emerge if research done in the past were repeated in the context of mutual knowledge and trust.

I have begun to explore the possibility of replicating typical psychological experiments, first in the impersonal way their designers conducted the studies, and then in the context of greater openness and mutual knowing between the psychologist and his subjects. Some of my students likewise are exploring in this vein. The remarks that follow give a more detailed consideration of the rationale for such replication and an introduction to some preliminary findings. At this stage, we are only beginning a project that may take many years and many collaborators to bring to fruition.

TWO KINDS OF ENCOUNTERS

Ultimately, we come to know something or somebody if that being *shows itself* to us. If we are dealing with stones, animals, stars, or viruses, the problem of knowing calls first for making contact with the object of study and then for devising means of getting it to disclose its mysteries. Natural scientists have shown incredible ingenuity in this task. They have devised gadgets which reveal previously inaccessible aspects of the being of all kinds of phenomena: x-rays, telescopes and microscopes, transducers, and recorders of light, sound, and movement. This equipment has enabled scientists to find answers to questions they pose about the being of things, objects, and processes in the world.

To know the being of *man* is a different problem. Existentialists have said that man is the being whose being is *in question*, i.e., not fixed. Man chooses his projects and thereby produces his own being. He chooses his ways to be in the world, and upon how he has chosen to be will depend the aspects of his being that he will show to anyone who happens to be looking. One choice open to him is whether he will show himself at all or choose to hide in a cave. Another option is whether he will aim to reveal his experience, his "being-for-himself," to another person or seek to conceal and misrepresent it.

If a man chooses to be fully known, he will show himself freely to another man, in all possible ways. His behavior, which is the "outside" of his being-for-himself (his experience), is unintelligible, however, unless he provides the observer with the key. Behavior is actually a code—or, better, a cipher—analogous to Etruscan writing or Egyptian hieroglyphics. It is the embodiment of a meaning assigned to it by the one who behaves. The observer can guess at this meaning, but the key rests with the behaver himself. The behavior carries but his intentions, his goals, and his projects. It is the goal of the action which gives it meaning. Yet it is precisely aims and goals that people seek most strongly to conceal from others, fearing that if the intentions were known, the other person might interfere. Machiavelli knew this when he advised his Prince to conceal his ultimate aims from his subjects. They were to be kept mystified. People will disclose their aims and the ways they construe the world only to those whom they have reason to trust. Without the trust and goodwill, a person will conceal or misrepresent his experience, hoping thus to mystify the other and to get him to misconstrue the action that is visible.

Encounters That Mystify

Suppose a young man is attracted to a pretty girl. At first, she is indifferent to his display of manly charms. He then tries to change her experience of him, in the hope that she will ultimately change her behavior toward him. What he does before her is the expression of his intent: "I want her to tumble for me." But he does not say this to her directly. If he did, it might frighten her away. Instead, he pretends he has no such wishes. He tries to appear as the kind of young man in whose physical presence she will want to stay. Once he wins her attention, he may start the next stage of his secret project. He will speak of jazz and Bach, philosophy and baseball. Then, he may remark about her lovely complexion and hair. His hand, apparently by accident, brushes against her shoulder, and she does not pull away. He suggests they go somewhere for a drink. There, he invites her to tell him about herself, and he seems to listen to every word with rapt attention.

Viewed from an abstract perspective, this encounter between the boy and the girl may seem a mystifying one. He tries to mislead her as to his intentions. He is "on the make," and he tries to manipulate her experience and action so that she will behave in the service of *his* goals, not her own. When a person is thus on the make, he will show aspects of himself that aim at persuading or influencing the other. The other person has been reduced from the status of a person to the status of an object, a manipulandum, something to be used if it is useful and neutralized or changed if it is not.

There is another kind of encounter that people may undertake in order to fulfill different aims. This is *dialogue*.

Encounters That Reveal

In genuine dialogue (Buber, 1958), each experiences the other as a person, as the origin and source of his intentional acts. Each participant aims to show his being to the other *as it is for him*. Transparency (Jourard, 1964), not mystification, is one of the goals. It matters little whether the dialogue is nonverbal or verbal or whether it occurs between a philosopher and his pupil, a therapist and his patient, a parent and child, or two friends. The aim is to show oneself in willful honesty before the other and to respond to the other with an expression of one's experience as the other has affected it. Dialogue is like mutual unveiling, where each seeks to be experienced and confirmed by the other as the one he is for himself. Such dialogue is most likely to occur when the two people each believe the other is trustworthy and of goodwill. The threat that motivates people to conceal their intentions and experience in manipulative encounters is absent in dialogue. The aims that make the action of each intelligible to the other will be fully revealed.

Now, I would like to examine the relationship between an experimenter and his subject in the light of these analyses of the two kinds of encounters.

EXPERIMENTER-SUBJECT RELATIONSHIP: MANIPULATION OR DIALOGUE?

The usual encounter between a psychological researcher and his subject has more in common with the example of the young man on the make than it has with dialogue. The experimenter wants something from the subject, but he wants to keep him partly mystified as to what it is. Moreover, he does not want to frighten the subject away, so the psychological researcher often cloaks his intentions with camouflage. If he "tips his hand," he may influence the subject and bias the findings. He tells the subject as little as he can when the latter appears in the laboratory.

Actually, in some ways a research psychologist tries to impersonate a machine by depersonalizing himself. He tries to be invisible or to be "constant." He seldom tries to find out from his subject just how that person experiences him, the researcher, either perceptually or in his fantasy.

Failure of the Impersonal Model

Increasingly, workers are finding that this effort to eliminate bias is failing. Rosenthal (1963) and Orne (1962), among others, are showing that when a psychologist is with a human subject he functions not unlike a subtle propagandist or attitude and action manipulator. They have shown that the data gotten from subjects (that is, the subjects' disclosures encoded in words or in nonverbal behavior) can be likened to expressions of compliance on the part of the subjects to confirm the psychologist's hypotheses about people of that sort. In fact, it seems to me that human subjects, to the extent that they are free, will please a researcher and confirm just about any of his hypotheses; witness the many confirmations of radically conflicting hypotheses. A person truly can choose a being, in the laboratory, that will uphold or refute his *experience* (fantasy or perceptual) of what the researcher wants him to show.

We researchers may be victims of the same myopia that has long afflicted physicians, preventing them from realizing that many diseases are actually *iatrogenic*—outcomes of the doctor-patient relationship. Laing and Esterson (1964) have shown, for example, that schizophrenia —its symptoms as recorded in textbooks—is (at least in part and perhaps fully) a function of the disconfirming attitudes of relatives and physicians toward the patient's experience of his world, as well as a way of being which is evoked by the mental hospital milieu itself. It is known that instances of invalidism have occurred because a doctor implied to a patient, "Your heart is not as healthy as it might be."

In research, we have recognized the "social-desirability" variable (Edwards, 1957). It has been investigated, and techniques have been proposed to bypass it or to make allowances for it. We have recognized subjects' tendencies to misrepresent their experiences in order to produce some desired image of themselves in the mind of the investigator. So we have invented tests and traps to catch their conscious and unconscious deceptions, e.g., the "Lie" and K scales on the MMPI (Minnesota Multiphasic Personality Inventory). We have utilized projective tests in the hope that a person will unwittingly reveal hidden aspects of himself. What we may not have realized is that a subject in a research project is no fool. He knows that many times his future career may depend upon how he appears through test and experimental findings. So he has a vested interest in such misrepresentation. It is very sane for him to protect himself. He has no guarantee, at least in his experience, that his responses will help the psychologist to help *him* (the subject) fulfill himself more fully. Our commitments as experimenters and as testers and the settings in which we work sometimes make it insane for a person to uncloak himself.

The Dyadic Effect

Research in self-disclosure (Jourard, 1964) has amply shown that what a person will disclose to another is a function of many variables, including the subject matter to be disclosed, the characteristics of the person, the setting in which disclosure is to take place, and—more important—the characteristics of the audience person. The most powerful "determiner" of self-disclosure appears to be the willingness of the audience person to disclose *himself* to the subject to the same extent that he expects the subject to confide his own experiences. I have termed this the *dyadic effect*. It asserts, as a general principle, that "disclosure begets disclosure." Now this is not, by any means, the only condition under which a man might reveal his experience to another. He will often disclose himself unilaterally, without reciprocation, when he believes that it serves his interests to do so. This is what happens, for example, in much psychotherapeutic interviewing. The patient discloses much more about himself than the therapist does, on the implicit promise that if he does so, his lot will be improved.

It is necessary to ask whether the relationship between the experimenter and his subject is such that a dyadic effect can occur. Is it anything like dialogue? Do the laboratory setting and the typical relationship between an investigator and his human subject provide the conditions for the fullest, most authentic disclosure of self by the latter, whether in words, in writing, or by means of action of unequivocal, revealed meaning?

In most psychological investigations, the psychologist is a stranger to the subject. It is hoped that the subject is naïve, unselfconscious, and willing to disclose himself, verbally or behaviorally and only through his responses, which are to be recorded on objective machines. Perhaps some people enter a laboratory in that spirit. Probably some infants and children are ready and willing to trust and to show themselves in that manner. However, I am convinced that the people who serve in psychological studies quickly become sophisticated and learn to play their parts. They are often taught what their part is by older, more experienced subjects who have served in many studies. This is also what happens to newcomers to a prison or mental hospital. The "old pros" show the ropes to the novices. I have ample reason to suspect that many subjects rattle off their performances before a researcher in a cynical way, giving him much "data" to carry off with him, away from people, to the calculating room. There the psychologist conducts complex analyses of variance and writes up his findings as part of his dialogue with his colleagues. But the people he is arguing about, the subjects, may be out in the pubs telling their cronies about how they "put one over."

Not only do we not provide human subjects with a setting and a relationship within which authentic self-disclosure can take place, but we also limit their vocabulary. Thus we limit our subjects' disclosures. We note only their GSR (galvanic skin response) reading or their questionnaire responses or the marks they leave on an event recorder. We ignore as irrelevant all the other possible means by which a person could show us what the laboratory conditions and the experiment have meant to him. We appear not to be interested in grounding our psychology on his experience. Rather, we want only to account for variance in the one kind of message we got from him and his fellow subjects. This message is just a response, serialized, fragmented, quantified. We assume that such responses have the same experiential meanings for each of the subjects or assume that whatever meanings the responses have for them are irrelevant. This is, I think, a mistake.

We can do something about this and, moreover, do it in the spirit of experimental inquiry. We can begin to change the status of the subject from that of an anonymous *object* of our study to that of a *person*, a *collaborator* in our enterprise. We can let him tell the story of his experience in our studies in a variety of idioms. We can let him show what our stimuli have meant to him through his manipulations of our gadgetry, through his responses to questionnaires, with drawings, and with words. We can invite him to reveal his being. We can prepare ourselves so that he will want to produce a multifaceted record of his experiencing in our laboratories. We can show him how we have recorded his responses and tell him what we think they mean. We can ask him to examine and then authenticate or revise our recorded version of the meaning of his experience for him. We can let him cross-examine us to get to know and trust us, to find out what we are up to, and to decide whether he wishes to take part. Heaven knows what we might find. We might well emerge with richer images of man.

PRELIMINARY DIALOGUE-BASED REPLICATIONS

My students and I have made a beginning in reperforming experiments in the kind of relationship climate I have been describing. However, I would like to see such studies done by more workers to see which "classes of response" and which "psychological functions" are affected by the interpersonal context of dialogue and which are not.

Here is a progress report on what we have done so far toward discovering whether the dialogic quality of the relationship between researcher and subject makes a difference.

One of my students, W. R. Rivenbark (1963–1964), varied the way in which he conducted interviews with subjects. Under one set of conditions, he responded to the subjects' self-disclosures with disclosures of his own which reported true experiences of his that were comparable to those of his subjects. Subjects interviewed under these conditions—as opposed to the conditions under which the interviewer was technically competent but impersonal and anonymous—reported that they liked the interviewer and the interview more and that they saw the interviewer as more human and more trustworthy, and they indicated that they would like to be interviewed by him again.

Rivenbark also conducted a simple word-association test, presenting words from the list given by Rapaport (1946) in his *Diagnostic Psychological Testing*. His procedure was as follows: He gave some general, impersonal instructions to his subjects, letting them know what he expected from them. Then, he gave them one-half of the words from the list. Next, he gave them an opportunity to disclose themselves to him in writing, in response to questions, or in mutually revealing dialogue. After this, he administered the rest of the words and secured the subjects' responses. Finally, he made a rating of the degree to which he judged that good rapport and willingness to be open existed in his relationship with each person. He did not ask the subjects to do this. Then, he studied the reaction times of the subjects in response to the stimulus words. There were no differences in mean reaction time or in the kind of responses given between groups differentiated in terms of the way they disclosed themselves to the experimenter, that is, in writing, in response to spoken questions, or in dialogue. Rivenbark did find, however, that there was a significant correlation (rho of .68) between his ratings of "goodness of rapport" and the mean *increase* in reaction time between the first administration of stimulus words and the last.

We have no idea just now of what this finding means in terms of psychodynamics. It does show that either the experimenter's or the subject's experience of the relationship between them—in this case, the experimenter's—was related to differences in the objective outcome of the experiment. True, there is much wrong, from a methodological viewpoint, with this study, but it is a beginning at the kind of replication discussed above.

Subject's Attitudes about Confiding

Rivenbark conducted still another exploratory study, this time directed toward people's views as to how trustworthy psychologists and their tools are. He prepared a list of fifteen possible confidants to whom, or settings within which, one might reveal intimate and personal data about himself. He asked twenty-five male and thirty female college students to rank these confidants or settings according to how willing they would be to confide fully under such circumstances. His findings, expressed as median ranks, are shown in Table 1–1.

Table 1–1   *Students' Readiness to Confide in Different Settings**

Setting	Male Rank	Female Rank
Tell a radio or TV audience	15	15
Tell a stranger on a bus or train	14	14
Tell at a cocktail party with friends and strangers present	13	12
Write on an application for a job or club membership	12	13
Write in an autobiography for publication	11	11
Tell in a bull session with friends	10	10
Tell an interviewer for scientific purposes	9	9
Write in a letter to a friend	8	8
Write in an anonymous questionnaire for scientific purposes	7	5
Tell a priest or minister	6	6
Tell a psychotherapist	5	2
Write in a secret diary	4	7
Tell closest parent	3	4
Tell best same-sex friend	2	3
Tell best opposite-sex friend or spouse	1	1

* Taken from Rivenbark, 1963–1964.

Significantly, the research psychologist was ranked ninth. Anonymous research questionnaires were ranked fifth by women and seventh by men. This investigation may be thought of as similar to the work of public relations firms engaged to determine the "public image" of the clients. Though I dislike the term "image" in this context, I feel justified, on the basis of these data, in urging all research psychologists to seek to earn an authentically higher rank as prospective recipients of the disclosures of their subjects.

Importance of Responsiveness

Another student, W. J. Powell, Jr. (1964), did a doctoral dissertation which was more carefully controlled than Rivenbark's exploratory study. He conducted interviews with college students, asking them to make themselves as fully known to him, the interviewer, as they cared to. He carefully controlled all extraneous variables and compared the increase in self-disclosure (using an operant-conditioning design) that occurred when, on the one hand, he responded to the students' disclosures with authentic disclosures of his own (in contrast to "reflecting" the feeling or content of their disclosures) and when, on the other hand, he responded with expressions of approval and support. He found that "approving, supporting" responses did not increase the students' disclosures at all. Reflection and restatement of their disclosures resulted in an increase in disclosures of negative self-statements, but did not affect positive, self-enhancing expressions. Self-disclosure from the researcher was associated with significant increases in the subjects' disclosures of both positive and negative self-references.

Another student, Miss Lee Reifel (1965–1966) conducted an interview with a girl whom she had never met, in the context of a game we invented, called "Invitations." The questions or topics for disclosure were typed on cards, and the rules were that the subject could ask the interviewer any question that she was willing to answer herself, and vice versa. In this interview, the girl became incredibly involved and revealed literally all she had to reveal. Miss Reifel disclosed much about herself, too. By the end of the interview, which lasted several hours, they knew each other very well indeed. In another interview, Miss Reifel began by using the cards as a guide, to "get acquainted" with a female student. However, for the first half of the session, she confined herself to asking questions only. The girl was to answer if she chose, but Miss Reifel would not explain or disclose more. Then Miss Reifel changed the rules and began to disclose herself truthfully regarding each question before she asked it of the student. The transformation in terms of openness and extent of self-disclosure on the part of the girl was remarkable.

TOWARD GREATER EXPERIMENTAL VALIDITY

We are continuing with this kind of research, still in the spirit of exploration. There are many technical problems to solve in a replication project of the sort we have begun. We shall need to learn better how to rate or measure the degree to which mutually self-revealing dialogue is being attained in any given relationship between a researcher and his subject. But we begin with a simple either-or discrimination between the impersonal researcher and the one who engages in a mutually revealing conversation before the experiment. More refined measures can be evolved with experience.

It would be helpful, in attempting replications in dialogue of representative experiments, if experimenters were trained to be more versatile in interacting with human beings. Perhaps we could insist that they be nice people, capable of entering into close, confiding relationships with a broad range of people. To be "nice" does not mean to be softheaded or unreliable in one's calculation of results. Training in experimental design, physiology, and statistics is no guarantee that one is qualified to interact in a confirming and evocative way with another person. I believe we can no longer afford to ignore the effect of the experimenter on the experience and behavior of the subject. We can no longer afford to divert nice, tenderhearted humanitarians into clinical work and leave the research for hard-nosed, hardhearted, impersonal folk. If an experimental psychologist is unpleasant and threatening in the eyes of others, it might be better to confine him to the calculating room or else let him contact human subjects only when the design for the experiment calls for an impersonal investigator. If a person has gone into psychology to get away from people, let him design experiments, build equipment, analyze data, run computers, and so on. We need all the versatility we can get in psychology.

At least, however, when we want to find out how people behave and disclose themselves under more permissive interpersonal conditions, let the one who encounters the subjects be someone who, by training and by commitment, is able to enter into dialogue. How strange that good animal psychologists view their animal subjects like individual persons, worthy of respect, while experimental psychologists frequently treat their human subjects as if they were anonymous animal objects! It is already known that "gentled," tame animals show different behavioral and physiological characteristics from those shown by nongentled or "wild" ones ("wild" means, here, defensive and hostile in the presence of humans). Yet many of our subjects are assumed to be tame and trusting when, in fact, they are wild. Genuine dialogue may prove to be the appropriate context for research in *human* (free) beings. When the experimenter-subject relationship varies, we might expect the subjects' responses to stimuli to vary. It is appropriate to consider the question: What will man prove to be like when he is studied by an investigator who consents to be studied by the subject?

If we do no more than study the effects of various modes of experimenter-subject relationship on the outcome of psychological experiments, and if we do this systematically, while including dialogue as one of the relationship modes, we shall have enriched our psychological knowledge considerably. Just as important, we may have taken a step toward reconciling the conflict between humanistic and nonhumanistic orientations to our discipline.

REFERENCES

BUBER, M. *I and thou.* New York: Scribner, 1958.

EDWARDS, A. L. *The social desirability variable in personality assessment and research.* New York: Dryden Press, 1957.

JOURARD, S. M. *The transparent self: Self-disclosure and well-being.* Princeton, N.J.: Van Nostrand, 1964.

LAING, R. D., & Esterson, A. *Sanity, madness and the family.* Vol. 1. *Families of schizophrenics.* London: Tavistock, 1964.

ORNE, M. T. On the social psychology of the psychological experiment: With particular reference to demand characteristics and their implications. *American Psychologist*, 1962, **17**: 776–783.

POWELL, W. J., Jr. A comparison of the reinforcing effects of three types of experimenter response on two classes of verbal behavior in an experimental interview. Unpublished doctoral dissertation, University of Florida, 1964.

RAPAPORT, D., et al. *Diagnostic psychological testing.* Vol. 2. Chicago: Year Book Publishers, 1946.

REIFEL, L. Unpublished research, Department of Psychology, University of Florida, 1965–1966.

RIVENBARK, W. R. Unpublished research, Department of Psychology, University of Florida, 1963–1964.

ROSENTHAL, R. On the social psychology of the psychological experiment. *American Scientist*, 1963, **51**: 268–283.

Duane P. Schultz

The Human Subject in
Psychological Research

In recent years, a number of psychologists have focused their research attention on the fundamental technique of their science: the experimental method. Articles and books have told us of experimenter effects in behavioral research (Rosenthal, 1966), the social nature of psychological research (Friedman, 1967), demand characteristics (Orne, 1962), and a host of other variables that may be confounding the data we continue to collect in such large quantities. We are warned, by the findings of this research on research, of the effect of unintended cues provided by our behavior, dress, speech, and commitment to a specific hypothesis; by the physical appearance of our laboratories; and by the general level of psychological research sophistication of the students who serve as our subjects. In short, this research suggests that the experimental situation may not be what we intend in our elaborately designed studies.

One essential aspect of the research process is the nature of the person who supplies our data: the human subject (usually known as the college sophomore). The common conception of the human subject seems to be that he (or, more aptly, it) functions as "a stimulus-response machine; you put a stimulus in one of the slots, and out comes a packet of reactions" [Burt, 1962, p. 232].

That such an image, no matter how devoutly believed, is totally incorrect and misleading, is a conclusion forced upon this researcher by his experience in personally "running" subjects in a three-year program of research on small-group behavior. That experience, together with an awareness of the growing literature on the human subject, has led to some sobering and alarming implications.

A hint of the seriousness of this problem is provided in the form of

From *Psychological Bulletin*, 1969, **72**: 214–228. Copyright © 1969 by The American Psychological Association, reprinted with permission of author and The American Psychological Association.

an imaginary letter from a subject to an experimenter in which Jourard (1968) noted what subjects have told him about their laboratory experiences. The letter is disturbing, for the subject says to the experimenter:

It's getting so I find it difficult to trust you. I'm beginning to see you as a trickster, a manipulator. . . . I lie to you a lot of the time. . . . When I don't lie, I will sometimes just answer at random, anything to get through with the hour, and back to my own affairs. . . . Did you ever stop to think that your articles, and the textbooks you write, the theories you spin—all based on your data (my disclosures to you)—may actually be a tissue of lies and half-truths (my lies and half-truths) or a joke I've played on you because I don't like you or trust you? That should give you cause for some concern [pp. 9, 11].

This is indeed cause for concern. The present paper looks critically at the human subject: what he was earlier in the history of psychology, what he is today, why his current image and role must change, and how such change might be brought about.

THE SUBJECT'S CHANGING ROLE IN PSYCHOLOGY'S HISTORY

The subjects (or, more properly, observers) who served in the laboratories of Wundt and Titchener bear little resemblance to today's subjects. First, they were either the psychologists themselves or psychologists-in-training (graduate students). As such, they were probably highly motivated in their roles as observers; surely, one would have had to be to perform the complex and time-consuming introspections required in that era. They were well trained for their task, having undergone long apprenticeships, and they knew exactly what to look for and what errors to avoid. Boring (1953) noted that observers in the Leipzig reaction experiments were required to perform some 10,000 introspective reactions before they were considered capable of providing data worthy of publication. Thus, the early subjects were highly skilled and motivated to pursue what Titchener called the "hard introspective labor."

It is interesting that the observers during this introspective era were sometimes referred to in journal articles as "reagents," which may be defined as any substance which, from its capacity for certain reactions, is used in detecting, examining, or measuring other substances (*Webster's New Collegiate Dictionary*, 1958, p. 704). This might suggest that a subject was considered to be of the nature of a chemical reagent: a constant which will elicit an invariant reaction from any substance or process to which it might be applied. It might be suggested, then, that subjects were thought of as rather like recording instruments, objectively noting the characteristics of their focus of observation. This "machine view" of observers was noted by Titchener (1912) when he spoke of the technique of observing becoming mechanized through training and practice, so that observation was not a conscious process.

In speaking of this mechanism of habit, Titchener (1912) quoted Wundt as saying that "*In his attention to the phenomena under observation, the observer in psychology, no less than the observer in physics, completely forgets to give subjective attention to the state of observing*" [p. 443]. Thus, we have an objective and detached observing mechanism who reports to the experimenter on the processes observed and attempts to mirror them accurately.

Could anyone be a reagent? Did everyone have this invariant capacity for certain reactions? The structuralists' answer was initially negative. Titchener (1895b) quoted Wundt as follows:

there are individuals who are entirely incapable of any steady concentration of the attention, and who will therefore never make trustworthy [reagents]. That should not be surprising. It is not everyone who has the capacity for astronomical or physical observation; and it is not to be expected either that everyone is endowed with the gifts requisite for psychological experimentation [p. 507].

Binet (1894) also noted that "the aptitude for introspection is not given to everyone; some possess it in high degree; these are the born psychologists" [p. 18].

It was thought, then, that there was a "disposition" (as Titchener called it) for psychological research. Precisely what constituted this disposition was never made explicit beyond describing it as specific habits, attitudes, and "characteristics of mind." Presumably, however, a master introspectionist would recognize this ability.

By 1912, perhaps due to a shortage of "born psychologists," Titchener modified the requirement of a disposition for introspection, noting that "any normal person, coming to the task with goodwill and application, may understand and acquire [it]" [p. 446]. Thus, a person could be trained to properly introspect. This training, Titchener argued, was similar to the kind of training required for reliable observations in biology or physics. In addition to the proper training, introspection required that the observers be in good health, free from anxiety and worry, and comfortable in their surroundings at the time of observation.

It was suggested previously that a subject was considered a constant eliciting an invariant reaction. If this were true, the research findings must have resulted in satisfyingly consistent data with no extreme scores to cause dismay. But surely Titchener's reagents, no matter how well trained and mechanized, could not have all produced highly similar reactions, considering the subjective nature of their task. It seems that they did not, but let us quote from Titchener on this point of data consistency.

In his famous reaction-time debate with James Mark Baldwin (1895–1896), Titchener noted that "The only results ruled out are those which are wholly irregular and inconstant" [1895b, p. 507]. In one research report, Titchener noted that "Seven participants in this investigation were found to be incapable of reacting with any degree of constancy: their results were therefore not employed" [1895a, p. 75]. Thus, out of the 10 reagents in this particular study, 7 gave inconsistent results, but the remaining 3 consistent reagents (no doubt "born psychologists") gave highly similar reaction times and so constituted the findings.

Small wonder that Baldwin engaged in such an active debate. In commenting on another Titchener study in which the results of six out of nine reagents were ruled out, Baldwin asked:

If one-third of mankind are to be taken to prove that a result is a universal principle, the rest being deliberately excluded because they cannot get the result that the one-third do, then what conclusions could not be proved in well-managed psychological laboratories? [1896, p. 82]

Baldwin favored the use of untrained and unpracticed observers, and the Titchener-Baldwin debate centering on the kinds of subjects to be used was really a debate between the older structuralist position and the newer American spirit of functionalism. Wundt and Titchener searched for general laws of the human mind and so the existence of individual differences among the reagents was, to them, a source of annoyance to be eliminated rather than investigated.

The functionalist spirit or attitude was able to accommodate the notion of individual differences; indeed, it fostered an active psychology of individual differences under the aggressive leadership of James McKeen Cattell. The functionalists were interested in studying the minds of untrained observers and so could turn to naïve subjects from the college and general populations. Earlier, a precursor of functional psychology, Sir Francis Galton, used naïve subjects from the general population in his famous anthropometric laboratory—and these subjects even paid for the privilege of being tested.

Thus, the functionalists' concern with individual differences brought about a change in the kind of human subject studied, from the trained and well-practiced professional of Titchener to the untrained and naïve amateur of Cattell and other functionalists.

There was another change taking place also, and that had to do with the decline of introspection with an attendant demotion in status of the human subject from observer to the one (or thing) observed. In the early years of this century, dissatisfaction was being expressed over introspection in this country (except, of course, at Cornell). For example, G. Stanley Hall said, in 1910, that "formerly everyone supposed that self-observation . . . was the oracle and muse of philosophic studies. Now, however, . . . it is coming to be seen that this method gives us access to but a very small part of the soul" [p. 621]. Hall urged the use of natural history methods involving careful observation and description of the actions of other people.

Even before John B. Watson and his behaviorist manifesto of 1913, there was a decided leaning among many American psychologists toward greater objectivity. At the functionalist base at the University of Chicago, much research was conducted in the early 1900s without recourse to introspection. Many of the subjects used in these studies were those most readily available—the graduate and undergraduate students.

Completing with a sharp finality the move away from introspection (of the classical variety) and toward the more exclusive use of the experimental observation of behavior was, of course, behaviorism. And it was this that brought about the total change of role of the human subject.

In classical introspection, the reagent was the observer and the observed at the same time. It was the reagent who observed the subject matter (his own conscious experience). As Boring (1953) commented, the observer "has the responsibility for the correctness of his descriptions of conscious data" [p. 184]. The observer, then, had a very important and responsible position. The experimenter set up the conditions and recorded the observations reported by the observer.

With behaviorism, this situation changed completely, for Titchener's observer became Watson's subject. In other words, with behaviorism, the true observer is the experimenter who observes the responses of the subject to the conditions the experimenter has set up. Thus, the human subject was demoted in status—he no longer observed, he merely behaved and became the object of observation. And almost anyone can behave—children, the mentally ill, animals, and even the college sophomore!

This image of the subject-as-object is reinforced by the mechanomorphic tendencies of behaviorism whose model of man is that of an organic machine—an inanimate, determined, reacting, empty organism. The tendency to view subjects as mechanical objects to be poked, prodded, manipulated, and measured causes the experimenter-subject dyad to be of the order of Buber's I-It relationship. The relationship is not that of person-to-person, but rather that of person-to-thing, with its attendant tendencies of domination, manipulation, and control.

This detachment and separation between experimenter and subject

means looking at something that is not you, not human, not personal, something independent of you the perceiver. It is something to which you are a stranger. . . . You the observer are, then, really alien to it, uncomprehending and without sympathy and identification [Maslow, 1966, p. 49].

In the same vein, Clark Hull suggested that we should consider "the behaving organism as a completely self-maintaining robot, constructed of materials as unlike ourselves as may be" [1943, p. 27].

Viewed in this manner, the sophomore in our laboratory is not a person, not an individual, but merely an anonymous, expendable object—and a sample object at that!

THE SUBJECT IN CONTEMPORARY PSYCHOLOGY

Bias in the Selection of Subjects

In reading our journals, one receives the distinct impression that the only kind of people of interest to psychologists are college students! If college students were truly representative samples of the population at large, there would be no problem in generalizing from the results of our studies. But (fortunately or unfortunately) they do differ in highly significant ways from the general population, and we cannot have a truly meaningful science of human behavior by studying such a restricted sample.

How biased in subject selection is our research? Smart (1966) examined the two largest journals of the American Psychological Association reporting research with human subjects: the *Journal of Abnormal and Social Psychology* (1962–1964, Vol. 64–67) and the *Journal of Experimental Psychology* (1963–1964, Vols. 65–68). The present author reviewed the same journals for the period 1966–1967 (the *Journal of Personality and Social Psychology*,[3] Vols. 3–7, and the *Journal of Experimental Psychology*, Vols. 71–75), and the data from both surveys is contained in Table 1–2. Both surveys dealt only with nonpsychiatric subject groups.

Inspection of Table 1–2 reveals a striking degree of similarity between the two sets of data with a heavy concentration of college students as subjects. In addition to the great reliance on college students, both surveys revealed an overrepresentation of male subjects. The extremely small percentage of studies sampling the general adult population was particularly disturbing; none of the studies published in the *Journal of Experimental Psychology* during those years used a sample of the general population. Further, this author's survey found that in this journal, the nature of the subjects studied was not specified in 3.6 percent of the articles for the two-year period. No mention could be found in these articles of where the subjects were obtained, who they were, or even if they were male or female. This certainly seems a serious omission in the reporting of research.

The fact that college students are our primary focus of research has a number of important and sobering consequences. For example, approximately 80 percent of our research is performed on the 3 percent of the population currently enrolled in college (U.S. Department of Commerce, 1967). Regardless of how much our college enrollments

Table 1-2   *Human Subject Sources in American Psychological Association Journals*

Subjects	JEP* Smart	JEP Schultz	JASP† Smart	JPSP‡ Schultz
Introductory Psychology	42.2%	41.2%	32.2%	34.1%
Other college	43.5%	42.5%	40.9%	36.1%
Precollege	7.0%	7.1%	16.9%	18.5%
Special adult	7.3%	5.6%	9.4%	10.1%
General adult	0	0	0.6%	1.2%
All male	22.3%	19.3%	33.6%	26.7%
All female	6.0%	6.0%	10.8%	10.6%

* *Journal of Experimental Psychology.*
† *Journal of Abnormal and Social Psychology.*
‡ *Journal of Personality and Social Psychology.*

may increase, college students most likely will never be truly representative of the total adult population, in terms of level of intelligence alone. Further, this pronounced emphasis on college students means that most of our research is conducted with a very young group, primarily aged eighteen to twenty-four.

Such students are probably at the peak of their learning and intellectual abilities and this could mean that many findings in learning, especially verbal learning, could be special to the college student with limited applicability to other groups [Smart, 1966, p. 119].

There is also the problem of social class representation for, as Smart noted, the college student population contains more upper- and middle-class people and fewer lower-class people than the general population.

There is a further biasing effect in much of our psychological research that further limits the degree of generalizability of our findings. While some students are required to serve as subjects as a part of their course work, others voluntarily agree to serve. Those who do volunteer to serve as subjects do so for a variety of reasons. Orne (1962), Riecken (1962), and Rosenthal and Rosnow (1969) suggested several reasons, such as pay, course credit, the opportunity to learn something about oneself, and a desire to contribute to science. Among volunteers for a sensory deprivation experiment Jackson and Pollard (1966) reported that 50 percent of the subjects said they volunteered out of curiosity, 21 percent for the money ($1.25 per hour), and only 7 percent in order to help science. Rosenthal and Rosnow noted that psychology majors appear to have a higher volunteer rate than non-psychology majors.

Differences in actual task performance as a function of the reason for volunteering remain to be determined. It seems plausible to suggest that a subject volunteering in the hope of learning something about himself might perform differently than one volunteering for, say, course credit.

Are there any significant and meaningful differences between those who volunteer for psychological research and those who do not? Rosenthal (1965) summarized the extensive research on this problem and reported some disturbing findings. The rates of volunteering vary widely within the same university (10 to 100 percent), even when the same recruiter is issuing the same invitation to participate in the same experiment. However, Rosenthal did find certain situational variables that tend to increase the likelihood of volunteering. These include (*a*) having only a relatively less attractive alternative to volunteering; (*b*) increasing the intensity of the request to volunteer; (*c*) increasing the perception that others in a similar situation would volunteer; (*d*) increasing acquaintanceship with, the perceived prestige of, and liking for, the experimenter; (*e*) having greater intrinsic interest in the subject matter being investigated; and (*f*) increasing the subjective probability of subsequently being favorably evaluated or not unfavorably evaluated by the experimenter (Rosenthal, 1965, p. 403).

Further, Rosenthal found that certain personal attributes were likely to be associated with a higher level of volunteering. He concluded that volunteers tend to have greater intellectual ability, interest, and motivation; greater unconventionality; lower age; less authoritarianism; greater need for social approval; and greater sociability (1965, pp. 403–404).

Thus, there is strong reason to suspect that in studies using only volunteer subjects, these subjects probably differ in various ways from those who do not volunteer. At the very least, this seems to violate the requirement of random sampling and thus places limitations on the statistical procedures used to analyze the data.

It might also be suggested that volunteers perform in the experimental situation in different ways than nonvolunteers as a function of their different personal characteristics. For example, Rosnow and Rosenthal (1966) reported exploratory research which suggested that volunteers, because of their greater need for social approval, were more highly motivated than nonvolunteers to verify the experimenter's hypothesis (or at least their interpretation of the hypothesis).

Another problem in the area of the volunteer subject is that some volunteers never show up for the experiment. The evidence suggests that in terms of personality test performance these "no shows" are more like nonvolunteers than volunteers who do show up. As a result, studies investigating volunteer-nonvolunteer differences are really comparing nonvolunteers with some unknown mix of true volunteers and other nonvolunteers. Thus, the results of volunteer-nonvolunteer comparisons may tend to underestimate differences between those who actually contribute data and those who do not.

And so we have the human subject who actually enters the laboratory and provides the data for our study of human behavior. He is primarily a male college student and is often enrolled in a psychology class. At least some of the time he will be a subject because he happened to be in class on the day volunteers were recruited or because his own personal characteristics and/or some aspect of the recruiting situation led him to volunteer. If a course requirement dictates that he serve as a subject, and if he has a choice among experiments, his own personal characteristics may lead him to choose one kind of experiment as opposed to another.

Are our subjects chosen at random? Are they representative of the general population, of the population of college students, of the population of college sophomores, or even of the sophomores of their own college? The answer to all of these questions, for much of our reported research, would seem to be a taunting and haunting No.

The Subject in the Laboratory

We now have our subject in the laboratory and are ready to instruct him in the experimental task. What is his set or attitude as he begins the experiment? Is he totally naïve with regard to psychological experimentation or does he approach the situation with certain predispositions and suspicions that can influence his task performance in ways not intended by the experimenter?

First, consider the attitudes of college students toward compulsory participation in experiments. Mention was made earlier of the policy of many psychology departments of requiring experimental participation as part of the introductory course. Gustav (1962) investigated the attitudes of 251 students at New York University toward their compulsory participation as subjects. At the time of this investigation, all students had participated in one experiment, though not all in the same study.

The results indicated that large numbers of required-service subjects may not be entering our laboratories with completely neutral feelings about the situation. Approximately 40 percent of the subjects expressed unfavorable attitudes, ranging from annoyance and irritation to fear and apprehension, toward their experiences as subjects, and 37 percent stated flatly that they would not have participated voluntarily.

The remaining subjects reported more positive attitudes of great interest, enthusiasm, curiosity, and eagerness.

Argyris (1968) reported on an evaluation of the general psychology course by 600 undergraduates at a large university and noted that an overwhelming majority of the students focused on the course requirement of research participation. "The students were very critical, mistrustful, and hostile to the requirement. In many cases they identified how they expressed their pent-up feelings by 'beating the researcher' in such a way that he never found out . . . ." [p. 188].

That such attitudes (either favorable or unfavorable) can influence the subjects' performance in a number of kinds of experimental tasks seems eminently possible. For example, those students who reported they were bored may well have performed the experimental task in a perfunctory fashion, going through the motions in order to get it over with as quickly as possible. Those who reported irritation at being required to serve might have deliberately distorted their responses in an attempt at revenge. The large number of subjects who reported apprehension and a fear of being measured and found wanting may have distorted results because of their high levels of tension and anxiety.

Holmes (1967) investigated the influence of performance in past experiments on performance in later experiments. It was found that subjects with a greater degree of experiment experience (more than six studies) tended to see the later experiment as more scientific and more valuable than those with low experience (one study). Further, the more experienced subjects made more of an attempt to cooperate with the experimenter but evidenced less interest in what the later experiment was about. Thus, subjects' perceptions of and behavioral intentions in experiments were influenced by their prior experience as research subjects.

One important requisite of psychological research is that the incoming subjects be naïve as to the nature and purpose of the experiment in which they are serving. With the large number of research studies being performed in the many universities with active graduate departments, the problem of subject naïveté may be assuming serious proportions.

With regard to specific experiments conducted over a long period of time, it seems very difficult to keep details of the experiment secret from potential future subjects. Despite our best intentions and attempts to secure pledges of secrecy, it seems that many subjects do talk about our research (in tones of ridicule or respect) to their fellow students. Even using signed pledges in connection with a well-established university honor code does not always prevent the arrival of new subjects who say, "Oh, I heard about this." Rokeach and Zemach (1966) suggested that highly interesting studies become so widely discussed and understood on a campus that the results are relatively useless. This is indeed a serious problem for long-term research projects.

On a more general level is the increasing sophistication of college students with regard to certain aspects of research methodology and attempts at deception. Surely many sophomores know by now that if they are given two questionnaires or tests with an activity or task in between, they are expected to change their answers on the second test.

As for deception, perhaps it is the researchers who are being deceived. Kelman (1967) noted that subjects "may not know the exact purpose of the particular experiment in which they are participating, but at least they know, typically, that it is *not* what the experimenter says it is" [p. 6]. Brown (1965) asked, "Does any of our subjects ever believe us?" [p. 580]. Orne (1962) noted that our attempts at concealing the true purpose of our studies are

so widely known in the college population that even if a psychologist is honest with the subject, more often than not he will be distrusted. As one subject pithily put it, "Psychologists always lie!" This bit of paranoia has some support in reality [pp. 778–779].

Argyris (1968) commented that subjects now come into the laboratory fully expecting to be deceived.

It would seem, then, that the subject does not enter the experiment as a tabula rasa but rather with a variety of positive and negative attitudes, expectations, and suspicions, any one of which can distort his performance. In some cases he knows the details of the specific experiment and, in many more cases, his sophistication with regard to laboratory techniques is such that the label, naïve, is a gross distortion of reality.

Performance in the Experimental Task

As we have seen, the subject brings certain attitudes and predispositions into the laboratory which may influence his behavior in the experimental task. The nature of his social interaction with the experimenter, as well as the conditions of the experiment, can also influence his behavior as a subject. His responses are being made not only to our manipulations of the independent variable, but to the host of cues that Orne (1962) called demand characteristics of the experimental situation. These demand characteristics include

the rumors or campus scuttlebutt about the research, the information conveyed during the original solicitation, the person of the experimenter, and the setting of the laboratory, as well as all explicit and implicit communications during the experiment proper [p. 779].

The experimental situation is one of social interaction, but the relationship has some of the characteristics of a superior-subordinate one. When a subject has crossed the threshold of the laboratory, he has implicitly agreed to come under the control of the experimenter, to do whatever the experimenter asks on the basis of limited (and probably false) information, with little, if any, opportunity to ask questions. Perhaps the only other such onesided relationships are those of parent and child, physician and patient, or drill sergeant and trainee.

Orne (1962) found, in several informal experiments, that people would tolerate high degrees of boredom and discomfort as long as the requests were phrased in terms of performing an experiment. For example, subjects were each given 2,000 sheets of paper filled with rows of random numbers and assigned a task that required 224 additions for each sheet of paper. The subjects' watches were taken away and they were cheered with the announcement that the experimenter would return "eventually." Orne noted that he gave up over 5 hours later but the subjects were still working.

Outside of the Army, where would we tolerate such an imposition? And yet our human subjects daily subject themselves to boredom, embarrassment, humiliation, fright, and, often, physical pain, because of the high degree of control in this situation.

The experimenter-subject relationship has a socially as well as historically defined character. As we have seen, the majority of subjects are college students. The experimenter, if not always a professor, is at least a deputy or representative of a professor (a graduate student). The experimenter is perceived by the subject as a member of the academic establishment that students are traditionally used to obeying; he represents another figure in the long line of those who have stood *in loco parentis*. As such, the experimenter

has responsibilities towards his students and is bound to protect as well as guide them . . . he is rational, serious and purposive. He may be eccentric; but he is not lunatic, a prankster or an idler. His behavior is explicable in terms of the scheme of motives, purposes and norms that govern the academic community [Riecken, 1962, p. 29].

But there is more to the experimenter than just his membership in a superordinate group. He is also a *psychologist*, reputed to have uncanny skills and techniques to probe and prod and poke into our innermost workings, to find out things about us which we would rather keep secret.

Thus, the experimenter is a powerful figure to the subject. He represents control over the student by his membership in the academic establishment, and he has a certain mystique about him by virtue of his alleged unique power or ability to see all.

Further, there is a one-sided distribution of information in this relationship. The experimenter presents a certain amount of information about the task which the subject may or may not believe. The subject may suspect that some information is being withheld, but he is not allowed to question the experimenter about this suspicion. As Riecken (1962) suggested, the experimenter plays:

> a serious game with the subject, inviting the latter to behave under specified conditions but revealing neither what the experimenter regards as the "right answer" nor even the criteria by which a particular answer will be judged . . . "the right answer" remains the property of the master of these ceremonies until the program is over [pp. 30–31].

Riecken suggested that because of the inadequate and possibly misleading information given the subject, he may look for meaning and purpose in the situation and try to discern the "right" answer or "right" behavior. As suggested earlier, the subject may begin the experiment with certain preconceptions or suspicions and these may be sharpened or modified in the light of information received in the laboratory, for example, instructions, behavior of the experimenter, physical and social environment, and other demand characteristics. The subject may be continuously redefining the situation until the experiment is completed, trying to determine what is expected of him so that he may behave accordingly.

Several reasons have been suggested as to why subjects may make such efforts. Orne (1962), for example, suggested that most subjects in psychological experiments have such a high regard for the aims of science that they

> tend to share (with the experimenter) the hope and expectation that the study in which they are participating will in some material way contribute to science. . . . Both subject and experimenter share the belief that whatever the experimental task is, it is important, and that as such no matter how much effort must be exerted or how much discomfort must be endured, it is justified by the ultimate purpose [p. 778].

The present author feels that such high and noble purpose can be attributed to only a minority of college student subjects. This is supported by the report of Jackson and Pollard (1966), cited previously, which found that only 7 percent of a group of volunteers gave as their motivation for volunteering a desire to help science. Perhaps even fewer nonvolunteers are concerned with making a contribution to science.

Orne (1962) did suggest that subjects were concerned about their own self-image as revealed by their task performance, but he felt that they were more concerned that their behavior serve to validate the experimenter's hypothesis and thus contribute to science.

Riecken (1962) felt that the subject attempted to uncover the rationale of the experiment for the purpose, not of contributing to science, but to present himself in the most favorable light—to "put his best foot forward." This seems a reasonable hypothesis, particularly if the experimenter is also the subject's instructor, or if he is particularly pleasant, or charming, or witty. Under these circumstances, the subject might not only want to be thought well of by the experimenter but also sincerely want to help the experimenter get "good" results, that is, the results the subject thinks the experimenter wants.

A third reason might be suggested for a subject's attempts to divine the nature of an experiment. He may want to foul up the experimenter's research by responding in the "wrong" way, in a manner opposite to what he thinks the experimenter wants—what Masling (1966) called "the screw you effect." As noted earlier, some subjects resent compulsory participation and so might wish to perpetrate revenge on the experimenter. Further, even some volunteer subjects may react in this way because the experimenter is their instructor, or because he is not pleasant, charming, or witty.

However, regardless of the reason for the subject's attempts to figure out the experiment, he does try to interpret it and responds according to his perception of the situation. Whether his perception is accurate or not is secondary to the fact that he is not a passive responder to the situation. He is an active participant in it, and this very activity changes the nature of the situation for him. His world, then, is not simply what the experimenter defines and presents to him. No matter how thoroughly we attempt to control and standardize the experimental situation, it is, in fact, neither controlled nor standardized to the subject. The resulting situation is one that is not intended and, more importantly, not known to the experimenter, and one that will vary among subjects.

Ethical Issues

Where is the line drawn between our responsibility to our discipline (and careers), and to those who enter our laboratories, willingly or unwillingly, to provide us with data? It seems that far too often, any concern for the well-being of our subjects is second to our interest in obtaining significance with clever new techniques of deception and probing. Perhaps this is something we really do not think about, or would prefer not to think about. Perhaps we are so used to the anonymity of subjects-as-objects and to their function as a mechanical source of data that we fail to recognize the need for concern about them as human beings.

The American Psychological Association has considered the problem of ethics in research. Principle 16, Research Precautions, of the "Ethical Standards of Psychologists" reads in part:

a. Only when a problem is of scientific significance and it is not practicable to investigate it in any other way is the psychologist justified in exposing research subjects . . . to physical or emotional stress as part of an investigation.
b. When a reasonable possibility of injurious aftereffects exists, research is conducted only when the subjects or their responsible agents are fully informed of this possibility and agree to participate nevertheless.
c. The psychologist seriously considers the possibility of harmful aftereffects and avoids them, or removes them as soon as permitted by the design of the experiment [American Psychological Association, 1963, pp. 59–60].

It is suggested that many of our experiments do involve potential emotional stress and that our subjects (volunteers and nonvolunteers) are rarely informed of this possibility. Further, we seldom bother to attempt to deal with any possible harmful aftereffects, for our interest in the subject ceases as soon as he leaves the laboratory. While there are exceptions to this seeming indifference to our subjects (and perhaps this is an important point in itself), they are indeed exceptions where they should be the rule.

Baumrind (1964) argued that researchers should insure that subjects do not leave the experimental laboratory more humiliated, insecure, or hostile than when they entered. This, she suggested, is part of the debt or obligation we have to our subjects in return for their participation in our many studies which manipulate, embarrass, and discomfort them.

Kelman (1967) expressed concern not only over the potentially harmful consequences of our experiments but also about the use of deception per se. He viewed such deception (even when there is little danger of harmful effects) as a violation of the basic respect and dignity to which every human being is entitled. Deception in the laboratory, he argued, is reinforcing an unfortunate trend in which man is increasingly considered as a manipulatable object and is therefore treated in a deliberate and highly systematic manner.

A further source of ethical concern relates to the invasion of privacy in cases where the subject is studied without his consent and/or where the data are not treated in full confidence. In our culture, the individual's right to privacy is being severely eroded to the point where it is cause for serious concern. In the laboratory, our subjects' inner feelings, fears, and fantasies are often exposed to view through deception and other techniques designed for such purposes. That we insist we are only interested in behavior may have no meaning to a subject who, through some overt action, feels that he has displayed cowardice, conformity, or some other characteristic he would rather not have displayed. "The right to privacy is the right of the individual to decide for himself how much he will share with others his thoughts, his feelings, and the facts of his personal life" [Panel on Privacy and Behavioral Research, 1967, p. 536].

Concern over the ethical use of human subjects in research has been increasing in recent years: In January 1966, the Panel on Privacy and Behavioral Research was appointed by the President's Office of Science and Technology; in July 1966, the United States Public Health Service adopted regulations dealing with the rights and welfare of human subjects; and in May 1967, the American Psychological Association devoted an entire issue of the *American Psychologist* to various aspects of this problem.

The Panel on Privacy and Behavioral Research noted that while most research does not violate the individual's right to privacy, there are enough serious exceptions to justify increased attention to the problem. The Panel strongly urged that subject participation be on a voluntary and informed consent basis wherever possible and that researchers take every precaution necessary to guarantee the subjects' privacy and the absence of permanent physical or psychological harm.

The fact that the Public Health Service had to institute regulations designed to protect the welfare of human subjects perhaps attests to our own lack of concern for the problem. Those who would seek research support from that agency are now compelled to be sensitive to the issue.

CONCLUSIONS

The present paper has discussed several problems relating to the selection of human subjects and the kinds of situations and tasks to which those subjects are exposed. There are serious methodological and ethical implications of the latter. The situation is cause for serious and constructive alarm within psychology, for if our source of data is open to question then surely one can legitimately question the validity of that data.

We cannot continue to base some 80 percent of our human subject data on college students and still call our work a science of human behavior. We cannot continue to use statistical techniques which are predicated in part on the random sampling and assignment of subjects when this requirement is not being fully met. We cannot continue to design elaborate studies based on deception when we may be the only ones being deceived. Our population of naïve and trusting subjects is running low and we can no longer assume that all subjects will respond to our experiments in the manner in which we define those situations. Finally, we cannot continue to ignore the welfare, dignity, and privacy of our subjects.

What can be done about these matters? An important part of any attempted resolution of the problem is an active awareness of its existence. As mentioned earlier, greater attention is being paid in recent years to the nature of experimentation in psychology, and part of the focus of this research on research has been the human subject. What actual impact this new area of research will have on future studies remains to be seen.

However, it is not possible to find noticeable changes in the nature of most subject groups as reported in our journals; the great majority continue to be college students. Will any such change require external pressures such as those imposed by the Public Health Service? If journal editors and grant agency referees started requiring more representative and more randomly chosen subjects, or evidence of differences between volunteers and nonvolunteers, then the subject selection situation would change rather rapidly.

In the absence of any such pressures, such changes will probably be a long time in developing because it may well be true that the majority of the psychologists who design experiments do not participate in the actual subject selection or data collection. Rosenthal (1966) noted that there is

a trend for less highly selected experimenters to collect data for serious scientific purposes. Not only more and more graduate students are collecting behavioral data but undergraduates as well. . . . The young postdoctoral psychologist can hardly wait to turn the burdens of data collection over to *his* graduate student assistants [pp. 335, 364].

As a result, many who design the studies may not see, for example, the subtle as well as the distinct demand characteristics in operation, nor do we hear the comments of subjects as they enter and leave the laboratory. Hence, although we may read the relevant articles and be aware of the problem on an intellectual level, we may lack direct experience with subjects and so may not be sensitive to the problem on a more visceral or working level.

The solution to the selection problem is an obvious one: more effort must be made to sample the noncollege population. And, just as obviously, this is much more easily said than done. There are few, if any, logistical difficulties in using our captive college students but there are numerous such problems in obtaining a noncollege group to participate, particularly if the experiment requires such a group to come to the university campus to serve. For example, it took the author several weeks of telephone and mail contact to finally secure 50 United States Naval Reservists to come to the laboratory to participate in an experiment. Even with these subjects, however, the problem of representativeness remains since they are a special group and not entirely representative of the general population. It is, nonetheless, a step in the right direction.

Smart (1966) suggested that more representative subject sampling could be accomplished through the establishment of large panels of subjects (necessarily volunteers) from the surrounding community, for example, industry, large clerical concerns, churches, and various other adult groups. This, of course, has the problem of using only volunteers, who may differ significantly from those who fail to volunteer. Also, these groups would not necessarily reflect the characteristics of the general population. Further, the subjects would probably have to be paid, presenting a problem for non-grant-supported research. These limitations notwithstanding, such groups would still supply data more generalizable than those supplied by the almost exclusive use of college students.

Rosenthal (1966) suggested that data collection centers or institutes be established with experiments being conducted by professionally trained data collectors. His concern is with the effects of the experimenter's behavior on the results of a study, and consequently he proposed standardized and thorough training for those whose sole task would be to collect data, such as a laboratory technician in medical research or an interviewer in survey research. The data collector would not be a scientist or scientist-in-training and hence would have no vested interest in the results.

Rosenthal does suggest that pilot studies still be performed by the individual investigator and his assistants, as is now the case, but the large-scale research study would then be turned over to an institute, just as survey research is turned over to a data collection organization such as the National Opinion Research Center.

At first glance, this might seem farfetched but "one can already have surveys conducted, tests validated, and experimental animals bred to order. What is proposed here simply extends the limits of the kind of data that could become available on a contract basis" [Rosenthal, 1966, p. 365]. (If one is skeptical of the need for the use of professional data collectors, one has only to read Rosenthal's account of the effects of the experimenter's hypotheses and behavior on the interpretation of his results).

The use of such centers would facilitate the collection of data from more representative samples of subjects; adult subjects could be obtained and paid for their participation. It is not farfetched to envision mobile data-collection centers housed in truck vans, taking the experiment virtually anywhere to secure subjects. With this mobility, there could be even greater success in getting a subject sample that would approximate the general population.

It is recognized that these centers or institutes would be expensive to establish and maintain, but they have the potential of providing us with a meaningful science of behavior, a science based more on the real world and less on the college campus.

Thus, it is within the realm of possibility to change our selection procedures so as to bring into the laboratory subjects who are more representative of the general population than is now the case. The procedures are admittedly expensive, time-consuming, difficult, and probably frustrating, but there seems no question that they would provide more valid and generalizable data.

It is suggested, however, that even if all research in psychology utilized perfectly random and representative samples, the results would still be highly questionable (indeed, some would say virtually worthless) without basic changes in our experimental procedures. The increasing sophistication of subjects has been discussed with regard to experimentation and their growing suspicion of what we say and do to them in our laboratories. Subjects seem "wise" to what we are doing and prone to respond in terms of their own interpretation of the situation, attitude toward us, and feeling about being used as subjects. Surely these, and the ethical considerations discussed above, justify the charge that some change in our methods of collecting data is necessary.

But there is a third, more basic, important, and compelling reason for such a change—our model or image of man as an organic stimulus-response machine, an inanimate, determined, reacting, empty organism, is obsolete. The image of the human subject-as-object is no longer appropriate, if, indeed, it ever was.

The model of man adopted by early scientific psychology was quite naturally that of the prevailing climate of thought induced by the mechanistic philosophers. In the so-called (and so long dominant) Newtonian world view, the image of the universe as a great machine was extended to man, and concepts such as determinism and mechanistic causation were applied to human nature.

One aspect of Newtonian classical physics of particular relevance to observation and experimentation is the notion that nature constitutes a unique reality independent of man. Derived from this is the assumption that nature is objectively observable and independent of the observer. Thus, there developed a dichotomy between man and nature, inner world and outer world, observer and observed. The observer is, as discussed earlier, detached, distant, aloof, and essentially different from what is being observed, be it the physical universe, the contents of consciousness, or the behavior of a subject.

This highly objective and detached spectator observation (by the experimenter) of a machinelike object (the subject) would be commendable, indeed necessary, if the underlying assumptions, that is, the Newtonian machine view of the universe and the consequent behaviorist machine view of man, were valid. But physics many years ago discarded this mechanical view, recognizing the ultimate subjectivity of all that which we would call objective, and that the very act of observing nature disturbs it, thus distorting or changing reality.

One important implication of this is the closing of the gap between the observer and the observed, and the change of focus of scientific inquiry from an independent and objectively knowable universe to man's observation of the universe. No longer the detached observer, the modern scientist is now cast in the role of participant-observer. The process of observation becomes an interaction, with both sides contributing to the observational transaction. There is no longer an independent fact and independent observer but rather an interaction and integration of the two in an observation.

Thus, a change in experimental technique is called for on empirical, ethical, as well as philosophical, grounds. Let us examine two recently proposed experimental approaches in the light of these considerations.

One approach, suggested by Brown (1965) and Kelman (1967), among others, is that of role playing. Instead of deliberately concealing the nature and purpose of the experiment, these would be explained to the subject and his cooperation sought. The intent is for the subject to directly and actively involve himself in the experiment, and to conscientiously participate in the experimental task. In this approach, the subject, hopefully, would have a more positive attitude toward the experiment and the experimenter if he felt that he was sharing with the experimenter in a collaborative endeavor rather than being used as a guinea pig.

This technique eliminates the questionable practice of deception which, as discussed earlier, is frequently ineffective. The subject, in role playing, is not considered as merely a mechanical responder to stimuli but is much more of an acting participant. How effectively subjects will role play, of course, may depend on a number of variables including the degree of intrinsic interest of the task, the face validity of the instructions, and the subject's perception of and attitude toward the experimenter. Of course, the latter point is also a serious problem in current research techniques.

Role playing would seem to offer two advantages: the elimination of deception and the involvement of the subject as more of a direct participant in the data collection. It must be remembered that the subject is a direct and influencing participant in data collection whether we recognize or like it. Such being the case, it would seem appropriate to make active use of this participation rather than to pretend that it does not exist.

Another approach, suggested by Jourard (1968), involves the conducting of experiments with a mutual self-disclosure between the experimenter and the subject. Instead of the impersonal, detached, and distrustful relationship that is now often the case, Jourard suggests a greater openness and mutual knowing in the experimenter-subject dyad. The subject would be encouraged to report what the stimuli and his behavioral responses really mean to him. The experimenter, in turn, would explain what he thinks the subject's responses mean, and the subject asked to respond. Thus, both experimenter and subject would be open and revealing to one another.

This approach, too, eliminates the problem of deception, and it involves the subject as an active participant and collaborator, perhaps even more fully than role playing. It might be suggested, however, that the subject's degree of self-disclosure and openness would depend in large measure on the "personality" of the experimenter and that this factor could influence the subject's responses more than the independent variables involved in the experiment. Of course, as we have seen, the subject's perception of and attitude toward the experimenter affects his behavior in contemporary research, but this influence of the experimenter would seem to be greater when he is more intrusive and interacting in the experiment.

Of less importance, but still a consideration, is the fact that such an approach would be tremendously time-consuming in experiments requiring relatively large numbers of subjects. Further, it would be difficult to adapt this technique to group research involving interaction and intermember influence.

These reservations notwithstanding, the technique is an interesting one and does offer certain advantages including the potential for changing "the status of the subject from that of an anonymous *object* of our study to the status of a *person*, a fellow seeker, a *collaborator* in our enterprise" [Jourard, 1968, p. 25]. Jourard and his students are performing very imaginative research to investigate the technique.

Both of these approaches have several points in common. They eliminate deception and "require us to *use* the subject's motivation to cooperate rather than to bypass it; they may even call for increasing the sophistication of potential subjects, rather than maintaining their naïveté" [Kelman, 1967, p. 10]. They both involve the subject as an active participant in the research process (which he always was) rather than assuming him to be an inanimate, mechanical responder to stimuli (which he *never* was).

For the various reasons discussed herein, it seems imperative that psychology adopt a more realistic image of the human subject—one that reflects and incorporates both the newer thinking in philosophy of science and the results of our own research on research. If we are able to cast off our prejudices and long-ingrained habits of thought and practice in research, we might even advance to the point of discovering "what everyone else already knows, that one can usually understand a person's behavior much better if one tries to find out what he thought

of the experiment and decided to do about it" [Farber, 1963, p. 187].
Perhaps, then, the best way of investigating the nature of man is to
ask him.

NOTES

1. Requests for reprints should be addressed to Duane P. Schultz, Department of Psychology, University of North Carolina at Charlotte, Charlotte, North Carolina 28205.
2. Preparation of this paper was supported by the Group Psychology Branch, Office of Naval Research, under Contract No. N00014-67-C-0131 (P001).
3. One of the journals created by splitting *JASP.*

REFERENCES

AMERICAN PSYCHOLOGICAL ASSOCIATION. Ethical standards of psychologists. *American Psychologist*, 1963, **18**: 56–60.

ARGYRIS, C. Some unintended consequences of rigorous research. *Psychological Bulletin*, 1968, **70**: 185–197.

BALDWIN, J. M. The "type-theory" of reaction. *Mind*, 1896, **5**: 81–90.

BAUMRIND, D. Some thoughts on ethics of research. *American Psychologist*, 1964, **19**: 421–423.

BINET, A. *Introduction à la psychologie expérimentale.* Paris: Alcan, 1894.

BORING, E. G. A history of introspection. *Psychological Bulletin*, 1953, **50**: 169–189.

BROWN, R. *Social psychology.* New York: Free Press, 1965.

BURT, C. The concept of consciousness. *British Journal of Psychology*, 1962, **53**: 229–242.

FARBER, I. E. The things people say to themselves. *American Psychologist*, 1963, **18**: 185–197.

FRIEDMAN, N. *The social nature of psychological research.* New York: Basic Books, 1967.

GUSTAV, A. Students' attitudes toward compulsory participation in experiments. *Journal of Psychology*, 1962, **53**: 119–125.

HALL, G. S. A children's institute. *Harper's Monthly Magazine*, 1910, CXX.

HOLMES, D. S. Amount of experience in experiments as a determinant of performance in later experiments. *Journal of Personality and Social Psychology*, 1967, **7**: 403–407.

HULL, C. L. *Principles of behavior.* New York: Appleton-Century-Crofts, 1943.

JACKSON, C. W., & Pollard, J. C. Some nondeprivation variables which influence the "effects" of experimental sensory deprivation. *Journal of Abnormal Psychology*, 1966, **71**: 383–388.

JOURARD, S. M. *Disclosing man to himself.* Princeton, N.J.: Van Nostrand, 1968.

KELMAN, H. C. Human use of human subjects: The problem of deception in social psychological experiments. *Psychological Bulletin*, 1967, **67**: 1–11.

MASLING, J. Role-related behavior of the subject and psychologist and its effects upon psychological data. *Nebraska Symposium on Motivation*, 1966, **14**: 67–103.

MASLOW, A. H. *The psychology of science.* New York: Harper & Row, 1966.

ORNE, M. T. On the social psychology of the psychological experiment: With particular reference to demand characteristics and their implications. *American Psychologist*, 1962, **17**: 776–783.

PANEL ON PRIVACY AND BEHAVIORAL RESEARCH. Privacy and behavioral research. *Science*, 1967, **155**: 535–538.

RIECKEN, H. W. A program for research on experiments in social psychology. In N. Washburne (Ed.), *Decisions, values and groups*. Vol. 2. New York: Pergamon Press, 1962.

ROKEACH, M., & Zemach, R. The pledge to secrecy: A method to assess violations. Paper presented at the meeting of the American Psychological Association, New York, August 1966.

ROSENTHAL, R. The volunteer subject. *Human Relations*, 1965, **18**: 389–406.

ROSENTHAL, R. *Experimenter effects in behavioral research*. New York: Appleton-Century-Crofts, 1966.

ROSENTHAL, R., & Rosnow, R. L. The volunteer subject. In R. Rosenthal & R. L. Rosnow (Eds.), *Artifact in behavioral research*. New York: Academic Press, 1969.

ROSNOW, R. L., & Rosenthal, R. Volunteer subjects and the results of opinion change studies. *Psychological Reports*, 1966, **19**: 1183–1187.

SMART, R. Subject selection bias in psychological research. *Canadian Psychologist*, 1966, **7a**: 115–121.

TITCHENER, E. B. Simple reactions. *Mind*, 1895, **4**: 74–81. (a)

TITCHENER, E. B. The type-theory of the simple reaction. *Mind*, 1895, **4**: 506–514. (b)

TITCHENER, E. B. Prolegomena to a study of introspection. *American Journal of Psychology*, 1912, **23**: 427–448.

U.S. DEPARTMENT OF COMMERCE. *200 million Americans*. Washington, D.C.: U.S. Government Printing Office, 1967.

WATSON, J. B. Psychology as the behaviorist views it. *Psychological Review*, 1913, **20**: 158–177.

Webster's new collegiate dictionary. Springfield, Mass.: G. & C. Merriam, 1958.

Kenneth Ring

Experimental Social Psychology:
Some Sober Questions about Some Frivolous Values

Thirty years ago, Kurt Lewin, emboldened by an almost heroic vision of psychology's potential contribution to the study of man in a social context, founded the Group Dynamics movement and thereby transformed and ultimately came to dominate the field of experimental social psychology. Through a complex interplay of theory, research, and social action, Lewin believed it possible for a discipline of social psychology not only to further the scientific understanding of man but also to advance the cause of human welfare at the same time. Even thirty years is too short a span to permit us to evaluate accurately the extent to which social psychology has actually made this dual contribution to science and society. As a substitute for this assessment, however, it may prove instructive to examine whether and to what extent social psychologists are nowadays guided by the same view of the field as moved Lewin originally to establish it. How widely shared is this Lewinian vision today? And if it is no longer the dominant conception of experimental social psychology (as I shall argue it is not), what conceptions and what values have supplanted it? These are the issues to which this paper is addressed.

Although a certain arbitrariness is necessarily entailed, I do not believe it is fundamentally misleading to distinguish at the outset three conceptions of social psychology which differ from one another primarily in terms of values that govern both the substance and the manner of research. I should like to mention and discuss relatively briefly two of these conceptions and then comment at some length on the third, which I believe embodies the ascendent values of the field today.

From *Journal of Experimental Social Psychology*, 1967, **3**: 113–123.
Reprinted with permission of author and Academic Press, Inc.

A *humanistic, action-oriented* social psychology was, of course, one of Lewin's legacies, and many social psychologists, even though their own research may not reflect it, are clearly sympathetic to and, possibly in a somewhat nostalgic way, proud of this research tradition. The large number of experimental social psychologists who are members of SPSSI (The Society for the Psychological Study of Social Issues) testifies to the "pull" of the values represented by this conception of social psychology. While this "pull" may not be sufficient to entice all of its members (including the author) out of their laboratories and into the "real world," it seems safe to assume that many social psychologists have been diverted from more academic or commercial preoccupations by the domestic unrest of the sixties and, of course, by the current Vietnam situation.

In spite of what seems to be a persisting (and possibly, in terms of numbers, a growing) concern with social issues, I question whether many experimental social psychologists would claim either that this humanistic, action-oriented conception of social psychology is regnant today or even that it ought to be. Doubtlessly in terms of conventional standards for evaluating the importance of an area, e.g., topics discussed in undergraduate social psychology courses or research studies appearing in the journals, there is scant evidence to justify the view that this is the dominant brand of contemporary social psychology. It may be objected with a certain feeling of righteousness that in the case of action-oriented research, the academic criteria cited as illustrative are strikingly irrelevant to the judgment in question. Whatever the appropriate criteria may be, I would nevertheless contend that these are *in fact* the sort of criteria in terms of which this judgment is made by most experimental social psychologists. Most of us, I submit, feel that the values represented by this conception of social psychology, while indisputably ingrained in the field, do not set the "tone" of experimental social psychology today. There is for most of us, I believe, a certain sense in which these values do not function to control much of our professional activity; I mean to return to this point in a moment.

Action research was only a part of Lewin's vision, a part, furthermore, that could not be separated from a theoretically oriented social psychology without its becoming formless and lacking in direction. Indeed, I think that one important reason why Lewin's conception of social psychology appealed to so many was precisely because it did represent a harmonious fusing of both applied and theoretical interests. The dicta commonly attributed to him—"no research without action, no action without research" and "nothing is so practical as a good theory"—clearly reveal that Lewin's intention was to effect a continuing and mutually beneficial union between these two sets of potentially antagonistic viewpoints. It is in this respect, among others, that Lewin's conception of social psychology now appears to be largely of historical interest with little correspondence to present-day realities.

It is my contention, furthermore, that social psychology circa 1967 no longer represents either an actual or a hoped-for fusion of applied and theoretical values, but that instead there is an increasing divergence between those who want social psychology to develop along humanistic, action-oriented lines and those who would prefer to see it become a more "scientific" discipline. It may well be that there is no fundamental incompatibility between these goals, but most social psychologists seem to act as if there were. Values which Lewin was able successfully to synthesize in his conception of the field now seem to be splitting social psychology into at least mildly hostile factions. Isidor Chein (1966), in fact, has recently commented on what appears to him to be a growing cleavage between scientifically oriented and practitioner-minded psychologists—a schism which, in his view, can be understood in terms of the development of certain social, political, and methodological conflicts between these two "subcultures."

While Chein's paper is an analysis of these divisive factors, my purpose here is merely to suggest that an analogous split has occurred within social psychology (we are not concerned here with the reasons for its having occurred). William McGuire, who is certainly among the most distinguished of the proponents of a *scientifically oriented* social psychology, has probably best expressed not only his own view of what social psychology ought to be, but also the low esteem in which a more humanistic social psychology is held by those who share his convictions. Speaking in 1961 at a Columbia University symposium celebrating the establishment of a department of social psychology there, McGuire said, in commenting on a paper delivered by William Schoenfeld:

> I can say of the Schoenfeld-suggested problems that they do represent the kind of work I would myself like to see done by social psychologists. In this regard, his suggestions contrast with the research suggestions of many of the other participants in this symposium. I find these suggestions too preoccupied with the Berlin wall, the urban blight, the population bomb, and the plight of the Negro in the South. Such action-oriented research strikes me as bad strategy. Approaching research from the perspective of application rather than theory, I regard as inelegant and inefficient as trying to push a piece of cooked spaghetti across the table from the back end. To these gentlemen who have suggested this applied approach, I would say quite emphatically: "We are not here to turn out consumer goods."
>
> What do I see us turning out? Let me explain with an authentic parable (adapted from Stephen Spender). I always ask an undergraduate inquirer why he feels his vocation lies in social psychology. Sometimes the student replies "I think maybe modern psychology has something to offer (or at least could be

made to offer something) on the problem of international tensions, on how to reduce them before we all blow ourselves up, and I'd like to work on it." To such I say gently: "My boy, you have a good heart. I admire you. But unfortunately I myself have little to offer you. Perhaps you should speak to one of my colleagues here. Or have you thought of the law or the ministry?" But sometimes I get that other kind of student who replies: "I'm interested because I've got a hunch that a person might be able to do neat things in social psychology by using a little matrix algebra and difference equations." To this one I say, "My boy . . . welcome home" [1965, pp. 138–139].

It is apparent that we have come a long way from Lewin. Although he would have regarded McGuire's quantitative aspirations with approbation, there is little question that Lewin would have deplored such a single-minded, even if hard-headed, approach to social psychology. The values embodied in McGuire's conception of social psychology represent, then, only one aspect of Lewin's vision. Science for science's sake was hardly Lewin's credo.

On the other hand, the conception of a scientifically oriented social psychology appeals strongly to tough-minded investigators who, while not necessarily denying an interest in problems of human welfare, feel that there is no reason why such problems must be an essential part of social psychology. For all its attractiveness, however, it is my impression that the ideal of the detached, scientifically oriented psychologist, content to refine his methods and to add systematically to our knowledge of human behavior, is not the one that is most highly relevant to the aspirations of the majority of present-day social psychologists. I am arguing that while there has indeed been a split between humanistically inclined and scientifically oriented social psychologists (each representing an aspect of Lewin's vision), in truth neither faction epitomizes the dominant values of social psychology today. I believe that whereas many investigators would claim (and quite sincerely, for the most part) that their sympathies lie with a scientifically oriented social psychology, their own professional *behavior* betrays an allegiance to a set of values quite foreign and, indeed, even antithetical to those to which they profess adherence.

These values, a consideration of which is one of the major purposes of this paper, have given rise to a brand of social psychology which I fear is likely to exert an increasingly baleful effect on the field unless it becomes openly recognized for what it is and thus becomes a legitimate issue for debate. It represents not an aspect of the Lewinian vision, but, in my judgment, a perversion of it. And because of its insidious character it is important, I think, to be as explicit as possible about not only the values underlying this view but also some of its likely consequences for the development of social psychology and the training of social psychologists. It is to these tasks that I now turn.

FUN AND GAMES IN SOCIAL PSYCHOLOGY

Experimental social psychology today seems dominated by values that suggest the following slogan: "Social psychology ought to be and is a lot of fun." The fun comes not from the learning, but from the doing. Clever experimentation on exotic topics with a zany manipulation seems to be the guaranteed formula for success which, in turn, appears to be defined as being able to effect a tour de force.[1] One sometimes gets the impression that an ever-growing coterie of social psychologists is playing (largely for one another's benefit) a game of "can you top this?" Whoever can conduct the most contrived, flamboyant, and mirth-producing experiments receives the highest score on the kudometer. There is, in short, a distinctly exhibitionistic flavor to much current experimentation, while the experimenters themselves often seem to equate notoriety with achievement.

The implicit values that produce this sort of research include the following:

1. Experiments should be as flashy and flamboyant as possible.
2. If you can think of an effective manipulation, fine; if you can think of an effective manipulation that is also amusing, even better.
3. If the topic selected for study is itself prosaic, you should reconsider; if you go ahead, at least study it cleverly.
4. Never make an obvious prediction.

Such values do make for entertaining APA presentations and jolly Ph.D. defense-of-thesis orals, but one wonders what the long-range consequences will be if this kind of social psychology continues to flourish. How likely is it, after all, that a social psychology with the implicit motto "games are the only things that ought to be taken seriously" will develop into a rigorous and respectable scientific discipline? Is it not more likely that a social psychology with frivolous values will simply remain frivolous, a source of in-group smugness and a cause of (justified) out-group derision? I should like now to consider some consequences of this fun-and-games approach to social psychology for three areas of concern to those in the field: (1) the teaching of social psychology to undergraduates, (2) graduate training in social psychology, and (3) the development of the field.

To the extent that the fun-and-games approach is reflected in our undergraduate courses in social psychology, it is likely eventually to lead to feelings of boredom, if not resentment, on the part of our students. The joke after a while begins to wear a bit thin; students are not so likely as we are to be impressed with our feats of ingenuity. They begin to wonder, with increasing impatience, whether social psychology is mainly a matter of style, not substance. What is the perceptive student to think, finally, of a field where the most renowned researchers apparently get their kicks from practicing sometimes unnecessary and frequently crass deceptions on their unsuspecting subjects? In my experience (which, though it may not be representative, is probably by no means unique), prolonged exposure to such a course is apt to breed a certain cynicism concerning the motivations of social psychologists, together with a lack of respect for the work that social psychologists do.[2] The fact that the fun-and-games approach tends to give the impression that social psychology is a field largely of fads and fashions (a point to which I shall return in another context) also contributes to these negative evaluations. In this connection, some observations made by MacLeod (1965) in his recent insightful critique of undergraduate teaching in psychology are relevant. MacLeod proposed that instead of asking ourselves whether a particular lecture was worth giving, we ought to worry whether an entire course was worthwhile. "The question I am asking," wrote MacLeod, "is in the last analysis an ethical question. Have we the moral right to ask our students to spend their time learning the stuff we teach as psychology?" [p. 345]. This, it would seem, is a question of particular pertinence to the field of social psychology these days.

There are somewhat different implications of the fun-and-games approach for the training of graduate students in social psychology. The principal dangers here are disenchantment and corruption.

Anyone who has had a hand in graduate education expects that a certain proportion of his students will sooner or later lose interest in the field and leave its ranks. Sometimes the student declares that he simply finds social psychology a good deal less relevant to his interests than he originally had thought; sometimes he claims (and this is not necessarily the same) that the field is preoccupied with trivial pursuits, or that it is too experimental, etc. One regrets losing a good student for any of these or similar reasons, of course, but one can usually console himself with the thought that it is merely a matter of noncoinciding tastes. When, however, a student justifies his departure by averring that social psychology seems to be little more than an amusing pastime to its practitioners, one feels not regret, but that acute twinge of shame that comes when he finds he has just been linked with an unrespectable enterprise, the character of which he had hitherto only dimly suspected. If it is true (as I have argued) that many uncommitted undergraduates react disdainfully to much of contemporary social psychology, is it not likely that increasing numbers of our graduate students will respond similarly and even more strongly? And how does one answer their not always implicit accusations?

Of course, there is another response that some graduate students can be expected to make to this brand of social psychology. If, somehow, their doubts concerning the value of what they are learning can be assuaged until a certain feeling of commitment to the field has been established, one would surely anticipate that they would come to share, rather than protest against, the values of their mentors. As graduate students in social psychology, they learn that rewards usually come to those who uphold the values of the group; and as the rewards increase in incidence and magnitude, it becomes more and more difficult to disavow those values, particularly when adherence to them is a prerequisite for continued success. This is a vicious cycle only if the values are perverse, of course, but it is a dangerous state of affairs in any case because of the subtlety of the entrapment process and because the consequences of the perpetuation of dubious values are far-reaching.

I should like, finally, to consider some implications of the fun-and-games approach for the development of social psychology.

Social psychology today, it seems to me, is in a state of profound intellectual disarray. There is little sense of progress; instead one has the impression of a sprawling, disjointed realm of activity where the movement is primarily outward, not upward. We approach our work with a kind of restless pioneer spirit: a new (or seemingly new) territory is discovered, explored for a while, and then usually abandoned when the going gets rough or uninteresting. We are a field of many frontiersmen, but few settlers. And to the degree that this remains true, the history of social psychology will be written in terms not of flourishing interlocking communities but of ghost towns.

I do not mean to suggest that the fun-and-games approach is itself necessarily responsible for this gadfly research tradition, but there is little doubt that it serves to perpetuate it. When the substance and manner of research are often determined by considerations of entertainingness and exotica,[3] we are almost guaranteed a social psychology in which the only continuity is one of amusement, and not purposeful direction. A *cumulative* social psychology is not likely to be a product or even a by-product of fun-and-games values. Instead, we can expect our field to continue its erratic and yet curiously stagnant course, saturated with "cute" experiments and petty quarrels between theorists who often seem more bent on establishing reputations than truth, and whose investment in their own theoretical position frequently outweighs their commitment to a (presumably) dispassionate inquiry into the nature of social behavior.[4]

The point of these remarks is a simple though important one: while nothing can guarantee that our research will be theoretically or practically significant or that it will lead to a systematic rather than a fragmented body of knowledge, fun-and-games values only divert (in a double sense) us from the attainment of these goals. Research guided by irrelevancies can only end up by being irrelevant.

Why these values should have come to pervade the field of experimental social psychology is a question that is best left for the historian of science. Nevertheless, one may at least speculate that some social psychologists share an essentially cynical view—though not necessarily always a conscious one—concerning the extent to which it is *in principle* possible to add significantly to our knowledge of social behavior through experimental methodology. This position, while hardly novel, has been expressed in a pessimistic, though not cynical, way by the philosopher of science Michael Scriven (1964), who has argued that the kind of discovery that transformed physics (e.g., quantum theory) is wholly impossible in psychology; we already know too much about human behavior for our conception of human nature to be radically altered by new data. And among social psychologists, one of the most scholarly, Fritz Heider (1958), has also commented, though again not in a cynical vein, on the extent of our prescientific knowledge of human behavior, particularly in regard to interpersonal relations. If many social psychologists do indeed share this view of their own field and feel that, because of the level of prior knowledge, their endeavors are largely refinements of this knowledge, it is understandable why *some of them* should attempt to mask the triviality of much of their research by approaching it with flamboyant *style*.[5] It is difficult for many of us to admit even the possibility that we may be spending most of our time filling in the details on a canvas already nearly complete.

CONCLUSIONS

To suggest that social psychology can be expected to make only limited contributions toward increasing our knowledge of man's social behavior should not be taken to mean that the enterprise is largely futile or is *bound* to be of trivial consequence. Even Scriven concedes that discoveries of great importance are now being made and will continue to be forthcoming. A realistic and frank assessment of what we can reasonably expect to achieve, however, would narrow the gap between professed aspirations and actual accomplishments, a gap that seems to breed cynicism as much as it does idealism. In this way (among others), one of the hypothesized roots of fun-and-games values would be undercut. There would still be plenty of room for idealism to flourish, since the fact that one cannot do all that one would hope is no reason not to do all that one can.

A periodic reassessment of the values and goals of social psychology is of course desirable, but in itself it will not necessarily rid the field of the values which, to my mind, plague it. If the reader shares my conviction that fun-and-games values are in the long run likely to be detrimental (whether or not he agrees that they are as pervasive as I have contended), there are at least three questions he ought to ask himself before initiating research:

1. Does this research really deal with a problem of some broad (not necessarily applied) human significance, or does it represent (be honest now!) merely an interest in one's own pet quiddities?
2. Is this research a part of a program of systematic inquiry (or likely to initiate one), or is it really likely to wind up a one-shot affair?
3. Does this research unavoidably entail using a deception-experiment paradigm?

Needless to say, "the appropriate" answers here do not insure that one's research will not be influenced by fun-and-games values, but it seems equally clear that such values are not *so likely* to affect systematic research directed toward significant questions concerning social behavior. I have argued that these values tend to creep in when real substance is lacking. The solution, while not foolproof, is obvious.

To sum up: whatever the reasons for their ascendence may be, the values of the fun-and-games approach are clearly out of character with the social psychology that Kurt Lewin envisaged thirty years ago. His conception, in my opinion, has not merely been compromised: it has been debased. It is time for us social psychologists to take stock of where our field is heading, and to ask ourselves whether the values for which Lewin argued so passionately are to remain only a part of the history of social psychology.

NOTES

1. It is pointless to name names here, or, what would amount to the same thing, to give specific examples to document my accusations. My purpose is not to attack particular individuals, but to call attention to certain values which seem now to permeate the field and which affect the research endeavors of many investigators. The verb "affect" was chosen in the last sentence in order to suggest that individuals may not endorse, indeed may even repudiate, these values and still be affected by them. No one who is familiar with the field of experimental social psychology will, in any case, have any difficulty in recalling examples that reflect the values under scrutiny here.

2. Although it is incidental here, there are indications that as students become more familiar with representative social psychological experimentation (through reading about it in their introductory psychology texts, for instance), they become singularly unsuitable as subjects. The short-run gains may be considerable, but it does not appear chimerical to suggest that the ultimate price of deception experiments may be the creation of extremely mistrustful and hostile subject pools. It would be ironic indeed if, by their very style of research, social psychologists were to put themselves out of business. While the issues involved are too complex to consider here, it seems to me that there is much wisdom in Brown's (1965) recent advocation of role-playing experiments: "The trouble with deception, morality aside, which it usually is, is that one cannot be sure who is being deceived. . . . Does any of our subjects ever believe us? Role-playing offers an alternative to deception. Instead of concealing experimental manipulations one can reveal them and ask subjects to help" [p. 580]. Kelman (1966), in an able and provocative paper in which he discusses some of the ethical and methodological consequences of deception experiments, has also recommended and outlined some nondeception experimental techniques that would appear to have considerable merit for the investigation of certain kinds of problems.

3. It would appear that the fun-and-games stylists assume a high correlation between the intrinsic interest of a study and its importance. While there is of course no necessary reason why this relationship should hold, it is easy to slip into an equally specious line of argument which denigrates any research that has either a high shock or high interest value. It should be clear that we are not objecting per se to studies of this kind, but only to the values which *often* (not always) give rise to them. Milgram's systematic work on destructive obedience (1963, 1964a, 1965a, 1965b), for example, although it raises serious ethical questions concerning the limits of laboratory experimentation (Baumrind, 1964; Milgram, 1964b), seems to me a good instance of research in social psychology which is both interesting and significant.

4. It should be apparent that many of the criticisms made in this paper of experimental social psychology apply to other branches of psychology as well—and, indeed, to some areas of the behavioral sciences, too. Social psychologists are hardly unique in their having come under the influence of fun-and-games values. For a pungent examination of these and related issues for psychology generally, see the recent paper by Dunnette (1966).

5. It is of interest to note that, in response to a question addressed to him after the talk in which this view of the inherent limits of psychology was propounded, Scriven remarked, "Pure research in social psychology is among the most unproductive fields of human endeavor today," ranking only "with mathematical economics as being a kind of exciting game for people that like exciting games in this particular field, i.e., nobody except those who do it" [p. 200].

REFERENCES

BAUMRIND, D. Some thoughts on ethics of research: After reading Milgram's "Behavioral study of obedience." *American Psychologist*, 1964, **19**: 421–423.

BROWN, R. *Social psychology*. New York: Free Press, 1965.

CHEIN, I. Some sources of divisiveness among psychologists. *American Psychologist*, 1966, **21**: 333–342.

DUNNETTE, M. D. Fads, fashions, and folderol in psychology. *American Psychologist*, 1966, **21**: 343–352.

HEIDER, F. *The psychology of interpersonal relations*. New York: Wiley, 1958.

KELMAN, H. C. The human use of human subjects: The problem of deception in social-psychological experiments. Unpublished mimeographed paper, University of Michigan, 1966.

MACLEOD, R. B. The teaching of psychology and the psychology we teach. *American Psychologist*, 1965, **20**: 344–352.

McGUIRE, W. J. Discussion of William N. Schoenfeld's paper. In O. Klineberg & R. Christie (Eds.), *Perspectives in social psychology*. New York: Holt, Rinehart, and Winston, 1965. Pp. 135–140.

MILGRAM, S. Behavioral study of obedience. *Journal of Abnormal and Social Psychology*, 1963, **67**: 371–378.

MILGRAM, S. Group pressure and action against a person. *Journal of Abnormal and Social Psychology*, 1964, **69**: 137–143. (a)

MILGRAM, S. Issues in the study of behavioral obedience: A reply to Baumrind. *American Psychologist*, 1964, **19**: 848–852. (b)

MILGRAM, S. Liberating effects of group pressure. *Journal of Personality and Social Psychology*, 1965, **1**: 127–134. (a)

MILGRAM, S. Some conditions of obedience and disobedience to authority. In M. Fishbein & I. Steiner (Eds.), *Current studies in social psychology*. New York: Holt, Rinehart, and Winston, 1965. Pp. 243–262. (b)

SCRIVEN, M. Views of human nature. In T. Wann (Ed.), *Behaviorism and phenomenology*. Chicago: University of Chicago Press, 1964. Pp. 163–183.

William J. McGuire

Some Impending Reorientations in Social Psychology:
Some Thoughts Provoked by Kenneth Ring

The creative tension between basic and applied research gives rise from time to time to feelings of uneasiness such as those recently expressed by Kenneth Ring (1967). Just as anxiety in the individual can have the beneficial function of signaling an imbalance among the contending aspects of his personality, so such expressions of concern about current emphases in our scientific establishment can be a useful warning sign that the dynamic equilibrium between basic and applied research has been disturbed by a temporary perturbation too far in one direction. Ring discerns a current stress in favor of basic, theory-oriented research. His choice of some paragraphs of mine to illustrate this overemphasis is apparently the reason why I have been asked to comment on his article, even though no offense was, I feel, implied and none certainly is inferred. It seems undeniable to me that, as Ring contends, the basic and applied streams of research in psychology have been flowing progressively further apart during the past ten or fifteen years, and that the emphasis on basic research has been increasing. I would also agree (though I recognize this point to be more debatable than the foregoing) that these trends have proceeded to an extent that is unfortunate. Indeed, I am in agreement with most of the substance of Ring's paper and differ mainly in that I regard the undesirable trends which he points out as less of a worry than he does. His comments do make me want to describe publicly some coming trends in social psychology that I have been urging privately for some time. Hence my comments constitute an extension, rather than a refutation, of Ring's remarks. My emphases fall on somewhat different points from his, and

From *Journal of Experimental Social Psychology*, 1967, **3**: 124–139.
Reprinted with permission of author and Academic Press, Inc.

58

I do not repeat all of his theses, so Ring's paper deserves a rereading in its own right lest these additional points of his be lost.

Where I would disagree with Ring is on his seeming expectation that the separation of the two streams of research and the overemphasis on basic research show signs of being continued and even accentuated for the foreseeable future in social psychology. I would like to argue here that, on the contrary, we shall in social psychology soon be witnessing a remelding of basic and applied research with increasing attention to the latter. I shall argue that social psychology is moving towards a "best of both worlds" solution in which we shall be doing theory-oriented research in natural settings. The trend which I discern and describe here is, I believe, due to technical and social forces, without conscious intent or even knowledge on the part of the social psychology researchers.

Tension between basic and applied research is no recent development. From a short historical perspective, it might seem that the very notion of basic research has only recently emerged, made possible in an affluent society that can seek knowledge for its own sake as well as knowledge for use (we must recognize, however, that even knowledge for its own sake has a use, an aesthetic use, as I was contending in the 1961 talk cited by Ring). However, from a longer historical perspective we see that, far from basic research's being an epiphenomenon of applied work which emerged only when the affluence brought about by practical technological advances made such a middle-class luxury possible, there are signs that basic research may have even preceded the applied. Such appears to have been the situation in the Ionian world that was the birthplace of Western scientific civilization. Thales, the first of the Greek thinkers, or at least the first of them who talked, and the other early physicists seem to be strictly speculative theorists whose work promised little practical dividends. Apparently the tension between basic and applied work was felt even in those pre-Socratic days, since legend has it that Thales once responded to the derision of his follow townsmen by using his astronomical knowledge to corner the olive market and make a small fortune during a bad weather year, just to show them that his neglect of action-oriented work was by choice and not necessity. Thales was then evidently allowed to go about his basic research until that accursed night when, as the Thracian maidens recited laughingly, "He fell to his death down a well while gazing at the nighttime sky." Perhaps the father of basic research, like many of his followers since, far from taking offense at the maidens' derisive remarks, would settle for them happily as his epitaph.

The anecdote illustrates the two-front war with which, even today, we social psychologists are confronted. If our work stays close to the basic, theory-oriented pole, we are liable to laymen's abuse for engaging in a Mandarin activity that is of interest only to our fellow social psychologists and consists in obscuring commonsense truths and fallacies behind professional jargon. If, on the other hand, we go too close to the applied, action-oriented pole, we are exposed to the abuse of the establishment who complain that we have been seeking narrow and possibly incorrect *ad hoc* solutions to specific problems, at a time when more basic, theoretically oriented research is necessary to allow a broader advance in the near future. The crux of the controversy seems to be whether one should choose his next step in research in order to clarify a theoretical issue or to guide action in the natural environment. It is this formulation of the problem which leads me to the optimistic prediction that we are converging towards a solution that involves testing theoretically derived hypotheses in natural settings. In such a solution the basic need of theory development would be served, in that problems for testing would be derived with the aim of developing and testing theory; while defining and testing the hypotheses in natural environments would clarify their relevance to the real world and provide directions for social action, either by forethought or at least by what is ludicrously termed "spin-off." Admittedly, this "compromise" admits the priority of theory-oriented research, and shows that my first loyalty lies with this side of the argument; however, it recognizes and provides a partial corrective for the current neglect of applied, action-oriented research in a social psychology in which only laboratory manipulated experimentation has been receiving the imprimatur of the establishment.

In brief, what I see coming for social psychology is a continuing emphasis on theory development and testing, but an increasing shift from regarding laboratory manipulated experiments on college sophomores as the only approved method of testing these theoretical deductions. Rather, I foresee that the ingenuity now exercised in creating laboratory surrogates for the real world will be steadily replaced by equal ingenuity exerted in utilizing the natural environment as a field in which to test these deductions. The solace that I see this prospect offering for those who are concerned with the social uses of science is that a theory tested in the real world is almost certain to prove relevant to the problems existing in the natural environment. Otherwise, the theory will wither away as untestable, or will be revealed as unrealizable under current conditions and hence will force its utilizers to decide whether it is sufficiently attractive to deserve continuing development even though it seems irrelevant to the currently available natural environment. What I will do here is review: first, some of the forces that I see making basic theory-oriented research possible and desirable in natural settings; and secondly, some forces of a more negative type that I see making research under artificial laboratory conditions less attractive to social psychologists in coming years.

ATTRACTIONS OF TESTING HYPOTHESES IN NATURAL ENVIRONMENTS

When I speak of hypothesis testing in natural environments, I have in mind several different types of studies. The least radical departure from the conventional laboratory experiment is carrying out manipulative experiments in natural settings, as described some time ago by French and often carried out by Sherif. But I include also more radical departures, such as observational work in natural settings where one does not have the possibility of manipulating the independent variable, and I look forward even to work with archival data. I shall review here some of the recent advances that make such an approach to hypothesis testing not only possible but attractive, though limitations of space will allow me only to indicate in general what I have in mind. We can pass quite briefly over doing manipulatory experiments in natural settings, since this involves only a slight extrapolation beyond our present methodology and allows employment of traditional statistics such as analysis of variance. Even here, however, it is useful and encouraging to note that the availability of sophisticated computer programs is allowing us to employ these traditional analytic techniques even within the limitations of controls that are imposed by having to work in the real world. Thus we can now do analyses of variance relatively conveniently, even when confronted by those onerous problems of unequal N's and contaminated variables that tend to arise in doing research in the "dirty" real world.

Current improvements are more obvious when we turn to more adventurous departures of hypothesis testing in natural environments, in which we can observe, but not manipulate, the independent variables. I have in mind here recent advances in research design and analysis that make possible the detection of causal direction in cases where the several factors in the situation are covarying due to factors beyond our control. Relevant here are such recent advances as the work by Campbell and Stanley on quasi-experimental designs, and work outside psychology such as cross-lag panel designs and other mathematical techniques proposed by Blalock and Coleman.

Still another line of methodological progress that allows us to do theory-oriented research in natural environments is provided by advances in mathematical modeling and computer simulation, illustrated elegantly in the work by Abelson on the resolution of community controversy over fluoridating water supplies. This work on mathematical modeling and especially on computer simulation in the social psychological area is described in the forthcoming chapters by Abelson in the new edition of the Lindzey and Aronson *Handbook of Social Psychology*, and in Volume III of Berkowitz's *Advances in Experimental Social Psychology*. It is interesting to note in the latter volume (as in the present *Journal*) that the magic word "experimental" is not defined narrowly to exclude hypothesis testing in natural settings, or even testing in natural settings without manipulation by the experimenter of the independent variables. It is a happy portent of the peaceful emergence of the new development that I am predicting here that "experimental" is taken in its etymologically correct meaning of "to test, to try"—rather than in the misuse of it sometimes found in the less perspicacious (or less classically educated) followers of the establishment, who interpreted it as referring only to manipulational research or, still more erroneously, only to manipulative research in the laboratory.

Still another opening to the real world for social psychological research is allowed by the greater availability of nationwide samples. In the area of survey research this greater availability is provided by at least two recent developments. One is the creation of caravan-type nationwide surveys in which a number of researchers, each of whom needs only a few minutes of data, can combine to test their notions at a manageable cost. Some of the better nationwide sampling agencies now conduct such composite nationwide surveys. A second line of progress along these lines, whose full realization is still a few years in the future, is the establishment of a standardized inventory for a continuing nationwide sampling and resampling to collect longitudinal data on some issues of basic social science significance. These developments are all still underdeveloped and so far have been discussed largely in terms of opinion surveys. However, as they become more utilized I believe that the opportunities they offer, not just to ask questions but also to vary experimentally the independent variables presented to the respondents, will become increasingly recognized.

A final technological advance to which I shall call attention in this review of modern developments facilitating hypothesis testing in natural settings is the increasing availability of data archives relevant to the social sciences. An adequate review of this resource would require considerable space. I need mention here only the several forms that these archives take. There is the interuniversity consortium of public opinion survey results from the United States and from several other parts of the world. Testing one's hypothesis against these data which were collected at an earlier time admittedly requires more efficient and sophisticated procedures for retrieval and analysis of the information contained in these massive archives, but work even on this topic is proceeding at a number of institutions (e.g., Stone's work on using the General Inquirer to retrieve data from opinionnaires). Besides the archives dealing with survey opinion data, other archives (such as ones at Yale and MIT) are collecting background data on national and subnational units that will also inevitably be exploited by social psychology theorists. Consumer panel records and other business data are being put to theory-testing use by Howard and others. Some are culling the United States Government's records for archival data that might be of use to social scientists. Except possibly in the latter development, and in some work on compiling county-by-county voting statistics since the beginning of the United States Government, one crying lack in these data archives is the neglect of a long-range historical perspective. Possibly this gap will also be filled in coming years, though providing satisfactory data of this type would require a cooperation by historians which they do not yet seem motivated to make. However, just as the psychologists, sociologists, and political scientists became progressively oriented towards massive data analysis for theory testing, so too, I believe, will the historian recognize as part of his discipline a speciality that tests historical theorizing against massive data as well as by incisive analysis of single cases. Meanwhile, we can make do, as McClelland has shown, by being our own Sunday historians. The adequate exploitation of these very expensively compiled archives requires that we make knowledge of their existence more widespread and that we develop techniques of analysis more sophisticated than are now available.

Besides these technological factors, which will make hypothesis testing in natural environments more feasible, there are some additional, metapsychological trends which are also making research in the real world somewhat more attractive to sensitive social psychologists. I have in mind here the increasing commitment among the intelligentsia in the United States, which is exhibited in the increased concern about social affairs visible in the current generation of students in contrast to the silent generation of the 1950s. The concern is seen even in their elders who are already part of the academic establishment, as Ring points out. It is not difficult to find a number of reasons for this trend. Certainly the development of nuclear weapons and the nuclear testing issue, and the terrifying war threat that they involve, played a part, as did the unignorable issues of equal rights, the Vietnamese war, etc. The role played by academic circles in our national administration became more visible if not actually greater during the Kennedy Administration than it had previously been. These trends in the United States have simply followed earlier movements in France and elsewhere in Europe, where during the Occupation the intelligentsia achieved an increasing degree of commitment and concern regarding social affairs which has been maintained during the postwar period.

Along this same line is the pressure of self-interest in obtaining research funds from the government. Just as, in the words of Francis Bacon, he who has wife and child has given hostages to fortune, so we social psychologists, who like other scientists, have grown accustomed to accepting and depending upon generous research funds from the government, now find ourselves having given hostages to the federal agencies that dole out these resources. Perhaps only a few of us would have the stamina and the ingenuity to continue our research efforts by other means, when pressures are put on us by these agencies to direct our current efforts more towards applied, action-oriented research. It takes no direct access to the inner circle of government to perceive increasing political interest in how and why research funds are being spent. As long as these funds were doled out largely on the advice of the scientific establishment itself, basic research fared very well. Now that the leadership in the Executive and Legislative branches of Government has taken a direct interest in the appropriation of these sizable research funds, there is more interest in the payoff to those outside the separate sciences themselves. While I do not despair of our being able to justify expenditures for basic research even on grounds of public interest, I do suggest as a compromise solution that we continue to do basic theory-oriented research, as far as hypothesis derivation is concerned, but that we think somewhat more of testing these hypotheses in natural settings rather than in laboratory situations.

A final attraction of doing research in natural settings, with its greater likelihood of applied fallout, is that such applied work offers the possibility of avoiding some of the mass frustrations of scientists. What I have in mind here is my suspicion that as far as basic research is concerned, good work is not enough. It simply clutters our journals and makes it harder to find the only thing that really counts in basic research, which is work of the first order of excellence. Unfortunately, even in social psychology most of the researchers are good rather than truly excellent. The result is that their work does little to advance basic theorizing, thus condemning them to a frustrated or self-deluding existence. It is my intuition that the practical, applied fallout of research in natural settings will have its social uses even if it is only good. This possibility for service gives a greater opportunity for those who cannot attain excellence to yet find satisfaction in social psychological research.

SOME GROWING PROBLEMS REGARDING LABORATORY RESEARCH

Above I have considered the more positive reasons for my prediction that the future would see more social psychological research being carried out in natural settings rather than in the laboratory even when this meant that nature, rather than the experimenter, would manipulate the independent variable. Now, I turn to the other side of the coin and consider the negative reasons for this prediction, reasons which have to do with some growing problems concerning the laboratory manipulational experimentation that constitutes the bulk of current good social psychological research. Probably the most important of the difficulties is the growing realization among laboratory experimenters that our work is troubled by artifacts that make generalization and interpretation difficult. Ring himself has expressed concern of this type. I merely have to mention such terms as "experimenter bias," "demand character," "evaluation apprehension," "guinea pig reaction," "social desirability," etc., to indicate to the reader what I have in mind here. A book being prepared by Robert Rosenthal and Ralph Rosnow is devoted entirely to artifacts in the social psychological laboratory. Usually correlated with laboratory experimentation is the problem of subject representativeness. We have almost grown used to the embarrassment occasioned by the concentration of our research on college students. The proverbial "psychology of the college sophomore" is more worrisome as to generalizability for the social psychologist than for those working in perception, learning, etc.

I must also mention, uncomfortable as it is, the ethical concerns that have been increasingly expressed regarding laboratory experimentation in social psychology. Most serious in my opinion is the use of noxious conditions in our experimental manipulations, including painful or dangerous physiological treatments or anxiety-producing and potentially harmful psychological manipulations. Other complaints, not without some justification, involve our lying to our subjects and the inevitable degrading interpersonal relations that develop in our deception experimentation. Still other criticism is aimed at the invasion of the subject's privacy in our research. The latter problem will by no means be solved and may even be aggravated by our doing our research in natural settings. However, the first two problems can be largely circumvented when the social psychology theorist develops the will and the skill to test his hypotheses in a real world that he never made, and takes experimental advantage of natural manipulations that he can neither produce nor control. It is also possible that the more obvious social relevance allowed by doing work in natural settings will offer more justification for the invasion of privacy that will inevitably occur in the field as well as in the laboratory. Many of us feel that the ethical problems here do not involve absolute answers. By this I mean that we must evaluate the possible benefits as well as the cost of the experimentation. I do not rule out absolutely the possibility that there are times when our work might be significant enough that we should be allowed to continue it even though some limited harm could possibly result. It is too easy to condemn current laboratory manipulational researchers, as has been done at a recent meeting which I attended, where someone complained that the very expression "we have run some subjects today" reveals an almost Eichmann-like abstraction about one's research and a failure to appreciate that the participants in one's experiment are real people. In response to this position, I feel we must also be concerned about an equally questionable ethical position epitomized by the words, "I have *not* run any subjects today." It seems to me all too simple to decide that it is safer to do no research. We must strictly censor our own work and find ways of maximizing gains and minimizing costs to some point at which we can ethically go ahead, perhaps inevitably with fear and trembling. But go on with our work we must, or else we must change our field. It seems to me that doing theoretically inspired work in natural settings furnishes some possibility that we can proceed ahead with somewhat less anguish than the more sensitive people in our field are now experiencing regarding our laboratory work.

At the risk of seeming somewhat facetious, I would suggest still a third reason for predicting a shift from the laboratory to the natural environment as the setting for social psychological research in the coming years. Laboratory work has become the "OK" approach in the psychological establishment and new people in the area are flocking to it, as Ring has himself pointed out with some concern regarding its consequents. I would venture the opinion that this concentration of work has reached the point of diminishing returns, and that inevitably the more adventurous people in the field are beginning to deviate into other approaches such as doing research in natural settings. Once these adventurous innovators (who are actually repelled by manipulatory lab work just because it has the establishment's acceptance as the current paradigm) try out the natural environment for their research, I feel that the favorable forces mentioned above will yield them considerably more success than was offered by previous deviations into the natural environment as recently as ten years ago. As the watchful waiters view the innovators' success from the acceptable premises of the laboratory, the premature elder statesmen and perspicacious Young Turks who are entrenched in the establishment will follow them into the natural environment and these stars will soon be followed by a partial redeployment into this new setting.

Let me stress, though, that the redeployment into the natural environment will be partial. It seems to me that the manipulational laboratory experiment is just too efficient to ever be dropped completely in social psychological research. Indeed, I think the bulk of our research will remain in the laboratory, though I may be prejudiced here by the fact that my own research has in the past involved the laboratory manipulational approach exclusively and I shall probably continue to stress this approach. Still, I am not so wedded to a methodology inspired by physics that I have become too biased to appreciate the methodology suggested by astronomy. In the next section, I would like to describe how our Ph.D. training programs in social psychology might be augmented to allow a more open methodology.

SOME NEEDED INNOVATIONS IN DOCTORAL PROGRAMS IN SOCIAL PSYCHOLOGY

Let me avail myself of the unpleasantly warlike analogue of the generals who unwisely trained their soldiers to fight the previous war, and point out that we social psychologists do not want to be in the position of training our doctoral students to carry out only the kind of research that predominated during the previous wave of progress in our field. In doctoral programs, we hope rather to train students to exploit possibilities for future advances. If the analysis I have given above is correct, then it seems we are in danger of playing the role of the backward-looking generals in the anecdote, in that our current doctoral programs are training students for the most part exclusively to do manipulatory laboratory experimentation. There may be a few centers where doctoral training also includes some hypothesis-testing research in natural settings, or at least survey research. It is my clinical judgment, however, that even in the latter departments, nonlaboratory experimentation is quickly perceived by the student as being taught as a secondary approach for second-class citizens when the royal road of manipulatory laboratory experimentation is somehow blocked. I propose that doctoral programs be strengthened in two directions in order to correct both for the growing separation of theory-oriented from action-oriented research and for the overemphasis on the former, so as to avoid some of the unfortunate features which Ring has cited in current social psychological research. Augmenting our programs to include hypothesis testing in natural settings and by means of archival data would hasten the solution I have proposed here—testing theoretically derived hypotheses in the real world—to allow the two streams of research to be reunited and attain, in a sense, the best of both worlds.

Such a new program would involve no derogation of laboratory manipulational research. But it would entail communicating to the students that basic research in natural settings, even without experimenter manipulations, is not only possible but praiseworthy. It would involve teaching new techniques for research in natural settings over and above those already taught regarding laboratory experimentation, and it would require also that we have worthy examples of research in these natural settings to demonstrate to students that work of the highest quality can be done using these techniques. Hence, to say that these procedures must be added to our pedagogical programs reveals only part of the burden that we must take on ourselves. In addition, we would also have to utilize and exploit these new procedures in our own research. Indeed, actually utilizing natural settings in our own research, must, I suspect, precede introducing such research techniques into our doctoral programs in which research apprenticeships now play a part. Here I shall only list succinctly the kinds of techniques I have in mind for these two areas of hypothesis testing: research in natural settings and research by means of archival data.

As regards techniques for testing hypotheses in natural settings, I have in mind training our students somewhat more fully than in the past in such techniques as participant observation (currently more emphasized in anthropology and sociology), and in using "unobtrusive measures," to use the term by Webb, Campbell *et al.*, that allow us to detect the impact of variables on subjects' responses in terms of the traces these responses leave without disturbing the subjects' ongoing behavior with our measuring instruments. Perhaps both basic and applied research would gain if we and our students exercised as much ingenuity in devising such unobtrusive measures as we now do in trying to simulate the real world in the laboratory. We also need to augment our courses in experimental design and statistics for social psychologists, to give more attention to techniques that allow us to tease our causal directions among covariants in situations where we do not have the resources to manipulate one of the factors. I have in mind here such procedures as the cross-lag panel analyses, quasi-experimental designs, etc., as described by Campbell, by Coleman, by Vroom, and others. Also, as mentioned above, we owe it to ourselves and our students to become more familiar with computer programs that allow us to analyze data involving dirty designs such as analysis of variance with unequal N's, covariance analysis to control for contamination factors, and trend analysis with unequally spaced intervals, all of which problems arise more often when we have to fit our research into natural settings than when we fashion the laboratory environment to fit our design. Procedures are now available that allow us to test hypotheses involving such nonideal conditions without resorting to an unacceptable amount of computational tedium.

We also owe it to at least some of our students that they become familiar with techniques for computer simulation of psychological and social situations, both prognostic and process simulation. If resources do not allow having a full-time specialist in this relatively esoteric technique in our own department, we might look for an interdepartmental consortium to support such a slot, perhaps in the computer center, in a department of applied mathematics, or even in the business school. At least we should be aware that the SSRC has a program allowing students and faculty members to visit centers that do have such resources for a brief period of time for pedagogic purposes. Again, when it comes to obtaining nationwide samples, it is hardly advisable that every Ph.D. program in social psychology set up its own apparatus for nationwide surveys such as currently exist at the SRC at Michigan or at the NORC at Chicago; however, we should acquaint ourselves and our students with the existence of the caravan-type surveys and with the impending creation of the reiterated nationwide survey to collect longitudinal data of interest to the behavioral sciences. Also, we should relax our thinking and communicate this relaxation to our students to the extent of considering testing our hypotheses in terms of such nationwide survey type research, rather than simply in terms of laboratory manipulations of college sophomores. We must also give thought to working miniature experiments into these "surveys."

As regards utilizing archival data for hypothesis testing, we again should augment our training programs to include such relatively quiescent techniques as content analysis, which shows renewed signs of life. We should also become aware of techniques for the statistical analysis of mass data such as seem now to have become almost exclusively the property of the econometricians. The perceptive social psychologists should be aware that certain advances have been made in the neighboring discipline of econometrics that deserve closer examination (though Ring seems perhaps to follow Scriven in disenchantment with some econometric work).

Again, we should acquaint ourselves and our students with the already accumulated archival resources that have been compiled at a number of universities at rather distressing expense. These archives are readily accessible not only at their home university but also to people at other institutions at relatively modest costs. Archives have already been set up for opinion data from both the United States and elsewhere at Centers established by Campbell at Michigan, Rossi at Chicago, Glock at Berkeley, and Hastings at Williams, to mention only some of the operational sites. Somewhat less relevant to the usual interests of social psychologists, but still worthy of consideration, are the archives of data other than public opinion, e.g., data in government archives and data on national characteristics, such as are contained in the Yale political data survey and the similar survey at MIT. Bauer has just edited a book dealing with such social indicators. No less useful than these somewhat impersonal institutional endeavors is the work of some individual entrepreneurs of social science who have established their own private data archives to test hypotheses on theoretical issues in which they are interested. I have in mind the data on national characteristics constructed by such individuals as Richardson, Rummel, and the Feierabends to test notions about interpersonal and international conflict. In a way, such smaller-scale efforts are perhaps a better pedagogic tool for showing students the useful interplay between theory testing and archival data amassing. I am not, of course, suggesting that every student be trained to amass his own data archive. I am suggesting that students be made aware of the existence of archival resources that would serve to test and sharpen their own theorizing, and that they also be presented with examples from our own work or the work of others that demonstrate the usefulness of this expensive resource. We should also give further thought to developing methodological techniques both tactical and strategic that would exploit the opportunities afforded by the availability of archival data.

It should be understood that I am not suggesting that each doctoral candidate be taught, in addition to all the techniques of manipulative laboratory experimentation that we now teach, all the techniques for hypothesis testing in natural settings and all those for testing hypotheses by means of archival data. The experienced teacher becomes aware that a technique is taught in a useable way only when the student experiences its utility by actual research and not simply by classroom presentation, and that the need for depth limits the possibility of breadth. What I am proposing is that both via classroom presentation and through the availability of apprenticeship training in these matters, we should give some attention to techniques for testing in natural environments and with archival data, as well as by means of laboratory manipulations. It will also be evident to the perspicacious reader that many of my suggested strengthenings require the reduction of the currently existing walls between conventional departments, including psychology on the one hand and sociology, economics, and even anthropology on the other. I do not apologize for or hide the fact that I am suggesting lowering the conventional barriers which now provide familiar and reassuring guidelines as to what we or our students are expected to know. Admittedly, good fences make good neighbors, and those who wish to be in a university that is as comfortable as an old shoe, rather than to feel the zest and pain of striving for excellence through leading new intellectual advances, should stand warned that the alterations I am suggesting here would to some extent involve disturbing the peace, and might also require that some old dogs learn some new tricks.

THE FUN-AND-GAMESMEN

My remarks above are occasioned by Ring's main contention, that the theory-oriented and action-oriented streams of social psychological research are growing progressively further apart with increasing emphasis on the former. While this theme underlies most of his paper, a secondary theme emerges much more explicitly in his later pages. Ring points out a trend that he seems to feel is one of the most objectionable by-products of the separation and of the emphasis on theory-oriented, laboratory manipulational work. Ring expresses considerable concern and chagrin about the increasing visibility in the area of social psychological laboratory research of the "fun-and-games" approach.

He seems to feel that some of the experimental social psychology establishment and a good number of their followers derive more gratification from their clever deceptions, ingenious laboratory manipulations, and flashy gimmicks, than from either the advancement of psychological theory or the providing of directives for action. Ring graciously does not point his finger at any individuals so I cannot be absolutely certain of what he does have in mind, but I think I get the message and agree that the spectacle he is describing does exist and is less than completely admirable. However, I do not feel as much concern about these developments as do he and some other commentators. When in the recent past I have heard similar complaints from my fellow social psychologists, it often seemed to me that their ire was directed less at the use of clever manipulations and ingenious deceptions than at the fact that the social psychologists using them derived some pleasure from their flamboyant happenings. In this reaction I am reminded of Mencken's description of the Puritan as someone who is worried that somewhere, somehow, someone might be enjoying himself. I wish that these fun-and-gamesmen would find motivation for their work in some nobler human impulse than play. However, if this must be their impulse then I am happy to see that they are happy.

Einstein has written, in an introduction to a book by Max Planck, something to the effect that in the temple of science there are many worshipers who come there for a great variety of motives, and that if somehow all those who come for financial gain or the pleasant life or social recognition were suddenly turned away, very few would remain to worship out of sheer love for the advancement of science *per se*, and that Max Planck would be among the very few in this latter category. I fear that the true believer would be as rare in psychology as in physics. But the lesson I draw is that we must be tolerant of the motivation that brings laborers to this vineyard. If a man is doing good work I refrain from asking whether he is doing it to develop theory, to solve the world's problems, to make a living, to stay out of the army, or to satisfy his impulse to play games. I am more obsessed by the need to see something worthwhile being done than by the need that it be done for the highest possible motivation. At the U.S. Infantry School at Fort Benning, Georgia, they used to teach as the final tactical decision, "In case of doubt, do anything, but do something." If there are some social psychology gamesmen who do their work only because of the play aspect, then let us say to them, "Social psychology, anyone?"

I must admit that some of those who express concern about the fun-and-gamesmen are motivated by more than the puritanical instinct of resenting the seeming enjoyment these people obtain from their work. There seems to be some fear that a Gresham's law might be operating and that the fun-and-gamesmen might be corrupting or driving out the sterling youth, especially by the gamesmen's claiming that the remainder of social psychology is floundering around in unimaginative, obvious research while they alone are doing the exciting, imaginative, and non-obvious work. Such a stance is indeed worrisome if we feel that students are likely to be permanently corrupted by displays of surface brilliance that sacrifice substantively lasting and important research. However, a number of pedagogic instincts lead me, first, to trust to quality in the long run and, secondly, to hesitate to attack a group of researchers with a different philosophy from my own.

I would urge, rather, that each of us try to do the best work he can and leave off attacking those whose predilections about what good work is are different from our own, even when these others take the offensive. I have confidence that there is a free market of ideas in which the best work wins out in the end and the best workers receive the most emulation. Furthermore, in my own experience with my fun-and-games colleagues and friends, I have found that argumentation only strengthens their stubbornness in their peculiar orientation, and I suspect that abuse causes them to cling to it longer than they might otherwise have done. On the other hand, it seems to me that those in the group who have been allowed to work in peace have tended to develop out of the gamesman approach. Furthermore, I am "no more enamored to" the notion that good research has to be dull than I am to the contention that only interesting flashy research is good. I would suggest as a therapeutic measure to those observers who are so dismayed by the spectacle of the gamesmen that they can no longer constrain themselves from comment that they merely speak with the words De Gaulle used when he confronted the revolting colonists of Algiers with the Delphic utterance, "Je vous comprends," and proceed with their own enterprises. In the long run, class will tell. Let each of us do his own work and leave negative comments about others' work for more desperate situations than the one that now confronts us.

In the last analysis, it must be admitted that as regards the issues with which we have dealt here, involving the yin and yang of basic and applied research, and particularly this last touchy issue which Ring has brought up about fun-and-gamesmen, there is much to be said on both sides. This is not to say that we must be neutral between good and evil but simply that we must expect no final solution. Rather, as one or another trend becomes overemphasized, we must be prepared to provide the corrective. It is not to be expected that the appropriate pressure to be applied in this decade will be the same as will be appropriate ten years from now. I must say that I personally am in sympathy with many of the opinions that Ring seems to express here (though one might wonder on reading my remarks whether, with a sympathizer like me, he needs opponents). However, for reasons I have tried to outline here, I am less worried than he by either the overemphasis of laboratory manipulative studies or by the visibility of the fun-and-gamesmanship approach. The correctives are already visible on the horizon.

Perhaps I have overreacted to Ring's comments on frivolous experimental social psychology because I have heard more complaints of late than I feel are called for about the purported dominance of our field by the fun-and-gamesmen. The ubiquity of these complaints makes me wonder whether the "dominant" group or the complainers are the persecuted minority. Still, I must admire Ring for taking a stance against what must seem to him to be the establishment consensus regarding social psychology. I see him assuming an important and risky role similar to that advocated by Simone Weil in her counterbalance notion, where she suggested that there are those whose vocation it is, when two forces appear in contention, to jump onto the scale on the weaker side and hope that the occasional incorrectness of their choice is excused by the purity of their motives. On this vital matter of purity of motives, I have learned, both in the psychological laboratory and outside of it, that the best policy is to impute the highest purity of motives to those who are working with us (or even against us) and to communicate this interpretation to the other. It seems to me that when we present the actor with a social reality in which we attribute his behavior to the purest of motives we create a "self-realizing prophesy" situation, in which the actor comes to accept this imputation as his own reality and aspires to adopt the imputed motives as his actual basis of action in the future. Perhaps by imputing to both the fun-and-games men and their attackers the purest of motives we can create a moral climate that will permit a rapprochement between them and an escalation in the quality of the research of both parties.

PART TWO

A Case Study: Milgram's Research on Obedience

The research of Stanley Milgram on obedience has achieved a degree of acclaim without precedent in experimental social psychology. Historically, his work represents an extension of the pioneering efforts of Asch, Sherif, and Festinger in the analysis of social influence and conformity. On its substantive merit, the research has received lavish praise, e.g., the 1965 prize awarded for the outstanding contribution to sociopsychological research by the American Association for the Advancement of Science. Yet, perhaps because of the popularity of his work, Milgram's experiments—and Milgram himself—have been the target of an imposing array of criticism, on ethical as well as methodological bases. A number of these problems are considered in their more general implications in Parts Three and Four of this book. There is, however, value in first encountering these issues in vivo—in the context of an original research report—and the reader may profit in his own attempt to anticipate the substantive, methodological, and ethical developments that have evolved from Milgram's report of his findings.

Ethical issues in psychological research can be discussed from a variety of perspectives—invasion of privacy (e.g., Ruebhausen & Brim, 1965), the use of deception (e.g., Kelman, Part Three), manipulation of the human being as research subject (e.g., Jourard, Part One), etc. The most predictable call for ethical debate, however, derives from those experiments which expose, either in fact or via deception, the subject to physical or mental anguish. Countless experiments can be cited in which subjects have received (or administered) electric shock, received fictitious or true reports of inadequacy on an intelligence or personality test, failed at a task, been exposed to the sight or sound of another in distress, been insulted or related to harshly by the experimenter or his accomplice, etc. Obviously there is a considerable range of such experimental treatment. From a substantive point of view, these conditions may be crucial in operationalizing one or more conceptual variables in the testing of an experimental hypothesis. The basic fact is that the psychologist, as well as the layman, is often vitally interested in behaviors which deal with ineffectiveness, with anxiety or stress, with interpersonal discord—in short, with man under less than optimal conditions. To create laboratory analogues for these behavioral processes, the investigator must employ the appropriate, and often unpleasant, experimental manipulations. To do otherwise might trivialize the research. The dilemma here is an obvious and very real one: The goals of meaningful scientific inquiry may be at odds with the value of treating man in a dignified and respectful manner.

The first paper is Milgram's report of a series of experimental investigations on obedience. The development of an original methodological paradigm is described, in addition to a number of empirical sequels, in which the basic strategy has been to vary systematically certain social psychological parameters in the design. The ethical controversy which this work has inspired seems to rest largely on the question of whether or not Milgram overextended the boundaries of experimental social psychology in evoking psychological stress in his subjects. The graphic vignettes in his report of subjects' reactions to their role as "teacher" in administering electric shock have undoubtedly contributed to this kind of reaction. But one also suspects that the data *per se* have proven irksome to many readers—the very fact that human beings, perhaps the reader himself, could be cruel and, in effect, so obedient. Indeed, this research, in method as well as findings, appears in direct contradiction to the values expressed in Jourard's writing. Yet Milgram's work seems to have a convincing vitality and significance.

The article by Baumrind was the first published reaction to Milgram's original report (1963). Her thesis is that there were too many unknowns in his conception and execution of the study to warrant the negative experiences of his subjects. Since the pronounced emotionality was one of the findings of Milgram's first experiment, rather than the object of inquiry, Baumrind's criticism would appear to be unjustified, at least in regard to the original work. Once it is established that the paradigm reliably evokes severe stress, discussion may well be in order. Baumrind was correctly dissatisfied with Milgram's cursory description of his debriefing procedure in the original report, and her warning on this matter has doubtless been responsible, in part, for subsequent interest and research on the debriefing process (Part Three).

Baumrind contends that only research with unquestionable relevance justifies potential harm to subjects, e.g., a medical breakthrough such as the Sabin vaccine. She finds Milgram's research lacking on this score. But one again is left uneasy with her concept of relevance, as with Ring's usage of significance. Most investigators, although less often their colleagues, consider their research relevant and significant, at least potentially so. Moreover, these are qualities that may become apparent years after the research is completed. One could argue that Milgram's effort to produce experimental analogues of a phenomenon even remotely related to the Nazi death camps constitutes a lofty and honorable task if social psychology is ever to see one. What research could be more relevant? Clearly, Baumrind has raised more questions than she has resolved, but that is the intrinsic value of her paper.

In his rebuttal, Milgram states that the discomfort displayed by his subjects, as well as the pronounced incidence of obedience, were surprise findings. He implies that because we may learn some distressing things about people from their performance in psychological research is not adequate justification for avoiding research. Acknowledging the need for more elaborate debriefing data, Milgram indicates that only a small percentage of his subjects experienced subsequent misgivings about their participation. The modal reaction was, in fact, highly favorable. Baumrind may be correct, however, in asserting that some of his subjects may be telling Milgram what they feel he wants to hear.[1] Milgram cannot be sure that some subjects ultimately realize that their behavior could be construed as characteristic of a rather unsavory class of people. It could, of course, be argued that people learn unpleasant things about themselves, quite unexpectedly, in a variety of life events. Must the social psychological laboratory necessarily be an exception?

This raises the general question of whether subjects should be told about their performance after their experimental participation, particularly when their behavior might be seen as antisocial, psychopathological, or unethical. A number of researchers (e.g., Kelman, Part Three) argue for immediate and complete debriefing, but could not a case be made to the effect that the truth, at times, is a rather bitter pill? Alan Elms counters with the thought that perhaps Milgram's debriefing made it too convenient for his obedient subjects to ignore the ethical implications of their behavior (Elms, reference in Part Three). One is reminded of the physician's conflict when faced with disclosing to his patient some disconcerting results of his diagnosis. Absolutist positions on this matter would seem unwarranted. An excellent discussion of this problem may be found in the chapter by Aronson and Carlsmith, noted in the previous section. These writers present the sound view that debriefing is as much a matter of style as it is of content, and that a sensitive and understanding experimenter will always prevail over a callous and threatening one—a clear recognition that the experiment is an interaction between *people*, as well as between experimenters and subjects.

The paper by Orne and Holland is a methodological critique of Milgram's research, based upon Orne's earlier exposition (1962) on the demand characteristics of experiments (Part Four). These authors argue that for a variety of reasons, Milgram's paradigm is not a plausible situation from the subjects' perspective—in short, the subjects do not perceive themselves to be in the precise experiment that Milgram describes. Focusing upon the discrepancy between the detachment of the experimenter and the agony of the "victim," Orne and Holland assert that most of the subjects do not believe that they are really shocking anyone. Why, then, the obedience and, perhaps more puzzling, why the pronounced affect associated with it? What seems to be involved is obedience of a different kind. The subjects go along with the experimenter and behave *as if* they did think they were shocking their victim. Orne and Holland are making a vital distinction between authority figures in general and the experimenter in particular. Subjects' responses toward the latter may not warrant extension to the former, for there are things about psychological experiments that define and delimit the behaviors which occur there.

Frankly, it is difficult to read Milgram's portrait of the anguish of his subjects and adhere to Orne and Holland's recasting of the entire experiment as a kind of unspoken role-playing venture. Consider the linear relationship between proximity of victim and mean shock level administered, shown in the figure on page 88. Orne and Holland's effort to account for this data is less than convincing. Their general argument seems to falter as they admit that some subjects might perceive the situation as genuine. Yet these authors speak from a position of strength, in that there is empirical support for the demand-characteristic dynamic in psychological experiments. Subjects can be aware of the deception and yet behave as if they are naïve (e.g., Levy, Part Four).

In terms of the ethical implications of Orne and Holland's reasoning, it would appear that there are social-psychological forces operating in the psychological experiment which *may* soften considerably the impact of noxious stimulation and which *may* make suspect expressions of affect or emotion—grief or joy—in subjects. While this might gladden the hearts of those who fear for the well-being of subjects in the laboratory, it poses overwhelming limitations on the generality of data obtained in such sterile laboratories. Stated more simply, the question is how realistic is the experiment from the subject's perspective, and can the experimenter successfully resolve the issue of the subject's awareness that, after all, it is an experiment and nothing more than that. Although Orne and Holland would certainly agree with this latter point—they are of the opinion that this is *the* pervasive set in psychological subjects—it is quite possible that it is a matter of the experimenter's skill in producing realism in the laboratory. It is of interest that Baumrind also noted the unique features of the laboratory, wherein the subject trusts and obeys the experimenter. She went so far as to suggest that the laboratory was an inappropriate setting for the study of obedience, since the baseline for such behavior was intrinsically high—an argument similar to Orne and Holland's position on the ecological validity of Milgram's paradigm. Yet Baumrind totally accepted the reality of the affective arousal in Milgram's subjects, with her resulting ethical misgivings.

Milgram's reply to Orne and Holland focuses upon a number of issues, some specific to the obedience experiments and others more general in their implications. Regarding the plausibility of the deception, Milgram not only documents his own questionnaire data but cites two independent replications of his basic findings (Ring, Wallston, & Corey, 1970; Rosenhan, 1969). It is evidence hard to deny. Because postexperimental interviews are fraught with difficulties in terms of assessing the cognitive states of subjects during the experiment proper (cf. Part Four), independent replication is a particularly convincing validity operation.

Milgram takes exception to Orne's general view of research subjects as suspicious, probing individuals, yet he takes obvious pleasure in referring to off-campus confirmations of his paradigm and to interesting extensions of the obedience design in naturalistic settings. It is true that several commentators, e.g., Jourard, Schultz, and Kelman, in addition to Orne, have promoted the view that naïve human subjects are becoming an extinct species. Perhaps this is an overreaction, in psychology's effort to clean house, ethically and methodologically. Milgram is correct in portraying the Orne and Holland paper as a post-facto utilization of the demand characteristic formulation. He is incorrect, however, when he states that "it is always post-facto" [p. 144], as an examination of the work of Page and Levy in Part Four will reveal.

What is perhaps most remarkable about the Orne-Milgram controversy is that although both display a profound appreciation for the power of social structure, they proceed in opposite directions regarding the generality of such influence as it appears in Milgram's experiments. The matter seems to rest, at least in part, on the notion of Orne and Holland that the experimental context gives the experimenter the implicit right to ask *anything* of the subject, with the implicit guarantee that no harm will be done, that it is in the interest of science, and that, further, no questions should be asked (p. 133). It is this experimenter-subject contract, as Aronson and Carlsmith have termed it, that puts constraints on the generality of behavior which occurs in the laboratory. Where else in life would such gross submissiveness, under *implicit* agreement, be found? Yet one wonders how subjects can be so inquisitive and sentient upon entering the laboratory and almost instantaneously, and without direct instruction, be transformed into the obedient and trusting individual that Orne and Holland describe.

It is pérhaps because both men share the same theoretical orientation that Milgram is unwilling to perceive the situation as merely two alternative interpretations of the same behavior. Rather he construes the Orne and Holland work as deprecating his own, as the product of an atmosphere in social psychology in which it is fashionable to debunk, in the comfort of one's armchair, another's research—to label it artifactual, unethical, or irrelevant. The fact is that most of the contributors to the social psychology of research, e.g., Barber, Kelman, Rosenberg, Rosenthal, and Orne himself, are prolific empiricists. But Milgram's point about seeing "no substance in things, only methodological wrinkles" [p. 151] is well taken, not because it is true (in the main it is not), but because it may appear to be so, and have unintended and undesired consequences.

NOTE

1. The matter of postexperimental questionnaires and interviews is a complex one and is considered in detail in Part Four.

FURTHER READING

AMERICAN PSYCHOLOGICAL ASSOCIATION, INC. *Casebook on ethical standards of psychologists*, Author, 1967. In terms of research precautions, the pronouncements are logical and benevolent, both to researcher and subject. They are somewhat vague, however, and it is difficult to imagine any researcher not being able to construe his research as ethical by some interpretation of these standards.

BAUMRIND, D. Further thoughts on ethics after reading Milgram's "A reply to Baumrind." Unpublished manuscript, University of California, Berkeley. Continues her critique of Milgram's research. She is particularly concerned about Milgram's claim that it was really the subject's choice rather than his passive trancelike adherence to the experimenter's command that resulted in obedience. Baumrind contends that the experimenter must assume more responsibility— although this does raise the specter of the phrase, "I was only following orders," heard at Nuremberg.

ELMS, A. C., & Milgram, S. Personality characteristics associated with obedience and defiance toward authoritative command. *Journal of Experimental Research in Personality*, 1966, 1: 282–289. Examines the personality test scores of twenty obedient and twenty defiant subjects in Milgram's obedience paradigm. Resemblances to previous work on authoritarianism are noted, although the writers stress that they have not identified a single personality dimension highly predictive of obedience or defiance.

ETZIONI, A. A model of significant research. *International Journal of Psychiatry*, 1968, 6: 279–280. An eminent sociologist gives high praise to Milgram's research, seeing it as a rapprochement between empirical and humanistic values. Etzioni expresses no misgivings about the methodological or ethical aspects of the research and boldly extends the data to indicate the latent Eichmann that resides in most men.

MILGRAM, S. Behavioral study of obedience. *Journal of Abnormal and Social Psychology*, 1963, **67**: 371–378. The original published report of the methodology and initial findings of Milgram's obedience research. Featured is a statement, often lost in a discussion of Milgram's work, of the importance of obedience as a substantive problem for analysis.

MILGRAM, S. Liberating effects of group pressure. *Journal of Personality and Social Psychology*, 1965, **1**: 127–134. Although conformity, as it has been investigated and as it is generally considered, connotes weakness or suggestibility, Milgram shows that it can have an altruistic effect. Accomplices who break off from the experimenter's authority are highly influential in inducing subjects to disobey as well.

RUEBHAUSEN, O. M., & Brim, O. G., Jr. Privacy and behavioral research. *Columbia Law Review*, 1965, **65**: 1184–1211. A sophisticated analysis of the concepts of privacy, consent, and confidentiality. Viewing these issues in a legal context gives the reader a new and stimulating perspective.

Stanley Milgram

Some Conditions of Obedience and Disobedience to Authority[1]

The situation in which one agent commands another to hurt a third turns up time and again as a significant theme in human relations. It is powerfully expressed in the story of Abraham, who is commanded by God to kill his son. It is no accident that Kierkegaard, seeking to orient his thought to the central themes of human experience, chose Abraham's conflict as the springboard to his philosophy.

War too moves forward on the triad of an authority which commands a person to destroy the enemy, and perhaps all organized hostility may be viewed as a theme and variation on the three elements of authority, executant, and victim.[2] We describe an experimental program, recently concluded at Yale University, in which a particular expression of this conflict is studied by experimental means.

In its most general form the problem may be defined thus: if X tells Y to hurt Z, under what conditions will Y carry out the command of X and under what conditions will he refuse? In the more limited form possible in laboratory research, the question becomes: if an experimenter tells a subject to hurt another person, under what conditions will the subject go along with this instruction, and under what conditions will he refuse to obey? The laboratory problem is not so much a dilution of the general statement as one concrete expression of the many particular forms this question may assume.

One aim of the research was to study behavior in a strong situation of deep consequence to the participants, for the psychological forces operative in powerful and lifelike forms of the conflict may not be brought into play under diluted conditions.

This approach meant, first, that we had a special obligation to protect the welfare and dignity of the persons who took part in the study; subjects were, of necessity, placed in a difficult predicament, and

From *Human Relations*, 1965, **18**: 57–76. Reprinted with permission of author and Plenum Press.

steps had to be taken to ensure their well-being before they were discharged from the laboratory. Toward this end, a careful, post-experimental treatment was devised and has been carried through for subjects in all conditions.[3]

TERMINOLOGY

If *Y* follows the command of *X* we shall say that he has obeyed *X*; if he fails to carry out the command of *X*, we shall say that he has disobeyed *X*. The terms *to obey* and *to disobey*, as used here, refer to the subject's overt action only, and carry no implication for the motive or experiential states accompanying the action.[4]

To be sure, the everyday use of the word *obedience* is not entirely free from complexities. It refers to action within widely varying situations, and connotes diverse motives within those situations: a child's obedience differs from a soldier's obedience, or the love, honor, and *obey* of the marriage vow. However, a consistent behavioral relationship is indicated in most uses of the term: in the act of obeying, a person does what another person tells him to do. *Y* obeys *X* if he carries out the prescription for action which *X* has addressed to him; the term suggests, moreover, that some form of dominance-subordination, or hierarchical element, is part of the situation in which the transaction between *X* and *Y* occurs.

A subject who complies with the entire series of experimental commands will be termed an *obedient* subject; one who at any point in the command series defies the experimenter will be called a *disobedient* or *defiant* subject. As used in this report, the terms refer only to the subject's performance in the experiment, and do not necessarily imply a general personality disposition to submit to or reject authority.

SUBJECT POPULATION

The subjects used in all experimental conditions were male adults, residing in the greater New Haven and Bridgeport areas, aged 20 to 50 years, and engaged in a wide variety of occupations. Each experimental condition described in this report employed 40 fresh subjects and was carefully balanced for age and occupational types. The occupational composition for each experiment was: workers, skilled and unskilled: 40 percent; white collar, sales, business: 40 percent; professionals: 20 percent. The occupations were intersected with three age categories (subjects in 20s, 30s, and 40s, assigned to each condition in the proportions of 20, 40, and 40 percent respectively).

THE GENERAL LABORATORY PROCEDURE

The focus of the study concerns the amount of electric shock a subject is willing to administer to another person when ordered by an experimenter to give the "victim" increasingly more severe punishment. The act of administering shock is set in the context of a learning experiment, ostensibly designed to study the effect of punishment on memory. Aside from the experimenter, one naïve subject and one accomplice perform in each session. On arrival each subject is paid $4.50. After a general talk by the experimenter, telling how little scientists know about the effect of punishment on memory, subjects are informed that one member of the pair will serve as teacher and one as learner. A rigged drawing is held so that the naïve subject is always the teacher, and the accomplice becomes the learner. The learner is taken to an adjacent room and strapped into an "electric chair."[5]

The naïve subject is told that it is his task to teach the learner a list of paired associates, to test him on the list, and to administer punishment whenever the learner errs in the test. Punishment takes the form of electric shock, delivered to the learner by means of a shock generator controlled by the naïve subject. The teacher is instructed to increase the intensity of electric shock one step on the generator on each error. The learner, according to plan, provides many wrong answers, so that before long the naïve subject must give him the strongest shock on the generator. Increases in shock level are met by increasingly insistent demands from the learner that the experiment be stopped because of the growing discomfort to him. However, in clear terms the experimenter orders the teacher to continue with the procedure in disregard of the learner's protests. *Thus, the naïve subject must resolve a conflict between two mutually incompatible demands from the social field. He may continue to follow the orders of the experimenter and shock the learner with increasing severity, or he may refuse to follow the orders of the experimenter and heed the learner's pleas. The experimenter's authority operates not in a free field, but against evermounting, countervailing pressures from the person being punished.*

A few technical points need to be considered before the findings of the study are described. For the purpose of delivering shock a simulated shock generator is used, with 30 clearly marked voltage levels that range from 15 to 450 volts (and each activated by one of 30 individual lever switches set in a horizontal line). The naïve subject is given a sample shock of 45 volts to convince him of the authenticity of the instrument. The generator bears verbal designations that range from "Slight Shock" to "Danger: Severe Shock."

The responses of the victim are standardized on tape, and each protest is coordinated to a particular voltage level on the shock generator. Starting with 75 volts the learner begins to grunt and moan.

At 150 volts he demands to be let out of the experiment. At 180 volts he cries out that he can no longer stand the pain. At 300 volts he refuses to provide any more answers to the memory test, insisting that he is no longer a participant in the experiment and must be freed. In response to this last tactic, the experimenter instructs the naïve subject to treat the absence of an answer as equivalent to a wrong answer, and to follow the usual shock procedure. The experimenter reinforces his demand with the statement: "You have no other choice, you must go on!" (This imperative is used whenever the naïve subject tries to break off the experiment.) If the subject refuses to give the next higher level of shock, the experiment is considered at an end. A quantitative value is assigned to the subject's performance based on the maximum intensity shock he administered before breaking off. Thus any subject's score may range from zero (for a subject unwilling to administer the first shock level) to 30 (for a subject who proceeds to the highest voltage level on the board). For any particular subject and for any particular experimental condition the degree to which participants have followed the experimenter's orders may be specified with a numerical value, corresponding to the metric on the shock generator.

This laboratory situation gives us a framework in which to study the subject's reactions to the principal conflict of the experiment. Again, this conflict is between the experimenter's demands that he continue to administer the electric shock, and the learner's demands, which become increasingly more insistent, that the experiment be stopped. The crux of the study is to vary systematically the factors believed to alter the degree of obedience to the experimental commands, to learn under what conditions submission to authority is most probable, and under what conditions defiance is brought to the fore.

PILOT STUDIES

Pilot studies for the present research were completed in the winter of 1960; they differed from the regular experiments in a few details. For one, the victim was placed behind a silvered glass, with the light balance on the glass such that the victim could be dimly perceived by the subject (Milgram, 1961).

Though essentially qualitative in treatment, these studies pointed to several significant features of the experimental situation. At first no vocal feedback was used from the victim. It was thought that the verbal and voltage designations on the control panel would create sufficient pressure to curtail the subject's obedience. However, this was not the case. In the absence of protests from the learner, virtually all subjects, once commanded, went blithely to the end of the board, seemingly indifferent to the verbal designations ("Extreme Shock" and "Danger:

Severe Shock"). This deprived us of an adequate basis for scaling obedient tendencies. A force had to be introduced that would strengthen the subject's resistance to the experimenter's commands, and reveal individual differences in terms of a distribution of break-off points.

This force took the form of protests from the victim. Initially, mild protests were used, but proved inadequate. Subsequently, more vehement protests were inserted into the experimental procedure. To our consternation, even the strongest protests from the victim did not prevent all subjects from administering the harshest punishment ordered by the experimenter; but the protests did lower the mean maximum shock somewhat and created some spread in the subject's performance; therefore, the victim's cries were standardized on tape and incorporated into the regular experimental procedure.

The situation did more than highlight the technical difficulties of finding a workable experimental procedure: it indicated that subjects would obey authority to a greater extent than we had supposed. It also pointed to the importance of feedback from the victim in controlling the subject's behavior.

One further aspect of the pilot study was that subjects frequently averted their eyes from the person they were shocking, often turning their heads in an awkward and conspicuous manner. One subject explained: "I didn't want to see the consequences of what I had done." Observers wrote:

. . . subjects showed a reluctance to look at the victim, whom they could see through the glass in front of them. When this fact was brought to their attention they indicated that it caused them discomfort to see the victim in agony. We note, however, that although the subject refuses to look at the victim, he continues to administer shocks.

This suggested that the salience of the victim may have, in some degree, regulated the subject's performance. If, in obeying the experimenter, the subject found it necessary to avoid scrutiny of the victim, would the converse be true? If the victim were rendered increasingly more salient to the subject, would obedience diminish? The first set of regular experiments was designed to answer this question.

IMMEDIACY OF THE VICTIM

This series consisted of four experimental conditions. In each condition the victim was brought "psychologically" closer to the subject giving him shocks.

In the first condition (Remote Feedback) the victim was placed in another room and could not be heard or seen by the subject, except that, at 300 volts, he pounded on the wall in protest. After 315 volts he no longer answered or was heard from.

The second condition (Voice Feedback) was identical to the first except that voice protests were introduced. As in the first condition the victim was placed in an adjacent room, but his complaints could be heard clearly through a door left slightly ajar, and through the walls of the laboratory.[6]

The third experimental condition (Proximity) was similar to the second, except that the victim was now placed in the same room as the subject, and 1½ feet from him. Thus he was visible as well as audible, and voice cues were provided.

The fourth, and final, condition of this series (Touch-Proximity) was identical to the third, with this exception: the victim received a shock only when his hand rested on a shockplate. At the 150-volt level the victim again demanded to be let free and, in this condition, refused to place his hand on the shockplate. The experimenter ordered the naïve subject to force the victim's hand onto the plate. Thus obedience in this condition required that the subject have physical contact with the victim in order to give him punishment beyond the 150-volt level.

Forty adult subjects were studied in each condition. The data revealed that obedience was significantly reduced as the victim was rendered more immediate to the subject. The mean maximum shock for the conditions is shown in Figure 2–1.

Expressed in terms of the proportion of obedient to defiant subjects, the findings are that 34 percent of the subjects defied the experimenter in the Remote condition, 37.5 percent in Voice Feedback, 60 percent in Proximity, and 70 percent in Touch-Proximity.

How are we to account for this effect? A first conjecture might be that as the victim was brought closer the subject became more aware of the intensity of his suffering and regulated his behavior accordingly. This makes sense, but our evidence does not support the interpretation. There are no consistent differences in the attributed level of pain across the four conditions (i.e., the amount of pain experienced by the victim as estimated by the subject and expressed on a 14-point scale). But it is easy to speculate about alternative mechanisms:

Empathic Cues

In the Remote and to a lesser extent the Voice Feedback condition, the victim's suffering possesses an abstract, remote quality for the subject. He is aware, but only in a conceptual sense, that his actions cause pain to another person; the fact is apprehended, but not felt. The phenomenon is common enough. The bombardier can reasonably suppose that his weapons will inflict suffering and death, yet this knowledge is divested of affect, and does not move him to a felt, emotional response to the suffering resulting from his actions. Similar observations have been made in wartime. It is possible that the visual cues associated with the victim's suffering trigger empathic responses in the subject and provide him with a more complete grasp of the victim's experience.

Or it is possible that the empathic responses are themselves unpleasant, possessing drive properties which cause the subject to terminate the arousal situation. Diminishing obedience, then, would be explained by the enrichment of empathic cues in the successive experimental conditions.

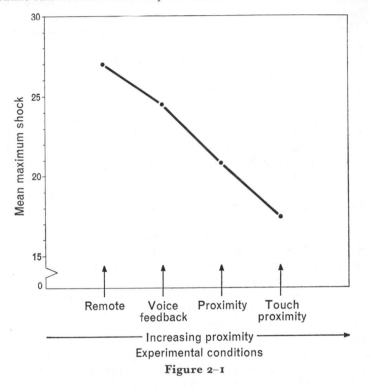

Increasing proximity
Experimental conditions
Figure 2–1

Denial and Narrowing of the Cognitive Field

The Remote condition allows a narrowing of the cognitive field so that the victim is put out of mind. The subject no longer considers the act of depressing a lever relevant to moral judgment, for it is no longer associated with the victim's suffering. When the victim is close it is more difficult to exclude him phenomenologically. He necessarily intrudes on the subject's awareness since he is continuously visible. In the Remote conditions his existence and reactions are made known only after the shock has been administered. The auditory feedback is sporadic and discontinuous. In the Proximity conditions his inclusion in the immediate visual field renders him a continuously salient element for the subject. The mechanism of denial can no longer be brought into play. One subject in the Remote condition said: "It's funny how you really begin to forget that there's a guy out there, even though you can hear him. For a long time I just concentrated on pressing the switches and reading the words."

Reciprocal Fields

If in the Proximity condition the subject is in an improved position to observe the victim, the reverse is also true. The actions of the subject now come under proximal scrutiny by the victim. Possibly, it is easier to harm a person when he is unable to observe our actions than when he can see what we are doing. His surveillance of the action directed against him may give rise to shame, or guilt, which may then serve to curtail the action. Many expressions of language refer to the discomfort or inhibitions that arise in face-to-face confrontation. It is often said that it is easier to criticize a man "behind his back" than to "attack him to his face." If we are in the process of lying to a person it is reputedly difficult to "stare him in the eye." We "turn away from others in shame" or in "embarrassment" and this action serves to reduce our discomfort. The manifest function of allowing the victim of a firing squad to be blindfolded is to make the occasion less stressful for him, but it may also serve a latent function of reducing the stress of the executioner. In short, in the Proximity conditions, the subject may sense that he has become more salient in the victim's field of awareness. Possibly he becomes more self-conscious, embarrassed, and inhibited in his punishment of the victim.

Phenomenal Unity of Act

In the Remote conditions it is more difficult for the subject to gain a sense of *relatedness* between his own actions and the consequences of these actions for the victim. There is a physical and spatial separation of the act and its consequences. The subject depresses a lever in one room, and protests and cries are heard from another. The two events are in correlation, yet they lack a compelling phenomenological unity. The structure of a meaningful act—*I am hurting a man*—breaks down because of the spatial arrangements, in a manner somewhat analogous to the disappearance of phi phenomena when the blinking lights are spaced too far apart. The unity is more fully achieved in the Proximity conditions as the victim is brought closer to the action that causes him pain. It is rendered complete in Touch-Proximity.

Incipient Group Formation

Placing the victim in another room not only takes him further from the subject, but the subject and the experimenter are drawn relatively closer. There is incipient group formation between the experimenter and the subject from which the victim is excluded. The wall between the victim and the others deprives him of an intimacy which the experimenter and subject feel. In the Remote condition, the victim is truly an outsider, who stands alone, physically and psychologically.

When the victim is placed close to the subject, it becomes easier to form an alliance with him against the experimenter. Subjects no longer have to face the experimenter alone. They have an ally who is close at hand and eager to collaborate in a revolt against the experimenter. Thus, the changing set of spatial relations leads to a potentially shifting set of alliances over the several experimental conditions.

Acquired Behavior Dispositions

It is commonly observed that laboratory mice will rarely fight with their litter mates. Scott (1958) explains this in terms of passive inhibition. He writes: "By doing nothing under ... circumstances [the animal] learns to do nothing, and this may be spoken of as passive inhibition ... this principle has great importance in teaching an individual to be peaceful, for it means that he can learn not to fight simply by not fighting." Similarly, we may learn not to harm others simply by not harming them in everyday life. Yet this learning occurs in a context of proximal relations with others, and may not be generalized to that situation in which the person is physically removed from us. Or possibly, in the past, aggressive actions against others who were physically close resulted in retaliatory punishment which extinguished the original form of response. In contrast, aggression against others at a distance may have only sporadically led to retaliation. Thus the organism learns that it is safer to be aggressive toward others at a distance, and precarious to be so when the parties are within arms' reach. Through a pattern of rewards and punishments, he acquires a disposition to avoid aggression at close quarters, a disposition which does not extend to harming others at a distance. And this may account for experimental findings in the remote and proximal experiments.

Proximity as a variable in psychological research has received far less attention than it deserves. If men were sessile it would be easy to understand this neglect. But we move about; our spatial relations shift from one situation to the next, and the fact that we are near or remote may have a powerful effect on the psychological processes that mediate our behavior toward others. In the present situation, as the victim is brought closer to the man ordered to give him shocks, increasing numbers of subjects break off the experiment, refusing to obey. The concrete, visible, and proximal presence of the victim acts in an important way to counteract the experimenter's power and to generate disobedience.[7]

CLOSENESS OF AUTHORITY

If the spatial relationship of the subject and victim is relevant to the degree of obedience, would not the relationship of subject to experimenter also play a part?

There are reasons to feel that, on arrival, the subject is oriented primarily to the experimenter rather than to the victim. He has come to the laboratory to fit into the structure that the experimenter—not the victim—would provide. He has come less to understand his behavior than to *reveal* that behavior to a competent scientist, and he is willing to display himself as the scientist's purposes require. Most subjects seem quite concerned about the appearance they are making before the experimenter, and one could argue that this preoccupation in a relatively new and strange setting makes the subject somewhat insensitive to the triadic nature of the social situation. In other words, the subject is so concerned about the show he is putting on for the experimenter that influences from other parts of the social field do not receive as much weight as they ordinarily would. This overdetermined orientation to the experimenter would account for the relative insensitivity of the subject to the victim, and would also lead us to believe that alterations in the relationship between subject and experimenter would have important consequences for obedience.

In a series of experiments we varied the physical closeness and degree of surveillance of the experimenter. In one condition the experimenter sat just a few feet away from the subject. In a second condition, after giving initial instructions, the experimenter left the laboratory and gave his orders by telephone; in still a third condition the experimenter was never seen, providing instructions by means of a tape recording activated when the subjects entered the laboratory.

Obedience dropped sharply as the experimenter was physically removed from the laboratory. The number of obedient subjects in the first condition (Experimenter Present) was almost three times as great as in the second, where the experimenter gave his orders by telephone. Twenty-six subjects were fully obedient in the first condition, and only nine in the second (chi square obedient vs. defiant in the two conditions, 1 d.f. = 14.7; $p < .001$). Subjects seemed able to take a far stronger stand against the experimenter when they did not have to encounter him face to face, and the experimenter's power over the subject was severely curtailed.[8]

Moreover, when the experimenter was absent, subjects displayed an interesting form of behavior that had not occurred under his surveillance. Though continuing with the experiment, several subjects administered lower shocks than were required and never informed the experimenter of their deviation from the correct procedure. (Unknown to the subjects, shock levels were automatically recorded by an Esterline-Angus event recorder wired directly into the shock generator; the instrument provided us with an objective record of the subjects' performance.) Indeed, in telephone conversations some subjects specifically assured the experimenter that they were raising the shock level according to instruction, whereas in fact they were repeatedly using the lowest shock on the board. This form of behavior is particularly interesting: although these subjects acted in a way that clearly undermined the avowed purposes of the experiment, they found it easier to handle the conflict in this manner than to precipitate an open break with authority.

Other conditions were completed in which the experimenter was absent during the first segment of the experiment, but reappeared at the point that the subject definitely refused to give higher shocks when commanded by telephone. Although he had exhausted his power via telephone, the experimenter could frequently force further obedience when he reappeared in the laboratory. Experiments in this series show that the physical *presence* of an authority is an important force contributing to the subject's obedience or defiance. Taken together with the first experimental series on the proximity of the victim, it would appear that something akin to fields of force, diminishing in effectiveness with increasing psychological distance from their source, have a controlling effect on the subject's performance. As the victim is brought closer, the subject finds it harder to administer shocks to him. When the victim's position is held constant relative to the subject, and the authority is made more remote, the subject finds it easier to break off the experiment. This effect is substantial in both cases, but manipulation of the experimenter's position yielded the more powerful results. Obedience to destructive commands is highly dependent on the proximal relations between authority and subject.

TENSIONS

The description of final scores does not fully convey the character of the subjects' performance, and it would be useful to interrupt our reporting of quantitative relationships to remark on the subjects' general reaction to the situation.

One might suppose that a subject would simply break off or continue as his conscience and temperament dictated. Yet this is very far from what happened. There were powerful reactions of tension and emotional strain in a substantial proportion of the participants. Persons were observed to sweat, tremble, stutter, bite their lips, and groan as they found themselves increasingly implicated in the experimental conflict. Some sense of the subjects' mood can be gotten from a transcript of their remarks at break-off point. Here are the remarks of two defiant subjects:

Is he banging? . . . Is he hurt out there? Well, I don't want to be responsible for anything that happens to him. No, I can't go on with it. I don't know whether he's all right or not. I mean he may have a heart condition or something; I wouldn't feel right doing it. He's banging for help. He's evidently in trouble or he wouldn't bang . . . I don't see any sense to this—to knocking him out or something. I just can't see it [*Subject 0108*].
[*Subject refuses to administer shocks*]
The man is banging. He wants to get out . . . I'm sorry. If the man wants to get out I'd just as soon stop . . . I don't want to administer any more [extremely excited] . . . I will gladly refund the check, but I will not harm this man . . . I'm sorry, I will not give him any more if he obviously wants to get out. There is no money in the world that will make me hurt another individual [*Subject 010X*].

And here is a transcript from an obedient subject. He began the experiment calmly, but became increasingly tense as the experiment proceeded. After administering the 150-volt shock, he began to address the experimenter in agitated tones:

150 volts delivered. You want me to keep going?
165 volts delivered. That guy is hollering in there. There's a lot of them here. He's liable to have heart condition. You want me to go?
180 volts delivered. He can't stand it! I'm not going to kill that man in there! You hear him hollering? He's hollering. He can't stand it. What if something happens to him? . . . I'm not going to get that man sick in there. He's hollering in there. You know what I mean? I mean I refuse to take responsibility. He's getting hurt in there. He's in there hollering. Too many left here. Geez, if he gets them wrong. There's too many of them left. I mean who is going to take responsibility if anything happens to that gentleman?
[*The experimenter accepts responsibility.*] All right.
195 volts delivered. You see he's hollering. Hear that. Gee, I don't know. [*The experimenter says: "The experiment requires that you go on."*]—I know it docs, sir, but I mean—hugh—he don't know what he's in for. He's up to 195 volts.
210 volts delivered.
225 volts delivered.

240 volts delivered. Aw, no. You mean I've got to keep going up with the scale? No sir. I'm not going to kill that man! I'm not going to give him 450 volts! [*The experimenter says: "The experiment requires that you go on."*]—I know it does, but that man is hollering in there, sir . . .

Despite his numerous, agitated objections, which were constant accompaniments to his actions, the subject unfailingly obeyed the experimenter, proceeding to the highest shock level on the generator. He displayed a curious dissociation between word and action. Although at the verbal level he had resolved not to go on, his actions were fully in accord with the experimenter's commands. This subject did not want to shock the victim, and he found it an extremely disagreeable task, but he was unable to invent a response that would free him from *E*'s authority. Many subjects cannot find the specific verbal formula that would enable them to reject the role assigned to them by the experimenter. Perhaps our culture does not provide adequate models for disobedience.

One puzzling sign of tension was the regular occurrence of nervous laughing fits. In the first four conditions 71 of the 160 subjects showed definite signs of nervous laughter and smiling. The laughter seemed entirely out of place, even bizarre. Full-blown, uncontrollable seizures were observed for 15 of these subjects. On one occasion we observed a seizure so violently convulsive that it was necessary to call a halt to the experiment. In the postexperimental interviews subjects took pains to point out that they were not sadistic types and that the laughter did not mean they enjoyed shocking the victim.

In the interview following the experiment subjects were asked to indicate on a 14-point scale just how nervous or tense they felt at the point of maximum tension (Figure 2-2). The scale ranged from "Not

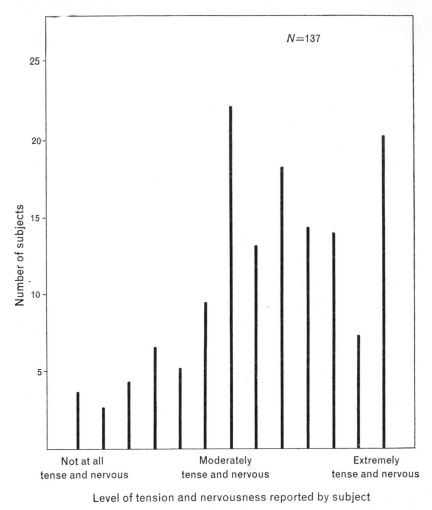

Figure 2-2

at all tense and nervous" to "Extremely tense and nervous." Self-reports of this sort are of limited precision, and at best provide only a rough indication of the subject's emotional response. Still, taking the reports for what they are worth, it can be seen that the distribution of responses spans the entire range of the scale, with the majority of subjects concentrated at the center and upper extreme. A further breakdown showed that obedient subjects reported themselves as having been slightly more tense and nervous than the defiant subjects at the point of maximum tension.

How is the occurrence of tension to be interpreted? First, it points to the presence of conflict. If a tendency to comply with authority were the only psychological force operating in the situation, all subjects would have continued to the end and there would have been no tension. Tension, it is assumed, results from the simultaneous presence of two or more incompatible response tendencies (Miller, 1944). If sympathetic concern for the victim were the exclusive force, all subjects would have calmly defied the experimenter. Instead, there were both obedient and defiant outcomes, frequently accompanied by extreme tension. A conflict develops between the deeply ingrained disposition not to harm others and the equally compelling tendency to obey others who are in authority. The subject is quickly drawn into a dilemma of a deeply dynamic character, and the presence of high tension points to the considerable strength of each of the antagonistic vectors.

Moreover, tension defines the strength of the aversive state from which the subject is unable to escape through disobedience. When a person is uncomfortable, tense, or stressed, he tries to take some action that will allow him to terminate this unpleasant state. Thus tension may serve as a drive that leads to escape behavior. But in the present situation, even where tension is extreme, many subjects are unable to perform the response that will bring about relief. Therefore, there must be a competing drive, tendency, or inhibition that precludes activation of the disobedient response. The strength of this inhibiting factor must be of greater magnitude than the stress experienced, else the terminating act would occur. Every evidence of extreme tension is at the same time an indication of the strength of the forces that keep the subject in the situation.

Finally, tension may be taken as evidence of the reality of the situations for the subjects. Normal subjects do not tremble and sweat unless they are implicated in a deep and genuinely felt predicament.

BACKGROUND AUTHORITY

In psychophysics, animal learning, and other branches of psychology, the fact that measures are obtained at one institution rather than another is irrelevant to the interpretation of the findings, so long as the technical facilities for measurement are adequate and the operations are carried out with competence.

But it cannot be assumed that this holds true for the present study.

The effectiveness of the experimenter's commands may depend in an important way on the larger institutional context in which they are issued. The experiments described thus far were conducted at Yale University, an organization which most subjects regarded with respect and sometimes awe. In postexperimental interviews several participants remarked that the locale and sponsorship of the study gave them confidence in the integrity, competence, and benign purposes of the personnel; many indicated that they would not have shocked the learner if the experiments had been done elsewhere.

This issue of background authority seemed to us important for an interpretation of the results that had been obtained thus far; moreover, it is highly relevant to any comprehensive theory of human obedience. Consider, for example, how closely our compliance with the imperatives of others is tied to particular institutions and locales in our day-to-day activities. On request, we expose our throats to a man with a razor blade in the barber shop, but would not do so in a shoe store; in the latter setting we willingly follow the clerk's request to stand in our stockinged feet, but resist the command in a bank. In the laboratory of a great university, subjects may comply with a set of commands that would be resisted if given elsewhere. *One must always question the relationship of obedience to a person's sense of the context in which he is operating.*

To explore the problem we moved our apparatus to an office building in industrial Bridgeport and replicated experimental conditions, without any visible tie to the university.

Bridgeport subjects were invited to the experiment through a mail circular similar to the one used in the Yale study, with appropriate changes in letterhead, etc. As in the earlier study, subjects were paid $4.50 for coming to the laboratory. The same age and occupational distributions used at Yale, and the identical personnel, were employed.

The purpose in relocating in Bridgeport was to assure a complete dissociation from Yale, and in this regard we were fully successful. On the surface, the study appeared to be conducted by Research Associates of Bridgeport, an organization of unknown character (the title had been concocted exclusively for use in this study).

The experiments were conducted in a three-room office suite in a somewhat run-down commercial building located in the downtown shopping area. The laboratory was sparsely furnished, though clean, and marginally respectable in appearance. When subjects inquired about professional affiliations, they were informed only that we were a private firm conducting research for industry.

Some subjects displayed skepticism concerning the motives of the Bridgeport experimenter. One gentleman gave us a written account of the thoughts he experienced at the control board:

. . . Should I quit this damn test? Maybe he passed out? What dopes we were not to check up on this deal. How do we know that these guys are legit? No furniture, bare walls, no telephone. We could of called the Police up or the Better Business Bureau. I learned a lesson tonight. How do I know that Mr. Williams [the experimenter] is telling the truth . . . I wish I knew how many volts a person could take before lapsing into unconsciousness . . . [*Subject 2414*].

Another subject stated:

I questioned on my arrival my own judgment [about coming]. I had doubts as to the legitimacy of the operation and the consequences of participation. I felt it was a heartless way to conduct memory or learning processes on human beings and certainly dangerous without the presence of a medical doctor [*Subject 2440 V*].

There was no noticeable reduction in tension for the Bridgeport subjects. And the subjects' estimation of the amount of pain felt by the victim was slightly, though not significantly, higher than in the Yale study.

A failure to obtain complete obedience in Bridgeport would indicate that the extreme compliance found in New Haven subjects was tied closely to the background authority of Yale University; if a large proportion of the subjects remained fully obedient, very different conclusions would be called for.

As it turned out, the level of obedience in Bridgeport, although somewhat reduced, was not significantly lower than that obtained at Yale. A large proportion of the Bridgeport subjects were fully obedient to the experimenter's commands (48 percent of the Bridgeport subjects delivered the maximum shock vs. 65 percent in the corresponding condition at Yale).

How are these findings to be interpreted? It is possible that if commands of a potentially harmful or destructive sort are to be perceived as legitimate they must occur within some sort of institutional structure. But it is clear from the study that it need not be a particularly reputable or distinguished institution. The Bridgeport experiments were conducted by an unimpressive firm lacking any credentials; the laboratory was set up in a respectable office building with title listed in the building directory. Beyond that, there was no evidence of benevolence or competence. It is possible that the *category* of institution, judged according to its professed function, rather than its qualitative position within that category, wins our compliance. Persons deposit money in elegant, but also in seedy-looking banks, without giving much thought to the differences in security they offer. Similarly, our subjects may consider one laboratory to be as competent as another, so long as it *is* a scientific laboratory.

It would be valuable to study the subjects' performance in other contexts which go even further than the Bridgeport study in denying institutional support to the experimenter. It is possible that, beyond a certain point, obedience disappears completely. But that point had not been reached in the Bridgeport office: almost half the subjects obeyed the experimenter fully.

FURTHER EXPERIMENTS

We may mention briefly some additional experiments undertaken in the Yale series. A considerable amount of obedience and defiance in everyday life occurs in connection with groups. And we had reason to feel in the light of many group studies already done in psychology that group forces would have a profound effect on reactions to authority. A series of experiments was run to examine these effects. In all cases only one naïve subject was studied per hour, but he performed in the midst of actors who, unknown to him, were employed by the experimenter. In one experiment (Groups for Disobedience) two actors broke off in the middle of the experiment. When this happened 90 percent of the subjects followed suit and defied the experimenter. In another condition the actors followed the orders obediently; this strengthened the experimenter's power only slightly. In still a third experiment the job of pushing the switch to shock the learner was given to one of the actors, while the naïve subject performed a subsidiary act. We wanted to see how the teacher would respond if he were involved in the situation but did not actually give the shocks. In this situation only three subjects out of forty broke off. In a final group experiment the subjects themselves determined the shock level they were going to use. Two actors suggested higher and higher shock levels; some subjects insisted, despite group pressure, that the shock level be kept low; others followed along with the group.

Further experiments were completed using women as subjects, as well as a set dealing with the effects of dual, unsanctioned, and conflicting authority. A final experiment concerned the personal relationship between victim and subject. These will have to be described elsewhere, lest the present report be extended to monographic length.

It goes without saying that future research can proceed in many different directions. What kinds of response from the victim are most effective in causing disobedience in the subject? Perhaps passive resistance is more effective than vehement protest. What conditions of entry into an authority system lead to greater or lesser obedience? What is the effect of anonymity and masking on the subject's behavior? What conditions lead to the subject's perception of responsibility for his own actions? Each of these could be a major research topic in itself, and can readily be incorporated into the general experimental procedure described here.

LEVELS OF OBEDIENCE AND DEFIANCE

One general finding that merits attention is the high level of obedience manifested in the experimental situation. Subjects often expressed deep disappoval of shocking a man in the face of his objections, and others denounced it as senseless and stupid. Yet many subjects complied even while they protested. The proportion of obedient subjects greatly exceeded the expectations of the experimenter and his colleagues. At the outset, we had conjectured that subjects would not, in general, go above the level of "Strong Shock." In practice, many subjects were willing to administer the most extreme shocks available when commanded by the experimenter. For some subjects the experiment provides an occasion for aggressive release. And for others it demonstrates the extent to which obedient dispositions are deeply ingrained, and are engaged irrespective of their consequences for others. Yet this is not the whole story. Somehow, the subject becomes implicated in a situation from which he cannot disengage himself.

The departure of the experimental results from intelligent expectation, to some extent, has been formalized. The procedure was to describe the experimental situation in concrete detail to a group of competent persons, and to ask them to predict the performance of 100 hypothetical subjects. For purposes of indicating the distribution of break-off points, judges were provided with a diagram of the shock generator, and recorded their predictions before being informed of the actual results. Judges typically underestimated the amount of obedience demonstrated by subjects.

In Figure 2-3, we compare the predictions of forty psychiatrists at a leading medical school with the actual performance of subjects in the experiment. The psychiatrists predicted that most subjects would not go beyond the tenth shock level (150 volts; at this point the victim makes his first explicit demand to be freed). They further predicted that by the twentieth shock level (300 volts; the victim refuses to answer) 3.73 percent of the subjects would still be obedient; and that only a little over one-tenth of 1 percent of the subjects would administer the highest shock on the board. But as the graph indicates, the obtained behavior was very different. Sixty-two percent of the subjects obeyed the experimenter's commands fully. Between expectation and occurrence there is a whopping discrepancy.

Why did the psychiatrists underestimate the level of obedience? Possibly, because their predictions were based on an inadequate conception of the determinants of human action, a conception that focuses on motives *in vacuo*. This orientation may be entirely adequate for the repair of bruised impulses as revealed on the psychiatrists's couch, but as soon as our interest turns to action in larger settings, attention must

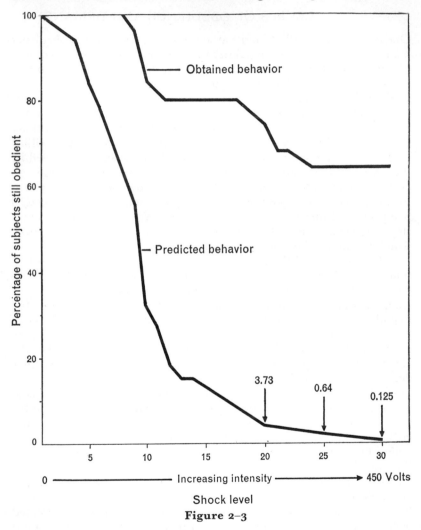

Figure 2–3

be paid to the situations in which motives are expressed. A situation exerts an important press on the individual. It exercises constraints and may provide push. In certain circumstances it is not so much the kind of person a man is, as the kind of situation in which he is placed, that determines his actions.

Many people, not knowing much about the experiment, claim that subjects who go to the end of the board are sadistic. Nothing could be more foolish as an overall characterization of these persons. It is like saying that a person thrown into a swift-flowing stream is necessarily a fast swimmer, or that he has great stamina because he moves so rapidly relative to the bank. The context of action must always be considered. The individual, upon entering the laboratory, becomes integrated into a situation that carries its own momentum. The subject's problem then is how to become disengaged from a situation which is moving in an altogether ugly direction.

The fact that disengagement is so difficult testifies to the potency of the forces that keep the subject at the control board. Are these forces to be conceptualized as individual motives and expressed in the language of personality dynamics, or are they to be seen as the effects of social structure and pressures arising from the situational field?

A full understanding of the subject's action will, I feel, require that both perspectives be adopted. The person brings to the laboratory enduring dispositions toward authority and aggression, and at the same time he becomes enmeshed in a social structure that is no less an objective fact of the case. From the standpoint of personality theory one may ask: What mechanisms of personality enable a person to transfer responsibility to authority? What are the motives underlying obedient and disobedient performance? Does orientation to authority lead to a short-circuiting of the shame-guilt system? What cognitive and emotional defenses are brought into play in the case of obedient and defiant subjects?

The present experiments are not, however, directed toward an exploration of the motives engaged when the subject obeys the experimenter's commands. Instead, they examine the situational variables responsible for the elicitation of obedience. Elsewhere, we have attempted to spell out some of the structural properties of the experimental situation that account for high obedience, and this analysis need not be repeated here (Milgram, 1963). The experimental variations themselves represent our attempt to probe that structure, by systematically changing it and noting the consequences for behavior. It is clear that some situations produce greater compliance with the experimenter's commands than others. However, this does not necessarily imply an increase or decrease in the strength of any single definable motive. Situations producing the greatest obedience could do so by triggering the most powerful, yet perhaps the most idiosyncratic, of motives in each subject confronted by the setting. Or they may simply recruit a greater number and variety of motives in their service. But whatever the motives involved—and it is far from certain that they can ever be known—action may be studied as a direct function of the situation in which it occurs. This has been the approach of the present study, where we sought to plot behavioral irregularities against manipulated properties of the social field. Ultimately, social psychology would like to have a compelling *theory of situations* which will, first, present a language in terms of which situations can be defined; then proceed to a typology of situations; and, finally, point to the manner in which definable properties of situations are transformed into psychological forces in the individual.[9]

POSTSCRIPT

Almost a thousand adults were individually studied in the obedience research, and there were many specific conclusions regarding the variables that control obedience and disobedience to authority. Some of these have been discussed briefly in the preceding sections, and more detailed reports will be released subsequently.

There are now some other generalizations I should like to make, which do not derive in any strictly logical fashion from the experiments as carried out, but which, I feel, ought to be made. They are formulations of an intuitive sort that have been forced on me by observation of many subjects responding to the pressures of authority. The assertions represent a painful alteration in my own thinking; and since they were acquired only under the repeated impact of direct observation, I have no illusion that they will be generally accepted by persons who have not had the same experience.

With numbing regularity good people were seen to knuckle under the demands of authority and to perform actions that were callous and severe. Men who are in everyday life responsible and decent were seduced by the trappings of authority, by the control of their perceptions, and by the uncritical acceptance of the experimenter's definition of the situation, into performing harsh acts.

What is the limit of such obedience? At many points we attempted to establish a boundary. Cries from the victim were inserted; not good enough. The victim claimed heart trouble; subjects still shocked him on command. The victim pleaded that he be let free, and his answers no longer registered on the signal box; subjects continued to shock him. At the outset we had not conceived that such drastic procedures would be needed to generate disobedience, and each step was added only as the ineffectiveness of the earlier techniques became clear. The final effort to establish a limit was the Touch-Proximity condition. But the very first subject in this condition subdued the victim on command, and proceeded to the highest shock level. A quarter of the subjects in this condition performed similarly.

The results, as seen and felt in the laboratory, are to this author disturbing. They raise the possibility that human nature, or—more specifically—the kind of character produced in American democratic society, cannot be counted on to insulate its citizens from brutality and inhumane treatment at the direction of malevolent authority. A substantial proportion of people do what they are told to do, irrespective of the content of the act and without limitations of conscience, so long as they perceive that the command comes from a legitimate authority. If in this study an anonymous experimenter could successfully command adults to subdue a fifty-year-old man, and force on him painful electric shocks against his protests, one can only wonder what government, with its vastly greater authority and prestige, can command of its subjects. There is, of course, the extremely important question of whether malevolent political institutions could or would arise in American society. The present research contributes nothing to this issue.

In an article entitled, "The Dangers of Obedience," Harold J. Laski wrote:

. . . civilization means, above all, an unwillingness to inflict unnecessary pain. Within the ambit of that definition, those of us who heedlessly accept the commands of authority cannot yet claim to be civilized men.

. . . Our business, if we desire to live a life not utterly devoid of meaning and significance, is to accept nothing which contradicts our basic experience merely because it comes to us from tradition or convention or authority. It may well be that we shall be wrong; but our self-expression is thwarted at the root unless the certainties we are asked to accept coincide with the certainties we experience. That is why the condition of freedom in any state is always a widespread and consistent skepticism of the canons upon which power insists.

NOTES

1. Stanley Milgram, Ph.D., Professor of Psychology, Graduate Center of the City University of New York, completed the study described here while an assistant professor of psychology at Yale University.

This research was supported by two grants from the National Science Foundation: NSF G-17916 and NSF G-24152. Exploratory studies carried out in 1960 were financed by a grant from the Higgins Funds of Yale University. The author is grateful to John T. Williams, James J. McDonough, and Emil Elges for the important part they played in the project. Thanks are due also to Alan Elms, James Miller, Taketo Murata, and Stephen Stier for their aid as graduate assistants. The author's wife, Sasha, performed many valuable services. Finally, a profound debt is owed to the many persons in New Haven and Bridgeport who served as subjects.

2. Consider, for example, J. P. Scott's analysis of war in his monograph on aggression: ". . . while the actions of key individuals in a war may be explained in terms of direct stimulation to aggression, vast numbers of other people are involved simply by being part of an organized society.

". . . For example, at the beginning of World War 1 an Austrian archduke was assassinated in Sarajevo. A few days later soldiers from all over Europe were marching toward each other, not because they were stimulated by the archduke's misfortune, but because they had been trained to obey orders." (Slightly rearranged from Scott, 1958, *Aggression*, p. 103.)

3. It consisted of an extended discussion with the experimenter and, of equal importance,

a friendly reconciliation with the victim. It is made clear that the victim did not receive painful electric shocks. After the completion of the experimental series, subjects were sent a detailed report of the results and full purposes of the experimental program. A formal assessment of this procedure points to its overall effectiveness. Of the subjects, 83.7 per cent indicated that they were glad to have taken part in the study; 15.1 per cent reported neutral feelings; and 1.3 per cent stated that they were sorry to have participated. A large number of subjects spontaneously requested that they be used in further experimentation. Four-fifths of the subjects felt that more experiments of this sort should be carried out, and 74 per cent indicated that they had learned something of personal importance as a result of being in the study. Furthermore, a university psychiatrist, experienced in outpatient treatment, interviewed a sample of experimental subjects with the aim of uncovering possible injurious effects resulting from participation. No such effects were in evidence. Indeed, subjects typically felt that their participation was instructive and enriching. A more detailed discussion of this question can be found in Milgram (1964).

4. *To obey* and *to disobey* are not the only terms one could use in describing the critical action of Y. One could say that Y is cooperating with X, or displays conformity with regard to X's commands. However, *cooperation* suggests that X agrees with Y's ends, and understands the relationship between his own behavior and the attainment of those ends. (But the experimental procedure and, in particular, the experimenter's command that the subject shock the victim even in the absence of a response from the victim, preclude such understanding.) Moreover, cooperation implies status parity for the coacting agents, and neglects the asymmetrical, dominance-subordination element prominent in the laboratory relationship between experimenter and subject. *Conformity* has been used in other important contexts in social psychology, and most frequently refers to imitating the judgments or actions of others when no explicit requirement for imitation has been made. Furthermore, in the present study there are two sources of social pressure: pressure from the experimenter issuing the commands, and pressure from the victim to stop the punishment. It is the pitting of a common man (the victim) against an authority (the experimenter) that is the distinctive feature of the conflict. At a point in the experiment the victim demands that he be let free. The experimenter insists that the subject continue to administer shocks. Which act of the subject can be interpreted as conformity? The subject may conform to the wishes of his peer or to the wishes of the experimenter, and conformity in one direction means the absence of conformity in the other. Thus the word has no useful reference in this setting, for the dual and conflicting social pressures cancel out its meaning.

In the final analysis, the linguistic symbol representing the subject's action must take its meaning from the concrete context in which that action occurs; and there is probably no word in everyday language that covers the experimental situation exactly, without omissions or irrelevant connotations. It is partly for convenience, therefore, that the terms *obey* and *disobey* are used to describe the subject's actions. At the same time, our use of the words is highly congruent with dictionary meaning.

5. A more detailed account of the laboratory procedure can be found in Milgram (1963). A similar and independently evolved experimental procedure, employing a shock generator, victim, and learning task, was reported by Buss (1961). Buss used the technique for studying aggression, not obedience, and did not make use of the fundamental measure employed in the present study: break-off points. His investigation promises to be a useful complement to the present research.

6. It is difficult to convey on the printed page the full tenor of the victim's responses, for we have no adequate notation for vocal intensity, timing, and general qualities of delivery. Yet these features are crucial to producing the effect of an increasingly severe reaction to mounting voltage levels. (They can be communicated fully only by sending interested parties the recorded tapes.) In general terms, however, the victim indicates no discomfort until the 75-volt shock is administered, at which time there is a light grunt in response to the punishment. Similar reactions follow the 90- and 105-volt shocks, and at 120 volts the victim shouts to the experimenter that the shocks are becoming painful. Painful groans are heard on administration of the 135-volt shock, and at 150 volts the victim cries out, "Experimenter, get me out of here! I won't be in the experiment any more! I refuse to go on!" Cries of this type continue with generally rising intensity, so that at 180 volts the victim cries out, "I can't stand the pain," and by 270 volts his response to the shock is definitely an agonized scream. Throughout, he insists that he be let out of the experiment. At 300 volts the victim shouts in desperation that he will no longer provide answers to the memory test; and at 315 volts, after a violent scream,

he reaffirms with vehemence that he is no longer a participant. From this point on, he provides no answers, but shrieks in agony whenever a shock is administered; this continues through 450 volts. Of course, many subjects will have broken off before this point.

A revised and stronger set of protests was used in all experiments outside the Proximity series. Naturally, new baseline measures were established for all comparisons using the new set of protests.

There is overwhelming evidence that the great majority of subjects, both obedient and defiant, accepted the victims' reactions as genuine. The evidence takes the form of: (a) tension created in the subjects (see discussion of tension); (b) scores on "estimated pain" scales filled out by subjects immediately after the experiment; (c) subjects' accounts of their feelings in postexperimental interviews; and (d) quantifiable responses to questionnaires distributed to subjects several months after their participation in the experiments. This matter will be treated fully in a forthcoming monograph.

(The procedure in all experimental conditions was to have the naive subject announce the voltage level before administering each shock, so that—independently of the victim's responses—he was continually reminded of delivering punishment of ever-increasing severity.)

7. Admittedly, the terms *proximity, immediacy, closeness,* and *salience-of-the-victim* are used in a loose sense, and the experiments themselves represent a very coarse treatment of the variable. Further experiments are needed to refine the notion and tease out such diverse factors as spatial distance, visibility, audibility, barrier interposition, etc.

The Proximity and Touch-Proximity experiments were the only conditions where we were unable to use taped feedback from the victim. Instead, the victim was trained to respond in these conditions as he had in Experiment 2 (which employed taped feedback). Some improvement is possible here, for it should be technically feasible to do a proximity series using taped feedback.

8. The third condition also led to significantly lower obedience than this first situation, in which the experimenter was present, but it contains technical difficulties that require extensive discussion.

9. My thanks to Prof. Howard Leventhal of Yale for strengthening the writing in this paragraph.

REFERENCES

Buss, A. H. *The psychology of aggression.* New York and London: John Wiley, 1961.

Kierkegaard, S. (1843). *Fear and trembling.* English edition. Princeton: Princeton University Press, 1941.

Laski, H. J. The dangers of obedience. *Harper's Monthly Magazine,* 1929, **159:** 1–10.

Milgram, S. Dynamics of obedience: Experiments in social psychology. Mimeographed report, National Science Foundation, January 25, 1961.

Milgram, S. Behavioral study of obedience. *Journal of Abnormal and Social Psychology,* 1963, **67:** 371–378.

Milgram, S. Issues in the study of obedience: A reply to Baumrind. *American Psychologist,* 1964, **19:** 848–852.

Miller, N. E. Experimental studies of conflict. In J. McV. Hunt (Ed.), *Personality and the behavior disorders.* New York: Ronald Press, 1944.

Scott, J. P. *Aggression.* Chicago: University of Chicago Press, 1958.

Diana Baumrind

Some Thoughts on Ethics of Research:
After Reading Milgram's "Behavioral Study of Obedience"

Certain problems in psychological research require the experimenter to balance his career and scientific interests against the interests of his prospective subjects. When such occasions arise the experimenter's stated objective frequently is to do the best possible job with the least possible harm to his subjects. The experimenter seldom perccives in more positive terms an indebtedness to the subject for his services, perhaps because the detachment which his functions require prevents appreciation of the subject as an individual.

Yet a debt does exist, even when the subject's reason for volunteering includes course credit or monetary gain. Often a subject participates unwillingly in order to satisfy a course requirement. These requirements are of questionable merit ethically, and do not alter the experimenter's responsibility to the subject.

Most experimental conditions do not cause the subjects pain or indignity, and are sufficiently interesting or challenging to present no problem of an ethical nature to the experimenter. But where the experimental conditions expose the subject to loss of dignity, or offer him nothing of value, then the experimenter is obliged to consider the reasons why the subject volunteered and to reward him accordingly.

The subject's public motives for volunteering include having an enjoyable or stimulating experience, acquiring knowledge, doing the experimenter a favor which may some day be reciprocated, and making a contribution to science. These motives can be taken into account rather easily by the experimenter who is willing to spend a few minutes

From *American Psychologist*, 1964, **19**: 421–423. Copyright © 1964 by The American Psychological Association and reprinted with permission of author and The American Psychological Association.

with the subject afterwards to thank him for his participation, answer his questions, reassure him that he did well, and chat with him a bit. Most volunteers also have less manifest, but equally legitimate, motives. A subject may be seeking an opportunity to have contact with, be noticed by, and perhaps confide in a person with psychological training. The dependent attitude of most subjects toward the experimenter is an artifact of the experimental situation as well as an expression of some subjects' personal need systems at the time they volunteer.

The dependent, obedient attitude assumed by most subjects in the experimental setting is appropriate to that situation. The "game" is defined by the experimenter and he makes the rules. By volunteering, the subject agrees implicitly to assume a posture of trust and obedience. While the experimental conditions leave him exposed, the subject has the right to assume that his security and self-esteem will be protected.

There are other professional situations in which one member—the patient or client—expects help and protection from the other—the physician or psychologist. But the interpersonal relationship between experimenter and subject additionally has unique features which are likely to provoke initial anxiety in the subject. The laboratory is unfamiliar as a setting and the rules of behavior ambiguous compared to a clinician's office. Because of the anxiety and passivity generated by the setting, the subject is more prone to behave in an obedient, suggestible manner in the laboratory than elsewhere. Therefore, the laboratory is not the place to study degree of obedience or suggestibility, as a function of a particular experimental condition, since the base line for these phenomena as found in the laboratory is probably much higher than in most other settings. Thus experiments in which the relationship to the experimenter as an authority is used as an independent condition are imperfectly designed for the same reason that they are prone to injure the subjects involved. They disregard the special quality of trust and obedience with which the subject appropriately regards the experimenter.

Other phenomena which present ethical decisions, unlike those mentioned above, *can* be reproduced successfully in the laboratory. Failure experience, conformity to peer judgment, and isolation are among such phenomena. In these cases we can expect the experimenter to take whatever measures are necessary to prevent the subject from leaving the laboratory more humiliated, insecure, alienated, or hostile than when he arrived. To guarantee that an especially sensitive subject leaves a stressful experimental experience in the proper state sometimes requires special clinical training. But usually an attitude of compassion, respect, gratitude, and common sense will suffice, and no amount of clinical training will substitute. The subject has the right to expect that the psychologist with whom he is interacting has some concern for his welfare, and the personal attributes and professional skill to express his goodwill effectively.

Unfortunately, the subject is not always treated with the respect he deserves. It has become more commonplace in sociopsychological laboratory studies to manipulate, embarrass, and discomfort subjects. At times the insult to the subject's sensibilities extends to the journal reader when the results are reported. Milgram's (1963) study is a case in point. The following is Milgram's abstract of his experiment:

This article describes a procedure for the study of destructive obedience in the laboratory. It consists of ordering a naïve S to administer increasingly more severe punishment to a victim in the context of a learning experiment. Punishment is administered by means of a shock generator with 30 graded switches ranging from Slight Shock to Danger: Severe Shock. The victim is a confederate of E. The primary dependent variable is the maximum shock the S is willing to administer before he refuses to continue further. 26 Ss obeyed the experimental commands fully, and administered the highest shock on the generator. 14 Ss broke off the experiment at some point after the victim protested and refused to provide further answers. The procedure created extreme levels of nervous tension in some Ss. Profuse sweating, trembling, and stuttering were typical expressions of this emotional disturbance. One unexpected sign of tension—yet to be explained—was the regular occurrence of nervous laughter, which in some Ss developed into uncontrollable seizures. The variety of interesting behavioral dynamics observed in the experiment, the reality of the situation for the S, and the possibility of parametric variation within the framework of the procedure, point to the fruitfulness of further study [p. 371].

The detached, objective manner in which Milgram reports the emotional disturbance suffered by his subject contrasts sharply with his graphic account of that disturbance. Following are two other quotes describing the effects on his subjects of the experimental conditions:

I observed a mature and initially poised businessman enter the laboratory smiling and confident. Within 20 minutes he was reduced to a twitching, stuttering wreck, who was rapidly approaching a point of nervous collapse. He constantly pulled on his earlobe, and twisted his hands. At one point he pushed his fist into his forehead and muttered "Oh God, let's stop it." And yet he continued to respond to every word of the experimenter, and obeyed to the end [p. 377].

In a large number of cases the degree of tension reached extremes that are rarely seen in sociopsychological laboratory studies. Subjects were observed to sweat, tremble, stutter, bite their lips, groan, and dig their fingernails into their flesh. These were characteristic rather than exceptional responses to the experiment.

One sign of tension was the regular occurrence of nervous laughing fits. Fourteen of the 40 subjects showed definite signs of nervous laughter and smiling. The laughter seemed entirely out of place, even bizarre. Full-blown, uncontrollable seizures were observed for 3 subjects. On one occasion we observed a seizure so violently convulsive that it was necessary to call a halt to the experiment ... [p. 375].

Milgram does state that,

After the interview, procedures were undertaken to assure that the subject would leave the laboratory in a state of well being. A friendly reconciliation was arranged between the subject and the victim, and an effort was made to reduce any tensions that arose as a result of the experiment [p. 374].

It would be interesting to know what sort of procedures could dissipate the type of emotional disturbance just described. In view of the effects on subjects, traumatic to a degree which Milgram himself considers nearly unprecedented in sociopsychological experiments, his casual assurance that these tensions were dissipated before the subject left the laboratory is unconvincing.

What could be the rational basis for such a posture of indifference? Perhaps Milgram supplies the answer himself when he partially explains the subject's destructive obedience as follows, "Thus they assume that the discomfort caused the victim is momentary, while the scientific gains resulting from the experiment are enduring" [p. 378]. Indeed such a rationale might suffice to justify the means used to achieve his end if that end were of inestimable value to humanity or were not itself transformed by the means by which it was attained.

The behavioral psychologist is not in as good a position to objectify his faith in the significance of his work as medical colleagues at points of breakthrough. His experimental situations are not sufficiently accurate models of real-life experience; his sampling techniques are seldom of a scope which would justify the meaning with which he would like to endow his results; and these results are hard to reproduce by colleagues with opposing theoretical views. Unlike the Sabin vaccine, for example, the concrete benefit to humanity of his particular piece of work, no matter how competently handled, cannot justify the risk that real harm will be done to the subject. I am not speaking of physical discomfort, inconvenience, or experimental deception per se, but of permanent harm, however slight. I do regard the emotional disturbance described by Milgram as potentially harmful because it could easily effect an alteration in the subject's self-image or ability to trust adult authorities in the future. It is potentially harmful to a subject to commit, in the course of an experiment, acts which he himself considers unworthy, particularly when he has been entrapped into committing such acts by an individual he has reason to trust. The subject's personal responsibility for his actions is not erased because the experimenter reveals to him the means which he used to stimulate these actions. The subject realizes that he would have hurt the victim if the current were on. The realization that he also made a fool of himself by accepting the experimental set results in additional loss of self-esteem. Moreover, the subject finds it difficult to express his anger outwardly after the experimenter in a self-acceptant but friendly manner reveals the hoax.

A fairly intense corrective interpersonal experience is indicated wherein the subject admits and accepts his responsibility for his own actions, and at the same time gives vent to his hurt and anger at being fooled. Perhaps an experience as distressing as the one described by Milgram can be integrated by the subject, provided that careful thought is given to the matter. The propriety of such experimentation is still in question even if such a reparational experience were forthcoming. Without it I would expect a naïve, sensitive subject to remain deeply hurt and anxious for some time, and a sophisticated, cynical subject to become even more alienated and distrustful.

In addition the experimental procedure used by Milgram does not appear suited to the objectives of the study because it does not take into account the special quality of the set which the subject has in the experimental situation. Milgram is concerned with a very important problem, namely, the social consequences of destructive obedience. He says,

Gas chambers were built, death camps were guarded, daily quotas of corpses were produced with the same efficiency as the manufacture of appliances. These inhumane policies may have originated in the mind of a single person, but they could only be carried out on a massive scale if a very large number of persons obeyed orders [p. 371].

But the parallel between authority-subordinate relationships in Hitler's Germany and in Milgram's laboratory is unclear. In the former situation the SS man or member of the German Officer Corps, when obeying orders to slaughter, had no reason to think of his superior officer as benignly disposed towards himself or their victims. The victims were perceived as subhuman and not worthy of consideration. The subordinate officer was an agent in a great cause. He did not need to feel guilt or conflict because within his frame of reference he was acting rightly.

It is obvious from Milgram's own descriptions that most of his subjects were concerned about their victims and did trust the experimenter, and that their distressful conflict was generated in part by the consequences of these two disparate but appropriate attitudes. Their distress may have resulted from shock at what the experimenter was doing to them as well as from what they thought they were doing to their victims. In any case, there is not a convincing parallel between the phenomena studied by Milgram and destructive obedience as that concept would apply to the subordinate-authority relationship demonstrated in Hitler's Germany. If the experiments were conducted "outside of New Haven and without any visible ties to the university," I would still question their validity on similar although not identical grounds. In addition, I would question the representativeness of a sample of subjects who would voluntarily participate within a noninstitutional setting.

In summary, the experimental objectives of the psychologist are seldom incompatible with the subject's ongoing state of well-being, provided that the experimenter is willing to take the subject's motives and interests into consideration when planning his methods and correctives. Section 4b in *Ethical Standards of Psychologists* (APA, undated) reads in part:

> Only when a problem is significant and can be investigated in no other way, is the psychologist justified in exposing human subjects to emotional stress or other possible harm. In conducting such research, the psychologist must seriously consider the possibility of harmful aftereffects, and should be prepared to remove them as soon as permitted by the design of the experiment. Where the danger of serious aftereffects exists, research should be conducted only when the subjects or their responsible agents are fully informed of this possibility and volunteer nevertheless [p. 12].

From the subject's point of view, procedures which involve loss of dignity, self-esteem, and trust in rational authority are probably most harmful in the long run and require the most thoughtfully planned reparations, if engaged in at all. The public image of psychology as a profession is highly related to our own actions, and some of these actions are changeworthy. It is important that as research psychologists we protect our ethical sensibilities rather than adapt our personal standards to include as appropriate the kind of indignities to which Milgram's subjects were exposed. I would not like to see experiments such as Milgram's proceed unless the subjects were fully informed of the dangers of serious aftereffects and his correctives were clearly shown to be effective in restoring their state of well-being.

REFERENCES

AMERICAN PSYCHOLOGICAL ASSOCIATION. *Ethical standards of psychologists: A summary of ethical principles*. Washington, D.C.: 1962.

MILGRAM, S. Behavioral study of obedience. *Journal of Abnormal and Social Psychology*, 1963, **67**: 371–378.

Stanley Milgram

Issues in the Study of Obedience:
A Reply to Baumrind

Obedience serves numerous productive functions in society. It may be ennobling and educative and entail acts of charity and kindness. Yet the problem of destructive obedience, because it is the most disturbing expression of obedience in our time, and because it is the most perplexing, merits intensive study.

In its most general terms, the problem of destructive obedience may be defined thus: If X tells Y to hurt Z, under what conditions will Y carry out the command of X, and under what conditions will he refuse? In the concrete setting of a laboratory, the question may assume this form: If an experimenter tells a subject to act against another person, under what conditions will the subject go along with the instruction, and under what conditions will he refuse to obey?

A simple procedure was devised for studying obedience (Milgram, 1963). A person comes to the laboratory, and in the context of a learning experiment, he is told to give increasingly severe electric shocks to another person. (The other person is an actor, who does not really receive any shocks.) The experimenter tells the subject to continue stepping up the shock level, even to the point of reaching the level marked "Danger: Severe Shock." The purpose of the experiment is to see how far the naïve subject will proceed before he refuses to comply with the experimenter's instructions. Behavior prior to this rupture is considered "obedience" in that the subject does what the experimenter tells him to do. The point of rupture is the act of disobedience. Once the basic procedure is established, it becomes possible to vary conditions of the experiment, to learn under what circumstances obedience to authority is most probable, and under what conditions defiance is brought to the fore (Milgram, 1965).

The results of the experiment (Milgram, 1963) showed, first, that it is more difficult for many people to defy the experimenter's authority

From *American Psychologist*, 1964, **19**: 848–852. Copyright © 1964 by The American Psychological Association and reprinted with permission of author and The American Psychological Association.

than was generally supposed. A substantial number of subjects go through to the end of the shock board. The second finding is that the situation often places a person in considerable conflict. In the course of the experiment, subjects fidget, sweat, and sometimes break out into nervous fits of laughter. On the one hand, subjects want to aid the experimenter; and on the other hand, they do not want to shock the learner. The conflict is expressed in nervous reactions.

In a recent issue of *American Psychologist*, Diana Baumrind (1964) raised a number of questions concerning the obedience report. Baumrind expressed concern for the welfare of subjects who served in the experiment, and wondered whether adequate measures were taken to protect the participants. She also questioned the adequacy of the experimental design.

Patently, "Behavioral Study of Obedience" did not contain all the information needed for an assessment of the experiment. But it is clearly indicated in the references and footnotes (pp. 373, 378) that this was only one of a series of reports on the experimental program, and Baumrind's article was deficient in information that could have been obtained easily. I thank the editor for allotting space in this journal to review this information, to amplify it, and to discuss some of the issues touched on by Baumrind.

At the outset, Baumrind confuses the unanticipated outcome of an experiment with its basic procedure. She writes, for example, as if the production of stress in our subjects was an intended and deliberate effect of the experimental manipulation. There are many laboratory procedures specifically designed to create stress (Lazarus, 1964), but the obedience paradigm was not one of them. The extreme tension induced in some subjects was unexpected. Before conducting the experiment, the procedures were discussed with many colleagues, and none anticipated the reactions that subsequently took place. Foreknowledge of results can never be the invariable accompaniment of an experimental probe. Understanding grows because we examine situations in which the end is unknown. An investigator unwilling to accept this degree of risk must give up the idea of scientific inquiry.

Moreover, there was every reason to expect, prior to actual experimentation, that subjects would refuse to follow the experimenter's instructions beyond the point where the victim protested; many colleagues and psychiatrists were questioned on this point, and they virtually all felt this would be the case. Indeed, to initiate an experiment in which the critical measure hangs on disobedience, one must start with a belief in certain spontaneous resources in men that enable them to overcome pressure from authority.

It is true that after a reasonable number of subjects had been exposed to the procedures, it became evident that some would go to the end of the shock board, and some would experience stress. That point, it seems to me, is the first legitimate juncture at which one could even start to wonder whether or not to abandon the study. But momentary excitement is not the same as harm. As the experiment progressed there was no indication of injurious effects in the subjects; and as the subjects themselves strongly endorsed the experiment, the judgement I made was to continue the investigation.

Is not Baumrind's criticism based as much on the unanticipated findings as on the method? The findings were that some subjects performed in what appeared to be a shockingly immoral way. If, instead, every one of the subjects had broken off at "slight shock," or at the first sign of the learner's discomfort, the results would have been pleasant, and reassuring, and who would protest?

PROCEDURES AND BENEFITS

A most important aspect of the procedure occurred at the end of the experimental session. A careful postexperimental treatment was administered to all subjects. The exact content of the dehoax varied from condition to condition and with increasing experience on our part. At the very least all subjects were told that the victim had not received dangerous electric shocks. Each subject had a friendly reconciliation with the unharmed victim, and an extended discussion with the experimenter. The experiment was explained to the defiant subjects in a way that supported their decision to disobey the experimenter. Obedient subjects were assured of the fact that their behavior was entirely normal and that their feelings of conflict or tension were shared by other participants. Subjects were told that they would receive a comprehensive report at the conclusion of the experimental series. In some instances, additional detailed and lengthy discussions of the experiments were also carried out with individual subjects.

When the experimental series was complete, subjects received a written report which presented details of the experimental procedure and results. Again their own part in the experiments was treated in a dignified way and their behavior in the experiment respected. All subjects received a follow-up questionnaire regarding their participation in the research, which again allowed expression of thoughts and feelings about their behavior.

The replies to the questionnaire confirmed my impression that participants felt positively toward the experiment. In its quantitative aspect (see Table 2-1), 84 percent of the subjects stated they were glad to have been in the experiment; 15 percent indicated neutral feelings, and 1.3 percent indicated negative feelings. To be sure, such findings are to be interpreted cautiously, but they cannot be disregarded.

Further, four-fifths of the subjects felt that more experiments of this sort should be carried out, and 74 percent indicated that they had learned something of personal importance as a result of being in the study. The results of the interviews, questionnaire responses, and actual transcripts of the debriefing procedures will be presented more fully in a forthcoming monograph.

Table 2–1 *Excerpt from Questionnaire Used in a Follow-up Study of the Obedience Research*

Now that I have read the report, and all things considered . . .	Defiant	Obedient	All
1. I am very glad to have been in the experiment	40.0%	47.8%	43.5%
2. I am glad to have been in the experiment	43.8%	35.7%	30.2%
3. I am neither sorry nor glad to have been in the experiment	15.3%	14.8%	15.1%
4. I am sorry to have been in the experiment	0.8%	0.7%	0.8%
5. I am very sorry to have been in the experiment	0.0%	1.0%	0.5%

Note—Ninety-two per cent of the subjects returned the questionnaire. The characteristics of the nonrespondents were checked against the respondents. They differed from the respondents only with regard to age; younger people were overrepresented in the nonresponding group.

The debriefing and assessment procedures were carried out as a matter of course, and were not stimulated by any observation of special risk in the experimental procedure. In my judgment, at no point were subjects exposed to danger and at no point did they run the risk of injurious effects resulting from participation. If it had been otherwise, the experiment would have been terminated at once.

Baumrind states that, after he has performed in the experiment, the subject cannot justify his behavior and must bear the full brunt of his actions. By and large it does not work this way. The same mechanisms that allow the subject to perform the act, to obey rather than to defy the experimenter, transcend the moment of performance and continue to justify his behavior for him. The same viewpoint the subject takes while performing the actions is the viewpoint from which he later sees his behavior, that is, the perspective of "carrying out the task assigned by the person in authority."

Because the idea of shocking the victim is repugnant, there is a tendency among those who hear of the design to say "people will not do it." When the results are made known, this attitude is expressed as "if they do it they will not be able to live with themselves afterward."

These two forms of denying the experimental findings are equally inappropriate misreadings of the facts of human social behavior. Many subjects do, indeed, obey to the end, and there is no indication of injurious effects.

The absence of injury is a minimal condition of experimentation; there can be, however, an important positive side to participation. Baumrind suggests that subjects derived no benefit from being in the obedience study, but this is false. By their statements and actions, subjects indicated that they had learned a good deal, and many felt gratified to have taken part in scientific research they considered to be of significance. A year after his participation one subject wrote:

This experiment has strengthened my belief that man should avoid harm to his fellow man even at the risk of violating authority.

Another stated:

To me, the experiment pointed up . . . the extent to which each individual should have or discover firm ground on which to base his decisions, no matter how trivial they appear to be. I think people should think more deeply about themselves and their relation to their world and to other people. If this experiment serves to jar people out of complacency, it will have served its end.

These statements are illustrative of a broad array of appreciative and insightful comments by those who participated.

The five-page report sent to each subject on the completion of the experimental series was specifically designed to enhance the value of his experience. It set out the broad conception of the experimental program as well as the logic of its design. It described the results of a dozen of the experiments, discussed the causes of tension, and attempted to indicate the possible significance of the experiment. Subjects responded enthusiastically; many indicated a desire to be in further experimental research. This report was sent to all subjects several years ago. The care with which it was prepared does not support Baumrind's assertion that the experimenter was indifferent to the value subjects derived from their participation.

Baumrind's fear is that participants will be alienated from psychological experiments because of the intensity of experience associated with laboratory procedures. My own observation is that subjects more commonly respond with distaste to the "empty" laboratory hour, in which cardboard procedures are employed and the only possible feeling upon emerging from the laboratory is that one has wasted time in a patently trivial and useless exercise.

The subjects in the obedience experiment, on the whole, felt quite differently about their participation. They viewed the experience as an opportunity to learn something of importance about themselves, and more generally, about the conditions of human action.

A year after the experimental program was completed, I initiated an additional follow-up study. In this connection an impartial medical examiner, experienced in outpatient treatment, interviewed 40 experimental subjects. The examining psychiatrist focused on those subjects he felt would be most likely to have suffered consequences from participation. His aim was to identify possible injurious effects resulting from the experiment. He concluded that, although extreme stress had been experienced by several subjects,

> none was found by this interviewer to show signs of having been harmed by his experience. . . . Each subject seemed to handle his task [in the experiment] in a manner consistent with well established patterns of behavior. No evidence was found of any traumatic reactions.

Such evidence ought to be weighed before judging the experiment.

OTHER ISSUES

Baumrind's discussion is not limited to the treatment of subjects, but diffuses to a generalized rejection of the work.

Baumrind feels that obedience cannot be meaningfully studied in a laboratory setting: The reason she offers is that "The dependent, obedient attitude assumed by most subjects in the experimental setting is appropriate to that situation" [p. 107]. Here, Baumrind has cited the very best reason for examining obedience in this setting, namely that it possesses "ecological validity." Here is one social context in which compliance occurs regularly. Military and job situations are also particularly meaningful settings for the study of obedience precisely because obedience is natural and appropriate to these contexts. I reject Baumrind's argument that the observed obedience does not count because it occurred where it is appropriate. That is precisely why it *does* count. A soldier's obedience is no less meaningful because it occurs in a pertinent military context. A subject's obedience is no less problematical because it occurs within a social institution called the psychological experiment.

Baumrind writes: "The game is defined by the experimenter and he makes the rules" [p. 107]. It is true that for disobedience to occur the framework of the experiment must be shattered. That, indeed, is the point of the design. That is why obedience and disobedience are genuine issues for the subject. *He must really assert himself as a person against a legitimate authority.*

Further, Baumrind wants us to believe that outside the laboratory we could not find a comparably high expression of obedience. Yet, the fact that ordinary citizens are recruited to military service and, on command, perform far harsher acts against people is beyond dispute. Few of them know or are concerned with the complex policy issues underlying martial action; fewer still become conscientious objectors. Good soldiers do as they are told, and on both sides of the battle line. However, a debate on whether a higher level of obedience is represented by (*a*) killing men in the service of one's country, or (*b*) merely shocking them in the service of Yale science, is largely unprofitable. The real question is: What are the forces underlying obedient action?

Another question raised by Baumrind concerns the degree of parallel between obedience in the laboratory and in Nazi Germany. Obviously, there are enormous differences: Consider the disparity in time scale. The laboratory experiment takes an hour; the Nazi calamity unfolded in the space of a decade. There is a great deal that needs to be said on this issue, and only a few points can be touched on here.

1. In arguing this matter, Baumrind mistakes the background metaphor for the precise subject matter of investigation. The German event was cited to point up a serious problem in the human situation: the potentially destructive effect of obedience. But the best way to tackle the problem of obedience, from a scientific standpoint, is in no way restricted by "what happened exactly" in Germany. What happened exactly can *never* be duplicated in the laboratory or anywhere else. The real task is to learn more about the general problem of destructive obedience using a workable approach. Hopefully, such inquiry will stimulate insights and yield general propositions that can be applied to a wide variety of situations.

2. One may ask in a general way: How does a man behave when he is told by a legitimate authority to act against a third individual? In trying to find an answer to this question, the laboratory situation is one useful starting point—and for the very reason stated by Baumrind—namely, the experimenter does constitute a genuine authority for the subject. The fact that trust and dependence on the experimenter are maintained, despite the extraordinary harshness he displays toward the victim, is itself a remarkable phenomenon.

3. In the laboratory, through a set of rather simple manipulations, ordinary persons no longer perceived themselves as a responsible part of the causal chain leading to action against a person. The means through which responsibility is cast off, and individuals become thoughtless agents of action, is of general import. Other processes were revealed that indicate that the experiments will help us to understand why men obey. That understanding will

come, of course, by examining the full account of experimental work and not merely the brief report in which the procedure and demonstrational results were exposed.

At root, Baumrind senses that it is not proper to test obedience in this situation, because she construes it as one in which there is no reasonable alternative to obedience. In adopting this view, she has lost sight of this fact: A substantial proportion of subjects do disobey. By their example, disobedience is shown to be a genuine possibility, one that is in no sense ruled out by the general structure of the experimental situation.

Baumrind is uncomfortable with the high level of obedience obtained in the first experiment. In the condition she focused on, 65 percent of the subjects obeyed to the end. However, her sentiment does not take into account that, within the general framework of the psychological experiment, obedience varied enormously from one condition to the next. In some variations, 90 percent of the subjects *dis*obeyed. It seems to be *not* only the fact of an experiment, but the particular structure of elements within the experimental situation that accounts for rates of obedience and disobedience. And these elements were varied systematically in the program of research.

A concern with human dignity is based on a respect for a man's potential to act morally. Baumrind feels that the experimenter *made* the subject shock the victim. This conception is alien to my view. The experimenter tells the subject to do something. But between the command and the outcome there is a paramount force, the acting person who may obey or disobey. I started with the belief that every person who came to the laboratory was free to accept or to reject the dictates of authority. This view sustains a conception of human dignity insofar as it sees in each man a capacity for *choosing* his own behavior. And as it turned out, many subjects did, indeed, choose to reject the experimenter's commands, providing a powerful affirmation of human ideals.

Baumrind also criticizes the experiment on the grounds that "it could easily effect an alteration in the subject's . . . ability to trust adult authorities in the future" [p. 109]. But I do not think she can have it both ways. On the one hand, she argues the experimental situation is so special that it has no generality; on the other hand, she states it has such generalizing potential that it will cause subjects to distrust all authority. But the experimenter is not just any authority: He is an authority who tells the subject to act harshly and inhumanely against another man. I would consider it of the highest value if participation in the experiment could, indeed, inculcate a skepticism of this kind of authority. Here, perhaps, a difference in philosophy emerges most clearly. Baumrind sees the subject as a passive creature, completely controlled by the experimenter. I started from a different viewpoint. A person who comes to the laboratory is an active, choosing adult, capable of accepting or rejecting the prescriptions for action addressed to him. Baumrind sees the effect of the experiment as undermining the subject's trust of authority. I see it as a potentially valuable experience insofar as it makes people aware of the problem of indiscriminate submission to authority.

CONCLUSION

My feeling is that viewed in the total context of values served by the experiment, approximately the right course was followed. In review, the facts are these: (*a*) At the outset, there was the problem of studying obedience by means of a simple experimental procedure. The results could not be foreseen before the experiment was carried out. (*b*) Although the experiment generated momentary stress in some subjects, this stress dissipated quickly and was not injurious. (*c*) Dehoax and follow-up procedures were carried out to insure the subjects' well-being. (*d*) These procedures were assessed through questionnaire and psychiatric studies and were found to be effective. (*e*) Additional steps were taken to enhance the value of the laboratory experience for participants, for example, submitting to each subject a careful report on the experimental program. (*f*) The subjects themselves strongly endorse the experiment, and indicate satisfaction at having participated.

If there is a moral to be learned from the obedience study, it is that every man must be responsible for his own actions. This author accepts full responsibility for the design and execution of the study. Some people may feel it should not have been done. I disagree and accept the burden of their judgment.

Baumrind's judgment, someone has said, not only represents a personal conviction, but also reflects a cleavage in American psychology between those whose primary concern is with *helping* people and those who are interested mainly in *learning* about people. I see little value in perpetuating divisive forces in psychology when there is so much to learn from every side. A schism may exist, but it does not correspond to the true ideals of the discipline. The psychologist intent on healing knows that his power to help rests on knowledge; he is aware that a scientific grasp of all aspects of life is essential for his work and is in itself a worthy human aspiration. At the same time, the laboratory psychologist senses his work will lead to human betterment, not only because enlightenment is more dignified than ignorance, but because new knowledge is pregnant with humane consequences.

REFERENCES

BAUMRIND, D. Some thoughts on ethics of research: After reading Milgram's "Behavioral study of obedience." *American Psychologist*, 1964, **19**: 421–423.

LAZARUS, R. A laboratory approach to the dynamics of psychological stress. *American Psychologist*, 1964, **19**: 400–411.

MILGRAM, S. Behavioral study of obedience. *Journal of Abnormal and Social Psychology*, 1963, **67**: 371–378.

MILGRAM, S. Some conditions of obedience and disobedience to authority. *Human Relations*, 1965, **18**: 55–76.

Martin T. Orne and Charles H. Holland

On the Ecological Validity of Laboratory Deceptions[1]

Oh what a tangled web we weave,
When first we practise to deceive!

(Sir Walter Scott, 1808)

In the last half of this century, social psychology has gained increasing significance and importance. In an age when technology has made the sudden extinction of man an all too real possibility, when we are witnessing a worldwide crisis of values and the only remaining social certainty is continuing change, the prospect of bringing relevant social psychological processes under scientific scrutiny is of major concern to all of us. The impressionistic, quasi-philosophical approaches which had long characterized writings about crowd behavior and group processes were not sufficient to form the body of a science, nor could the technology of evaluating attitudes and public opinion, regardless of its methodological sophistication, provide for the development of basic new insights into the nature of man. Rather the pioneering work, particularly by Lewin, Asch, and Sherif, showed how the techniques of experimental psychology could also be applied to the study of social psychological phenomena. The use of the psychological experiment as a tool has made it possible to systematically manipulate a wide range of variables, and increasing ingenuity has been devoted to the application of this tool to an ever wider range of problems. The experiments by Festinger and his students (e.g., Brehm & Cohen, 1962) in support of the cognitive dissonance theory are particularly ingenious examples of what has recently become known as experimental social psychology.

Conceptual and methodological issues that had been skirted by much of the research in this exciting new discipline have been brought to a head by Milgram's studies in obedience. He has addressed himself

From *International Journal of Psychiatry*, 1968, 6: 282–293. Reprinted with permission of authors and Science House, Inc.

to one of the most compelling questions of our time: What are the conditions under which man will inflict pain and suffering upon another individual? In a series of apparently crucial experiments Milgram seems to have shown that subjects (hereinafter designated *S*s) can be required to inflict pain up to and beyond intensities clearly designated as dangerous merely by legitimizing this behavior as part of a scientific experiment. Such findings are uncomfortably reminiscent of the concentration camp "medical experiments" reported to have been carried out by Schumann, Mengele, and others (Manvell & Fraenkel, 1967). Milgram has also tried to demonstrate that this behavior is lawful in that it can be shown to vary, depending upon the proximity between the *S* and his victim and the extent to which the experimental situation as a whole is legitimized, i.e., carried out within the confines of a university campus versus a rented office in a slightly disreputable office building.

The implications of Milgram's work are clear. It would appear that with little effort most individuals can be induced to carry out destructive and aggressive actions bringing severe pain, possible permanent injury, or even death to their victim. The fact that the *S*'s behavior is in the name of science provides little reassurance and suggests at the very least a horrifying callousness as a characteristic of modern man. The studies seem to provide convincing empirical support for Freud's belief in the death instinct and the philosophic position on man put forth by Hobbes, Nietzsche, and others. One may even conceive of these studies as laboratory analogs to the Genovese murder (Rosenthal, 1964).

As has often been pointed out, the extent to which scientific findings become generally accepted is only partly a function of the care with which they are obtained. In large part, acceptance depends upon the extent to which results fit the *Zeitgeist* and the prejudices of the scientific community. The flair with which Milgram presents his findings and the affect they generate tend to obscure serious questions about their validity. In evaluating research which has broad implications and is of practical importance, there is a tendency to minimize concern for methodological rigor. Yet it is because of its importance that this research demands thoughtful consideration.

ECOLOGICAL VALIDITY OF DECEPTION STUDIES

In some areas, the bases for evaluating the methodological adequacy of research have been worked out in considerable detail. A judgment is usually made by evaluating the controls, the manner in which data are collected and how they are handled statistically. By these criteria,

Milgram's work appears to have been carefully carried out. Unfortunately there is an entirely different set of problems requiring consideration, which Brunswik (1947) has subsumed under the concept of ecological validity.

Experiments are carried out to make inferences to other—usually nonexperimental—situations. They make it possible to observe events in a standard situation, ideally holding constant everything other than the particular independent variable under investigation. For this technique to allow valid inference it is essential that the experimental situation adequately reflect the process under investigation. This crucial step is taken when the general process is translated into specific experimental terms by an operational definition. Milgram, for example, has operationally defined the concept of obedience as whether or not in the experiment the S continues to administer ever increasing levels of electric shock. Then by studying the conditions under which the specific behavior may be obtained, the ease with which it can be elicited, the percentage of individuals who obey, etc., he tries to investigate the generic problem of obedience. The validity of his findings for legitimate generalizations to nonexperimental contexts where the concept of obedience applies depends upon the appropriateness of the experimental situation and the adequacy of the operational definition—questions central to the issue of ecological validity. Unfortunately, while the rules of statistical inference have received a great deal of attention in recent years, no such consensus exists about how to evaluate the ecological validity of research findings.

As a solution to the problem of ecological validity, Brunswik suggested running Ss with differing demographic, personality and I.Q. characteristics and extending the study to a wide variety of contexts. Milgram's work is of special interest because he, more than most other investigators, has systematically tried to vary both subject population and the institutional setting in which his studies are carried out, implicitly recognizing the crux of the issues confronting his work. These attempts do not, however, successfully deal with the two issues addressed in this discussion: the methodological problems common to all psychological deception studies and the unique social psychological attributes of the psychological experiment itself.

PROBLEMS OF DECEPTION STUDIES

Conceptually, the Milgram situation is closely related to the conformity situation developed by Asch. In his classic research on conformity, Asch (1952) placed Ss in a group situation, ostensibly to investigate perception. The Ss were required to carry out simple perceptual tasks such as judging the length of lines and to reach agreement about their perceptions. Starting out with very ambiguous stimuli, the perceptual qualities became more and more clear-cut. The situation was so devised, however, that there was only one real S while the other Ss were confederates. They were instructed to agree on perceptions which were in fact inaccurate, and matters were so arranged that the actual S was required to make his judgment after most of the others. In the beginning, with stimuli which were very ambiguous, it was not difficult for him to agree but, as the experiment continued, he found himself confronted with agreement among his peers about perceptions that were clearly at odds with his own, an experience which many Ss found extremely frightening and disturbing. They were forced either to conform to group pressure and deny what they could plainly see or to maintain their perceptual judgment against the group.

Asch used this situation to explore the kinds of factors that determined the S's conformity response. Recognizing the importance of not allowing the S to suspect that the other Ss were actually confederates, he was careful to keep the situation plausible. The stimuli were chosen to be ambiguous at first, and only gradually was the S forced to recognize the increasing discrepancy between his perceptions and those of his peers. The extent to which Ss accepted the situation was checked by careful postexperimental interviews which allowed Asch to evaluate their degree of suspicion. In this way he was able to determine the limits within which the experiment had to be conducted without becoming obvious—a formidable problem when Swarthmore students were used as Ss!

The development of a new paradigm of this kind is usually followed by a large number of studies using the technique in order to relate conformity to a wide variety of other parameters. While Asch himself paid close attention to the plausibility of his situation, later investigators showed less concern about this problem, often changing the perceptual stimuli abruptly and excessively. Rather than checking carefully whether Ss were taken in by the deception they tended to define conformity in simple behavioral terms, either omitting postexperimental discussion or carrying it out in a perfunctory fashion.

Unless a postexperimental inquiry is carried out with great persistence and sensitivity a "pact of ignorance" tends to develop (Orne, 1962). It is important to Ss that their experimental participation prove useful. If the S sees through the deception in an experiment, he may also realize that this might destroy the value of his performance. Since neither he nor the experimenter (E) wants to discard his data, their interests collaborate to make the S appear naïve even after extremely transparent procedures.

The use of deception in social psychological studies has become extremely popular in recent years.[2] It is obviously felt that deception is needed to make it possible to explore the process under investigation. Experimenters implicitly realize that *S*s are active, sentient beings who are influenced not only by the immediate stimuli in the experimental situation but also by their symbolic meaning in a broader sense: the context in which the studies are carried out, their aims, purposes, and so forth. The deception, then, is an attempt on the part of the investigator to circumvent those cognitive processes of the *S* which would interfere with his research. When such an experiment is carried out, however, it is vital that the investigator determine whether it is the *S* or he himself who is being deceived!

Milgram's studies use deception to create what seems to be a compelling conflict situation. Because of the ingenuity of the deception, the reader is drawn to assume with Milgram that the *S*s accepted the situation at face value. It is unfortunate that no data are presented to indicate whether this was in fact the case. Yet the extent to which the deception actually was accepted by the *S* determines how the results should be interpreted. Had quasi-control procedures been included in obedience studies, they would have shed light on the adequacy of the deception manipulation, but in the absence of data on this crucial issue, the only way we can evaluate the experiment's plausibility is to analyze the congruence of the cues available to the *S*.

THE MILGRAM DESIGN

In all the variations of Milgram's obedience research, *S*s are told that they are participating in an experiment to study the effect of punishment on memory. Each *S* always draws straws with the other *S* (confederate) and by "chance" ends up with the teacher's role. The other "*S*" is always strapped into an awesome looking electric chair and both are always shown a shock generator by means of which shocks from a very low voltage up to 450 volts can be administered. This machine is made all the more awesome by labeling the high end of the scale in red letters, "Danger—Severe Shock—XXX."

Before beginning the experiment a shock described as 45 volts is administered to the *S*, presumably so that he knows what the shocks are like. This, incidentally, is an extremely uncomfortable shock. The teacher's role is then explained to the *S*—how to present a paired-associates learning task to the learner, how it is the teacher who determines the duration of the punishment, and how a higher level of shock must be administered for each failure. Initially the learner is able to answer correctly two out of three times, but he rapidly begins to fail more and more frequently, requiring the *S* to administer ever higher levels of shock to the victim.

Starting with 75 volts the learner begins to grunt and moan. At 150 volts he demands to be let out of the experiment. At 180 volts he cries out that he can no longer stand the pain. At 300 volts he refuses to provide any more answers to the memory test, insisting that he is no longer a participant in the experiment and must be freed [Milgram, 1965, p. 60].

The *E* throughout this procedure remains calm and instructs the *S* to continue. If the teacher says that the learner is no longer responding and therefore there is no point in going on, he is told, "Treat the absence of an answer as equivalent to a wrong answer, and follow the usual shock procedure." If the *S* does not wish to do so, he is told, "You have no other choice, you must go on!" Regardless of the degree of agitation shown by the *S* or the anguished screams of the victim, the *E* remains imperturbable and demands that the *S* continue.

HOW PLAUSIBLE IS THIS PARADIGM?

*S*s participating in psychological experiments have considerable awareness of the implicit rules which govern the situation. They have learned to distrust the *E* because they know that the true purpose of the experiment may be disguised. Many *S*s view their task as a problem-solving situation which requires them to determine the "real" situation and respond appropriately. This process has been analyzed elsewhere (Orne, 1962b; Riecken, 1962). Of particular relevance here is that the *S*'s perception of the purpose of an experiment will depend only in part on what he is told explicitly. He will then evaluate this information in terms of his prior knowledge, using whatever cues are available in the situation. These cues include not only the manner in which instructions are communicated but also scuttlebutt about the experiment, the setting in which it is carried out, the person of the *E* and, most important of all, the experimental procedure itself. The congruence of all of these cues with the instructions that the *S* is explicitly given will determine the plausibility of the experimental situation. When the procedure suggests one experimental intent and the explicit instructions another, what the *S* believes becomes difficult to determine and very slight changes in the procedure may lead to radical changes in the *S*'s hypotheses and subsequent behavior. In a conflict situation when the instructions are at odds with other cues, the *S* is apt, however, to rely preferentially on those cues stemming from the experimental procedure, because, as the old adage says, "Actions speak louder than words."

To successfully carry out a deception study is exceedingly difficult because subtle practical problems, often dealt with in some fashion by research assistants, assume crucial importance. In arranging the schedule, for example, the *S* may inquire whether he might be run at the same time as a friend. Considerable ingenuity is required to explain in a plausible fashion why no suitable time exists for the *S*s to be run together in a study apparently requiring two *S*s. The task of preventing *S*s from communicating with each other is also formidable, especially in an experiment that makes such ideal cocktail party conversation. There are moreover innumerable subtle cues that can give away the true status of a confederate, stemming not only from the confederate's behavior but also from that of the *E*. (It is exceedingly difficult to treat the confederate and the *S* in a similar fashion.) In the absence of evidence it does not seem justified to assume that the performance was carried out flawlessly in each instance. Plausible deceptions are not easily achieved, but no hint of difficulties or *S* disqualifications appears in any of Milgram's reports.

Beside the myriad technical problems, even if we were to assume that everybody played his role to perfection, the experimental procedure itself contains serious incongruities. The experiment is presented as a study of the effect of punishment on memory. The investigator presumably is interested in determining how the victim's rate of learning is affected by punishment, yet there is nothing that he requires of the *S* (teacher) that he could not as easily do himself. Those *S*s who have some scientific training would also be aware that experimental procedures require more care and training in administering stimuli than they have been given. The way in which the study is carried out is certainly sufficient to allow some *S*s to recognize that they, rather than the victim, are the real *S*s of the experiment.

The most incongruent aspect of the experiment, however, is the behavior of the *E*. Despite the movie image of the mad scientist, most *S*s accept the fact that scientists—even behavioral scientists—are reasonable people. No effort is made to emphasize the world-shaking importance of the learning experiment; rather it is presented as a straightforward, simple study. Incongruously the *E* sits by passively while the victim suffers, demanding that the experiment continue despite the victim's demands to be released and the possibility that his health may be endangered. This behavior of the *E*, which Milgram interprets as the demands of legitimate authority, can with equal plausibility be interpreted as a significant cue to the true state of affairs —namely that no one is actually being hurt. Indeed, if the *S* believes that the experiment is a legitimate study, the very fact that he is being asked to continue a relatively trivial experiment while inflicting extreme suffering upon his victim clearly implies that no such suffering or danger exists.

The incongruity between the relatively trivial experiment and the imperturbability of the *E* on the one hand, and the awesome shock generator able to present shocks designated as "Danger—Severe

Shock" and the extremity of the victim's suffering on the other, should be sufficient to raise serious doubts in the minds of most *S*s.

ANOTHER WAY TO CONCEPTUALIZE
MILGRAM'S FINDINGS

In considering the incongruities of the situation, one may wonder how different this experiment is from the stage magician's trick where a volunteer from the audience is strapped into the guillotine and another volunteer is required to trip the release lever. The magician is careful to do a professional job of deception. He demonstrates that the guillotine will split a head of cabbage and allows the volunteer to satisfy himself about the genuineness of the guillotine. Though releasing the lever will lead to the apparently inevitable decapitation of the victim, he has little difficulty in obtaining "obedience" because the *S* knows full well that everything is going to be all right. This does not, of course, prevent the *S* from being somewhat uncomfortable, perhaps showing nervous laughter, when he is actually required to trip the lever, if only because such behavior is appropriate in this context.

The lawfulness which Milgram demonstrates in the relationship of obedience to physical proximity can be accounted for by the cues that different procedures communicate to the *S*—albeit implicitly—that things are not what they seem. Sixty-six percent obedience is obtained when the victim is in another room and the only communication between him and the teacher is his banging the wall at 300 volts, ostensibly wanting to be let out. When we consider the most striking cues available to the *S* at this point—the victim's protestations and the *E*'s calmly continuing to take notes and ignoring these pleas—it would seem more plausible to assume not that the *E* is some fanatic with a cause which justifies his behavior but rather that the *E* is still a responsible scientist whose behavior is clearly communicating that the alleged victim is not really a victim at all. One need not assume undue intellectual ability on the part of the *S* to postulate that he may be able to surmise the true state of affairs. To us the high rate of compliance would seem less due to the *S*'s "putting the victim out of mind" (as Milgram suggests) than to the relatively low cue value of the victim's behavior when compared with that of the *E*'s unswerving imperturbability. The addition of auditory feedback (the victim's screams) results in a remarkably small decrement in obedience—to 62.5 percent. We would suspect this is partly due to the technical problems; namely, the *S* tends to scream only in response to the immediate punishing stimuli while sitting quietly and continuing to cooperate in response to the verbal stimuli. Regardless of the quality of the screams, the situation is not very plausible. Apparently by using good actors in close proximity it is easier to convince *S*s that the situation might be real. Here the degree of compliance drops to 40 percent, and when the *S* is required to actually hold the victim's hand, to 30 percent.

In contrast to many other investigators, Milgram is aware of some of the difficulties inherent in social psychological laboratory research and, for this reason, he used the ingenious modification of renting an office in downtown Bridgeport and making the research appear unrelated to a major university. Under these circumstances the cue value of the *E*'s imperturbability would diminish and, as one might expect, the degree of obedience also diminishes. Even in this situation, however, the *E* is still carrying out an experiment in an apparently professional manner.

RELEVANT DATA FROM OTHER STUDIES

The problems inherent in this research are illustrated in the long-standing controversy about whether *S*s in hypnosis can be compelled to carry out antisocial actions. Already, in 1889, Janet reports that before a distinguished group of jurists and medical men a deeply hypnotized patient stabbed individuals with rubber daggers, poisoned their tea with sugar, and carried out any other type of murder or mayhem required of her. This demonstration was very impressive, and after the distinguished guests had left, the *S* was left to be awakened by students who wished to end the experiment on a lighter note. They suggested to the patient that she was alone, about to take a bath, and should undress. Her response to the suggestion was to awaken immediately, greatly disturbed. It is one thing to "kill" people during an experimental situation with means that cannot really do damage; it is quite another to be asked to undress in a context that transcends the experimental situation.

More recently, Rowland (1939) carried out a seemingly definitive experiment by showing that *S*s in deep hypnosis could be compelled to carry out antisocial and destructive acts, such as throwing fuming nitric acid at a research assistant, a finding which was subsequently replicated by P. C. Young (1952). In both studies *S*s were "obedient" in deep hypnosis, but when asked in the waking state whether they would carry out these actions, they indicated in horror that they would not. In a careful replication of these experiments, Orne and Evans (1965) found that five out of six deeply hypnotized *S*s could in fact be compelled to carry out an action as antisocial as throwing fuming nitric acid at another individual. In addition, however, it was found that six out of six nonhypnotized individuals, who had been required to simulate hypnosis for a "blind" *E*, would also carry out these actions. Depending upon the degree of social pressure, moreover, various degrees of "obedience" were obtained from other groups of *S*s who were merely asked to participate in a previously unspecified experiment. The crucial difference seemed to be that instead of *asking* Ss whether they would carry out the action, the *E* clearly communicated to them that they *were* to do so. In an experiment, when it is clearly communicated to the *S* that he is to carry out an action which appears very destructive and dangerous, it is thereby concurrently communicated that it will be safe to do so. In contrast, when the *S* is questioned as to whether he would carry out such an action, it does nothing to alter what is patently obvious—that someone would be severely hurt— thereby eliciting vehement denial.

Thus far we have only described the part of the experiment which is analogous to the seeming antisocial aspects of Milgram's work. More illuminating perhaps is that Ss were also required to carry out apparently self-destructive actions; in particular, to pick up and place in a bag a snake known to be poisonous and to remove a penny from the jar of fuming nitric acid with their bare fingers. In Milgram's terms, there was little trouble in eliciting obedience from our Ss. Our findings in this regard did not, however, lead us to conclude that outside the experimental situation Ss can be instructed to walk off the roof, in some other way to injure themselves or even to commit suicide. On the contrary, when we asked our Ss about their behavior, they clearly indicated that despite perceptual evidence to the contrary they did not have the slightest doubt that every care had been taken to protect them from serious harm. Without having to be told, Ss were quite aware of the reality constraints governing research in our society and, correctly we might add, assumed that as long as we really intended them to carry out these behaviors, we would have made certain no serious injury would befall anyone—neither them nor our research assistants.

It was essential for the *S* to be in an actual subject-experimenter relationship in order to have him carry out these actions; despite repeated attempts, not one of our colleagues could be induced to attempt any of these acts. We would like to attribute their refusal not to a lack of trust in us, but to the absence of the experimental relationship that legitimized the behavior. Our colleagues were also convinced, much like the group of psychiatrists polled by Milgram, that few if any Ss would comply with the demands of the experiment. It would appear that even expertise in nonexperimental human behavior does not allow accurate prediction of what Ss will do in an actual experimental situation.

Holland (1967) extended Milgram's studies in an attempt to explore the demand characteristics of the situation. The substantive findings will be reported elsewhere and only some observations are relevant here. Initially it was intended to replicate precisely the verbal feedback condition where the victim refuses to answer further after having received a 300-volt shock. It became clear, however, that it would be necessary to add additional auditory feedback in the form of moans or groans each time a substantial shock was administered, because, during the pilot studies, *S*s run in the original condition indicated after the experiment that they had been certain that the victim had either escaped or been released! Even with additional auditory feedback and meticulous attention to perfecting the deception aspects of the situation, three-quarters of the *S*s run in the analog of Milgram's situation indicated that they did not really believe the deception when carefully questioned after the experiment.

Holland added two additional groups of *S*s in his study and a "blind" second *E*. The first *E* told one group that they were control *S*s and suggested that there would be something "fishy" about the experiment in which they were about to participate. They were instructed not to "let on" but rather to act as though they were regular *S*s. In this manner it was hoped to raise their level of suspicion, making it virtually certain that they would become aware of the incongruities of the situation. The other group was told before the experiment that the level of shock which would be administered to the *S* was really only one-tenth of what was indicated on the shock generator. Though the experimental manipulation made certain that these latter two groups would be relatively aware that things were not as they seemed, their obedience behavior was not significantly different from the group run under the Milgram condition. Other aspects of their behavior also failed to separate these groups: *S*s exposed to each treatment appeared to become uncomfortable and show signs of severe anxiety conflict. As a result, the "blind" *E* was unable to judge at better than chance levels the experimental group to which *S*s belonged. These findings suggest that *S*s run in the Milgram condition could easily have become aware of the deception and still behave as if they were naïve. Neither the extent of the *S*'s obedience nor his objective signs of discomfort necessarily reflect what he experiences. Thus, in the final post experimental inquiry it became clear that much of the *S*'s disturbed behavior was purposive and occurred because the individual felt that such behavior was demanded by the situation.

It would seem that the simple behavioral response of obeying instructions cannot tell us much about why the *S* obeys. We are dealing with a highly complex situation where *S*s may perceive that no real hurt is being inflicted upon anyone and yet not be certain what constitutes the desired response on their part. They are placed in a dilemma where the only definitely appropriate response seems to be discomfort. Whether continued obedience or conformity is seen as the successful response seems to depend upon many as yet obscure and subtle aspects of the total situation.

It seems that in the Milgram-type experiment one may encounter two groups of *S*s that do not necessarily differ in their overt behavior. Usually the majority of *S*s assume that the situation is essentially safe while a much smaller group may accept the situation at its face value. Logically these two groups of *S*s take part in quite different experiments. Obedience by the first group that is (correctly) convinced the situation is essentially safe allows inference about what they would do in other experimental situations but not about what they would do outside of such a context. For the experiment to have any significance for other contexts, it is essential that the *S*s believe in its reality. To ignore the *S*s' perceptions and merely focus upon their overt behavior by saying it matters only whether the *S* is in fact obedient according to an arbitrary operational definition ignores a vital issue: To what are they obedient? Only by answering this question can an experiment of this kind have broader meaning.

THE PSYCHOLOGY OF THE PSYCHOLOGICAL EXPERIMENT

For most psychological studies involving deception it is sufficient to make certain that the situation is accepted, but Milgram's paradigm raises an additional problem. There are some issues which cannot readily be examined in an experimental context since they are context-specific or at least context-related. This is particularly true when an experimental situation is used to study compliance or obedience.

Milgram appropriately points out that we expose our neck to the barber and remove our shoes in the shoe store because these constitute legitimate requests. In everyday life the individual is able to determine what constitutes a legitimate request and rather clearly defined, implicit rules govern what one individual may ask of another. However, the agreement to participate in an experiment gives the *E carte blanche* about what may legitimately be requested. In asking the *S* to participate in an experiment, the *E* implicitly says, "Will you do whatever I ask for a specified period of time? By so doing you may earn a fee, contribute to science, and perhaps even learn something of value to yourself. In return I promise that no harm will befall you. At the completion of the experiment you will be no better or worse off than you are now and though you may experience temporary inconvenience, this is justified by the importance of the undertaking." A corollary to this agreement is that the *S* may not ask why certain things are required of him. He must assume that these actions are legitimate and appropriate for the needs of the experiment.

The *S*'s willingness to comply with unexplained or unreasonable requests in an experimental context does not permit inference to be drawn beyond this context. For example, a study required Ss to carry out a boring and tedious task—serial addition. After completing each page of work Ss were instructed to destroy their own product and continue working (Orne, 1962b). To our surprise, Ss were willing to carry out this task for long periods of time and do so with a high rate of speed and accuracy. Anyone who believes direct inference about obedience in real life can be drawn from an experimental context should ask his secretary to type a letter, and after making certain there are no errors, ask her to tear it up and retype it. With rare exceptions, two or three such trials should be sufficient to ensure that the E will require a new secretary! It should be noted that the activity required of the secretary is no different in kind from what she is normally required to do. She is paid for the work at her usual rate, no one is hurt and yet as long as she has an option, there is little question about her behavior in real life. Incidentally, the same individual would likely be "obedient" if she had agreed to participate in an experiment.[3]

The S's unquestioning compliance with the E's requests depends in part upon his awareness of the total experimental situation and the safeguards built into it. The Milgram paradigm runs, therefore, into an inevitable paradox. There are some things which the S would not do but these are behaviors that he knows the E cannot require of him. Therefore, when the E asks him to carry out an action which would lead to serious harm either to himself or to someone else and communicates that the S is intended to carry out these actions, he inevitably also communicates that these actions will *not* lead to their apparent consequences. That the S will in an experiment carry out behaviors that appear destructive either to himself or others reflects more upon his willingness to trust the E and the experimental context than on what he would do outside of the experimental situation.

It can be argued that Ss will carry out behaviors which appear dangerous and that an unscrupulous investigator could utilize this to inflict serious harm on either the S or other individuals. This is, of course, true but lest we be concerned about breeding a nation of sheep who will unsuspectingly carry out dangerous actions, it is well to remember that in our complex but still basically cooperative society it is impossible to function without trust in reasonable situations. We take our car to have the brakes repaired and assume without personally checking that they have been put back together properly; we take a plane without personally subjecting the pilot to physical examination, trusting in his competence and soundness of mind; when a physician prescribes green pills, we blithely assume that the medication is for our good although, of course, if he had chosen to give us arsenic we would have taken it and died. Therefore, a demonstration that a situation that can legitimately be expected to contain all possible safeguards for the participants could conceivably be perverted cannot at the same time be used to prove that man is either gullible or, when on guard, easily deceived. Unfortunately, as important as the problem of obedience is in modern society, it is unlikely to be resolved by using the psychological experiment as a tool in a situation where the *S* can recognize and define it as such.

CONCLUSION

Ignoring the questions we have raised thus far, one might try to set up a situation where *S*s must stop being obedient; for example, having the victim complain of heart trouble and showing signs of having a coronary attack. Certainly no learning experiment would justify continuing at the risk of bringing about the *S*'s death. It is difficult under these circumstances to imagine either an *E* calmly saying, "Continue—you must go on—the experiment requires that you continue" or a *S* actually continuing to administer shock to a victim who had passed out after complaining of chest pain. If some other investigator reported such a caricature of the Milgram situation it might be considered a scientific practical joke. A finding that in the face of an apparent coronary by the victim, *S*s continued to administer shock would have to be explained by assuming that *S*s did not believe in the reality of the events and, therefore, would most likely be dismissed as a poorly executed piece of laboratory work. Yet it is Milgram himself who reports such findings! The fact that he elicits obedience from a significant proportion of *S*s even under the threat of an impending heart attack must throw serious doubt on the manner in which the deception was handled in all of his other studies. Thus, by pushing the psychological deception experiment *ad absurdum*, Milgram forces us to come to terms with issues of ecological validity.

What can be said about the ease with which man can be forced to abuse his fellow man? To show that Milgram's empirical findings do not allow him either to prove or disprove his conclusions does not help us to draw any meaningful inferences about the true nature of man. Rather, the news media, more validly and, alas, more eloquently than any experimental data, attest to the scope of the problem and the urgent need to understand the forces that govern violence. Appropriate ecologically valid techniques must be developed to study this and related problems. The difficulties of research in these areas do not mean that we can afford to abandon either the scientific method or the experimental technique; rather, to attack some problems we will have to devise experiments that are not recognized as such by the *S*s.[4] In doing so, moreover, we must make certain that this is in fact the case while being careful to keep in mind the ethical strictures which must govern research in a free society.

Milgram's studies in obedience, though they fail to provide a viable model for the scientific investigation of violence, are nonetheless a milestone in social psychology. By demonstrating that it is possible to stay within currently accepted scientific conventions and yet push the psychological experiment beyond its limits, the obedience studies force us to consider what these limits are and hasten the day when issues of ecological validity will receive the kind of careful attention currently devoted to statistical inference. Finally, Milgram has dared to attempt the systematic scientific study of an urgent problem currently facing our society. While new means will be required for this purpose, by focusing on vital issues Milgram has provided new impetus to an exciting field.

NOTES

1. The substantive work upon which the theoretical outlook presented in this paper was based was supported in part by contract # Nonr 4731 from the Group Psychology Branch of the Office of Naval Research.

We wish to thank our colleagues, Frederick J. Evans, Edgar P. Nace, Emily C. Orne, David A. Paskewitz, and David L. Rosenhan, for their helpful comments and criticisms.

2. For an excellent discussion of the ethical problems as well as other issues concerning the use of deception in psychological studies see Kelman, "Human Use of Human Subjects," 1967.

3. A secretary would regard this kind of request as intolerable only in the context of her continuing activities but would be relatively untroubled by such a request if it was "episodic" in the sense of Garfinkel (1967) and legitimized in an appropriate fashion, e.g. necessary for science.

4. For an extended discussion of these issues, see Orne (1962b) and Orne (1969). A particularly elegant example of a method which allows systematic scientific study without the *S*'s recognizing that he is participating in an experiment is the lost-letter technique developed by Milgram, et al. (1965).

REFERENCES

Asch, S. E. *Social psychology.* Englewood Cliffs, N.J.: Prentice Hall, 1952.

Brehm, J. W., & Cohen, A. R. *Explorations in cognitive dissonance.* New York: Wiley, 1962.

Brunswik, E. *Systematic and representative design of psychological experiments with results in physical and social perception.* (Syllabus Series No. 304) Berkeley: University of California Press, 1947.

Garfinkel, H. *Studies in ethnomethodology.* New York: Prentice-Hall, 1967.

Holland, C. H. Sources of variance in the experimental investigation of behavioral obedience. Unpublished doctoral dissertation, University of Connecticut, 1967.

Janet, P. *L'automatisme psychologique; essai de psychologie expérimentale sur les formes inférieures de l'activité humaine.* Paris: Alcan, 1889.

Kelman H. C. Human use of human subjects: The problem of deception in social psychological experiments. *Psychological Bulletin,* 1967, **67,** 1–11.

Manvell, R., & Fraenkel, H. *The incomparable crime.* New York: Putnam's, 1967.

MILGRAM, S. Some conditions of obedience and disobedience to authority. *Human Relations*, 1965, **18**: 57–76.

MILGRAM, S., Mann, L., & Harter, S. The lost-letter technique: A tool of social research. *Public Opinion Quarterly*, 1965, **29**, 437–438.

ORNE, M. T. Antisocial behavior and hypnosis: Problems of control and validation in empirical studies. In G. H. Estabrooks (Ed.), *Hypnosis: Current problems*, New York: Harper & Row, 1962. Pp. 137–192 (a).

ORNE, M. T. On the social psychology of the psychological experiment: With particular reference to demand characteristics and their implications. *American Psychologist*, 1962, **17**: 776–783 (b).

ORNE, M. T. Demand characteristics and quasi-controls. In R. Rosenthal & R. Rosnow (Eds.), *Artifact in behavioral research*. New York: Academic Press, 1969. Pp. 143–179.

ORNE, M. T., & Evans, F. J. Social control in the psychological experiment: Antisocial behavior and hypnosis. *Journal of Personality and Social Psychology*, 1965, **1**: 189–200.

RIECKEN, H. W. A program for research on experiments in social psychology. In N. F. Washbourne (Ed.), *Decisions, values and groups*, Vol. 2. New York: Pergamon Press, 1962. Pp. 25–41.

ROSENTHAL, A. M. *Thirty-eight witnesses*. New York: McGraw-Hill, 1964.

ROWLAND, L. W. Will hypnotized persons try to harm themselves or others? *Journal of Abnormal and Social Psychology*, 1939, **34**: 114–117.

YOUNG, P. C. Antisocial uses of hypnosis. In L. M. LeCron (Ed.), *Experimental hypnosis*. New York: Macmillan, 1952. Pp. 376–409.

Stanley Milgram

Interpreting Obedience: Error and Evidence
A Reply to Orne and Holland[1]

*Thus far we have been singularly unsuccessful in finding an
experimental task which would be discontinued, or indeed refused
by subjects in an experimental situation.* . . . (M. Orne, 1962)

In the October 1968 issue of the *International Journal of Psychiatry*, Orne
and Holland sought to reinterpret the findings of my experimental
studies of obedience and disobedience to authority. In this paper, I shall
discuss their comments and, beyond this, address myself to some of the
related questions that have formed part of Orne's thinking, and which
have found their way into his critique.[2]

To begin, I note that Orne does not question the behavioral outcomes obtained in the obedience experiments, but focuses on the
psychological meaning behind them. This point of agreement on
behavior is important. First, it gives us a common empirical starting
point for our discussion. Second, it places a burden on the critic. Let us
leave open for the moment whether the subject's state of mind is characterized by the suspiciousness and disbelief that Orne postulates, assuming only that the subject complies outwardly with the experimenter.
The critic must still ask *why* subjects respond with a show of outward
compliance. The forces in a situation that constrain a person to adhere
to required external forms cannot be dismissed as inconsequential.
Nor in my view is such compliance most profitably seen as a methodological wrinkle but rather as a social fact of interest in its own right.
An orientation in terms of demand characteristics, then, is questionable
on two counts: (1) it treats compliance merely as if it were an impediment to research, thereby deflecting attention from the substantive
issues underlying such compliance; and (2), it is presented as an
explanation while it functions mainly as a depreciatory label.

There is a further implication in the locus of Orne's criticism. It is certainly legitimate to accept the behavioral facts and carry out arguments in regard to the psychological attitudes that lie behind them. However, a warning is in order: namely, this shift in no way diminishes the need for evidence in support of argumentation. I am afraid Orne has assumed that once he has moved the argument off the level of behavioral evidence, he is free to proceed on the basis of speculation and anecdote. In this he is quite wrong. Systematic evidence is of decisive importance and must be brought to bear on the argument.

II

What characterizes Orne's piece is gross overstatement of a point that has an element of validity, is corrected for with relative ease by control procedures, and ought to be seen in its proper place. Orne's first major argument is that subjects do not accept the experimental situation at face value. To make matters perfectly clear, let us state explicitly what subjects may fail to believe: (1) they may not believe the experiment is about memory and learning; (2) they may not believe the learner is getting painful shocks; (3) they may not believe the learner is the focus of experiment. Only the second of these points is critical, for as long as the subject believes he is transmitting painful shocks to the learner on command of the experimenter, the essential manipulatory intent of the experiment is achieved. The fact is that most subjects do believe that the shocks are painful, some subjects are unsure about it, and a few subjects do not believe it. This has been assessed at points during the experiment, immediately after the experiment, and in questionnaire and interview studies a year after the experiment. Orne asserts that no evidence has been presented on this question. This is false. The first published report states:

With few exceptions subjects were convinced of the reality of the experimental situation, that they were administering shocks to another person, and the most potent shocks were extremely painful. In the post-experimental interview subjects were asked: "How painful to the learner were the last few shocks that you administered to him?" Subjects were instructed to indicate their answers on a printed 14-point scale, ranging from "Not at all painful" to "Extremely painful." The modal response was 14 (Extremely painful) with the mean at 13.42 [1963, p. 375].

Moreover, the occurrence of tension provided striking evidence of the subject's genuine involvement in the experimental conflict, and this has been observed and reported throughout in the form of representative transcripts (1963), scale data (1965b), and filmed accounts (1965a). In the course of a recent debate with Orne (1969), a member of the audience pointed out that he would be willing to consider Orne's interpretation a possibility if, indeed, subjects gave evidence of a wry, tongue-in-cheek attitude, but that Orne's view was untenable in view of the formidable tension and strain observed. Orne's suggestion that the subjects only *feigned* sweating, trembling, and stuttering to please the experimenter is pathetically detached from reality, equivalent to the

Table 2-2   *Subjects' Estimate of Pain Felt by Victim*

Condition	Obedient Ss $\bar{x}$	n	Defiant Ss $\bar{x}$	n	$\bar{x}$
Remote victim	13.50	(20)	13.27	(11)	13.42
Voice feedback	11.36	(25)	11.80	(15)	11.53
Proximity	12.69	(16)	11.79	(24)	12.15
Touch proximity	12.25	(28)	11.17	(12)	11.93
Coronary tape (a)	11.40	(26)	12.25	(14)	11.70
Coronary tape (b)	11.98	(20)	12.05	(20)	12.02
Bridgeport replication	11.79	(19)	11.81	(18)	11.80
Women as subjects	12.88	(26)	12.07	(14)	12.60
Experimenter departs	11.67	(31)	12.39	(9)	11.83

statement that hemophiliacs bleed to keep their physicians busy. To be sure, I could certainly improve my image with D. Baumrind (1964) and others who have criticized the experiment because of the tension it induced, constructing a defense on Orne's interpretation, but this would be utterly false, for the conflict *was* present, intensely experienced, and cannot be wished or theorized away.

In all experimental conditions the level of pain was interpreted as very high, bordering on the upper extreme. In condition (02), Voice Feedback (when the victim is audible but not visible), the mean on the 14-point scale for obedient subjects is 11.36 and falls within the "Extremely painful" zone of the scale. More than half the obedient subjects use the extreme upper point on the scale, and at least one subject indicated by a + sign that "Extremely painful" was not a strong enough designation. Of the 40 subjects in this condition, two indicate on the scale (with scores of 1 and 3) that they did not think the victim received painful shocks, and both subjects were obedient. These subjects, it would appear, were not successfully exposed to the manipulatory intent of the experimenter. But even this is not so simple, since denial of an unpleasant action can serve a defensive function, and some subjects come to view their performance in a favorable light only by reconstructing what their state of mind was when they were administering shocks. The question is: Did they hold their disbelief as a firm hypothesis or as a fleeting notion among many other notions?

The broad quantitative picture of subjects' testimony on belief can be examined, among other ways, by scrutinizing responses to a follow-up questionnaire distributed about a year after subjects participated in the study. Item 4 of the questionnaire is reprinted below, along with the distribution of responses to it.

Table 2-3   *Response to Question on Belief in Follow-up Questionnaire*

During the Experiment	Defiant	Obedient	All Subjects
1. I fully believed the learner was getting painful shocks.	62.5% (230)	47.9% (139)	56.1% (369)
2. Although I had some doubts, I believed the learner was *probably* getting the shocks.	22.6% (83)	25.9% (75)	24.0% (158)
3. I just wasn't sure whether the learner was getting the shocks or not.	6.0% (22)	6.2% (18)	6.1% (40)
4. Although I had some doubts, I thought the learner was probably not getting the shocks.	7.6% (28)	16.2% (47)	11.4% (75)
5. I was certain the learner was not getting the shocks.	1.4% (5)	3.8% (11)	2.4% (16)

There are several ways to describe the results. Emphasizing the positive side, one could say that only 4 percent of the subjects were certain the learner was *not* getting any shocks, while 96 percent, in some degree or other, felt the learner was receiving the shocks. Or one could put the most negative interpretation possible on the results by asserting that only half of the subjects fully accepted the experimental deception. But the fairest treatment of the data is to say that three-quarters of the subjects (the first two categories), by their own testimony, acted under the belief that they were administering painful shocks. It would have been an easy out at this point to have denied that the hoax had been accepted. But only a fifth of the group indicated having had serious doubts.

David Rosenhan of Swarthmore College carried out a replication of the obedience experiment in order to obtain a base measure for further studies of his own. He took elaborate interviewing steps. Among other things, he established the interviewer as a person independent of the experiment who demands a detailed account of the subject's experience, and probes the issue of belief even to the point of asking, "You really mean you didn't catch on to the experiment?" On the basis of highly stringent criteria of full acceptance, Rosenhan reports that (according to the determination of independent judges), 68.9 percent of the subjects thoroughly accepted the authenticity of the experiment. Examining the performance of these subjects, he reports that 85 percent are fully obedient. (Rosenhan, it must be pointed out, employed a subject population that was younger than that used in the original experiments, and this, I believe, accounts for the higher level of obedience).[3]

When my experimental findings are subjected to a comparable type of analysis, they are not altered in any substantial manner. For example, in condition (02), Voice Feedback, of those subjects who indicated acceptance of the deception (categories 1 and 2), 58 percent are obedient; of those who indicated category 1, 60 percent are obedient. Over all experimental conditions this manner of controlling the data slightly reduced the proportion of obedient-to-defiant subjects. The changes leave the relations among conditions intact and are inconsequential for interpreting the meaning or import of the findings.

In sum, the majority of subjects accept the experimental situation as genuine; a few do not. Within each experimental condition it was my estimate that two to four subjects did not think they were administering painful shocks to the victim, but I adopted a general rule that no subject be removed from the data, because selective removal of subjects on somewhat imprecise criteria is the quickest way to inadvertently shape hypotheses. Even now I am not willing to dismiss those subjects, because it is not clear that their rejection of the technical illusion was a cause of their obedience or a consequence of it. Does it not occur to Orne that cognitive processes may serve to rationalize behavior that the subject has felt compelled to carry out? It is simple indeed for a subject to explain his behavior by stating he did not believe the victim received shocks, and some subjects come to this position as a post facto explanation of their actions. The explanation has no cost to them and goes a long way toward preserving their positive self-conception. It has the additional benefit of demonstrating how astute and clever they were to penetrate a carefully laid cover story.

More important, however, is to be able to see the role of denial in the total process of obedience and disobedience, for denial is not a *deus ex machina* that descends on the laboratory and sweeps away all else. It is rather one specific cognitive adjustment of several that occur in the experiment, and needs to be properly placed in terms of its functioning in the performance of some subjects.

III

Leaving the evidential basis of this discussion, let us now consider the arguments Orne offers to support his idea that subjects see through the experimental illusions. Orne says, first, that the subjects of psychological experiments tend to "view their task as a problem-solving situation which requires them to determine the 'real' situation and respond appropriately." I do not share the belief that people by and large are suspicious, distrustful and given to outguessing scientific authorities; nor do I think that among postal clerks, high-school teachers, salesmen, engineers, and laborers—our typical subjects—a great deal is known about psychological experiments. It is true, as Orne says, that within university circles a certain "scuttlebutt" develops about such endeavors, but it is very much a matter of local campus culture and, as Orne must surely know, not relevant to this study, which relied on a general not a campus population (1963, 1965b). Some of our subjects were highly intelligent, others of very limited intellectual ability. Very few of them approached the experiment with implicit distrust of the experimenter. Rather than trying to outwit him, subjects occasionally wanted to engage him in personal problems and probably held the idea of a psychiatric interview in their image of psychology. What kind of world does Orne postulate? It is a world populated with mutually suspicious persons, each with concealed motives and working at cross-purposes. I do not believe this corresponds to reality, not even the reality of a psychological experiment. I am struck by the fact that Orne not only approaches the question of experimentation from an acutely suspicious point of view, but assumes experimental subjects possess a similar outlook. He supposes that they, too, are searching for concealed motives and hidden meanings, while, in fact, this is true for only a small fraction of subjects of characteristically paranoid outlook.

Orne contends that there are incongruities in the experimental process that give away the deception. He says that a subject would find it implausible that he be required to administer shocks to an individual to test a presumed relation between punishment and learning when the experimenter could as easily give the shocks himself. Yet Orne could determine, by reading that portion of the instructions reprinted in the initial report of the experiment (1963), that a role was assigned to the subject and a reason for his administering the shocks was given. Each subject was told:

We don't know how much punishment is best for learning, and we don't know how much difference it makes as to who is giving the punishment, whether an adult learns best from a younger or an older person than himself, or many things of that sort. So in this study we are bringing together a number of adults of different occupations and ages. And we're asking some of them to be teachers and some of them to be learners. We want to find out just what effect different people have on each other as teachers and learners, and also what effect punishment will have on learning in this situation.

Another source of doubt, according to Orne, is "The incongruity between the relatively trivial experiment and the imperturbability of the *E* on the one hand . . . and the extremity of the victim's suffering.

. . ." One could argue with equal conviction that people usually do not assess the relative importance of scientific studies and that the cool, competent stance of the experimenter is the typical posture of authority in modern times, so that casting him in this role contributes to the plausibility of the situation. But the argument can only be resolved by assessment of the subject's acceptance of the situation.[4]

A major problem with the demand characteristic approach is that it is always post facto. Orne is quite incapable of knowing what the results of a scientific experiment will be. He only knows how to argue after the results are in. Moreover, he forgets that from the standpoint of a "demand characteristic" analysis, virtually all of the cues in the obedience experiment communicate the necessity to break off the experiment, yet many subjects are unable to do so.

Finally, at times Orne describes the experiment backwards, implying that the subject is told right off to administer dangerous shocks to a screaming person. Far from it, there is an important developmental aspect to the experiment which comes to constrain and control the subject's behavior. The early stages of the experiment are quite proper, even uneventful; it is only gradually as the shock levels intensify that conflict arises. The earlier parts of the experiment, in which any reasonable person would participate, only gradually ease the subject into a conflict; when conflict arises the subject has already routinized his behavior, committed himself to the procedure and, in consequence, is locked into the situation. The shifting, step by step, and piecemeal escalation of shocks plays an important part in exacting obedience, and, moreover, sets the experiment apart from other studies, such as the nitric acid study, which lack this temporal component.

IV

Since Orne makes frequent reference to the experiments he has carried out, some comments ought to be made about them. Many of them are not experiments at all, but only incidents involving one or two individuals. Orne rarely carries his incidents out in sufficient numbers to view the full range of responses to them. Yet they represent, relatively speaking, strong points in Orne's style of inquiry, for often he dispenses with evidence altogether and turns with an air of authority to anecdotes. The anecdotal method does not have much standing in science and has never, to my knowledge, settled anything. Nonetheless, we may critically examine some of Orne's stories, if only to expose the flawed logic with which they are applied to present issues.

Orne tells us that about eighty years ago a hypnotized woman was induced to perform many seemingly antisocial acts, such as stabbing a victim, but could not be induced to undress before an assemblage of males. Orne concludes that the woman did not believe she was inflicting stab wounds. First, this is a gratuitous assumption. Neither Orne nor I have the slightest idea of what went through this woman's mind, and there is no evidence now to help us decide.

But there is a more significant point. Orne asserts that an act such as undressing possesses an irreducible meaning that "transcends the context" [Orne, 1968, p. 288] and, therefore, cannot be elicited by a hypnotist. One imagines the hypnotist standing, Svengali-like over the poor girl, intoning, "You are in my power: Undress! Undress!" All very fine, but it is hard to see what this has to do with the exercise of authority through ordinary channels of social structure, which is the subject matter of the experiments on obedience.

A military officer does not need to rely on animal magnetism or Svengali-like poses to exact compliance from his subordinates. The parties are embedded in a socially defined hierarchical structure and this fact dominates their behavior. Social structure is not a mysterious thing. From the standpoint of the participating subject it is the conviction that another person, by virtue of his status, has the right to prescribe behavior for him.

Let us return to undressing the girl, but now shift from the irrelevant issue of hypnotism to the pertinent question of social structure. It is well known that under a proper set of role relationships, e.g., when visiting a gynecologist, a woman not only undresses but allows her body to be thoroughly inspected. So we are left to conclude that not even hypnotism can bring about what is readily and routinely accomplished by legitimized societal roles. And that is precisely what we have investigated: our subjects are not hypnotized, but they are defined into social roles that place them in a position of subordination vis-à-vis the experimenter.

Let us note a further point. The woman taking part in her medical checkup does not deny that she is undressing before a male stranger, but she defines the meaning of the act in a manner that permits it. In the experiment the subject does not deny he is shocking the victim, but he defines the meaning of his act in terms of the constructive purposes outlined by the experimenter. This is not an alternative to complying with authority, but is the typical cognitive concomitant of such compliance.[5]

Orne asserts that direct inferences about obedience in real life cannot be drawn from an experimental context. His documentation consists of a speculative anecdote that is offered as a parallel to the obedience experiment, but which on analysis proves to be misleading and without pertinence.

Orne states:

Anyone who believes direct inference about obedience in real life can be drawn from an experimental context should ask his secretary to type a letter, and after making certain there are no errors, ask her to tear it up and retype it. With rare exceptions, two or three such trials should be sufficient to ensure that the *E* will require a new secretary.

It is hard to see that this anecdote has anything to do with my obedience experiment or real life. In the experiment, the act of shocking the victim is coordinated to a set of rational purposes concerning advancement of knowledge about the effects of punishment on learning. Nor does the anecdote have much to do with obedience in other settings. Not even in the army are individuals ordered to perform a destructive act for its own sake. The burning of a village containing innocent civilians is carried out with the explanation that it is to impress the populace, or to frighten the inhabitants into cooperating, or to enforce a system of military justice. Were the secretary in Orne's anecdote provided a set of rational purposes for the destructive act, Orne's story would end differently.

The criminal-act experiments on which Orne rests much of his argument also bear little resemblance to the obedience experiment or to life outside the laboratory. In these experiments, the subject is simply told to stab or throw nitric acid at a human target. Orne contends that the subject knows that no one really will be harmed and therefore obeys. It is the same in the obedience experiment, Orne says. But it is not the same. An important feature of the nitric acid experiment is that a meaningless act is arbitrarily demanded of the subject. In the obedience experiments, the act of shocking the victim is tightly embedded in a set of socially constructive purposes, namely, the furtherance of knowledge in regard to memory and learning processes. Obedience occurs not as an end in itself, but as an instrumental element in a situation that the subject construes as significant and meaningful. Further, in contrast to the nitric acid study, in the obedience experiment the experimenter explicitly denies the possibility of harm. He states, "Although the shocks can be extremely painful, they cause no permanent tissue damage." (The subject also watches, after the electrode is attached to the victim's wrist, the application of a paste "to avoid blisters and burns.") The indications of harm come from other sources, and the subject must weigh information from his own senses against his trust in and dependence on the experimenter. Most of Orne's analysis ignores this critical aspect of the experiment and is simply not relevant to it.[6]

In summary, the several points on which the obedience experiment differs from the models provided by Orne are: First, we are not dealing with the *personal* power of the experimenter as in the case of hypnosis but, quite explicitly, with the consequence of social structure for action.

A clearly defined hierarchical relationship exists between subject and authority. Second, the purposes which authority defines are not senseless and stupid (as in the nitric acid study) but are readily accepted by the subject as worthwhile. Third, the experiment has an important temporal aspect to it. It begins with the mutual consent of all parties, and only gradually leads into conflict.

V

The issue of ecological validity comes down to two very different though equally important points that are not kept clearly distinct in Orne's thinking. The first question is: Within the context of a psychological experiment, will a subject accept that he is administering painful shocks to another person against his will? The question must be resolved by resorting to evidence and not simply rhetoric. The second question, which is analytically quite separate, is: Does the behavior established in the laboratory have any generality beyond the circumstances in which it was observed, or is the experimental situation so special that nothing that was observed can contribute to a general view of the functions of obedience in wider social life?

Orne observes that behavior is legitimized in the subject-experimenter relationship. He sees this only as getting in the way of establishing general truths, while in actuality, it is precisely an understanding of behavior *within* legitimized social relationships that the investigation seeks to attain. What Orne can construe only as an impediment is in fact a strategic research opportunity.

Orne wishes to show the uniqueness of the psychological experiment as a context for eliciting behavior, but his manner of supporting the view is specious. Thus he informs us that "it was essential for the subject to be in an actual subject-experimenter relationship in order to have him carry out these actions; despite repeated attempts not one of our colleagues could be induced to attempt any one of these acts." This merely says that the presence of legitimized, hierarchical role relations in needed for exacting compliance. And this is correct. But the further implication that only the subject-experimenter relationship possesses this quality is not merely gratuitous, but blind to the reality of social life, which is replete with hierarchical structures, and which in significant measure is composed of them. Orne's colleagues did not comply for the same reason that, during a parade, when the marshal shouts "left face" the military band turns left but the onlooking pedestrians do not. One group consists of subordinates in a hierarchical structure and the other does not. We can in a despairing moment conclude that this establishes the uniqueness of a parade as a social situation, or we can see through to the deeper principle that only persons defined into a hierarchical structure will respond to it. It is precisely those situations in which a person is defined into a hierarchical structure that constitutes the subject matter of the obedience experiment.

Perhaps the main source of confusion in Orne's thinking is his failure to keep clearly in mind the distinction between social occasions that are hierarchically organized and those that are not. To move from a discussion of one into the other, without taking account of the critical change, can only lead to muddled thought.

The occasion we term a psychological experiment shares its essential structural properties with other situations composed of subordinate-superordinate roles. In all such circumstances the person responds not so much to the content of what is required but on the basis of his relationship to the person who requires it. Indeed, I am tempted to assert this principle in more drastic form: where legitimate authority is the source of action, *relationship overwhelms content*. That is what is meant by the importance of social structure and that is what is demonstrated in the present experiment.

VI

The obedience experiment makes use of a technical illusion, namely, that the learner was receiving shocks, when in fact he was an actor. Orne asserts that, according to his analysis, cues in the experiment would not allow the subject to accept this illusion. In fact, observation and data show that Orne's conjecture is wrong, that most subjects do accept the illusion.

There are, to be sure, many alternative methods for accruing evidence, and if the use of a technical illusion is the stumbling block to confidence in the results, then the investigator who wishes to study obedience can do two things. First, he can study the performance of only those subjects who fully accept the illusion. We have already discussed how the data of Milgram and Rosenhan, controlled in this manner, continue to yield levels of obedience comparable to those reported in the original articles. A second approach is to study situations in which no illusion is required because the naïve subject himself serves as the victim. Even when subjects cannot possibly deny the genuineness of what they are doing, because it is happening to them, they comply in extraordinary degree. Thus Turner and Solomon (1962) and Shor (1962) have reported that subjects willingly accept near traumatizing shocks when serving in their experiments. Kudirka (1965) presents an experiment of unusual interest in which subjects were instructed to perform a highly noxious, although not dangerous, task, namely, eating bitter crackers (they were soaked in strong quinine solution). The crackers were extremely distasteful and gave rise to facial distortions, grunts, groans, and in some subjects feelings of nausea. Since in this experiment the subject is himself the victim, none of Orne's criticism relating to deception is applicable. The question is whether compliance with the experimenter will occur in any significant degree. The first finding was that the requirement of obedience was so powerful that the experiment could not be done with the experimenter present: virtually all subjects obeyed. Kudirka, therefore, consciously weakened the experimenter's authority by removing him from the laboratory. Even under these circumstances 14 of the 19 subjects continued to the end of the experiment, each one ingesting, frequently with considerable disgust, 36 quinine soaked crackers.

Orne himself (1962b) has used the example of subjects carrying out extremely boring, stupid, and meaningless tasks (such as performing endless serial additions, then tearing up answer sheets) to show the power of the experimenter to induce action in his subjects. He says that although these actions may appear stupid, subjects perform them because they occur within a psychological experiment. When Orne moves on to the obedience experiment, however, he shifts his argument. The power of the experimenter, which Orne so carefully demonstrated, suddenly evaporates. Whereas his subjects genuinely did carry out actions prescribed by the experimenter, Orne would have us believe that my subjects did not. This is, at best, twisted logic, and Orne really cannot have it both ways. On the one hand he asserts an extreme degree of control over the subject, and on the other hand he denies this control exists in the present experiment. It is far more logical to see the obedience experiment as climaxing a consistent line of research demonstrating the power of authority, a line that can be traced to Frank (1944), through Orne (1962b), and into the present research.

His argument is further weakened by his failure to come to grips with the Bridgeport variation of the experiment in which the university setting was eliminated. For years Orne has pointed to the benignity of the university and hospital setting and the manner in which these specific contexts invalidate experimental studies of antisocial behavior. Insofar as Orne's general position is concerned, the implication of the Bridgeport experiment would seem to be that the university context may be less important than thought in the elicitation of antisocial behavior and that whatever elementary social structure is required for its elicitation can function independently of established, benevolent organizations.

At the conclusion of his critical evaluation, Orne calls for "experiments that are not recognized as such by the subjects" to elucidate the true nature of man. I call his attention, then, to a study in which a group of nurses, on duty in hospital wards, were the unknowing subjects (Hofling *et al.*, 1966). The nurses were given over the telephone an irregular order to administer medication. The voice of the caller, purporting to be a known physician, was unfamiliar to the nurse; the medicine was not on the ward stocklist and thus unauthorized; the dose requested was double the maximum dose shown on the pill box; and the procedure of ordering medication by telephone was in violation of hospital policy. Yet of the 22 nurses tested in this fashion, 21 gave the medication as ordered. In reply to a questionnaire, a majority of a control group of nurses said that they would not have given the medication. The parallel results found in Hofling's results in a naturalistic setting and those found in my laboratory study are striking and lend support to the ecological validity of my laboratory findings.

Ecological validity refers to mapping the range of conditions under which a phenomenon will appear. If Orne is saying there are more experiments to be done, and the present experiments do not give all the answers, I entirely agree with him. But the ultimate effect of Orne's work seems to be the denial of scientific knowledge.

Orne does a disservice to his high methodological ideals when he pursues his doctrines so zealously that, in order to make them fit, he misstates the manner in which the obedience study was conducted (p. 143), or continues to insist on his presuppositions in the face of contrary evidence (p. 139). For we must then ask whether this theory is a useful scientific analysis or shades into an autistic construction in which the themes of conspiracy, distrust, contaminants, and concealed motives play a commanding part. Without question, one may legitimately ask whether the subjects believed the victim received painful shocks, but the answer resides in evidence, not the infallibility of Orne's presuppositions.

Orne's arguments, built largely on anecdotes, are slippery and shift to meet the needs of a limited intellectual orientation. Their aim seems to be to deny the reality of a phenomenon, whether it be hypnosis (1959, 1965), sensory deprivation (1964), general experimentation (1962b), or obedience (1968). Orne's doctrine begins with a population of subjects who are actively suspicious and distrustful, except when trust is the ingredient that will render the experiment invalid; then they are trustful (Orne, 1968, p. 291). Demand characteristics come next: the experimenter is not really studying what he wants to study, for the subject has thwarted the possibility of objective inquiry by giving him only what he wants to hear. Evidence for this view is nonexistent, and indeed, Sigall, Aronson, and Van Hoose (1970) have recently reported a study showing it does not hold up.

In any case, Orne realizes that the argument of the "cooperating subject" cannot invalidate the obedience experiment, since the experimenter makes quite explicit to the subject what he "wants," and the degree to which the subject gives him what he "wants" constitutes the actual experimental measure. Accordingly, Orne again shifts his argument, arguing that outward behavior is not what it seems to be, and there are hidden meanings beneath the surface. One might note that Orne's interest in the hidden meaning is pursued in disregard of the manifest meaning of the behavior and, indeed, is employed to discount what is most apparent.

Orne does not hesitate to use the obedience experiment to discredit hypnotic phenomena (1965); having done this he next turns to discredit the obedience experiment, introducing irrelevant arguments and misstatements of fact along the way. He next asserts the unqualified uniqueness of psychological experiments, so that nothing found within them has relevance to anything else. The overall pattern of this work does not point to the possibilities for studying phenomena, but only the possibility for discrediting them. Orne does not see a possible link between the compliance found in his studies and the compliance observed in the obedience experiments, for his aim in reporting his findings of compliance is to show how impossible the experimental situation was for determining scientific truth. Finally, there is no substance in things, only methodological wrinkles. This seems to me the history of the school of social psychology which Orne has assiduously cultivated. I do not believe that, in its present one-sided form, it constitutes a contribution to our understanding of human behavior. While specific details of this viewpoint are sometimes plausible, the rigid presuppositions animating such ideology invariably deform the total picture until it no longer corresponds with reality.

Certain methodological correctives derived from this point of view can, I believe, be of value. Increased experimental sophistication in the form of careful interviewing and avoidance of obvious pitfalls (e.g., employing psychology majors as subjects) can enhance the quality of experimentation. But these steps are only helpful when detached from the tunnel vision of conspiratorial thought and applied with a sense of balance to the problem at hand.

VII

Despite the rhetorical vigor of the Orne and Holland piece, it contains a good deal of error and much that is irrelevant. Let me summarize its major deficiencies:

1. Orne's case rests on the supposition that subjects do not believe they are administering painful shocks to the learner. He builds this case not by looking at evidence, but by anecdote and by weaving a speculative analysis not based on fact. In doing so he disregards information obtained by direct observation, interviewing, quantitative scales, and questionnaire studies, all of

which indicate that most subjects accept the experiment at face value.

2. If we are uneasy about the degree to which the authenticity of the experiment was experienced by a fraction of the subjects, we may take the step of considering only those subjects for whom we are certain the manipulatory intent was most fully achieved. For the critical question is not whether some subjects disbelieved, but whether, among those who did fully believe, performance was such that the major conclusions are altered. The data of several investigators show that the phenomenon of obedience holds up for subjects who fully accepted the experiment at face value.

3. Orne mechanically applies a critique of the experiments based on his criticism of hypnotic phenomena. This is the wrong model. Obedience to authority explicitly treats of the consequences of social structure for behavior. The experimental situation is constructed of hierarchically defined role relations. All of Orne's illustrations showing the power of social structure do not, as he believes, invalidate the findings, but only serve to show how general is the phenomenon.

4. If deception is the key issue, then all that the investigator interested in obedience needs to do is to study behavior in which the subject himself is the victim, in which case Orne's criticism of plausibility cannot apply. Studies of this sort have been reported. All the evidence, including that obtained by Orne, points to the extreme compliance of subjects in obeying the experimenter and carrying out acts that are stupid, tedious, noxious, and painful. Orne himself writes he could not find any task which subjects would refuse to do. That was an insight he ought to have taken seriously and pursued to its logical conclusion.

5. Orne asserts that the university context invalidates studies of antisocial behavior, but fails to come to grips with a replication of the experiment run with no visible university affiliation.

6. The trouble with "demand characteristics" is that those who rely on the concept are incapable of predicting the results of an experiment and only know how to apply the label after the facts are in. Then, any number of "demand characteristic" analyses can be formulated. Indeed, the strongest case can be made for the view that all of the cues in the study tell the subject of the necessity to break off. Yet many of them are unable to break with authority.

7. The basic logical contradiction in Orne's argument is that at one moment he argues for the extreme compliance of subjects to experimental commands, and at the next he argues against the

reality of such compliance. A set of shifting arguments is employed in the service of nihilistic outlook. With far greater logic, one can set the obedience experiment in a context of research that shows, with increasing clarity and force, the profound consequences of submission to authority, a line of research to which Orne's early work (1962b) has contributed in an important way.

NOTES

1. The author wishes to thank Barbara Kline, Mary Englander, and Lynne Steinberg for assistance in preparing this paper.

2. For brevity of reference I shall employ Orne's name exclusively in dealing with the above paper. This is not in any way meant to diminish the contribution of Dr. Holland to the paper, but rather is used to be concise and to focus my criticism on a well-known body of methodological philosophy which has appeared under Orne's name.

3. Holland's thesis (1969), though it contains many serious flaws of procedure which are fatal to the successful replication of the experiment, nonetheless offers supporting data on this issue. By Holland's own calculation, only a quarter of the subjects were successfully subjected to the manipulatory intent of the experiment. He would be perfectly correct, then, in looking at these subjects and determining the proportion of obedient subjects. It turns out that 70 percent of his "good" subjects are obedient, a figure that slightly exceeds my own figures, but is nonetheless of the same order of magnitude. Unfortunately, Holland carried out the study in 1967, and employed as his subjects students in an introductory psychology class. The author should have steered as far clear from psychology undergraduates as possible, for they would constitute the worst possible subjects for an experiment in which prior knowledge of the experiment is a fatal contaminant.

4. Recently, Ring, Wallston, and Corey (1970) carried out an obedience experiment in which the experimenter's behavior was made more animated and responsive, and this does not lead to any decrement in obedience. Instead of electric shock, the authors substituted excruciatingly painful noise fed to the subject's ear. Ninety-one percent of the subjects were maximally obedient.

5. Orne may properly pose the question: Can one devise an *experiment* in which women will undress? Of course it is possible to devise such an experiment. Naturally, the act of undressing would have to be coordinated to a set of rational purposes that the subject could accept. Indeed, an experiment has already been carried out by Masters and Johnson (1966) at Washington University in which, in the course of studies of sexual response, women—some prostitutes but others ordinary girls—not only undressed before the investigators but masturbated and engaged in coitus as well. Can we expect Orne to write an article arguing that the women did not really think they were engaging in coitus because of the imperturbable quality of the investigators?

6. Incidentally, Orne believes that if unhypnotized subjects throw nitric acid at individuals it is because they believe they will not really harm the other individual. My guess is that there is more to it than this, that in some degree they do not feel accountable for what they are doing.

REFERENCES

BAUMRIND, D. Some thoughts on ethics of research: After reading Milgram's "Behavioral study of obedience." *American Psychologist*, 1964, **19**: 421-423.

FRANK, J. D. Experimental studies of personal pressure and resistance. *Journal of General Psychology*, 1944, **30**: 23-64.

HOFLING, C. K., Brotzman, E., Dalrymple, S., Graves, N., & Pierce, C. M. An experimental study in nurse-physician relationships. *The Journal of Nervous and Mental Disease*, 1966, **143** (2): 171-180.

HOLLAND, C. H. *Sources of variance in the experimental investigation of behavioral obedience.* Unpublished doctoral dissertation, University of Connecticut, 1967.

KUDIRKA, N. K. *Defiance of authority under peer influence.* Unpublished doctoral dissertation, Yale University, 1965.

MASTERS, W. H., & Johnson, V. E. *Human sexual response,* Boston: Little, Brown and Co., 1966.

MILGRAM, S. Behavioral study of obedience. *Journal of Abnormal and Social Psychology,* 1963, **67:** 371–378.

MILGRAM, S. *Obedience* (a filmed experiment). Distributed by the New York University Film Library. Copyright 1965 (a).

MILGRAM, S. Some conditions of obedience and disobedience to authority. *Human Relations,* 1965, **18:** 57–75 (b).

ORNE, M. T. The nature of hypnosis: Artifact and essence. *Journal of Abnormal and Social Psychology,* 1959, **58:** 277–299.

ORNE, M. T. Antisocial behavior and hypnosis: Problems of control and validation in empirical studies. In G. H. Estabrooks (Ed.), *Hypnosis: Current problems.* New York: Harper and Row, 1962 (a).

ORNE, M. T. On the social psychology of the psychological experiment: With particular reference to demand characteristics and their implications. *American Psychologist,* 1962, **17** (11): 776–783 (b).

ORNE, M. T., & Evans, F. J. Social control in the psychological experiment: Antisocial behavior and hypnosis. *Journal of Personality and Social Psychology,* 1965, **1,** 189–200.

ORNE, M. T., & Holland, C. C. On the ecological validity of laboratory deceptions. *International Journal of Psychiatry,* 1968, **6** (4): 282–293.

ORNE, M. T. & Milgram, S. Obedience or demand characteristics. A debate held at the University of Pennyslvania on February 19, 1969.

ORNE, M. T., & Scheibe, K. E. The contribution of nondeprivation factors in the production of sensory deprivation effects. *Journal of Abnormal and Social Psychology,* 1964, **68** (1): 3–12.

ORNE, M. T., Sheehan, P. W., & Evans, F. J. Occurrence of post-hypnotic behavior outside the experimental setting. *Journal of Personality and Social Psychology,* 1968, **9** (2, Pt. 1): 189–196.

RING, K., Wallston, K. & Corey, M. Mode of debriefing as a factor affecting subjective reaction to a Milgram-type obedience experiment—an ethical inquiry. *Representative Research in Social Psychology,* 1970, **1** (1): 67–88.

ROSENHAN, D. Some origins of concern for others. In P. Mussen, J. Langer, & M. Covington (Eds.), *Trends and issues in developmental psychology.* New York: Holt, Rinehart & Winston, 1969.

ROSENHAN, D. Obedience and rebellion: Observations on the Milgram three-party paradigm. In preparation.

SHOR, R. E. Physiological effects of painful stimulation during hypnotic analgesia under conditions designed to minimize anxiety. *International Journal of Clinical and Experimental Hypnosis,* 1962, **10:** 183–202.

SIGALL, H., Aronson, E., & Van Hoose, T. The cooperative subject: Myth or reality? *Journal of Experimental Social Psychology,* 1970, **6:** 1–10.

TURNER, L. H., & Solomon, R. L. Human traumatic avoidance learning: Theory and experiments on the operant-respondent distinction and failures to learn. *Psychological Monographs,* 1962, **76** (40, whole no. 559).

PART THREE

The Deception and Debriefing Dilemma

The subject in a psychological experiment is almost certain to be deceived at one or more junctures. In Milgram's obedience experiments, for example, there are at least three distinct occurrences of deception: During the rationale for the experiment, in alleging that the study deals with the effects of punishment on learning; at the independent-variable level, e.g., using confederates to influence the subject; and at the dependent-variable level, e.g., having subjects believe that they are shocking the learner when, in fact, they are not. The use of stooges or accomplices—commonplace in experimental social psychology—is deception *par excellence*. But deception is used in other more subtle ways, e.g., refusing to answer questions about the experiment before its completion or not telling the subject the truth or all he may wish to know after he has participated—deception by omission rather than commission. This portrait lends credibility to the reasoning of Jourard, Schultz, and others that the experimenter-subject relationship is a unique kind of affair and, at first glance, a rather unsavory one.

How prevalent is deception in the contemporary literature? Two recent reviews indicate the percentage of studies reporting deception in the areas of personality and social psychology to be extraordinarily high—around 40 percent (Seeman, 1969), with specific research problems, e.g., conformity, approaching 100 percent use of deception (Stricker, 1967). Deception is not confined to these areas, however, and the problem of debriefing or phasing out subjects from their research participation is familiar to most research psychologists.

Why is deception used as an experimental method? There are many answers to this question, for deception, itself, is a variable having qualitative and quantitative dimensions. One general kind of answer is that deception can be a practical and efficient means of conducting an experiment. The laboratory, for example, is often regarded as superior to the natural field, at least in the respect that conditions can be created for analysis rather than the experimenter having to wait for their occurrence under undefined circumstances. To the extent that these "created conditions" are to appear realistic to the subject, deception may well be a prerequisite. Deception, paradoxically, can be an ethically superior methodology. In Milgram's research it was certainly more advantageous to deceive subjects into thinking that they were shocking the learner than it would have been actually to shock the learner. Some of the difficulties in achieving a successful or effective deception have been noted by Orne and Holland in the previous section.

Another facet of the deception issue involves the roles of experimenter and subject. Traditionally, the goals of the experimenter are the prediction and explanation of behavior. It is generally considered, however, that these activities must not cause, determine, or influence the behavior with which they deal. Hence, subjects must not be equipped with the same predictive or conceptual information about the experiment as held by the experimenter. Were he to have such information, the subject's behavior might largely reflect his disposition, or lack thereof, to corroborate the experimenter's hypothesis—quite different from assuming behavior to be solely a function of the variables of experimental interest. The fact is that subjects often do obtain or invent directives for their experimental performance (Parts Four and Five). Of considerable interest in their own right, these phenomena should not mask recognition of what stands as a tenable rationale for deception: that there be, of necessity, an information gap between the predictor and the object of his prediction regarding the conceptual structure of the experiment. That this is but one view of the experimenter-subject relationship, and the justification for deception, is clear after a reading of Jourard's views.

Kelman recognizes the logic of deception but takes a decidedly negative position regarding its use, on ethical as well as methodological grounds. He is one of a growing number of psychologists (cf. Part One) who argue that research methods must exist in conjunction with human values rather than adhering only to the statutes in a text on experimental design. In the reasoning by Kelman—and Jourard, Schultz, and Ring as well—one senses a kind of moral distaste directed at the prospect of the experimenter exerting control over the subject's behavior. Witness, for example, Kelman's reference to the legitimization of deception as a "holiness of sin," and his assertion that such procedures mirror and possibly further the trends of contemporary society toward the manipulation and dehumanization of man.

Could not one argue, however, that as pain administered by a physician is not to be equated with criminal assault, neither should deception by the research psychologist be likened to unfaithful activity on the part of one's spouse. The ethical parallels appear superficial. Although seemingly engaged in a kind of self-defeating moral absolutism, what Kelman may be pointing to, really, is the psychological researchers' lack, or potential loss, of public trust. Thus, a highlight of his paper is his admonition that psychology keep its house in order, that it attend to its complex research dilemmas "lest we leave their resolution to others who have no understanding of what we are trying to accomplish" [p. 165].

Crawford points out that deception and stress are hardly unique to Milgram's research, both phenomena having been traditional features of psychological research. Of course the established way of doing things should not be considered in itself moral justification for the acts in question. Yet it is of interest that Milgram's research has seemingly become a scapegoat for moral criticism. The criticism appears to be of a discriminating nature, for although quite willing to accept Milgram's account of the emotional discomfort in his subjects, the critics do not appear equally receptive to his evidence that no harmful aftereffects of the deception were observed (e.g., Baumrind; Kelman, p. 167).

Crawford extends Kelman's ethical theses by showing them to be consistent with Milgram's *findings* as opposed to his methods. The realization of human values, Crawford argues, may depend ultimately upon the kind of understanding that can only be provided by forceful, empirical inquiry, often requiring deception as the means to a, hopefully, more noble end. This would seem to be Crawford's ethic, and he is not alone in holding it. The esteem that Crawford holds for Milgram's research, illuminating in itself, has been echoed by others (e.g., Elms), and serves as an appropriate counterweight to Kelman's influential argument. The proposal with which Crawford closes his paper is a valuable exercise, perhaps exemplary of what Kelman has in mind when he calls for an active awareness of these issues.

Kelman recommends that role playing be explored as an alternative to laboratory deception. A major feature of role playing is that it brings the subject into the experimenter's confidence, decreasing the interpersonal distance between the two research participants. Implicit in Kelman's reasoning is the assumption that role playing immunizes the subject against many of the harms that may befall him in the deception experiment. The idea seems to be that "if you know it isn't real, it can't hurt you."

A number of investigations have recently explored the utility of role playing in the manner suggested by Kelman. The basic strategy involves selecting a successful deception experiment and replicating it without the deception. If the obtained results are similar to the original data, the fruitfulness of the role-playing approach is documented. Greenberg's study is an excellent illustration. In this experiment, Greenberg replicated the finding by Schachter that birth order and anxiety interact in their effects on individuals' dispositions to affiliate with others. A crucial aspect to this study, however, is the lack of a successful experimental induction of anxiety. It is *perceived* or self-rated anxiety rather than *manipulated* anxiety that interacts with birth order in the predicted direction. This result, an extremely informative one, casts a shadow on the power of role-playing designs. One of the primary purposes of role playing is to replace a seemingly real event with an imaginary or pretended version. In Greenberg's experiment, neither a check on the effectiveness of the anxiety manipulation nor the dependent variable itself (affiliation score) validates this rationale for role playing. The fact that perceived anxiety interacts with birth order under a role-playing set is, of course, interesting in its own right and certainly extends one's faith in Schachter's original work. But we are still left with the conclusion that one cannot attribute the results to the subjects' ability to play the roles assigned to them.

Freedman, in a particularly forceful paper, argues against role playing as an alternative to deception. He contends that any form of a "let's pretend" set on the part of subjects makes their subsequent behavior unique to that set—what they *think* they would do if circumstances were, in fact, realistic. The problem is a central one in the social psychology of research: the generalizability of data. Freedman argues that as behavior in the nonexperimental world has an intrinsic element of spontaneity, so must laboratory behavior be enveloped in an atmosphere of realism. This, of course, will often presume the use of deception.

Although the main thrust of Freedman's paper is epistemological and methodological, there are certain values or beliefs implicit in his writing. Consider his commentary upon man as a predictor:

They are only fallible humans who are for better or worse not very good at telling what they would do in a given situation unless they have just been in that very situation—and not even very well then [p. 204].

Or the following, on the viability of experimental social psychology:

Carefully designed experiments, skilled experimenters, and ingenious manipulations can make laboratory experiments extremely realistic and cause the subject to respond spontaneously [p. 206].

This is quite a departure in tone from that of Kelman or Ring. His optimistic and receptive posture toward the very concept of human experimentation bears scant resemblance to the renovative views of Jourard and Schultz.

The debate is not a simple one, however. Ring (Part One, p. 57) has some flattering comments regarding Milgram's work, as does

Kelman for that of Rosenthal—research which is based intrinsically on deception. Freedman's position, as is that of Crawford, is one of a commitment to the acquisition of scientific data which will permit a maximum of inference or generality. Whether or not the price is too high seems to be the critical issue.

The debriefing process, in which subjects are disengaged from the experiment, presents conflictual demands upon the experimenter rivaling those of deception. Implicit in many discussions of debriefing is the question of whether or not the experimenter and subject should abandon their roles and establish a more conventional and communicative relationship. Ethical considerations regarding the disclosure of possibly disquieting results to subjects have been noted previously. Kelman proposes that the subject should leave the experiment enriched in some manner and in no case should the postexperimental feedback itself involve deception. Crawford, however, contends that the disclosure that subjects behaved in an aberrant fashion can satisfy Kelman's plea for a debriefing which is truthful as well as enlightening.

There are critical methodological problems associated with debriefing in addition to ethical factors. One of these—the "contamination" of the subject pool—pertains to future subjects learning of the essentials of an experiment from those who have received a full description during debriefing. Most commentators (e.g., Aronson & Carlsmith, 1968) recognize the scope of this issue but feel that it can be minimized by instilling in subjects an awareness of how crucial it is that they honor their pledge of secrecy. Donald T. Campbell, the noted methodologist, offers a different view:

> While debriefing has come to be a standard part of deception experiments in the laboratory, it has many ethical disadvantages. It is many times more of a comfort to the experimenter for his pain at deceiving than to the respondent who may learn in the process of his own gullibility, conformity, cruelty, or bias. It provides modeling and publicity for deceit and thus serves to debase language for the respondent as well as for the experimenter. It reduces the credibility of the laboratory and undermines the utility of deceit in future experiments [1969, p. 371].

A related issue concerns the common practice of using the same subjects in more than one experiment. There is a fair amount of empirical information available on this matter, but with mixed results. Some investigators find that a subject's research history is a critical determinant of his subsequent experimental behavior (e.g., Holmes & Appelbaum, 1970; Silverman, Shulman, & Wiesenthal, 1970); others do not (e.g., Brock & Becker, 1966; Fillenbaum & Frey, 1970). What is particularly disconcerting is the apparent ability of some subjects to behave as if they were naïve—when in fact they are quite suspicious or even knowledgeable (e.g., Levy, Part Four). The experimenter who presumes but fails to confirm naïveté in his subjects—and it is not an easy task—may well obtain data which are simply not indicative of the truth or falsity of his hypothesis. This issue is reconsidered in Part Four.

One of the primary purposes of debriefing is to return the subject to what might be termed his state of psychological normalcy, particularly if the experimental conditions have subjected him to a form of stress or noxious stimulation. In addition to ethical discussion, this matter is fortunately susceptible to empirical inquiry. The study by Walster and her associates is the first major effort in this direction. Their central hypothesis does not receive support, suggesting that experimental deceptions do not necessarily "add insult to injury" in individuals who might be especially prone to the deceptive message. Although these investigators are distressed by the presence of lingering effects and the suggestion of individual differences in this recovery period, there is the optimistic note that the effects of deception, in fact, dissipate over time—an ethically comforting finding. Recently, Lowin and his associates have confirmed and extended the findings of Walster *et al.* These researchers again document short-term effects of deception, but no lasting ones—measured in terms of days and months after the deception. As in the study by Walster *et al.*, this experiment involved an emotionally severe deception. Finally, a recent experiment by Ring, Wallston, and Corey (1970) failed to disclose any serious negative after-effects in a Milgram-type obedience study.

The empirical evidence regarding the emotional aftereffects of experimental manipulations must now be regarded as favorable and supportive of the advocates of deception. Of course, three experiments do not resolve an issue of this complexity. But perhaps no amount of research—no matter how favorable the results—will ever completely justify the pursuit of an ethically questionable manipulation, partly because experimental findings of this nature are limited in their generality, and partly because, for some, ethical problems will not be resolved solely by empirical procedures. There is, however, considerable logic in the thought expressed by Lowin *et al.*:

> The emergent literature which is so critical of deceptive research partly because of the possibility of lasting effects surely implies that these exist and can be documented. . . . The absence of the expected in the data is, therefore, prominent and demands attention [p. 22–23].

FURTHER READING

BEM, D. J. Self-perception: An alternative interpretation of cognitive dissonance phenomena. *Psychological Review*, 1967, **74**: 183–200. An interesting utilization of role playing as a methodological device for challenging cognitive dissonance theory. Individuals are asked to take the role of subjects in several classic dissonance experiments. When given what Bem (although not his critics) considers to be the relevant stimulus information, his simulators are able to produce data compatible with dissonance theory without, of course, experiencing cognitive dissonance itself. Bem then theorizes that the behavior of actual subjects in dissonance experiments may similarly be accounted for without recourse to internal constructs.

BROCK, T. C., & Becker, L. A. Debriefing and susceptibility to subsequent experimental manipulations. *Journal of Experimental Social Psychology*, 1966, **2**: 314–323. One of the first empirical investigations of the effects of deception and debriefing on subsequent experimental behavior. Among their findings is the tendency for intensive debriefing *not* to affect reactions to an immediately succeeding experiment unless there is a marked similarity between the two experiments. The investigators are generally optimistic regarding the repeated use of subjects, although this practice requires that limiting conditions be met.

CAMPBELL, D. T. Prospective: Artifact and control. In R. Rosenthal & R. L. Rosnow (Eds.), *Artifact in behavioral research*. New York: Academic Press, 1969. Pp. 351–382. A valuable summarizing chapter by an outstanding methodologian in social psychology. Included is an extensive commentary on research in nonlaboratory settings, particularly the use of unobtrusive measures.

DARROCH, R. K., & Steiner, I. D. Role-playing: An alternative to laboratory research? *Journal of Personality*, 1970, **38**: 302–311. An investigation which features a more theoretical conception of role-playing than has previously been available. Whose role subjects are asked to play appears critical, in addition to the experimenter's ability to identify the crucial information that must be conveyed to the role-playing subjects.

ELMS, A. C. Obedience as a personal response. Experimental ethics. Unpublished manuscripts, University of California, Davis. A provocative analysis of Milgram's work from both a substantive and ethical perspective. Elms' view essentially parallels that of Crawford. He takes a decidedly negative stance on the role-playing issue.

FILLENBAUM, S., & Frey, R. More on the "faithful" behavior of suspicious subjects. *Journal of Personality*, 1970, **38**: 43–51. An experiment assessing the effects of deception upon subsequent performance in groups of trusting and suspicious subjects. As in the Brock and Becker study, deception appears to have little influence. Unlike the research of Stricker, Messick, and Jackson, suspiciousness does not appear as a significant predictor. These investigators stress the docility of subjects and its implication for the generality of experimental data.

HOLMES, D. S., & Appelbaum, A. S. Nature of prior experimental experience as a determinant of performance in subsequent experiments. *Journal of Personality and Social Psychology*, 1970, **14**: 195–202. Subjects are exposed to a positive, a negative, or no experimental history, and then participate in a criterion experiment. A variety of indices show history to be a significant determinant of behavior in the criterion study, particularly the tendency for positive experience to enhance performance.

HOROWITZ, I. A., & Rothschild, B. H. Conformity as a function of deception and role playing. *Journal of Personality and Social Psychology*, 1970, **14**: 224–226. An Asch-type conformity experiment which includes a deception group, a completely pre-briefed group, and a forewarned group—the latter similar to Greenberg's role-playing group in which subjects are asked to play the role of an experimental subject but are given little added information about the experiment itself. The forewarned and deceived groups perform comparably, both showing significantly more conformity than the prebriefed group. The authors suggest that forewarning may avoid some of the ethical shortcomings of deception without a serious loss of experimental realism.

LOWIN, A., Walsh, J. A., Klieger, D. M., Sandler, B., & Wilkes, R. L., Are there any lasting effects of a deceptive manipulation? Unpublished manuscript, State University of New York, Albany, 1968. An elaborate and well-controlled investigation, viewing deception as a message and debriefing as a countermessage in an attitude-change theoretical analysis. No lasting effects of deception are found.

MCGUIRE, W. J. Suspiciousness of experimenter's intent. In R. Rosenthal & R. L. Rosnow (Eds.), *Artifact in behavioral research*. New York: Academic Press, 1969. Pp. 13–57. A sophisticated review of the role of suspiciousness and awareness by a leading theorist and researcher in the area of attitude change. McGuire sees deception as involving a moral cost, but one that is likely to be worth paying in terms of the consequences of not performing research. Role playing is not seen as a promising solution.

RING, K., Wallston, K., & Corey, M. Mode of debriefing as a factor affecting subjective reaction to a Milgram-type obedience experiment: An ethical inquiry. *Representative Research in Social Psychology*, 1970, 1: 67–88. An important replication of the essential features of Milgram's paradigm. High levels of obedience and distress are found, but no significant negative aftereffects are reported.

ROGERS, C. R., & Skinner, B. F. Some issues concerning the control of human behavior: A symposium. In R. Ulrich, T. Stachnik, & J. Mabry (Eds.), *Control of human behavior*. Glenview: Scott, Foresman & Company, 1966. Pp. 300–316. A classic debate between two dominant influences in contemporary psychological thought. Although not focusing on the pros and cons of experimentation per se this debate exposes a variety of crucial issues, particularly as these relate to the ties between human values and scientific inquiry.

SEEMAN, J. Deception in psychological research. *American Psychologist*, 1969, 24: 1025–1028. A review of deception in contemporary psychological journals. Seeman argues passionately against the use of deception, viewing it as *antitherapy* in the sense of fostering distrust, incongruence, and unreality. Essentially an endorsement of Jourard's position.

SILVERMAN, I., Shulman, A. D., & Wiesenthal, D. L. Effects of deceiving and debriefing psychological subjects on performance in later experiments. *Journal of Personality and Social Psychology*, 1970, 14: 203–212. Unlike Brock and Becker, and Fillenbaum and Frey, these investigators find strong effects of deception on a variety of criterion measures separated from the treatment experiment by one week. Deception increases social-desirability responding and reduces compliance with demand characteristics, as in Sigall, Aronson, and Van Hoose. The authors advocate the utilization of subject populations other than college students.

STRICKER, L. J. The true deceiver. *Psychological Bulletin*, 1967, 68: 13–20. A useful empirical review of deception in psychological research. Featured are a series of classification tables illustrating the types of deception used in various kinds of research, the percentage of suspicious subjects reported, etc.

WILLIS, R. H., & Willis, Y. A. Role playing vs. deception: An experimental comparison. Paper presented at the meeting of the Midwestern Psychological Association, Chicago, 1969. An ingenious experiment showing the inadequacy of role-playing methodology in reproducing subtle and complex aspects of behavior that are achieved in deception designs.

Herbert C. Kelman

Human Use of Human Subjects:
The Problem of Deception in Social Psychological Experiments[1]

In 1954, in the pages of the *American Psychologist*, Edgar Vinacke raised a series of questions about experiments—particularly in the area of small groups—in which "the psychologist conceals the true purpose and conditions of the experiment, or positively misinforms the subjects, or exposes them to painful, embarrassing, or worse, experiences, without the subjects' knowledge of what is going on" [p. 155]. He summed up his concerns by asking, "What . . . is the proper balance between the interests of science and the thoughtful treatment of the persons who, innocently, supply the data?" [p. 155]. Little effort has been made in the intervening years to seek answers to the questions he raised. During these same years, however, the problem of deception in social psychological experiments has taken on increasingly serious proportions.[2]

The problem is actually broader, extending beyond the walls of the laboratory. It arises, for example, in various field studies in which investigators enroll as members of a group that has special interest for them so that they can observe its operations from the inside. The pervasiveness of the problem becomes even more apparent when we consider that deception is built into most of our measurement devices, since it is important to keep the respondent unaware of the personality or attitude dimension that we wish to explore. For the present purposes, however, primarily the problem of deception in the context of the social psychological experiment will be discussed.

The use of deception has become more and more extensive, and it is now a commonplace and almost standard feature of social psychological experiments. Deception has been turned into a game, often played with great skill and virtuosity. A considerable amount of the creativity and ingenuity of social psychologists is invested in the

From *Psychological Bulletin*, 1967, **67**: 1–11. Copyright © 1967 by The American Psychological Association and reprinted with permission of author and The American Psychological Association.

development of increasingly elaborate deception situations. Within a single experiment, deception may be built upon deception in a delicately complex structure. The literature now contains a fair number of studies in which second- or even third-order deception was employed.

One well-known experiment (Festinger & Carlsmith, 1959), for example, involved a whole progression of deceptions. After the subjects had gone through an experimental task, the investigator made it clear—through word and gesture—that the experiment was over and that he would now "like to explain what this has been all about so you'll have some idea of why you were doing this" [p. 205]. This explanation was false, however, and was designed to serve as a basis for the true experimental manipulation. The manipulation itself involved asking subjects to serve as the experimenter's accomplices. The task of the "accomplice" was to tell the next "subject" that the experiment in which he had just participated (which was in fact a rather boring experience) had been interesting and enjoyable. He was also asked to be on call for unspecified future occasions on which his services as accomplice might be needed because "the regular fellow couldn't make it, and we had a subject scheduled" [p. 205]. These newly recruited "accomplices," of course, were the true subjects, while the "subjects" were the experimenter's true accomplices. For their presumed services as "accomplices," the true subjects were paid in advance—half of them receiving $1, and half $20. When they completed their service, however, the investigators added injury to insult by asking them to return their hard-earned cash. Thus, in this one study, in addition to receiving the usual misinformation about the purpose of the experiment, the subject was given feedback that was really an experimental manipulation, was asked to be an accomplice who was really a subject, and was given a $20 bill that was really a will-o'-the-wisp. One wonders how much further in this direction we can go. Where will it all end?

It is easy to view this problem with alarm, but it is much more difficult to formulate an unambiguous position on the problem. As a working experimental social psychologist, I cannot conceive the issue in absolutist terms. I am too well aware of the fact that there are good reasons for using deception in many experiments. There are many significant problems that probably cannot be investigated without the use of deception, at least not at the present level of development of our experimental methodology. Thus, we are always confronted with a conflict of values. If we regard the acquisition of scientific knowledge about human behavior as a positive value, and if an experiment using deception constitutes a significant contribution to such knowledge which could not very well be achieved by other means, then we cannot unequivocally rule out this experiment. The question for us is not simply whether it does or does not use deception, but whether the amount and type of deception are justified by the significance of the study and the unavailability of alternative (that is deception-free) procedures.

I have expressed special concern about second-order deceptions, for example, the procedure of letting a person believe that he is acting as experimenter or as the experimenter's accomplice when he is in fact serving as the subject. Such a procedure undermines the relationship between experimenter and subject even further than simple misinformation about the purposes of the experiment; deception does not merely take place *within* the experiment, but encompasses the whole definition of the relationship between the parties involved. Deception that takes place while the person is within the role of subject for which he has contracted can, to some degree, be isolated, but deception about the very nature of the contract itself is more likely to suffuse the experimenter-subject relationship as a whole and to remove the possibility of mutual trust. Thus, I would be inclined to take a more absolutist stand with regard to such second-order deceptions—but even here the issue turns out to be more complicated. I am stopped short when I think, for example, of the ingenious studies on experimenter bias by Rosenthal and his associates (e.g., Rosenthal & Fode, 1963; Rosenthal, Persinger, Vikan-Kline, & Fode, 1963; Rosenthal, Persinger, Vikan-Kline, & Mulry, 1963). These experiments employed second-order deception in that subjects were led to believe that they were the experimenters. Since these were experiments about experiments, however, it is very hard to conceive of any alternative procedures that the investigators might have used. There is no question in my mind that these are significant studies; they provide fundamental inputs to present efforts at reexamining the social psychology of the experiment. These studies, then, help to underline even further the point that we are confronted with a conflict of values that cannot be resolved by fiat.

I hope it is clear from these remarks that my purpose in focusing on this problem is not to single out specific studies performed by some of my colleagues and to point a finger at them. Indeed, the finger points at me as well. I too have used deception, and have known the joys of applying my skills and ingenuity to the creation of elaborate experimental situations that the subjects would not be able to decode. I am now making active attempts to find alternatives to deception, but still I have not forsworn the use of deception under any and all circumstances. The questions I am raising, then, are addressed to myself as well as to my colleagues. They are questions with which all of us who are committed to social psychology must come to grips, lest we leave their resolution to others who have no understanding of what we are trying to accomplish.

What concerns me most is not so much that deception is used, but precisely that it is used without question. It has now become standard operating procedure in the social psychologist's laboratory. I sometimes feel that we are training a generation of students who do not know that there is any other way of doing experiments in our field—who feel that deception is as much *de rigueur* as significance at the .05 level. Too often deception is used not as a last resort, but as a matter of course. Our attitude seems to be that if you can deceive, why tell the truth? It is this unquestioning acceptance, this routinization of deception, that really concerns me.

I would like to turn now to a review of the bases for my concern with the problem of deception, and then suggest some possible approaches for dealing with it.

IMPLICATIONS OF THE USE OF DECEPTION IN SOCIAL PSYCHOLOGICAL EXPERIMENTS

My concern about the use of deception is based on three considerations: the ethical implications of such procedures, their methodological implications, and their implications for the future of social psychology.

1. Ethical Implications

Ethical problems of a rather obvious nature arise in the experiments in which deception has potentially harmful consequences for the subject. Take, for example, the brilliant experiment by Mulder and Stemerding (1963) on the effects of threat on attraction to the group and need for strong leadership. In this study—one of the very rare examples of an experiment conducted in a natural setting—independent food merchants in a number of Dutch towns were brought together for group meetings, in the course of which they were informed that a large organization was planning to open up a series of supermarkets in the Netherlands. In the High Threat condition, subjects were told that there was a high probability that their town would be selected as a site for such markets, and that the advent of these markets would cause a considerable drop in their business. On the advice of the executives of the shopkeepers' organizations, who had helped to arrange the group meetings, the investigators did not reveal the experimental manipulations to their subjects. I have been worried about these Dutch merchants ever since I heard about this study for the first time. Did some of them go out of business in anticipation of the heavy competition? Do some of them have an anxiety reaction every time they see a bulldozer? Chances are that they soon forgot about this threat (unless, of course, supermarkets actually did move into town) and that it became just one of the many little moments of anxiety that must occur in every shopkeeper's life. Do we have a right, however, to add to life's little anxieties and to risk the possibility of more extensive anxiety purely for the purposes of our experiments, particularly since deception deprives the subject of the opportunity to choose whether or not he wishes to expose himself to the risks that might be entailed?

The studies by Bramel (1962, 1963) and Bergin (1962) provide examples of another type of potentially harmful effects arising from the use of deception. In the Bramel studies, male undergraduates were led to believe that they were homosexually aroused by photographs of men. In the Bergin study, subjects of both sexes were given discrepant information about their level of masculinity or femininity; in one experimental condition, this information was presumably based on an elaborate series of psychological tests in which the subjects had participated. In all of these studies, the deception was explained to the subject at the end of the experiment. One wonders, however, whether such explanation removes the possibility of harmful effects. For many persons in this age group, sexual identity is still a live and sensitive issue, and the self-doubts generated by the laboratory experience may take on a life of their own and linger on for some time to come.

Yet another illustration of potentially harmful effects of deception can be found in Milgram's (1963, 1965) studies of obedience. In these experiments, the subject was led to believe that he was participating in a learning study and was instructed to administer increasingly severe shocks to another person who after a while began to protest vehemently. In fact, of course, the victim was an accomplice of the experimenter and did not receive any shocks. Depending on the conditions, sizable proportions of the subjects obeyed the experimenter's instructions and continued to shock the other person up to the maximum level, which they believed to be extremely painful. Both obedient and defiant subjects exhibited a great deal of stress in this situation. The complexities of the issues surrounding the use of deception become quite apparent when one reads the exchange between Baumrind (1964) and Milgram (1964) about the ethical implications of the obedience research. There is clearly room for disagreement, among honorable people, about the evaluation of this research from an ethical point of view. Yet, there is good reason to believe that at least some of the obedient subjects came away from this experience with a lower self-esteem, having to live with the realization that they were willing to yield to destructive authority to the point of inflicting extreme pain on a fellow human being. The fact that this may have provided, in Milgram's (1964) words, "an opportunity to learn something of importance about themselves, and more generally, about the conditions of human action" [p. 850] is beside the point. If this were a lesson from life, it would indeed constitute an instructive confrontation and provide a valuable insight. But do we, for the purpose of experimentation, have the right to provide such potentially disturbing insights to subjects who do not know that this is what they are coming for? A similar question can be raised about the Asch (1951) experiments on group pressure, although the stressfulness of the situation and the implications for the person's self-concept were less intense in that context.

While the present paper is specifically focused on social psychological experiments, the problem of deception and its possibly harmful effects arises in other areas of psychological experimentation as well. Dramatic illustrations are provided by two studies in which subjects were exposed, for experimental purposes, to extremely stressful conditions. In an experiment designed to study the establishment of a conditioned response in a situation that is traumatic but not painful, Campbell, Sanderson, and Laverty (1964) induced—through the use of a drug—a temporary interruption of respiration in their subjects. "This has no permanently harmful physical consequences but is nonetheless a severe stress which is not in itself painful . . ." [p. 628]. The subjects' reports confirmed that this was a "horrific" experience for them. "All the subjects in the standard series said that they thought they were dying" [p. 631]. Of course the subjects, "male alcoholic patients who volunteered for the experiment when they were told that it was connected with a possible therapy for alcoholism" [p. 629], were not warned in advance about the effect of the drug, since this information would have reduced the traumatic impact of the experience.[3] In a series of studies on the effects of psychological stress, Berkun, Bialek, Kern, and Yagi (1962) devised a number of ingenious experimental situations designed to convince the subject that his life was actually in danger. In one situation, the subjects, a group of Army recruits, were actually "passengers aboard an apparently stricken plane which was being forced to 'ditch' or crash-land" [p. 4]. In another experiment, an isolated subject in a desolate area learned that a sudden emergency had arisen (accidental nuclear radiation in the area, or a sudden forest fire, or misdirected artillery shells—depending on the experimental condition) and that he could be rescued only if he reported his position over his radio transmitter, "which has quite suddenly failed" [p. 7]. In yet another situation, the subject was led to believe that he was responsible for an explosion that seriously injured another soldier. As the authors pointed out, reactions in these situations are more likely to approximate reactions to combat experiences or to naturally occurring disasters than are reactions to various laboratory stresses, but is the experimenter justified in exposing his subjects to such extreme threats?

So far, I have been speaking of experiments in which deception has potentially harmful consequences. I am equally concerned, however, about the less obvious cases, in which there is little danger of harmful effects, at least in the conventional sense of the term. Serious ethical issues are raised by deception per se and the kind of use of human beings that it implies. In our other interhuman relationships, most of us would never think of doing the kinds of things that we do to our subjects— exposing others to lies and tricks, deliberately misleading them about the purposes of the interaction or withholding pertinent information, making promises or giving assurances that we intend to disregard. We would view such behavior as a violation of the respect to which all fellow humans are entitled and of the whole basis of our relationship with them. Yet we seem to forget that the experimenter-subject relationship—whatever else it is—is a *real* interhuman relationship, in which we have responsibility toward the subject as another human being whose dignity we must preserve. The discontinuity between the experimenter's behavior in everyday life and his behavior in the laboratory is so marked that one wonders why there has been so little concern with this problem, and what mechanisms have allowed us to ignore it to such an extent. I am reminded, in this connection, of the intriguing phenomenon of the "holiness of sin," which characterizes certain messianic movements as well as other movements of the true-believer variety. Behavior that would normally be unacceptable actually takes on an aura of virtue in such movements through a redefinition of the situation in which the behavior takes place and thus of the context for evaluating it. A similar mechanism seems to be involved in our attitude toward the psychological experiment. We tend to regard it as a situation that is not quite real, that can be isolated from the rest of life like a play performed on stage, and to which, therefore, the usual criteria for ethical interpersonal conduct become irrelevant. Behavior is judged entirely in the context of the experiment's scientific contribution and, in this context, deception—which is normally unacceptable—can indeed be seen as a positive good.

The broader ethical problem brought into play by the very use of deception becomes even more important when we view it in the light of present historical forces. We are living in an age of mass societies in which the transformation of man into an object to be manipulated at will occurs "on a mass scale, in a systematic way, and under the aegis of specialized institutions deliberately assigned to this task" (Kelman, 1965). In institutionalizing the use of deception in psychological experiments, we are, then, contributing to a historical trend that threatens values most of us cherish.

2. Methodological Implications

A second source of my concern about the use of deception is my increasing doubt about its adequacy as a methodology for social psychology.

A basic assumption in the use of deception is that a subject's awareness of the conditions that we are trying to create and of the phenomena that we wish to study would affect his behavior in such a way that we could not draw valid conclusions from it. For example, if we are interested in studying the effects of failure on conformity, we must create a situation in which the subjects actually feel that they have failed, and in which they can be kept unaware of our interest in observing conformity. In short, it is important to keep our subjects naïve about the purposes of the experiment so that they can respond to the experimental inductions spontaneously.

How long, however, will it be possible for us to find naïve subjects? Among college students, it is already very difficult. They may not know the exact purpose of the particular experiment in which they are participating, but at least they know, typically, that it is *not* what the experimenter says it is. Orne (1962) pointed out that the use of deception "on the part of psychologists is so widely known in the college population that even if a psychologist is honest with the subject, more often than not he will be distrusted." As one subject pithily put it, " 'Psychologists always lie!' " Orne added that "This bit of paranoia has some support in reality" [p. 237]. There are, of course, other sources of human subjects that have not been tapped, and we could turn to them in our quest for naïveté. But even there it is only a matter of time. As word about psychological experiments gets around in whatever network we happen to be using, sophistication is bound to increase. I wonder, therefore, whether there is any future in the use of deception.

If the subject in a deception experiment knows what the experimenter is trying to conceal from him and what he is really after in the study, the value of the deception is obviously nullified. Generally, however, even the relatively sophisticated subject does not know the exact purpose of the experiment; he only has suspicions, which may approximate the true purpose of the experiment to a greater or lesser degree. Whether or not he knows the *true* purpose of the experiment, he is likely to make an effort to figure out its purpose, since he does not believe what the experimenter tells him, and therefore he is likely to operate in the situation in terms of his own hypothesis of what is involved. This may, in line with Orne's (1962) analysis, lead him to do what he thinks the experimenter wants him to do. Conversely, if he resents the experimenter's attempt to deceive him, he may try to throw a monkey wrench into the works; I would not be surprised if this kind of Schweikian game among subjects became a fairly well-established part of the culture of sophisticated campuses. Whichever course the subject uses, however, he is operating in terms of his own conception of the nature of the situation, rather than in terms of the conception that the experimenter is trying to induce. In short, the experimenter can no longer assume that the conditions that he is trying to create are the ones that actually define the situation for the subject. Thus, the use of deception, while it is designed to give the experimenter control over the subject's perceptions and motivations, may actually produce an unspecifiable mixture of intended and unintended stimuli that make it difficult to know just what the subject is responding to.

The tendency for subjects to react to unintended cues—to features of the situation that are not part of the experimenter's design—is by no means restricted to experiments that involve deception. This problem has concerned students of the interview situation for some time, and more recently it has been analyzed in detail in the writings and research of Riecken, Rosenthal, Orne, and Mills. Subjects enter the experiment with their own aims, including attainment of certain rewards, divination of the experimenter's true purposes, and favorable self-presentation (Riecken, 1962). They are, therefore, responsive to demand characteristics of the situation (Orne, 1962), to unintended communications of the experimenter's expectations (Rosenthal, 1963), and to the role of the experimenter within the social system that experimenter and subject jointly constitute (Mills, 1962). In any experiment, then, the subject goes beyond the description of the situation and the experimental manipulation introduced by the investigator, makes his own interpretation of the situation, and acts accordingly.

For several reasons, however, the use of deception especially encourages the subject to dismiss the stated purposes of the experiment and to search for alternative interpretations of his own. First, the continued use of deception establishes the reputation of psychologists as people who cannot be believed. Thus, the desire "to penetrate the experimenter's inscrutability and discover the rationale of the experiment" [Riecken, 1962, p. 34] becomes especially strong. Generally, these efforts are motivated by the subject's desire to meet the expectations of the experimenter and of the situation. They may also be motivated, however, as I have already mentioned, by a desire to outwit the experimenter and to beat him at his own game, in a spirit of genuine hostility or playful one-upmanship. Second, a situation involving the use of deception is inevitably highly ambiguous since a great deal of information relevant to understanding the structure of the situation must be withheld from the subject. Thus, the subject is especially motivated to try to figure things out and likely to develop idiosyncratic interpretations. Third, the use of deception, by its very nature, causes the experimenter to transmit contradictory messages to the subject. In his verbal instructions and explanations he says one thing about the purposes of the experiment; but in the experimental situation that he has created, in the manipulations that he has introduced, and probably in covert cues that he emits, he says another thing. This again makes it imperative for the subject to seek his own interpretation of the situation.

I would argue, then, that deception increases the subject's tendency to operate in terms of his private definition of the situation, differing (in random or systematic fashion) from the definition that the experimenter is trying to impose; moreover, it makes it more difficult to evaluate or minimize the effects of this tendency. Whether or not I am right in this judgment, it can, at the very least, be said that the use of deception does not resolve or reduce the unintended effects of the experiment as a social situation in which the subject pursues his private aims. Since the assumptions that the subject is naïve and that he sees the situation as the experimenter wishes him to see it are unwarranted, the use of deception no longer has any special obvious advantages over other experimental approaches. I am not suggesting that there may not be occasions when deception may still be the most effective procedure to use from a methodological point of view. But since it raises at least as many methodological problems as any other type of procedure does, we have every reason to explore alternative approaches and to extend our methodological inquiries to the question of the effects of using deception.

3. Implications for the Future of Social Psychology

My third concern about the use of deception is based on its long-run implications for our discipline and combines both the ethical and methodological considerations that I have already raised. There is something disturbing about the idea of relying on massive deception as the basis for developing a field of inquiry. Can one really build a discipline on a foundation of such research?

From a long-range point of view, there is obviously something self-defeating about the use of deception. As we continue to carry out research of this kind, our potential subjects become more and more sophisticated, and we become less and less able to meet the conditions that our experimental procedures require. Moreover, as we continue to carry out research of this kind, our potential subjects become increasingly distrustful of us, and our future relations with them are likely to be undermined. Thus, we are confronted with the anomalous circumstance that the more research we do, the more difficult and questionable it becomes.

The use of deception also involves a contradiction between our experimental procedures and our long-range aims as scientists and teachers. In order to be able to carry out our experiments, we are concerned with maintaining the naïveté of the population from which we hope to draw our subjects. We are all familiar with the experimenter's anxious concern that the introductory course might cover the autokinetic phenomenon, need achievement, or the Asch situation before he has had a chance to complete his experimental runs. This perfectly understandable desire to keep procedures secret goes counter to the traditional desire of the scientist and teacher to inform and enlighten the public. To be sure, experimenters are interested only in temporary secrecy, but it is not inconceivable that at some time in the future they might be using certain procedures on a regular basis with large segments of the population and thus prefer to keep the public permanently naïve. It is perhaps not too fanciful to imagine, for the long run, the possible emergence of a special class in possession of secret knowledge— a possibility that is clearly antagonistic to the principle of open communication to which we, as scientists and intellectuals, are so fervently committed.

DEALING WITH THE PROBLEM OF DECEPTION IN SOCIAL PSYCHOLOGICAL EXPERIMENTS

If my concerns about the use of deception are justified, what are some of the ways in which we, as experimental social psychologists, can deal with them? I would like to suggest three steps that we can take: increase our active awareness of the problem, explore ways of counteracting and minimizing the negative effects of deception, and give careful attention to the development of new experimental techniques that dispense with the use of deception.

1. Active Awareness of the Problem

I have already stressed that I would not propose the complete elimination of deception under all circumstances, in view of the genuine conflict of values with which the experimenter is confronted. What is crucial, however, is that we always ask ourselves the question whether deception, in the given case, is necessary and justified. How we answer the question is less important than the fact that we ask it. What we must be wary of is the tendency to dismiss the question as irrelevant and to accept deception as a matter of course. Active awareness of the problem is thus in itself part of the solution, for it makes the use of deception a matter for discussion, deliberation, investigation, and choice. Active awareness means that, in any given case, we will try to balance the value of an experiment that uses deception against its questionable or potentially harmful effects. If we engage in this process honestly, we are likely to find that there are many occasions when we or our students can forego the use of deception—either because deception is not necessary (that is, alternative procedures that are equally good or better are available), because the importance of the study does not warrant the use of an ethically questionable procedure, or because the type of deception involved is too extreme (in terms of the possibility of harmful effects or of seriously undermining the experimenter-subject relationship).

2. Counteracting and Minimizing the Negative Effects of Deception

If we do use deception, it is essential that we find ways of counteracting and minimizing its negative effects. Sensitizing the apprentice researcher to this necessity is at least as fundamental as any other part of research training.

In those experiments in which deception carries the potential of harmful effects (in the more usual sense of the term), there is an obvious requirement to build protections into every phase of the process. Subjects must be selected in a way that will exclude individuals who are especially vulnerable; the potentially harmful manipulation (such as the induction of stress) must be kept at a moderate level of intensity; the experimenter must be sensitive to danger signals in the reactions of his subjects and be prepared to deal with crises when they arise; and, at the conclusion of the session, the experimenter must take time not only to reassure the subject but also to help him work through his feelings about the experience to whatever degree may be required. In general, the principle that a subject ought not to leave the laboratory with greater anxiety or lower self-esteem than he came with is a good one to follow. I would go beyond it to argue that the subject should in some positive way be enriched by the experience, that is, he should come away from it with the feeling that he has learned something, understood something, or grown in some way. This, of course, adds special importance to the kind of feedback that is given to the subject at the end of the experimental session.

Postexperimental feedback is, of course, the primary way of counteracting negative effects in those experiments in which the issue is deception as such, rather than possible threats to the subject's well-being. If we do deceive the subject, then it is our obligation to give him a full and detailed explanation of what we have done and of our reasons for using this type of procedure. I do not want to be absolutist about this, but I would suggest the following as a good rule of thumb to follow: Think very carefully before undertaking an experiment whose purposes you feel unable to reveal to the subjects even after they have completed the experimental session. It is, of course, not enough to give the subject a perfunctory feedback, just to do one's duty. Postexperimental explanations should be worked out with as much detail as other aspects of the procedure and, in general, some thought

ought to be given to ways of making them meaningful and instructive for the subject and helpful for rebuilding his relationship with the experimenter. I feel very strongly that to accomplish these purposes, we must keep the feedback itself inviolate and under no circumstance give the subject false feedback or pretend to be giving him feedback while we are in fact introducing another experimental manipulation. If we hope to maintain any kind of trust in our relationship with potential subjects, there must be no ambiguity that the statement "The experiment is over and I shall explain to you what it was all about" means precisely that and nothing else. If subjects have reason to suspect even that statement, then we have lost the whole basis for a decent human relationship with our subjects and all hope for future cooperation from them.

3. Development of New Experimental Techniques

My third and final suggestion is that we invest some of the creativity and ingenuity, now devoted to the construction of elaborate deceptions, in the search for alternative experimental techniques that do not rely on the use of deception. The kind of techniques that I have in mind would be based on the principle of eliciting the subject's positive motivations to contribute to the experimental enterprise. They would draw on the subject's active participation and involvement in the proceedings and encourage him to cooperate in making the experiment a success—not by giving the results he thinks the experimenter wants, but by conscientiously taking the roles and carrying out the tasks that the experimenter assigns to him. In short, the kind of techniques I have in mind would be designed to involve the subject as an active participant in a joint effort with the experimenter.

Perhaps the most promising source of alternative experimental approaches are procedures using some sort of role playing. I have been impressed, for example, with the role playing that I have observed in the context of the Inter-Nation Simulation (Guetzkow, Alger, Brody, Noel, & Snyder, 1963), a laboratory procedure involving a simulated world in which the subjects take the roles of decision-makers of various nations. This situation seems to create a high level of emotional involvement and to elicit motivations that have a real-life quality to them. Moreover, within this situation—which is highly complex and generally permits only gross experimental manipulations—it is possible to test specific theoretical hypotheses by using data based on repeated measurements as interaction between the simulated nations develops. Thus, a study carried out at the Western Behavioral Sciences Institute provided, as an extra, some interesting opportunities for testing hypotheses derived from balance theory, by the use of mutual ratings made by decision-makers of Nations A, B, and C, before and after A shifted from an alliance with B to an alliance with C.

A completely different type of role playing was used effectively by Rosenberg and Abelson (1960) in their studies of cognitive dilemmas. In my own research program, we have been exploring different kinds of role-playing procedures with varying degrees of success. In one study, the major manipulation consisted of informing subjects that the experiment to which they had just committed themselves would require them (depending on the condition) either to receive shocks from a fellow subject or to administer shocks to a fellow subject. We used a regular deception procedure, but with a difference: We told the subjects before the session started that what was to follow was make-believe, but that we wanted them to react as if they really found themselves in this situation. I might mention that some subjects, not surprisingly, did not accept as true the information that this was all make-believe and wanted to know when they should show up for the shock experiment to which they had committed themselves. I have some question about the effectiveness of this particular procedure. It did not do enough to create a high level of involvement, and it turned out to be very complex since it asked subjects to role-play subjects, not people. In this sense, it might have given us the worst of both worlds, but I still think it is worth some further exploration. In another experiment, we were interested in creating differently structured attitudes about an organization by feeding different kinds of information to two groups of subjects. These groups were then asked to take specific actions in support of the organization, and we measured attitude changes resulting from these actions. In the first part of the experiment, the subjects were clearly informed that the organization and the information that we were feeding to them were fictitious, and that we were simply trying to simulate the conditions under which attitudes about new organizations are typically formed. In the second part of the experiment, the subjects were told that we were interested in studying the effects of action in support of an organization on attitudes toward it, and they were asked (in groups of five) to role-play a strategy meeting of leaders of the fictitious organization. The results of this study were very encouraging. While there is obviously a great deal that we need to know about the meaning of this situation to the subjects, they did react differentially to the experimental manipulations and these reactions followed an orderly pattern, despite the fact that they knew it was all make-believe.

There are other types of procedures, in addition to role playing, that are worth exploring. For example, one might design field experiments in which, with the full cooperation of the subjects, specific experimental variations are introduced. The advantages of dealing with motivations at a real-life level of intensity might well outweigh the disadvantages of subjects' knowing the general purpose of the experiment. At the other extreme of ambitiousness, one might explore the effects of modifying standard experimental procedures slightly by informing the subject at the beginning of the experiment that he will not be receiving full information about what is going on and asking him to suspend judgment until the experiment is over.

Whatever alternative approach we try, there is no doubt that it will have its own problems and complexities. Procedures effective for some purposes may be quite ineffective for others, and it may well turn out that for certain kinds of problems there is no adequate substitute for the use of deception. But there *are* alternative procedures that, for many purposes, may be as effective or even more effective than procedures built on deception. These approaches often involve a radically different set of assumptions about the role of the subject in the experiment: They require us to *use* 'the subject's motivation to cooperate rather than to bypass it; they may even call for increasing the sophistication of potential subjects, rather than maintaining their naïveté. My only plea is that we devote some of our energies to active exploration of these alternative approaches.

NOTES

1. Paper read at the symposium on "Ethical and Methodological Problems in Social Psychological Experiments," held at the meetings of the American Psychological Association in Chicago, September 3, 1965. This paper is a product of a research program on social influence and behavior change supported by United States Public Health Service Research Grant MH-07280 from the National Institute of Mental Health.

2. In focusing on deception in *social* psychological experiments, I do not wish to give the impression that there is no serious problem elsewhere. Deception is widely used in most studies involving human subjects and gives rise to issues similar to those discussed in this paper. Some examples of the use of deception in other areas of psychological experimentation will be presented later in this paper.

3. The authors reported, however, that some of their other subjects were physicians familiar with the drug; "they did not suppose they were dying but even though they knew in a general way what to expect, they too said that the experience was extremely harrowing" [p. 632]. Thus, conceivably, the purposes of the experiment might have been achieved even if the subjects had been told to expect the temporary interruption of breathing.

REFERENCES

Asch, S. E. Effects of group pressure upon the modification and distortion of judgments. In H. Guetzkow (Ed.), *Groups, leadership, and men*. Pittsburgh: Carnegie Press, 1951. Pp. 177–190.

Baumrind, D. Some thoughts on ethics of research: After reading Milgram's "Behavioral study of obedience." *American Psychologist*, 1964, **19**: 421–423.

Bergin, A. E. The effect of dissonant persuasive communications upon changes in a self-referring attitude. *Journal of Personality*, 1962, **30**: 423–438.

BERKUN, M. M., Bialek, H. M., Kern, R. P., & Yagi, K. Experimental studies of psychological stress in man. *Psychological Monographs*, 1962, **76** (15, Whole No. 534).

BRAMEL, D. A dissonance theory approach to defensive projection. *Journal of Abnormal and Social Psychology*, 1962, **64**: 121–129.

BRAMEL, D. Selection of a target for defensive projection. *Journal of Abnormal and Social Psychology*, 1963, **66**: 318–324.

CAMPBELL, D., Sanderson, R. E., & Laverty, S. G. Characteristics of a conditioned response in human subjects during extinction trials following a single traumatic conditioning trial. *Journal of Abnormal and Social Psychology*, 1964, **68**: 627–639.

FESTINGER, L., & Carlsmith, J. M. Cognitive consequences of forced compliance. *Journal of Abnormal and Social Psychology*, 1959, **58**: 203–210.

GUETZKOW, H., Alger, C. F., Brody, R. A., Noel, R. C., & Snyder, R. C. *Simulation in international relations*. Englewood Cliffs, N.J.: Prentice-Hall, 1963.

KELMAN, H. C. Manipulation of human behavior: An ethical dilemma for the social scientist. *Journal of Social Issues*, 1965, **21**(2): 31–46.

MILGRAM, S. Behavioral study of obedience. *Journal of Abnormal and Social Psychology*, 1963, **67**: 371–378.

MILGRAM, S. Issues in the study of obedience: A reply to Baumrind. *American Psychologist*, 1964, **19**: 848–852.

MILGRAM, S. Some conditions of obedience and disobedience to authority. *Human Relations*, 1965, **18**: 57–76.

MILLS, T. M. A sleeper variable in small groups research: The experimenter. *Pacific Sociological Review*, 1962, **5**: 21–28.

MULDER, M., & Stemerding, A. Threat, attraction to group, and need for strong leadership. *Human Relations*, 1963, **16**: 317–334.

ORNE, M. T. On the social psychology of the psychological experiment: With particular reference to demand characteristics and their implications. *American Psychologist*, 1962, **17**: 776–783.

RIECKEN, H. W. A program for research on experiments in social psychology. In N. F. Washburne (Ed.), *Decisions, values and groups*. Vol. 2. New York: Pergamon Press, 1962. Pp. 25–41.

ROSENBERG, M. J., & Abelson, R. P. An analysis of cognitive balancing. In M. J. Rosenberg et al. (Eds.), *Attitude organization and change*. New Haven: Yale University Press, 1960. Pp. 112–163.

ROSENTHAL, R. On the social psychology of the psychological experiment: The experimenter's hypothesis as unintended determinant of experimental results. *American Scientist*, 1963, **51**: 268–283.

ROSENTHAL, R., & Fode, K. L. Psychology of the scientist: V. Three experiments in experimenter bias. *Psychological Reports*, 1963, **12**: 491–511. (Monogr. Suppl. 3-V12)

ROSENTHAL, R., Persinger, G. W., Vikan-Kline, L., & Fode, K. L. The effect of early data returns on data subsequently obtained by outcome-biased experimenters. *Sociometry*, 1963, **26**: 487–498.

ROSENTHAL, R., Persinger, G. W., Vikan-Kline, L., & Mulry, R. C. The role of the research assistant in the mediation of experimenter bias. *Journal of Personality*, 1963, **31**: 313–335.

VINACKE, W. E. Deceiving experimental subjects. *American Psychologist*, 1954, **9**: 155.

Thomas J. Crawford

In Defense of Obedience Research:
An Extension of the Kelman Ethic

In recent years social scientists have shown a somewhat belated concern with the ethics of social research, and with moral dilemmas arising from the application of social science findings. Such concerns are not unique to social scientists. Nuclear physicists have debated responsibility for the application of their knowledge for decades, but they have not been able to agree upon ethical guidelines for allocating obligations and blameworthiness for the uses of their research products. Unresolved controversy also characterizes the attempts of medical researchers to resolve ethical problems that arise in the process of gathering data from human subjects. Thus, we are left to devise our own normative formulas. Among social psychologists, Herbert Kelman has provided the most penetrating and thoughtful consideration of research ethics. The present paper is an attempt to apply two ethical guidelines suggested by Kelman to the social psychological experiment that has probably generated more controversy than any other: Stanley Milgram's study of destructive obedience.

TWO ETHICS

In "The Manipulation of Human Behavior" Kelman (1965) proposes and partially resolves the conflict arising from the fact that, on the one hand, effective behavior change in processes such as education and psychotherapy involves some degree of manipulation and control, but, on the other hand, *any* manipulation of human behavior inherently violates a fundamental value and intrudes on the essential humanity of the individual being manipulated. Kelman takes the position that manipulations are legitimate provided that they serve to increase the individual's freedom of choice. He suggests that:

The purpose of education and of the arrangement of the social order, as I see it, is to enable men to live in a society while at the same time enhancing their freedom to choose and widening their areas of choice . . . valuing free individual choice is a vital protection against tyranny . . . attempts designed to enhance the client's freedom of choice and techniques that are consistent with this goal are ethically superior, and we should continue to push and explore in this direction [Kelman, 1965].

This principle is very helpful as a guideline for resolving ethical conflicts such as those discussed in the Skinner vs. Rogers (1956) debate. Family planning practitioners have expressed a similar idea, pointing out that the term "birth control" may erroneously connote manipulative intent. The family planners argue that when contraceptives are made available to people their range of possible choices in the area of family planning is increased. Of course, it can be argued that "increased freedom of choice" needs to be modified before it provides a completely satisfactory ethic. Perhaps it is best applied in situations in which the new choices are "good" or at least neutral in some utilitarian sense. Thus, for example, providing an individual with the means for harming others may increase his freedom of choice, but may be morally objectionable on other grounds. However, even though other and often conflicting values must be considered, Kelman's principle is a potentially powerful standard for resolving and clarifying dilemmas connected with manipulation.

Although the increased-choice criterion was apparently conceived in reference to the application of social science findings, it may also clarify moral ambiguities that occur in the process of conducting research. In a subsequent article, Kelman (1966) dealt more directly with ethical problems that arise in the process of gathering the data of social science. In the latter treatment, however, he did not apply the increase in freedom of choice standard, but instead suggested that:

. . . a good principle to follow is that a subject ought not to leave the laboratory with greater anxiety or lower self-esteem than he came with. I would go beyond it to argue that the subject should in some positive way be enriched by the experience—he should come away from it with the feeling that he has learned something, understood something, or grown in some way [Kelman, 1966].

Indeed this is a laudable standard, and perhaps it should be included as an explicit principle in the APA Code of Ethics even though it would be difficult or impossible to enforce. It seems that social scientists, because of the nature of their subject matter and methodology, almost automatically violate the Kantian ethic. The injunction that we should never treat any person as a means, but only as an end in himself, may be incompatible with conducting research with the *primary* purpose of testing a theory or of increasing our understanding of some general behavioral phenomenon. In that process, individuals who participate in the research are means to an end and, regardless of the nobility of the end, a certain dehumanizing and distancing between the researcher and his subjects often results. This disinterested attitude carries with it a potentially dangerous propensity to ignore the rights and the welfare of the individuals from whom we obtain our data. Thus an explicit statement of Kelman's "No Less Self-Esteem or More Anxiety" principle may help to keep these dangers more salient in the minds of social scientists designing research.

To summarize thus far: Kelman has presented us with two ethical guidelines. The first is that manipulations which serve to increase freedom of choice are ethically superior, and the second is that the participants in our studies should not leave the experience with less self-esteem or more anxiety than they brought to it. However, as I will attempt to demonstrate in what follows, there are certain circumstances in which these two values are mutually exclusive. Indeed, the juxtaposition of these two principles may be an illustration of the essence of tragedy—the opposition of two conflicting and incompatible goods (Abel, 1964).

OBEDIENCE RESEARCH AND ITS CRITICS

For reasons that are not entirely clear, a great deal of concern over research ethics has focused upon Stanley Milgram's studies of obedience. These studies have been described in detail elsewhere in this volume. In the opinion of the present writer Milgram's research on destructive obedience is one of the most important studies ever done in social psychology. Unlike many social psychological experiments, it is not a watered-down analogue of the process supposedly being simulated, and it is not merely a demonstration of methodological expertise for one's peers. It is an allegory for our times. What interpersonal process could be of more relevance to contemporary America than that in which B inflicts injury upon C at the command of A? By simulating this process in a simple but elegant experimental paradigm, Milgram was able to examine the social, situational, and personal correlates and causes of obedience *and disobedience*. The results of the victim proximity and authority figure prestige manipulations are particularly compelling, and the liberating effect of the example provided by a dissenting "fellow subject" is loaded with implications.

With what aspects of this study do the critics find fault? Is it the deception? Hardly! As a routine part of experimental procedure, psychologists have been deceiving subjects for years. For example, in "prestige suggestion" and "communicator credibility" studies, attitude researchers frequently attribute the same message to different sources, depending upon the experimental condition. This routinization of deception has been ably described by Kelman (1967). A more plausible source of the objection is sympathy for the discomfort and conflict which the subject experiences, as manifested by the sweating, twitching, and nervous laughter. The problem with that explanation is that we have been subjecting subjects to stress for years—and not merely as an unanticipated side effect, as it was in Milgram's study (Milgram 1964), but as the deliberately induced key variable.

As middle-class American social scientists we may have become adept at avoiding direct physical sources of pain and fear, and for this reason we may be less able to identify with subjects in stress and fear experiments. But the anxiety Milgram's "teachers" felt may be more familiar to us. It is possible that many of us have faced the conflict that arises when someone in a position of authority asks us to perform an ethically questionable act or to refrain from taking a morally sound but "disruptive" step, and perhaps we have not always resolved such conflicts in an entirely independent and ethical manner. From this interpretation it could be argued that more identification with the *victims* of destructive obedience, and perhaps less empathy with obedient functionaries, would lead to a more positive evaluation of the Milgram studies.

But the "Identification with the Teacher" explanation does not account for all of the criticism levelled at this study. The more thoughtful critics seem to be primarily concerned with the danger that there will be permanent psychological damage to the obedient subjects when they learn what the nature of the experiment was. It certainly does seem possible that some of the subjects will experience at least a temporary feeling of guilt and lowered self-esteem during the debriefing sessions. However, Milgram has not shown any lack of concern for the welfare of his subjects. At his request a psychiatrist interviewed forty of the participants and found no evidence that any of them had been harmed by the experience. In fact the overwhelming majority of subjects reacted very favorably to the experience. Similarly, positive reactions were reported by the subjects in a recent obedience experiment conducted by Ring, Wallston, and Corey (1970). The Ring *et al.* study was explicitly designed to investigate possible harmful effects of subject participation in obedience research. If comparable data were available on subject reaction to other psychological experiments, the reported effects of participating in the obedience research would probably look even more positive by comparison.

In spite of these assurances, the possible arousal of guilt and anxiety in the obedient subjects remains a critical moral issue for most of the obedience research critics. Perhaps because of our Freudian heritage, most American psychologists would be likely to agree with Kelman that guilt and anxiety are emotions to be avoided whenever possible. But Kelman has also proposed that we should "set enhancement of freedom of choice as a positive goal" and that we should "study conditions for enhancement of freedom of choice and maximization of individual values." Unfortunately, however, the experience of freedom of choice and the concomitant feeling of responsibility may be incompatible with the total absence of anxiety. The anguish of freedom —of a man, as Sartre puts it, condemned to be free, and therefore, responsible—is not always a pleasant burden. Submissive authoritarianism may be one way to escape from this freedom, as Fromm (1941) has suggested. This seems to be precisely what many of Milgram's subjects did when they obeyed the experimenter. But the postexperimental debriefing served to *heighten their awareness that choice was possible* in a situation in which they had been willing to relinquish autonomy. Therefore, the study performs the very service which Kelman says justifies manipulations of human behavior—it enhances awareness of freedom of choice and thereby maximizes the attainment of individual values.

Kelman (1967) has replied to a similar point made by Milgram, i.e., that the participants learned something of importance about themselves and about the determinants of human behavior. Kelman asks if researchers have the right to provide such potentially disturbing insights to subjects who do not know that this is what they volunteered for? To counter this by asking the same question about educators, therapists, and social science practitioners would obscure the issue here. The end or goal of the research is an increase in our understanding of destructive obedience. It is not conducted to provide self-knowledge to the participants. This is merely a by-product of the procedures, but it happens to be a by-product that meets Kelman's criterion for the justification of manipulation.

The most important justification for obedience research is that it makes an important contribution to "the body of certified knowledge" about human behavior. But almost equally important is the particular nature of that contribution. Kelman (1965) tells us that "In order to build some protection against manipulation into the social structure, we will have to extend our research on processes of resistance to control." From the series of obedience studies, we have learned a great deal about the relationship between destructive obedience and factors such as authoritarianism, education, proximity of the victim, surveillance by the authority figure, conflicting authority demands, and the liberating effects of group pressure. I submit that Milgram's research, along with the studies of Asch and Sherif on conformity and McGuire's work on inoculation and resistance to persuasion, is precisely aimed at achieving the admirable goal which Kelman sets before us. We can hardly read the study without becoming more sensitized to analogous conflicts in our own lives.

A PROPOSAL AND A DILEMMA FOR THE READER

The foregoing discussion underscores Kelman's observation that problems in research ethics cannot be resolved by invoking absolute norms and values. Controversies over research ethics are difficult to settle precisely because they involve conflicts between important values such as individual rights and science or community interest. Perhaps a "hedonic calculus" in the form of Rosenberg's (1956) value-instrumentality technique would be useful for making moral judgments concerning a research project. The problem is that judges will differ in the *values* they assign to research consequences such as increased freedom of choice, increased anxiety, increased distrust of authority figures, etc. Judges will also differ in their *beliefs* about the probability that the research will lead to a given consequence such as increased subject anxiety, or increased public understanding of an important interpersonal process. Given these unresolvable differences in values and beliefs, perhaps the only practical solution for arriving at a binding moral decision about a study is to rely upon the consensus or majority evaluation of a group of informed judges.

There is something artificial about discussing the ethical implications of research that has already been completed. Even though we may learn some important lessons, the research is a *fait accompli* and for this reason we may be somewhat uninvolved in our evaluations. Perhaps asking for an ethical decision on a specific experiment that has not yet been conducted will help to make the issues more exigent and less "academic." I would like to propose a study and to ask the reader to imagine that he is serving as a member of an Advisory Committee to the Ford Foundation or to the National Science Foundation and that the Committee's task is to decide whether the proposed study is ethically objectionable. Stanley Milgram began his research career as Solomon Asch's assistant, and Milgram's first major research project was a cross-cultural replication of Asch's conformity studies in Norway and in France (Milgram, 1961). The study I am proposing is a cross-cultural replication of Milgram's obedience research, and one of the countries involved would be West Germany. Such a study would make an important contribution to our knowledge of national character. In their article on "National Character" in the 1954 *Handbook of Social Psychology*, Alex Inkeles and Daniel Levinson suggested that the issue of *relation to authority* is one that has universal psychosocial relevance, and is, therefore, a very promising research topic. Inkeles and Levinson mention several expressions of relation to authority, including:

1. Personal ideology, i.e., beliefs, values and attitudes regarding authority and authority-subordinate relationships; and

2. Ways of adapting behaviorally in interaction with authority. We have some data on cross-cultural differences in beliefs and attitudes regarding authority. For example, 25 years ago McGranahan (1946) measured attitudes toward authority in what he felt were two roughly comparable groups of high-school students—one group in West Germany, and the other in a Chicago suburb. He found the German students to be more authoritarian. According to some observations, this difference may have declined or disappeared, at least among the postwar generation. Of course, a replication of the McGranahan survey would supply a partial answer to the question. But as attitude researchers from LaPiere (1934) to Festinger (1964) have stressed: the relationship between attitudes and behavior is far from perfect correspondence and consistency. Fortunately, Milgram has provided us with a paradigm for the systematic and controlled study of behavioral interaction with authority. Are there strong ethical arguments against conducting this important cross-national research? If so, I would like to hear them.

NOTE

1. The author wishes to acknowledge his indebtedness to Richard Willis for his helpful comments and suggestions.

REFERENCES

ABEL, L. Is there a tragic sense of life? *Commentary*, December, 1964.

FESTINGER, L. Behavioral support for opinion change. *Public Opinion Quarterly*, 1964, **28**: 404–417.

FROMM, E. *Escape from freedom*. New York: Farrar & Rinehart, 1941.

INKELES, A., & Levinson, D. J. National character: The study of modal personality and sociocultural systems. In G. Lindzey (Ed.), *Handbook of social psychology*. Reading, Mass. · Addison-Wesley, 1954.

KELMAN, H. C. Manipulation of human behavior: An ethical dilemma for the social scientist. *Journal of Social Issues*, 1965, **21**: 31–46.

KELMAN, H. C. Deception in social research. *Trans-action*, 1966, **3**: 20–24.

KELMAN, H. C. Human use of human subjects: The problem of deception in social psychological experiments. *Psychological Bulletin*, 1967, **61**: 1–11.

LAPIERE, R. Attitudes vs. actions. *Social Forces*, 1934, **13**: 230–237.

McGRANAHAN, D. V. A comparison of social attitudes among American and German youth. *Journal of Abnormal and Social Psychology*, 1946, **41**: 245–257.

MILGRAM, S. Nationality and conformity. *Scientific American*, 1961, **205**: 45–51.

MILGRAM, S. Behavioral study of obedience. *Journal of Abnormal and Social Psychology*, 1963, **67**: 371–378.

MILGRAM, S. Issues in the study of obedience: A reply to Baumrind. *American Psychologist*, 1964, **19**: 848–852.

MILGRAM, S. Some conditions of obedience and disobedience to authority. *Human Relations*, 1965, **18**: 57–76.

RING, K., Wallston, K., & Corey, M. Mode of debriefing as a factor affecting subjective reaction to a Milgram-type obedience experiment: An ethical inquiry. *Representative Research in Social Psychology*, 1970, **1**: 67–88.

ROGERS, C. R., & Skinner, B. F. Some issues concerning the control of human behavior. *Science*, 1956, **124**: 1057–1066.

ROSENBERG, M. J. Cognitive structure and attitudinal affect. *Journal of Abnormal and Social Psychology*, 1956, **53**: 367–372.

Martin S. Greenberg

Role Playing:
An Alternative to Deception?

In recent years there has been a growing concern with the ethical and methodological implications of the use of deception in social psychological research. For example, Baumrind (1964), Kelman (1967), and Vinacke (1954) have questioned whether the information derived from studies employing deception justifies the harm that might be done to the subject and to the subject-experimenter relationship. Others, however, have taken a more sanguine view of deception. Milgram (1964) reported that in spite of the deception involved in his experiments, subjects felt quite positive about their participation and viewed it "as an opportunity to learn something of importance about themselves, and more generally, about the conditions of human action" [p. 850]. As regards methodological considerations, Brock and Becker (1966) reported that the debriefing of subjects who have experienced deception did not impair their usefulness as subjects in future psychological research.

However, Kelman (1967), Orne (1962), and Riecken (1962) have taken a different view concerning the methodological liabilities inherent in the use of deception. While presenting no original data to support their conclusions, all three cogently argued that subjects are usually aware of attempts at deception and, therefore, substitute their own hypotheses in place of the experimenter's. The presence of these demand characteristics (Orne, 1962) often makes it difficult to arrive at an unambiguous interpretation of the results.

In light of the ethical and methodological questions raised by the use of deception in social psychological experiments, Kelman (1967) and Vinacke (1954) have called for the exploration of alternative techniques. One such technique proposed by Kelman is that of role playing. Until 1957 there was a paucity of social psychological studies

From *Journal of Personality and Social Psychology*, 1967, **7**: 152–157.
Copyright © 1967 by The American Psychological Association and reprinted with permission of author and The American Psychological Association.

which used role playing, and as Mann (1956) pointed out, "Perhaps the most striking impression to be gained from a review of the experimental studies of role playing is their scarcity" [p. 233].

It was the advent of Festinger's (1957) theory of cognitive dissonance, with its emphasis on the subject playing the role of an advocate of a position which he privately opposes, that greatly stimulated the employment of role playing in social psychological research. Yet much of the research generated by dissonance theory and related approaches (Elms & Janis, 1965; Festinger & Carlsmith, 1959; Rosenberg, 1965; Scott, 1957) used role playing as an *adjunct* rather than as a *substitute* for deception.

Those studies in which an attempt has been made to substitute role playing for some form of deception have produced inconsistent results. The works of Rosenberg and Abelson (1960) and Guetzkow, Alger, Brody, Noel, and Snyder (1963) support the utility of the device. At least two investigations, however, have found that the performance of subjects who act *as if* they are in a certain situation differs in several respects from the performance of subjects who are placed in the situation through either deception (Deutsch, 1960) or hypnosis (Rosenberg, 1960).

In summary, the results are equivocal as to the efficacy of role playing as a substitute for deception; it is the purpose of the present investigation to shed further light on the utility of the role-playing approach. In order to accomplish this purpose, a role-playing procedure was used to test the hypothesis that affiliative behavior is related to birth order and level of anxiety. Recent investigations using deception to create high- and low-anxiety states support the conclusions that: (*a*) high anxiety produces a greater tendency to prefer affiliation than low anxiety only among firstborn and only child subjects and not among later-born subjects (Gerard & Rabbie, 1961; Schachter, 1959); (*b*) firstborn and only child subjects have a greater desire to affiliate with others than later-born subjects only under conditions of high anxiety but not under conditions of low anxiety (Sarnoff & Zimbardo, 1961; Schachter, 1959).

The procedure in each of these investigations was essentially similar and involved the creation of high- and low-anxiety states by instructing subjects that they were about to receive either a series of rather severe and painful electrical shocks (high anxiety) or a series of mild electrical shocks (low anxiety) "that would resemble more a tickle or a tingle than anything unpleasant." Subjects in both groups were subsequently informed that it would take a few minutes to prepare the apparatus and that each subject would have the opportunity of spending this waiting period alone or in the company of others. Each subject was then presented with two scales which measured his willingness to wait alone or in the company of others (i.e., his need for affiliation). No shocks were ever administered, as the experiments were terminated at this point.

METHOD

The present investigation replicated Schachter's (1959) experiment in a classroom setting with the major difference being that each subject was asked to assume the role of a subject who was about to receive electrical shocks. Instead of using deception to create in the subject the impression that he was going to receive shocks, the experimenter relied solely upon each subject's imagination and upon his willingness to assume the role to create such a cognitive state.

Subjects and Design

The subjects consisted of 88 undergraduate students (51 males and 37 females) enrolled in an introductory psychology course at Washington University.

Approximately half the subjects were randomly assigned to the high-anxiety condition and half to the low-anxiety condition. On the basis of birth-order data obtained from each subject, subjects were further classified according to whether they were firstborn or only children or whether they were later born. The foregoing procedure yielded a 2 × 2 design consisting of the following four conditions; high anxiety—firstborn and only children; high anxiety—later born; low anxiety—firstborn and only children; low anxiety—later born.

Procedure

The experiment was performed during a regularly scheduled class meeting. Each subject was given a test booklet and was told that the booklet should remain face down. The experimenter then read aloud the following instructions:

I'd like your cooperation in an experiment involving role playing. In role playing the persons involved act or make believe that they are in a particular situation. What I'd like you to do is to play the role of subjects in an experiment, and I will play the role of the experimenter. It's very important that you take your role seriously and that you act *as if* this were a real situation. O.K.? Are there any questions?

Subsequently, the experimenter donned a white laboratory coat and proceeded to wheel into view a cart prominently displaying a shock apparatus. From this point on, the instructions and procedure were essentially identical to those of Schachter (1959).

The experimenter then addressed the subjects in the following manner:

Allow me to introduce myself. I am Dr. Greenberg of the Medical School's Department of Neurology and Psychiatry. I have asked you to come today in order to serve as subjects in an experiment concerned with the effects of electrical shock. As you may know, this type of research is very important. Data from this experiment and experiments like this will help increase man's knowledge of the effects of electroshock therapy, as well as help us treat large numbers of victims of accidents due to electricity. Now that you understand the importance of this research, please turn over your booklets and read the instructions on the first page.

These instructions were designed to produce either high or low anxiety. The subjects in the high-anxiety condition received the following instructions:

What I will ask each of you to do is very simple. I would like to give each of you a series of electric shocks. Now, I feel I must be completely honest with you and tell you exactly what you are in for. These shocks will hurt, they will be painful. As you can guess, if, in research of this sort, we're to learn anything at all that will really help humanity, it is necessary that our shocks be intense. What I will do is put an electrode on your hand, hook you into apparatus such as you see on the desk, give you a series of electric shocks, and take various measures such as your pulse rate, blood pressure, and so on. Again, I do want to be honest with you and tell you that these shocks will be quite painful but, of course, they will do no permanent damage.

The subjects in the low-anxiety condition received a much milder communication:

What I will ask each of you to do is very simple. I would like to give each of you a series of very mild electric shocks. I assure you that what you will feel will not in any way be painful. It will resemble more a tickle or a tingle than anything unpleasant. I will put an electrode on your hand, give you a series of mild shocks, and measure such things as your pulse rate and bood pressure, measures with which I'm sure you are all familiar from visits to your family doctor.

The experimenter continued:

Before we begin I'd like to have you tell me how you feel about taking part in this experiment and being shocked. We need this information in order to understand fully your reactions to the shock apparatus. I ask you, therefore, to be as honest as possible in answering and to describe your feelings as accurately as possible.

Page 2 of the booklet contained a single item designed to measure the success of the anxiety manipulation. Subjects indicated how anxious they felt by choosing one alternative from six which ranged from "I feel completely calm" to "I feel extremely uneasy."

The experimenter then read aloud the following instructions:

Before we begin with the shocking proper there will be about a ten minute delay while I get this room in order. I have several pieces of equipment to bring in and get set up. With this many people in the room, this would be very difficult to do, so I will have to ask you to leave the room.

Here is what I will ask you to do for this ten minute period of waiting. We have in this building a number of additional rooms, so that each of you, if you like, can wait alone in your own room. These rooms are comfortable and spacious; they all have armchairs, and there are books and magazines in each room. It did occur to me, however, that some of you might want to wait for these ten minutes together with some of the other people here. If you would prefer this, of course, just let me know. I'll take some of the empty classrooms on this floor and you can wait together with some of the other students here. If you do choose to wait with others, these others must not be acquaintances of yours. In the past we have found that putting close friends together interferes with the physiological measures which we are trying to obtain. [The latter instruction was included so that friendship should not confound the measurement of the subject's willingness to be with others.] With a group this size and with the number of additional rooms we have, it's not always possible to give each person exactly what he'd like. So be perfectly honest and let me know how much you'd like to be alone or together with other students. Let me know just how you feel, and I'll use this information to come as close as possible to putting you into the arrangement of your choice. Please answer the items on pages 3 and 4.

Page 3 contained the same instrument used by Schachter (1959) to measure the intensity of the subject's willingness to be alone or with others. This scale, to be called the "affiliation scale," consisted of six alternatives with the zero point eliminated. It read as follows:

(0) I prefer very much being alone
(1) I prefer being alone
(2) I slightly prefer being alone
(4) I slightly prefer being together with others
(5) I prefer being together with others
(6) I very much prefer being together with others

The figures in parentheses represent the values used in scoring this scale and were not included in the questionnaire.

On the final page subjects were asked to indicate their order of birth.

RESULTS

The success of the experimental manipulation of anxiety was tested by comparing the mean anxiety scores of the four conditions. The mean was 3.81 for firstborns and only children in the high-anxiety condition and 2.85 for the low-anxiety group of firstborns and only children. The difference between the two was statistically significant[1] ($t = 2.29$, $p < .05$). The mean for the high-anxiety group of later borns was 3.32, and the mean for the low-anxiety group of later borns was 2.88. The difference between the two did not approach statistical significance ($t = 1.14$). In effect, the anxiety manipulation was only partially successful.

The mean affiliation scores for the four conditions are reported in Table 3-1. Because of the unequal distribution of subjects, differences between each of the four conditions were tested by Student's t. Although the differences between conditions were in the predicted direction, none proved to be statistically significant.

In light of the fact that the anxiety manipulation was only partially successful, it was decided to recast subjects into a high- or low-perceived

Table 3-1   *Mean Affiliation Scores for Between-Condition Comparisons When Subjects are Classified According to Level of Manipulated Anxiety*

| Level of Manipulated Anxiety | Birth Order | | | |
| | FIRSTBORN AND ONLY CHILDREN | | LATER BORN | |
	N	M	N	M
High	21	4.19	22	3.64
Low	20	3.85	25	3.60

anxiety group on the basis of their responses to the questionnaire item measuring perceived anxiety. Those subjects whose responses fell into one of the upper three categories (i.e., I feel extremely uneasy; I feel very uneasy; I feel quite uneasy) were placed in the high-perceived-anxiety condition. Those whose responses fell into one of the lower three categories (i.e., I feel a little uneasy; I feel relatively calm; I feel completely calm) were placed in the low-perceived-anxiety condition.

Table 3-2   *Mean Affiliation Scores for Between-Condition Comparisons When Subjects are Classified According to Level of Perceived Anxiety*

| Level of Perceived Anxiety | Birth Order | | | |
| | FIRSTBORN AND ONLY CHILDREN | | LATER BORN | |
	N	M	N	M
High	17	4.94	13	3.85
Low	24	3.53	34	3.38

The mean affiliation scores for the four groups thus formed are presented in Table 3-2. According to Table 3-2, the high-perceived-anxiety group of firstborns and only children had a higher mean affiliation score than either the low-perceived-anxiety group of first-borns and only children ($t = 3.71$, $p < .001$) or the high-perceived-anxiety group of later borns ($t = 2.27$, $p < .05$). No significant differences were obtained in comparisons between the (a) low-perceived-anxiety–firstborn and only children and low-perceived-anxiety–later-born groups; and (b) high-perceived-anxiety–later-born and low-perceived-anxiety–later-born groups.

The data in Table 3-2 support Schachter's finding that high anxiety produces a greater tendency to prefer affiliation than low anxiety only among the firstborn and only-child subjects and not among the later-born subjects. The data also support Schachter's other finding that only under conditions of high anxiety do firstborn and only-child subjects have a greater tendency to prefer affiliation than later-born subjects.

In order to assess further the significance of the data, comparisons were made between the four conditions in terms of the number of subjects preferring to wait together and the number preferring to wait alone. The data for this analysis were derived from the affiliation scale and are reported in Table 3–3. Here it can be seen that all 17 of the

Table 3–3 *Number of Subjects Choosing Together and Alone Condition*

	Together	Alone
High perceived anxiety—firstborn and only children	17	0
Low perceived anxiety—firstborn and only children	14	10
High perceived anxiety—later born	9	4
Low perceived anxiety—later born	22	12

subjects in the high-perceived-anxiety–firstborn and only-child condition preferred waiting together, whereas only 14 out of 24 (58 percent) of the subjects in the low-perceived-anxiety–firstborn and only-child condition preferred waiting together. The difference between the two was statistically significant ($p = .003$) as determined by the Fisher exact-probability test. In the high-perceived-anxiety–later-born condition 9 of the 13 (69 percent) subjects preferred waiting together. The difference between the high-perceived-anxiety group of firstborn and only children and high-perceived-anxiety group of later borns was statistically significant ($p - .05$, Fisher test).

Additional evidence for the relationship between anxiety and affiliation and birth order comes from a correlation analysis using Pearson's r. Correlations between anxiety scores and affiliation scores were calculated separately for the firstborn and only-child subjects and later-born subjects. For the first-born subjects, the relationship was highly significant ($r = .56$, $p < .01$), whereas a corresponding r of .16 ($p > .05$) was obtained for the later-born subjects. These correlations support the prediction that the greater the amount of anxiety experienced by a firstborn subject, the greater is his desire to wait together (affiliate) with others. No such statement could be made concerning the later-born subjects.

DISCUSSION

The present study employed a role-playing technique in order to test the proposed relationship between anxiety, birth order, and affiliation. Although the results with regard to manipulated anxiety were not significant, the data based on perceived anxiety strongly supported the predictions. These results should not be interpreted as supporting the utility of the role-playing approach in all or even most social psychological experiments. Rather, this study confirms the utility of role playing under a set of specifiable conditions, and it remains the task of future research to delineate further the conditions under which it is optimally useful.

Implicit in the role-playing approach is the assumption that an individual can vicariously experience and empathize with the situation of another. Such a line of reasoning is strongly supported by the research of Bandura (1965) and his co-workers. If the success of the role-playing approach is dependent upon the subject's ability to empathize with another's situation (regardless of whether the other is physically present) then it would have at least one important implication with regard to the choice of subjects for experiments involving role playing: as suggested by Kelman (1967), role playing would stimulate the search for sophisticated rather than naive subjects.

The degree of active involvement in the role would appear to be another pivotal variable determining the success of a role-playing approach. The involvement required of a role player may range from a questionnaire item asking the subject to imagine what he would do if he were in a particular situation to a Moreno-type psychodrama, the latter being analogous to Level III of Sarbin's (1954) seven levels of organismic involvement.

One of the goals of future empirical research is to determine for each particular experimental problem how actively a subject must be involved in the role-playing situation in order for him to perceive and respond to the subtle cues that are ordinarily responded to in the real life situation.

The qualified success of the role-playing approach in the present study may have an important implication regarding Festinger's (1953) distinction between cognitively real situations and cognitively experimental situations. The data tentatively support the hypothesis that cognitively experimental situations can be further divided into those that are cognitively *real* experimental situations (i.e., involve direct experience) and those that are cognitively *vicarious* experimental situations (i.e., involve indirect or *as if* experience).

NOTE

1. All tests of significance reported in this paper are two-tailed.

REFERENCES

BANDURA, A. Vicarious processes: A case of no-trial learning. In L. Berkowitz (Ed.), *Advances in experimental social psychology*. Vol. 2. New York: Academic Press, 1965. Pp. 1–55.

BAUMRIND, D. Some thoughts on ethics of research: After reading Milgram's "Behavioral study of obedience." *American Psychologist*, 1964, **19**: 421–423.

BROCK, T. C., & Becker, L. A. "Debriefing" and susceptibility to subsequent experimental manipulations. *Journal of Experimental Social Psychology*, 1966, **2**: 314–323.

DEUTSCH, M. The pathetic fallacy: An observer error in social perception. *Journal of Personality*, 1960, **28**: 317–332.

ELMS, A. C., & Janis, I. L. Counter-norm attitudes induced by consonant versus dissonant conditions of role-playing. *Journal of Experimental Research in Personality*, 1965, **1**: 50–60.

FESTINGER, L. Laboratory experiments. In L. Festinger & D. Katz (Eds.), *Research methods in the behavioral sciences*. New York: Holt, Rinehart & Winston, 1953. Pp. 136–172.

FESTINGER, L. *A theory of cognitive dissonance*. Evanston, Ill.: Row, Peterson, 1957.

FESTINGER, L., & Carlsmith, J. M. Cognitive consequences of forced compliance. *Journal of Abnormal and Social Psychology*, 1959, **58**: 203–210.

GERARD, H. B., & Rabbie, J. M. Fear and social comparison. *Journal of Abnormal and Social Psychology*, 1961, **62**: 586–592.

GUETZKOW, H., Alger, C. F., Brody, R. A., Noel, R. C., & Snyder, R. C. *Simulation in international relations*. Englewood Cliffs, N.J.: Prentice-Hall, 1963.

KELMAN, H. C. The human use of human subjects: The problem of deception in social psychological experiments. *Psychological Bulletin*, 1967, **67**: 1–11.

MANN, J. H. Experimental evaluations of role playing. *Psychological Bulletin*, 1956, **53**: 227–234.

MILGRAM, S. Issues in the study of obedience: A reply to Baumrind. *American Psychologist*, 1964, **19**: 848–852.

ORNE, M. T. On the social psychology of the psychological experiment: With particular reference to demand characteristics and their implications. *American Psychologist*, 1962, **17**: 776–783.

RIECKEN, H. W. A program for research on experiments in social psychology. In N. F. Washburne (Ed.), *Decisions, values, and groups*. Vol. 2. New York: Pergamon Press, 1962. Pp. 25–41.

ROSENBERG, M. J. Cognitive reorganization in response to the hypnotic reversal of attitudinal affect. *Journal of Personality*, 1960, **28**: 39–63.

ROSENBERG, M. J. When dissonance fails: On eliminating evaluation apprehension from attitude measurement. *Journal of Personality and Social Psychology*, 1965, **1**: 28–42.

ROSENBERG, M. J., & Abelson, R. P. An analysis of cognitive balancing. In M. J. Rosenberg, C. I. Hovland, W. J. McGuire, R. P. Abelson, & J. W. Brehm (Eds.), *Attitude organization and change*. New Haven: Yale University Press, 1960. Pp. 112–163.

SARBIN, T. R. Role theory. In G. Lindzey (Ed.), *Handbook of social psychology*. Vol. 1. Cambridge, Mass.: Addison-Wesley, 1954. Pp. 223–255.

SARNOFF, I., & Zimbardo, P. G. Anxiety, fear, and social affiliation. *Journal of Abnormal and Social Psychology*, 1961, **62**: 356–363.

SCHACHTER, S. *The psychology of affiliation*. Stanford, Calif.: Stanford University Press, 1959.

SCOTT, W. A. Attitude change through reward of verbal behavior. *Journal of Abnormal and Social Psychology*, 1957, **55**: 72–75.

VINACKE, W. E. Deceiving experimental subjects. *American Psychologist*, 1954, **9**: 155.

Jonathan L. Freedman[1]

Role Playing:
Psychology by Consensus[2]

For thousands of years men have observed themselves and others and have developed ideas about how humans behave. Many brilliant men recorded their insights into these matters. Many are still doing so. It is only in recent years, however, that scientific principles were applied to the study of human behavior. Over the past few hundred years psychology has slowly emerged as a science, or at least as scientific. This new psychology does not differ very much from the old. They both deal with the same problems, use many of the same terms, and often produce the same answers. There is one critical difference—whereas previous writings on psychology consisted primarily of intuition and speculations, the core of the science is research.

This dependence on the results of research is what makes modern psychology part of the scientific world. The scientist understands that no matter how strongly he believes something, his opinion is only an opinion. Similarly, no matter how many men agree with him, they are still only expressing their opinions. Opinions of this kind are by no means worthless. They are often interesting; they sometimes form the basis for research. But these opinions have no scientific value beyond this. They can never be used as evidence of what would happen in the real situation. We must always go to the trouble of finding out what actually occurs rather than depending on one man's or a million men's intuitions. We still use speculations; we still value intuitions. But we trust data.

Unfortunately, collecting these data is not always easy. Research in social psychology is fraught with difficulties and possibilities for error. Manipulating independent and measuring dependent variables often require great ingenuity, extensive pretesting of a trial and error

From *Journal of Personality and Social Psychology*, 1969, **13**: 107–114. Copyright © 1969 by The American Psychological Association, and reprinted with permission of author and The American Psychological Association.

nature, and huge amounts of time and effort. Even with all of this the experimenter is rarely certain that he has produced exactly the effect he desired or has measured precisely what he was interested in. In addition, the social psychologist must be aware of such factors as demand characteristics, experimenter bias, and suspicion, which can cast doubt on the validity of his results. He deals with these problems by keeping himself blind as to the subject's experimental condition, by being attuned to possible demands that may inadvertently creep into the situation, by constructing any necessary deception so as to minimize suspicion, and by whatever other means he can devise. All of this means that research in this field is difficult and uncertain, and that great amounts of energy, ingenuity, and hard work are necessary in order to do it well. And despite all of his best efforts, the experimenter still may not be successful in conducting a valid and meaningful study. His results may be questionable, ambiguous, or even worthless. Perhaps we can derive some consolation from the thought that all of this is true of most scientific endeavors and there is no particular reason to expect our kind of research to be easier than that in other fields.

Most social psychologists recognize these difficulties and accept them as inevitable. In the last few years, however, a number of social psychologists (e.g., Greenberg, 1967; Kelman, 1967) have become so concerned with the difficulties and weaknesses of experimental research that they have proposed an alternative. They have suggested that the so-called role-playing technique be substituted for traditional methods of research, that instead of trying to manipulate and measure variables the experimenter merely describe a situation to a subject and ask him how he would behave if he were in that situation. Although I can sympathize with many of their complaints about experimental research, I think it is a very serious mistake to consider role playing an acceptable substitute. On the contrary, the use of role playing under most circumstances constitutes a return to the prescientific days when intuition and consensus took the place of data. Since the use of role playing strikes at the very root of psychology as a science, it seems appropriate to subject this technique to a thorough analysis. The arguments in its favor have been presented in some detail elsewhere; this paper is an attempt to argue against its use as a substitute for experimental research.

To begin with, let me be clear what I am talking about. I am *not* talking about studies which deal with role playing as an independent variable. There has been a great deal of work on forced compliance (e.g., Festinger & Carlsmith, 1959), in which someone is induced to take a position or assume a role discrepant from his own opinion. Major interest in this research is in how much opinion change results from taking the discrepant position. There has also been work (e.g., Janis &

Mann, 1965) in which subjects are encouraged to play a role such as imagining that they are dying of lung cancer as a means of getting them involved in and concerned about a given issue. All of this very interesting research is studying role playing itself. It is not using role playing as a substitute for a standard experimental manipulation and it, therefore, lies outside the scope of this paper.

What I am talking about is research which uses role playing *instead* of some other kind of manipulation. A subject is asked to pretend that he is going to receive an electric shock or that he has been paid $10 for telling a lie rather than being told that he *is* going to be shocked or be paid $10. The basic difference between this and the usual method is that the subject in the role-playing study is trying to tell you how he would behave if he were in a particular situation, while the subject in the regular study is behaving. The data from the former are the subject's opinions or guesses; the data from the latter are the subject's actual responses.

It should be made clear that there are degrees of role playing. At one extreme are studies conducted in a classroom with written or taped instructions under circumstances that bear little or no relation to the situation that the subject is trying to imagine. He is told, for example, to imagine that he is in a frightening room with a sinister doctor who is about to administer strong electric shocks to him. But in fact he is sitting quietly in a large classroom surrounded by many other students with no doctor, apparatus, or anything else present. At the other extreme might be a study (I know of none exactly like this, but it is certainly feasible) in which the subject is run through the whole fear-arousing situation just as if he were a real subject in a real experiment. The only difference is that he is told ahead of time that he will not actually receive the electric shock, but should pretend he is going to. This situation is much like an actor playing a role with all of the props; while the stripped-down type of study described previously is acting on an empty stage. Presumably the more realistic the situation is made, the closer it is to reality, the better able the subject should be to imagine what he would actually do if he were in the real situation. But regardless of where on this continuum the particular role-playing study falls, the critical factor is that the subject is pretending rather than actually behaving.

The next important point is that various ways of utilizing role playing are possible. The most extreme use is simply to substitute it for more traditional experimental methods. Instead of producing fear through a complex manipulation, merely tell the subject to imagine he is afraid; instead of making him angry and seeing how aggressive he acts, tell him to pretend he is angry and then ask him how aggressive he would be. This use of the method is based on the notion that role playing is equivalent to traditional methods, that the two are interchangeable.

A second possible use of role playing involves performing a series of studies in which role playing and experimental techniques are used side by side. This is done presumably in an attempt to discover when role playing produces the same results and when it does not. Eventually, when role playing is thoroughly understood in this particular situation, further research can be done with role playing alone if it is established fairly well that the results it produces will be the same as those that would have been produced by traditional methods. This use of role playing gives us additional knowledge about role playing itself, about people's assumptions about the world and how they differ from reality, and may allow us to do the relatively easy role-playing research instead of experimental work and still have some confidence in the results. As far as I know, no one has ever done such a series of studies, but it is certainly a possibility.

Then there is the idea of using role playing only in those circumstances for which traditional methods are impossible. The effect of extreme fear on aggression cannot be studied experimentally because we cannot or will not induce extreme fear in human beings. If we were interested in this effect, thought that extreme fear was different from moderate fear, and could not find a natural situation in which to study this difference, role playing would be a technique for studying it. Just how useful it would be is open to question, but this limited use of the technique does not depend on the claim that it is equivalent to experimental methods. Rather, when the latter is not possible, the former may be of some use.

Finally, there is a very specialized use of role playing as a means of testing a theory. The only example of this I know was provided by Bem, who suggested an explanation of dissonance results in terms of the subjects' perceptions of how they have been behaving. In essence he argued that subjects define their feelings only after knowing how they have behaved; and that their behavior in a forced compliance situation tells them that they must have believed what they said or they would not have said it. As support for this notion, Bem then demonstrated that other subjects to whom the situation was only described (i.e., role-playing subjects) were able to predict how the real subjects felt. He argued that this was support for his explanation. Used in this way, role playing is not a substitute for experimental research, but rather a tool for gathering the specific kind of data that is desired.

There are thus four different ways of utilizing role playing—as a straight substitute for experimental research, alongside experimental research with the eventual intention to use it as a substitute should it prove to produce equivalent results, as a substitute only when experimental research on the problem is impossible, and to produce data specifically designed to test a theory. Let us begin by discussing the first and broadest use of role playing and then turn to the relatively specialized, limited uses.

There is no question that role playing is easy, convenient, and efficient. It avoids many of the difficulties of experimental work. Ingenuity in devising manipulations of independent and measures of dependent variables, and pretesting to be certain that they are successful, are unnecessary. Instead, the intrepid investigator merely writes out a description of the situation, reads it to the subject, and asks him how he would behave if he were in such a situation. Nothing could be simpler and more appealing. The only question is whether the responses obtained from a role-playing subject are meaningful, whether they reflect how he would behave in the actual situation. And it is here that the argument in favor of role playing breaks down completely.

For some reason advocates of role playing think that cooperative, helpful subjects who are pretending to be in a situation are capable of telling the experimenter how they would have responded in the real situation. These supporters of role playing argue that data from real experiments and from role-playing studies are of comparable validity. Roger Brown (1962) went further than that. He wrote: "We believe that a role-playing subject will behave in a way that corresponds more closely to the life situation than a hoodwinked subject will" [p. 74]. In other words, Brown suggested that data from role playing was more realistic than that from true experiments.

This is difficult to understand. No amount of discussion of other aspects of role playing can conceal the one simple fact that this procedure provides information about what people think they would do, not necessarily what they would do. And experimental results are not always easy to predict; people do not always behave the way that they or we expect them to.

Consider some well-known experiments. How many subjects would say that they would conform to a unanimous majority when their own eyes tell them that the answer is incorrect? Surely very few. Yet Asch (1951) and others have shown that subjects do conform more than 30 percent of the time. How many subjects would say that they would deliver dangerous shocks to innocent people just because the experimenter told them to press the lever? Very few. Milgram (1963) asked people, including trained psychologists, to predict these results and they were extremely inaccurate. I have asked a large class of students to tell me how they would respond and none ever says he would deliver shocks of 450 volts. Even after I describe the experiment and present the results, they refuse to believe it of themselves. They believe the results but they say they would not do it. Yet subjects just like themselves have delivered 450 volts (Milgram, 1963).

These examples could be continued indefinitely. Sometimes subjects can guess accurately how they would behave; sometimes they cannot. Anytime subtle factors or interactions are involved, anytime actual behavior runs counter to what is considered socially desirable or acceptable, guesses will probably tend to be wrong. But, most important, one can never know ahead of time whether the guess is right or wrong until the people are observed in the real situation, because their actual behavior is the only standard of truth.

To put it another way, when I get an idea about how a particular variable affects behavior, I sometimes have a considerable amount of confidence in it. Sometimes it sounds right; it fits in with other knowledge I have; and it makes sense to me. This intuition of mine is the beginning of my research—it is not the end. I would certainly not suggest that it is data on how people actually behave—it is just my guess. I would not think of publishing it (except in a speculative article) and no one would think of accepting it for publication in a serious journal.

The next step in my research is to discuss this idea with some of my colleagues. These are extremely able psychologists and graduate students who have all had considerable experience thinking about, observing, and speculating about social situations. They are sophisticated and talented. Sometimes they all agree with my intuition. When this happens, my confidence soars because I think a great deal of these colleagues. If they all agree, it seems that we must be right. In fact, if most of them agree, that's pretty good too because often we don't find much agreement. When they do agree, I am encouraged. I do not, however, stop there and write up the article. Once again, no one thinks of this as data. The fact that, let's say, 10 highly skilled, experienced people say it will work in a particular way is not proof that it will.

Now let us suppose that I go to an introductory class in psychology (or history, for that matter) and pose the problem to them. I may do this in a clever way so that half of the class is shown one situation and the other half is shown the other. Then I can compare their responses under the two situations. But it boils down to asking the class what they think. Suppose they all agree with me. Do I stop there and publish it? I wouldn't think of it. Yet apparently this is now acceptable in some people's eyes. But why? Why do the opinions of these relatively naïve, untrained observers count more than those of my talented, sophisticated colleagues? Surely it is not just the numbers that make the difference. If so, I should simply poll the American Psychological Association or Division 8 and publish the answers.

There is no reason to trust the subjects' responses more than those of anyone else. In fact, I trust them much less. If my class disagrees with me, it means much less than if my colleagues do. After all, when I teach a class, I do not *ask* them what the facts of psychology are; I *tell* them. I tell them what experimental research has found. Sometimes, after describing an experimental design, I ask them to guess what happened. Often they guess wrong—that is, they disagree with the actual results. This does not cause me to question the results; it merely shows the class how little their own intuitions are worth. So I do not publish their responses; and I would not publish the responses of any other group that I asked to role-play a situation.

The argument comes down to the simple truth that data from role-playing studies consist of what some group of subjects guesses would be their reaction to a particular stimulus. The subjects are giving their estimates, their intuitions, their insights, and introspections about themselves or others. If we are studying the myths and values of a society, these data would be useful. If we want to know how people actually behave, they are, at best, suggestive. If we are interested in people's intuitions, fine; if we are interested in their behavior (other than guessing behavior), we must ordinarily use the experimental method. Just because a significant number of subjects have the same intuition about something does not make them correct. We must rely on real data, not on opinion surveys. Consensus is not truth.

All of these arguments are directed primarily against the somewhat extreme idea that role playing is an acceptable substitute for experimental research. To some extent, the arguments also apply to the other three uses, but with somewhat less force. If a series of say 10 studies on a particular problem employing both role playing and experimental techniques were actually done, and if the two methods produced identical results or at least the differences that did appear were systematic and understandable, then an eleventh study employing only role playing might have some value. Perhaps we could have some confidence that in this situation, with these subjects, and with various limitations, the subjects' guesses were equivalent to their behavior. Personally this sounds like a great deal of effort for a rather small payoff. If the eleventh study were quite different from the others, we would have little confidence in the results. If it were similar, presumably the experimental method is not all that difficult and could be used for the eleventh also.

More important, however, is that confidence would still be much lower than if the experimental method were used. After all, if I make 10 accurate predictions, should the journal publish my eleventh without data? Of course not. So why do we trust subjects just because their peers were accurate predictors previously? It is more likely that any problem on which subjects can predict accurately 10 times in a row is simple enough and probably uninteresting enough so that most of us would no longer want to work on it. Frankly I cannot imagine anyone even bothering, nor can I imagine the role-playing and experimental results being so similar in anything except the simplest study. Nevertheless, if anyone really did all of this work, and if the other criteria listed above were met, I think the role-playing data would have some meaning. The data would always evoke somewhat less confidence than experimental data, but this seems to me to be a marginally legitimate use of the role-playing method.

This lack of confidence would disappear if such a series of side-by-side studies led to a theory of role playing which would specify in detail when role-playing results will and will not be the same as experimental results. If such a theory were proposed, extensively tested, and supported by data, it would presumably be possible to have considerable confidence in appropriate role-playing studies. If we trusted the theory, we would trust the data that came from those role-playing studies which it predicted would coincide with experimental studies. Under these circumstances, role playing could substitute for experimental procedures.

It should be perfectly clear, however, that such an eventuality is highly unlikely in the foreseeable future. No such theory, or one remotely approaching it, exists at the moment. In addition, it is a rare theory in psychology, and particularly in social psychology, that is so well supported and so widely accepted that one would have perfect confidence in its predictions. For most theories, this is not absolutely crucial. They make probabilistic predictions, most of which are independently verifiable. But the role-playing theory would have to make predictions which were so certain that psychologists would not need to verify them —that is, they would accept the results of a role-playing study without comparing them to experimental results. If they felt they still had to compare them, of course, the whole purpose of the role-playing study would be lost. Such a theory, with such good support, is not impossible. It *is* improbable and it certainly is not available at the present time.

Using role playing when traditional methods are impossible is obviously a legitimate technique of research. If you want extreme hunger, fear, or anger as your independent variable, you cannot produce this by a deliberate experimental manipulation. Even if there were no ethical problems, it would be exceedingly difficult. Instead, you can try to find a natural situation in which people are extremely hungry or afraid. This would be ideal, but these are few and far between, and it is almost impossible to mobilize a research project fast enough to study them. Therefore, lacking any other method of studying the problem, you can ask people to role-play the situation and hope that their guesses as to their behavior are roughly equivalent to what they would actually do.

This is certainly a reasonable way to proceed. The only question is how valuable the data are. All of the arguments against role playing discussed above makes us doubt the validity of such guesses when role playing is simply substituted for experimental work, and unfortunately they also apply here. Yes, it is a legitimate way of studying the problem; but the results are probably not worth much.

People are poor at predicting their behavior in reasonably familiar situations such as being ordered to do something or facing a unanimous majority which holds an incorrect opinion. It must be much more difficult for them to predict their behavior in unusual, unique, unfamiliar situations. That is the core of the problem. They can try, they can put all their effort into the attempt, they can be honest and spontaneous, they can even, perhaps, avoid being influenced by cultural norms and social desirability. But all of this will only eliminate sources of error—it will not, and I am afraid nothing can, make the subjects able to predict their behavior accurately. They are only fallible humans who are for better or worse not very good at telling what they would do in a given situation unless they have just been in that very situation and not even very well then. Thus, although using role playing to study these special problems may be the only feasible way of studying them, I fear that it is not a very useful way. Instead, I feel we must wait until natural situations produce the effect we want, and then study them.

All of the arguments we have presented up to now refer primarily to the use of role playing as a substitute for traditional research methods. There is one special and somewhat unusual use of role playing that deserves special consideration. This is the use of role playing as a "simulation" of the real situation. A model or theory is constructed to explain experimental results and the model is then "tested" by having subjects role-play the original situation. However, the description of the situation that is given to the subjects includes only those factors which are assumed by the theory to be critical. If under these circumstances the role-play subjects reproduce the results of the original study, the model is supposedly supported.

Bem (1967), for example, has used this technique in connection with his alternative explanation of various results which have previously been interpreted in terms of cognitive dissonance. He demonstrated that subjects who role-played the experimental situations and were given only minimal information gave results similar to those obtained by experimental methods. In contrast, a number of authors (Jones *et al.*, 1968) have shown that describing the situation more fully caused role-play subjects to give results different from those of subjects who actually took part in the experiment. In other words, making the descriptions correspond more closely to the original situation made the role-play results deviate; whereas the skeleton description produced replications of the experimental results.

These authors argued that this result refuted Bem's explanation by demonstrating that his studies involved situations extremely dissimilar to the original experiments. Bem (1968) replied that his explanation was actually supported by their findings. His model stated which factors were critical. Giving subjects only those factors reproduces the experimental results. Giving irrelevant information should change the results and it does. True, those irrelevant factors were present in the original situation, but Bem suggested that describing them to the subjects in the rarefied atmosphere of role playing made them overly important, whereas they were of minor importance in the original situation.

I think that keeping entirely within his own framework, Bem had the better of this controversy. If the point is to show that Facts A and B are critical to the results, then only those facts should be given. If giving other facts washes out the results, in a sense this does support the model rather than refute it. On the other hand, the basic question is whether you really are showing anything about the importance of Facts A and B or any other facts.

Bem (1968) admitted that role playing is a simulation and not equivalent to the real situation. As he said: "No 'as if' methodology . . . is an adequate substitute for the intensive study of the actual situation . . ." [p. 273]. So what he appears to be interested in is how various facts change people's guesses about other people's behavior or attitudes. If subjects know A and B about someone, they guess one way; if they know A, B, and C, they guess another way. What it all comes down to is that Bem and the others are studying what affects people's guesses in this particular setting. They are not studying what affects their behavior or attitudes. No amount of data on their guesses will tell us much, if anything, about what affects their behavior. If we are interested in peoples' estimates, perceptions of others, guesses, or views of the world, role playing is a reasonable method of investigation. But if we really want to know why they behave in a particular way, we must use real situations.

The use of role playing as a simulation may, however, have considerable utility. It cannot be used to test hypotheses because guesses just are not equivalent to actual behavior. On the other hand, studying what affects people's guesses may be one way of getting ideas about what is important. If giving Facts A and B produces opposite results from giving A, B, and C, the investigator may want to turn his attention to C by varying it in a real experiment. In other words, role-playing studies may be a fruitful technique for gathering intuitions (other people's) and ideas about human behavior. Employed in this way, as a source of ideas rather than a test of hypotheses, role playing may turn out to be very effective.

There is one argument concerning role playing which, while it is not directly relevant to the central theme of this paper, should be considered. Harold Kelley recently suggested[3] that role playing is to laboratory experiments as laboratory experiments are to field studies. He argued that these three methods fall on a continuum ranging from quite unrealistic and unspontaneous (role playing) to realistic and spontaneous (field), with laboratory work falling in the middle.

This is an interesting and provocative proposal and in most respects I agree with it. Role-playing studies are certainly unrealistic and unspontaneous; most field studies are realistic and spontaneous, and many laboratory experiments tend to be somewhat unrealistic. I disagree with Kelley, however, in the feeling that this problem is inherent in laboratory work. Laboratory experiments do pose serious problems for the experimenter in terms of producing realism and spontaneity. Because they occur in a laboratory, because the subject knows he is a subject, it is difficult to produce realism and spontaneity in the laboratory. But it is not impossible. Carefully designed experiments, skilled experimenters, and ingenious manipulations can make laboratory experiments extremely realistic and cause the subject to respond spontaneously. It is not easy, but it can be done. Field studies tend to be but are not always realistic. Assuming we are discussing field *experiments*, the manipulations used in the field can be unrealistic and behavior unspontaneous just as in poor laboratory experiments. It is easier to get realism in the field, but not certain. In other words, the problem of producing realism is greater in the laboratory than in the field, but is present in both settings and is not insurmountable in either.

Thus, although I agree that field studies tend to be more realistic than laboratory experiments, I disagree with the implication that the former are more valid in general. The basic issue is how realistic the research is, and realism is possible in the laboratory just as it is in the field. In other words, I would argue very strongly that laboratory and field experiments are not inherently or basically different. And most important, the data collected in good laboratory experiments are essentially comparable to those collected in good field experiments. (A more extensive and profound discussion of this issue may be found in Aronson and Carlsmith's [1968] excellent chapter in the new *Handbook of Social Psychology.*)

In contrast, role-playing studies are not comparable to experiments of either kind. There is no possibility of producing realism or spontaneity since the essence of role playing is the lack of these qualities. Therefore, and for all of the other reasons I have discussed in this paper, data from role-playing studies are not equivalent to data from experiments. The position I have taken in this paper and the arguments for it can be summarized very briefly. Role playing is not a substitute for experimental research. It is totally unacceptable when used instead of experiments; it is marginally useful when used in conjunction with experiments in a series of studies; it is legitimate but probably futile when employed to study problems not accessible to traditional methods; and when used as a simulation of a real situation it cannot test hypotheses but may provide them. There is essentially only one basis for these somewhat bald and uncompromising statements. The data from role playing are people's guesses as to how they would behave if they were in a particular situation; they are not data on how they actually would behave; and people's guesses as to future or hypothetical situations are not the stuff of which a science of human behavior is made. Role playing tells us what men think they would do. It does not tell us what men would actually do in the real situation. Despite all of its difficulties, experimental research is the foundation of the science of psychology and must remain so.

NOTES

1. Requests for reprints should be sent to the author, who is now at the Department of Psychology, Columbia University, New York, New York 10027.
2. The preparation of this paper was supported in part by a grant from the National Science Foundation.
3. Informal remarks at a conference on "Alternatives to Laboratory Research," University of California, Los Angeles, 1968.

REFERENCES

ARONSON, E., & Carlsmith. J. Experimentation in social psychology. In G. Lindzey & E. Aronson (Eds.), *Handbook of social psychology*, Vol. 4. Reading, Mass.: Addison-Wesley, 1968.

ASCH, S. E. Effects of group pressure upon the modification and distortion of judgments. In H. Guetzkow (Ed.), *Groups, leadership, and men*. Pittsburgh: Carnegie Press, 1951.

BEM, D. J. Self-perception: An alternative interpretation of cognitive dissonance phenomena. *Psychological Review*, 1967, **74**: 183–200

BEM, D. J. The epistemological status of interpersonal simulations: A reply to Jones, Linder, Kiesler, Zanna, and Brehm. *Journal of Experimental Social Psychology*, 1968, **4**: 270–274.

BROWN, R. Models of attitude change. In R. Brown, E. Galanter, E. H. Hess, & G. Mandler (Eds.), *New directions in psychology*. Vol. 1, New York: Holt, 1962.

FESTINGER, L., & Carlsmith, J. Cognitive consequences of forced compliance. *Journal of Abnormal and Social Psychology*, 1959, **58**: 203–210.

GREENBERG, M. S. Role playing: An alternative to deception? *Journal of Personality and Social Psychology*, 1967, **7**: 152–157.

JANIS, I. L., & Mann, L. Effectiveness of emotional role playing in modifying smoking habits and attitudes. *Journal of Experimental Research in Personality*, 1965, **1**: 84–90.

JONES, R. A., Linder, D. E., Kiesler, C. A., Zanna, M., & Brehm, J. W. Internal states or external stimuli: Observers' attitude judgements and the dissonance-theory–self-persuasion controversy. *Journal of Experimental Social Psychology*, 1968, **4**: 247–269.

KELMAN, H. C. Deception in social research. *Trans-Action*, 1966, **3**: 20–24.

MILGRAM, S. Behavioral study of obedience. *Journal of Abnormal and Social Psychology*, 1963, **67**: 371–378.

Elaine Walster, Ellen Berscheid,
Darcy Abrahams, and Vera Aronson[1]

Effectiveness of Debriefing
Following Deception Experiments

In order to investigate many social psychological questions, it is often
necessary to deceive subjects within the experimental context. Deception generally serves two purposes: First, in many experiments the
experimenter's hypothesis would be all too apparent to the subjects
if a false explanation of the experimenter's purposes were not provided. If the purpose of the experiment were clear to subjects,
they might try to assist or thwart what they believe to be the experimenter's aims (Orne, 1965). A false explanation eliminates this problem, for even if subjects try to help or hurt the experimenter, they will
in fact be responding to an irrelevant hypothesis. Second, deception
might be required in order to manipulate the independent variable.
Such deception permits the laboratory study of variables which would
otherwise not be accessible to investigation.

In spite of, or perhaps because of, the regularity with which deception is used in experimentation, several reservations have been expressed about the use of this experimental technique (e.g., Kelman, 1965;
Orne, 1965, Silverman, 1965). Critics of deception experiments seem
to be primarily concerned with the possibility that deception might
cause the subject permanent harm. In partial response to this criticism,
defenders of the deception technique have pointed out that subjects in
deception experiments are almost always thoroughly debriefed at the
end of the experiment. In the debriefing, the subjects are usually told
the nature of the deception, the true purpose of the experiment, and the
reasons why deception was necessary. Kelman (1965) suggested that "in
general, the principle that a subject ought not to leave the laboratory
with greater anxiety or lower self-esteem than he came with is a good
one to follow." Most experimenters seem to operate under the convic-

From *Journal of Personality and Social Psychology*, 1967, **6**: 371–380.
Copyright © 1967 by The American Psychological Association and
reprinted with permission of authors and The American Psychological
Association.

tion that a thorough debriefing will accomplish the goal of returning the subject to his preexperimental state.

Yet the fact that experimenters who employ deception usually take a great deal of time and care to debrief their subjects has not entirely allayed fears concerning the use of deception. The obvious question which remains is how can the researcher be certain that his debriefing has been successful? How can he be sure that when the subject walks out the door, he does not do so with lower self-esteem than when he came in? In spite of the fact that it is of crucial importance to experimenters that debriefing remove the effects of the deception, there is no experimental evidence that debriefing, in fact, does so.

Deception experiments differ so greatly from one another in the nature and degree of deception used that even the harshest critic of this technique would be hard pressed to state unequivocally that all deception has potentially harmful effects. There are, however, two frequently mentioned dangers of deception experiments, to which some experiments are more liable than others. First, some critics have voiced their concern that lying to people may lead them to lose faith in their fellow human beings. Because scientists are ordinarily highly respected, the discovery that a scientist would lie might upset subjects even more than lies told by others. Second, and perhaps more importantly, it has been pointed out that some deception manipulations are emotionally disturbing to a subject, and that some disturbances might not be entirely amendable by debriefing. Consider, for example, an experiment dealing with the differences between task performance of high self-esteem and low self-esteem people. High self-esteem might be manipulated by telling subjects that they are virile, creative, and personable individuals. Low self-esteem might be manipulated by telling subjects they have negative qualities. It is evident that for the duration of the experiment the subjects in the low self-esteem condition are likely to be upset. But what about *after* they are debriefed? It has been suggested by Kelman that if one is a normal person, it is probable that such a shock to one's self-concept can be overcome and the assurances of the experimenter in the debriefing session can be readily accepted. However, Kelman points out that there are undoubtedly instances in which simply telling the subject that the results of his virility-creativity-personableness test were falsified will not erase the effects of the deception.

Under what conditions might we expect debriefing to fail? Suppose that a subject is told that his test results indicate that he is not very creative. In fact, the experimenter reports, few people tested have ever scored so low on creativity. Further suppose that this subject happened to be a budding poet who picked up his mail on his way to the experimental session and discovered the fourteenth publisher's rejection slip for his first serious effort. While pursuing his way to the experiment, the subject might quite naturally wonder if the series of rejections should be attributed to his lack of talent or to the possibility that the uncultured masses are not clamoring for sonnets about the Crimean War.

It seems quite possible that the experimenter's authoritative evaluation of the subject's creative talents would initiate in this particular subject some independent thinking during the course of the experiment. It is quite likely, for example, that this subject would try to reach some consistency between the content of the experimenter's report and his own original ideas about his level of creativity. To do this, he might well reexamine his self-concept and selectively recall past incidents, most notably the 14 rejection slips, which would agree with the experimenter's information. Memories of criticisms from friends and family, the recollection of some low grades in English composition, would, when interpreted in the light of the test results, strengthen his belief in his supposed low creativity. Consequently, at some point in the course of the experiment, the subject might decide that since his own cognitions augment the experimental evidence, what the experimenter said was true. He might even come to the conclusion that he himself had been imperceptive not to realize his lack of creativity before.

At the completion of the experiment, of course, the subject-poet would be informed that the negative evaluation he received was chosen at random, and it would be explained that it was just as likely that he could have received a neutral or favorable evaluation of his creative talents. As previously mentioned, there is ordinarily little reason for the subject not to accept completely the notion that he has been deceived, that he is not the unimaginative dullard he thought he was, and be none the worse for wear. It even seems quite probable that the subject might believe the debriefing message in its entirety, that is, that the creativity test was not genuine. In this case, however, his own supporting and freshly organized cognitions might remain. It is still true that he *has* gotten 14 consecutive rejection slips and that he *did* receive those low grades. Consequently, it is possible that, though the specific anxieties produced by the deception might be completely removed by the debriefing, his general opinion about himself might well be lowered, and his life turned upon a new course, because of the extra thinking the manipulation initiated.

When the deception happens to strike an area of deep concern and worry to the individual, when it is likely to initiate a train of thought which would not be altered by the revelation of the deception, it is possible that the damage done to a subject by the deception might be irreversible.

The authors will report in this paper an experiment which tests the hypothesis that it will be more difficult to successfully debrief (i.e., return to his preexperimental state) a subject who has received false information on some aspect of himself about which he is currently concerned, than it will be to debrief a subject who has received information which is irrelevant to his current concerns. While the preceding discussion focused on the possible residual effects of receiving negative information, a parallel result could be expected to occur when the subject has received positive information. That is, it might also be more difficult to debrief someone who receives positive information in an area of current concern. This experiment, then, was designed to test for the existence of both positive and negative residual effects after debriefing.

METHOD

Overview

Three steps were required to test our hypothesis. It was necessary that: (*a*) some subjects be very concerned about their characteristics in a given area while other subjects be unconcerned. Subjects either could be selected because they did or did not manifest this concern, or concern could be experimentally manipulated. We chose both to measure preexperimental concern and to manipulate concern experimentally; (*b*) subjects participate in a deception experiment in which false information relevant to the area of concern is provided; (*c*) subjects have time to think about the false information and an opportunity to use it to organize events in their past life. We, of course, expect subjects to be more inclined to relate the false material to previous life experiences when they are deeply concerned about the area than when they are not; (*d*) subjects be thoroughly debriefed and, following the debriefing, success or failure be measured.

Procedure

The 80 subjects who participated in this study were freshmen and sophomore women enrolled at the University of Minnesota.[2] Subjects were recruited from an introductory psychology course and from the university library. All subjects had taken the MMPI as part of the freshman testing program.

In an initial contact, subjects agreed to participate in two separate experiments. They were told that the first experiment would have an hour's delay between the first and second part. Therefore, a second experiment had been scheduled during this hour for their convenience. They were told they could either participate in this experiment or not as they chose. In fact, all subjects chose to participate in both experiments. In reality, of course, the two experiments were both parts of the same experiment.

The purpose of Experiment 1 was twofold: (*a*) to *measure* the subject's preexperimental concern about the kind of social impression she makes, and (*b*) to randomly assign the subject to an experimental group and *manipulate* her concern about the kind of social impression she makes. We wanted half of our subjects to be highly concerned and curious about their social abilities and the other half to be little concerned about these abilities.

Subjects arrived at Experiment 1 in groups of four, and each subject's concern about her social abilities was measured as soon as all had arrived at the experimental room. Each subject completed the Fear of Rejection Scale. According to Rosenfeld (1964), this scale measures one's concern or fears about social rejection.

The remainder of Experiment 1 was designed to manipulate subjects' concern about their social skills. This was done in the following way: Experimenter 1 told the subjects that the purpose of Experiment 1 was to find out "something about how people make first impressions and how they react to a first-impression situation." She explained to them that two college seniors would interview each subject for about 10 minutes, asking her several questions. Following the interview, the seniors would evaluate the subject. The seniors were described as outstanding students, both academically and socially, who had been doing such interviews for about a year. The subjects were then introduced to our two interviewers, a very attractive male and female.

Subjects were interviewed one at a time, while the other subjects continued filling out forms in an adjoining room. The interviewers stood behind a one-way mirror, so that the subject could not see their facial reactions. It was the confederates' job, by the tone of their voices and their comments, to make each subject very unsure about how well she had done. In pretests the authors selected several interview questions which were difficult for subjects to answer (e.g., "How do you feel towards people who are better looking than yourself?" or "What is your favorite joke?"). The two confederates by their manner approved some answers and disapproved of other answers.

At the completion of each subject's interview, the experimenter checked to see whether the subject had been randomly assigned to a group that should have *high concern* with how they had done in the interview situation or to a group that should have *low concern* with their performance. If the subject had been assigned to a *high-concern* group, the experimenter made several comments designed to impress the subject with the fact that her performance in the ambiguous interview situation was extremely important. To point out how important interviews are in daily life, the experimenter cited statistics concerning the importance of first impressions. She explained that since automation could take over many routine jobs but could replace only a few jobs requiring personal contacts, the ability to create a good first impression would be even more important in the future. Finally, the experimenter attempted to refute any arguments that the subject might come up with to challenge her claim that the first impression she made in the interview situation was important. She noted that some subjects had felt that because they had not been warned in advance that the interview was important, or because the interview was too short, or because they were nervous, the impression they made was not a valid one. Experimenter 1 explained that since these factors were present in real life interviews, they actually increased the validity of the evaluation. If the subject had been assigned to the low-concern condition, Experimenter 1 made totally different comments after her interview. She explained that although her performance would be of interest, one could not tell too much about a person on the basis of just one interview. She said such a situation was not a very good predictor of how one did in real life and commented that at present she was just pretesting the procedure. Finally, she presented all the reasons why a person might argue that her interview performance was not a valid indicator of her personality, but this time she agreed that these objections were valid ones.

When all four subjects had completed their interviews, Experimenter 1 explained that during the next 20 minutes the interviewers would be busy evaluating the subjects' performance. She told the subjects that they could leave for the second experiment, but that those who had given an unusually good or an unusually poor performance would be called back to Experiment 1 for more extensive interviewing after Experiment 2 had been completed. The remaining subjects would come back simply to complete a brief questionnaire. She said that she would send a note to them sometime during the second experiment, telling them whether to plan on a long interview or a short one.

The purpose of Experiment 2 was to lead one-half of the unconcerned and one-half of the concerned subjects to believe for the duration of Experiment 2 that they possessed good social skills, and the remainder of the subjects to believe that they possessed poor social skills. To impart these beliefs to subjects, Experimenter 2 told them, when they arrived at Experiment 2, that she was interested in several aspects of sociability or "the ability of a person to enter into warm, long-lasting and meaningful relationships with other people." She said she already had secured MMPI sociability scores for all of them. After briefly discussing the omniscience of the MMPI's sociability scale, the experimenter told the subjects that many researchers were now engaged in developing a shorter test than the MMPI to measure sociability, and also a test more easily utilized with youthful test takers. The experimenter explained that today they would take a newly developed test, the "Social Aptitude-Achievement Test." The test booklet which the experimenter then proceeded to pass out was designed simply to appear to be a valid measure of sociability. It presented several social situations in which one might find oneself and asked the subject how she would respond to each situation. After approximately half an hour the experimenter collected the tests, and announced she would score them immediately so that she could see to what extent the results agreed with those of the MMPI. Before leaving the room to score the test, Experimenter 2 gave each subject what was purported to be her MMPI report to read, while she was out scoring the tests "in case she was interested." Of course, all subjects were interested.

The MMPI report which the subject received was false. Only two alternate forms existed. By random assignment, one-half of the subjects were to receive a positive social assessment in their report. Their reports specified that the subject had scored near the 90th percentile on the "Sociability Scale" of the MMPI and contained a two-page personality assessment, supposedly written by a clinician at the University of Minnesota. This assessment indicated that they were "natural and balanced" in their relations with others, that they played the ascendant role in relationships with others without being overbearing, but that possibly they were not aware of the "potential richness of their skills" in the social area. Subjects assigned to the negative condition received profiles indicating that they had scored near the 18th percentile in sociability. The written portion of their profiles claimed that they were reluctant to become involved with others, that they could not express their real feelings to others, and that they lacked self-insight to the point of being largely unaware of these shortcomings.

The subjects were then given time to read and to think about these clinical reviews. It was the authors' expectation that those subjects who were very concerned about how they had performed in the interview in Experiment 1 would use the MMPI personality information in an attempt to resolve the ambiguity they felt concerning their interview performance. It was thought that unconcerned subjects would be less interested in their performance (which they had been told was not a good indicator of their real personality), and thus less concerned about resolving any ambiguity they felt.

To remind subjects of Experiment 1, and to reinforce the ambiguity of evidence concerning their interview performance, Experimenter 1 walked in the room while Experimenter 2 was out of the room scoring the sociability tests, and handed a message to each subject. Presumably, this note was to tell subjects whether or not they had given an unusual performance in Experiment 1 (and thus had to return for a long interview at the end of Experiment 2) or had done about average. Actually, each subject received a note saying that her performance had been unusual. Whether it was unusually good or unusually poor was not specified. Experimenter 1 then supervised subjects until Experimenter 2 returned.

When Experimenter 2 returned she handed each subject her test scores on the Social Aptitude-Achievement Test. In all cases, the scores agreed with those provided in the false MMPI report. A subject assigned to the positive condition was told that she had received a percentile of score 94. A subject in the negative condition was told that she had received a score of only 20.

Once subjects had had a chance to consider the deceptive material we had provided, we were ready to debrief them. However, before we could do so, a bit more deception, designed to increase the plausibility of the situation, was necessary. We wanted Experiment 2 to seem complete in and of itself to the subject. We certainly did not want any subjects to connect Experiment 2 with Experiment 1. If we had simply explained to subjects at this point that we had been lying to them about their personality reports, many of them would have wondered what we had accomplished by lying to them. Consequently, the next step was designed to provide a rationale for Experiment 2 and to make it seem complete in and of itself by the time of debriefing.

Thus, Experimenter 2 asked the subjects to read and evaluate two case reports. In these case reports, a great deal of personality information was provided about two girls. Interspersed with the information was the fact that one of the girls was very sociable and outgoing, while the other was a very introverted person, lacking in social skills. Subjects were asked to comment upon their own reactions to the girls. Specifically, they were asked to indicate on a series of 20-point scales how much they liked the girls, to evaluate various personality characteristics of the girls, and to indicate how similar each of the girls seemed to themselves. After the subjects had finished rating the two girls, the stage was set for the debriefing. Experimenter 2 explained that the MMPI and Social Aptitude-Achievement Test scores she had given the subjects had been entirely false. She explained that she had never seen the subjects' MMPI tests, and that in fact there was no such thing as an MMPI sociability scale nor a Social Aptitude-Achievement Test. Subjects were shown both the high sociability and the low sociability MMPI reports, and it was pointed out that which report the subject received had been determined by chance. This explanation took a minimum of twenty minutes. Experimenter 2 then briefly explained to subjects why they had received a false personality report. She told the subjects that the experiment was actually concerned with how high or low self-esteem individuals felt about other people with the same traits. She explained that by raising the self-esteem of some subjects and lowering the self-esteem of others and then asking them to rate similar or dissimilar stimulus girls, she could answer this question in a clear-cut way.

Any questions asked by the subjects were answered and the whole procedure was discussed with subjects until Experimenter 2 felt confident that subjects understood that the false personality reports they had received were not their own.

Measuring of Postdebriefing Effects

The relative effectiveness or ineffectiveness of our debriefing procedures was measured in the following ways:

1. Immediately after the false debriefing, Experimenter 2 explained that a knowledge of what the subjects' personalities were *really* like would be valuable to her in analyzing the data. Thus, subjects were asked to fill out a questionnaire which they believed to be anonymous. They were asked to describe how plausible the personality information they had received had been, and, more importantly, to rate themselves on several personality traits. The traits on which subjects rated themselves were: their "ability to make deep, close, lasting, mature friendships," their "popularity," their "sensitivity to the feelings of others," and their "naturalness and spontaneity with others." Subjects utilized 4-point rating scales. The higher the score, the more "sociable" the subject indicated she was. The subject's scores on each trait were summed and the total score gave us a *Sociability Index*.

2. After being released from Experiment 2, all subjects reported back to Experiment 1. Since all had been told that they had done "unusually" in Experiment 1, they all believed that they would be required to answer a great number of questions for Experimenter 1. Undoubtedly, most subjects assumed that the other subjects were "average", and were returning to Experiment 1 simply to answer a few questions. All subjects were given a questionnaire to complete. The first question asked, "How well do you think you scored on your interview in Experiment 1?" Question 2 asked, "How well do you generally do in first impression situations?" Possible answers to these questions ranged from 0 ("I guess I did extremely poorly") to 18 ("I guess I did extremely well"). Answers on these two questions were combined to form the *Interview Performance Index*, a measure of the extent to which a subject felt that she had done well in the initial interview.

The final question on this questionnaire was essentially a manipulation check. It asked, "Is this [the interview] a good example of what you are like in real life?" Subjects could answer either "Yes" or "No." It will be recalled that subjects in the high-concern condition had been told that their interview performance was important since it was representative of them, while low-concern subjects had been told that their performance was unimportant and unrepresentative of them. Subjects were debriefed at great length after all of these measures were collected. Since subjects viewed this experiment as an effort to find out the extent to which deception might or might not be harmful to them, virtually all of them indicated that they were happy to have participated.

RESULTS AND DISCUSSION

All of the F tests in this paper are $2 \times 2 \times 2$ analyses involving selected concern, manipulated concern, and type of personality report provided to subjects.

Manipulation Checks

In Experiment 1, we tried to make half of our subjects concerned with the quality of their interview performance, and half unconcerned with their performance. This manipulation appears to have been effective. On their final questionnaire, subjects were asked to state whether or not the interview situation was a good example of what they were like in real life. More of the manipulated high-concern than low-concern subjects felt that the interview *was* representative $(F = 3.40, df = 1/56, p = .07)$.[3]

During Experiment 2, some subjects were led to believe that they had received high scores on two tests of sociability, and others were led to believe that they had received low sociability scores. Did our subjects accept this information? The evidence indicates they did. It will be recalled that as part of Experiment 2, subjects were asked how similar they were to each of the girls described in the two case reports. Girls in the high-sociability condition indicated that they were much more similar to the high-sociability stimulus girl $(F = 31.04, df = 1/56, p < .001)$, and that they were much less similar to the low-sociability stimulus girl $(F = 80.13, df = 1/56, p < .001)$ than did girls in the low-sociability condition.

Results

It was hypothesized that it would be more difficult to debrief the high-concern subjects than low-concern subjects. Thus, we expected high-concern subjects who were told they possessed good skills in Experiment 2 to overestimate their performance, even after debriefing, to a greater extent than would those low-concern subjects who were also told they possessed good social skills. Similarly, we expected high-concern subjects who were told they possessed poor social skills to underestimate their social skills, even after debriefing, to a greater extent than low-concern subjects.

In this experiment, subjects were classified as high concern in two ways: (*a*) *Selected concern*: concerned and unconcerned subjects were selected on the basis of their scores on Rosenfeld's Fear of Rejection test. Those subjects who scored from 35 to 65 on this test were classified as high in their concern about social rejection. Those subjects who scored from 0 to 34 were classified as low in their concern about social rejection; (*b*) *manipulated concern*: concern was manipulated in Experiment 1 as has been previously described.

Table 3-4   *Subjects' Estimates of Their Sociability and Interview Performance after Debriefing in Various Conditions*

Degree of Concern	Deceptive Personality Information Given	N	Sociability Index*	Interview Performance Index†
Selected concern				
High concern	Told sociable	16	9.86	20.54
	Told unsociable	20	8.70	17.62
Low concern	Told sociable	16	10.19	20.64
	Told unsociable	12	9.83	23.20
Manipulated concern				
High concern	Told sociable	16	9.93	20.70
	Told unsociable	16	8.93	19.78
Low concern	Told sociable	16	10.12	20.49
	Told unsociable	16	9.31	19.64

* A high score indicates the subject reported high ability to make friends, popularity, sensitivity, and spontaneity.

† A high score indicates the subject estimated that she did well in the initial interview and that she generally makes a good first impression.

How much social skill a subject believed she possessed *after debriefing* was measured by her self-ratings on the Sociability Index.

From Table 3-4 it is clear that regardless of whether we deal with manipulated concern or selected concern, and regardless of whether we consider self-estimates on the sociability index or on the interview performance index, high-concern subjects do *not* seem to be more difficult to debrief than low-concern subjects. Selected concern and type of deception do not interact in affecting subjects' estimates of their sociability ($F = 1.52$, $df = 1/56$) or of their interview performance ($F = 5.76$, $df = 1/56$) as we predicted they would. Though the last interaction F is significant, the mean estimates are clearly not in the predicted direction. We will discuss this interaction later in the paper. When we consider manipulated concern, the results are the same. After debriefing, high-concern subjects do not seem to be more difficult to debrief than low-concern subjects, whether we consider the Sociability Index ($F = .12$, $df = 1/56$) or the Interview Performance Index ($F = .00$, $df = 1/56$).[4]

The data obtained from this experiment lead us to believe that our hypothesis is incorrect. This belief is further strengthened by information that we have not yet presented to the reader. The study presented here is not the first time that this hypothesis was tested. In a very lengthy pilot study conducted by Abrahams (1967), the hypothesis of this paper was tested with only minor variations. (Ostensibly the Abrahams study was concerned with "problem solving ability" and "creativity" rather than with "interview performance" and "sociability.") The data from the Abrahams experiment also failed to provide any evidence that highly concerned subjects are more difficult to debrief than unconcerned subjects.

Although we feel that our hypothesis is incorrect, this does not mean that we have concluded that debriefing is uniformly effective with all subjects. Our data indicate that subjects in the various conditions do exhibit lingering aftereffects of the deception, although they are not the effects we predicted.

Let us first consider the estimates subjects made of their own sociability immediately after having been debriefed. For all subjects, it appears that the personality report had an impact which lasted at least for a few moments beyond the occurrence of debriefing. Regardless of whether concern was manipulated or selected, and regardless of level of concern, subjects who were given favorable sociability reports rated themselves significantly higher on the sociability index than did those subjects who received an unfavorable personality report (main effect $F = 6.12$, $df = 1/56$, $p < .05$). Since the type of sociability report a girl received was determined by chance, we must assume these differences are due to the fact that the subjects were not entirely disabused of the information they received in Experiment 2.

It is possible, of course, that these aftereffects are due to the fact that our experimenters were simply poor debriefers. However, this possibility does not reduce our concern about these results for two reasons: (*a*) In the Abrahams (1967) experiment, four different experimenters conducted the variation of the study reported here. These experimenters also got similar debriefing aftereffects. Those subjects who were told in Experiment 2 that they were immature and uncreative rated themselves as less mature after debriefing ($F = 3.25$, $df = 1/63$, $p = .08$) than did subjects who were told they were mature and creative. The creativity differences were not significant. Since the results of the Abrahams study are so similar to those obtained in this experiment, and since four experimenters were involved in the Abrahams experiment, it is hard for us to believe that our results are simply due to poor debriefing techniques; (*b*) we, like many other experimenters, believe that we make an unusual effort to instruct our students in debriefing procedures. The six experimenters participating

in the two studies discussed in this paper were all graduate students
who had been trained to debrief subjects and who had conducted
several other experiments. Obviously, doing a good job of debriefing
was of unusual importance to them in this experiment, and it will be
recalled that Experimenter 2 followed a lengthy debriefing procedure.

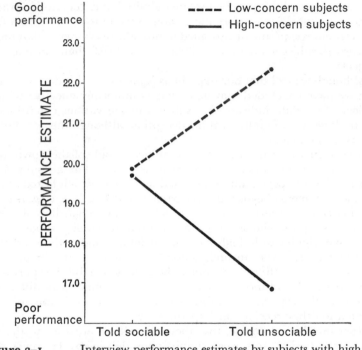

Good
performance
23.0

PERFORMANCE ESTIMATE

22.0
21.0
20.0
19.0
18.0
17.0

Poor
performance

Told sociable   Told unsociable

---- Low-concern subjects
—— High-concern subjects

Figure 3-1   Interview performance estimates by subjects with high
or low fear of rejection scores.

When we look at the difference in the interview performance
estimates between those subjects who received good sociability reports
in Experiment 2 and those subjects who received poor reports, we see
that the high-sociability-condition subjects do not think that they
performed better than do subjects in the low-sociability condition
($F = .22$, $df = 1/56$). Debriefing does not seem to be ineffective here. This
interview performance estimate differs in two main ways from the
sociability estimate. First, the interview estimates were taken a longer
period of time after debriefing than the sociability estimates. Perhaps
it takes a few minutes for debriefing to "sink in." Secondly, the Interview Performance Index may measure a different aspect of sociability
than the Sociability Index.

In addition to the aftereffects previously discussed, there is one additional finding that seems worth commenting upon; though our manipulated-concern measure seemed to have little impact upon the success or failure of debriefing, there is some evidence that selected concern may be of importance.

From Figure 3-1 and Table 3-4 it is clear that a subject's initial degree of concern (with her social abilities) has a marked effect on her postdebriefing estimate of her interview performance.

When we consider only the data from *selected high-concern* subjects, we see that even after the passage of time, debriefing does not seem to be totally effective. Selected high-concern subjects who received good sociability reports in Experiment 2, even after being told these reports were false, estimated that they did better in the interview situation than did subjects who received poor sociability reports. *Selected low-concern* subjects who received good sociability reports estimated their interview performance very much as did high-concern subjects who received the good report. However, the interview performance estimates of the low-concern subjects who received a poor sociability report are markedly different from the estimates of comparable high-concern subjects. These low-concern subjects guessed they did *better* in the interview situation than did subjects in any other group. This finding is peculiar.

In an attempt to explain this result, our first thought was to consider carefully what selected high concern and selected low concern must mean. According to Rosenfeld, the Fear of Rejection test was constructed to parallel the structural form of Mandler and Sarason's Test Anxiety Questionnaire and, presumably, measures the extent to which a subject is concerned with social rejection. From an analysis of our data, however, it appears that in many ways the Fear of Rejection test is a general measure of self-esteem. Subjects classified as low-concern subjects by this test tend to say better things about themselves than do high concern subjects. For example, on both the Sociability Index and on the Interview Performance Index there is a main effect due to initial level of selected concern of the subject. Subjects low in fear of rejection claim to be more sociable ($F = 6.06$, $df = 1/56$, $p < .05$) and to have done better in the interview situation ($F = 6.20$, $df = 1/56$, $p < .05$) than do subjects high in fear of rejection.

If low concern does in fact reflect high self-esteem, perhaps we can find an explanation for these findings. The apparent failure of debriefing for high-concern subjects is disturbing, but comprehensible. What is peculiar is the high performance estimates made by low-concern subjects who were given low personality results. Perhaps this simply demonstrates that high self-esteem individuals are especially likely to reject unpleasant information about themselves. Cohen (1959) suggested that:

different self-esteem groups are differentially able to fulfill the important acquired motive of maintenance of self-esteem at the highest possible level. Through their use of avoidance defenses . . . the highs are able to maintain a high-level equilibrium . . . whereas the lows are more dependent upon experimental variation [p. 117].

Cohen further noted that the high self-esteem individual may "emphasize enhancing experiences, thereby preserving an insulated but positive self-picture" [p. 117]. Perhaps our low-concern (high self-esteem) subjects, when faced with a low personality report, simply enhanced their performance in the interview situation in order to maintain their self-esteem.

This explanation is not entirely satisfactory. If Cohen's formulation is applicable there should be *some* evidence in our experiment that the selected low-concern subjects were "less receptive to experimental variations" than selected high-concern subjects, as Cohen suggests is the case. Low-concern subjects seem, during Experiment 2, to accept the negative personality reports to the same extent as do high-concern subjects. Acceptance of the negative or positive evaluations was measured by the extent to which subjects indicated that they were similar to a sociable or unsociable stimulus girl. Low-concern subjects who were told they had low sociability scores were just as likely to agree that they were similar to a low sociability girl as were high-concern subjects (interaction $F = .03$, $df = 1/56$). Further, even immediately after debriefing, there is no evidence that low-concern subjects, who were told in Experiment 2 that they had low sociability scores, were especially anxious to inflate their estimates of their own sociability (interaction $F = .62$, $df = 1/56$). It was not until they were quizzed several minutes after debriefing about their performance in another situation that low-concern–poor-evaluation subjects overestimated their performance.

We conclude two things from the preceding study:

1. The question of whether or not it is more difficult to successfully debrief concerned subjects than unconcerned subjects of information relevant to their current concerns remains unanswered. We can only say that two lengthy attempts to demonstrate this effect have been unsuccessful. Whether or not a stronger manipulation would produce the effect is, of course, a moot question, but we have been unable to produce evidence of even a slight tendency for subjects to behave in the predicted manner.

2. We have presented evidence that debriefing might not be as immediately effective as experimenters have hoped and assumed. This evidence is distressing for a number of reasons. First of all, it is disturbing that in the present experiment and in the Abrahams experiment, even after a very lengthy and thorough debriefing (probably atypical in thoroughness), subjects still

behaved to some extent as though the debriefing had not taken place. Subjects behaved in this manner even though they had voiced to the experimenter their understanding that the manipulation was false, their understanding of the true purpose of the experiment, and even though, by their manner and replies, the experimenter had been satisfied that they did indeed understand the nature of the deception.

Even more disturbing is the evidence that the aftereffects of debriefing might be complex, unpredictable, and might depend in part upon the personality traits of the subjects. The nature of the effect of personality traits in the present experiment were not totally explicable to us. Aftereffects in the Abrahams experiment were also present and somewhat inexplicable. The success of debriefing in that experiment was influenced by several significant interactions between sex of subject, sex of experimenter, and treatments. At the time the Abrahams experiment was run, we were willing to conclude that the significant interactions obtained were perhaps due to chance, to experimental error, to measurement error, and so on. The results of the present experiment, however, combined with the results of the Abrahams experiment, have aroused our suspicions and anxiety that there are often residual effects of debriefing, and that these effects appear to be complex and not easily interpreted. What is needed now is the generation of hypotheses and experimentation which would help us predict exactly what effects can be expected, with what kinds of people, under what types of conditions, as well as an investigation of the effectiveness of various types of debriefing procedures.

NOTES

1. The authors would like to express great appreciation to Bill Walster and Raymond O. Collier (who analyzed our data), and to Susan Boye, Shirley Damrosch, David Landy, and Darwyn Linder, who helped to conduct the studies reported in this paper and wish to acknowledge the many helpful comments and suggestions made by Dr. John M. Darly. This study was supported in part by National Science Foundation Grant GS 1056.

2. Sixteen of these subjects were discarded from our analysis: 1 subject had recently received an MMPI report in counseling, 1 subject could not understand the procedure, 2 subjects failed to answer all questions, 1 subject was very suspicious that we were deceiving her, and 11 subjects were slightly suspicious of the procedure for reasons they could not specify. We discarded any subjects who were in the least suspicious. We did, however, reanalyze the data including all subjects, and it is clear that including the data of the suspicious subjects would not have altered our conclusions in any way.

3. The reader might feel that a multiple-contingency test is a more appropriate method of analysis (Sutcliffe, 1957). Such an analysis gives us almost identical results to those reported above ($\chi^2 = 3.33$, $df = 1$, $.10 > p > .05$). Recent research would indicate that with a reasonable sample size there is no appreciable difference between a chi-square or an F test on discrete data (Cochran, 1950).

4. On both the Sociability index and the Interview Performance index, the three-way interaction (Selected Concern × Manipulated Concern × Type of Personality Report) is insignificant as is the two-way interaction between selected concern and manipulated concern.

All four interaction *F*s are below .20, $df = 1$ and 56. No significant interaction was present for these variables, and it would have been difficult to know what to make of these interactions if they had been significant.

REFERENCES

ABRAHAMS, D. The effect of concern on debriefing, following a deception experiment. Unpublished master's thesis, University of Minnesota, 1967.

COCHRAN, W. G. The comparison of percentages in matched samples. *Biometrika*, 1950, **37**: 256–266.

COHEN, A. R. Some implications of self-esteem for social influence. In I. L. Janis & C. I. Hovland (Eds.), *Personality and persuasibility*. New Haven: Yale University Press, 1959. Pp. 102–137.

KELMAN, H. C. The human use of human subjects: The problem of deception in social psychological experiments. Paper presented at the meeting of the American Psychological Association, Chicago, 1965.

ORNE, M. T. Demand characteristics and their implications for real life: The importance of quasi controls. Paper presented at the meeting of the American Psychological Association, Chicago, 1965.

ROSENFELD, H. M. Social choice conceived as a level of aspiration. *Journal of Abnormal and Social Psychology*, 1964, **68**: 491–499.

SILVERMAN, I. Motives underlying the behavior of the subject in the psychological experiment. Paper presented at the meeting of the American Psychological Association, Chicago, 1965.

SUTCLIFFE, J. P. A general method of analysis of frequency data for multiple classification designs. *Psychological Bulletin*, 1957, **54**: 134–137.

PART FOUR

Subject Reactions to the Psychological Laboratory

How do individuals react to being research subjects in psychological experiments? In this section, attention is directed to an intriguing line of inquiry concerning the thoughts, feelings, and expectations which reside in subjects as they participate in research. All of these may affect their behavior, in addition to—or perhaps in spite of—the particular stimulus array or psychological atmosphere constructed by the investigator to pursue his research. A major theme in this section, and the one to follow, is that the subject and the experimenter are partners in a dynamic social interaction, a process which may figure heavily in the outcome of the research.

In the first selection, Orne characterizes the subject role as a compliant or yielding one, the experimental setting essentially evoking and legitimizing submissiveness (cf. Orne & Holland, Part Two). This stance may reflect a modal disposition to be a *good* subject, in the manner of contributing to a successful scientific enterprise. How is this achieved? One logical strategy is to behave as predicted. This involves the subject divining the purpose of the experiment and responding to "the totality of cues which convey [the] experimental hypothesis" [p. 237]—what Orne terms the "demand characteristics" of the experiment. To the extent that demand characteristics determine the experimental data, one is limited in making inferences to nonexperimental settings in which such demands may not be operative, i.e., the problem of ecological validity. Contrary to those who might argue for an exodus from the laboratory, however, Orne seeks a more precise understanding of what occurs in experimentation with human beings. In short, the experimental context is less an artificial one than it is a misunderstood one.

If the experiment has a high degree of realism or plausibility for the subject—often the result of a successful deception—there may be little difficulty. Here the demand characteristics perceived by subjects may exist as a relatively weak and unsystematic set of stimuli, not a significant distraction from what the experimenter intends to be the subject's view of things. The problem becomes acute when these cues guide behavior in the predicted direction but are yet unknown to the experimenter and discrepant from his conception of the causal variables in his design. This begins to look like deception in the wrong party. The situation assumes chaotic proportions when considering that subjects may increasingly be entering research in a skeptical posture (Jourard, Part One) and that neither the subject nor the experimenter may wish to acknowledge the presence of demand characteristics—what Orne terms their "pact of ignorance." Subjects may, of course, be expected to differ in initial suspiciousness and in their candor after the experiment is completed (Stricker, Messick, & Jackson, 1967).

Orne suggests a number of methodological innovations for clarifying the presence and impact of demand characteristics. A general strategy, analogous to the placebo control in pharmaceutical research, is to expose a group of subjects to conditions which closely approximate those of the experimental or treatment group but which omit the treatment itself. If subsequent performances are similar in both groups, one may have evidence for the activation of demand characteristics. Orne is careful to note that such results do not, in themselves, prove the absence of experimental effects. Rather, they detract from the plausibility of such an interpretation. There are interesting parallels in this discussion to distinctions between role-playing and deception experiments cited by Freedman.

Rosenberg sees the experimental context as a potentially threatening one in terms of the subject's self-esteem. He defines evaluation apprehension as "an active, anxiety-toned concern that he [the subject] win a positive evaluation from the experimenter, or at least that he provide no grounds for a negative one" [p. 248]. The rationale here is that people generally have a desire to appear competent, normal, or mentally adjusted—particularly if their behavior is under scrutiny by a psychologist. Rosenberg asserts that this goal, when pursued by subjects in an experiment, may constitute a significant determinant of their behavior. As in the case of demand characteristics, this phenomenon may easily escape detection by the experimenter.

Rosenberg selects a well-known investigation from the cognitive dissonance literature to document the influence of evaluation apprehension. He challenges the assertion that counterattitudinal advocacy for a large reward produces less attitude change than for a small reward because of a low degree of cognitive dissonance in the high reward condition. Rather, the large reward induces disbelief or skepticism in subjects, leading them to suspect that their persuasibility is on the line

—preconditions for evaluation apprehension. Rosenberg modifies the procedure to eliminate evaluation apprehension and obtains a reinforcement effect—opposite to that predicted by dissonance theory and congruent with his own affective cognitive-consistency theory of attitude change.

The interaction of evaluation apprehension with the independent variable—it occurs only in the high reward condition—is of particular interest, for it suggests that variables associated with the social psychology of research may be closely interwoven in the theoretical and methodological design of experiments. They are not simply general characteristics with similar effects on all subjects or experimental conditions. Rosenberg's findings have, understandably, been received with considerable interest and resistance, particularly in cognitive dissonance circles (e.g., Linder, Cooper, & Jones, 1967). Rosenberg has recently engaged in an elaborate theoretical and empirical development of the evaluation apprehension construct (1969).

Are subjects disposed to pleasing the experimenter, as Orne suggests, or are they primarily in pursuit of a favorable self-image, as Rosenberg would have it. Sigall, Aronson, and Van Hoose note that often either goal can be realized by the same behavior. In an ingenious experiment, however, these investigators impose a condition in which the pursuit of one of these goals conflicts with attaining the other. Their results suggest that the need to "look good" overrides that of corroborating the experimenter's hypothesis. The question remains, however, whether the Decreased-Output condition in fact produced a demonstrable conflict for subjects, which was resolved by increasing their performance, or whether the achievement motive was the only salient force in that condition. This would seem to be a logical next step in the comparative analysis of the Orne and Rosenberg formulations.

The role of the individual's awareness in verbal learning and attitude formation (and change) has long been a matter of intense debate, particularly between those partisan to behavioristic and cognitive formulations of human behavior. Part of the complexity rests on the fact that the experimental methodologies in these research areas often present to subjects a rather obvious problem-solving occasion in which the experimenter's intent or expected outcome may be difficult to mask. A considerable amount of empirical evidence is available, for example, which suggests that manipulating the consequences of an individual's verbal behavior will result in systematic changes in that behavior. Controversy has emerged, however, in accounting theoretically for this behavior change—specifically, whether it can occur without the individual's awareness, as an automatic consequence of reinforcement, or whether such change is the result of the individual's awareness of the relationship between his verbal utterances and their effect on his environment. To the extent that awareness is a critical precondition for learning or performance and is not thus acknowledged by the investigator, his data are open to a demand characteristic interpretation. The epistemological features of this problem have been elegantly outlined by Spielberger (1965). The primary concern, however, has been methodological, that of measuring awareness and specifying when it occurs in the verbal "conditioning" paradigm. Attempts to detect awareness by means of a postexperimental interview have difficulty in distinguishing between awareness as an antecedent or as a consequence of the conditioning procedure. There is the further danger that the interview may induce what it is attempting to assess.

In an ingenious deception experiment, Levy instills immediate awareness of the essentials of the experiment in one of the experimental groups prior to their entrance into the laboratory. What follows is a truly fascinating documentary in the social psychology of research. A particularly noteworthy aspect of Levy's data is the "learning curve" for the informed subjects. What surely must exist as demand characteristics for extremely rapid learning (to say the least) nevertheless result in a group performance suggestive of an incremental growth process, in which reinforcement gradually increases the strength of the response in question. Levy thus shows that subjects, although perceiving demand characteristics early in the experiment, may act upon them with considerable individual variation, or perhaps not act upon them at all—an important extension of Orne's thesis. Levy's data raise once again the central theme of this section: Experimental behavior, although quite in line with the experimenter's hypothesis, may in fact be the result of one or more factors of which the experimenter is totally unaware.

Levy's experiment calls for a reappraisal of the postexperimental inquiry period. What is *post*experimental for the experimenter may well be *experimental* for his subject, even if this procedure is enacted by someone other than the experimenter himself. In a recent experiment, related to and supportive of Levy's, Golding and Lichtenstein note: "It may be that changes in the subjects' honesty behavior during postexperimental interviews cannot be expected unless the usual experimenter-subject role relationship is fundamentally altered" [1970, p. 221]—a suggestion quite in the spirit of Jourard's views. Levy remains optimistic, stating that "there is no intrinsic reason . . . why the study of awareness need place the experimenter entirely at the mercy of his subjects' testimony" and that "Converging operations are possible" [p. 286]. It is a bold task that Levy offers.

In a 1957 issue of the *Journal of Experimental Psychology*, Carolyn and Arthur Staats published an experiment in which subjects were exposed to numerous pairs of verbal stimuli, each pair containing a nonsense syllable and a word having connotative meaning in Osgood's sense of that term. Subjects later indicated that connotative meaning had been transferred to the nonsense syllables, apparently via contiguous association with the meaningful words. The Staats interpreted their results as "meaning established by classical conditioning." Since this model was supported after rejecting 9 of the 86 total subjects for their ability to verbalize "the relationship between certain words and syllables" [p. 77], the investigators concluded that the "meaning of stimuli may be learned without awareness" [p. 79]. It was an assertion not to be ignored.

Twelve years later, the Staats' experiment is resurrected in the *Journal of Personality and Social Psychology*. Page contends that Orne's concept of demand characteristics provides a more compelling explanation for the observed results than does the Pavlovian conditioning model. It should be noted, as Page himself recognizes, that in principle the hypothesis of attitudes or affective meaning being established by classical conditioning is a tenable one. The problem is that the methodological arrangement for classical conditioning in the laboratory—and operant conditioning as well--is also the occasion for a kind of relational or concept learning in the human subject, learning which might be equated with awareness of the experimenter's intent rather than viewed as the result of the continuous exposure to pairs of conditioned and unconditioned stimuli. Awareness must be ruled out as a primary causal variable if classical conditioning is to remain as the most straightforward explanation for the change in behavior. That Staats and Staats (1957) are in agreement is clear, for they used deceptive orienting instructions to prevent their subjects from attending to the pairing of stimuli and they discarded their aware subjects prior to the analysis of their data.

The highlight of Page's study from a methodological point of view is his extensive postexperimental questionnaire. Although he views awareness as a dichotomous state—"A subject either knows it [the experimenter's hypothesis] or he doesn't" [p. 297]—he doubts the likelihood of one question being able to tap the subject's knowledge. This is quite in line with Levy's position. Page confirms Levy's distinction between subjects perceiving demand characteristics and acting upon them—the latter, understandably, turns out to be a somewhat more powerful predictor. In terms of his general view of the inquiry period, however, Page appears to take his subjects' verbal reports at face value. He notes, for example, that orienting instructions were used "to enlist the honesty and cooperation of subjects while releasing them from the demand characteristics of the experiment proper" [p. 296]. This is in striking contrast to Levy's conception of the postexperimental inquiry as having its own peculiar demand characteristics and his caution against adopting a testimonial view of the subjects' verbalizations. Is the experimenter, in the final analysis, doomed to believing his subjects? It is far from being a closed issue.

Staats' reply to Page gives the reader a classic portrait of a theorist faithful to his position. He contends that awareness is the result of, rather than the precondition for, conditioning and, further, that the extended questionnaire itself demands awareness. He advocates the brief form of postexperimental inquiry, but, of course, Levy's data are very negative on this point. Page's questionnaire is certainly extensive enough to break through the reticence of beneficent subjects, to use Levy's phrase, but it is unclear as to the degree to which it might have induced awareness that was not present during the experiment *per se*. A problem in Page's study is that he does not specify *exactly* when it is that subjects became aware. Questions 11 and 12—which Page regards as crucial—contain the phrase "during the experiment." But this constitutes a period of some duration, with different implications for the role of awareness resting on when, exactly, it did occur during the experiment. It would seem in fact that Question No. 5 is the critical one, but it is not clear how responses to this question in particular were used in the final judgment of awareness. It would seem that the same theoretical explanation need not apply to *all* subjects in these experiments—a possibility not stated by Page or Staats. Gregory Kimble's elegant (1962) formulation of the problems involved in the issue of awareness and classical conditioning provides an illuminating background for the Page-Staats controversy, particularly for the reader interested in the methodological complexities of classical conditioning.

Staats might have cited the factor of experimenter expectancy, to be reviewed in the next section. Perhaps investigators who are committed to a theoretical orientation which focuses on awareness and, as with Page, have an empirical history of showing awareness to be crucial, in fact are prone to discover awareness by covertly communicating this expectancy to their subjects. Such cues would not have to be present on the printed questionnaire itself, of course, but could be transmitted in some manner during the interaction. Since in Page's experiment the questionnaire was apparently administered by the same person who conducted the experiment, his study would seem open to this speculative kind of criticism. At this point, it is largely conjecture. Page's data are highly convincing, but Staats' contention that awareness can be "produced" by vigorous questioning warrants empirical attention. Some of the quasi-control techniques discussed recently by Orne (1969) appear particularly well suited to this problem.

Finally, there is the issue of autonomic responses. In several experiments cited by Staats, significant correlations are shown to exist between the intensity of conditioned meaning ratings and the extent to which the conditioned stimuli elicit galvanic skin response (GSR) activity. Since the GSR is allegedly impervious to voluntary control— subjects may not even be aware that such a response is in their repertoire—a demand characteristic or awareness explanation for its role in these studies seems unjustified. Although recent evidence indicates that the GSR may be susceptible to cognitive variables (e.g., Kiesler, Collins, & Miller, 1969, pp. 149–150), this is a converging operation that may prove useful in distinguishing between social-psychological, and conditioning effects—particularly in organisms, e.g. adult humans, to whom it is logical or reasonable to apply awareness or demand characteristics as explanatory concepts. A recent study by Zanna, Kiesler, and Pilkonis (1970) appears to circumvent the more obvious effects of demand characteristics during both conditioning and post-experimental inquiry. Their results, including physiological evidence of conditioning, are favorable for Staats' position.

FURTHER READING

GOLDING, S. L., & Lichtenstein, E. Confession of awareness and prior knowledge of deception as a function of interview set and approval motivation. *Journal of Personality and Social Psychology*, 1970, **14**: 213–223. An interesting extension of Levy's study, showing low confession rates among informed subjects and their ability to behave as if they were naïve.

KIESLER, C. A., Collins, B. E., & Miller, N. *Attitude change*. New York: Wiley, 1969. Ch. 3 A brilliant review and critique of theoretical positions in the areas of attitude change and formation. An exceptionally strong treatment is given to the awareness problem.

KIMBLE, G. A. Classical conditioning and the problem of awareness. In C. W. Eriksen (Ed.), *Behavior and awareness: A symposium of research and interpretation*. A noted methodologist in classical conditioning outlines the complexities of the process and the possible role of a variety of verbal or cognitive events.

LINDER, D. E., Cooper, J., & Jones, E. E. Decision freedom as a determinant of the role of incentive magnitude in attitude change. *Journal of Personality and Social Psychology*, 1967, **6**: 244–254. Argues that Rosenberg's procedure for reducing evaluation apprehension committed his subjects to perform the task before they learned of its nature or the amount of reward involved. This no-choice aspect of Rosenberg's study does not, according to these writers, make it an appropriate challenge to dissonance theory.

MASLING, J. Role-related behavior of the subject and psychologist and its effects upon psychological data. *Nebraska symposium on motivation*. Lincoln, Nebraska: University of Nebraska Press, 1966. Pp. 67–103. A stylistic and somewhat entertaining review of subject and experimenter effects, particularly as they occur in projective testing.

ORNE, M. T. Demand characteristics and the concept of quasi-controls. In R. Rosenthal & R. L Rosnow (Eds.), *Artifact in behavioral research*. New York: Academic Press, 1969. Pp. 143–179. A recent review of the concept of demand characteristics with a particularly strong consideration of methodological procedures for controlling and understanding the effects of this phenomenon.

ORNE, M. T. Hypnosis, motivation, and the ecological validity of the psychological experiment. In W. J. Arnold & M. M. Page (Eds), *Nebraska symposium on motivation*. Lincoln: University of Nebraska Press, 1970. Pp. 187–265. An extension and elaboration of Orne's view that "the single most important variable which must be taken into account in psychological research with man in his recognition that he is under observation, that he is the object of study" (p. 259).

ROSENBERG, M. J. The conditions and consequences of evaluation apprehension. In R. Rosenthal & R. L. Rosnow (Eds.), *Artifact in behavioral research*. New York: Academic Press, 1969. Pp. 279–349. A clear and highly promising account of the construct validity of evaluation apprehension. Of particular interest are Rosenberg's views relating this variable to the work of Orne and Rosenthal, and his general feelings on a variety of issues in experimental social psychology.

ROSNOW, R. L., & Rosenthal, R. Volunteer effects in behavioral research. In *New directions in psychology*, 4. New York: Holt, Rinehart & Winston, 1970. Pp. 211–277. Bias in the selection of subjects is a significant problem in contemporary research, as noted by Schultz. These writers present a thorough and well-organized review of the empirical research dealing with differences between volunteer and nonvolunteer research subjects.

SPIELBERGER, C. D. Theoretical and epistemological issues in verbal conditioning. In S. Rosenberg (Ed.), *Directions in psycholinguistics*. New York: Macmillan, 1965. Pp. 149–200. An extensive analysis of research in verbal operant conditioning, distinguishing between theoretical orientations which do, and which do not, focus upon awareness as a key variable. Spielberger speaks for the cognitive view—pro awareness.

STAATS, C. K., & Staats, A. W. Meaning established by classical conditioning. *Journal of Experimental Psychology*, 1957, 54: 74–80. One of the early experiments purporting to document learning without awareness. Most noteworthy, perhaps, is the monumental amount of theoretical and empirical activity that was generated by this and similar research.

STRICKER, L. J., Messick, S., & Jackson, D. N. Suspicion of deception: Implications for conformity research. *Journal of Personality and Social Psychology*, 1967, 5: 379–389. A study showing high incidence of suspicion about experimental procedures in a high-school population. Suspiciousness is shown to correlate negatively with the amount of conformity, is higher in boys than in girls, and relates to various personality variables, including social desirability response styles.

ZANNA, M. P., Kiesler, C. A., & Pilkonis, P. A. Positive and negative attitudinal affect established by classical conditioning. *Journal of Personality and Social Psychology*, 1970, 14: 321–328. A study which attempts to rule out a demand characteristic interpretation of the classical conditioning of affect by separating the conditioning procedure from the test for conditioning itself and by making explicit—thereby reducing suspicion—a highly plausible rationale for the pairing of conditioned and unconditioned stimuli. The results clearly keep the issue of learning without awareness an open one.

Martin T. Orne[1]

On the Social Psychology
of the Psychological Experiment:

With Particular Reference to
Demand Characteristics and
Their Implications[2]

> It is to the highest degree probable that the subject['s] . . . general
> attitude of mind is that of ready complacency and cheerful willing-
> ness to assist the investigator in every possible way by reporting to
> him those very things which he is most eager to find, and that the
> very questions of the experimenter . . . suggest the shade of reply
> expected. . . . Indeed . . . it seems too often as if the subject were
> now regarded as a stupid automaton. . . .   A. H. Pierce, 1908[3]

Since the time of Galileo, scientists have employed the laboratory
experiment as a method of understanding natural phenomena.
Generically, the experimental method consists of abstracting relevant
variables from complex situations in nature and reproducing in the
laboratory segments of these situations, varying the parameters
involved so as to determine the effect of the experimental variables.
This procedure allows generalization from the information obtained in
the laboratory situation back to the original situation as it occurs in
nature. The physical sciences have made striking advances through the
use of this method, but in the behavioral sciences it has often been
difficult to meet two necessary requirements for meaningful experimentation: reproducibility and ecological validity.[4] It has long been
recognized that certain differences will exist between the types of
experiments conducted in the physical sciences and those in the
behavioral sciences because the former investigates a universe of
inanimate objects and forces, whereas the latter deals with animate

From American Psychologist, 1962, 17: 776–783. Copyright © 1962 by
The American Psychological Association and reprinted with
permission of author and The American Psychological Association.

organisms, often thinking, conscious subjects. However, recognition of this distinction has not always led to appropriate changes in the traditional experimental model of physics as employed in the behavioral sciences. Rather the experimental model has been so successful as employed in physics that there has been a tendency in the behavioral sciences to follow precisely a paradigm originated for the study of inanimate objects, i.e., one which proceeds by exposing the subject to various conditions and observing the differences in reaction of the subject under different conditions. However, the use of such a model with animal or human subjects leads to the problem that the subject of the experiment is assumed, at least implicitly, to be a *passive responder* to stimuli—an assumption difficult to justify. Further, in this type of model the experimental stimuli themselves are usually rigorously defined in terms of what *is done* to the subject. In contrast, the purpose of this paper will be to focus on what the human subject *does* in the laboratory: what motivation the subject is likely to have in the experimental situation, how he usually perceives behavioral research, what the nature of the cues is that the subject is likely to pick up, etc. Stated in other terms, what factors are apt to affect the subject's reaction to the well-defined stimuli in the situation? These factors comprise what will be referred to here as the "experimental setting."

Since any experimental manipulation of human subjects takes place within this larger framework or setting, we should propose that the above-mentioned factors must be further elaborated and the parameters of the experimental setting more carefully defined so that adequate controls can be designed to isolate the effects of the experimental setting from the effects of the experimental variables. Later in this paper we shall propose certain possible techniques of control which have been devised in the process of our research on the nature of hypnosis.

Our initial focus here will be on some of the qualities peculiar to psychological experiments. The experimental situation is one which takes place within the context of an explicit agreement of the subject to participate in a special form of social interaction known as "taking part in an experiment." Within the context of our culture the roles of subject and experimenter are well understood and carry with them well-defined mutual role expectations. A particularly striking aspect of the typical experimenter-subject relationship is the extent to which the subject will play his role and place himself under the control of the experimenter. Once a subject has agreed to participate in a psychological experiment, he implicitly agrees to perform a very wide range of actions on request without inquiring as to their purpose, and frequently without inquiring as to their duration.

Furthermore, the subject agrees to tolerate a considerable degree of discomfort, boredom, or actual pain, if required to do so by the experimenter. Just about any request which could conceivably be asked of the subject by a reputable investigator is legitimized by the quasi-magical phrase, "This is an experiment," and the shared assumption that a legitimate purpose will be served by the subject's behavior. A somewhat trivial example of this legitimization of requests is as follows:

A number of casual acquaintances were asked whether they would do the experimenter a favor; on their acquiescence, they were asked to perform five push-ups. Their response tended to be amazement, incredulity and the question, "Why?" Another similar group of individuals was asked whether they would take part in an experiment of brief duration. When they agreed to do so, they too were asked to perform five push-ups. Their typical response was, "Where?"

The striking degree of control inherent in the experimental situation can also be illustrated by a set of pilot experiments which were performed in the course of designing an experiment to test whether the degree of control inherent in the *hypnotic* relationship is greater than that in a waking relationship.[5] In order to test this question, we tried to develop a set of tasks which waking subjects would refuse to do, or would do only for a short period of time. The tasks were intended to be psychologically noxious, meaningless, or boring, rather than painful or fatiguing.

For example, one task was to perform serial additions of each adjacent two numbers on sheets filled with rows of random digits. In order to complete just one sheet, the subject would be required to perform 224 additions. A stack of some 2,000 sheets was presented to each subject—clearly an impossible task to complete. After the instructions were given, the subject was deprived of his watch and told, "Continue to work; I will return eventually." Five and one-half hours later, the experimenter gave up! In general, subjects tended to continue this type of task for several hours, usually with little decrement in performance. Since we were trying to find a task which would be discontinued spontaneously within a brief period, we tried to create a more frustrating situation as follows:

Subjects were asked to perform the same task described above but were also told that when finished with the additions on each sheet, they should pick up a card from a large pile, which would instruct them on what to do next. However, every card in the pile read:

> You are to tear up the sheet of paper which you have just completed into a minimum of thirty-two pieces and go on to the next sheet of paper and continue working as you did before; when you have completed this piece of paper, pick up the next card which will instruct you further. Work as accurately and as rapidly as you can.

Our expectation was that subjects would discontinue the task as soon as they realized that the cards were worded identically, that each finished piece of work had to be destroyed, and that, in short, the task was completely meaningless.

Somewhat to our amazement, subjects tended to persist in the task for several hours with relatively little sign of overt hostility. Removal of the one-way screen did not tend to make much difference. The post-experimental inquiry helped to explain the subjects' behavior. When asked about the tasks, subjects would invariably attribute considerable meaning to their performance, viewing it as an endurance test or the like.

Thus far, we have been singularly unsuccessful in finding an experimental task which would be discontinued, or, indeed, refused by subjects in an experimental setting.[6,7] Not only do subjects continue to perform boring, unrewarding tasks, but they do so with few errors and little decrement in speed. It became apparent that it was extremely difficult to design an experiment to test the degree of social control in hypnosis, in view of the already *very high degree of control in the experimental situation itself.*

The quasi-experimental work reported here is highly informal and based on samples of three or four subjects in each group. It does, however, illustrate the remarkable compliance of the experimental subject. The only other situations where such a wide range of requests are carried out with little or no question are those of complete authority, such as some parent-child relationships or some doctor-patient relationships. This aspect of the experiment as a social situation will not become apparent unless one tests for it; it is, however, present in varying degrees in all experimental contexts. Not only are tasks carried out, but they are performed with care over considerable periods of time.

Our observation that subjects tend to carry out a remarkably wide range of instructions with a surprising degree of diligence reflects only one aspect of the motivation manifested by most subjects in an experimental situation. It is relevant to consider another aspect of motivation that is common to the subjects of most psychological experiments: high regard for the aims of science and experimentation.

A volunteer who participates in a psychological experiment may do so for a wide variety of reasons ranging from the need to fulfill a course requirement, to the need for money, to the unvoiced hope of altering his personal adjustment for the better, etc. Over and above these motives, however, college students tend to share (with the experimenter) the hope and expectation that the study in which they are participating will in some material way contribute to science and perhaps ultimately to human welfare in general. We should expect that many of the characteristics of the experimental situation derive from the peculiar role relationship which exists between subject and experimenter. Both subject and experimenter share the belief that whatever the experimental task is, it is important, and that as such no matter how much effort must be exerted or how much discomfort must be endured, it is justified by the ultimate purpose.

If we assume that much of the motivation of the subject to comply with any and all experimental instructions derives from an identification with the goals of science in general and the success of the experiment in particular,[8] it follows that the subject has a stake in the outcome of the study in which he is participating. For the volunteer subject to feel that he has made a useful contribution, it is necessary for him to assume that the experimenter is competent and that he himself is a "good subject."

The significance to the subject of successfully being a "good subject" is attested to by the frequent questions at the conclusion of an experiment, to the effect of, "Did I ruin the experiment?" What is most commonly meant by this is, "Did I perform well in my role as experimental subject?" or "Did my behavior demonstrate that which the experiment is designed to show?" Admittedly, subjects are concerned about their performance in terms of reinforcing their self-image; nonetheless, they seem even more concerned with the utility of their performances. We might well expect then that as far as the subject is able, he will behave in an experimental context in a manner designed to play the role of a "good subject" or, in other words, *to validate the experimental hypothesis.* Viewed in this way, the student volunteer is *not* merely a passive responder in an experimental situation but rather he has a very real stake in the successful outcome of the experiment. This problem is implicitly recognized in the large number of psychological studies which attempt to conceal the true purpose of the experiment from the subject in the hope of thereby obtaining more reliable data. This maneuver on the part of psychologists is so widely known in the college population that even if a psychologist is honest with the subject, more often than not he will be distrusted. As one subject pithily put it, "Psychologists always lie!" This bit of paranoia has some support in reality.

The subject's performance in an experiment might almost be conceptualized as problem-solving behavior; that is, at some level he sees it as his task to ascertain the true purpose of the experiment and respond in a manner which will support the hypotheses being tested. Viewed in this light, the totality of cues which convey an experimental hypothesis to the subject become significant determinants of subjects' behavior. We have labeled the sum total of such cues as the "*demand characteristics of the experimental situation*" [Orne, 1959a]. These cues include the rumors or campus scuttlebutt about the research, the information conveyed during the original solicitation, the person of the experimenter, and the setting of the laboratory, as well as all explicit and implicit communications during the experiment proper. A frequently overlooked, but nonetheless very significant source of cues for the subject lies in the experimental procedure itself, viewed in the light of the subject's previous knowledge and experience. For example, if a test is given twice with some intervening treatment, even the dullest college student is aware that some change is expected, particularly if the test is in some obvious way related to the treatment.

The demand characteristics perceived in any particular experiment will vary with the sophistication, intelligence, and previous experience of each experimental subject. To the extent that the demand characteristics of the experiment are clear-cut, they will be perceived uniformly by most experimental subjects. It is entirely possible to have an experimental situation with clear-cut demand characteristics for psychology undergraduates which, however, does not have the same clear-cut demand characteristics for enlisted army personnel. It is, of course, those demand characteristics which are perceived by the subject that will influence his behavior.

We should like to propose the heuristic assumption that a subject's behavior in any experimental situation will be determined by two sets of variables: (a) those which are traditionally defined as experimental variables, and (b) the perceived demand characteristics of the experimental situation. The extent to which the subject's behavior is related to the demand characteristics, rather than to the experimental variable, will in large measure determine both the extent to which the experiment can be replicated with minor modification (i.e., modified demand characteristics) and the extent to which generalizations can be drawn about the effect of the experimental variables in nonexperimental contexts [the problem of ecological validity (Brunswik, 1947)].

It becomes an empirical issue to study under what circumstances, in what kind of experimental contexts, and with what kind of subject populations, demand characteristics become significant in determining the behavior of subjects in experimental situations. It should be clear that demand characteristics cannot be eliminated from experiments; all experiments will have demand characteristics, and these will always have some effect. It does become possible, however, to study the effect of demand characteristics as opposed to the effect of experimental variables. However, techniques designed to study the effect of demand characteristics need to take into account that these effects result from the subject's *active* attempt to respond appropriately to the *totality* of the experimental situation.

It is perhaps best to think of the perceived demand characteristics as a contextual variable in the experimental situation. We should like to emphasize that, at this stage, little is known about this variable. In our first study which utilized the demand characteristics concept (Orne, 1959b), we found that a particular experimental effect was present only in records of those subjects who were able to verbalize the experimenter's hypothesis. Those subjects who were unable to do so did not show the predicted phenomenon. Indeed, we found that whether or not a given subject perceived the experimenter's hypothesis was a more accurate predictor of the subject's actual performance than his statement about what he thought he had done on the experimental task. It became clear from extensive interviews with subjects that response to the demand characteristics is not merely conscious compliance. When we speak of "playing the role of a good experimental subject," we use the concept analogously to the way in which Sarbin (1950) describes role playing in hypnosis, namely, largely on a nonconscious level. The demand characteristics of the situation help define the role of "good experimental subject," and the responses of the subject are a function of the role that is created.

We have a suspicion that the demand characteristics most potent in determining subjects' behavior are those which convey the purpose of the experiment effectively but not obviously. If the purpose of the experiment is not clear, or is highly ambiguous, many different hypotheses may be formed by different subjects, and the demand characteristics will not lead to clear-cut results. If, on the other hand, the demand characteristics are so obvious that the subject becomes fully conscious of the expectations of the experimenter, there is a tendency to lean over backwards to be honest. We are encountering here the effect of another facet of the college student's attitude toward science. While the student wants studies to "work," he feels he must be honest in his report; otherwise, erroneous conclusions will be drawn. Therefore, if the subject becomes acutely aware of the experimenter's expectations, there may be a tendency for biasing in the opposite direction. (This is analogous to the often observed tendency to favor individuals whom we dislike in an effort to be fair.)[9]

Delineation of the situations where demand characteristics may produce an effect ascribed to experimental variables, or where they may obscure such an effect and actually lead to systematic data in the opposite direction, as well as those experimental contexts where they do not play a major role, is an issue for further work. Recognizing the contribution to experimental results which may be made by the demand characteristics of the situation, what are some experimental techniques for the study of demand characteristics?

As we have pointed out, it is futile to imagine an experiment that could be created without demand characteristics. One of the basic characteristics of the human being is that he will ascribe purpose and meaning even in the absence of purpose and meaning. In an experiment where he knows some purpose exists, it is inconceivable for him not to form some hypothesis as to the purpose, based on some cues, no matter how meager; this will then determine the demand characteristics which will be perceived by and operate for a particular subject. Rather than eliminating this variable then, it becomes necessary to take demand characteristics into account, study their effect, and manipulate them if necessary.

One procedure to determine the demand characteristics is the systematic study of each individual subject's perception of the experimental hypothesis. If one can determine what demand characteristics are perceived by each subject, it becomes possible to determine to what extent these, rather than the experimental variables, correlate with the observed behavior. If the subject's behavior correlates better with the demand characteristics than with the experimental variables, it is probable that the demand characteristics are the major determinants of the behavior.

The most obvious technique for determining what demand characteristics are perceived is the use of postexperimental inquiry. In this regard, it is well to point out that considerable self-discipline is necessary for the experimenter to obtain a valid inquiry. A great many experimenters, at least implicitly, make the demand that the subject not perceive what is really going on. The temptation for the experimenter in, say, a replication of an Asch group pressure experiment, is to ask the subject afterwards, "You didn't realize that the other fellows were confederates, did you?" Having obtained the required, "No," the experimenter breathes a sigh of relief and neither subject nor experimenter pursues the issue further.[10] However, even if the experimenter makes an effort to elicit the subject's perception of the hypothesis of the experiment, he may have difficulty in obtaining a valid report because the subject as well as he himself has considerable interest in appearing naïve.

Most subjects are cognizant that they are not supposed to know any more about an experiment than they have been told and that excessive knowledge will disqualify them from participating or, in the case of a postexperimental inquiry, such knowledge will invalidate their performance. As we pointed out earlier, subjects have a real stake in viewing their performance as meaningful. For this reason, it is commonplace to find a pact of ignorance resulting from the intertwining motives of both experimenter and subject, neither wishing to create a situation where the particular subject's performance needs to be excluded from the study.

For these reasons, inquiry procedures are required to push the subject for information without, however, providing in themselves cues as to what is expected. The general question which needs to be explored is the subject's perception of the experimental purpose and the specific hypotheses of the experimenter. This can best be done by an open-ended procedure starting with the very general question of, "What do you think that the experiment is about?" and only much later asking specific questions. Responses of, "I don't know" should be dealt with by encouraging the subject to guess, use his imagination, and in general, by refusing to accept this response. Under these circumstances, the overwhelming majority of students will turn out to have evolved very definite hypotheses. These hypotheses can then be judged, and a correlation between them and experimental performance can be drawn.

Two objections may be made against this type of inquiry: (*a*) that the subject's perception of the experimenter's hypotheses is based on his own experimental behavior, and therefore a correlation between these two variables may have little to do with the determinants of behavior, and (*b*) that the inquiry procedure itself is subject to demand characteristics.

A procedure which has been independently advocated by Riecken (1958) and Orne (1959a) is designed to deal with the first of these objections. This consists of an inquiry procedure which is conducted much as though the subject had actually been run in the experiment, without, however, permitting him to be given any experimental data. Instead, the precise procedure of the experiment is explained, the experimental material is shown to the subject, and he is told what he would be required to do; however, he is not permitted to make any responses. He is then given a postexperimental inquiry as though he had been a subject. Thus, one would say, "If I had asked you to do all these things, what do you think that the experiment would be about, what do you think I would be trying to prove, what would my hypotheses be?" etc. This technique, which we have termed the pre-experimental inquiry, can be extended very readily to the giving of preexperimental tests, followed by the explanation of experimental conditions and tasks, and the administration of postexperimental tests. The subject is requested to behave on these tests as though he had been exposed to the experimental treatment that was described to him. This type of procedure is not open to the objection that the subject's own behavior has provided cues for him as to the purpose of the task. It presents him with a straight problem-solving situation and makes explicit what, for the true experimental subject, is implicit. It goes without saying that these subjects who are run under the preexperi-mental inquiry conditions must be drawn from the same population as the experimental groups and may, of course, not be run subsequently in the experimental condition. This technique is one of approximation rather than of proof. However, if subjects describe behavior on the preinquiry conditions as similar or identical to that actually given by subjects exposed to the experimental conditions, the hypothesis becomes plausible that demand characteristics may be responsible for the behavior.

It is clear that pre- and postexperimental inquiry techniques have their own demand characteristics. For these reasons, it is usually best to have the inquiry conducted by an experimenter who is not acquainted with the actual experimental behavior of the subjects. This will tend to minimize the effect of experimenter bias.

Another technique which we have utilized for approximating the effect of the demand characteristics is to attempt to hold the demand characteristics constant and eliminate the experimental variable. One way of accomplishing this purpose is through the use of simulating subjects. This is a group of subjects who are not exposed to the experimental variable to which the effect has been attributed, but who are instructed to act *as if* this were the case. In order to control for experimenter bias under these circumstances, it is advisable to utilize more than one experimenter and to have the experimenter who actually runs the subjects "blind" as to which group (simulating or real) any given individual belongs.

Our work in hypnosis (Damaser, Shor, & Orne, 1963; Orne, 1959b; Shor, 1959) is a good example of the use of simulating controls. Subjects unable to enter hypnosis are instructed to simulate entering hypnosis for another experimenter. The experimenter who runs the study sees both highly trained hypnotic subjects and simulators in random order and does not know to which group each subject belongs. Because the subjects are run "blind," the experimenter is more likely to treat the two groups of subjects identically. We have found that simulating subjects are able to perform with great effectiveness, deceiving even well-trained hypnotists. However, the simulating group is not exposed to the experimental condition (in this case, hypnosis) to which the given effect under investigation is often ascribed. Rather, it is a group faced with a problem-solving task, namely, to utilize whatever cues are made available by the experimental context and the experimenter's concrete behavior in order to behave as they think that hypnotized subjects might. Therefore, to the extent that simulating subjects are able to behave identically, it is possible that demand characteristics, rather than the altered state of consciousness, could account for the behavior of the experimental group.

The same type of technique can be utilized in other types of studies. For example, in contrast to the placebo control in a drug study, it is equally possible to instruct some subjects not to take the medication at all, but to act as if they had. It must be emphasized that this type of control is different from the placebo control. It represents an approximation. It maximally confronts the simulating subject with a problem-solving task and suggests how much of the total effect could be accounted for by the demand characteristics—assuming that the experimental group had taken full advantage of them, an assumption not necessarily correct.

All of the techniques proposed thus far share the quality that they depend upon the active cooperation of the control subjects, and in some way utilize his thinking process as an intrinsic factor. The subject does *not* just respond in these control situations but, rather, he is required *actively* to solve the problem.

The use of placebo experimental conditions is a way in which this problem can be dealt with in a more classic fashion. Psychopharmacology has used such techniques extensively, but here too they present problems. In the case of placebos and drugs, it is often the case that the physician is "blind" as to whether a drug is placebo or active, but the patient is not, despite precautions to the contrary; i.e., the patient is cognizant that he does not have the side effects which some of his fellow patients on the ward experience. By the same token, in psychological placebo treatments, it is equally important to ascertain whether the subject actually perceived the treatment to be experimental or control. Certainly the subject's perception of himself as a control subject may materially alter the situation.

A recent experiment (Orne & Scheibe, 1964) in our laboratory illustrates this type of investigation. We were interested in studying the demand characteristics of sensory deprivation experiments, independent of any actual sensory deprivation. We hypothesized that the overly cautious treatment of subjects, careful screening for mental or physical disorders, awesome release forms, and, above all, the presence of a "panic (release) button" might be more significant in producing the effects reported from sensory deprivation than the actual diminution of sensory input. A pilot study (Stare, Brown, & Orne, 1959), employing preinquiry techniques, supported this view. Recently, we designed an experiment to test more rigorously this hypothesis.

This experiment, which we called Meaning Deprivation, had all the *accoutrements* of sensory deprivation, including release forms and a red panic button. However, we carefully refrained from creating any sensory deprivation whatsoever. The experimental task consisted of sitting in a small experimental room which was well lighted, with two comfortable chairs, as well as ice water and a sandwich, and an optional task of adding numbers. The subject did not have a watch during this time, the room was reasonably quiet, but not soundproof, and the duration of the experiment (of which the subject was ignorant) was four hours. Before the subject was placed in the experimental room, 10 tests previously used in sensory deprivation research were administered. At the completion of the experiment, the same tasks were again administered. A microphone and a one-way screen were present in the room, and the subject was encouraged to verbalize freely.

The control group of 10 subjects was subjected to the identical treatment, except that they were told that they were control subjects for a sensory deprivation experiment. The panic button was eliminated for this group. The formal experimental treatment of these two groups of subjects was the same in terms of the objective stress—four hours of isolation. However, the demand characteristics had been purposively varied for the two groups to study the effect of demand characteristics as opposed to objective stress. Of the 14 measures which could be quantified, 13 were in the predicted direction, and 6 were significant at the selected 10 percent alpha level or better. A Mann-Whitney U test has been performed on the summation ranks of all measures as a convenient method for summarizing the overall differences. The one-tailed probability which emerges is $p = .001$, a clear demonstration of expected effects.

This study suggests that demand characteristics may in part account for some of the findings commonly attributed to sensory deprivation. We have found similar significant effects of demand characteristics in accounting for a great deal of the findings reported in hypnosis. It is highly probable that careful attention to this variable, or group of variables, may resolve some of the current controversies regarding a number of psychological phenomena in motivation, learning, and perception.

In summary, we have suggested that the subject must be recognized as an active participant in any experiment, and that it may be fruitful to view the psychological experiment as a very special form of social interaction. We have proposed that the subject's behavior in an experiment is a function of the totality of the situation, which includes the experimental variables being investigated and at least one other set of variables which we have subsumed under the heading, demand characteristics of the experimental situation. The study and control of demand characteristics are not simply matters of good experimental technique; rather, it is an empirical issue to determine under what circumstances demand characteristics significantly affect subjects' experimental behavior. Several empirical techniques have been proposed for this purpose. It has been suggested that control of these variables in particular may lead to greater reproducibility and ecological validity of psychological experiments. With an increasing understanding of these factors intrinsic to the experimental context, the experimental method in psychology may become a more effective tool in predicting behavior in nonexperimental contexts.

NOTES

1. I wish to thank my associates Ronald E. Shor, Donald N. O'Connell, Ulric Neisser, Karl E. Scheibe, and Emily F. Carota for their comments and criticisms in the preparation of this paper.

2. This paper was presented at the Symposium, "On the Social Psychology of the Psychological Experiment," American Psychological Association Convention, New York, 1961. The work reported here was supported in part by a Public Health Service Research Grant, M-3369, National Institute of Mental Health.

3. See reference list (Pierce, 1908).

4. Ecological validity, in the sense that Brunswik (1947) has used the term: appropriate generalization from the laboratory to nonexperimental situations.

5. These pilot studies were performed by Thomas Menaker.

6. Tasks which would involve the use of actual severe physical pain or exhaustion were not considered.

7. This observation is consistent with Frank's (1944) failure to obtain resistance to disagreeable or nonsensical tasks. He accounts for this "primarily by *S*'s unwillingness to break the tacit agreement he had made when he volunteered to take part in the experiment, namely, to do whatever the experiment required of him" [p. 24].

8. This hypothesis is subject to empirical test. We should predict that there would be measurable differences in motivation between subjects who perceive a particular experiment as "significant" and those who perceive the experiment as "unimportant."

9. Rosenthal (1961) in his recent work on experimenter bias, has reported a similar type of phenomenon. Biasing was maximized by ego involvement of the experimenters, but when an attempt was made to increase biasing by paying for "good results," there was a marked reduction of effect. This reversal may be ascribed to the experimenters' becoming too aware of their own wishes in the situation.

10. Asch (1952) himself took great pains to avoid this pitfall.

REFERENCES

ASCH, S. E. *Social psychology.* Englewood Cliffs, N.J.: Prentice Hall, 1952.

BRUNSWIK, E. *Systematic and representative design of psychological experiments with results in physical and social perception.* (Syllabus Series, No. 304) Berkeley: University of California Press, 1947.

DAMASER, E. C., Shor, R. E., & Orne, M. T. Physiological effects during hypnotically-requested emotions. *Psychosomatic Medicine*, 1963, **25**: 334–343.

FRANK, J. D. Experimental studies of personal pressure and resistance: I. Experimental production of resistance. *Journal of General Psychology*, 1944, **30**: 23–41.

ORNE, M. T. The demand characteristics of an experimental design and their implications. Paper read at American Psychological Association, Cincinnati, 1959. (a)

ORNE, M. T. The nature of hypnosis: Artifact and essence. *Journal of Abnormal and Social Psychology*, 1959, **58**: 277–299. (b)

ORNE, M. T., & Scheibe, K. E. The contribution of nondeprivation factors in the production of sensory deprivation effects: The psychology of the "panic button." *Journal of Abnormal and Social Psychology*, 1964, **68**: 3–12.

PIERCE, A. H. The subconscious again. *Journal of Philosophy, Psychology, and Scientific Methodology*, 1908, **5**: 264–271.

RIECKEN, H. W. A program for research on experiments in social psychology. Paper read at Behavioral Sciences Conference, University of New Mexico, 1958.

ROSENTHAL, R. On the social psychology of the psychological experiment: With particular reference to experimenter bias. Paper read at American Psychological Association, New York, 1961.

SARBIN, T. R. Contributions to role-taking theory: 1. Hypnotic behavior. *Psychological Review*, 1950, 57: 255–270.

SHOR, R. E. Explorations in hypnosis: A theoretical and experimental study. Unpublished doctoral dissertation, Brandeis University, 1959.

STARE, F., Brown, J., & Orne, M. T. Demand characteristics in sensory deprivation studies. Unpublished seminar paper, Massachusetts Mental Health Center and Harvard University, 1959.

Milton J. Rosenberg

When Dissonance Fails:

On Eliminating Evaluation Apprehension from Attitude Measurement[1]

Certain studies that have been important in advancing the dissonance-theory explanation of attitude-change phenomena seem to be open to a particular kind of reinterpretation. After an explanatory discussion of some general considerations from which this reinterpretation derives we shall turn to an experiment that attempts to put it to a critical test.

Theorists from Thomas and Znaniecki (1918) to Lewin (1935) have contended that the person's "definition of the situation" is the ground from which behavior emerges and takes its direction. But psychologists have tended to miss the relevance of this nearly banal proposition as it might apply to the understanding of psychological research itself. For most human subjects psychological experiments are ambiguous situations, sometimes exhilarating, sometimes provocative of curiosity or anxiety; and all these forms of arousal are likely to set them searching for the possibly veiled meanings of the experimental situation. Just how the subject *does define* the situation, and thus how he is likely to behave in it, may often be affected by those differences in treatment manipulations or in instructions that distinguish one experimental condition from another. When such intercell differences in definition of the situation are not intended, they may contaminate the design and lead to false confirmation or, for that matter, to false disconfirmation of hypotheses. Two separate ways in which this may happen will be explicated here.

Evaluation Apprehension as a Research Contaminant

It is proposed that the typical human subject approaches the typical psychological experiment with a preliminary expectation that the

From *Journal of Personality and Social Psychology*, 1965, **1**: 28–42. Copyright © 1965 by The American Psychological Association and reprinted with permission of author and The American Psychological Association.

psychologist may undertake to evaluate his (the subject's) emotional adequacy, his mental health or lack of it. Members of the general public, including students in introductory psychology courses, have usually learned (despite our occasional efforts to persuade them otherwise) to attribute special abilities along these lines to those whose work is perceived as involving psychological interests and skills.[2] Even when the subject is convinced that his adjustment is not being directly studied he is likely to think that the experimenter is nevertheless bound to be sensitive to any behavior that bespeaks poor adjustment or immaturity.

In experiments the subject's initial suspicion that he may be exposing himself to evaluation will usually be confirmed or disconfirmed (as he perceives it) in the early stages of his encounter with the experimenter. Whenever it *is* confirmed, or to the extent that it is, the typical subject will be likely to experience *evaluation apprehension*; that is, an active, anxiety-toned concern that he win a positive evaluation from the experimenter, or at least that he provide no grounds for a negative one. Personality variables will have some bearing upon the extent to which this pattern of apprehension develops. But equally important are various aspects of the experimental design such as the experimenter's explanatory "pitch," the types of measures used, and the experimental manipulations themselves.

Such factors may operate with equal potency across all cells of an experiment; but we shall focus upon the more troublesome situation in which treatment differences between experimental groups make for differential arousal and confirmation of evaluation apprehension. The particular difficulty with this state of affairs is that subjects in groups experiencing comparatively high levels of evaluation apprehension will be more prone than subjects in other groups to interpret the experimenter's instructions, explanations, and measures for what they may convey about the kinds of responses that will be considered healthy or unhealthy, mature or immature. In other words, they will develop *hypotheses* about how to win positive evaluation or how to avoid negative evaluation. And usually the subjects in such an experimental group are enough alike in their perceptual reactions to the situation so that there will be considerable similarity in the hypotheses at which they separately arrive. This similarity may, in turn, operate to systematically influence experimental responding in ways that foster false confirmation of the experimenter's predictions.

Let us consider one example of a situation in which some well-known findings might be accounted for in these terms. It seems quite conceivable that in certain dissonance experiments the use of surprisingly large monetary rewards for eliciting counterattitudinal arguments may seem quite strange to the subject, may suggest that he is being treated disingenuously. This in turn is likely to confirm initial expectations that evaluation is somehow being undertaken. As a result the typical subject, once exposed to this manipulation, may be aroused to a comparatively high level of evaluation apprehension; and, guided by the figural fact that an excessive reward has been offered, he may be led to hypothesize that the experimental situation is one in which his autonomy, his honesty, his resoluteness in resisting a special kind of bribe, are being tested. Thus, given the patterning of their initial expectations and the routinized cultural meanings of some of the main features of the experimental situation, most low-dissonance subjects may come to reason somewhat as follows: "they probably want to see whether getting paid so much will affect my own attitude, whether it will influence me, whether I am the kind of person whose views can be changed by buying him off."

The subject who has formulated such a subjective hypothesis about the real purpose of the experimental situation will be prone to resist giving evidence of attitude change; for to do so would, as he perceives it, convey something unattractive about himself, would lead to his being negatively evaluated by the experimenter. On the other hand, a similar hypothesis would be less likely to occur to the subject who is offered a smaller monetary reward and thus he would be less likely to resist giving evidence of attitude change.

Affect toward the Experimenter as a Research Contaminant

Yet another and even simpler type of possible systematic bias should be noted. This involves the unsuspected affective consequences of designs which call for the experimenter to behave differently toward persons in different conditions of an experiment. Under certain circumstances such differences may generate further differences in how subjects feel toward the experimenter or toward his experiment; and these intercell affective differences too may have the final consequence of influencing experimental responses in ways which make for false confirmation of hypotheses. Thus, turning again to dissonance studies in which subjects are offered large rewards for the writing of counterattitudinal essays, this manipulation, instead of creating low dissonance, may establish comparatively high arousal of the suspicion that one is being deceived; and this in turn may generate anger. A possible consequence is that the low-dissonance subject, provoked to hostility by the suspected duplicity, may find emotional release in refusing to show the response (attitude change) that he perceives the experimenter to be after.

Contaminant Control by Altered Replication

One way of checking upon the presence of these types of contamination is to ask the subject how he interpreted the purpose and meaning of the experiment. This will often be possible but it may sometimes involve one major hazard: such interviewing in itself can be open to the very kinds of contamination it seeks to disclose. Another approach is to conduct an altered replication of the original experiment, one in which we redesign those of its aspects that are presumed to have fostered the contaminating processes. Not only does such an approach enable application of the law of parsimony in interpreting the relation of data to theoretical claims, it also facilitates further study of the social psychology of the psychological experiment.[3] In pursuit of these goals much of this paper will report and discuss an altered replication of one important study that has been presented as confirming the prediction that counterattitudinal advocacy will generate greater attitude change when undertaken for a small reward than when undertaken for a large one. First it will be necessary to consider the background, design, and results of the original study upon which the present altered replication is based.

From the dissonance point of view counterattitudinal behavior, or even the commitment to undertake it, will lead to attitude change in inverse proportion to the strength and number of cognitions that could be used to justify such behavior (Brehm, 1960). Of the many conceivable types of counterattitudinal performance the one that has been most frequently studied both by dissonance theorists and others has been advocacy, in oral or written form, of an attitude position opposite to the subject's actual private attitude (Carlson, 1956; Culbertson, 1957; Janis & King, 1954; Kelman, 1953; Scott, 1957, 1959).

In most of the relevant dissonance studies the justification variable has been operationalized in one of three ways: subjects are given high or low choice in deciding whether to undertake counterattitudinal advocacy (for example, Cohen & Latané in Brehm & Cohen, 1962); they are told that their performances will be of great or little value for interested other parties (for example, Cohen, Brehm, & Fleming, 1958); or they are given or promised large or small monetary, or other, rewards (for example, Festinger & Carlsmith, 1959).

The study upon which the present paper is focused was conducted by Cohen and is one of the many recently reported by Brehm and Cohen (1962). Its general design was similar to earlier dissonance studies except that it used four levels of monetary reward, instead of the usual two. The prediction was that with this graded range of monetary rewards the resulting attitude change would be monotonically and inversely related to the size of the reward.

The subjects were Yale undergraduates. The issue concerned the actions of the New Haven police in a campus riot that had occurred a few weeks earlier. The experimenter, appearing at randomly chosen dormitory rooms, introduced himself as a "member of an Institute of

Human Relations research team," ascertained by verbal inquiry that the subject disapproved of the actions of the police, and asked him to write an essay in support of the actions of the police.[4] The request for the counterattitudinal essay was explained in this way:

It has been shown that one of the best ways to get relevant arguments, on both sides of an issue, is to ask people to write essays favoring only one side. . . . What we really need now are some essays favoring the police side. I understand that you have very different views on the matter, but as you can see it's very interesting to know what kinds of arguments people bring up in their essays if they have different opinions about it.

The reward manipulation was then introduced by telling the subject that he would receive a particular sum for "writing the essay against your own position." Eight subjects were offered $.50, 6 were offered $1, 10 others were offered $5, 6 others were offered $10. The subject wrote his essay on a blank sheet headed "Why the New Haven Police Actions Were Justified." He was then told:

Now that you have looked at some of the reasons for the actions of the New Haven police, we would like to get some of your reactions to the issue: *you may possibly want to look at the situation in the light of this.* So, would you please fill out this questionnaire.

The questionnaire on which the subject was invited to indicate approval of the New Haven police, if so inclined, began with this query: "Considering the circumstances, how justified do you think the New Haven police actions were in the recent riot?" An a priori 31-point scale was used with labels at every fifth point and ranging from "completely justified" to "not at all justified." Additional questionnaire items were used to check that the subject correctly perceived the amount of payment that he had been promised and that he had understood that he was to write a strong essay opposite to his own attitude. A control group was given the attitude questionnaire but received neither the manipulation nor the other measures.

It was found that the $5 and $10 groups did not differ significantly from the control group in expressed attitude toward the New Haven police. However, the subjects in the $.50 group were less negative toward the New Haven police than the $1 subjects ($p < .05$) who in turn were less negative than the $10 subjects ($p < .05$); and both the $.50 and $1 groups differed significantly from the control group.

Thus in the main the data appeared to confirm the original prediction. However, the point of view outlined above would suggest that in this study, as in others of similar design, the low-dissonance (high-reward) subjects would be more likely to suspect that the experimenter had some unrevealed purpose. The gross discrepancy between spending a few minutes writing an essay and the large sum offered, the fact that this large sum had not yet been delivered by the time the subject was handed the attitude questionnaire, the fact that he was virtually invited to show that he had become more positive toward the New Haven police: all these could have served to engender suspicion and thus to arouse evaluation apprehension and negative affect toward the experimenter. Either or both of these motivating states could probably be most efficiently reduced by the subject refusing to show anything but fairly strong disapproval of the New Haven police; for the subject who had come to believe that his autonomy in the face of a monetary lure was being assessed, remaining "antipolice" would demonstrate that he *had* autonomy; for the subject who perceived an indirect and disingenuous attempt to change his attitude and felt some reactive anger, holding fast to his original attitude could appear to be a relevant way of frustrating the experimenter.[5] Furthermore, with each *step* of increase in reward we could expect an increase in the proportion of subjects who had been brought to a motivating level of evaluation apprehension or affect arousal.

How can such an interpretation be tested? If it is correct it points to the importance of the fact that the experimenter conducts both the dissonance arousal and the attitude measurement. Evaluation apprehension and negative affect, if they exist, have been focused upon the experimenter; and it would be either to avoid his negative evaluation or to frustrate him, or both, that the high-reward subject would hold back (from the experimenter and possibly even from himself) any evidence of having been influenced by the essay he had just completed.

The most effective way, then, to eliminate the influence of the biasing factors would be to separate the dissonance arousal phase of the experiment from the attitude measurement phase. The experiment should be organized so that it appears to the subject to be two separate, unrelated studies, conducted by investigators who have little or no relationship with each other and who are pursuing different research interests. In such a situation the evaluation apprehension and negative affect that are focused upon the dissonance-arousing experimenter would probably be lessened and, more important, they would not govern the subject's responses to the attitude-measuring experimenter and to the information that he seeks from the subject.

This was the main change introduced into the original design.[6] A second change was that the reward manipulation involved not only telling the subject that he would be paid a certain amount, but also the actual delivery of that amount to him immediately after he completed the essay. It was assumed that this change too would work to reduce the likelihood that the high-reward subjects would develop suspicions concerning the experimenter's possible duplicity and unrevealed purposes.

Adherence to the dissonance view would suggest that under these altered conditions the results would still show an inverse relationship between magnitude of reward and extent of attitude change. Indeed the significance of the dissonance-confirming relationship might be expected to increase; for now with each subject having actually received a monetary reward the cognitions concerning reasons for undertaking the counterattitudinal performance would be less variable within experimental groups than could have been the case in the original experiment.

However, the consistency theory developed by the present author (Rosenberg, 1956, 1960) suggests the opposite prediction. It holds that the most usual basis for attitude change is the establishment of new beliefs about the attitude object, beliefs that are inconsistent with the original affective orientation toward that object. In this view the significance of a reward received for writing a counterattitudinal essay (that is, for improvising or rehearsing inconsistency-generating cognitions) would be different from that claimed in dissonance theory: such a reward would, in proportion to its magnitude, be likely to have a positive effect both upon the development and the stabilization of the new cognitions. From this it would be predicted that with the removal of the biasing factors the degree of attitude change obtained after the subjects have written counterattitudinal essays will vary directly, rather than inversely, with the amount of reward. Thus the altered design outlined here may afford something approximating a critical test between this approach and the dissonance approach as regards their applicability to predicting the attitude-change effects of counterattitudinal advocacy.

METHOD

Attitude Issue and Subjects

To replicate as closely as possible, except for the major changes that distinguish the present study from its model, the author sought an issue comparable to "the actions of the New Haven police." Late in 1961 the Ohio State University football team, having won the Big Ten championship, received an invitation to the Rose Bowl. Concerned with the extent to which its reputation as the "football capital of the world" weakened OSU's academic reputation and performance, the faculty council of the University voted to reject the invitation and thereby engendered, both in the student body and the surrounding community, a sense of incredulous outrage. This, through the promptings of local news media, was rapidly turned toward active protest. The immediate result was a riot in which a large crowd of undergraduates (estimates varied between one to three thousand) stormed through University buildings shouting pro-Rose-Bowl and antifaculty slogans. The more longlasting result was the stabilization among the undergraduates of an attitude of disapproval toward any limitation upon Rose Bowl participation. This attitude remained salient during the following year and even in the face of the fact that during that year the faculty council, by a close vote, reversed its original decision. In general, interested students felt that future faculty interference with participation in bowl games continued to be a real possibility.

With a pilot questionnaire administered early in 1963 it was confirmed that opposition to a Rose Bowl ban remained a consensual position among the undergraduate body; more than 94 percent of the sample indicated strong disapproval toward any restoration of the ban in the future. Upon completion of this pilot study a new group of male subjects was recruited from sections of introductory psychology for participation in the present study. In all, 51 subjects were finally used. Ten were randomly assigned to each of three experimental conditions and 21 to a control condition.

Dissonance Arousal

As each experimental subject arrived at the author's office he found him busily engaged either in writing or in a conversation with another "student." The experimenter then told the subject:

> I'm sorry but I'm running late on my schedule today and I'll have to keep you waiting for about fifteen or twenty minutes. Is this all right?

Most subjects simply said it was though a few expressed concern about getting to their next class on time. All of the latter, when assured that the work the experimenter wanted them to do would take no more than twenty minutes, accepted the situation with equanimity. The experimenter then said:

> Oh, I've just thought of something; while you are waiting you could participate in another little experiment that some graduate student in education is doing.

The experimenter explained that he had had a call the previous day from the "graduate student" who needed volunteers in a hurry for

> some sort of study he's doing—I don't know what it's about exactly except that it has to do with attitudes and that's why he called me, because my research is in a similar area as you'll see later. [The experimenter went on to say] Of course he can't give you any credit [the usual research credit point used to keep up experimental participation rates in introductory psychology courses] but I gather they have some research funds and that they are paying people instead. So if you care to go down there you can.

All but three subjects indicated that they did want to participate in the other study. (The three who did not were eliminated from the experiment.) With some show of effort and uncertainty the experimenter then recalled the name of the education graduate student and the room, actually located in the education department, where he could be found.

Upon reporting to the "education graduate student" the subject received an explanation modeled word-for-word upon that used in the earlier experiment reported by Brehm and Cohen. Also, as in that experiment, it was determined by verbal inquiry that the subject held an attitude position opposite to the one he was to argue for in the essay. Subjects were randomly assigned to one of three reward conditions ($.50, $1, $5), and the amount that each subject was to receive was made clear to him before he undertook to write an essay on why the OSU football team should not be allowed to participate in the Rose Bowl. After the subject had completed the essay he was *paid* the amount that he had been promised, then thanked for his participation and dismissed. He then returned to the experimenter's office and, under the guise of participating in another study, his attitudes toward the Rose Bowl ban and toward various other issues were ascertained.

Attitude Measurement

This phase of the study began by the experimenter telling the subject that the study for which his participation had originally been solicited was a continuing survey on student attitudes "that I run every semester as a sort of Gallup poll to keep a check on opinion patterns on different University issues." (The experimenter, of course, did not know at this point which of the three magnitudes of reward the subject had received for writing the essay). The subject then filled out an attitude questionnaire dealing with eight different issues. One of these read, "How would you feel if it were decided that from now on the OSU football team would not be allowed to participate in the Rose Bowl?" Following the procedure in the earlier study the subject responded on a 31-point graphic scale, marked at every fifth point by these labels: I think this decision would be not justified at all; very little justified; little justified; slightly justified; rather justified (instead of "quite justified" as in the earlier study); very justified; completely justified.

The same scale form was used with the other seven issues. One of these dealt with the area of varsity athletics and read, "How would you feel if it were decided that the University would no longer give any athletic scholar-ships?" This issue was included to provide another and more indirect test of the attitude-change consequences of writing the anti-Rose-Bowl essay under varying conditions of reward. The other six issues dealt with nonathletic matters such as dormitory regulations, University admission policies, library rules, etc.

When the subject had completed this questionnaire he was asked what he thought the experiment was really about. His responses during a period of subsequent inquiry were transcribed and these were to be analyzed for the extent to which they reflected any suspicion that the two experiments were actually related to one another. The subject then filled out a follow-up questionnaire. The first item asked, "while you were filling out the opinion questionnaire did it occur to you that there might be some connection between this experiment and the one you worked on in the education department?" After he had answered this item the subject was told that in fact there had been "a connection between the two experiments" and that it would all be explained after he completed the questionnaire. The subject then proceeded to answer the other questions which asked how strong an essay he had agreed to write, how strong an essay he did write, how free he had felt in his decision to write the essay, how getting paid for the essay had made him feel, etc. Each of the questions was answered by choosing one of a number of alternative positions.

The experimenter then told the subject about the nature (but not the purpose) of the deception that had been used and proceeded to engage him in an interview designed to elicit further evidence of any doubts or suspicions that the subject might have felt during the experiment. The experimenter then explained the actual purpose of the experiment, commenting both upon its basic hypothesis and its design, and then answered all of the subject's questions. Before the subject was thanked and dismissed he was urged not to speak of the experiment to any fellow students during the remainder of the academic semester. All subjects promised to comply with this request.

In distinction to the experimental subjects each of the control subjects, upon reporting for his appointment, was merely told that the experimenter was conducting "a sort of Gallup poll on University issues" and then filled out the attitude questionnaire.

RESULTS

In all, 62 subjects were originally run through the experiment. Eleven were discarded from the final analysis because on one basis or another they failed to meet necessary conditions that had been specified in advance. Six subjects (two originally assigned to the control condition and four to the experimental conditions) were rejected because postexperimental questioning revealed that they were members of varsity athletic teams. It had been decided that persons in this category would not be used since their pro-Rose-Bowl attitudes could be assumed to be considerably stronger, more firmly anchored, than those of other students. Two other subjects, originally assigned to experimental groups, were discarded from the analysis because they evidenced virtually complete and spontaneous insight into the deception that had been employed. One other subject was discarded because he reported, on the postexperimental questionnaire, that he had been asked to write a "weak" rather than a "strong" essay. Two additional experimental subjects were discarded because they impressed both the experimenter and his assistant as showing psychotic tendencies. However, when the analysis reported below is repeated with the last three rejected subjects *included* the findings are in no wise altered.

Except for the manipulated independent variable, other factors that might influence attitudinal response appear to have remained constant across experimental groups. Thus on the postexperimental questionnaire the subjects in the three experimental groups do not differ in their perceptions as to how strong an essay they were asked to write or actually did write; nor do they differ in their self-reports on how free they felt to refuse. From the postexperimental interview data it appears that though a few subjects were surprised to find the Rose Bowl situation featured in the "two different experiments," the groups were equally lacking in insight both as regards the deception that was used and as regards the real purpose of the experiment.[7]

It will be remembered that the measurement phase of the present study consisted of a questionnaire concerned with eight different University issues. On the six issues concerning matters unrelated to athletic policy, and thus not subjected to manipulation through the essay-writing procedure, statistical analysis reveals no overall differences and no differences between any specific groups taken two at a time.

Table 4-1   *Group Means and Differences between Groups on Attitude toward the Rose Bowl Ban*

		GROUP DIFFERENCES*			
Group	M	$.50	$1	$.50 and $1	$5
Control	1.45	z = 1.97	z = 1.80	z = 2.31	z = 3.93
		p < .03	p < .04	p < .015	p < .0001
$.50	2.24		z = .11		z = 1.77
					p < .04
$1	2.32				z = 1.81
					p < .04
$.50 and $1	2.28				z = 2.11
					p < .02
$5	3.24				

Note.—Overall difference between groups as assessed by Kruskal-Wallis test: $H = 17.89$, $p < .001$.
* Tested by Mann-Whitney z, one-tailed.

On the main matter of experimental interest, whether attitude change on the Rose Bowl and athletic-scholarship issues varies directly or inversely with the magnitude of monetary reward, the data reviewed below reveal that the former is the case; that is, the prediction drawn from a consistency-theory interpretation appears to be confirmed and the opposite prediction based upon dissonance theory appears thereby to be disconfirmed.

Scoring the 31-point attitude scale from 1.0 (for the banning of Rose Bowl participation would be "not justified at all") through 1.2, 1.4 . . . to 6.8, 7.0 (banning Rose Bowl participation would be "completely justified") we find the following mean scores: 1.45 for the control group, 2.24 for the $.50 reward group, 2.32 for the $1 reward group, and 3.24 for the $5 reward group. The attitude score ranges are 1–3 for the control group, 1–4 for the $.50 group, 1–5 for the $1 group, and 2–6 for the $5 group.

The significance of the reward variable in its influence upon attitude toward a Rose Bowl ban was assessed by computing the Kruskal-Wallis one-way analysis of variance from the ranked scores of all groups. *H*, which is distributed as chi square, equals 17.89 and has a chance probability of less than .001 (see Table 4–1). In addition to this overall confirmation of the original prediction it is desirable to test the significance of differences between the specific groups.

Analysis by the Mann-Whitney rank sum test (computing *z*; see Mosteller & Bush, 1954) reveals that there is no significant difference between the \$.50 and \$1 groups. Accordingly in some of the additional analyses these two groups were combined. As Table 4–1 indicates the combined \$.50–\$1 group is significantly more favorable toward banning Rose Bowl participation than is the control group ($p < .015$) and significantly less favorable than the \$5 group ($p < .02$). When the \$.50 and \$1 groups are analyzed separately, each is found to be significantly different from both the control and \$5 conditions (see Table 4–1). As would be expected, the difference between the control and \$5 groups is of very large significance ($p < .0001$).

Thus the only deviation from the original prediction in this set of findings is the absence of a significant difference between the \$.50 and \$1 groups. Since these groups do differ as predicted from both the control and \$5 groups, respectively, it might be conjectured that the \$.50 difference between them does not generate a large enough *subjective* difference in the magnitude of payment. However, the alternative possibility that even this small magnitude of difference in reward does have some subtler influence upon attitude is suggested by the additional data regarding the issue of abandoning the policy of giving athletic scholarships.

This issue was used as a second test of the basic hypothesis. The expectation was that attitude change on the Rose Bowl issue should tend to *generalize* toward a similar issue, one that suggests another way of deemphasizing the role of varsity sports in university life. It would of course be expected that the group differences would be of lesser magnitude on this issue than on the Rose Bowl issue since the latter served as the actual topic for the counterattitudinal essay.

Analysis of the subjects' responses on the athletic-scholarship issue reveals again a pattern of findings that supports the original hypothesis. Responding on a 31-point scale from 1.0 to 7.0 (with higher scores indicating greater approval for "abandoning athletic scholarships") the groups yield the following mean scores: 2.28 for the control group, 2.26 for the \$.50 group, 3.04 for the \$1 group, and 3.88 for the \$5 group. The score ranges are 1–7 for the control group, 1–4.8 for the \$.50 group, 1–6 for the \$1 group, and 1.2–7 for the \$5 group.

Application of the Kruskal-Wallis test indicates a significant main effect ($H = 14.50, p < .005$); thus the extent to which the writing of the essay affects an attitude *related* to the topic of the essay is shown to be a positive monotonic function of the amount of reward.

Analysis of the differences between the specific groups as reported in Table 4–2 clarifies certain interesting details. While the mean attitude scores of the control and $.50 groups are virtually identical,

Table 4-2 *Group Means and Differences between Groups on Attitude toward Ending Athletic Scholarships*

			GROUP DIFFERENCES*	
Group	M	$.50	$1	$5
Control	2.28	z = .95	z = 1.33	z = 2.45
		p < .20	p < .10	p < .01
$.50	2.26		z = 1.09	z = 2.36
			p < .15	p < .01
Control and $.50	2.27		z = 1.44	z = 2.67
			p < .08	p < .005
$1	3.04			z = 1.24
				p < .12
$5	3.88			

Note.—Overall difference between groups as assessed by Kruskal-Wallis test; $H = 14.50$, $p < .005$.
* Tested by Mann-Whitney z, one-tailed.

there is a slight and insignificant trend ($p < .20$) toward a greater concentration of extreme negative scores in the control group. The difference between the control and $1 groups comes closer to an acceptable probability level ($p < .10$), reflecting the greater differences in means (control = 2.28, $1 = 3.04) reported above.

As predicted, the control and $.50 groups do show significantly less approval of abandoning athletic scholarships than does the $5 group; $p < .01$ in both cases. When the control and $.50 groups are combined the difference from the $5 group has a probability of less than .005 as compared to less than .08 when the difference between the combined group and the $1 group is assessed. The $1 group clearly stands in an intermediate position. While its mean attitude score reflects greater endorsement of the antiathletic scholarship view than does the $.50 group and less endorsement than the $5 group, neither of these differences ($p < .15$ and $p < .12$, respectively) reaches significance.

Thus in comparison to the $.50 group the $1 group is less clearly differentiated from the $5 group and more clearly differentiated from the control group. From this it is apparent that the difference in size of reward between the $.50 and $1 groups does have some influence upon the extent to which the writing of the essay affected the subjects' attitudes on a related issue; and that influence too is consistent with the prediction that attitude change following counterattitudinal performance will be a *positive* function of the degree of reward received for such performance.

A question of considerable interest is why the difference between the $.50 and $1 groups shows up more clearly on a related issue rather than on the issue with which the essay was directly concerned. One possible interpretation emerges when we recall that the $.50 group does differ significantly from the control group on the Rose Bowl issue but does not show such a difference on the athletic-scholarship issue. With this small amount of reward there may be a minimal likelihood that the induced attitude change will generalize to a similar issue; with the somewhat larger reward of $1 a somewhat stronger tendency toward generalization may be operative.

On the basis of the findings that have so far been presented, the following conclusion seems warranted: when the design of the original study reported by Brehm and Cohen is altered so as to eliminate aspects that were likely to have generated evaluation apprehension and unsuspected affect arousal, the prediction that guided the present study is confirmed and the original dissonance prediction is disconfirmed.

DISCUSSION

This paper has combined two purposes: to present some propositions about how subjects' perceptions of experimental situations may affect their experimental performances; and, on this basis, to report an experimental reexamination of the dissonance-theory interpretation of attitude change due to counterattitudinal advocacy.

As regards the first purpose, the confirmation of the predictions in the present study lends support to the original propositions about evaluation apprehension and affect arousal; for it was in part on the basis of those propositions that the experimental predictions were formulated. However, more direct investigation of these contaminating processes is possible and desirable. For example, in two recent studies the author has, by intention rather than by inadvertence, supplied cues to the subjects about types of responding that might connote maturity and immaturity. In one of these studies some subjects were led to believe that mature persons like strangers more than immature people do while other subjects were led to believe the opposite. In a second study some subjects were led to believe that mature people perform well on dull arithmetic tasks while others were led to believe that immature people do better at such tasks. The results of these studies, to be reported elsewhere, strongly demonstrate the power of evaluation apprehension in controlling experimental responding.

However, it is necessary that we go beyond such demonstration studies if these contaminating processes are to be better understood and thus more effectively controlled. A number of questions remain to be investigated. Do such personality variables as passivity, low self-esteem, and the need for social approval predict to the likelihood that evaluation apprehension will be aroused in the experimental situation? Does evaluation apprehension, once aroused, interact with experimenter bias (see Rosenthal, 1963) in a way that guides the subject in his hypothesizing about the kinds of responding that will win approval? Will exposure to psychological perspectives, as in the introductory courses from which so many subjects are drawn, tend to heighten the likelihood of experiencing evaluation apprehension in the experimental situation? Is there a minority of subjects who seek *negative* evaluation for masochistic purposes or as a way of asking for help, and will this affect their experimental responding? Can the presence of evaluation apprehension be uncovered by postexperimental inquiry? Comparable questions about the arousal of aggressive and other contaminating affective states could just as readily be formulated. Indeed, it would seem desirable in further studies to attempt an operational separation of the two types of contamination that have been stressed in this paper.

In general, the recently developed interest in investigating the experimenter-subject interaction as a source of bias in psychological research is a long-needed innovation. The work of Orne (1962), Riecken (1962), Rosenthal (1963), and others has provided a most useful beginning. To the list of research contaminating processes that they have investigated, might well be added those that have been discussed here.

As regards the second major focus of this paper, do the present findings call the validity of dissonance theory into question? Recently, there have been reported many challenging studies testing that theory's pertinence not only to attitude change but also to perceptual and motivational processes and even to learning phenomena.[8] Thus the present study, taken alone, cannot be interpreted as challenging the general theory as such. However, it does seem to indicate that, at least in its account of the attitude-change consequences of counterattitudinal advocacy, dissonance theory has been overextended.

In the author's view, the kind of counterattitudinal performance that best fits the dissonance paradigm is a simple overt act that directly violates one's private attitude (for example, eating or agreeing to eat a disliked food; expressing approval of a disliked proposal or candidate; merely *committing* oneself to develop counterattitudinal arguments; etc.). But when a person actually *does* elaborate a set of arguments opposite to his own attitude, the dissonance he experiences is probably of much wider scope than dissonance analysis would have it; it encompasses considerably more than merely realizing that he has argued against his own position. The broader pattern of inconsistency that he encounters is that between the content and apparent plausibility, on the one hand, of the new arguments that he has developed and, on the other hand, his original affective judgement of the attitude object.

Thus, the subject who opposes the Rose Bowl ban and then argues in favor of it may come up with some good arguments (for example, "If we ban going to the Rose Bowl we will improve our reputation as a serious University . . . we will draw better students," etc.). In so doing he may become convinced of the validity of those arguments. This will produce intraattitudinal inconsistency; that is, the newly established beliefs relating the Rose Bowl ban to positive ends and values will be inconsistent with the original negative affect toward the ban.

As was suggested earlier, the author's theoretical model (Rosenberg, 1956, 1960) takes this sort of inconsistency to be a basic condition for the occurrence of attitude change. It will be useful to show how this alternative model may be applied to interpreting the process of counter-attitudinal advocacy. From this standpoint, attitudes normally are stable, affective-cognitive structures and feature considerable internal consistency. It is assumed that the production of *inconsistency* through change in either the affective or cognitive component (the latter being more usual and likely) will, if it transcends the individual's tolerance limits, motivate further symbolic activity. This may lead either to the restoration of the original attitude or, if this line of defense is not available, to its reorganization in the opposite direction.

For the sequence that begins with cognitive alterations, what is required is that the new cognitions be sufficiently internalized and difficult to reverse; then the most likely outcome will be for the affective disposition toward the attitude object to move in the direction consistent with the newly established cognitions. Thus attitude change in its conventional sense will have occurred.

In this context, a basic question is: what will render the new, inconsistency-generating cognitions sufficiently internalized and difficult to reverse? Many variables could have this influence; but in the present study the necessary suggestion would be that the most important is the amount of reward expected and received for *developing* such cognitions. Putting this another way, it may be hypothesized that the demonstrated influence of the magnitude of payment upon ultimate attitude change is mediated through its effects upon the cognitive processes that are activated during the essay-writing task.

Broadly speaking, two separate kinds of mediation are easily conceivable: the *expectation* of payment for counterattitudinal advocacy may operate as an incentive and thus affect the quality of the arguments advanced in support of the new cognitions; the *receipt* of payment may operate as a reinforcement that further fosters the internalization of the counterattitudinal cognitions; and of course the scope of these two processes would be expected to vary as a function of the actual amount of payment.

A subsidiary analysis of the essays themselves tends to support and clarify this view. One unequivocal finding is that the $.50 and $1 groups differ in the actual number of words per essay, the latter group writing the longer ones ($p < .05$).[9] However, the $1 and $5 groups do not show any such difference. Considering that the $.50 and $1 groups do not differ on the Rose Bowl issue while the $1 and $5 groups do, sheer verbal productivity does not seem to mediate the main effect. Furthermore, separate analyses within each of the three experimental groups reveal absolutely no relationship between essay length and the post-essay attitude toward the Rose Bowl ban.

But do the essays vary in quality, in the actual *persuasiveness* with which they are written; and if so does this relate to the postessay attitude score? Two judges, working without knowledge of the different reward conditions and using a 5-point scale, rated all the essays for their basic persuasiveness. As part of their instructions they were asked to ignore the length of essays "because a long one may often be less persuasive than a short one." The interjudge reliability of these ratings proved quite adequate: for 80 percent of the essays, the two ratings were either identical or within 1 point of each other.

Six of the 20 subjects in the combined $.50 and $1 group had persuasiveness scores that were lower (1 and 1.5, based on the pooled ratings of the two judges) than any that occurred in the $5 group. Four of these 6 subjects also had extreme negative attitudes. A comparable finding is obtained when we split the $.50–$1 group into approximately equal low persuasiveness and high persuasiveness halves. Those who wrote comparatively unpersuasive essays show significantly more attitudinal negativism toward the Rose Bowl ban than those who wrote comparatively persuasive essays ($p < .03$). When this same sort of analysis is separately performed with the $.50 and $1 groups, respectively, similar findings are obtained with borderline significance ($p < .10$ in both instances). On the other hand within the high-reward group a division of the subjects into those who got the five lowest (though not as low as the comparable subjects in the low-reward group) and the five highest persuasiveness ratings does not yield any corresponding difference in attitudes toward the Rose Bowl ban.

An exactly similar finding is obtained when we use as the estimate of persuasiveness not the judges' ratings but the subjects' own post-experimental judgments of "how strong" their essays actually were. In the combined low-reward group, those below the median in their self-ratings are less favorable to the Rose Bowl ban than those above the median ($p < .05$). Again no such effect is discovered in the high-reward group.

From these findings it may be concluded that one mediating source of the overall difference between the low- and high-reward groups is that some of the subjects in the former group were insufficiently motivated by the small reward that had been promised them: in consequence, they wrote insufficiently developed essays, essays that were essentially unpersuasive to themselves. Thus it would seem appropriate to conclude that the overall positive relationship between reward and attitude change reflects the operation of an incentive or effort variable.

However, our analysis need not stop at this point. While some low-reward subjects wrote essays that are rated as extremely low on persuasiveness, others did not. Thus it is possible to match the low- and high-reward groups on this factor and by so doing we can test for the presence of some other process that may also play a role in mediating the overall relationship between reward and attitude change. This was done by simply excluding from the analysis those low-reward subjects who got extremely low ratings (1 and 1.5) on the 5-point persuasiveness scale. With persuasiveness thus equalized (actually the mean persuasiveness score is then slightly *higher* for the remaining low-reward subjects than for the high-reward subjects), the high-reward group *still* shows significantly greater acceptance of the Rose Bowl ban ($p < .05$) and also of the proposal that athletic scholarships be abandoned ($p < .05$). These last findings do thus seem to confirm the expectation that, in addition to the incentive effect of variations in promised reward, there is yet another factor that contributes to the positive relationship between reward and attitude change. It would seem reasonable to interpret this other factor as based not upon the *promise* of reward but rather upon its *receipt*; thus our original conjecture that a reinforcement dynamic may be operative seems, on these grounds, to be rendered more plausible.

The use here of the term reinforcement should not, of course, be taken as referring solely to the kinds of relationships emphasized in conventional models of instrumental learning. In the present study the $5 payment, once received, could have increased the habit strength of the improvised counterattitudinal cognitions by directly increasing their attractiveness and credibility. Similarly, working for an expected large reward could have made the essay-writing a more ego-involving task and thus could have sensitized the subject to pay close attention to the persuasive worth of his own arguments or to find greater merit in them. Furthermore, the amount of payment may also have affected the very clarity with which the new counterattitudinal arguments were remembered after the essay writing session.

In this discussion we have attempted to state, and also to present some additional data in support of, a consistency theory view of how counterattitudinal advocacy produces attitude change. That view can be summarized in the following set of propositions: the counterattitudinal improvisation establishes new cognitions that are inconsistent with the original attitudinal affect; the extent to which the affective judgment of the object will move toward the content of these new cognitions will depend upon the degree of affective-cognitive inconsistency they generate; this in turn will depend upon the strength and stability of the new cognitions; the strength and stability of the new cognitions are influenced, among other things, by the degree of reward received for their improvisation—and this is probably due both to the promised reward operating as an incentive and the received reward as a reinforcement; in consequence, when counterattitudinal advocacy is investigated in a way that circumvents certain biasing factors it will be found, as in the present study, that it produces attitude change in proportion to the magnitude of the reward for such advocacy.

Turning again to dissonance theory and shifting from its approach to one type of attitude change to its approach toward attitude change *generally*, the author would venture the judgment that dissonance research in this area has been complicated by certain difficult methodological and interpretive issues. Thus, as Chapanis and Chapanis (1964) have noted, it is common to many of these studies that they do not investigate the subject's personal reactions to the dissonance-arousing situation, that the magnitudes of attitude change are often quite small, and that often a rather large number of subjects is, for one or another theory-based reason, eliminated from analysis. To this must be added the present demonstration that, in experiments on counterattitudinal advocacy, certain data-biasing processes may be invoked to account for reported findings. Indeed, since dissonance studies on other types of attitude change also place some, but not other, subjects in highly puzzling and unexpected situations it should be recognized that in these studies, as well, biased contamination may often affect the results obtained. In the light of all these points, it would seem desirable to undertake an empirical reexamination of some of the major studies that have been offered as confirming the dissonance analysis of attitude change. In the opinion of the present author, the consequence of such reexamination would not be the disconfirmation of the dissonance view of attitude processes but the discovery that its generality is of somewhat smaller scope than its advocates have estimated and that certain kinds of attitude change are better predicted and accounted for by other theories.

NOTES

1. This study was carried out while the author was a member of the Psychology Department at Ohio State University. It was supported by Contract 495 (24) with the Group Psychology Branch of the Office of Naval Research. The author is indebted to Frederick Weizmann

for his assistance in executing the experiment and to David Glass and Irving Janis who raised a number of useful questions.

2. As used in this paper the term "psychologist" is merely a convenient categorical simplification. It denotes anyone who "runs" subjects through an experimental or interview procedure and is perceived as being at least somewhat skilled at, and professionally interested in, figuring people out. For example, this is certainly the case when undergraduate subjects participate in a study conducted by an advanced psychology major or graduate student.

3. For a programmatic statement that defines some outstanding prospects and problems in this area see the useful article by Riecken (1962). In his comments on the subject's desire to "put his best foot forward" Riecken is speaking of something rather like the concept of "evaluation apprehension" that has been developed here and more briefly treated earlier (Rosenberg, 1961, 1963). However, for Riecken this is basically a source of "unintended variance" in data and the possibility that it will exert systematic influence making for false validations of hypotheses is not directly examined. Orne (1962) and Rosenthal (1963) have suggested other types of systematic bias. The former has argued that subjects are often motivated to help the experimenter "prove his hypothesis" while the latter has presented evidence that the experimenter's hypotheses or expectations are often indirectly communicated in ways that shape the subject's experimental responding. These views are not in conflict with, nor are they particularly close to, the interpretations offered here. More directly related are the studies on "social desirability" by Edwards (1957) and Crowne and Marlowe (1960). However, these investigators have been basically concerned with sources of invalidity in psychological testing rather than with systematic bias in experiments.

4. It is not clear from the research report whether the experimenter actually referred to himself as a psychologist. But belonging to an "Institute of Human Relations research team" would have been sufficient to establish that he was some sort of psychologist or advanced psychological trainee who would be reporting back to a more senior colleague. This was because the "Institute of Human Relations" was the name of the building that housed the Yale psychology department; no other department that gave undergraduate courses was located there and the research organization for which it was named had long since ceased to exist. The experimenter also described himself as a "fellow student." This may have worked to further heighten the arousal of evaluation apprehension, since the Yale undergraduate culture places great emphasis upon the competitive show of maturity, sophistication, and "all around balance." It would probably be particularly important to the subject that the evaluation of him formed by a psychologically trained "fellow student" be a positive one.

5. Some other reasons (see Footnote 4 for the first) why the experimenter calling himself a "fellow student" might have increased the potency of these biasing processes are worth noting here. Given the fact that the antipolice attitude was highly normative among Yale undergraduates at this time many subjects would have been likely to assume that the experimenter was also antipolice. Thus among the high-reward subjects who made this attribution to the experimenter any tendency to inhibit showing themselves capable of being "bought off" would be further strengthened by the expectation that the experimenter would personally disapprove of the subject's new attitude. On the other hand, if the experimenter was perceived, as he might have been by some subjects, to actually be propolice, the fact that he was a "fellow student" would lead to his being seen as violating an important group standard; and this, particularly for high-reward subjects who might interpret the experimenter as trying to "buy them off" for the propolice side, would have engendered even more anger toward the experimenter than would otherwise have been the case. In turn this would have increased the likelihood that the high-reward subject would resist showing any change in the propolice direction. Thus, both the evaluation apprehension and affect arousal patterns of contamination might well have been intensified by the experimenter being perceived as a fellow student.

6. The author is aware of only one dissonance study in which some attempt was made to separate counterattitudinal advocacy from subsequent attitude measurement; this is the experiment by Festinger and Carlsmith (1959). However, the degree of separation may well have been insufficient. That experiment did not involve, as did the present one, disguising the two phases as two different studies conducted in two different departments. Furthermore, the dependent variable was not change in a previously stable social attitude but rather a momentary rating of how much the subject liked or disliked an experiment just completed.

7. It has been already suggested that in interviews, as in experiments, subjects' responses may often be influenced by their private interpretations of the situation. Thus the post-experimental data collected in this study cannot necessarily be taken at simple face value.

But there is at least one important consideration (probably relevant whenever the credibility of an experimental deception is being assessed) that suggests that the subjects were not holding back evidence of having discerned the true design of the experiment or of having doubted the explanations that were given them. Experienced experimenters will probably agree that college student subjects usually desire to represent themselves as sophisticated and as not easily misled. Thus when the postexperimental interview situation is a permissive one the subjects are likely to disclose, rather than withhold, promptings toward insight. *Yet none of the present subjects revealed any such insights when, after completion of the experiment, they were asked, "What do you think the experiment was really about?"* Later on when *told* by the experimenter that the "two experiments" were really one or still later when the full explanation was given, only a few subjects (two or three per group) claimed to have had suspicions suggestive of what had now been revealed. However, in their attitudinal responses on the two athletic issues these subjects do not differ from others in their groups (that is, they are not clustered in the low, middle, or high portions of the within-group attitude score rankings). Thus it seems likely that most of these particular subjects were exaggerating, and some perhaps were even imagining, their earlier doubts and in so doing were seeking positive evaluation from the experimenter after they had been shown capable of being "taken in." As intended, then, the procedures of the present experiment seem to have achieved their basic purpose which was to avoid, or at least to minimize, the kind of suspicion and disturbing confusion that tends to activate such biasing processes as affect arousal and evaluation apprehension.

8. For example, and despite the fact that the author has found it possible to reinterpret one of the experiments reported by them, the work of Brehm and Cohen (1962) does seem to establish the relevance of the dissonance approach to the study of certain aspects of motivation and does so with considerable inventiveness and concern for methodological issues. Similarly, the work of Lawrence and Festinger (1962) has opened a very interesting new line of inquiry on some problems in the psychology of learning.

9. All probability estimates reported in this discussion are based on a one-tailed interpretation of the Mann-Whitney statistic; in each case it was possible to make a unidirectional prediction about the attitude-change effects of the mediational variable under study.

REFERENCES

BREHM, J. W. A dissonance analysis of attitude-discrepant behavior. In M. J. Rosenberg, C. I. Hovland, W. J. McGuire, R. P. Abelson, & J. W. Brehm (Eds.), *Attitude organization and change.* New Haven: Yale University Press, 1960. Pp. 164–197.

BREHM, J. W., & Cohen, A. R. *Explorations in cognitive dissonance.* New York: Wiley, 1962.

CARLSON, E. R. Attitude change and attitude structure. *Journal of Abnormal and Social Psychology,* 1956, **52**: 256–261.

CHAPANIS, N. P., & Chapanis, A. C. Cognitive dissonance: Five years later. *Psychological Bulletin,* 1964, **61**: 1–22.

COHEN, A. R., Brehm, J. W., & Fleming, W. H. Attitude change and justification for compliance. *Journal of Abnormal and Social Psychology,* 1958, **56**: 276–278.

CROWNE, D. P., & Marlowe, D. A new scale of social desirability independent of psychopathology. *Journal of Consulting Psychology,* 1960, **24**: 349–354.

CULBERTSON, F. M. Modification of an emotionally held attitude through role playing. *Journal of Abnormal and Social Psychology,* 1957, **54**: 230–233.

EDWARDS, A. L. *The social desirability variable in personality assessment and research.* New York: Dryden Press, 1957.

FESTINGER, L., & Carlsmith, J. M. Cognitive consequences of forced compliance. *Journal of Abnormal and Social Psychology,* 1959, **58**: 203–210.

JANIS, I. L., & King, B. T. The influence of role playing on opinion change. *Journal of Abnormal and Social Psychology,* 1954, **49**: 211–218.

KELMAN, H. C. Attitude change as a function of response restriction. *Human Relations*, 1953, 6: 185–214.

LAWRENCE, D. H., & Festinger, L. *Deterrents and reinforcement: The psychology of insufficient reward.* Stanford: Stanford University Press, 1962.

LEWIN, K. *Dynamic theory of personality.* New York: McGraw-Hill, 1935.

MOSTELLER, F., & Bush, R. R. Selected quantitative techniques. In G. Lindzey (Ed.), *Handbook of social psychology.* Vol. 1. *Theory and method.* Cambridge, Mass.: Addison-Wesley, 1954. Pp. 289–334.

ORNE, M. T. On the social psychology of the psychological experiment: With particular reference to demand characteristics and their implications. *American Psychologist*, 1962, 17: 776–783.

RIECKEN, H. W. A program for research on experiments in social psychology. In N. F. Washburne (Ed.), *Decisions, values and groups.* Vol. 2. New York: Pergamon Press, 1962. Pp. 25–41.

ROSENBERG, M. J. Cognitive structure and attitudinal affect. *Journal of Abnormal and Social Psychology*, 1956, 53: 367–372.

ROSENBERG, M. J. An analysis of affective-cognitive consistency. In M. J. Rosenberg, C. I. Hovland, W. J. McGuire, R. P. Abelson, & J. W. Brehm (Eds.), *Attitude organization and change.* New Haven: Yale University Press, 1960. Pp. 15–64.

ROSENBERG, M. J. A research program on consistency and change in social attitudes. Columbus: Ohio State University, 1961. (Mimeo.)

ROSENBERG, M. J. Simulated man and the humanistic criticism. In S. S. Tomkins & S. J. Messick (Eds.), *Computer simulation of personality.* New York: Wiley, 1963. Pp. 113–124.

ROSENTHAL, R. On the social psychology of the psychological experiment: The experimenter's hypothesis as unintended determinant of experimental results. *American Scientist*, 1963, 51: 268–283.

SCOTT, W. A. Attitude change through reward of verbal behavior. *Journal of Abnormal and Social Psychology*, 1957, 55: 72–75.

SCOTT, W. A. Attitude change by response reinforcement: Replication and extension. *Sociometry*, 1959, 22: 328–335.

THOMAS, W. I., & Znaniecki, F. *The Polish peasant in Europe and America.* Boston: Badger, 1918. 5 vols.

Harold Sigall, Elliot Aronson, and
Thomas Van Hoose

The Cooperative Subject:
Myth or Reality?

The validity of findings in some psychological experiments, especially those using human subjects, has recently been questioned. In particular, it has been suggested by various commentators that results thought to be attributable to an experimental manipulation are frequently artifactual and due to the demands of the experimental situation resulting from the nature of the experimenter-subject interaction (Orne, 1962; Orne & Scheibe, 1964; Riecken, 1962; Rosenberg, 1965). What are the relevant factors that contribute to or produce these artifacts? Examination of the references cited above would indicate that although different points and emphases are made, the views offered tend to be complementary and supportive of one another, rather than contradictory. But this may be illusory. To elaborate, let us review some of these writings.

Riecken (1962) was concerned more with random error than systematic error; he suggested that subjects care about how they appear to an experimenter and that they want to appear in the best possible light. Therefore, subjects "put their best foot forward." How to put one's best foot forward, however, is not a simple question. The subject is confronted with a task and will be evaluated on his performance. In addition, since experimenters can either be defied or cooperated with, the subject is open to evaluation on his cooperativeness.

Riecken points out that in order to know what can be done to succeed in making a favorable impression, the subject must know what is going on in the experiment. He tries to find out what is going on by progressively defining the experimental situation. The cues used to accomplish this definition include the subject's preexperimental expectations, features of the scene (e.g., apparatus), and what the experimenter says and/or expects.

Orne (1962) takes a slightly different approach to the same general problem. His position is that subjects, above all, want to be "good sub-

From *Journal of Experimental Social Psychology*, 1970, **6**: 1–10. Reprinted with permission of authors and Academic Press, Inc.

jects" and that they satisfy this desire by cooperating with the experimenter. He states, "Admittedly, subjects are concerned about their performance in terms of reinforcing their self image; nonetheless, they seem even more concerned with the utility of their performances" [p. 778].

Thus, whereas Riecken (1962) named the two dimensions on which a subject may be evaluated—on the task and on "cooperativeness," Orne orders the importance of the two, concluding that cooperativeness is the more salient. In addition, much like Riecken's "progressive definition" concept, Orne suggests that "at some level he [the subject] sees it as his task to ascertain the true purpose of the experiment and respond in a manner which will support the hypothesis being tested" [p. 779].

The third position presented here is the one advanced by Rosenberg (1965). Rosenberg is concerned with systematic error introduced through the subject-experimenter interaction. He says that a subject in an experimental situation, confronted by a psychologist, suffers from "evaluation apprehension," which he defines as "anxiety-toned concern that he [the subject] win a positive evaluation from the experimenter, or at least that he provide no grounds for a negative one" [p. 29]. Rosenberg goes on to point out that there is no conflict between his notions and those put forth by Orne.

It should be clear, however, that there is no conflict between Orne and Rosenberg *only if* the evaluation apprehension experienced by subjects is over an evaluation of their cooperativeness. If on the other hand, evaluation apprehension refers to an evaluation of the subject's performance—his ability or personality characteristics, for example— then the two positions can be in conflict. Under certain circumstances, in order to cooperate by confirming the experimenter's hypothesis, the subject may be forced to appear to be stupid, slow, or strange. Conversely, a subject may have to disconfirm the experimenter's expectations (be uncooperative) in order to impress him as being intelligent, above average, or clever.

These seemingly congruent but differing approaches bring us to the present problem. Specifically, the question we are asking is: If, in fact, a subject alters his "natural" behavior due to the nature of the experimental situation, is it because he is trying to please the experimenter, and therefore opts to cooperate with him in an effort to confirm the hypothesis, or is it because he is trying to appear in a good light— intelligent, attractive, efficient, etc.—regardless of what the experimenter's hypothesis may be?

What is the nature of the evidence on this question? The conclusions reached by Orne (1962), that subjects are cooperative and try to help the experimenter to verify his hypothesis, were in part based on research in which it was demonstrated that subjects would continue to do page after page of arithmetic problems, even when they were made to destroy each page upon completion before tackling the succeeding page. Is this cooperation in the technical meaning of the word? That is, do these results demonstrate that subjects attempt to help the experimenter to verify his hypothesis? Hardly. What they do show is that subjects are obedient –i.e., they will do what an experimenter tells them to do (see Milgram, 1963).

Additional evidence, in the form of informal data (a personal communication from Zajonc), is cited by Riecken (1962). Zajonc found that when the experimenter told the subjects he believed the hypothesis to be true, the data supported that hypothesis; when he indicated that he felt the hypothesis was false, the obtained data did not support the hypothesis. The results would seem to support Orne, but the findings may be confounded. It is not clear whether the subjects *really* cooperated with the experimenter, or if they were attempting to present themselves as able people. If, instead of deciphering the experimenter's hypothesis, the subject is told "point blank" what the experimenter wants, he may feel that the experimenter is really trying to find out how nice he (the subject) is. Thus, he may comply with the experimenter's explicitly stated wishes as a way of putting his best foot forward.

Similarly, Rosenthal's (1966) work, while demonstrating experimenter bias, is not unequivocal regarding cooperativeness. For example, in one study (Rosenthal & Fode, 1963) subjects were instructed to rate people pictured in photographs on a success-failure continuum. Some experimenters were led to believe that the ratings would be high, others that the ratings would be low. Those that expected high ratings obtained significantly higher ratings than those who expected low ratings. Somehow the experimenter affected the data. Moreover, the cues emitted by the experimenter were extremely subtle, i.e., the cues were not discernible to investigators attempting to define them. It is difficult to know whether these cues suggested to the subject how to cooperate or how to put his best foot forward. For example, the experimenters who expected high ratings may have believed and conveyed to the subjects that perception of success was a good thing. Of course, there are numerous other possibilities, but our point is that one definite interpretation is not possible.

Thus, clear evidence demonstrating the cooperative nature of subjects does not seem to exist. Our own hypothesis is that subjects would rather look good than cooperate with the experimenter. Underlying our hypothesis in the present experiment is the notion that the subject's concern about "looking good" is centered around how he will appear on an ability dimension. His concern about being evaluated as a cooperative subject is secondary, if present at all. Thus, we predict that if a subject knows the experimenter's hypothesis, he will not try to be consistent with those expectations if his cooperation will fail to put him in a good light.

A test of this hypothesis has important methodological consequences. In building an experiment, there are literally scores of problems that an experimenter must solve and potential pitfalls that he must avoid. Some of these avoidance attempts are mutually antagonistic; e.g. in a specific situation, the kind of precautions that we take to guard against the cooperative subject may weaken the impact of the experimental variable or may result in a situation which increases a subject's evaluation apprehension or lead to other sources of variance. Thus, while it is a good general rule for the experimenter to be cautious (even overly cautious when possible) a superabundance of caution is not always reasonable. For this reason it is essential to know whether the cooperative subject presents a real problem, or whether his supposed existence is a myth due to a tendency to confuse cooperativeness with obedience or a desire to look good.

METHOD

Subjects and Design

It was necessary to allow subjects the opportunity to cooperate with the experimenter. Therefore, in the experimental conditions the experimenter had to make a hypothesis known. In addition, it was necessary that in one situation (*a*) both the experimenter and subject would profit from the subject's cooperation, and in the other situation (*b*) cooperation would benefit the experimenter but not the subject, while lack of cooperation would satisfy the subject's needs at the expense of the experimenter's. Moreover, we wanted to eliminate a direct "achievement" alternative, and therefore situation (*a*), above, took on two forms: one in which both the experimenter and subject would gain by an increase in output, and the other in which a decrease in output would fulfill the goals of both. A control condition was also employed to provide a baseline with which to compare the experimental conditions. Subjects were 40 undergraduates enrolled in introductory psychology at the University of Texas. They were randomly assigned to one of the four conditions and were tested individually.

Procedure

The experimenter greeted the subject and explained that the experiment was one with implications for industrial psychology. He told the subjects that their task would consist of copying a list of telephone numbers. After acknowledging that this task was not exciting, he pointed out that it was selected because it was related to several industrial types of tasks, and at the same time had been shown to be independent of intelligence and related abilities. The experimenter then supplied blank sheets of paper and a long strip of telephone numbers, and set a timer to ring after seven minutes. He told the subjects that he wanted them to have a practice trial first, and that he would return after seven minutes. The experimenter instructed the subjects not to rush, to work at a normal rate, and to stop when the timer sounded. He then left the room. When seven minutes had passed, the experimenter returned, collected the practice trial paper, and told the subjects to rest for a few moments while he left to get the forms for the "real trial." Again, the experimenter left the room.

It should be clear that up until this point subjects had received very little information; nor had they been assigned to a condition. This was done to reduce the possibility of experimenter bias during the presentation of the initial instructions. In addition, we used blank paper and one extremely long list of telephone numbers, rather than ruled paper and numbers as they appear in a telephone book, in order to minimize the possibility that subjects would be aware of the extent of their output.

When the experimenter left to get the "real trial" forms, he totaled the numbers copied. Then he randomly drew a card, thereby assigning the subject to one of the four conditions. The experimenter returned to the room with the "real trial" forms. These forms were merely sheets of paper made up with a series of lines, each of which provided space for one telephone number. Each line was preceded by a number, so that the subject would be aware of how many telephone numbers he had copied at any given time.

In the Control condition the experimenter merely said: "Here are the forms for the real trial." He provided a second list of telephone numbers, reset the timer, told subjects to begin, and left.

In the Increased-Output condition the experimenter added 20 to the total amount copied during "practice," rounded that number to the nearest five, and said: "Before we begin, let me tell you a little more about what we're doing. We have a theory relating the amount of illumination in a room to a person's performance in a room such as this." Pointing out that only half the available illumination was turned on, he continued, "With this amount of light, and a trivial, boring task, and given this time limit of seven minutes, we feel that if you don't rush you'll do about X numbers, or about $X/7$ per minute." "X" was equal to the amount done in practice (unknown to the subject) plus 20, and rounded off, and "$X/7$" was that amount divided by seven. The experimenter then said, "You may look at the clock from time to time to see how you're doing." Again, the experimenter left, returning after seven minutes to collect the data and explain the true purpose of the experiment to the subject.

The Decreased-Output condition was identical to the Increased-Output condition in every way, except that the quantity of telephone numbers given in the experimental hypothesis was arrived at by subtracting 20 from the practice total and rounding off this number rather than adding 20.

The fourth condition was the Decreased-Output-Obsessive-Compulsive condition. Here the experimenter, after subtracting 20 from the practice trial and rounding that total to the nearest five, said, "Before we begin, let me tell you a little more about what we're doing. There is a personality type called obsessive-compulsive. People who possess this characteristic are overly meticulous and overly concerned with detail. We have a theory that this task is a good indication of the obsessive-compulsive because people who feel compelled to rush at a trivial, boring task (like the copying of phone numbers) tend to be obsessive-compulsive. Given this time limit of seven minutes, we expect that you'll do about X numbers or $X/7$ per minute. You may look at the clock from time to time to see how you're doing." As before, after collecting the dependent measure, i.e., the phone numbers copied on the real trial, the experimenter debriefed the subjects.

Summarizing the three experimental conditions, we see that in the Increased-Output condition the experimenter "hypothesized" increased production. Since high output would also satisfy achievement needs of the subject, we can infer that "cooperation" on the part of the subject would be rewarding to both. In the Decreased-Output-Obsessive-Compulsive condition, the experimenter "hypothesized" decreased output. Here, too, if we assume that subjects did not want to be classified as obsessive-compulsive, "cooperation" would benefit both subject and experimenter. However, in the Decreased-Output condition the experimenter "hypothesized" a decrease, while subjects could demonstrate competence by increasing output. Thus, in the latter situation, "cooperation" with the experimenter would hinder the subject from satisfying his own aims, while satisfying his own aims would prevent him from aiding the experimenter.

RESULTS AND DISCUSSION

The means of the differences between the two trials for the four conditions are presented in Table 4–3. As expected, the least amount of change was manifested in the Control condition; subjects increased their output by 1.9 units (telephone numbers). Subjects in the Increased-Output condition increased their performance by 5.7 units, while those in the Decreased-Output condition increased by 6.2. Subjects in the Decreased-Output-Obsessive-Compulsive condition *decreased* their

Table 4–3   *Mean Change in Output from "Practice" to "Real" Trial*

Condition	Mean Change
Control	+1.9
Increased-Output	+5.7
Decreased-Output	+6.2
Decreased-Output-Obsessive-Compulsive	−8.0

output by 8.0 units. Analysis of variance yielded an $F = 6.28$, 3 and 36 df, demonstrating the differences between the means to be statistically significant beyond the .005 level. Moreover, Duncan's Multiple Range Test showed that every pair of means differed significantly ($p < .01$) with the exception of the Increased-Output and Decreased-Output pair.

Thus, it may be seen that our hypothesis has been supported; i.e., subjects looked as though they were cooperating with the experimenter only when such "cooperation" also resulted in good, effective behavior. When the experimenter expected increased output (Increased-Output condition), he was "assisted." When he expected decreased output and behavior to the contrary would indicate obsessive-compulsiveness (Decreased-Output-Obsessive-Compulsive condition), he was "assisted." Thus, subjects either speeded up or slowed down, depending on which mode of behavior would make them appear as more effective people. Simultaneously, the behavior exhibited also served to support their experimenter's "hypothesis."

One may ask how we can be sure that the important process involved was self-enhancement and that the incidental covariant was cooperativeness, rather than vice versa. To answer this question, we must examine the nature and results of the crucial Decreased-Output condition. In this condition subjects were, in effect, presented with a choice. We know from the results of the Decreased-Output-Obsessive-Compulsive and Increased-Output conditions that subjects do adjust their behavior as a function of the information they are given. Considering this and the results of the Control condition, we can assume that in the Decreased-Output condition subjects' behavior was affected by the instructions. Consequently, the subjects' alternatives were (a) to decrease output and thereby help the experimenter confirm his hypothesis, or (b) to work as fast as possible, thereby impressing the experimenter with ability, at the cost of disconfirming the experimenter's "hypothesis." Thus, the subject could either cooperate or make himself appear effective. Unlike the other two experimental conditions, in the Decreased-Output condition it was impossible to do both at the same time. The results are unequivocal: Subjects *increased* their output, thereby appearing "good," while the experimenter's hypothesis was disconfirmed. It should be noted that the increased output was virtually identical regardless of whether the experimenter hypothesized an increase or a decrease in output.

After running these conditions, it was suggested to us that if our subjects were truly motivated to look good, then subjects who were merely told by the experimenter that he was interested in the relationship between illumination and productivity, but not given a specific hypothesis regarding output, should manifest greater increases in output than control subjects. In order to follow up this possibility 24 additional subjects were tested.[1] Half of them were randomly assigned to virtually an exact replication of the Control condition. The remainder received treatment identical to the Increased-Output and Decreased-Output conditions, except that they were not presented with any particular hypothesis. The mean changes, from practice to real trial (T_2-T_1), were -0.1 in the replicated control condition, and $+2.9$ in the new unspecified-hypothesis condition—a differcnce between groups of 3.0 telephone numbers. Analysis of variance resulted in an $F = 3.81$, 1 and 22 df, indicating that this difference is significant at the .07 level. This suggests that the simple fact that subjects are aware of the existence of a hypothesis regarding output will lead them to attempt to impress the experimenter, even if the attempt requires that they ignore some instructions (which, in this particular case, directed subjects not to rush).

Before elaborating on our data we must comment on the theoretical difficulties involved in this type of research. To use a social psychological experiment to investigate problems (indeed, artifacts) that plague social psychological experiments is somewhat akin to placing two mirrors face-to-face and trying to point out the original image in one of them. How do we know that the data we are using to discuss possibly biased data are not, in and of themselves, biased? We cannot be absolutely certain that this trap was avoided. However, certain evidence does bear on the issue. At the conclusion of the experimental session, each subject received a thorough interview (see Aronson & Carlsmith, 1968). One of the aims of this interview was an attempt to detect any suspicion on the part of the subject. In this interview, the experimenter discussed the terrible consequences which would befall him if he published data which were at all tainted. In this vein, he pleaded with the subject to *cooperate* by providing the experimenter with any evidence that might be relevant. Accordingly, the subject was carefully probed for his own hypotheses and encouraged to venture wild guesses. There was no evidence whatever that any subject suspected the true hypothesis. To argue that subjects (*a*) guessed our true hypothesis and behaved congruently in order to be cooperative, and (b) refused to cooperate with the experimenter's request in the postexperimental interview is to say the least somewhat far-fetched. As Aronson and Carlsmith (1968) point out, if the subject is really trying to be helpful, then why should he suddenly stop being so? Moreover, the sense of satisfaction achieved by a freshman upon discovering a ruse perpetrated by an experimenter would seem to be very great. Thus, whether the subject is trying to be cooperative or attempting to present himself as bright, disclosure of his own hypotheses during the postexperimental interviews should be forthcoming.

Assuming that the present set of data is unbiased, we must reach the conclusion that, in this experiment, subjects were not cooperative, and that when they appeared to be cooperative, this behavior on closer examination can be seen to be a covariant of behavior by the subject designed to impress the experimenter with his ability. These findings suggest that evaluation apprehension does occur, and that subjects do adjust their performances in light of the hypotheses. The nature of this adaptation seems, however, to be more in line with Rosenberg's (1965) formulation than with those of Riecken (1962) or Orne (1962). Riecken's belief that the subject's concern was over being evaluated on cooperativeness seems unwarranted. Moreover, our data provide no substantiation whatever for Orne's belief that subjects are *more* concerned over the utility of their performances than with reinforcing their self-images. This is not to say that subjects are disobedient. Subjects are obedient in the sense that if they are instructed to do something, they fulfill that request. Our data indicate that this concept may have been overextended to include subjects trying to make the experimenter's data turn out well. Our results show that subjects *refuse* to cooperate in this manner if such behavior goes against their self-interest.

Obviously, we cannot conclude on the basis of this single experiment that subjects never manifest cooperative behavior per se. It is possible that under certain circumstances cooperativeness would occur. However, the inducements to be cooperative in the present experiment were powerful indeed. Considering both the lack of clear evidence on cooperativeness in the literature and the results of the present experiment, we must conclude that the large amount of concern spent over the "cooperative subject" problem has been disproportionate. Although the problem of subject cooperativeness should not be ignored, it seems that the experimenter's energy would be better directed toward solving other methodological problems.

NOTE

1. The authors would like to thank Phyllis Baunach for her assistance in collecting the data.

REFERENCES

ARONSON, E., & Carlsmith, J. M. Experimentation in social psychology. In G. Lindzey and E. Aronson (Eds.), *Handbook of social psychology*. (Rev. ed.) Vol. II. Reading, Mass.: Addison-Wesley, 1968.

MILGRAM, S. Behavioral study of obedience. *Journal of Abnormal and Social Psychology*, 1963, **67**: 371–378.

ORNE, M. T. On the social psychology of the psychological experiment. *American Psychologist*, 1962, **17**: 776–783.

ORNE, M. T., & Scheibe, K. E. The contribution of non-deprivation factors in the production of sensory deprivation effects: The psychology of the "panic button." *Journal of Abnormal and Social Psychology*, 1964, **68**: 3–12.

RIECKEN, H. W. A program for research on experiments in social psychology. In N. F. Washburne (Ed.), *Decision, values and groups*. Vol. II. New York: Pergamon Press, 1962. Pp. 25–41.

ROSENBERG, M. J. When dissonance fails: On eliminating evaluation apprehension from attitude measurement. *Journal of Personality and Social Psychology*, 1965, 1: 28–42.

ROSENTHAL, R. *Experimenter effects in behavioral research.* New York: Appleton-Century-Crofts, 1966.

ROSENTHAL, R., & Fode, K. L. Psychology of the scientist: V. Three experiments in experimenter bias. *Psychological Reports*, 1963, 12: 491–511.

Leon H. Levy

Awareness, Learning, and the Beneficent Subject as Expert Witness[1]

There are certain issues in psychology for which it appears that even the most rigorous and behavioristically inclined researchers are apt to turn to their experimental subjects as expert witnesses. One such issue is the role of awareness in human learning (Adams, 1957). Beginning with Thorndike's (1932) assertion that learning can occur without awareness, and continuing through to the current controversy over the role of awareness and cognition in verbal conditioning (Spielberger, 1965), psychologists have based their positions in large part upon the verbal testimony of their subjects. Those who would dismiss awareness as a scientifically useful concept (Verplanck, 1962), no less than those who would embrace it (Dulany, 1962; Spielberger, 1962), have turned to their subjects' verbal reports in support of their positions. Farber (1963), for example, has said that awareness cannot be disregarded in the study of behavior and that one excellent approach is to "ask the subjects what they are doing or think they are doing and why" [p. 195] As straight-forward as this approach might be, it is obviously not without its problems.

It seems to be generally accepted that awareness is a private event of which only the subject has knowledge: while the experimenter may gather data on learning via response frequencies, latencies, and the like, only the subject has access to data on awareness. Thus, to the extent that his verbal reports of awareness are taken as veridical or given the same weight as the experimenter's summary statistics, the subject may be said to be cast in the role of coinvestigator or expert witness (Buck, 1961). This is a role which he has not formally played since the days of introspectionist psychology, and because so many

From *Journal of Personality and Social Psychology*, 1967, **6**: 365–370. Copyright © 1967 by The American Psychological Association and reprinted with permission of author and The American Psychological Association.

crucial theoretical issues have been made to rest upon his testimony, it becomes a proper subject of investigation.

The present study was conducted within a verbal conditioning framework for both theoretical and methodological reasons. Verbal conditioning has come to occupy a focal position in theoretical controversies over the nature of complex human learning and psychotherapy (Krasner, 1958, 1962; Spielberger & Levin, 1962), and in the test of a variety of hypotheses in personality and psychotherapy (Williams, 1964). To a large degree, the issues hinge upon whether the learning curves are interpreted as manifesting the unconscious and automatic effects of reinforcement upon S-R contingencies, or whether they are a consequence of awareness and the hypotheses (Dulany, 1961) held by the subject as to what he should do in order to obtain reinforcement. While it has appeared that verbal conditioning is only found in those subjects who were inferred to be aware of the S-R reinforcement contingencies (Spielberger, 1965), this has not been true in all cases (Farber, 1963), and an element of ambiguity remains since (*a*) judgments of awareness have been shown to be dependent upon the thoroughness of the postexperimental interview (Levin, 1961), and (*b*) it is possible to argue that awareness may be a consequence of conditioning rather than a cause (Postman & Sassenrath, 1961). The present experiment attempts to reduce these ambiguities through experimental manipulation of awareness: it investigates the extent to which learning curves are a function of awareness.

Methodologically, the use of verbal conditioning provides a convenient vehicle for the study of the subject in his role as expert witness. Orne (1962) has presented persuasive evidence for the effects of the "demand characteristics" of experiments on the subject's performance. Simply put, these are the effects of the subject's hypotheses or beliefs about the nature of the experiment and his attempt to be a "good subject" and provide the data sought for by the experimenter. But because not all subjects necessarily perform as they think the experimenter wishes them to (Farber, 1963), it seems reasonable to refer to those who do, or those who have been subjected to some experimental treatment which may be expected to increase the likelihood that they would, as "beneficent subjects." The verbal conditioning task permitted the author to manipulate awareness directly by either informing or not informing subjects how the experimenter wanted them to perform. Because of certain sociocultural aspects of the experimental situation, to be described below, it seemed reasonable to assume that the informed subjects would also be beneficent. Thus it was possible to compare not only their performance in verbal conditioning as a function of awareness and beneficence, but also the quality of their testimony in the postexperimental awareness interview. If demand characteristics enter into the subjects' performance in the experiment proper, there seems to be no reason why they would not also affect their performance as expert witnesses in the postexperimental interview.

In summary, the purpose of this experiment was to contribute data relevant to the question of the role of awareness in verbal conditioning and also to study the behavior of subjects in postexperimental awareness interviews, where both awareness and demand characteristics have been experimentally manipulated.

METHOD

Subjects

The subjects were 32 male students enrolled in an introductory psychology course for which participation in four experiments was a requirement.

Stimulus Materials

A Taffel (1955) conditioning procedure was used for which one hundred 3- by 5-inch white index cards, each containing a past-tense verb and the pronouns I, WE, YOU, HE, SHE, and THEY, provided the stimuli. The verb was typed in the center of the card and the pronouns beneath it, in a different sequence from one card to the next.

Procedure

The subjects were randomly assigned in equal numbers according to a predetermined schedule to either an informed or an uninformed group. The experimental personnel consisted of a male undergraduate confederate, whose job it was to either inform or not inform each subject of what the experiment was all about; a female graduate student, who acted as the experimenter and whose physical endowments and manner were such as to leave little doubt concerning her ability to elicit beneficence from the typical male undergraduate; and an undergraduate female who conducted the postconditioning interview.

Each subject was identified throughout the experiment by a code number based upon his order of arrival for the experiment. The schedule followed by the confederate which determined whether or not a subject was to be informed was not known to either the experimenter or to the interviewer. Thus, each subject was run and interviewed blind so far as knowledge of which group he was in. Additionally, the interviewer had no knowledge of the subject's performance in verbal conditioning at the time that she conducted her awareness interview.

Upon arriving for the experiment, each subject found the confederate sitting outside the laboratory with a vacant chair beside him. A sign by the laboratory door requested all subjects for the experiment to be seated until called by the experimenter. The confederate engaged in small talk with all subjects so that when the experimenter arrived to bring the subject into the lab she found them all engaged in conversation and could not determine which group they were in. For those subjects in the informed group, the confederate began his conversation with the following remarks delivered in a well-rehearsed, *entre nous* fashion:

> Are you waiting to be in the experiment "words?" I just got through with it and I have to wait for a second part or something. I think the girl who is running it is doing it for her doctor's dissertation. Boy, I'll bet she's worried about getting the right results. It's a funny experiment. You have to sit there and make up sentences using these words she has on a card and it seems she wants you to make up sentences using *I* or *We* as the pronoun. I think I did pretty well once I caught on. Better not say that I told you about it.

In this way awareness was provided the informed group, and, given the aforementioned characteristics of the experimenter, it seemed likely that these subjects would also be beneficent.

Subjects were run individually by the experimenter, who gave them the conventional Taffel instructions to the effect that they were to make up a sentence for each card using the verb and one of the six pronouns beneath it, saying the first sentence that came to mind. The experimenter, who was separated from the subject by a small wooden partition resting on a table, presented the stimuli on a stimulus holder in front of the subject, recorded his pronoun choice, and, during the conditioning trials, reinforced each sentence beginning with *I* or *We* by saying "good." The first 20 sentences, which the subjects were told would be for practice, were used to determine the subject's operant level, and the remaining 80 constituted the conditioning trials. The experimenter knew that half of the subjects were in each group, and immediately after the subject left the room recorded her guess as to whether or not he had been informed.

Following completion of conditioning the experimenter thanked the subject for his cooperation, asked him not to tell anyone else about the experiment, and then led him into another room in the laboratory suite and introduced him to the interviewer who, she said, wished to ask him a few questions. The interviewer then administered a 12-question postconditioning interview for awareness used by Spielberger and Levin (1962). The questions in this interview began in a nonleading way with, "Did you usually give the first sentence that came to your mind?" and became increasingly direct and to the point with the last question being, "While going through the cards, did you think that her saying 'good' had anything to do with the words you chose to begin your sentences? What?" When awareness was judged on the basis of the subjects' answers to the entire interview, Spielberger and Levin found a highly significant difference in the number of conditioned responses between aware and unaware subjects, and no difference between unaware subjects and those in a nonreinforced control group. Our interest in using this interview was not only as a means of inferring awareness; by noting the question number on which the subject indicated awareness it seemed also to offer a way of investigating the effects of demand characteristics and beneficence upon the subject's candor.

If the subject reported awareness at any point during these 12 questions he was then asked to identify the trial block in which he first became aware. Finally, as the last question all subjects were asked: "Did you know anything about the experiment before you participated in it?" The interviewer recorded all answers verbatim and the early interviews were tape-recorded as a check on the interviewer's performance. The interviewer proved so competent that it was not felt necessary to tape all of her interviews.

RESULTS

Interview Data and Detection of Beneficence

The experimenter's ability to identify which subjects had been informed and which had not was evaluated by comparing her judgments against their actual treatment. She correctly identified 56 percent of the informed subjects and 75 percent of the uninformed subjects, but her overall hit rate of 66 percent was not any better than expected by chance ($\chi^2 = 2.07$, $df = 1$). Hence, the experimenter was not able to detect the beneficent subject on the basis of his performance alone.

A subject was classified as aware if any of his answers during the postconditioning interview could be taken as statements of the reinforcement contingency of "good" for sentences beginning with I alone, with We alone, or with I or We. Subjects were classified without knowledge of their preexperimental treatment or their performance in verbal conditioning. By definition, it would be expected that a larger proportion of the informed subjects would be aware than would the uninformed. Actually, 81 per cent of the informed subjects were classified as aware, compared to 44 percent of the uninformed subjects. Thus the subjects' verbal reports did reflect their preexperimental treatment with some degree of accuracy ($\chi^2 = 3.33$, $df = 1$, $p < .05$, one-tailed). There were no differences between the aware subjects in the two groups, however, in the trial block which they designated as the one on which they first became aware of the contingency (informed, $M = 2.2$; uninformed, $M = 2.1$).

The number of questions it was necessary to ask in the postconditioning interview before the subject gave an answer from which awareness might be inferred was taken as a measure of his readiness to report awareness or his candor. While it might seem that it should take relatively little persistence to elicit a report of awareness from an informed subject since he ostensibly came into the experiment with it, considering the fact that he possesses guilty knowledge—the confederate asked him not to tell the experimenter that he had told him about the experiment—it would seem reasonable to predict on the basis of his possible conflict over this knowledge, as well as his beneficence toward the experimenter, that he would be more reluctant to reveal awareness as compared with an innocent uninformed subject. Giving each aware subject a score based upon the number of questions asked before he revealed awareness, the mean for the 13 aware, informed subjects was 5.3 and for the 7 aware, uninformed subjects, 3.3. This difference was evaluated by a procedure suggested by Edwards (1960, pp. 106–107) for unequal n's and found to be statistically significant ($t = 2.02, p < .05$, one-tailed). Thus, as compared with the innocent subject, the beneficent subject appears less likely to give evidence revealing awareness unless pressed for it.

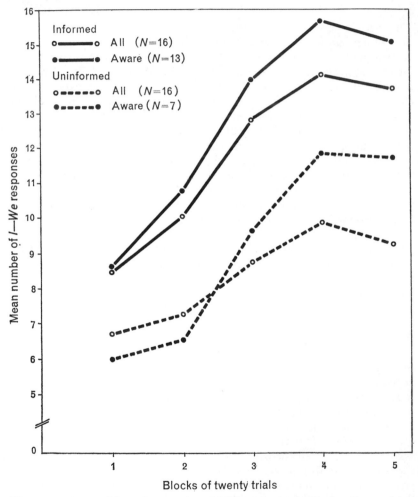

Figure 4–1   Mean frequencies of *I-We* sentences in blocks of 20 each.

It will be recalled that the last question asked of all subjects was whether they had any knowledge of the experiment before taking part in it. Only 1 of the 16 informed subjects reported that he had been fully informed by the confederate, and 3 others only that the confederate had told them that they would have to make up sentences but nothing more. It is noteworthy that one of the partial reporters also said that he thought the interviewer might have known about the confederate—apparently he didn't want to be considered dishonest. Thus, 75 percent of the informed group denied any prior knowledge of the experiment, and *none* spontaneously volunteered his knowledge to the experimenter during the experiment.

Verbal Conditioning

The 100 trials were divided into five blocks of 20 each. Because the groups were not found to differ significantly in their frequency of *I-We* responses during the operant period, all analyses included this period as the first block of trials and were based upon frequencies rather than difference scores. These data are presented in Figure 4–1 for all subjects in the informed and uninformed groups and separately for only the aware subjects in these groups.

An analysis of variance comparing frequency of *I-We* responses for all subjects in the informed and uninformed groups indicated that the informed group was superior to the uninformed group ($F = 6.06$, $df = 1/30$, $p < .05$). It also produced a significant main effect for trials ($F = 13.19$, $df = 4/120$, $p < .01$), but no significant interaction between groups and trials, confirming the impression gained from Figure 4–1 that both groups showed the same rate of increase in frequency and differed only in level. A similar analysis conducted only on the performance of the aware subjects in each group showed the informed subjects still tending to be superior to the uninformed subjects ($F = 3.56$, $df = 1/18$, $p < .10$), with a highly significant effect for trials ($F = 17.49$, $df = 4/72$, $p < .01$), but again no significant Groups × Trials interaction. Thus, informed subjects inferred to be aware of the response-reinforcement contingency appear to differ from their uninformed counterparts only in their level of performance and not in the shape of their acquisition curve.

DISCUSSION

Because the rationale in so many human experiments assumes a naïve subject to begin with, perhaps the most common operational thread running through human research is the request made by the experimenter just before the subject leaves the experiment that he not tell anyone about it. How often this request is honored has seen little investigation, but it seems unlikely, college students being what they are, that it is anywhere near 100 percent. For this reason many experimenters also ask their subjects whether they knew anything about the experiment before taking part in it. It seems to be common practice to accept the subject's word on this. The data cast serious doubt on the validity of this practice.

For a variety of social psychological and other reasons, well discussed by Orne (1962) and others, the finding that 75 percent of the subjects in the present experiment did not give any indication that they had been told anything about it is not too surprising. But it is distressing. Given a beneficent subject, neither naïveté nor complete candor may be assumed.

These data strongly suggest that when subjects' verbal reports provide the evidential basis for hypothesis testing, demand characteristics may be expected to enter no less than when their performance, verbal or otherwise, is the source of data. For this reason studies in verbal conditioning, particularly of the Taffel type, must always be doubly suspect with respect to demand characteristics when the question is one of learning without awareness. Although more subjects in the informed than in the uninformed group indicated awareness during the postconditioning interview, it required a larger number of questions on the average to elicit this indication from them. Indeed, had they been subjected to one of the briefer types of awareness interviews, not at all uncommon in verbal conditioning studies (Levin, 1961), less than half of the informed aware subjects would have been so classified.

By definition, awareness implies the ability to verbalize. But although awareness may be a necessary condition for verbalization, it is obviously not a sufficient one. Nevertheless, the present study should not be taken to mean either that no faith may be put in subjects' verbalizations or that awareness is beyond the reach of scientific investigation. (It was true that those subjects who were classified as unaware, in the informed as well as in the uninformed group, showed very little change in performance as compared with aware subjects.) Rather, it demonstrates that these verbalizations, like any other form of behavior, cannot be adequately understood without knowledge of their antecedent conditions. Like any other hypothetical construct, the meaning of awareness resides in the nomological net of which it is a part (Cronbach & Meehl, 1955) and in the corresponding converging operations (Campbell & Fiske, 1959; Garner, Hake, & Eriksen, 1956) by which it is defined. But there is no intrinsic reason, as Dulany (1962), as well as the present experiment have shown, why the study of awareness need place the experimenter entirely at the mercy of his subjects' testimony, whether they be beneficent, innocent, expert, or otherwise. Converging operations are possible and the study cannot be based upon subjects' verbal reports alone. For the present experiment makes it obvious that to rely upon the subject as an expert witness would be to betray as much naïveté on the part of the experimenter as that which he hopes exists in his subject; without corroborative, independent data the subject's verbal testimony possesses no greater (or lesser) validity than does an unstandardized test.

Given that a subject is aware of the reinforcement contingency or what the experimenter wishes him to do, as Dulany (1962) and Farber (1963) have observed, it does not necessarily follow that he will behave accordingly. The verbal conditioning data appear to be consistent with these observations. Although all of the informed subjects in the present experiment had been provided with information which would have permitted them to obtain 100 percent reinforcement from the first trial onward, none did. While the first block of unreinforced trials might have been confusing and account for part of this, the gain in *I-We* responses in the informed group during conditioning was of the same order as that for the uninformed group, only their level of responding was higher. Awareness, whether defined by directly informing subjects or by inference from interview protocols, appeared to be associated with the same kind of growth curve commonly taken as reflecting the continuous incremental effects of reinforcement upon habit strength. But to interpret these curves in this fashion seems obviously inappropriate. For this reason, the conditioning data of this experiment would seem to have important implications for the conceptualization of the processes involved in verbal conditioning.

Most generally, they tend to make suspect interpretations of verbal conditioning data within an operant conditioning framework. While it would certainly be gratuitous to argue that the curves obtained in the present study simply reflect the subjects' beneficent responses to the demand characteristics of the experiment, it would be just as unfounded to view them as representing the operation of the same principles of learning and conditioning as is believed operative in rats and pigeons. And if this is true in the present experiment, it may well be true in others. Thus it seems obvious that the shape of a response curve plotted over trials is, by itself, a weak basis upon which to infer the nature of the underlying process.

The great similarity between the curves for the informed and uninformed groups, while startling, is not uninterpretable. That the pre-experimental treatment of informing or not informing subjects had an effect upon them is obvious from both the difference in height between the two curves, and the differences found in the number of aware subjects in each group and their readiness to admit awareness. However, when Dulany (1962) instructed subjects in the correct response and the reinforcement contingency, their response rate increased abruptly; in the present experiment with essentially the same kind of information it did not. One possible explanation for this may be that in Dulany's experiment such an abrupt increase was socially sanctioned; the subject was acting upon legitimately obtained information. In the present experiment, it is possible that the informed subjects were deterred from acting upon their knowledge and showing a similar abrupt increase in response frequency because of their fear that it would reveal their illicitly obtained information. Thus, one interpretation of the shape of the curve for the informed group is that it reflects the rate of change among the subjects in their decisions to act consistently with their knowledge, in order to obtain reinforcement or to satisfy the experimenter. And if this is true for the informed group, it is also a plausible explanation for the similarly shaped curve produced by the uninformed group. Although their awareness was not based upon illgotten knowledge, when they obtained it during the conditioning series it may be expected to have varied from one subject to another just as when they decided to act upon it.

What this suggests, of course, is that the curves obtained in verbal conditioning studies may reflect the operation of cognitive and volitional processes, or hypotheses and intentions as Dulany (1962) would have it, rather than the direct, automatic, and unconscious consequences of reinforcement. If this is the case, then it would seem to be misleading to speak of these studies as demonstrating verbal conditioning. They demonstrate the modification of verbal behavior to be sure, but many of them may owe their data more to the beneficence of their subjects than to the potency of their theory or reinforcement. This is not to say that reinforcement is unimportant. It provides the subject with information; it tells him what to do, albeit in a most inefficient way, and he may do it if he wishes to. But if he does, the question remains whether he should be considered conditioned or beneficent.

NOTE

1. This study was supported in part by Grant MH 11081 from the National Institute of Mental Health, United States Public Health Service. The author wishes to express his thanks to Martha Henderson, Estelle Resnick, and Steve Barkley for their excellent performance in their respective roles in this experiment.

REFERENCES

ADAMS, J. K. Laboratory studies of behavior without awareness. *Psychological Bulletin,* 1957, 54: 383–405.

BUCK, R. Comments on Buchwald's "verbal utterances as data." In H. Feigl & G. Maxwell (Eds.), *Current issues in the philosophy of science.* New York: Holt, Rinehart & Winston, 1961. Pp. 468–472.

CAMPBELL, D. T., & Fiske, D. W. Convergent and discriminant validation by the multitrait-multimethod matrix. *Psychological Bulletin,* 1959, 56: 81–105.

CRONBACH, L. J., & Meehl, P. E. Construct validity in psychological tests. *Psychological Bulletin*, 1955, **52**: 281–302.

DULANY, D. E. Hypotheses and habits in verbal "operant conditioning." *Journal of Abnormal and Social Psychology*, 1961, **63**: 251–263.

DULANY, D. E. The place of hypotheses and intentions: An analysis of verbal control in verbal conditioning. In C. Eriksen (Ed.), *Behavior and awareness—a symposium of research and interpretation*. Durham, N. C.: Duke University Press, 1962. Pp. 102–129.

EDWARDS, A. L. *Experimental design in psychological research*. New York: Rinehart, 1960.

FARBER, I. E. The things people say to themselves. *American Psychologist*, 1963, **18**: 185–197.

GARNER, W. R., Hake, H. W., & Eriksen, C. W. Operationism and the concept of perception. *Psychological Review*, 1956, **63**: 149–159.

KRASNER, L. Studies of the conditioning of verbal behavior. *Psychological Bulletin*, 1958, **55**: 148–171.

KRASNER, L. The therapist as a social reinforcement machine. In H. H. Strupp & L. Luborsky (Eds.), *Research in psychotherapy*. Vol. II. Washington, D.C.: American Psychological Association, 1962. Pp. 61–94.

LEVIN, S. M. The effects of awareness on verbal conditioning. *Journal of Experimental Psychology*, 1961, **61**: 67–75.

ORNE, M. T. On the social psychology of the psychological experiment: With particular reference to demand characteristics and their implications. *American Psychologist*, 1962, **17**: 776–783.

POSTMAN, L., & Sassenrath, J. M. The automatic action of verbal rewards and punishments. *Journal of General Psychology*, 1961, **65**: 109–136.

SPIELBERGER, C. D. The role of awareness in verbal conditioning. In C. W. Eriksen (Ed.), *Behavior and awareness—a symposium of research and interpretation*. Durham, N.C.: Duke University Press, 1962. Pp. 71–101.

SPIELBERGER, C. D. Theoretical and epistemological issues in verbal conditioning. In S. Rosenberg (Ed.), *Directions in psycholinguistics*. New York: Macmillan, 1965. Pp. 149–200.

SPIELBERGER, C. D., & Levin, S. M. What is learned in verbal conditioning? *Journal of Verbal Learning and Verbal Behavior*, 1962, **1**: 125–132.

TAFFEL, C. Anxiety and the conditioning of verbal behavior. *Journal of Abnormal and Social Psychology*, 1955, **51**: 496–501.

THORNDIKE, E. L. *The fundamentals of learning*. New York: Teachers College, 1932.

VERPLANCK, W. S., Unaware of where's awareness: Some verbal operants—notates, monents, and notants. In C. W. Eriksen (Ed.), *Behavior and awareness—a symposium of research and interpretation*. Durham, N.C.: Duke University Press, 1962. Pp. 130–158.

WILLIAMS, J. H. Conditioning of verbalization: A review. *Psychological Bulletin*, 1964. **62**: 383–393.

Monte M. Page[1]

Social Psychology of a Classical Conditioning of Attitudes Experiment[2]

Staats and Staats (1957, 1958) introduced a complex deception experiment which they claim results in the classical conditioning of an evaluative meaning or attitudinal response. Their subjects were told that they were participating in a learning experiment designed to study the ability to learn two lists of words simultaneously. One list of six words was presented visually and was repeated many times. Immediately after each visual word, a word was spoken from another much longer list. Each of the spoken words was repeated only once. This procedure was intended to disguise the repeated contiguous association of spoken words having strong positive evaluative meaning (beautiful, healthy) with one of the visual words; and the association of strong negative evaluative meaning (ugly, sick) with another visual word. The other four visual words were included to disguise the associations and were always followed by spoken words of neutral evaluative meaning.

After "conditioning," subjects rated the six visual words on pleasant-unpleasant semantic differential scales. Instructions as to the purpose of the ratings were deceptive. Then subjects wrote down what they thought the purpose of the experiment was. Subjects verbalizing awareness of the relationship between the two lists were dropped from the analysis. The Staats' concern as to subjects' awareness of the association between the lists was a recognition that such awareness might invalidate a classical conditioning interpretation of the results.

Two studies (Cohen, 1964; Insko & Oakes, 1966) have subsequently challenged the Staats' conclusion that their result occurred "without awareness—without cognition" [Staats & Staats, 1957]. The issue raised by these studies was in the context of the learning and contingency awareness controversy (Spielberger, 1962; Spielberger & DeNike, 1966). Cohen used the Staats' single-question awareness

From *Journal of Personality and Social Psychology*, 1969, **11**: 177–186. Copyright © 1969 by The American Psychological Association and reprinted with permission of author and The American Psychological Association.

measure with a more stringent criterion for classifying a subject as unaware. Insko and Oakes used a more extended postexperimental questionnaire. Both studies found strong relationships between post-experimental assessment of awareness of the relation between the two lists (contingency awareness) and the so-called conditioned attitudes. These studies seem to challenge sufficiently the Staats' conclusion as to learning without contingency awareness. However, since neither study obtained evidence as to when the contingency awareness occurred, the correlations by themselves are consistent with two interpretations. Awareness could be causally linked to the marking of the rating scales, or the experimental effect (conditioning) could be causing the post-experimental awareness. What is still needed is evidence as to which came first, the awareness or the conditioning.

Assuming for the moment that contingency awareness precedes the marking of the rating scales, and this can be tested by asking aware subjects to pinpoint the time during the experiment when they became aware, there is a broader context in which the attitude conditioning effect may be interpreted. That context is the social psychology of experiments (Orne, 1962; Page, 1968; Silverman, 1968). Contingency awareness may be only the first step in the complex sequence which brings about the "conditioned ratings." Perhaps the crucial factor in mediating the ratings is awareness of demand characteristics, or discovery of the purpose of the experiment, bringing about compliant or cooperative role behavior on the part of the subject (Page, 1968). That such factors are potentially very powerful mediators of behavior in human experiments is implicitly recognized by many experimenters (including the Staats) in that they often go to great lengths to disguise the true purpose of the experiment. In this context the important question with regard to attitude conditioning has to do with whether the deception was effective on all subjects; and if not, did those who saw through the deception behave any differently than those who did not (Kelman, 1967).

In the context of Orne's (1962) demand characteristics formulation, there could be an alternative explanation of why the Staats obtained their results. While their subjects were told to learn two separate lists of words, some of them did not follow directions; instead they learned or noted the consistent relation between pleasant and unpleasant spoken words and the visually presented syllables. For these contingency aware subjects the situation changed so that they no longer perceived themselves as participating in a rather dull and routine learning experiment. The experimenter had not fully explained; he must have something subtle and deceptive in mind. With this appraisal of the situation, they may have been set to search for other unexplained relations and to mistrust further instructions; they may even have conceived of the experiment as a test of their intelligence or problem-solving ability. With this or a similar set of expectancies, the aware subjects were presented the rating scales. At that point the purpose of the experiment became apparent to most of them; that is, "The experimenter wants to know if I caught on to the pleasant or unpleasant syllables and this is his way of testing," or "He was trying to condition my feelings," etc. In any case, some of the contingency aware subjects came to believe that the purpose of the experiment was for them to rate the crucial syllables in opposite directions and to the extremes of the scales. Having this knowledge of the purpose of the experiment (demand awareness) each subject then was faced with the problem of whether to cooperate with the experimenter and respond in the way that so obviously was demanded by the situation, or to resist the influence. In the majority of cases, the decision was made to cooperate (Page, 1968) and hence the "conditioned response."

Two previous studies (Cohen, 1964; Page, 1964) have found the distribution of subjects' ratings in attitude conditioning to be peculiarly bimodal. Subjects either rated the critical syllables as negatively or positively as possible or appeared, as a group, not to be affected. The difference between group means was produced by a few subjects conditioning a good deal rather than most of them conditioning a little. In another study (Page, 1968) concerned with awareness of demand characteristics in a deceptive learning situation, a similar bimodal distribution was found. The upper mode of the distribution in that study was populated entirely by subjects claiming to have been aware of and cooperating with demand characteristics. It may be that the bimodal distribution is typical of data mediated by demand characteristics. If so, the Staats' data is suspect. Also, not all subjects who verbalized contingency awareness in the previous studies showed the extreme conditioned rating. This suggests that something in addition to contingency awareness, possibly demand awareness plus motivation to cooperate, is necessary to produce the extreme ratings.

Insko and Oakes (1966) included measures of both contingency and demand awareness in their study. On the basis of their data they concluded that the concept of demand awareness does not add anything beyond simple contingency awareness. They go on to offer an explanation of the Staats' effect in terms of an aware concept formation rather than affective conditioning. Since their measure of demand awareness did not account for all the variance, they suggested that the Staats' phenomenon was not entirely an artifact of demand characteristics. In light of postexperimental interviews conducted earlier by the present author (Page, 1964) a "concept-formation only" interpretation seemed incomplete and a further investigation was considered worthwhile. For example, one female subject in that study said, "I don't really dislike the name Bill, that's my husband's name, but for purposes of this experiment, I marked Bill bad." Other subjects who were also extreme in their "conditioned attitudes" gave similar indications that their ratings were pure artifacts of demand characteristics.

Based on the above considerations, the present experiment was designed. Several predictions consistent with a demand-characteristics explanation were made. First, a strong association between carefully assessed postexperimental reports of having been contingency aware (knew the interlist association) during training and before marking the rating scales and the high conditioning scores was predicted. This is suggested by the Insko and Oakes correlations, but because they did not ask subjects to pinpoint the time at which they noted the contingency, they had no evidence as to direction of causation. Second, the awareness and conditioning association should be strengthened if demand awareness (knew the experimenter expected pleasant and unpleasant ratings) was separated from contingency awareness. This prediction is contradicted by Insko and Oakes, but in this study the questionnaire and scoring procedures were designed on the assumption that demand awareness is basically an either-or dichotomy, rather than attempting to measure awareness as a continuum as did Insko and Oakes. Third, a new "second learning test," which was a direct test of interlist associations given immediately after the rating scales, was predicted to correlate highly with the postexperimental awareness measures and the conditioned ratings.

In addition, two predictions were made with regard to independent variables. First, subject sophistication might significantly facilitate the conditioned rating behavior. This was a significant variable in a previous experiment (Page, 1968), and it is reasonable that subjects who have spent a semester listening to a psychologist lecture, reading a text-book, and participating in experiments (Holmes, 1967) would do better at figuring out what a psychologist might expect them to do in an experiment. This prediction is not necessarily required by the demand-characteristics formulation, but it is consistent with it. If evidence is found in support of this prediction, it would be difficult for the "conditioning" and the "concept-formation only" interpretations to account for.

The last hypothesis concerned a direct manipulation of the difficulty of learning the interlist associations. If this were possible, then it should reduce contingency awareness and consequently the probability of becoming aware of the correct demand characteristics, which in turn should reduce the conditioning. The rationale for this manipulation is similar to that of the color-naming manipulation of Insko and Oakes, although operationally the variables are quite different. For the Staats' interpretation of their experiment, since subjects supposedly didn't know the associations anyway and since the strength of response depends on number of pairings of the syllables with meaningful words, increasing the difficulty of noting interlist associations should have no effect on conditioning as long as the number of trials is held constant.

METHOD

Subjects

Subjects were 288 introductory psychology students at the University of Nebraska at Lincoln. They were run in 12 groups of 24 each. Actually 19 other subjects were also run, but they were randomly eliminated, before the data were analyzed, to equalize the Ns in the 12 groups.

Experimental Design

For an overall description of the basic experimental design, the reader is referred to Staats and Staats (1957, 1958). The present independent variables were: psychological sophistication of subjects (naïve versus sophisticated), difficulty of interlist association (2, 4, and 10 filler syllables), and direction of conditioning (reversal of the syllable-meaning association), making a $2 \times 3 \times 2$ design. In addition, there were the assessed variables of interlist association (second learning test) and postexperimental measures of contingency and demand awareness.

Subject sophistication was varied by running half the subjects (naïve) during the first two weeks of the university semester. The other half of the subjects (sophisticated) were run eleven weeks later in the semester. To control for possible biasing effects of early and late volunteers, subjects were not allowed to volunteer. The class rolls of three introductory sections were randomly divided and half were asked to participate early and the other half later. A plausible cover story was given for this procedure so as not to arouse suspicion, that is, that some learning experiments require random samples of subjects. Subjects run at the first of the semester were carefully sworn to secrecy until the end of the semester.

Association difficulty was manipulated by varying the number of neutrally paired or filler syllables included with the two crucial nonsense syllables. The crucial syllables were yof and wuh. In the easy condition (AD_1) only 2 filler syllables (laj and giw) were included with the crucial syllables. It was expected that with a list of only 4 nonsense syllables it would be rather easy to discover the relationship between the two lists. For the moderate difficulty condition (AD_2), 4 filler syllables were included (laj, giw, xeh, and qug). For the difficult condition (AD_3), 10 filler syllables were included (laj, giw, xeh, qug, meq, sij, vaf, vec, yim, and xad). It was expected that this amount of extra diversionary material would make the interlist association rather obscure. The effectiveness of this manipulation was checked by the "second learning test" of interlist association. Number of conditioning trials (18 pairings of pleasant or unpleasant words with yof and wuh) was held constant for all three groups.

Procedure

Through the presentation of the semantic differential rating scales the procedure was essentially the same as that of Staats and Staats in their many conditioning experiments. Beyond that point the procedure was changed to accommodate the second learning test and the postexperimental questionnaire. The experiment was conducted in a large classroom and subjects were seated with at least one empty seat between them so as to discourage either talking or copying.

The same deceptive orienting instructions were read to all groups. These were similar, but not identical, to those of Staats and Staats (1957); that is, "This is an experiment to see how well we can learn two separate lists simultaneously through two different sensory modalities." The nonsense syllables were presented by means of a slide projector. Each syllable appeared for four seconds with a one-second change time. The lists of syllables (4, 6, or 12 in length for the three difficulty groups) were repeated eighteen times in unsystematic order. One second after a syllable appeared the experimenter gave a spoken word and subjects repeated it in unison. For the crucial syllables (yof or wuh) the spoken words were consistently pleasant for one and unpleasant for the other. The order was reversed for half of the groups. The remainder of the spoken words were of neutral connotation.

Following learning, subjects were given the same deceptive orientation used by Staats and Staats, that is, "How we learn lists of words may be affected by how we feel toward the various words." They then read instructions for marking semantic differential scales. The first learning test consisted of 24 nonsense syllables each on a separate page of a small booklet. Beside each syllable was a blank line and below it was a pleasant-unpleasant semantic differential scale. Subjects rated all 24 syllables and made a check mark on the blank line if the syllable was one they had learned.

Up to this point the procedure was essentially a replication of the Staats and Staats procedure with the exception of the manipulation of association difficulty and the extra syllables added to the rating booklet so as to make it less obvious. The second learning test, consisting of a sheet of paper containing six syllables with large blank spaces below them, was then introduced. Instructions were as follows:

Now, I also want to find out how many of the spoken words you can remember. We are passing out a recall test of the spoken words. We want to know how many associations between the spoken words and the written syllables you learned. So, for each nonsense syllable listed, write below it as many spoken words as you remember going with it. You may guess. This is a timed test and you will have only five minutes.

This measure represents an indirect index of awareness of the interlist contingency with considerable face validity.[3] It also has the advantage of being presented in the form of a test within the context of the experiment itself, rather than being postexperimental. The rationale is this: If subjects learned or formed the concept "good and bad words go with certain syllables," then they should be able to demonstrate it by writing down many more good and bad associates to the correct syllables than subjects depending on rote recall of something they had not been instructed to learn.

Finally, the postexperimental written questionnaire was introduced with orienting instructions, like those used in a previous study (Page, 1968), to enlist the honesty and cooperation of subjects while releasing them from the demand characteristics accompanying the experiment proper. Since there are many forms of postexperimental questionnaires currently in use, and since the resolution of the contradiction between the data of Insko and Oakes (1966) and those of the present study may involve differences in questioning and scoring, the entire postexperimental interview is reported in Table 4–4. Each question appeared on a separate sheet of a small booklet.

Table 4–4   *Postexperimental Questionnaire*

1. What was the purpose of this experiment and what were you supposed to do?
2. During the experiment did you ever have the idea that its purpose might be something other than what I was telling you? What?
3. Thinking back to the experiment, did you notice at the time any relationship between certain syllables on the screen and the words that were spoken? What?
4. If you noticed any relationship between the lists, is this something you were actually aware of during the experiment or is it something you thought of while filling out these questions?
5. Do you remember approximately when it was that you noticed this? (1) right away, (2) first one-third of learning, (3) second one-third, (4) last one-third, (5) while taking the first learning test, (6) while taking the second learning test.
6. What did you think was the purpose of the rating scales at the time you were filling them out, if anything?
7. How did you go about deciding what rating to give the various nonsense syllables?
8. Did you think that the experimenter might have expected that you would rate certain of the nonsense syllables in any certain way? Explain.
9. Was your answer to Question 8 something you were actually aware of before or during the marking of the rating scales or something that you thought of afterwards?
10. What syllable was always or usually paired with travel words?
    a. How certain are you of this or are you guessing?
        Guessing——:——:——:——:——:——:——Certain
    b. Is this something you were aware of during the experiment or something you thought of since? Please explain if necessary.
11. What syllable was always or usually paired with words of pleasant meaning?
    a. How certain are you of this or are you guessing?
        Guessing——:——:——:——:——:——:——Certain
    b. Is this something you were aware of during the experiment or something you thought of since? Please explain if necessary.
12. What syllable was always or usually paired with words of unpleasant meaning?

Table 4-4—contd.

a. How certain are you of this or are you guessing?
Guessing——:——:——:——:——:——:——Certain
b. Is this something you were aware of during the experiment or something you thought of since? Please explain if necessary.

13. Were you ever aware during the experiment that yof [wuh for the other group] was always paired with words of pleasant meaning or connotation and that wuh [yof] was always paired with words of unpleasant meaning? And, if so, were you aware of any effect this might have had on you as you marked the rating scales? Explain.

14. Assuming that you knew the pleasant and unpleasant words and what was expected on the marking of the rating scales, rate your attitude while marking the rating scales.
Resist the influence——:——:——:——:——:——:——Mark the right answers.

15. Please make any other comments that you feel might help us understand your reaction to this experiment.

16. Have you had any previous courses in psychology such as in high school?

17. Do you know the meaning of the term conditioning? If so, did you think about it during this experiment?

The assumption behind this questionnaire is that awareness, like problem solving, is basically a dichotomy. A subject either knows it or he doesn't. Also, subjects aren't likely to tell about such things as demand awareness unless specifically and carefully asked. The use of brief or vague questions may lead to either too many false positives or false negatives or both. These incorrectly scored subjects of either type would reduce any association that might actually be present. Questionnaires should have multiple indicators of awareness, and judges should score in terms of the total context of the questionnaire. Notice Questions 11 and 12, which are crucial questions for contingency awareness. Not only does a subject have to write down the correct contingency, but he has to be reasonably certain without guessing and willing to say he knew it earlier and isn't reflecting back now that the experiment is over. With this type of multiple-criteria approach, one should be able to separate most of the aware from the unaware subjects.

Scoring Procedures

It was not possible to use the original Latin-square analysis (Staats & Staats, 1957) based on each subject having two scores. Because this study added two extra factors, it was more convenient to assign each subject a single conditioning score (yof rating minus wuh rating) which is equivalent to the previous scoring. This score can vary from -6 to $+6$ and should average approximately 0 for neutral nonsense syllables if there is no conditioning.

The second learning test of interlist associates was scored so as to maximize the measurement of learning of the correct concept (good words with yof and bad with wuh, or the reverse). Subjects who wrote down several guesses that were neither pleasant nor unpleasant had not learned the correct concept.

Therefore, the most sensitive measure of interlist association would be total correct associates for the two crucial syllables minus total incorrect. Because this task proved to be impossible for subjects who hadn't formed the concept, this scoring resulted in a minus number (which depended on amount of guessing) for those who hadn't, and a large positive number for those who had. Actually, a cutoff score of 4 (2 for each syllable) was selected as a minimum criterion for considering a subject to have formed the concept.

Table 4-5   *Mean Conditioning (Disregarding Direction of Conditioning) for the Six Groups of the Experiment*

S.	ASSOCIATION DIFFICULTY			M
	AD₁	AD₂	AD₃	
Naïve	1.43	1.15	.23	.94
Sophisticated	2.11	2.21	1.08	1.80
M	1.77	1.68	.66	1.37

Table 4-6   *Summary of the Analysis of Variance Performed on Conditioning Scores for Two Levels of Sophistication, Three Levels of Association Difficulty, and Two Directions of Conditioning*

Source	df	MS	F
Sophistication (A)	1	24.50	2.74
Difficulty (B)	2	25.45	2.84
Conditioning (C)	1	539.01	60.22*
A × B	2	4.03	–
A × C	1	53.39	5.97†
B × C	2	36.70	4.10†
A × B × C	2	1.94	–
Error	276	8.95	

* $p < .001$.   † $p < .05$.

The postexperimental questionnaires were read and scored by two independent judges. The judges scored for contingency awareness (did the subject say he was aware, during learning, of the interlist association) on a 4-point scale of (1) clearly aware, (2) probably aware, (3) probably unaware, and (4) clearly unaware. Most subjects fell in either Categories 1 or 4. Only questions from 1 to 12 were considered. The judges made an overall evaluation of the consistency and clarity of the subjects' responses to all questions, but keyed on Questions 11 and 12, one of which had to be answered correctly and with certainty for the subjects to be considered contingency aware. The judges' ratings correlated $r = .96$ and they disagreed as to the dichotomy aware-unaware on only 5 of 288 subjects.

The judges then scored for demand awareness (did the subject say he was aware, before marking the rating scales, of how the experimenter expected him to rate the syllables) on the same 4-point scale. Any subject who was not contingency aware could not logically be considered to have been aware of correct demand characteristics. This may be an important difference between the present measure and the Insko and Oakes measure of demand awareness, because in the present data several subjects knew that the experimenter expected something, but they didn't know what. Also, some contingency aware subjects reported that they realized what was expected too late for it to affect their ratings; these were not considered demand aware. The judges correlated $r = .91$ on their ratings of this variable. While this is a high reliability, the difference in reliability between contingency and demand awareness suggests that the latter was more difficult to judge from the protocols. There were 20 disagreements for aware-unaware for this variable. For both demand and contingency awareness the average of both judges' ratings was used as the index of awareness in the analysis. Cooperation-resistance was scored keying on Questions 13 and 14. Knowing about conditioning and thinking about it during the experiment were scored separately for Question 17.

RESULTS

Results for the independent variables of subject sophistication and association difficulty are presented in Tables 4–5 and 4–6. The analysis of variance was performed on the signed conditioning scores described earlier. In Table 4–5 the data were collapsed over the two syllable-sign conditions so as to give a clearer picture of the differences between the two more important variables. In Table 4–5, conditioning is indicated by a positive deviation from zero, otherwise the scores used in Tables 4–5 and 4–6 are equivalent. The means in each of the cells of Table 4–5 are based on Ns of 48.

In Table 4–6, notice first the strong conditioning effect ($F = 60.22$, $p < .001$) showing that a replication of the Staats' results was obtained. Because of the nature of the experimental design (half of the subjects conditioned in one direction and the other half in the other), the hypotheses regarding subject sophistication and association difficulty are tested by the interactions of these variables with the conditioning effect. In Table 4–6 the interaction between sophistication and conditioning is significant ($F = 5.97$, $p < .05$). Notice (see Table 4–5) that the sophisticated subjects showed more conditioning ($\bar{X} = 1.80$) than the naïve subjects ($\bar{X} = .94$) as predicted. The interaction between association difficulty and conditioning is also significant ($F = 4.10$, $p < .05$). From Table 4–5 we see a marked attenuation of conditioning in the difficult condition ($\bar{X} = .66$) relative to the other two conditions ($\bar{X}s = 1.77$ and 1.68) as predicted. Scores on the second learning test paralleled the pattern of results in Table 4–5, indicating that an attenuation of interlist association did occur in Group AD_3.

Recall the predictions concerning the relationships between the conditioned rating responses, the test for interlist association, and the measures of awareness. Since these variables were all eithei dichotomies or sharply bimodal, they were made into dichotomies before testing the association between them. Chi-squares were computed and converted into phi coefficients (see Table 4–7) to obtain a measure of strength of

Table 4–7 *Summary of phi Coefficients (over Their Appropriate phi$_{max}$ Values) of Associations between Four Dichotomized Variables*

Variable	2	3	4
1. Conditioned ratings	.67/.90	.81/.93	.69/1.00
2. Contingency awareness		.86/.88	.79/ .88
3. Demand awareness			.76/1.00
4. Association learning			

association. All of the relationships were very strong and highly significant as predicted. Under each phi coefficient is given the appropriate phi$_{max}$. This provides a basis for comparing strengths of association as phi$_{max}$ is the maximum value of phi obtainable with the given marginal proportions (Guilford, 1956).

The tight association between all of the variables in Table 4–7 is striking. This means that if a subject had a high conditioning score (+ 4 or greater difference between positive and negative syllable), there is a high probability that he also did well on the test of association. He also was able to state postexperimentally the interlist contingencies and claimed to have been rather certain of them during the learning and before the rating. He also claimed that he knew, before marking the rating scales, how the experimenter expected him to mark them. This is very strong support for the explanation of the Staats' results presented earlier.

While all the variables in Table 4–7 are tightly bound together, the smaller differences in strength of association are meaningful. The best predictor of conditioning is demand awareness, not contingency awareness as claimed by Insko and Oakes. In fact, 18 subjects were contingency aware who weren't demand aware, and these subjects did not show high conditioning. The mean for this group, when conditioning was scored as a positive deviation from 0, was .11, which was not significantly different from 0 ($t = .03$, ns). The mean of the unaware group was also almost exactly 0 ($-.02$). The mean for the subjects who were both contingency and demand aware was 4.6, which was quite significantly different from 0 ($t = 37.33$, $p < .0001$). While demand awareness is closely associated with contingency awareness (the first criterion for demand awareness was contingency awareness), the slight discrepancy between these measures makes demand awareness a stronger correlate of the conditioned ratings.

Figure 4-2 presents the distributions for conditioning scores of demand aware and cooperating versus unaware subjects. The direction of conditioning is folded over in this figure so that positively signed

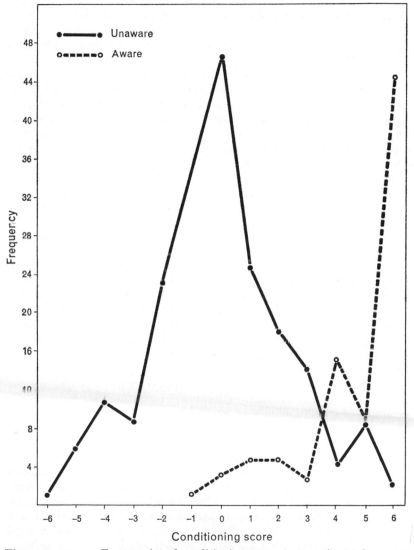

Figure 4-2 Frequencies of conditioning scores on experimental syllables yof and wuh (positive minus negative syllable) for the unaware (*n* = 195) versus the demand aware and cooperating subjects (*n* = 86).

scores mean behavior in the direction of conditioning. Notice the symmetrical distribution of scores for unaware subjects; only two had conditioning scores of 6 while more than 50 percent of the demand awares had scores of 6. In Figure 4–3, notice that a distribution of "conditioning" scores artificially generated on control syllables looks just like the distribution for unawares on experimental syllables. Only demand awares rated the experimental syllables any differently than control syllables.

What of the demand aware subjects with positive but not extreme scores? A few at 4 were aware of both contingencies, but did not use the ends of the scales. Most demand aware subjects with conditioning scores of 5 or less were only aware of one contingency. If a subject was aware that extreme ratings were expected for only one syllable and rated it accordingly while rating the other syllable according to his actual feelings about a nonsense syllable, then his conditioning score should be positive and would vary according to how he rated the syllable on which he was unaware. This is exactly what happened. All aware subjects with conditioning scores of 6 were aware of both contingencies; most with lower scores were aware of only one. These findings are very consistent with the general formulation which generated the experiment.

Cooperation-resistance has not been discussed in this paper because the number of resistors ($n = 7$) was much smaller than found in a previous study (Page, 1968). However, these few who reported resisting did not show conditioning, corresponding to the previous results.

Recall that subjects were asked whether they knew the meaning of conditioning and if they had thought about it during the experiment. The argument of this paper does not depend upon aware subjects knowing or thinking about conditioning; consequently no predictions were made, but it would be interesting support for the argument if some of them did. The association between sophistication and knowing the meaning of conditioning was highly significant ($\chi^2 = 70.6$, $df = 1$, $p < .001$). Only 10 of 144 sophisticated subjects did not know the meaning of conditioning while this was true for 75 of the naïves. Most introductory students apparently do learn something during a semester. What is more interesting is that almost half of the naïve group also knew about conditioning, and therefore "naïve" wasn't an entirely correct description of this group. The association between knowing the meaning of conditioning and demand awareness was also significant ($\chi^2 = 9.65$, $df = 1$, $p < .01$), though it doesn't account for a large amount of total variance. Of those ($n = 203$) who knew the meaning of conditioning there was a highly significant association ($\chi^2 = 36.55$, $df = 1$, $p < .001$) between thinking about conditioning during the experiment and demand awareness. Perhaps these data should not be overinterpreted, but they seem to suggest that while knowing about conditioning (and probably other psychology-related concepts) and thinking about it are not required for becoming demand aware in this situation, they do facilitate it.

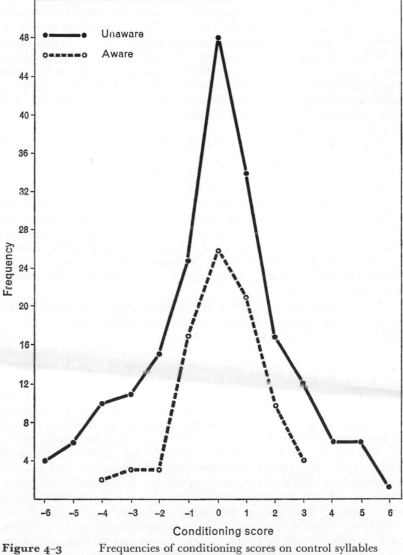

Figure 4-3   Frequencies of conditioning scores on control syllables laj and giw (first minus second syllable with order reversed for half the subjects) for the unaware versus the demand aware and cooperating subjects.

DISCUSSION

Every hypothesis of this study was clearly supported and all the converging evidence seems to attest to the essential correctness of the formulation which generated the predictions. It appears that the Staats' (1958) classical conditioning of evaluative affect or attitudes interpretation of their data is incorrect. The reaction they evoked in their subjects was far too complex, and apparently cognitively mediated, to be labeled classical conditioning. This critique says nothing about the general theory which they believe was demonstrated by their experiment (Staats, 1967). Attitudes certainly are learned and perhaps sometimes through a process similar to classical conditioning. But this neat little deception experiment, using college sophomores as subjects, does not seem to demonstrate it.

The present study supports the idea that the so-called conditioned attitudes are entirely artifacts of demand characteristics. This is not to say that the social perception, social influence, and other social psychological variables present in the total laboratory situation were not genuine and interesting psychological phenomena, but they are artifactual sources of variance from the point of view of what the original experiments were designed to study. Perhaps the demand-characteristics problem is such a limiting factor on deception experiments that the kinds of hypotheses the Staats were interested in testing simply cannot be tested in the psychological laboratory at the present stage of development.

From the present vantage point it seems that while attitudes are learned phenomena, it is rather naïve to suppose that a brief, deceptive, and highly artificial laboratory experiment could induce genuine attitudes towards neutral stimuli. Perhaps psychologists would do better in the future to recognize the limitations of "quick and easy" deception experiments such as here described. The popularity of such methodology in our discipline seems symptomatic of a kind of worship of experimental manipulations for their own sake (Bakan, 1967) without due regard for the complexities or the actualities of the social context in which these manipulations occur (Sherif, Sherif, & Nebergall, 1965).

The conflict between the present results and those of Insko and Oakes (1966) as to the relative importance of contingency and demand awareness remains to be clarified by further empirical investigation. While they found that demand awareness could not account for all of the variance (Insko, 1967, p. 29), the present study suggests that it can. There are many procedural differences between these two studies, most specifically the different questionnaires and scoring techniques used in assessing awareness. In addition to differences in specific operations, there were basic differences in assumptions about the nature of so-called "awareness." In the present study an elaborate and multifaceted written questionnaire was used to answer a simple question: Did the subjects know the approximate purpose of the experiment while it was going on? Insko and Oakes used a simpler oral questionnaire to answer a more difficult question. Under the assumption that demand awareness is a continuum, they attempted to quantify that continuum. They assumed that individual differences in clarity of expression in responding to questions was an accurate reflection of the so-called "continuum of demand awareness," and then classified degrees of clarity on an ordinal scale. If in fact demand awareness is more accurately thought of as a dichotomy, and Insko and Oakes were actually quantifying something only roughly correlated with awareness, then this could account for the lower correlation between their demand-awareness scale and the rating scales. However, which of these sets of assumptions about the nature of demand awareness is more adequate remains a question for further investigation.

NOTES

1. Requests for reprints should be sent to Monte Page, Department of Psychology, University of Nebraska, Lincoln, Nebraska 68508.
2. This research was supported in part by a grant from the University of Nebraska Research Council.
3. The author is indebted to Katherine E. Baker for suggesting this measure.

REFERENCES

BAKAN, D. *On method: Toward a reconstruction of psychological investigation.* San Francisco: Jossey-Bass, 1967.

COHEN, B. H. Role of awareness in meaning established by classical conditioning. *Journal of Experimental Psychology,* 1964, **67**: 373–378.

GUILFORD, J. P, *Fundamental statistics in psychology and education.* (3rd ed.) New York: McGraw-Hill, 1956.

HOLMES, D. S. Amount of experience in experiments as a determinant of performance in later experiments. *Journal of Personality and Social Psychology,* 1967, **7**: 403–407.

INSKO, C. A. *Theories of attitude change.* New York: Appleton-Century-Crofts, 1967.

INSKO, C. A., & Oakes, W. F. Awareness and the "conditioning" of attitudes. *Journal of Personality and Social Psychology,* 1966, **4**: 487–496.

KELMAN, H. C. Human use of human subjects: The problem of deception in social psychological experiments. *Psychological Bulletin,* 1967, **67**: 1–11.

ORNE, M. T. On the social psychology of the psychological experiment: With particular reference to demand characteristics and their implications. *American Psychologist,* 1962, **17**: 776–783.

PAGE, M. M. Role of awareness in the classical conditioning of meaning. Unpublished master's thesis, University of Oklahoma, 1964.

PAGE, M. M. Modification of figure-ground perception as a function of awareness of demand characteristics. *Journal of Personality and Social Psychology,* 1968, **9**: 59–66.

SHERIF, C. W., Sherif, M., & Nebergall, R. E. *Attitude and attitude change.* Philadelphia: Saunders, 1965.

SILVERMAN, I. Role-related behavior of subjects in laboratory studies of attitude change. *Journal of Personality and Social Psychology*, 1968, **8**: 343–348.

SPIELBERGER, C. D. The role of awareness in verbal conditioning. In C. W. Eriksen (Ed.), *Behavior and awareness.* Durham, N.C.: Duke University Press, 1962.

SPIELBERGER, C. D., & DeNike, L. D. Descriptive behaviorism versus cognitive theory in verbal operant conditioning. *Psychological Review*, 1966, **73**: 306–326.

STAATS, A. W. An outline of an integrated learning theory of attitude formation and function. In M. Fishbein (Ed.), *Readings in attitude theory and measurement.* New York: Wiley, 1967.

STAATS, C. K., & Staats, A. W. Meaning established by classical conditioning. *Journal of Experimental Psychology*, 1957, **54**: 74–80.

STAATS, A. W., & Staats, C. K. Attitudes established by classical conditioning. *Journal of Abnormal and Social Psychology*, 1958, **57**: 37–40.

Arthur W. Staats[1]

Experimental Demand Characteristics and the Classical Conditioning of Attitudes

As previously indicated, the issue of awareness versus conditioning in the context of learning experiments is the type of conflict in interpretation which arises in a science (Finley & Staats, 1967). That is, it is not unusual for the same experimental results to be interpreted in two different ways, in the context of two different theories. Sometimes such controversies are resolved by conducting a "crucial" experiment which clearly verifies one theory and refutes the other. Certainly, this is one of the dreams of many scientists.

More usually, however, the issue is resolved in other ways. One theory is found to have greater advantages in that its principles are extended to a greater number of events; the theory presents greater possibility for prediction and control of events, and thus it thereby generates more successful experimentation; and so on. It has been the author's plan to concentrate his efforts in the realm of developing the general goodness of a competitive theory rather than to criticize competitors. That is, the author's emphasis has been on the development and extension of his learning theory in a comprehensive experimental and theoretical manner to various aspects of human behavior (see Staats, 1963, 1964, 1968a, 1968b; in press).

However, it is felt that it would be unfortunate if aspects of the learning theory and experimental methods were to be weakened because a criticism was successful through the absence of a rebuttal. This brief note is thus being written in response to the interpretation Page (1969) has made of his experimental results and, in so doing, to other suggestions (see Cohen, 1964) that the classical conditioning of meaning may

From *Journal of Personality and Social Psychology*, 1969, **11**: 187–192.
Copyright © 1969 by The American Psychological Association and reprinted with permission of author and The American Psychological Association.

be attributed to "awareness" in the subjects, rather than to the conditioning process.

Thus, it seems worthwhile to indicate that Page's points arc not crucial challenges to the author's learning theory of attitudes (see Staats, 1968a, 1968b) or to the experimental methods of the author which have been employed in a series of studies by the author and associates, as well as by other investigators. In beginning, it should be indicated that Page's results are not contested—the study appears to be very well conducted. It is the interpretation of the results that is in question.

Page says that a bimodal distribution of scores is the giveaway. In such cases of bimodal distribution he suggests that one must suspect that conditioning is not involved, but rather the demand characteristics of the procedures get the subjects to respond in a way that looks as if conditioning had occurred. The view that a bimodal distribution is inconsistent with the operation of learning principles in the present experimental procedure arises because Page did not consider the learning task in detail in learning terms. A bimodal distribution is not anomalous. While the principle involved is that of classical conditioning, the experimental situation is actually a complex one.

One must distinguish between the operation of the simple principle of classical conditioning and the complex behaviors necessary to get the conditioning. The conditioning occurs when the subject looks at the CS syllable and listens to the UCS word which elicits the attitude response to be conditioned to the CS. Simple as this may be diagrammed, in the actual experimental procedure some rather complex behaviors are required of the subject for the CS-UCS pairings to occur as they are supposed to. The subject must look at the CS and listen to the UCS. If he does not attend to both, conditioning will not occur. Some subjects do not attend; the language conditioning procedure is repetitious, boring, and seemingly fairly senseless. With 6 syllables paired each with 18 UCS words there are 108 presentations in the conditioning phase. Some subjects do not attend, daydream, and so on.

Moreover, some subjects also employ various strategies for attempting to memorize the CS syllables together as a word-association chain. Or the subject may attempt this with the UCS words, although the author developed the instructions to prevent these interfering behaviors. Thus, although the presentation of a CS syllable and UCS word may be considered to be a classical conditioning trial, it is not possible to strap the human subject into a harness where the stimuli may be reliably presented and the organism will not engage in the interfering activities. The author has been confronted with cases of other investigators who did not get the attitude conditioning because of deficient analysis of the experimental task, and consequent deficient procedures.

At any rate, it would be expected that there would be subjects who attend well and are highly conditioned, others who attend partially and are partially conditioned, and others who do not attend, or participate in interfering mnemonic behaviors, and who do not evidence conditioning. That is, the subjects who attend well and do not engage in mnemonic behaviors will receive the clearest-cut conditioning. The bimodality characteristics of the conditioning procedures are determined in part by the percentage of subjects who are in the first category. It would be expected that differences in instructions and procedures (individual versus group conditioning, the manner in which UCS words are presented, and so on) would affect the extent and distribution of conditioning and awareness. For example, the author has observed that if the positive attitudinal words are pronounced in a positive manner and the negative words in a negative manner, there will be much greater conditioning and awareness—a sharper bimodality. It is interesting to note that $8\frac{1}{2}$ percent of the subjects scored extreme conditioning in the author's original attitude (evaluative meaning) conditioning procedure employing nonsense syllables. In the latest study with which the author is acquainted,[2] the same procedures were followed except that the order of the CS and UCS was reversed in a backward-conditioning method. With this method, conditioning was significant, but less, and there were only 7 percent of the subjects who had maximal scores. Page's results, it may be noted, show about twice this percentage maximally conditioned, perhaps due to procedural variables which would enhance extreme conditioning and thus awareness. At any rate, the bimodality of the distribution is no evidence for or against a conditioning interpretation. Bimodality arises because of the extraconditioning behaviors the subjects display in the experiment, and the other variables mentioned.

Page also makes a point of finding a relationship between what he calls the naïveté-sophistication variable and the conditioning. The variable here is between early in the semester versus late in the semester participation—ample opportunity for the students to be informed about the experiment from other students or from reading about the experiment itself if certain introductory psychology textbooks are employed. This result is thus really not consequential as a verification of either the cognitive or conditioning interpretation.

Page also finds that recall of the CS and UCS associations depends on the "difficulty" of the task (number of irrelevant nonsense syllables in the task), and recall is related to the extent of conditioning and awareness. None of these findings contradicts the present author's conditioning theory, however, as was assumed. That is, Page's addition of nonsense syllables increases the repetitive, boring nature of the task, not its difficulty. (Page's interpretation of the difficulty variable is actually based upon an implicit assumption that the subjects are really attempting to divine the actual purpose of the experimenter.) This increase means that fewer of the subjects will continue to attend well, and fewer will be conditioned. Since fewer will experience the CS and UCS pairings, fewer will be able to indicate later that UCS words went with what CS. Let us assume, as will be elaborated below, that extent of awareness depends upon extent of conditioning. In that case, Page's manipulation of "difficulty" will produce fewer conditioned subjects and thus fewer aware subjects. As the learning analysis of the task indicates, the "difficulty" variable in Page's experiment would be expected to produce just the results obtained.

At this point, it appears germane to challenge more directly the whole rationale of the demand-characteristic procedures employed, and thus the demand-characteristic position. That is, Page suggests that the instructions and conditioning task the present author developed actually "demand" from the subject that he rate the syllables in a certain way irrespective of a conditioning process. This demand characteristic is thought to function even though the instructions, and so on, were composed to be deceptive. It may be suggested, in contrast, that Page's questionnaire has far greater "demand characteristics" than the original procedures. (This is also true of the study by Insko & Oakes, 1966, which Pages cites in his article.) The questionnaire actually *demands* that the subject indicate that he saw through the purpose of the experiment. This demand confronts the subject from the beginning item, with no deception involved. The item states: "What was the purpose of this experiment and what were you supposed to do?" From here on the subject is exposed item by item (if the subjects encountered the items sequentially) to additional stimuli that would effectively program him to the desired position—if he has made some of the necessary observations and can recall them.

The demand-characteristic rationale also assumes that the subjects are in some manner reticent about revealing that they know the purpose of the experiment and what they were "supposed" to do in response to the question the author originally posed to them. This item was: "Would you write down anything you thought about the experiment, especially anything you thought about the purpose of the experiment *while* you were participating in the experiment." The author still feels that this item pretty effectively elicits the subjects' thoughts about the experiment while they were participating. If anything, it probably elicits *more* awareness than that which occurred during the conditioning procedure. That is, rating the pleasantness or unpleasantness of the CS word probably also leads some otherwise unaware subjects to become aware when they later encounter the question concerning purpose.

In this context it is interesting to note that Cohen (1964), whom Page refers to, altered the original item to test awareness of the subjects —although this point was not clearly brought out in his study. That is, he changed the item by deleting the phrase "while you were participating in the experiment." Cohen obtained a greater number of aware subjects than in the original study as would be expected from the procedural difference. This should have been taken into account in his interpretation.

In any event, the variation of Cohen's results from the original results indicates how the questions asked after the experiment will influence the subjects' responses. On this basis, one has to challenge the questionnaire procedure itself. Depending upon how it is conducted, it will *produce* varying levels of "awareness" as well as measure it. The extent of influence on awareness is difficult to judge.

In his introduction, Page characterizes the process he feels occurs in the present author's attitude-conditioning procedures. That is, he suggests that the subjects become aware of the demands of the situation and respond accordingly. A contrasting view may be presented. This may be done by describing the response of one of the subjects to the question concerning the purpose of the experiment. She said that as she was participating in the study, she was thinking that she did not like the name Dutch (a CS word), and that at this moment the name flashed on the screen and was followed by a negative attitudinal word. The subject stated that she then realized what had been occurring and why she did not like the name Dutch. It seems quite likely that subjects could be conditioned to "awareness" in this manner and yet be led later to respond to a questionnaire in a manner that would corroborate the demand-characteristic interpretation.

At any rate, it is suggested that a usual subject, who had been conditioned to a positive emotional response to a syllable and who had learned some of the UCS words paired with the syllables, could on the questionnaire come to be scored as an aware subject, even though he might not have been aware in any causative sense. Actually, an analysis which considered the conditioned attitude (emotional response) capable of mediating similar-attitude word responses would not even have to assume the subject had *learned* any syllable word pairs, even though he could cite them when questioned. Along this line, it is interesting that Pollio (1963) found that the words given as associates of the CS syllables had in many cases never been presented to the subjects in the conditioning procedures. However, even in those cases these word associates tended to be of the correct attitudinal meaning. Pollio concluded that the conditioned attitude mediated the occurrence of these word responses.

The preceding discussion suggests that we have a circumstance in which the same empirical events are interpreted differently within the two theoretical contexts. It is thus also relevant in presenting the learning theory to summarize some of the supporting evidence which has not been included in Page's paper. There are several experimental findings that should be brought to bear upon the matter.

First, the classical conditioning of attitudes in the first-order situation is well documented. A CS word paired with an aversive UCS will come to be rated as unpleasant, and also to be responded to emotionally as indexed by physiological measures of emotional response such as the GSR (Staats, Staats, & Crawford, 1962). Such emotional responses could not be considered as voluntary responses to the demand characteristics of the experiment, it should be noted. In this experiment the subjects after the conditioning also rated the CS word on an attitude scale (again, a 7-point pleasant-unpleasant scale.) The subjects who had been in the conditioning procedure rated the word as significantly more negative than did control subjects. This rating, it should be recalled, would be interpreted by Page to be a result of the demand characteristics of the experimental procedure. Thus, it is important to see also that the intensity of the involuntary emotional conditioning was significantly correlated with the intensity of the attitudinal conditioning as measured by the rating scale. Subjects who were more intensely conditioned to an emotional response to the stimulus gave a more intense attitudinal response (rating) to the stimulus.

It may be added that Maltzman, Raskin, Gould, and Johnson (1965) have replicated these findings using the same type of procedure. It is interesting to note that in their study the intensity of the conditioning was varied over three groups of subjects by varying the intensity of the aversive UCS. The important point here is that the subjects could not be demand aware, or aware in any way, that they were receiving different intensities of conditioning, yet they were conditioned physiologically and by attitude rating in accord with the intensity of the conditioning. (The present author has also verified the first-order conditioning of attitudinal responses to words in both animals and preverbal children [Staats, 1968a]. Moreover, much of the literature on counterconditioning in behavior therapy is a verification of the classical conditioning theory of attitudes as indicated in Staats, in press.)

Results relevant to the awareness versus conditioning positions are also available from the higher-order attitude-conditioning studies, where attitude words are used as the UCS. For example, Pecjak and Smith (in press) have employed a modification of the author's original procedure in an interesting study. Two types of conditioned stimuli were employed, color stimuli or geometric forms. Four of each kind were used so there were eight conditioned stimuli. These stimuli were each paired with either positive, negative, or neutral attitudinal stimuli for each subject; two with positive attitudinal words, two with negative, and four with neutral words. The purpose of the experiment was to condition attitudinal responses to the separate color and form stimuli and then to combine pairs of colors and forms into compound stimuli, and then measure the type of attitude response made to the compounds. The various combinations of compounds were made and the extent of conditioned positive or negative attitudinal responses was tested. The results expected from the classical conditioning attitude theory occurred. Two positively conditioned stimuli when combined elicited the most positive attitude responses, the positive-neutral compound elicited the next most positive attitude responses, the neutral-neutral compound was neutral, the neutral-negative compound elicited a mildly negative attitude, and the negative-negative compound stimulus elicited a more intense conditioned negative attitude response. It is difficult to conclude that the subjects would have been *aware* of the complex conditioning they were subjected to, the complex combinations of conditioned stimuli with which they were presented, and the summation of conditioned attitudes which a demand-awareness interpretation would suggest they were "supposed" to display when the separate conditioned stimuli were compounded.

One other experiment will be cited in which the classical conditioning of attitudes occurred where the influence of demand characteristics can be negated. Yavuz and Bousfield (1963) conducted a study in which subjects had the deceptive task of learning English response words to Turkish stimulus words. Each English word was supposed to be the equivalent of the Turkish word with which it was paired. Criterion performance was three correct recalls of each of the English words upon presentation of the Turkish stimulus words. Actually, the putative English equivalents had been chosen to be either positive, neutral, or negative attitude words and thus to serve as potential UCS words, in the present terminology. The Turkish words may be considered to be the CS words which should come to elicit the attitude response elicited by the English word with which the Turkish word was paired. One week after this learning procedure the subjects were tested for knowledge of the "translations," and they also had to rate the Turkish words on a good-bad attitude scale. The rating was done *whether or not the subject could remember the English word he had learned in response to the Turkish word.* As expected on the basis of conditioning theory, the subjects had been conditioned to respond to the Turkish word with the attitude elicited by the English word that had been paired with the Turkish word. The important thing, however, is that *the subjects showed the attitude conditioning even when they could not remember the English word that had been paired with the Turkish word.* By the criterion which is set by cognitive psychologists, including Page, the subjects were not aware—but they were conditioned to the attitude, nevertheless. In terms of the social psychology of psychological experiments, it is interesting to note that Bousfield's theoretical orientation was one which would have expected the conditioned attitude to depend upon recall of the English word, not upon the classical conditioning of attitudes.

Other related experiments which support the classical conditioning theory of attitude formation and change could also be cited here (for example, Lott & Lott, 1960; Razran, 1938, 1940; Schutz & Naumoff, 1964). A very interesting experiment has also been published by Early (1968). In this study, the present author's attitude-conditioning procedures were employed with fourth- and fifth-grade children. After positive attitudinal conditioning to the *names* of "isolate" children, these isolates were themselves approached more in the free play situation by the conditioned children than were control isolate children. This study begins to show that classically conditioned attitudes affect behaviors other than the behavior of scoring a rating scale—a very important demonstration.

There is a point, related to the last one, which is germane here. That is, according to the author's general learning theory of attitudes a stimulus which is a CS for an attitude response should also have other learning functions (see Staats, 1964, 1968a, 1968b; in press). For one thing, a stimulus which elicited a positive attitude should function as a positive reinforcer; one eliciting a negative attitude should function as a negative reinforcer (or punishment). Thus the words used which elicited attitude responses in the classical conditioning procedures should also serve as reinforcing stimuli in an instrumental conditioning situation.

Finley and Staats (1967) have shown this to be the case with sixth-grade children. Using the same words that were shown to elicit positive attitudes in the experiments under discussion, it was found that a motor response could be learned by the children if the words were employed as reinforcing stimuli. When a positive-attitude word like VACATION, JOY, FAMILY, SUNSHINE was presented after the motor response for one group of subjects the response increased in frequency. For another group, negative attitudinal words such as HURT, POISON, BITTER, THIEF, on the other hand, acted as punishments and weakened the response. Neutral words had an intermediate effect. This study begins to explore the vast power that attitude stimuli have in molding our instrumental behaviors—an effect that has long been recognized in social psychology, albeit not within the context of explicitly stated empirical principles of behavior. The learning theory thus yields this expectation, and many others, which the cognitive position would not suggest.

This study is supplemented by another recent experiment (Pihl &

Greenspoon, in press). That is, a word was paired, for different groups of subjects, with UCSs which had varying levels of positive attitude. The CS word for the different subjects should come to elicit different levels of positive attitude and this should be shown by the extent to which the word would reinforce an instrumental response. This expectation of the present *learning* attitude theory was supported. It is difficult to see how "demand characteristics" could have affected the extent to which the subjects were later instrumentally conditioned as a function of the intensity of the original classical conditioning of the attitude response.

This summary by no means exhausts the studies supporting the classical conditioning analysis of attitude formation, in contrast to the "demand aware" interpretation. It may be suggested, however, that the evidence is very substantial and much of it has been influenced by the original experiments.

In conclusion, it may be noted that criticism of methodology may be very productive. The criticism may lead to improvements in the methodology developed in the substantive study. The criticism may, however, have its drawbacks also in cases where it dissuades individuals from accepting a productive theory or a productive experimental procedure. The present note is written to prevent the unjustified weakening of the learning theory of attitudes which in its elaborated form (see Staats, 1968b; in press) extends to a wide variety of human behavior in a manner important to the theorist, the experimentalist, and the practicing psychologist.

NOTES

1. Requests for reprints should be sent to Arthur W. Staats, Department of Psychology, University of Hawaii, Honolulu, Hawaii 96822.
2. B. A. Brewer and M. C. Gross. Unpublished study, University of Hawaii.

REFERENCES

COHEN, B. H. Role of awareness in meaning established by classical conditioning. *Journal of Experimental Psychology*, 1964, **67**: 373–378.

EARLY, C. J. Attitude learning in children. *Journal of Educational Psychology*, 1968, **59**: 176–180.

FINLEY, J. R., & Staats, A. W. Evaluative meaning words as reinforcing stimuli. *Journal of Verbal Learning and Verbal Behavior*, 1967, **6**: 193–197.

INSKO, C. A., & Oakes, W. Awareness and the "conditioning" of attitudes. *Journal of Personality and Social Psychology*, 1966, **4**: 487–496.

LOTT, B. E., & Lott, A. J. The formation of positive attitudes toward group members. *Journal of Abnormal and Social Psychology*, 1960, **61**: 297–300.

MALTZMAN, I., Raskin, P. C., Gould, J., & Johnson, O. Individual differences in the orienting reflex and semantic conditioning and generalization under different UCS intensities. Paper presented at the meeting of the Western Psychological Association, Honolulu, 1965.

PAGE, M. M. The social psychology of classical conditioning of attitude experiments. *Journal of Personality and Social Psychology*, 1969, **11**: 177–186.

PECJAK, V., & SMITH, S. Influence of induced evaluations and of codability upon the cognitive interaction of colors and forms. *Journal of Experimental Psychology*, in press.

PIHL, R. O., & Greenspoon, J. The effect of amount of reinforcement on the formation of the reinforcing value of a verbal stimulus. *Journal of Verbal Learning and Verbal Behavior*, in press.

POLLIO, H. R. Word associations as a function of conditioned meaning. *Journal of Experimental Psychology*, 1963, **66**: 454–460.

RAZRAN, G. H. S. Conditioning away social bias. *Psychological Bulletin*, 1938, **35**: 693.

RAZRAN, G. H. S. Conditioning response changes in rating and appraising sociopolitical slogans. *Psychological Bulletin*, 1940, **37**: 481.

SCHUTZ, R. E., & Naumoff, H. An application of Mowrer's sentence conditioning paradigms in developing evaluative meaning. *Journal of Verbal Learning and Verbal Behavior*, 1964, **1**: 459–462.

STAATS, A. W. (With contributions by C. K. Staats) *Complex human behavior*. New York: Holt, Rinehart & Winston, 1963.

STAATS, A. W. *Human Learning*. New York: Holt, Rinehart, & Winston, 1964.

STAATS, A. W. *Learning, language and cognition*. New York: Holt, Rinehart, & Winston, 1968. (a)

STAATS, A. W. Social behaviorism and human motivation: Principles of the attitude-reinforcer-discriminative system. In A. G. Greenwald, T. C. Brock, & T. M. Ostrom (Eds.), *Psychological foundations of attitudes*. New York: Academic Press, 1968. (b)

STAATS, A. W. Social behaviorism, human motivation, and the conditioning therapies. In B. Maher (Ed.), *Progress in experimental personality research*. New York: Academic Press, in press.

STAATS, A. W., Staats, C. K., & Crawford, H. L. First-order conditioning of meaning and the parallel conditioning of a GSR. *Journal of General Psychology*, 1962, **67**: 159–167.

YAVUZ, H. S., & Bousfield, W. A. Recall of connotative meaning. *Psychological Reports*, 1959, **5**: 319–320.

PART FIVE

Experimenter Reactions to the Psychological Laboratory

To what extent does the experimenter unknowingly contribute to his data? This question, although challenging the caricature of the scientist as a stoic and virtuous seeker of truth, is a fair one, for it could be as naïve to regard the experimenter as a passive administrator of his research as it would be to regard his subject as a passive responder. Rosenthal's portrait of the experimenter parallels Orne's conception of the subject. Both stress the essential *human condition* of these roles, in addition to their more formal or prescribed qualities.

There are several dimensions to the problem of "experimenter effects." One deals simply with what kind of person the experimenter is. Subjects may, for example, react differently to a male or female, white or black, anxious or relaxed experimenter. Closely related to this is the likelihood that the kind of person the experimenter is will influence his behavior toward subjects, or particular types of subjects. Again the issue of the generality of experimental results arises. To the extent that the experimenter *per se* is a determining factor in the experiment, that fact must be considered in interpreting and extending the findings. Sattler (1970) has reviewed an interesting manifestation of this matter in connection with the race of the experimenter in experimental and clinical settings.

The experimenter, as with the mystery writer, has the complex task of carrying out a substantial portion of his activities as if he had no idea of the outcome, when, in fact, he often has a very clear picture of—and perhaps precious stake in—what that outcome will be. In this context, it is Rosenthal's empirical citation of the experimenter as a covert communicator of his hypothesis that has captured the attention and critical interest of his colleagues. It appears that the experimenter's expectancy or hypothesis leads him to behave differentially toward subjects, depending upon their assignment to experimental conditions. Resulting group differences, then, may reflect differential treatment by the experimenter, regardless of the validity of the hypothesis itself. It is in this sense that the experimenter effect is a bias or artifact, for it may be responsible for data which appear to verify the prediction but which in fact may not be doing so. This phenomenon assumes added credibility, considering that subjects appear to be highly receptive to the kinds of cues or demand characteristics which, Rosenthal asserts, experimenters are prone to emit. It should be recognized, of course, that expectancy effects are not limited to the experimenter's interaction with his subjects, but may occur elsewhere—in the recording or analysis of data, in the experimenter's interaction with consultants from the computing center, etc.

Rosenthal is particularly interested in the processes by which hypotheses are conveyed to subjects. A recent study by Minor (1970) presents a new line of inquiry concerning this question of the mediation of expectancies. Minor used Rosenthal's paradigm experiment in which two groups of *experimenters* were given contradictory hypotheses of how their subjects should rate a series of photographs. Within each of these conditions, however, *subjects* were given high or low evaluation apprehension instructions. Minor observed that

the overall positive experimenter-expectancy effect . . . was entirely mediated by the high-evaluation apprehension group, in that it was only in this group that the expectancy held by an experimenter appeared to make a difference in the photo rating behavior of his subjects [p. 331].

Minor's study is a striking demonstration of the interactive quality of the experimenter-subject relationship and signals the necessity for conceptualizing their joint contribution to psychological data.

What procedures are there to circumvent the effects of the experimenter's expectancy? There are several dimensions to this question. One relates to the issue of student experimenters, as might typically be found in undergraduate courses in experimental psychology. Rosenthal (1966, Ch. 3) has pointed to a pervasive tendency for students—as the result of their instruction—to become outcome-oriented rather than process-oriented in their approach to psychological research. Rosenthal has not been reticent to admit the likelihood of cheating—the fabrication of data—as one response to this pressure for "correct results," nor does he suppose that such effects are unique to novice experimenters in quest of a good grade. Of greater significance, however, is the fact that most psychological researchers will have their orientation to research in such an atmosphere and it is likely that some of their values will be born here. Rosenthal urges laboratory instructors—and indeed all research supervisors—to avoid an emphasis on replicating the outcome of "classic studies" and to imbue in students an appreciation for "the thrill of the hunt."

In terms of specific methodological procedures, any technique which will focus the subject's attention on intended communication should reduce the amount or influence of unintended information conveyed by the experimenter. Making the rationale for the experiment convincing and reducing the arousal of evaluation apprehension are likely to be effective. Another set of techniques, elaborated upon by Rosenthal elsewhere (1966), involves the use of expectancy-control groups, analogous to Orne's quasi-control groups in regard to demand characteristics. Here one assesses the actual impact of the experimenter's expectancy, independent of the effects of the experimental treatment. Other strategies acknowledge the inevitability of the experimenter having an expectation, but recommend that he be ignorant of the assignment of subjects to the specific experimental conditions—or as ignorant as is feasible. Interestingly, the strategy of using more than one experimenter is one which may be useful in reducing experimenter bias, as in Levy's study, as well as reducing evaluation apprehension, as in Rosenberg's experiment. This is particularly true when the experiment features the role of a postexperimental interview.

Barber and Silver question the widespread and apparently uncritical acceptance of the experimenter-expectancy phenomenon. What motivated these investigators to undertake their prodigious review? One answer is found in a recent paper by Barber and his associates:

After failing to show the effect in five investigations, we (Barber & Silver, 1968a) looked very closely at all of the extant investigations that had attempted to demonstrate that the expectancy-biases of student-*E*s influence their *S*s' responses [Barber, Calverly, Forgione, McPeake, Chaves, & Bowen, 1969, p 6].

It was thus a personal and negative encounter with the expectancy effect that, at least in part, instigated the Barber and Silver critique. While it is tempting to speculate that Barber and Silver were operating under an expectancy for negative features in the experiments they reviewed, this is a moot question. The data are there for anyone to probe. Yet few would be inclined to be as thorough as these writers obviously were, and that is what is unique and imposing about their paper.

There are innumerable points of interest in the Barber and Silver review, as well as in Rosenthal's rebuttal, yet there is little agreement expressed in these papers on matters of substance. There does not seem to be one study or even a series of experiments that would substantially resolve the controversy expressed here. This is particularly true in matters of statistical design and the philosophical underpinnings of the null hypothesis decision procedure. Of interest in its own right, one would hope that this kind of argumentation will not result in a degeneration of scientific inquiry into the phenomenon, for example, in the manner of ESP—one investigator claiming it, another refuting it, ad infinitum. Barber and Silver certainly suggest that the expectancy effect is difficult to replicate, and there is other evidence as well (e.g., Jacob, 1968). Yet there are data to indicate that the phenomenon is indeed obtainable (e.g., Duncan, Rosenberg, & Finkelstein, 1969; Minor, 1970).

The issue of the replication of experiments is a central one in the Barber and Silver—Rosenthal debate. Levy has commented on this matter in an articulate fashion:

> The demonstration of the EBE [experimenter bias effect] in the Rosenthal and Fode experiment and others might be likened to a wife's discovery of a strange shade of lipstick on her husband's shirt collar. Whether or not she had suspected him of infidelity in the past, it seems unlikely that any number of unblemished shirt collars in the future will completely remove her concerns about his conjugal constancy. Thus it seems unlikely that the five failures to reject the null hypothesis by Barber *et al.* will in itself convince many of the rarity of the EBE or that it need not be taken into account in the design and interpretation of experiments [1969, p. 16].

What is needed, Levy argues, more than new instances of the expectancy effect, or its absence, is a theoretically oriented program of research in which each new empirical finding could be systematically located into a theoretical network. Minor's study, noted previously, is a good example. It was guided by the theoretical assertion that the expectancy effect would be facilitated in conditions where subjects were particularly sensitive to the experimenter's verbal behavior. Had this study failed to confirm this hypothesis, there would have still been informational value to the research—more than if one attempts solely to replicate the effect, does not find it, is criticized for not really replicating the original study *exactly*, etc. Although the concept of replication is basically sound, Levy's notion that "the perfect replication is a fiction" [p. 15] is well taken.

To what extent may one generalize from the findings concerning the experimenter expectancy effect? Barber and Silver argue persuasively that many of the experiments purporting to document this phenomenon are gross distortions of what might be termed professional psychological research. How often does one encounter journal reports in which there is a contingency between the results obtained and the amount of payment given to experimenters? Also it is rare to find experiments in which experimenters are assigned to only one of the conditions and, hence, have but one expectation concerning the directionality of results as they run subject after subject. Although not mentioned by Barber and Silver, one wonders about the numerous experiments which have as their central hypothesis a rather complex outcome—for example, an interaction between two or more independent variables or a complex matrix of correlation coefficients. Are unintended communications by the experimenter likely to produce these results? Aronson (1968) has distinguished between demonstrating that experimenter bias *can* intrude into experiments and demonstrating that it *does* in fact intrude into experiments, a distinction that would apply to evaluation apprehension and demand characteristics, as well. Although Rosenthal has shown the expectancy effect in situations beyond those having an obvious "pull" for the phenomenon, Barber and Silver justifiably add credence to the point Aronson is making.

Rosenthal and Jacobson, in the final selection, illustrate the expectancy effect in a setting far removed from its empirical development. This research is an excellent example of the fact that social psychological forces in research are by no means unique to the experimental laboratory. Completely arbitrary predictions regarding the achievement potential of students appear to be reflected in actual performance gains, quite in line with the predictions. This research, as with expectancy data in the laboratory, has been the subject of intense interest on methodological as well as substantive bases (e.g., Snow, 1969; Thorndike, 1968). The importance of checking on the effectiveness of the expectancy manipulation itself, noted by Barber and Silver, is dramatically illustrated by the teachers appearing unable to recall accurately the "bloomers" from a provided list of student names. Although this would seem to suggest that the expectancy effect was covert or unintended—if not miraculous—more evidence will be required before this aspect of the process of mediation is confirmed. Postresearch interviews regarding the role of expectancies would, in this context, seem to share some of the methodological difficulties involved in detecting the role of awareness or demand characteristics, noted in the previous section.

One basis for the popular acclaim that this research has received relates undoubtedly to its potential significance in explaining certain deficiencies in the educational progress of underprivileged children. Clark (1965), for example, has contended that a critical problem in educating ghetto children is that their teachers do not expect them to learn. The problem is not one of motivation in the learner but rather one of expectancies in the teacher. An underlying assumption here is that teachers form expectations concerning the competence of students *before* they have adequate grounds for making these judgments. It is the communication of these unjustified expectations—i.e., stereotypes— that results in the insidious self-fulfilling prophecy. This raises the question of when, if ever, expectations for low or poor performance are justified. If by having simply been made, such prophecies are fulfilled, perhaps it is better that they not be made at all. Given the evaluative nature of the educational process, however, this prospect is quite unlikely. It is, of course, of great theoretical interest whether the expectations are *self*-fulfilling or whether teachers quite consciously practice educational discrimination. In a practical sense, however, what is crucial is that expectancies have demonstrable consequences. Teachers can be alerted and perhaps the disconcerting results averted, or desired effect facilitated. The expectancy effect—a methodological "spoiler" variable for some—could have considerable pedagogical value.

Rosenthal and Jacobson have investigated only one side of the expectancy regarding intellectual promise. Elsewhere they note, "on ethical grounds . . . it was decided to test only the proposition that favorable expectations by teachers could lead to an increase in intellectual competence" [1968, p. 175]. However, in a study by Beez (cited in Rosenthal, 1969, p. 265), teachers were led to expect good or poor learning in a group of Headstart pupils. Striking expectancy effects were observed. In addition, there was evidence that teacher effort was strongly influenced by their expectations—in line with Clark's thesis noted previously. Beez' data, in addition to numerous recent investigations (e.g., Meichenbaum, Bowers, & Ross, 1969; Rosenthal, 1969), portray expectancy effects in nonexperimental contexts as an extremely vital derivative of the experimental work on this phenomenon and worthy of the considerable interest that the Rosenthal and Jacobson effort has generated.

FURTHER READING

ARONSON, E. Running and pushing the experimental subject. *Contemporary Psychology*, 1968, **13**: 5–7. An insightful review of Rosenthal's *Experimenter effects in behavioral research*.

BARBER, T. X., Calverly, D. S., Forgione, A., McPeake, J. D., Chaves, J. F., & Bowen, B. Five attempts to replicate the experimenter bias effect. *Journal of Consulting and Clinical Psychology*, 1969, **33**: 1–10. Five failures to replicate the expectancy effect—followed by interesting reactions by Rosenthal, Barber, and Levy.

CLARK, K. *Dark ghetto*. New York: Harper and Row, 1965. Regarding the academic failure of ghetto school children, Clark gives an analysis of cultural deprivation by focusing upon the concept of the self-fulfilling prophecy.

DUNCAN, S., Rosenberg, M. J., & Finkelstein, J. The paralanguage of experimenter bias. *Sociometry*, 1969, **32**: 207–219. An empirical demonstration that voice quality cues may transmit the experimenter's hypothesis to his subject. As in the study by Minor (1970), low-evaluation apprehension inhibits the expectancy phenomenon.

JACOB, T. The experimenter bias effect: A failure to replicate. *Psychonomic Science*, 1968, **13**: 239–240. A methodological note that experimenters, in expectancy research, may become suspicious of the manipulations. Since this study differed in *some* respects from Rosenthal's procedure, the failure to replicate is of limited informational value—in line with Levy's remarks.

LEVY, L. H. Reflections on replications and the experimenter bias effect. *Journal of Consulting and Clinical Psychology*, 1969, **33**: 15–17. A provocative commentary on the concept of experimental replications.

MEICHENBAUM, D. H., Bowers, K. S., & Ross, R. R. A behavioral analysis of teacher expectancy effect. *Journal of Personality and Social Psychology*, 1969, **13**: 306–316. A demonstration of the expectancy effect in a group of adolescent females institutionalized in a training school. As in Rosenthal and Jacobson, effects are noted for objective but not subjective examinations. Four different teachers were given the same expectancy concerning the same subjects. Marked individual differences in the probable mediation of the expectancy effect were observed.

MINOR, M. W. Experimenter-expectancy effect as a function of evaluation apprehension. *Journal of Personality and Social Psychology*, 1970, **15**:326–332. Supports the Sigall, Aronson, and Van Hoose thesis that subjects' evaluative needs may have priority over altruistic concerns for the experimenter's hypothesis. The expectancy phenomenon occurs only in subjects who are sensitized to the evaluative aspects of the study.

ROSENTHAL, R. *Experimenter effects in behavioral research*. New York: Appleton, Century-Crofts, 1966. A comprehensive account of the expectancy effect and other experimenter contributions to psychological research, from an historical, methodological, and substantive point of view.

ROSENTHAL, R. Interpersonal expectations: Effects of the experimenter's hypothesis. In R. Rosenthal & R. L. Rosnow (Eds.), *Artifact in behavioral research*. New York: Academic Press, 1969. Pp. 181–277. An updating of the above reference, this chapter focuses upon the expectancy effect and extensions from laboratory work to nonexperimental settings.

ROSENTHAL, R. & Jacobson, L. *Pygmalion in the classroom*. New York: Holt, Rinehart and Winston, 1968. A full report on their pioneering research relating teacher expectations to intellectual change.

SATTLER, J. M. Racial "experimenter effects" in experimentation, testing, interviewing, and psychotherapy. *Psychological Bulletin*, 1970, **73**: 137–160. A thorough and well-organized review of race as a social psychological factor in experimental and clinical psychology.

SNOW, R. E. Unfinished *Pygmalion*, *Contemporary Psychology*, 1969, **14**: 197–199. A critical, if not vitriolic, review of Rosenthal and Jacobson's research, essentially from a methodological viewpoint. Snow is particularly concerned—with justification—about the immediate and widespread acceptance of this work, especially in the mass media, and urges a more conservative approach toward research with this kind of excitatory appeal.

THORNDIKE, R. L. Review of "Pygmalion in the classroom." *American Educational Research Journal*, 1968, **5**: 708–711. Thorndike, as with Snow, takes issue with several methodological features of *Pygmalion*. He is particularly concerned with the psychometric properties of the IQ test used in the research. This is followed by a rebuttal from Rosenthal.

Robert Rosenthal

Covert Communication in the
Psychological Experiment[1]

Psychological laboratories and the psychological experiments conducted there are not the only scenes or means whereby we learn of
human behavior. There is no doubt, however, that in our discipline as
in others, the laboratory experiment is a preferred mode for the
observation of nature. It is so preferred because of the greater control
it gives us over the inputs to the experimental subject. Unlike the usual
situation in the field or in the "real world," when we observe the
behavior of the subject of a psychological experiment we are in a
position to attribute his behavior to the antecedent conditions we have
ourselves arranged.

In the paradigm psychological experiment, there is a subject whose
behavior is to be observed and an experimenter whose functions
include the control of inputs to the subject. (The experimenter also
often functions as recorder of the subject's output, but this function of
the experimenter is not important to the present discussion. It may be
assumed for present purposes that the subject's response is recorded
directly by an error-free automated system.) As part of the experimenter's function of controlling the subject's inputs, he engages in a
variety of intended, programmed, overt communications with the
subject. Such communications include the "instructions to subjects."
Although the instructions are highly programmed, they, along with
aspects of the physical scene (Riecken, 1962) and the overall design
of the experiment as perceived by the subject, may unintentionally
communicate to the subject something of what the experimenter is
after. Such unintended information transmission has been discussed
most fully by Orne (1962), who referred to such sources of cues as the
demand characteristics of the experimental procedures. To the extent that
these unintended cues tend to be systematic for a given experiment, and
do not depend for their operation on *differential* communication to
subjects by experimenters, they are not discussed here. Instead, the
focus will be on variations in the covert and unintended communications that occur in the psychological experiment. Such variations are

From *Psychological Bulletin*, 1967, **67**: 356–367. Copyright © 1967 by
The American Psychological Association and reprinted with permission
of author and The American Psychological Association.

not random and are predictable to some extent from a knowledge of various characteristics of the experimenter and the subject.

One purpose of this paper is to illustrate the fact that unintended covert communications are the norm in psychological experiments. To the extent that the experimenter communicates unintentionally and differentially with his subjects he has lost some measure of control over the inputs. Since such control is a major reason for our reliance on the experimental method, there are serious implications. Serious as these implications may be for our interpretation of the results of experiments, it should not surprise us that different experimenters engage in different covert communication with different subjects. We should, in fact, be more surprised if such covert communication did not occur. Covert communications occur routinely in all other dyadic interactions; why then, should they not occur in the dyad composed of the experimenter and his subject?

The evidence for the experimenter's covert communication with his tacitly understanding subject comes from a program of experiments on experiments (Rosenthal, 1964). One purpose of this research program is primarily methodological. By taking account of the covert communication processes in the psychological experiment, techniques may be developed which will permit the drawing of more valid substantive conclusions about those experimental inputs whose effects on the subject's behavior we want to learn. Another purpose of this research program is less methodological and more substantive. What we learn about the covert communication between experimenter and subject may teach us something about covert communication processes in other dyadic interactions as well. Laboratories need not simply be those places where we test, in simplified form, the hypotheses derived from the "real world." Laboratories, as Mills (1962) has pointed out, are just as "real" as the rest of the world.

THE EXPERIMENTER AS COVERT COMMUNICATOR

Covert communication between experimenter and subject could be demonstrated simply by showing that different experimenters behave differently toward their subjects in their conduct of a specific experiment and that these individual differences in behavior affect the subject's response. But it seems late in the history of psychology simply to demonstrate individual differences in behavior even when the people happen to be experimenters. It seems more useful, therefore, to concentrate on those cases of covert communication in which we can predict, more or less, just how he will communicate covertly with his subjects, before the experimenter even enters the laboratory.

Experimenter's Sex

There is a good deal of evidence that the sex of the experimenter can affect the responses of the experimental subject (Rosenthal, 1966; Sarason, 1965; Stevenson, 1965). What we have not known, however, is whether the effect of the sex of the experimenter was passive or active. By "passive effect" is meant that subjects respond differently to and for male and female experimenters simply because they are male or female. By "active effect" is meant that subjects respond differently to and for male and female experimenters because male and female experimenters treat the subjects differently. The best way to determine the extent to which any effects of the experimenter are active or passive is to make observations of the experimenter as he or she conducts an experiment.

In our research program we have employed two types of observers. One type of observer has been the subject himself. In several experiments, subjects have been asked to describe the behavior of their experimenter during the experimental transaction. An advantage of such observations by the subject himself is that there is no one closer to the experimenter during the experiment than the subject, and he is in a good position to see what the experimenter does. A disadvantage of such observations by the subjects themselves is that they may be contaminated by the responses they made during the experiment itself. Thus, if a subject has made conforming responses during an experiment in verbal conditioning, he may describe his experimenter as a more forceful, dominant person, not because the experimenter really was, but because that would justify to the subject and to others the subject's having conformed.

Another type of observer has been employed who was not a participant in the experiment itself. Instead, graduate and undergraduate students have observed sound motion pictures made of experimenters interacting with their subjects. Neither experimenters nor subjects knew that their interaction was being observed. The films were of five different samples of experimenters and subjects involving altogether 29 experimenters (5 of whom were females) and 86 subjects (of whom 21 were males). The details of the experiments which were filmed are given elsewhere (Rosenthal, Persinger, Mulry, Vikan-Kline, & Grothe, 1964a, 1964b). It is enough to know that in all of the experiments filmed the task was the same. The experimenters presented to each of their subjects a series of 10 standardized photos of faces. Each face was to be judged as to how successful or unsuccessful the person appeared to be. All experimenters were to read the same instructions to their subjects and this reading lasted about a minute, on the average. Before reading the instructions, experimenters asked subjects for their name, age, major field, and marital status. This brief preinstructional period lasted on the average about half a minute.

Analysis of the films showed that even during this brief preinstructional period, male and female experimenters treated their subjects in a significantly different manner. Male experimenters interacting with either male or female subjects were a good deal more friendly in their interaction than were female experimenters ($r_{pb} = .47$; $p < .05$). Support for this finding comes from a different study employing the same experimental task. This time the observers of the experimenters' behavior were the subjects themselves. Suzanne Haley made the data available for this analysis. Her 86 female subjects judged their 12 male experimenters to be more friendly during the course of the experiment than their 2 female experimenters ($r_{pb} = .32$, $p < .005$). Regardless of whether we ask external observers or the subjects themselves, male experimenters are observed to behave differently than female experimenters. Such systematic differences in the treatment of subjects suggest that though experimenters may read the same instructions to their subjects, subjects contacted by male experimenters and subjects contacted by female experimenters are simply not in the same experiment. It should not surprise us, therefore, when male and female experimenters obtain different responses from their subjects. Whenever the warmth or friendliness of the experimenter can affect the subject's response, and that happens often (Gordon & Durea, 1948; Luft, 1953; Reece & Whitman, 1962), we may look also for the effect of the experimenter's sex.

The effect of the experimenter's sex is complicated by the effect of the subject's sex. Male and female subjects evoke different behavior from their experimenters. Neil Friedman (1964) made observations of the smiling behavior of the experimenters who had been filmed, which were made available for this analysis. During the brief half-minute preceding the reading of the instructions, female subjects evoked more smiling behavior from their experimenters than did male subjects ($p < .05$). Only 12 percent of the experimenters smiled even a little at any male subject, but 70 percent of the experimenters smiled at least a little at their female subjects. From this evidence and from some more detailed analyses which suggest that female subjects may be more protectively treated by their experimenters (Rosenthal, 1966), it might be suggested that in the psychological experiment, chivalry is not dead. This news may be heartening socially, and it is interesting social psychologically, but it is very disconcerting methodologically. Sex differences are well established for many kinds of behavior. But a question must now be raised as to whether sex differences which emerge from psychological experiments are due to the subject's genes, morphology, enculturation, or simply to the fact that the experimenter treated his male and female subjects differently so that, in a sense, they were not really in the same experiment at all.

Male and female experimenters remember and respond to their subject's sex. They also remember their own sex. Female experimenters show a pattern of behavior which might be called "interested modesty" when interacting with their male subjects, while male experimenters show a pattern which might more simply be called "interested" when interacting with their female subjects. An indirect assessment of this interest comes from an analysis of the time spent in performing the preparations to show the subject the next stimulus photo. The timing of these portions was done by Richard Katz (1964), who made the data available for the present analysis. When male experimenters were contacting female subjects, it took them 16 percent longer to prepare to present the next stimulus than when they were contacting male subjects ($p < .01$). When female experimenters were contacting male subjects, it took them 13 percent longer to prepare the next stimulus for presentation than when they were contacting female subjects, though this difference was not significant statistically. Though the absolute amounts of time involved were measured in a few seconds, it appeared that among male experimenters especially, there was a tendency to stretch out the interaction with the opposite-sexed subject. This same finding of a prolongation of opposite sex experimental interactions has also been reported recently by Shapiro (1966) in an experiment on verbal conditioning.

Among our own female experimenters, evidence for their "modesty" in the motor channel of communication comes from observations of the degree to which experimenters leaned toward their subjects during the experimental transaction. (These observations were made by R. Katz, who made them available for this analysis.) Male and female experimenters leaned toward their female subjects to about the same degree. However, when the subjects were males, female experimenters did not lean as close as did their male colleagues ($p < .05$).

Further evidence for this relative modesty of female experimenters when contacting male subjects comes from a different, still preliminary sort of analysis. Observations of experimenters' friendliness were now made by two different groups of observers. One group watched the films but did not hear the sound track. Another group listened to the sound track but did not see the films. From this, a measure of motor or visual friendliness and an independent measure of verbal or auditory friendliness were available. (The correlation between ratings of friendliness obtained from these independent channels was only .29.) The results of this analysis are shown in Table 5–1. Among male experimenters, there was a tendency, not statistically significant, for their movements to show greater friendliness than their tone of voice, and to be somewhat unfriendly toward their male subjects in the auditory channel of communication. It was among the female experimenters that the more striking effects occurred. They were quite friendly toward their female subjects in the visual channel but not in the auditory channel. With male subjects, the situation was reversed significantly ($p < .05$). Though not friendly in the visual mode, female experimenters showed remarkable friendliness in the auditory channel when contacting male subjects.

Table 5-1   *Experimenter Friendliness in Two Communication Channels as a Function of Experimenter and Subject Sex*

| Experimenter Sex | Subject Sex | COMMUNICATION CHANNEL | | |
		Visual	Auditory	Difference
Male	Male	3.00	−0.50	3.50
	Female	2.81	1.32	1.49
	Mean	2.90	0.41	
Female	Male	0.44	2.96	−2.52
	Female	1.75	0.25	1.50
	Mean	1.10	1.60	

The quantitative analysis of sound motion pictures is not yet far enough developed that we can say whether such channel discrepancy in the communication of friendliness is generally characteristic of women in our culture, or only of advanced women students in psychology, or only of female experimenters conducting experiments in person perception. Perhaps it would not be farfetched to attribute the obtained channel discrepancy to an ambivalence over how friendly they ought to be. Quite apart from considerations of processes of covert communication in the psychological experiment, such findings may have some relevance for a better understanding of communication processes in general.

Other Attributes

We have seen that the sex of the experimenter, a variable shown often to affect subjects' responses, is associated with different patterns of communication in the psychological experiment, patterns which may account in part for the effects on the subjects' responses. Further, we have seen that the sex of the subject affects the experimenters' behavior, so that it is hard to tell whether different responses obtained from male and female subjects are due to the subjects' difference in sex or to the differences in the behavior of their experimenters. There are many other characteristics of experimenters and of subjects which should be analogously investigated. Some beginnings have been made and some results have been reported (Rosenthal, 1966). Here we present brief examples of differences in the experimenter's behavior toward the subject of the experiment, differences which are predictable from a knowledge of various attributes of the experimenter. The examples are chosen from only those experimenter variables which have been shown by various investigators to affect the subjects' responses.

There is considerable evidence that the anxiety of the experimenter, as measured before he enters the laboratory, can be a significant determinant of his subjects' responses (e.g., Rosenthal, 1966; Sarason, 1965). But what does the more anxious experimenter do in the experiment that leads his subjects to respond differently? We might expect more anxious experimenters to be more fidgety, and that is just what they are. Experimenters scoring higher on the Taylor (1953) Manifest Anxiety scale are observed from their films to show a greater degree of general body activity ($r = .41, p = .09$) and in addition, to have a less dominant tone of voice ($r = -.43, p = .07$). What effects just such behavior on the part of the experimenter will have on the subjects' responses depend no doubt on the particular experiment being conducted and, very likely, on various characteristics of the subject as well. In any case, we must assume that a more anxious experimenter cannot conduct just the same experiment as a less anxious experimenter. It appears that in experiments which have been conducted by just one experimenter, the probability of successful replication by another investigator is likely to depend on the similarity of his personality to that of the original investigator.

Anxiety of the experimenter is just one of the experimenter variables affecting the subjects' responses in an unintended manner. Crowne and Marlowe (1964) have shown that subjects who score high on their scale of need for approval tend to behave in such a way as to gain the approval of the experimenter. Now there is evidence that suggests that experimenters who score high on this measure also behave in such a way as to gain approval from their subjects. Analysis of the filmed interactions showed that experimenters scoring higher on the Marlowe-Crowne scale spoke to their subjects in a more enthusiastic tone of voice ($r = .39, p < .10$) and in a more friendly tone of voice ($r = .47, p < .05$). In addition, they smiled more often at their subjects ($r = .44, p = .07$) and slanted their bodies more toward their subjects than did experimenters lower in the need for approval ($r = .39, p < .10$).

THE EXPERIMENTER AS REACTIVE COMMUNICATOR

Experimenter's Experience

The kind of person the experimenter is *before* he enters his laboratory can in part determine the responses he obtains from his subjects. From the observation of experimenters' behavior during their interaction with their subjects there are some clues as to how this may come about. There is also evidence that the kind of person the experimenter becomes *after* he enters his laboratory may alter his behavior toward his subjects and lead him, therefore, to obtain different responses from his subjects.

In the folklore of psychologists who do experiments, there is the notion that sometimes, perhaps more often than we might expect, subjects contacted early in an experiment behave differently from subjects contacted later in an experiment. There may be something to this bit of lore even if we make sure that subjects seen earlier and later in an experiment come from the same population. The difference may be due to changes over the course of the experiment in the behavior of the experimenter. From what we know of performance curves we might, in fact, predict both a practice effect and a fatigue effect on the part of the experimenter. There is evidence for both. In the experiments which were filmed, experimenters became more accurate $(r = .25, p = .07)$ and also faster $(r = .31, p = .03)$ in the reading of their instructions to their later-contacted subjects. That seems simply to be a practice effect. In addition, experimenters became more bored or less interested over the course of the experiment as observed from their behavior in the experimental interaction $(r = .31, p = .02)$. As we might also predict, experimenters became less tense with more experience $(r = -.26, p = .06)$. The changes which occur in the experimenters' behavior during the course of their experiment affect their subjects' responses. In the experiments which were filmed, for example, subjects contacted by experimenters whose behavior changed as described rated the stimulus persons as less successful $(r - .31, p = .02)$.

Subjects' Behavior

The experimenter-subject communication system is a complex of intertwining feedback loops. The experimenter's behavior, we have seen, can affect the subject's next response. But the subject's behavior can also affect the experimenter's behavior, which in turn affects the subject's behavior. In this way, the subject plays a part in the indirect determination of his own next response. The experimental details are given elsewhere (Rosenthal, 1966; Rosenthal, Kohn, Greenfield, & Carota, 1965). Briefly in one experiment, half the experimenters had their experimental hypotheses confirmed by their first few subjects, who were actually accomplices. The remaining experimenters had their experimental hypotheses disconfirmed. This confirmation or disconfirmation of their hypotheses affected the experimenters' behavior sufficiently so that from their next subjects, who were bona fide and not accomplices, they obtained significantly different responses not only to the experimental task, but on standard tests of personality as well.

These responses were predictable from a knowledge of the responses the experimenters had obtained from their earlier-contacted subjects.

There is an interesting footnote on the psychology of the accomplice which comes from the experiment alluded to. The accomplices had been trained to confirm or to disconfirm the experimenter's hypothesis by the nature of the responses they gave the experimenter. These accomplices did not, of course, know when they were confirming an experimenter's hypothesis or, indeed, that there were expectancies to be confirmed at all. In spite of the accomplices' training, they were significantly affected in the adequacy of their performance as accomplices by the expectancy the experimenter had of their performance, and by whether the experimenter's hypothesis was being confirmed or disconfirmed by the accomplices' responses. We can think of the accomplices as experimenters and the experimenters as their targets or "victims". It is interesting to know that experimental targets are not simply affected by experimental accomplices. The targets of our accomplices, like the subjects of our experimenters, are not simply passive responders. They "act back."

Experimental Scenes

One of the things that happens to the experimenter which may affect his behavior toward his subject and thus the subject's response, is that he falls heir to a specific scene in which to conduct his experiment. Riecken (1962) has pointed out how much there is we do not know about the effects of the physical scene in which an experimental transaction takes place. We know little enough about how the scene affects the subject's behavior, we know even less about how the scene affects the experimenter's behavior.

The scene in which the experiment takes place may affect the subject's response in two ways. The effect of the scene may be direct, as when a subject judges others to be less happy when his judgments are made in an "ugly" laboratory (Mintz, 1957). The effect of the scene may also be indirect, as when the scene influences the experimenter to behave differently and this change in the experimenter's behavior leads to a change in the subject's response. The evidence that the physical scene may affect the experimenter's behavior comes from some data collected with Suzanne Haley. We had available eight laboratory rooms which were varied as to the "professionalness," the "orderliness," and the "comfortableness" of their appearance. The 14 experimenters of this study were randomly assigned to the eight laboratories. Experimenters took the experiment significantly more seriously if they had been assigned to a laboratory which was both more disordered and less comfortable ($R = .73$, $p = .02$). These experimenters were graduate students in the natural sciences or in law school. Perhaps they felt that scientifically serious business is carried on best in the cluttered and severely furnished laboratory which fits the stereotype of the scientist's ascetic pursuit of truth.

In this same experiment, subjects described the behavior of their experimenter during the course of the experiment. Experimenters who had been assigned to more professional appearing laboratories were described by their subjects as significantly more expressive-voiced ($r = .22$, $p = .05$), more expressive-faced ($r = .32$, $p = .005$), and as more given to the use of hand gestures ($r = .32$, $p = .005$). There were no films made of these experimenters interacting with their subjects, so we cannot be sure that their subjects' descriptions were accurate. There is a chance that the experimenters did not really behave as described but that subjects in different appearing laboratories perceive their experimenters differently because of the operation of context effects. The direct observation of experimenters' behavior in different physical contexts should clear up the matter to some extent.

Principal Investigators

More and more research is carried out in teams and groups so that the chances are increasing that any one experimenter will be collecting data not for himself alone. More and more there is a chance that the data are being collected for a principal investigator to whom the experimenter is responsible. The basic data are presented elsewhere (Rosenthal, 1966), but here it can be said that the response a subject gives his experimenter may be determined in part by the kind of person the principal investigator is and by the nature of his interaction with the experimenter.

More specifically, personality differences among principal investigators, and whether the principal investigator has praised or reproved the experimenter for his performance of his data-collecting duties, affect the subjects' subsequent perception of the success of other people and also affect subjects' scores on standardized tests of personality (e.g., Taylor Manifest Anxiety scale).

In one experiment, there were 13 principal investigators and 26 experimenters. When the principal investigators collected their own data it was found that their anxiety level correlated positively with the ratings of the success of others (pictured in photographs) they obtained from their subjects ($r = .66$, $p = .03$). Each principal investigator was then to employ two research assistants. On the assumption that principal investigators select research assistants who are significantly like or significantly unlike themselves, the two research assistants were assigned to principal investigators at random. That was done so that research assistants' scores on the anxiety scale would not be correlated with their principal investigator's anxiety scores. The randomization was successful in that the principal investigators' anxiety correlated only .02 with the anxiety of their research assistants.

The research assistants then replicated the principal investigators' experiments. Remarkably, the principal investigators' level of anxiety also predicted the responses obtained by their research assistants from their new samples of subjects ($r = .40$, $p = .07$). The research assistants' own level of anxiety, while also positively correlated with their subjects' responses ($r = .24$, ns) was not as good a predictor of their own subjects' responses as was the anxiety level of their principal investigator. Something in the covert communication between the principal investigator and his research assistant altered the assistant's behavior when he subsequently contacted his subjects. We know the effect of the principal investigator was mediated in this indirect way to his assistant's subjects because the principal investigator had no contact of his own with those subjects.

Other experiments show that the data obtained by the experimenter depend in part on whether the principal investigator is male or female, whether the principal investigator makes the experimenter self-conscious about the experimental procedure, and whether the principal investigator leads the experimenter to believe he has himself performed well or poorly at the same task the experimenter is to administer to his own subjects. The evidence comes from studies in person perception, verbal conditioning, and motor skills (Rosenthal, 1966).

As we would expect, these effects of the principal investigator on his assistant's subjects are mediated by the effects on the assistant's behavior toward his subjects. Thus, experimenters who have been made more self-conscious by their principal investigator behave less courteously toward their subjects, as observed from films of their interactions with their subjects ($r = -.43$, $p = .07$). In a different experiment, involving this time a verbal conditioning task, experimenters who had been given more favorable evaluations by their principal investigator were described by their subsequently contacted subjects to be more casual ($r = .33$, $p < .01$), and more courteous ($r = .27$, $p < .05$). These same experimenters, probably by virtue of their altered behavior toward their subjects, obtained significantly more conditioning responses from their subjects. All 10 of the experimenters who had been more favorably evaluated by their principal investigator showed conditioning effects among their subjects ($p = .001$) but only 5 of the 9 experimenters who felt unfavorably evaluated obtained any conditioning ($p = 1.00$).

THE EXPERIMENTER AS HYPOTHESIS COMMUNICATOR

Ever since Pfungst's (1911) brilliant series of experiments with Clever Hans, we have known that the experimenter's hypothesis can be communicated quite unintentionally to his subject. Hans, it will be remembered, was that clever horse who could solve problems of mathematics and musical harmony with equal skill and grace, simply by tapping out the answers with his hoof. A committee of eminent experts testified that Hans, whose owner made no profit from his horse's talents, was receiving no cues from his questioners. Of course, Pfungst later showed that this was not so, that tiny head and eye movements were Hans's signals to begin and to end his tapping. When Hans was asked a question, the questioner looked at Hans's hoof, quite naturally so, for that was the way for him to determine whether Hans's answer was correct. Then, it was discovered that when Hans approached the correct number of taps, the questioner would inadvertently move his head or eyes upward—just enough that Hans could discriminate the cue, but not enough that even trained animal observers or psychologists could see it.

The "Clever Hans" phenomenon has also been demonstrated to occur in more ordinary and more recent experiments. The details are found elsewhere (Rosenthal, 1966). Briefly, the expectancy or hypothesis of the experimenter has been shown to be a significant determinant of the results of his research in studies of person perception, verbal conditioning, personality assessment, and animal learning. The basic paradigm for such studies has been to divide a sample of experimenters into two equivalent groups and to create in each an expectancy for the data they would obtain which was opposite in direction to the expectancy induced in the other group of experimenters. Thus in the animal learning studies, half the experimenters were told that their rats were from the special "Berkeley Stock" and were specially bred for maze brightness or "Skinner-box brightness." The remaining experimenters were told that their animals had been specially bred for maze or "Skinner-box dullness." The rats run by experimenters expecting good performance performed significantly better than did the rats run by experimenters expecting poor performance. This was equally true in maze learning and in operant learning experiments.

In the person perception studies, half the experimenters were told that their subjects (humans now) had been selected because they tended to see photos of people as reflecting a great deal of past success, while the remaining experimenters were told that their subjects had been selected for the perception of failure in other people's faces. Subjects were then randomly assigned to their experimenters who subtly communicated their expectancies to their subjects in such a way that subjects expected to be success perceivers became success perceivers while subjects expected to be failure perceivers became failure perceivers. We can safely say that the communication process whereby subjects learned of experimenter expectations were subtle ones because for the last five years we have been analyzing films of such experiments and we have yet to find the specific cues that mediate the Clever Hans phenomenon to human subjects. This is not for want of careful observation. The films have been observed by dozens of psychologists, graduate students, and undergraduate students; and two doctoral dissertations were based on the analysis of these films (Friedman, 1964; Katz, 1964). We all wish Pfungst were here to help us now, though there is some experimental evidence that human subjects are not using the same sort of cues that Clever Hans employed.

What we do know of the communication to subjects of the experimenter's expectancy has been learned as much from experiments as from the analysis of films. The details of the research are available elsewhere (Rosenthal, 1966). To summarize briefly, we know that both visual and auditory cues are helpful to the subjects in their tacit understanding of the experimenter's covertly communicated messages. We know that the communication of expectancies can occur before the subject makes even his first response so that verbal or nonverbal reinforcements of desired responses will not do as an explanation. There are not yet sufficient data to be sure of this point, but there are indications that experimenters learn during the course of an experiment how better to communicate their expectancies to their subjects. Subjects contacted later in the experiment, therefore, tend to give responses more biased in the direction of their experimenter's hypothesis.[2]

Such a finding makes good sense. It may be asked, if the experimenter is learning to communicate unintentionally, who is the teacher? Most likely, the subject is the teacher. It seems to be rewarding to have one's expectations confirmed (Aronson, Carlsmith, & Darley, 1963; Carlsmith & Aronson, 1963; Harvey & Clapp, 1965; Sampson & Sibley, 1965). Therefore, whenever the subject responds in accordance with the experimenter's expectancy, the likelihood is increased that the experimenter will repeat any covert communicative behavior which may have preceded the subject's confirming response. Subjects, then, may quite unintentionally shape the experimenter's unintended communicative behavior. Not only does the experimenter influence his subjects to respond in the expected manner, but his subjects may well evoke just that unintended behavior which will lead subjects to respond as expected. As the work of Hefferline (1962) suggests, such communication may not fall under what we commonly call "conscious control."

When it was mentioned earlier that the observation of the films of experimenters interacting with their subjects had not solved the modern riddle of Clever Hans, it was not meant that the films had not been worthwhile. There has already been frequent reference to things learned about experiments and experimenters from these movies. There is a good deal more. One of the most exciting findings was that it was possible to predict whether an experimenter would subsequently influence his subjects to respond in accordance with his hypothesis from the experimenter's behavior during the first half-minute of his interaction with the subject. Experimenters who were more likeable, dominant, personal, relaxed, and important-acting during these initial seconds of the interaction and less given to leg movements, later obtained data significantly biased in the direction of their hypothesis (all the correlations exceeded .30 but were less than .43 and all p's were less than .05).

Observations were made of the sound films by one group of observers, of the silent films by another group, and of the sound track alone by a third group. Interestingly, during this phase of the experiment, it did not help the observers at all to have access to the sound track. None of the observations made by the group with access only to the sound track was predictive of subsequent effects of the experimenter's expectancy. The group of observers with access only to the silent films did just as well in predicting subsequent biasing as did the observers who had access to the sound films. During this brief pre-instructional phase, then, tone of voice variables seemed to be of little consequence.

Observations of the experimenter's behavior during the instruction-reading period showed much the same pattern of variables to be predictive of subsequent biasing of the subject's responses. Only now there were a great many more predictor variables which reached significance, and the correlations became larger. (The largest of the newly significant predictors of subsequent biasing was the variable of professionalism of manner, $r = .45$, $p < .005$). The details are presented elsewhere (Rosenthal, 1966), but one interesting phenomenon must be mentioned. During the instruction-reading period of the experiment, a number of tone of voice variables became significant predictors of the experimenter's subsequent unintended biasing effects. Very often, the direction of the predictive correlation with a variable judged from the sound track alone was in the opposite direction from the correlation with the same variable judged from the films without sound track. One example must do. Experimenters who later biased their subjects' responses more were *seen* as more honest ($r = .40$, $p < .01$) in the films but were *heard* as less honest ($r = -.30$, $p < .05$). Current work in the search for the cues mediating the Clever Hans phenomenon has turned to a closer examination of the implications for unintended communication processes of such channel discrepancy. Such an examination may have consequences for areas other than the social psychology of the psychological experiment. It is, for example, part of clinical lore, though the evidence is scanty (Ringuette & Kennedy, 1966), that such channel discrepancies may have important consequences for the development of psychopathology (Bateson, Jackson, Haley, & Weakland, 1956). The clinical and social importance of a better understanding of discrepancies among communication channels has been recently implied in a study of the treatment of alcoholism. Tape recordings were made of nine physicians' voices as they talked about their experiences with alcoholic patients. There was no relationship between the amount of hostility judges perceived in the doctors' speech and the doctors' effectiveness in getting alcoholics to accept treatment. However, when the content was filtered out of the tape recordings, the degree of hostility found in the doctors' tone of voice alone was found to correlate significantly and negatively with his success in influencing alcoholics to accept treatment ($r = -.65$, $p = .06$; Milmoe, Rosenthal, Blane, Chafetz, & Wolf, 1967).

BEYOND THE EXPERIMENTER-SUBJECT DYAD

The particular patterns of covert communication which have been described as relevant to the experimenter's communication of his expectancy to his subject are no doubt specific to the type of experiment being performed. We are in no position to speak for the generality of any of these findings across different experiments, much less for their generality in the other "real world," that one outside the laboratory. But there are some conclusions to be drawn from the data presented here and from the program of research which has investigated the effects of the experimenter's expectancy.

Perhaps the most compelling and most general conclusion is that human beings can engage in highly effective and influential unprogrammed and unintended communication with one another. If such communication is responsible in the psychological experiment for the fulfillment of the experimenter's expectancy, it might also be responsible for the fulfillment of other expectancies held by humans outside the laboratory. If rats learn better when their experimenter thinks they will, then children may learn better if their teachers think they will.

The experiment, a longitudinal one, is not yet completed, but the results for the first year can be given (Rosenthal & Jacobson, 1966). The procedure was exactly as in the experiments on the effects of the experimenter's expectancy. All the children in an elementary school were given an intelligence test which was disguised as a test which would predict academic "blooming." There were 18 classes, 3 at each of six grade levels. By the use of a table of random numbers, about 20 percent of the children in each class were chosen for the experimental condition. The experimental treatment consisted of telling their teachers that they had scored on the predictive achievement test such that they would show unusual intellectual development within the next academic year. At the end of the academic year the children were retested with the same test of intelligence. For the 18 classes combined, children whose teachers expected them to gain in performance showed significantly greater gain in IQ than did the control children ($p < .02$), though the mean relative gain in IQ was small (3.8 points). Teachers' expectancies, it turned out, made little difference in the upper grades. But at the lower levels the effects were dramatic. First graders purported to be bloomers gained 15.4 IQ points more than did the control children ($p = .002$), and the mean relative gain in one classroom was 25 points. In the second grade, the relative gain was 9.5 IQ points ($p < .02$), with one of the classes showing a mean gain of 18 points. These effects were especially surprising in view of the large gains in IQ made by the control group, which had to be surpassed by the experimental groups. Thus first graders in the control group gained 12 IQ points and second graders gained 7 IQ points, somewhat larger than might simply be ascribed to practice effects. More likely, the entire school was affected to some degree by being involved in an experiment with consequent good effects on the children's performance.[3]

Experimenters, teachers, probably psychotherapists, and probably "ordinary" people can affect the behavior of those with whom they interact by virtue of their expectations of what that behavior will be. Of course, we must now try to learn how such communication takes place—how teachers communicate their expectations to their pupils. Considering the difficulties we have had in trying to answer that same question for the case of experimenters, whose inputs into the experimenter-subject interaction could be much more easily controlled and observed, we should not expect a quick or an easy solution. But there may be consolation drawn from the conviction that, at least, the problem is worth the effort.

NOTES

1. The research described in this paper has been supported by research grants (G-17685, G-24826, GS-177, GS-714) from the Division of Social Sciences of the National Science Foundation. An earlier version of this paper was presented at the symposium "Ethical and Methodological Problems in Social Psychological Experiments," American Psychological Association, Chicago, September 1965.

2. For 3 experiments with a total of 54 experimenters, the combined p was less than .001, but it must be pointed out that in these studies we could not always be sure that there were no systematic subject differences which could have accounted for a greater effect of the experimenter's expectancy among later-contacted subjects.

3. These findings raise the question of what proportion of the effects of contemporary educational programs are due to the content of the programs rather than to the administrators' and teachers' expectancies. The social importance of these programs, to say nothing of the financial costs, make it appear important that program evaluations employ some form of "expectancy control group" [Rosenthal, 1966].

REFERENCES

Aronson, E., Carlsmith, J. M., & Darley, J. M. The effects of expectancy on volunteering for an unpleasant experience. *Journal of Abnormal and Social Psychology*, 1963, **66**: 220–224.

Bateson, G., Jackson, D. D., Haley, J., & Weakland, J. H. Toward a theory of schizophrenia. *Behavioral Science*, 1956, **1**: 251–264.

Carlsmith, J. M., & Aronson, E. Some hedonic consequences of the confirmation and disconfirmation of expectancies. *Journal of Abnormal and Social Psychology*, 1963, **66**: 151–156.

Crowne, D. P., & Marlowe, D. *The approval motive*. New York: Wiley, 1964.

Friedman, N. The psychological experiment as a social interaction. Unpublished doctoral dissertation, Harvard University, 1964.

Gordon, L. V., & Durea, M. A. The effect of discouragement on the revised Stanford Binet Scale. *Journal of Genetic Psychology*, 1948, **73**: 201–207.

Harvey, O. J., & Clapp, W. F. Hope, expectancy, and reactions to the unexpected. *Journal of Personality and Social Psychology*, 1965, **2**: 45–52.

Hefferline, R. F. Learning theory and clinical psychology—An eventual symbiosis? In A. J. Bachrach (Ed.), *Experimental foundations of clinical psychology*, New York: Basic Books, 1962. Pp. 97–138.

Katz, R. Body language: A study in unintentional communication. Unpublished doctoral dissertation, Harvard University, 1964.

Luft, J. Interaction and projection. *Journal of Projective Techniques*, 1953, **17**: 489–492.

Mills, T. M. A sleeper variable in small groups research: The experimenter. *Pacific Sociological Review*, 1962, **5**: 21–28.

Milmoe, S., Rosenthal, R., Blane, H. T., Chafetz, M. E., & Wolf, I. The doctor's voice: Postdictor of successful referral of alcoholic patients. *Journal of Abnormal Psychology*, 1967, **72**: 78–84.

Mintz, N. On the psychology of aesthetics and architecture. Unpublished manuscript, Brandeis University, 1957.

Orne, M. T. On the social psychology of the psychological experiment: With particular reference to demand characteristics and their implications. *American Psychologist*, 1962, **17**: 776–783.

Pfungst, O. *Clever Hans (the horse of Mr. von Osten): A contribution to experimental, animal, and human psychology.* (Trans. by C. L. Rahn) New York: Holt, 1911. (Republished: 1965).

Reece, M. M., & Whitman, R. N. Expressive movements, warmth, and verbal reinforcements. *Journal of Abnormal and Social Psychology*, 1962, **64**: 234–236.

Riecken, H. W. A program for research on experiments in social psychology. In N. F. Washburne (Ed.), *Decisions, values and groups*. Vol. 2. New York: Pergamon Press, 1962. Pp. 25–41.

Rinquette, E. L., & Kennedy, T. An experimental study of the double bind hypothesis. *Journal of Abnormal Psychology*, 1966, **71**: 136–141.

Rosenthal, R. The effect of the experimenter on the results of psychological research. In B. A. Maher (Ed.), *Progress in experimental personality research*. Vol. 1. New York: Academic Press, 1964. Pp. 79–114.

Rosenthal, R. *Experimenter effects in behavioral research.* New York; Appleton-Century-Crofts, 1966.

ROSENTHAL, R., & Jacobson, L. Teachers' expectancies: Determinants of pupils' IQ gains. *Psychological Reports*, 1966, **19**: 115–118.

ROSENTHAL, R., Kohn, P., Greenfield, P. M., & Carota, N. Experimenters' hypothesis-confirmation and mood as determinants of experimental results. *Perceptual and Motor Skills*, 1965, **20**: 1237–1252.

ROSENTHAL, R., Persinger, G. W., Mulry, R. C., Vikan-Kline, L., & Grothe, M. Changes in experimental hypotheses as determinants of experimental results. *Journal of Projective Techniques and Personality Assessment*, 1964, **28**: 465–469. (a)

ROSENTHAL, R., Persinger, G. W., Mulry, R. C., Vikan-Kline, L., & Grothe, M. Emphasis on experimental procedure, sex of subjects, and the biasing effects of experimental hypotheses. *Journal of Projective Techniques and Personality Assessment*, 1964, **28**: 470–473. (b)

SAMPSON, E. E., & Sibley, L. B. A further examination of the confirmation or non-confirmation of expectancies and desires. *Journal of Personality and Social Psychology*, 1965, **2**: 133–137.

SARASON, I. G. The human reinforcer in verbal behavior research. In L. Krasner & L. P. Ullman (Eds.), *Research in behavior modifications: New developments amd implications*. New York: Holt, Rinehart & Winston, 1965. Pp. 231–243.

SHAPIRO, J. L. The effects of sex, instructional set, and the problem of awareness in a verbal conditioning paradigm. Unpublished master's thesis, Northwestern University, 1966.

STEVENSON, H. W. Social reinforcement of children's behavior. In L. P. Lipsitt & C. C. Spiker (Eds.), *Advances in child development and behavior*. Vol. 2. New York: Academic Press, 1965. Pp. 97–126.

TAYLOR, J. A. A personality scale of manifest anxiety. *Journal of Abnormal and Social Psychology*, 1953, **48**: 285–290.

Theodore X. Barber and Maurice J. Silver

Fact, Fiction, and the Experimenter Bias Effect[1]

Introductory psychology texts state that (a) researchers have recently performed "a substantial number of experiments [which] indicate that the experimenter in good faith can influence unconsciously and in subtle ways the outcome of experiments" [Morgan & King, 1966, p. 17], (b) "the phenomenon is, apparently, reliable as well as general, [and (c)] the most obvious explanation . . . is that in some subtle way, presumably in nonverbal fashion, E influences S to act in the way he would prefer" [Lyons, 1965, pp. 212–213]. These contentions seem to imply that experimenters bias their results even though they consciously and conscientiously try to avoid doing so. The purpose of the present paper is twofold: (a) to evaluate studies purporting to demonstrate that experimenters subtly and unconsciously bias their subjects' responses even when they conscientiously try to follow programmed procedures and to use standardized methods of assessment, and (b) to deduce conclusions from the review that are generally applicable to research methodology in the behavioral sciences.

Rosenthal (1966) delineated several ways that an experimenter might inadvertently influence the results of his research ("experimenter effects"). These include, for example, an experimenter personal attributes effect (due to the experimenter's sex, age, personality traits, and other personal characteristics) and an experimenter bias effect (produced by the experimenter's expectancies, desires, or biases). Since the present paper focuses on only one of these two types of experimenter effects, they need to be carefully distinguished.

Experimenter Personal Attributes Effect

Irrespective of their expectancies, desires, or biases, experimenters differing on such attributes as sex, age, race, status, ethnic characteris-

From *Psychological Bulletin*, 1968, **70** (6, Pt. 2): 1–29. Copyright © 1968 by The American Psychological Association and reprinted with permission of authors and The American Psychological Association.

tics, or personality traits may at times obtain different responses from comparable groups of subjects (Masling, 1960, 1966; Rosenthal, 1966, Chs. 4 & 5). There is also suggestive evidence that the experimenter's sex and other personal attributes may at times interact with the attributes of the subjects. For example, using a marble sorting task, Stevenson and Allen (1964) found that significantly more marbles were sorted when experimenters and subjects were of the opposite sex rather than of the same sex.

To clarify the scope of the present review, it is necessary to discriminate between the main effects and the interactive effects of experimenters' personal attributes. The main effects of experimenters' personality characteristics, sex, age, race, etc., are not the major topic of the present paper. However, the experimenters' personal attributes will enter the discussion peripherally, when we discuss their possible interaction with the independent variable that is of major interest, namely, the experimenters' biases.

Experimenter Bias Effect

The present review focuses on the effect exerted on the experimental outcome by the experimenters' expectancies, hypotheses, desires, or biases. In various places, Rosenthal has labeled this effect as the experimenter bias effect, the experimenter expectancy effect, the experimenter outcome-orientation effect, and the "Clever Hans Phenomenon." We will henceforth label this effect simply the experimenter bias effect.

There is little doubt that experimenters often expect or desire different responses from subjects assigned to different experimental treatments and that they rarely rigorously exclude the possibility that their results are affected by their biases. If the experimenter bias effect is generally valid—if experimenters often obtain spurious results which confirm their expectancies, hypotheses, or desires—a substantial proportion of the facts" of present day psychology are open to question and many earlier psychological investigations need to be redone to determine if the results were a function of the experimenters' biases. Furthermore, as Rosenthal (1966, Chs. 19–23) has emphasized, if the effect is robust, we must henceforth either (a) institute rather expensive control procedures to rule out the effects of the experimenters' biases, or (b) exclude human beings from the conduct of research (replacing them by automated procedures).

A series of earlier reviews (Rosenthal, 1963, 1964a, 1966, 1967) seems to imply that the experimenter bias effect is rather easy to demonstrate and is rather pervasive and robust, for example, "The [bias] phenomenon occurred in varying degrees in all twelve studies [that had been conducted as of 1963], the weakest p level being .08 and the median p level being .02" [Rosenthal, 1963, p. 270] and the effect "may well be a fairly general one" [Rosenthal, 1966, p. 310]. Our own review of the literature, however, indicates that these conclusions may be misleading. It is our opinion that approximately 19 of the 31 pertinent studies that were available for critical analysis as of early 1967 did not clearly demonstrate an experimenter bias effect.

In the first part of the paper we cover, more or less in chronological order, the 19 studies which, in our opinion, did not clearly show the effect. The procedures and analyses used in many of these studies are presented in detail. We hope that our detailed critique of these studies will serve two purposes. First, we hope that it will place the topic in proper focus by showing that the experimenter bias effect is more difficult to demonstrate and appears to be less pervasive than was implied in previous reviews in this journal (Kintz, Delprato, Mettee, Persons, & Schappe, 1965; Rosenthal, 1964b, 1967). Second, we hope that by painstakingly pointing out methodological deficiencies and pitfalls in data analysis, we will stimulate more rigorous research in this and also in other areas of psychology.

In the second part of the paper, we review the 12 remaining studies which apparently showed an experimenter bias effect. Our detailed analysis of the ostensibly successful studies raises several important issues pertaining to the mode of action of the effect and generates a series of questions to be answered in further research.

Since we are concerned with the effects of expectancy biases in the formal experimental situation (in which there are standardized treatment procedures and standardized methods of assessment), we do not review the literature pertaining to expectancy effects in psychotherapy, in clinical investigations, or in "real life." For similar reasons we do not cover a recent interesting study by Rosenthal and Jacobson (1966) in which elementary school teachers were led to expect that unusual potential for intellectual gain was present in some of their students but not in others. (The latter study did not include standardized treatment procedures—the teachers were permitted to treat the "unusual" children differently than the others.)

Although clinical investigations, which test new treatment methods or new drugs, are not within the purview of this paper, it is worth noting that (*a*) such investigations have at times yielded results that seemed to be related to the investigators' expectancies, and (*b*) placebos and double-blind controls have recently been instituted in this area in order to minimize possible bias effects. Some of the broad literature pertaining to the effects of expectancies in clinical investigations, in psychotherapy, and in real life has been reviewed by Goldstein (1962) and Rosenthal (1966).

NINETEEN STUDIES THAT DID NOT
CLEARLY DEMONSTRATE THE
EXPERIMENTER BIAS EFFECT

Many of the 19 studies discussed in this section were cited in review papers (Rosenthal, 1963, 1964a, 1966) as supporting the conclusion that experimenters' expectancies and desires exert an important influence on the experimental outcome. We do not believe that this conclusion clearly follows from the data presented. Specifically, it is our opinion that the 19 studies fall into two sets: those that failed to demonstrate an experimenter bias effect, and those that do not lend themselves to clear-cut conclusions because of one or more of the following inadequacies in the analysis of data:

1. An overall statistical analysis was not performed to exclude chance findings.

2. The authors performed a large number of post hoc statistical tests after the overall analysis had failed to reject the null hypothesis at a conventional level of significance. The authors failed to make clear that the results of such postmortem analyses are far from definitive and can, at best, only suggest new hypotheses to be validated in further research.

3. Problems of "probability pyramiding" were not avoided; for instance, there was a failure to take account of changing levels of significance when many statistical tests were performed on a single set of data.

4. The authors "strained for significance" by accepting questionable p values (e.g. p values $> .10$) as substantiating the experimental hypothesis.

5. "Negative" data (data which were significantly opposite to the experimental hypothesis) were not used in the statistical analysis that ostensibly showed the experimenter bias effect. The decision not to use the negative data was made after inspection of the results and on the basis of the dependent variable criterion alone.

6. The authors failed to perform a multivariate statistical analysis, such as multiple-discriminant analysis or canonical correlation, in studies which included many independent and many dependent variables. Instead, a multitude of comparisons were made on overlapping data by individual t tests and Spearman rho correlation coefficients.

We point out in various places in the review why we believe that these deficiencies in data analysis can give rise to misleading conclusions. The pitfalls in such procedures are also discussed in texts by Hays (1963) and Cattell (1966) and are illustrated in recent papers by Chapanis and Chapanis (1964) and Neher (1967).

Overview of Procedure

Most of the studies in this area used a person-perception task as the criterion instrument. In this task, the subject is shown a series of photographed faces and is asked to rate on a scale whether each of the persons depicted has been "experiencing failure" or has been "experiencing success." The rating scale employed ran from −10 (extreme failure) to +10 (extreme success) with intermediate labeled points. Prior to the critical studies, the person-perception task had been administered under a "no-expectancy condition" to a large number of student subjects. The average ratings given to the photographs were very close to 0; that is, when the experimenter did not have special expectancies, subjects perceived the persons depicted as "neutral" with respect to having experienced failure or success.

In the experiments reviewed in the following section all experimenters and all subjects were students. Before running their subjects, the student experimenters were typically told (by the principal investigator) that "The subjects you are running should average about +5 ratings" or that the subjects should give ratings averaging about −5. In addition, the student experimenters were typically told that (*a*) the expected results had been "well established" in previous studies which used the person-perception task, (*b*) they would conduct the experiment to obtain practice in "duplicating experimental results," (*c*) if their results came out "properly—as expected" they would be paid $2 per hour, and (*d*) if their results did not come out "properly" they would be paid $1 per hour (Rosenthal & Fode, 1963b, p. 507). Thus, the dependent variable in these studies was the subjects' ratings on the person-perception task and the independent variable was the experimenters' desires, expectancies, or biases to obtain high (usually +5) or low (usually −5) ratings from their subjects.

Studies 1–4 (Persinger, 1963; Marcia, 1961; Pflugrath, 1962; and Wartenberg-Ekren, 1962)

We shall first briefly discuss four master's theses that apparently failed to show the experimenter bias effect.

In a thesis by Persinger (1963) six student experimenters were instructed (by the principal investigator) to expect high (+5) ratings from their subjects on the person-perception task, and six additional student experimenters were instructed to expect low (−5) ratings. Subjects who proffered ratings in the direction of the experimenters' expectancies received a plus "bias score" and those who gave ratings in the opposite direction from the experimenters' expectancies received a minus bias score. The author of this thesis did not perform an overall statistical analysis to ascertain if he had demonstrated the experimenter bias effect. (Apparently, the author judged an overall analysis to be unnecessary because he "was not interested in a differential bias between the two conditions per se" [p. 26] but was interested in testing the hypothesis that "*E*s would bias acquainted *S*s significantly more than unacquainted *S*s" [p. 27].) However, the overall mean bias score (which we computed from Table 4 of the thesis) was −.17, which was slightly in the *opposite* direction from the experimenters' expectancies; thus, the study failed to show the experimenter bias effect. (A brief critique of other data included in Persinger's thesis will be presented later—see Footnote 3.)

In a thesis by Marcia (1961), 13 student experimenters ran 83 student subjects on the person-perception task. Six of the experimenters (Group 1) were asked to formulate their own hypotheses concerning the average ratings they expected to obtain from their subjects. These expectations ranged from −4 to +4. The remaining 7 experimenters (Group 2) were told that they should expect specified ratings (ranging from −4 to +4) from their subjects. One of the hypotheses of the study was that "those *E*s who made their own hypotheses concerning their *S*s' average ratings would show more bias than those *E*s to whom the expected rating was ready-made and given" [p. 9]. However, an overall statistical analysis was not performed to ascertain if the experimenter bias effect was present in the study. We carried out the overall analysis, using the raw data presented in the thesis. First, we found that experimenters (in Groups 1 and 2 combined) who expected low (from −4 to −1) ratings obtained a mean rating of +.31, whereas experimenters (in the same groups) who expected high (from +1 to +4) ratings obtained a mean rating of +.17. These mean ratings, which tend to be slightly in the opposite direction from the experimenters' expectations, are not significantly different. Next, we analyzed the data separately for experimenters in Group 1 and in Group 2; again, we found that the means, which were far from significantly different, tended to be slightly in the opposite direction from the experimenters' expectancies. In brief, this study failed to show the experimenter bias effect.

Marcia also hypothesized that experimenters with high "need for approval" (as measured by the Marlowe-Crowne Social Desirability scale) obtain ratings more in line with their expectancy biases than experimenters with low need for approval. Although the data presented in the thesis appeared to support the hypothesis, a series of subsequent studies typically found no significant relationship between experimenters' need for approval and the experimenter bias effect and, of those few correlations that were significant, some were positive and some were negative (Rosenthal, 1966, p. 238).

In another thesis (Pflugrath, 1962) three sets of experimenters administered the Taylor Manifest Anxiety scale to 142 subjects. The first and second set of experimenters were instructed to expect high- and low-anxiety scores, respectively, from their subjects. The third set of experimenters were not given any expectancies. The overall analysis of the results failed to show significant differences in anxiety scores earned by the subjects of the three groups of experimenters; that is, the study failed to show the experimenter bias effect.

In another thesis (Wartenberg-Ekren, 1962) 8 student experimenters administered the Block Design subtest from the Wechsler Adult Intelligence Scale to 32 student subjects. The experimenters were instructed to expect that half of their subjects would perform well and half would perform poorly. The experimenters' expectancies failed to influence the results.

Study 5 (White, 1962)

This doctoral dissertation involved 18 student experimenters and 108 student subjects. The experimenters were divided into six groups and each groups was instructed to expect that subjects would proffer one of six types of ratings on the person-perception task (either -6, -3, $-.5$, $+.5$, $+3$, or $+6$ ratings). Within each of these conditions of experimenter expectancy, the subjects were divided into six groups and each group was told that the particular photos they would be shown had been found earlier to elicit one of the six types of ratings. The results were as follows:

1. When subjects were told that the photos had previously evoked high ($+.5$ to $+6$) ratings, experimenters expecting high ratings and experimenters expecting low ratings did not elicit significantly different ratings.
2. When subjects were told that the photos had previously elicited low (-6 to $-.5$) ratings, the experimenters obtained results significantly opposite to their expectancies (experimenters expecting low ratings obtained high ratings and experimenters expecting high ratings obtained low ratings).
3. Overall, the results were not significant and they were slightly in the opposite direction from the experimenters' expectancies; thus, this study also did not clearly demonstrate an experimenter bias effect.

Study 6 (Rosenthal, Persinger, Vikan-Kline, & Mulry, 1963)

We now turn to a widely quoted study which aimed to demonstrate that "a biased E might communicate his bias to his As [assistants] without his telling them the nature and magnitude of his bias" [p. 313]. The salient features of this study were as follows. There were 14 experimenters who ran 76 subjects on the person-perception task. Each experimenter later trained two assistants. The assistants in turn ran 154 subjects. The *major* antecedent variables were apparently as follows:

1. The experimenters were first asked to predict the mean photo ratings they expected to obtain from their subjects. These predictions constituted the experimenters' "idiosyncratic expectancies or biases."

2. Before running the study, half of the experimenters were told to expect high ($+5$) ratings and half were told to expect low (-5) ratings from their subjects. These expectations were termed "induced expectancies."

3. Subsequently, the experimenters were led to expect that their assistants would obtain the same high or low ratings from their subjects that they (the experimenters) had been originally led to expect. However, the experimenters were "warned not to tell their *S*s [assistants] of the type of data they could expect" [p. 316].

Among the *major* dependent variables were the photo ratings given by (*a*) the experimenters' subjects, and (*b*) their assistants' subjects. The authors reported that "The 2×2 analysis of variance, based on *Es*' *Ss*' ratings as a function of *Es*' induced and idiosyncratic bias yielded no *F* with an associated $p < .15$" [p. 321]. In other words, the experimenter bias effect was not demonstrated in this study—the experimenters did not obtain ratings in line with what they were told to expect or in line with what they themselves had predicted that they would obtain. In addition, the authors reported that there were no significant main effects, and no significant interaction effect ($p = .12$), for the assistants' subjects' ratings as a function of their experimenters' experimentally induced or idiosyncratic expectancies. In other words, the assistants were not significantly influenced by their experimenters to obtain ratings in accord with the experimenters' expectancies.

The conclusion indicated by the aforementioned analysis of variance is that the study had failed to demonstrate that either the experimenters or the assistants had biased the subjects' ratings. However, the authors of the paper did not draw this conclusion and they went on to perform a large number of statistical tests (Spearman rho correlations and *t* tests) among the variables mentioned above and many other variables. We feel that the conclusions drawn from the further statistical tests are not justified. Furthermore, it seems to us that our differing interpretations of the results of this study may be the occasion to make explicit markedly different perspectives with respect to appropriate data analysis. We now present a detailed analysis of this study with the hope that our critique will clarify some of the basic methodological issues which underlie research in this area.

Predictor (independent) variables. Approximately 52 predictor variables were measured in this study. Apparently, 30 of these (pertaining to experimenters' characteristics, such as friendliness, tension, and gesturing) were not used in the statistical analyses. The remaining 22 or so predictor variables that were considered in the analyses included the following: (1) experimenters' awareness of the true intent of the experiment; (2) assistants' prior acquaintanceship with their subjects. For experimenters and also for assistants: (3–4) prediction of their subjects' average photo ratings (idiosyncratic expectancies); (5–6) experimentally induced expectancy for +5 or −5 ratings; (7–8) observed versus unobserved (experimenter-subject or assistant-subject) interactions; (9–10) early-run versus later-run subjects. For experimenters, for assistants, and for subjects: (11–13) anxiety scores from the Taylor scale; (14–16) social desirability scores from the Marlowe-Crowne scale; (17–19) birth order; and (20–22) sex.

Criterion (dependent) variables. The criterion variables included (a) photo ratings of experimenters' subjects; (b) photo ratings of assistants' subjects; (c) bias scores for the experimenters (derived from their subjects' photo ratings); and (d) bias scores for the assistants (also derived from their subjects' photo ratings).

Significant statistics. Although this study included many independent and many dependent variables, the authors did not perform a multivariate analysis (e.g., multiple-discriminant analysis, canonical correlation, factor analysis, multiple analysis of variance or covariance). Instead, the data were analyzed primarily by individual t tests and Spearman rhos. The authors reported 21 statistics (5 ts, 15 rhos, and 1 F) which were significant ($p \leq .05$, one-tailed or two-tailed). Did these 21 nominally significant statistics exceed the number that can be expected to be significant by chance alone? To approach an answer to this question we have to determine how many statistical tests were made explicitly and how many could have been made but apparently were not made (implicit statistics).

Explicit statistical comparisons. The authors of the paper apparently calculated approximately 125 explicit statistics. (Our estimate is approximate because the authors at times stated that certain variables were not significantly related but it is not clear how many statistical tests were computed among the nonrelated variables.) If one were to make 125 planned comparisons, each of which was independent, one would expect at least 6 to be significant at the .05 level by chance alone. However, if, as in this study, the comparisons (a) are not planned (only some of the many possible comparisons are made and clear reasons are not given for selecting some and not others) and (*b*) are not independent (involve overlapping data), it is necessary to determine how many possible comparisons are actually present in the data before we can attempt to assign an expected probability to the results of any one comparison. Let us now look at the statistical comparisons that were actually present in the data.

Implicit statistical comparisons. The authors calculated some of the many possible statistics that could have been calculated among the 22 independent variables and 4 dependent variables. They reported several statistics which imply third-order interactions; for example, one statistical analysis involved one dependent variable and three independent variables (experimenters' idiosyncratic expectancies, experimenters' induced expectancies, and observed versus unobserved experimenter-subject interactions). The authors also reported statistics which aimed to delineate fourth-order interactions; for example, one set of comparisons involved two dependent variables (bias scores for experimenters and bias scores for assistants) and four independent variables (assistants' birth order, subjects' birth order, assistants' sex, and subjects' sex).[2] However, only some of the many possible main effects and interactions were reported. Many other main effects and interactions that were present in the data were not computed or, if computed, were not reported, and clear reasons were not given for considering only some of the many possible comparisons. The question now arises: What would have happened if the authors had made all of the comparisons that were imbedded in the data (instead of choosing only some comparisons for analysis in a *post hoc* manner)? Since the authors did not consider comparisons that included more than four independent variables, this question can be worded more precisely: How many statistics would need to be computed for this study if one were to consider only the main effects and the first-, second-, third-, and fourth-order interactions of the 22 independent variables? Although no precise answer to this question is possible, we can approximate an answer by considering the following. If the study had been set up as a 2^{22} factorial (with each of the independent variables at just two levels) and analyzed only for one dependent variable, a total of 9,107 F tests would have to be computed to determine the significance of the main effects and the first-, second-, third-, and fourth-order interactions (Guilford, 1954, p. 80). Of the total of 9,107 statistics that would need to be computed for 22 independent variables and just 1 dependent variable (there were apparently 4 dependent variables in this study), we would expect 455 to be significant at the .05 level by chance alone.

Let us now summarize and draw out the implications of the above analysis: (a) The authors made about 125 statistical comparisons of which about 21 were nominally significant. (*b*) If the authors had made planned comparisons (i.e., if they had clearly specified in advance which comparisons were to be made), we would expect about 6 of the 125 to be "significant" by chance. (*c*) However, since the authors apparently were not using the technique of planned comparisons and since a rather large number of the possible comparisons that were imbedded in the data could be expected to be spuriously "significant," it is difficult to determine exactly how many of the 125 comparisons (that were chosen by unclear criteria from the thousands of possible comparisons) might be "significant" by chance but this number may have exceeded 21 (cf., Hays, 1963, Ch. 14).

The above considerations highlight the importance of keeping the number of variables in a study to manageable proportions, using relevant variables, and making specific predictions in advance. As Hays (1963) has cogently stated:

In planning an experiment, it is a temptation to throw in many experimental treatments, especially if the data are inexpensive and the experimenter is adventuresome. However, this is *not* always good policy if the psychologist is interested in finding meaning in his results; other things being equal, the simpler the psychological experiment the better will be its execution, and the more likely will one be able to decide what actually happened and what the results actually mean [p. 411].

Even if we disregard the above critique, we would still find it difficult to interpret the 21 significant statistics obtained in the study for the following reasons:

1. Some of the significant statistics are not independent of each other. Specifically, of the 21 significant statistics, 15 were Spearman rhos that often involved overlapping data. (For instance, 2 of the significant statistics were correlations between experimenters' anxiety and subjects' photo ratings. One of these 2 correlations used all experimenters and all subjects and the other used only half of the experimenters and half of the subjects.)

2. Five of the remaining 6 significant statistics were *t*s that were performed upon data which had been first tested for significance by overall *F* tests. The *F* tests did not permit rejection of the null hypothesis. When the preliminary analysis of variance does not show overall significance, postmortem analyses of the same data by means of *t* tests can lead to misleading results (Hays, 1963, p. 483).

Before leaving this study, we must emphasize that one of its isolated findings has been widely quoted in the recent literature. This finding, which has been interpreted as indicating that experimenters unintentionally transmit their biases to their assistants, was apparently based on the following analyses: (*a*) The authors transformed the experimenters' subjects' ratings of the photos and derived a set of scores (experimenters' "bias scores") which they viewed as reflecting the degree to which the experimenters had biased their subjects' ratings. (*b*) Similarly, the ratings given by the assistants' subjects were transformed and a second set of scores (assistants' "bias scores") were derived. (*c*) Experimenters' bias scores were then correlated with assistants' bias scores and the Spearman rho (.67) was found to be significant.

The authors interpreted the obtained rho as indicating that the degree to which the experimenters biased their subjects was related to the degree to which their respective assistants had biased their subjects and, more broadly, that the experimenters had unintentionally transmitted their biases to their assistants and had consequently influenced the responses of their assistants' subjects. This conclusion has been generalized by other writers; for instance, a recent review in this journal (Kintz *et al.* 1965) interpreted this finding as indicating that

directors of laboratory research who use student *E*s, must be aware of the extremely great effect of their personal biases which can be perceived by the student *E*s and translated into practically any significant experimental effect [p. 231].

This interpretation of the significant correlation between experimenters' bias scores and assistants' bias scores is questionable for the following reasons:

1. As stated previously, the total number of significant results that were obtained in this study may not have exceeded the number that might have been significant by chance alone.
2. Since the overall analyses did not clearly show that the experimenters had biased their subjects' ratings or that the assistants had biased their subjects' ratings, we cannot be certain that either the experimenters' "bias scores" or the assistants' "bias scores" actually reflect bias. Since both sets of "bias scores" may consist of sets of chance fluctuations, we cannot be certain that the correlation between the two sets of scores indicates that bias had been unintentionally transmitted from the experimenters to their assistants and from the assistants to their subjects.[3]

Study 7 (Rosenthal & Fode, 1963b, Experiment 3)

Twelve graduate students served as experimenters in this investigation. First, each experimenter was instructed to expect that his subjects would give ratings around +7 on the person-perception task. However, before the experimenters ran their subjects they were asked to predict what ratings they actually expected to obtain. (Apparently, a substantial proportion of the experimenters predicted that they would obtain ratings that differed from those +7 ratings that they had been told originally to expect.) There were also other independent variables in this investigation: Half of the experimenters were told they would be paid $5 per hour if their results came out "properly—as expected" and half were told they would be paid $2 per hour for "proper" results; also, half of the subjects were unpaid and half were paid $.50.

The study failed to confirm the following hypotheses made by the authors: (*a*) experimenters paid $5 per hour would bias their subjects' ratings more than those paid $2, (*b*) subjects paid $.50 would be more influenced by the experimenters' expectancies than unpaid subjects, and (*c*) experimenters paid $5 and running paid subjects would bias the most, whereas experimenters paid $2 and running unpaid subjects would bias least.

The authors also hypothesized that experimenters' predictions of the ratings they would obtain from their subjects would be positively correlated with the ratings they actually obtained. It seems to us that the way to test this hypothesis would be to perform a Pearson or a Spearman correlation between the experimenters' predicted and obtained ratings, using all of the original ratings. However, it is not clear from the report whether the authors computed this correlation. First, the authors computed Spearman correlations between the experimenters' predicted and obtained ratings separately for the male subjects and the female subjects. Neither of the obtained rhos (.32 for males and .30 for females) differed significantly from zero. Next, a correlation was computed by a method which is not quite clear to us; in this instance, the authors stated that "male and female subjects were pooled using average ranks" and the obtained rho (.56) fell short of significance by a two-tailed test but was significant at the .05 level by a one-tailed test. At this point, the authors concluded that the original hypothesis—that the experimenters' predicted and obtained ratings are correlated—was "tentatively confirmed though the obtained significance level suggests that this could well bear repetition" [p. 502]. Next, the authors corrected each of the aforementioned correlations for restriction of range and reported that these corrections made all of the correlations significant by a one-tailed test. Subsequently, a document containing four additional correlations, performed on the same data, was filed by the authors with the American Documentation Institute. This document contains four Spearman correlations between experimenters' predicted and obtained ratings, computed separately for experimenters paid $5, testing unpaid subjects, and testing paid subjects, and for experimenters paid $2, testing unpaid subjects, and testing paid subjects. The four correlations average out to .04. Three of the four correlations (two in the negative direction and one in the positive direction) are not significantly different from zero while the fourth correlation (in the positive direction) differs from zero.

We do not know what to make of the aforementioned correlations. For instance, we are not sure whether a correlation coefficient around .04, or one around .30-.32, or one around .56 would have been obtained if a Pearson or Spearman correlation had been performed upon all of the original (nontransformed) predicted and obtained ratings. In brief, since a series of correlations were performed upon overlapping data and since each calculation yielded a different rho, we find it difficult to state with confidence at what level of significance the experimenter bias effect was supported in this study (cf., Neher, 1967, p. 259).

Study 8 (Rosenthal, Persinger, Vikan-Kline, & Fode, 1963b)

In this study 18 graduate student experimenters administered the person-perception task to 65 undergraduates. The experimenters were instructed to say "good" whenever a subject gave a rating of from $+1$ to $+4$ to a photograph and to say "excellent" whenever a subject gave a rating of $+5$ or higher. Half of the experimenters were told that their subjects had personality test scores such that on postexperimental inquiry they would be aware of having been verbally conditioned to give $+$ ratings; the remaining experimenters were told that their subjects would not be aware of having been conditioned. Also, "half of the *Es* in each of these two groups read instructions to their *Ss* informing them that they would later be asked to state the true intent of the experiment. The remaining *Es* did not so inform their *Ss*" [p. 276]. The dependent variable was subjects' awareness of having been conditioned as measured by two postexperimental questionnaires. Questionnaire 1 asked simply, "The purpose of this experiment was ———," and "My evidence for this is ———." Questionnaire 2 included 15 items that probed much more intrusively into the subjects' awareness. With respect to Questionnaire 2, the authors reported that the 2×2 analysis of variance (experimenters' expectations for awareness by subjects' set for awareness) yielded no significant Fs. With respect to Questionnaire 1, the 2×2 analysis of variance yielded a nonsignificant F for subjects' set for awareness and an F of 2.15 for the effect of experimenters' expectancies. Although all F tables give an associated probability around .16 for the latter F with its associated degrees of freedom, the authors stated that they had performed a "one-tailed F test" and halved the probability value to .08. It seems to us that this procedure— converting a p value of .16, as given in an F table, to a p value of .08 by referring to a one-tailed F test—may misrepresent the actual probability because the F ratio in an analysis of variance always provides a one-tailed test of the null hypothesis in terms of the sampling distribution of F (Hays, 1963, pp. 349–351, p. 369). In brief, we see the results of this study as suggesting but not conclusively demonstrating an experimenter bias effect and we believe that the major hypothesis of the study—pertaining to the effects of experimenters' expectancies on subjects' awareness in a verbal conditioning experiment—should be tested again in future research.

Study 9a (Rosenthal, Persinger, Mulry, Vikan-Kline, & Grothe, 1964b)

In this study, 20 student experimenters tested 73 student subjects on the person-perception task. All experimenters were told that on the basis of personality tests given to the subjects it could be predicted that some of their subjects would rate the photographed persons as successful (+5 ratings) and others would rate them as unsuccessful (−5 ratings). Thirteen of the twenty experimenters were also told that they would obtain the expected results "if [they] follow [ed] instructions and the proper experimental procedure." The dependent variable was the difference between the mean photo ratings obtained by each experimenter from those subjects who were expected to give +5 ratings and those subjects expected to give −5 ratings.

The authors reported that 3 of the 20 experimenters showed a "reversal of the biasing effect of expectancy, i.e., they obtained data significantly opposite to what they had been led to expect" [p. 472] and that the remaining 17 experimenters showed a significant experimenter bias effect. There are two interrelated reasons why we find it difficult to accept the latter analysis, which included 17 of the 20 experimenters, as clearly showing the effect: (*a*) Apparently, the authors excluded from the analysis the "negative" data (in the opposite direction) obtained by three experimenters after inspection of the results and on the basis of the dependent variable criterion alone. (*b*) The authors were *not* using the acceptable procedure of predetermining, prior to the experiment, which subjects or experimenters were to be used in the analysis by a criterion that enabled test of the experimental hypothesis. In another connection, Chapanis and Chapanis (1964) presented several considerations that appear relevant to the statistical procedures used in this study:

> Unfortunately, this line of reasoning [exclusion of "negative" data after inspection of the results] contains one fundamental flaw: *it does not allow the possibility that the null hypothesis may be correct.* The experimenter, in effect, is asserting that his . . . prediction is correct and that *S*s who do not conform to the prediction should be excluded from the analysis. This is a foolproof method of guaranteeing positive results.

> Some people may feel that no matter how questionable the selection procedure, it must still mean something if it leads to significant results. This point

of view, however, cannot be reconciled with the following facts of life: it is always possible to obtain a significant difference between two columns of figures in a table of random numbers provided we use the appropriate scheme for rejecting certain of these numbers. . . .

We strongly recommend that *S*s not be discarded from the sample *after* data collection and inspection of the results. Nor is it methodologically sound to reject *S*s whose results do not conform to the prediction. . . . If there are any theoretical grounds for suspecting that some *S*s will not show the predicted . . . effect, the characteristics of such *S*s, or the conditions, should be specifiable in advance. It should then be possible to do an analysis on all *S*s by dividing them into two groups, those predicted to show [the effect], and those predicted not to show it [pp. 16–17].

In brief, it is our opinion that a significant experimenter bias effect was obtained in this study when the data were inappropriately analyzed. When we carried out the statistical analysis which we deem appropriate (using all of the ratings), the mean difference between the ratings obtained under the +5 and −5 expectancy condition was −.11 (in the opposite direction, since plus signs indicate the experimenter bias effect) and the obtained *t* was far from significant.

The authors of this paper (Study 9a) also performed several further analyses which did not include the negative data that were in the opposite direction from the experimenters' expectancies. The criticisms delineated above are also applicable to these additional analyses.

Study 9b (Friedman, 1964, 1967; and Friedman, Kurland, & Rosenthal, 1965)

A total of 73 subjects participated in the investigation described in the previous section (Study 9a). A carefully concealed motion picture camera was used to film 53 of these 73 experimenter-subject interactions. The filmed portion of this study is the subject of a doctoral dissertation by Friedman (1964) and also of a book (Friedman, 1967) and of a paper (Friedman, Kurland, & Rosenthal, 1965) which are derived from the dissertation.

Friedman stated in the dissertation that each of the experimenters participating in Study 9a (discussed previously) also tested a group of subjects under a no-expectancy (control) condition. According to Friedman (1964, p. 92), the mean ratings (proffered under the three types of expectancy conditions by those subjects whose participation was filmed) were as follows:

Expectancy Condition	*Mean* Photo Ratings
High (+5)	−.11
No Expectancy (Control)	+.79
Low (−5)	+.23

The reader should note that these data fail to demonstrate an experimenter bias effect; that is (*a*) under the high-expectancy (+5) condition, subjects tended to give slightly lower ratings than under the low-expectancy (−5) condition; (*b*) the no-expectancy (control) condition tended to yield the highest ratings; and (*c*) the differences among the three means are not statistically significant.

Although the ratings were not shown to be biased in these experimenter-subject interactions, the authors treated the ratings as if bias had been demonstrated. That is, a "bias score" was derived for each subject as follows:

When *E* had a +5 expectancy, the *S*'s bias score was his mean rating of the photos minus the grand mean photo rating of all the *S*s for whom that *E* had a −5 expectancy. When *E* had a −5 expectancy that *S*'s bias score was his mean photo rating subtracted from the grand mean photo rating of all the *S*s for whom that *E* had a +5 expectancy [Friedman *et al.*, 1965, p. 483].

These "bias scores" were then correlated with various facets of the experimenters' behavior (derived from the films), such as the number of times that the experimenter smiled or glanced toward the subject. Some of the correlations were found to be significant. The significant correlations were interpreted as indicating that more "professional" experimenters exert the most bias. Two considerations are relevant here:

1. Since the student experimenters did not bias their subjects' ratings in this study—the subjects' ratings under the high- and low-expectancy condition tended to be slightly in the *unexpected* direction but did not differ significantly—the "bias scores" that were derived from the subjects' ratings may be random fluctuations (may consist of a set of scores that differ from each other by chance). Since it is questionable that the "bias scores" actually reflect bias, it is difficult to interpret the correlations between the "bias scores" and the experimenters' behaviors.

2. Even if the experimenter bias effect had been demonstrated in this study, and thus the "bias scores" could be considered to reflect unequivocally the degree of bias, we still could not clearly interpret the correlations presented by the authors. The dissertation stated that 2,888 correlations were computed and it was not clearly shown that the number of significant correlations that were obtained exceeded the 144 that can be expected to be "significant" among 2,888 correlations by chance alone.

In summary, the original study (Study 9a) from which the filmed portion was derived did not clearly show an experimenter bias effect, the subsample of experimenter-subject interactions that were filmed did not show the effect, the "bias scores" were not clearly shown to reflect bias, and the correlations between the "bias scores" and various facets of the experimenters' behavior appear to be difficult to interpret.

Study 10a (Rosenthal, Persinger, Mulry, Vikan-Kline, & Grothe, 1964a, Experiment 1)

Five student experimenters and fifty-two student subjects participated in this study. The experimenters were told to expect (on the basis of personality tests given to the subjects) that some of their subjects would give high ($+5$) ratings on the person-perception task and that other subjects would give low (-5) ratings. Half of the experimenter-subject interactions were observed by one of the authors of the paper (monitored condition) and half were unobserved (unmonitored condition). We doubt that this study clearly demonstrated an experimenter bias effect: The differences between the ratings obtained under the high- and low-expectancy conditions were in the expected direction but fell short of significance ($F = 3.60$, $df = 1/4$, $p = .15$).[4]

The authors reclassified the ratings in terms of experimenters' sex and subjects' sex and performed another analysis of variance. This analysis yielded nonsignificant main effects (male experimenters did not exert more or less bias than female experimenters, and male subjects were not more or less biased than female subjects). The authors considered the interaction between the experimenters' sex and subjects' sex to be significant ($p = .10$) and they performed t tests upon the four cell means that entered into the interaction. One of the t tests indicated that, "Among the female Es contacting male Ss there was a nonsignificant trend for the data obtained to be opposite to that expected" [p. 467] ($p = .66$). These data, which showed an opposite trend, were not included in the subsequent analysis. The authors reported that the subsequent analysis, which included the remaining data (data obtained by female experimenters contacting female subjects and male experimenters contacting male and female subjects), showed a significant experimenter bias effect. We cannot accept the latter analysis as clearly showing the effect. It seems to us that investigators can show practically any effect they wish to show by not including in the analysis those data which show "a nonsignificant trend . . . opposite to that expected."

This study (Study 10a) actually included three analyses of variance. The third analysis was designed to evaluate the effects of monitoring. (The main effect for monitoring was not significant, but the interaction effect—Experimenters × Monitoring—was significant.) This appears to be an appropriate place to note that when several analyses of variance are performed on overlapping data, as in this study, the probability of obtaining a spuriously "significant" finding increases much more rapidly than is commonly supposed. The problems involved in such "probability pyramiding" have been thoroughly discussed in an important recent paper by Neher (1967).

Study 11a (Rosenthal, Persinger, Mulry, Vikan-Kline, & Grothe, 1964a, Experiment 2)

This study included 6 student experimenters and 35 student subjects. The experimenters were instructed to expect that some of their subjects would give high ($+5$) ratings on the person-perception task and that the other subjects would give low (-5) ratings. Analysis of variance showed that the ratings obtained under the high- and low-expectancy conditions did not differ significantly ($F<0.5$, $df = 1/5$, $p>60$); that is, the study did not show an experimenter bias effect.

Although the ratings under the high- and low-expectancy condition were not significantly different ($p>.60$), the authors did not conclude that the study had failed to demonstrate the experimenter bias effect. Instead, they reclassified the ratings by experimenters' sex and subjects' sex and performed another analysis of variance. The F ratios for the main effects indicated that male experimenters exerted more bias than female experimenters and female subjects were more influenced by the experimenters' bias than male subjects. The interaction effect (Experimenters' Sex × Subjects' Sex) was not significant ($p = .20$). The authors next performed t tests among the four means that entered into the (nonsignificant) interaction and ostensibly showed that a (significant) interaction had occurred; that is, they ostensibly showed that three combinations of experimenters' sex with subjects' sex yielded results in the direction of the experimenters' expectancies, whereas the fourth combination (female experimenters testing male subjects) yielded results in the opposite direction. It is our opinion that the latter analysis by means of t tests is open to question: When the analysis of variance shows a nonsignificant interaction, it appears inappropriate to compute t tests among the means that enter into the interaction and to conclude, explicitly or implicitly, from the results of the t tests, that a significant interaction has occurred. It seems to us that, at best, the t tests performed in this study (Study 11a) and in the previous study (Study 10a) suggest a hypothesis that needs to be tested in further research, namely, that results opposite to those expected may be obtained when female experimenters test male subjects.

Study 10b–11b (Rosenthal, Friedman, & Kurland, 1966)

In Studies 10a and 11a, discussed previously, approximately three of every eight experimenter-subject interactions were filmed by a carefully concealed motion picture camera. The films were analyzed in a supplementary study reported by Rosenthal, Friedman, and Kurland (1966). Although neither of the two studies from which the films were derived had clearly demonstrated the experimenter bias effect, the subjects' ratings were treated in the supplementary study as if the effect had been demonstrated. That is, "bias scores" were derived from the subjects' original ratings and these "bias scores" were then correlated with various behaviors manifested by the experimenters (as derived from the films) such as the number of times the experimenter glanced toward the subject and his accuracy in reading the instructions. Some of the correlations were found to be significant. However, as we noted above in evaluating Study 9b, it is very difficult to interpret correlations computed between (*a*) various facets of the experimenters' behavior and (*b*) "bias scores" which are derived from a set of original ratings that may have differed by chance, that is, were not clearly shown to be biased.

Let us assume, for the moment, that the "bias scores" actually reflected the degree to which the experimenters biased their subjects' ratings. If we make this assumption, we can compare the results obtained in this study (Study 10b–11b) with the results of a very similar study which we discussed previously (Study 9b). In Study 9b (Friedman, 1964; Friedman *et al.*, 1965), three significant correlations were obtained between the "bias scores" and the ratings of the behaviors manifested by the male experimenters (derived from the films); the "bias scores" were (*a*) positively correlated with "experimenters' accuracy in reading the instructions," (*b*) negatively correlated with "time required for experimenters to read the first paragraph of the instructions," and (*c*) negatively correlated with "number of exchanged glances between experimenter and subject." With respect to the male experimenters participating in Study 10b–11b (Rosenthal, Friedman, & Kurland, 1966, Table 1), a contradictory finding (a significant negative correlation) was obtained with respect to the first variable, and confirming findings (negative correlations) were obtained with respect to the second and third variables. However, the correlations with respect to the second and third variables for female experimenters (participating in the second study) were in the opposite (positive) direction.

In light of our previous criticisms of Study 9b and Study 10b–11b, we view the two replicated correlations with male experimenters as suggestive at best. That is, we believe that further research is needed to test the hypothesis (suggested by the two studies) that male experimenters (but not female experimenters) who exert the most bias tend to read the first paragraph of the instructions quickly and tend to exchange few mutual glances with their subjects.

Study 12 (Rosenthal, Friedman, Johnson, Fode, Schill, White, & Vikan, 1964)

This study was conducted in a group setting and included 30 experimenters and 150 subjects. The 30 experimenters (undergraduate students) were subdivided into 5 groups of 6 experimenters each. One of these five groups of experimenters was instructed to expect low (-5) ratings from their subjects on the person-perception task; the remaining four groups of experimenters were instructed to expect high ($+5$) ratings. There were two additional independent variables in this experiment: explicitness of instructions to bias (half of the experimenters expecting high ratings were told, and the other half were not told, to do whatever they could to obtain the expected ratings); and motivation to bias (half of the experimenters expecting high ratings were told, and the other half were not told, that they would be given extra money if they obtained the expected high ratings).

The photo ratings obtained by each of the four groups of experimenters expecting high ($+5$) ratings (means $= -.23$, $-.35$, $-.02$, and $-.17$) tended to be lower than the ratings obtained by the experimenters expecting low (-5) ratings (mean $= +.14$). However, these means did not differ significantly ($p = .13$). Although the authors interpreted these data as suggesting a "reverse bias effect," we believe that the appropriate conclusion is as follows: Since the ratings obtained under the high- and low-expectancy condition were not significantly different, the study failed to demonstrate an experimenter bias effect. (A 2×2 analysis of variance that took into account all of the ratings obtained by the four groups of experimenters expecting high ratings showed that the main effects and the interaction of the other two independent variables, explicitness of instructions to bias and motivation to bias, were also not significant; all $Fs < 1.0$.)

Study 13 (Rosenthal, Kohn, Greenfield, & Carota, 1965)

This complex study, which included 26 undergraduate student experimenters and 115 subjects, had 4 independent variables: (*a*) experimenter expectancy for high ($+5$) ratings versus expectancy for low (-5) ratings; (*b*) confirmation versus disconfirmation of the experimenters' expectancies (by the first two subjects who were actually stooges); (*c*) praise versus reproof of the experimenters for the manner in which they were conducting the experiment; and (*d*) praise or reproof given by one of the authors of the paper versus praise or reproof given by another author. The dependent variable was the mean photo ratings on the person-perception task obtained by the experimenters from their real subjects (excluding the stooges). Analysis of variance showed that the first independent variable—experimenter expectancy—was not significant either as a main effect or in interaction with any of the other independent variables. The authors, however, failed to draw the conclusion indicated by this analysis, namely, that the study had failed to demonstrate an experimenter bias effect.

Although the analysis of variance showed that the experimenters' expectancies did not significantly interact with any of the other three variables, the authors went on to compute t tests among the means that entered into these interactions. For instance, they presented t tests which purported to show that the first independent variable (experimenters' high-low expectancies) interacted with the second independent variable (confirmation versus disconfirmation of the expectancies) as follows: Experimenters having their expectancies confirmed (by "early returns" from the stooges) obtained higher ratings from their subjects when they expected high ($+5$) ratings (mean $= -1.16$) than when they expected low (-5) ratings (mean $= -1.94$) but experimenters having their expectancies disconfirmed (by early returns from the stooges) did not subsequently obtain different ratings when they expected high and low ratings. The results of these t tests were interpreted (Rosenthal, 1966, Ch. 12) as supporting an early data returns hypothesis which states, in part, that experimenters obtaining good early returns (data in line with their expectancies) subsequently obtain more data which confirm their original expectancies. However, since the overall analysis of variance showed that the interaction was not significant, it is our opinion that the results of the t tests, performed upon the four means that entered into the (nonsignificant) interaction, cannot be clearly interpreted.[5]

Study 14 (McFall, 1965)

This doctoral dissertation showed that student experimenters expecting high ($+5$) or low (-5) ratings on a person-perception task did not obtain significantly different ratings from their student subjects. Also, experimenters expecting that their subjects would rate each photograph quickly or slowly did not obtain significantly different response times. The author concluded from these results that "there were no expectancy effects demonstrated—at least not of the magnitude previously reported" [p. 60]. The author then performed a postmortem analysis upon the response times and the ratings obtained from those subjects who had been run during the first half of the experiment. These analyses with half of the subjects indicated that experimenters expecting fast or slow responses did not obtain significantly different response times but experimenters expecting high ratings obtained significantly higher ratings than those expecting low ratings. Since the latter analysis of the ratings, which yielded a significant finding, was applied only to half of the subjects and was *post hoc* (was performed after an overall test had failed to reject the null hypothesis), it can, at best, be viewed as suggestive and subject to test in further research.

Studies 15–19 (Barber, Calverley, Forgione, McPeake, Chaves, & Bowen, 1966)

This report includes five investigations (conducted at five different universities) that were designed to demonstrate the experimenter bias effect. These 5 investigations included a total of 51 student experimenters and 501 student subjects. The procedure in each of the investigations was patterned as closely as possible after that used in an earlier study (to be discussed in the next section of this paper) which had shown an experimenter bias effect (Rosenthal & Fode, 1963b, Experiment 1). However, instead of including only experimenters given high (+5) or low (−5) expectancies, an additional (control) group of experimenters was included that was not given any expectancies. Each of the five investigations failed to demonstrate the effect; in each investigation, experimenters expecting high ratings, experimenters expecting low ratings, and experimenters not given expectancies did not differ significantly in the ratings they obtained. In each of the five investigations, the *F* ratio for the experimenter bias effect was less than 1.0 or very close to 1.0. The overall average ratings obtained in the five investigations under the high-expectancy (+5) condition, the control condition, and the low-expectancy (−5) condition were almost identical (+.3, +.1, and +.2, respectively). The authors concluded from these five investigations that the bias effect appears to be very difficult to demonstrate.[6]

VARIABLES MAXIMIZING THE EXPERIMENTER BIAS EFFECT

In addition to hypothesizing a main effect for experimenters' biases, Rosenthal (1966, Ch. 14) hypothesized that the bias effect is maximized by or interacts with a large number of variables, for example, with the experimenters' level of anxiety, the subjects' level of anxiety, and the experimenters' need for social approval. We first summarize briefly the data presented in support of these hypotheses and then present our general criticisms.

Experimenters' Anxiety

Rosenthal (1966, p. 234) concluded from the results of six studies that experimenters' level of anxiety is related to the occurrence of the experimenter bias effect. Three of these studies indicated that medium-anxious experimenters exert the most bias, two indicated that high-anxious experimenters exert the most bias, and one indicated that low-anxious experimenters exert the most bias (p values in each of these studies were $<.13$).

Subjects' Anxiety

To support the hypothesis that the experimenters' biases differentially affect subjects of high, low, and medium anxiety, Rosenthal (1966, p. 234) presented the following results obtained in six studies: The experimenter bias effect was maximized in subjects of low anxiety (one study), in subjects of medium anxiety (two studies), in subjects of high anxiety (two studies), and in subjects of high and low anxiety (one study). (The p values in each of these six studies were $<.12$).

Experimenters' Need for Approval

To support the hypothesis that experimenters' need for approval is related to the occurrence of bias effects, Rosenthal (1966, p. 238) presented 20 correlation coefficients (obtained in seven studies). These correlations between the degree of experimenter bias effect and the experimenters' need for approval were tabulated separately for experimenters rated as high, medium, and low anxious. With respect to the 12 correlations presented for the high- and low-anxious experimenters, only 2 differed significantly from zero. However, 4 of the 8 correlations pertaining to medium-anxious experimenters differed from zero; 3 of these significant correlations were in the positive direction and 1 was in the negative direction.

There are at least two possible interpretations of these contradictory but significant or near significant findings. One is that the experimenter bias effect is related to experimenters' and subjects' level of anxiety and to experimenters' need for approval in very complex ways and there are additional variables which are interacting to produce the complexity and the contradictions. An alternative interpretation is that the results are due to chance and there is no noticeable relationship between these variables. The latter interpretation is supported by the following considerations:

1. Most of the data summarized above, which ostensibly relate the experimenter bias effect to anxiety and to need for approval, derive from the studies which we criticized in the preceding section of this paper. In these studies, which did not clearly demonstrate an experimenter bias effect, anxiety and need for approval were correlated with a set of scores ("bias scores") that may have varied by chance.

2. Even if bias had been unequivocally demonstrated in these studies, the data which purportedly relate the bias effect to anxiety or to need for approval could quite likely be due to

chance because of the following: In many instances, the data came from studies in which many overlapping (nonindependent) explicit and implicit statistical tests were performed among a large number of predictor and criterion variables and in which, consequently, it was very difficult to assign an expected probability to the results of any one statistical test (see, for example, our discussion of Study 6 by Rosenthal, Persinger, Vikan-Kline, & Mulry, 1963).

In brief, it is our judgment that the data which purportedly relate the experimenter bias effect to anxiety or to need for approval may be chance findings (cf., Neher, 1967). Before we hypothesize complex interactions that might explain the contradictory results, we believe that further research is necessary to determine if the results can be replicated.

The general criticisms delineated above also apply to data presented in a recent text (Rosenthal, 1966, Chs. 6, 13, 14) to support the contentions that (*a*) male experimenters exert greater expectancy effects upon acquainted than upon unacquainted subjects; (*b*) experimenters' sex interacts with subjects' sex to determine the effects of experimenters' biases (see our discussion of Studies 10a and 11a); and (*c*) the experimenter bias effect is maximized when rewards offered to experimenters to obtain expected responses are not excessive. A recent paper (Silver, 1967) raises similar criticisms with respect to the hypothesis that subjects perform on an experimental task in the way their experimenters originally performed on the same task (experimenter modeling effect, Rosenthal, 1966, Ch. 7).

TWELVE STUDIES THAT APPARENTLY SHOWED THE EXPERIMENTER BIAS EFFECT

We will now review 12 investigations that apparently demonstrated an experimenter bias effect. The major question at issue will be: What factors mediated the effect? To answer this question, it will be necessary to present a rather detailed analysis of the procedures and results of each study.

Before we delineate the many possible ways that the effect can be mediated, we must emphasize that, in almost all investigations in this area, student experimenters were not simply told to expect certain results; they were also told explicitly or implicitly that they should obtain the results. In other words, in practically all of the investigations, expectancy for certain results was apparently confounded with the desire or wish to obtain the results.

There are at least 11 possible ways that an experimenter's expectancies and desires can influence the results of his research:

(a) The experimenter may unintentionally influence his subjects to give expected-desired responses through unintentional paralinguistic cues, for example, by variations in his tone of voice. (b) The experimenter may influence his subjects to give expected-desired responses by means of unintentional kinesic cues, for example, by changes in his posture or by changes in his facial expression. (c) The experimenter may influence his results by unintentionally reinforcing his subjects verbally when they give expected-desired responses. (d) The experimenter may unintentionally misjudge his subjects' responses. (e) The experimenter may unintentionally misrecord the subjects' responses.

Each of the above modes of mediation could also be intentional. That is, the experimenter may obtain expected-desired data by (f) intentionally transmitting paralinguistic cues, (g) intentionally transmitting kinesic cues, (h) intentionally administering verbal reinforcement, (i) intentionally misjudging the subjects' responses, and (j) intentionally misrecording the responses. Finally, (k) the experimenter may simply fabricate his data.

The 11 possible models of mediation of the experimenter bias effect can be more generally classified into two sets. One set includes those modes of mediation that do not affect the subjects' responses; these comprise unintentional or intentional misjudgment or misrecording of the responses on the part of the experimenter and fabrication of the data by the experimenter. The remaining modes of mediation (unintentional or intentional paralinguistic cues, kinesic cues, and verbal reinforcement) may affect the responses of the subjects. In the discussion to follow we will ask: When experimenters' biases affected the results, did they do so by affecting the subjects' responses or by affecting the experimenters' scoring or reporting of the responses?

Rosenthal (1964a, 1966) has focused on the first 2 of the 11 possible ways that an experimenter's results may be related to his expectancies and desires. That is, Rosenthal has hypothesized that experimenters' biases influence their subjects' responses through unintentional paralinguistic and kinesic cues. In the analysis to follow we attempt to judge whether the evidence supports this hypothesis.

We first review studies that were concerned with the effects of experimenters' biases on animal learning or animal conditioning and then we turn to studies that used human subjects.

Animal Studies

Study 1 (Rosenthal & Fode, 1963a) and Study 2 (Rosenthal & Lawson, 1964). The 12 experimenters participating in the study by Rosenthal and Fode (1963a) were undergraduate students enrolled in an experimental psychology laboratory. Each student experimenter was told that, to obtain "further experience in duplicating experimental findings," he would run five rats through a simple maze 10 times a day for a period of five days. Half of the experimenters were told that their rats were "bright" and should show rapid learning and the remaining half were told that their rats were "dull" and should show "very little evidence of learning." The rats were actually drawn at random from a homogeneous animal colony. Each experimenter recorded on each of 250 trials if his rats made the correct response of "go[ing] to the darker of two platforms."

The average number of correct responses obtained from each animal on any one day was 2.3 for "bright" animals and 1.5 for "dull" animals. Since the difference between these means was statistically significant, the study showed an experimenter bias effect.

Although the student experimenters in this study "worked alone and were much of the time unobserved by the laboratory supervisor" [Rosenthal, 1966, p. 169], the authors stated that there were "five observed instances of cheating in which an *E* prodded an *S* to run the maze." (Three of these instances of cheating occurred among experimenters running "dull" animals and two among experimenters running "bright" animals.) Whether the student experimenters cheated or conducted the experiment honestly when they were unobserved is, of course, unknown.

In a subsequent study (Rosenthal & Lawson, 1964), 39 undergraduate students, enrolled in an experimental psychology laboratory, were divided into 14 research teams. Each team worked with one rat. Eight of the teams were told that their rat had been bred for brightness and should show rapid learning. The remaining six teams of experimenters were told that their rat had been bred for dullness and should show very little evidence of learning. All rats were in fact randomly drawn from a homogeneous colony of animals. Over a period of two months the experimenters ran their animals through seven learning tasks (magazine training, operant acquisition, extinction and spontaneous recovery, secondary reinforcement, stimulus discrimination, stimulus generalization, and response chaining).

Experimenters told that their rat should learn rapidly and those told that their rat should show little learning did not obtain significantly different performance from their animals on five of the seven learning tasks. However, experimenters running supposedly bright rats obtained significantly faster learning from their animals on the remaining tasks (stimulus discrimination and stimulus generalization). Taking all seven tasks in combination, the "bright" rats showed slightly faster learning than the "dull" rats (normalized mean ranks equaled 4.5 and 5.5, respectively) and the differences were statistically significant.

Again, as in the preceding study, the student experimenters were not closely observed during the two-month experimental period to determine whether they ran the rats in the way specified in the laboratory manual and whether they correctly recorded the responses. Even though the students were not closely observed, one of the authors subsequently stated (without presenting further details) that, in this study, "several instances of data fabrication came to light" [Rosenthal, 1964a, p. 83]. There is no reason to believe that the fabricated data were used in the overall statistical analysis. However, there is no way of knowing whether the remaining students, who were not caught in the act of fabricating data and whose data were used in the analysis, carried out the experiment honestly or dishonestly.

How was the experimenter bias effect mediated in these two studies with rats? It appears possible, as Rosenthal has hypothesized, that the effect was mediated by tactual cues transmitted to the animals during handling. There is presumptive evidence supporting this hypothesis: Experimenters who worked with "bright" animals, as compared with those who worked with "dull" animals, reported after completion of the study that they had handled the animals more often or more gently. An alternative hypothesis is that the effect was due to "cheating" (prodding the animals), to misrecording of responses, or to data fabrication on the part of the student experimenters who were enrolled in the experimental psychology laboratory. Additional studies are needed to decide among these alternative modes of mediation.

Further attempts to replicate the study by Rosenthal and Lawson (1964) should also control a potentially contaminating variable. In the Rosenthal and Lawson study, the rats labeled as dull were confined to one cage and the rats labeled as bright were confined to another cage. Early in the experiment 25 percent (two of eight) of the "dull" rats died. None of the "bright" rats died. It thus appears possible that an illness may have been present among the "dull" rats who were confined together in one cage and this may have led to their poorer performance.

Study 3 (Cordaro & Ison, 1963). In this experiment, students in an introductory psychology course were asked to record the number of "contractions" and "head turns" manifested by tiny flatworms during a two-second period when the worms were exposed to a conditioned stimulus (a light). Some of the students were told that their flatworms had "already been conditioned and will probably show a high response rate" and the others were told that their flatworms had not been conditioned and they "shouldn't expect too much from them." The students had not had prior experience with the tiny animals and they were not told what criteria to use in judging contractions and head turns. The students told (by the instructor) that their flatworms should show a high response rate reported significantly more contractions and head turns than those told they should not expect too much from their flatworms.

Cordaro and Ison presented a further trial-by-trial analysis which indicated that the results were due to the use of different criteria for judging the responses by experimenters expecting many and those expecting few responses. In addition, the authors noted that (a) the judgment asked of the students, which required "separating an anticipatory response from spontaneous activity at one end and the unconditioned response at the other end of a short 2-sec. interval" [p. 789] is a very difficult one to make, and (b) in further studies with flatworms, what is to be judged as a contraction or a head turn should be specified unambiguously by establishing a critical deflection point.

Study 4 (Ingraham & Harrington, 1966). This study, involving learning in rats, resembled the study discussed above (by Cordaro & Ison) in that undergraduate students, without previous laboratory experience, were asked to score an ambiguous response. Over a five-day experimental period, the student experimenters judged the number of times that rats pressed a bar but what was to be judged as a "bar press" was not defined for them (each student was required to "set his own criterion"). Six students ran rats which the teacher labeled as bright, six ran rats labeled as dull, and fifteen ran both "bright" and "dull" rats. (The rats were actually assigned at random without regard to brightness.)

The students running "bright" rats recorded more bar presses than those running "dull" rats during the first part of the experiment (Days 1-3) but not during the latter part (Days 4-5). The authors interpreted these results as follows: (a) The response that was to be judged (bar pressing) was ambiguous to the students especially during the first days of the experiment; however, (b) as the students became better acquainted with the behavior of rats, those who perceived the rats as bright and those who perceived them as dull converged on similar criteria for judging bar pressing and their results during the latter part of the experiment were practically identical.

In brief, the studies by Cordaro and Ison and by Ingraham and Harrington appear to indicate that, when undergraduate students without prior experience in running laboratory animals are given ambiguous criteria for judging multifaceted animal responses, their judgments will be influenced by the teacher's statement that their animals will show either many or few of the (ambiguous) responses.

Human Studies

Studies 5-7 (Rosenthal & Fode, 1963b, Experiments 1 and 2; and Laszlo & Rosenthal, 1967). In the first study by Rosenthal and Fode (1963b, Experiment 1), one group of experimenters was told that their subjects should average about +5 ratings on the person-perception task and a second group of experimenters was told that the subjects should average about −5. Also, the experimenters were informed that if their results came out "properly—as expected" they would be paid $2 per hour and if their results did not come out "properly" they would be paid $1. Significantly higher ratings were obtained by experimenters expecting +5 rather than −5 ratings.

How was the experimenter bias effect mediated in this study? It appears possible, as Rosenthal has hypothesized, that the effect was mediated by unintentional paralinguistic or kinesic cues. However, there are alternative possibilities; for example, the experimenters (undergraduate students enrolled in an experimental psychology laboratory) may have unintentionally or intentionally misrecorded or misreported their results. It should be noted that (*a*) the students were told they would earn more money if they obtained the proper results; (*b*) no attempt was made to ascertain if the student experimenters ran their subjects in accordance with the programmed procedure and if they correctly recorded and reported the data; and (*c*) a series of investigations by other workers indicate that some students and also some nonstudents who are asked to serve as experimenters or as interviewers do not conduct their studies in accordance with the experimental protocol and at times misrecord, misreport, or falsify their results (Azrin, Holz, Ulrich, & Goldiamond, 1961; Crespi, 1946; Guest, 1947; Hansel, 1966; Hyman, 1954, pp. 238–242; Symposium, 1947).

Three experimenters (law school students) participated in a recent study by Laszlo and Rosenthal (1967). Each experimenter was instructed to expect high (+5) ratings from some of his subjects and low (−5) ratings from other subjects. The mean photo ratings obtained by the three experimenters were −.53 when expecting +5 ratings and −.99 when expecting −5 ratings. Although both means were in the negative direction, the mean obtained when experimenters expected high ratings was significantly higher than the mean obtained when experimenters expected low ratings; thus, the study apparently demonstrated an experimenter bias effect. How was the effect mediated? Although the data presented in the original paper do not provide a definite answer, one of the authors (Rosenthal, 1966, p. 13) noted that, in this study, (*a*) all three experimenters made errors in adding their subjects' ratings; (*b*) although one experimenter erred only 6 percent of the time, the others erred in 22 percent and 26 percent of their computations; and (*c*) 75 percent of the errors were in the direction of the experimenters' expectancies. Although there is every reason to believe that the errors in addition were corrected by the authors of the paper prior to analyzing the data, the fact that the student experimenters made biased errors in adding the ratings also raises the possibility that they may have made biased errors in originally recording their subjects' ratings.

However, another study by Rosenthal and Fode (1963b, Experiment 2) provided evidence that the experimenter bias effect can be mediated by unintentional or intentional verbal and visual cues. This study involved four groups of student experimenters. Experimenters in Group I were told that they would earn more money if they obtained low (−5) ratings from their subjects on the person-perception task. Experimenters in Groups II, III, and IV were told that they would earn more money if they obtained high (+5) ratings. The latter three groups differed as follows: Experimenters in Group II sat behind a screen when they administered the person-perception task to their subjects; experimenters in Group III were visible but they did not speak to their subjects (presenting all instructions in writing); and experimenters in Group IV ran the subjects in the usual way presenting instructions orally and in full view of the subjects. The major findings were as follows:

1. Group II experimenters (nonvisible and expecting +5) elicited significantly higher ratings than Group I experimenters (expecting −5) and significantly lower ratings than Group IV experimenters (expecting +5). This outcome appeared to indicate that visual cues play a role but are not necessary in transmitting the experimenters' expectancies.

2. The ratings elicited by Group III experimenters (nonverbal and expecting +5) did not differ significantly from those elicited by Group I experimenters (expecting −5). This result appeared to indicate that, if the experimenters' expectancies are to be transmitted successfully, it may be necessary for the experimenters to speak to their subjects.

Study 8 (Masling, 1965, 1966). This study was first presented in 1965 and then was further amplified (Masling, 1966, pp. 80–82). The author told seven graduate students that

a good measure of their skill in administering the Rorschach test was the extent to which they could secure many animal responses from their *S*s; a similar group of examiners was told that if they were skilled, they would produce many human responses. [The author] cited evidence for this relationship between expertness and content for each group of examiners by reading abstracts of journal articles proving this point; needless to say, the evidence was all fabricated [Masling, 1966, p. 81].

Each student examiner then tested two subjects on the Rorschach, with tape recordings made of each session. Significantly more animal responses were obtained by examiners told to show their skill by obtaining such responses. Analysis of the tape recordings indicated that the student examiners did not obtain the desired responses by verbally reinforcing their subjects. Masling (1965, 1966, pp. 80–82) suggested two ways that the examiners could have influenced the subjects to give the responses that were desired:

1. When a subject gave a desired response on any one Rorschach card, the examiner could take the card away from the subject. However, when the subject did not give a desired response, the examiner could allow the subject to continue to hold the card and to respond to it until he gave a response that was wanted.

2. By posture, gesture, or facial expression the examiners could have communicated their approval when the subjects gave responses that were desired and could have communicated their disapproval when they gave unwanted responses.

Study 9 (Silverman, 1966). In this investigation, 20 student experimenters administered a word-association test to 333 student subjects. Ten of the experimenters were told that the purpose of the study was to establish norms for association time (base-line condition). The remaining 10 experimenters were told that half of their subjects were scheduled to take an examination later on the day of the experiment (exam condition) and their other subjects were not scheduled to take an examination (no-exam condition). The latter experimenters were also led to expect that subjects under the exam condition, as compared to those under the no-exam condition, would show a greater latency of association time to exam-related words. (The subjects were in fact randomly assigned to the exam and no-exam conditions, without regard for course examination schedules.) All experimenter-subject interactions were recorded on tape.

The results were generally in the expected direction: The latencies to examination-related words were significantly higher under the exam condition than under the base-line condition, and tended to be higher under the exam condition than under the no-exam condition.

A possible mode of mediation of the effect was suggested by a further analysis. A research assistant, who did not have knowledge of the hypothesis under investigation, used the tape recordings to time the response latencies to the key words in the exam and no-exam conditions for the two experimenters who obtained the greatest differences between these conditions. Systematic scoring errors by the experimenters (either in timing the responses or in recording the responses) were found. The scoring errors were in the direction of the experimenters' expectancies; that is, under the exam condition the experimenters incorrectly timed or improperly recorded the latencies to the key (exam-related) words as significantly longer than they actually were ($p < .01$). In brief, the analyses of the tape recordings suggested that the experimenter bias effect may have been mediated by intentional or unintentional scoring or recording errors on the part of the student experimenters. (Unfortunately, due to the poor quality of the remaining tapes, the author was unable to determine if systematic errors by the student experimenters could account for all of the results.)

Study 10 (Adair & Epstein, 1967). There were two parts to this experiment:

Part 1. Six student experimenters were told they would earn a higher rate of pay if they obtained expected high ($+5$) or low (-5) ratings from subjects on a person-perception task. Each experimenter tested 10 subjects. (When each experimenter was administering the task to each of his subjects, his procedure was recorded by means of a carefully concealed tape recorder.) The experimenter bias effect was demonstrated: Experimenters obtained significantly higher ratings when they expected high rather than low ratings.

Part 2. The person-perception task was administered to a new group of 60 subjects by means of the tape recordings that had been made in Part 1; that is, the instructions for the task, which had been taped in Part 1, were played to another group of subjects by one of the authors of the paper. Significantly higher ratings were obtained from subjects who were exposed to the taped instructions that derived from experimenters who had expected high ratings. Since the experimenter bias effect was obtained from the taped instructions, the study strongly indicated that vocal cues, for example, variations in the experimenters' tone of voice, are sufficient to transmit the effect.

Study 11 (Shames & Adair, 1967). These authors examined the effects of experimenters' expectancies on responses to a more ambiguous task (the person-perception task) and to a less ambiguous, more "factual" task (number estimation). The number-estimation task was patterned after the person-perception task in that it included 10 stimulus cards, and the subjects were asked to make a judgment about each card on a 20-step rating scale.

Ten student experimenters administered the number-estimation task to 38 student subjects. Each of the 10 stimulus cards contained 200 dots, in designs of varying density. The subjects were required to estimate the number of dots on each card and the experimenters were led to expect that their subjects would either overestimate (210 dots) or underestimate (190 dots). An additional 10 student experimenters administered the person-perception task to 41 subjects; these experimenters were led to expect that their subjects would either give high ($+5$) or low (-5) ratings. An experimenter bias effect was obtained with the person-perception task but not with the number-estimation task. The authors interpreted these results as follows:

1. The person-perception task requires the subject to make an abstract, evaluative judgment of the person depicted. That is, the subject is asked to rate whether the person depicted has been "experiencing failure" (− ratings) or has been "experiencing success" (+ ratings) on an arbitrary − 10 to + 10 scale. Thus, the judgment asked of the subject tends to be ambiguous and the subject typically turns to the experimenter for cues as to how he should respond.

2. The judgment required in the number-estimation task is much less ambiguous. Since the subject is abundantly familiar with the number system, he has well-established norms on which to base his estimate of the number of dots on the card and, thus, does not find it necessary to turn to the experimenter for cues as to how he should respond.

The authors concluded from these data that ambiguous tasks appear to be more conducive to experimenter bias effects than more factual, objective tasks. Further studies using a larger sampling of ambiguous and factual tasks are needed to determine the generalizability of this conclusion.

Study 12 (Marwit & Marcia, 1967). The experimenters participating in this recent study were 36 undergraduate students. Each student experimenter administered a modified form of the Holtzman Inkblot Test to one or two subjects. Prior to administering the test, half of the experimenters were asked whether they expected to obtain many or few responses to the inkblots from their subjects and the other experimenters were told to expect either many or few responses. Both sets of experimenters (those formulating their own expectancies and those given expectancies) obtained results significantly related to their expectancies. In a further analysis of the data, the authors found a general tendency for the bias effect to increase during the course of the experimenters' interaction with each subject. They interpreted the latter datum as suggesting the possibility that a "form of verbal conditioning" may have occurred; that is, the student experimenters may have administered verbal reinforcement to the subjects when they gave expected responses.[7]

CONCLUSIONS AND RECOMMENDATIONS

One conclusion indicated by this review is as follows: Since most of the studies in this area did not clearly demonstrate that experimenters' expectancies, desires, or biases significantly influence the outcome of their research, the experimenter bias effect appears to be more difficult to demonstrate and less pervasive than was implied in previous reviews in this journal (Kintz *et al.*, 1965; Rosenthal, 1967). However, in many studies in which it is questionable that the student experimenters biased their results, the principal investigators concluded that an experimenter bias effect had in fact been demonstrated. What is the basis for these differing conclusions? It seems to us that the contradictory interpretations derive from different criteria for appropriate data analysis. We first discuss these criteria and then turn to other conclusions and methodological implications of this review.

Data Analysis

It is our opinion that certain procedures in analyzing data can easily give rise to misleading conclusions. We set forth these procedures explicitly with the hope that the basis of our disagreement with other workers in this area may be clarified.

We believe that further research in this area will avoid misleading conclusions if it adheres to the following principles of data analysis:

1. If the particular comparisons that the investigator is interested in are not specified in advance (that is, the technique of planned comparisons is not being used, Hays, 1963, Ch. 14), an overall statistical test will be performed that includes *all* of the data.
2. The probability value (p) required for rejection of the null hypothesis will be specified in advance.
3. Conclusions will not be drawn from the results of *post hoc* tests performed upon the data after an overall test has failed to reject the null hypothesis. The results of such post-mortem tests will be "substantiated in independent research in which they are specifically predicted and tested" [Kerlinger, 1964, p. 621].
4. The analysis will avoid errors of "probability pyramiding" [Neher, 1967], for example, the error of "finding some significant F ratios in an experiment by complicating the experiment with more and more irrelevant variables, while continuing to base the error rate upon the individual F" [Ryan, 1959].
5. If many independent and many dependent variables are used in one study, they will be clearly specified beforehand and they will be analyzed by multivariate procedures such as multiple-discriminant analysis, canonical correlation, factor analysis, or multivariate analysis of variance or covariance. The analysis of multivariate studies will not be carried out by individual t tests, Spearman rhos, and chi-squares (Cattell, 1966).

It is our belief that, at the present time, psychologists should adhere to these principles of data analysis even if they find merit in the Bayesian approach to statistical inference. As Binder (1964) has aptly stated,

At some future date perhaps we will shift to Bayesian logic (although I personally doubt it), when it is much more fully developed both logically and practically, but it is perfectly clear that experimenters should not presently throw away their traditional significance testing procedures and methods of setting confidence intervals, the current standards for good design and competent analysis, the generally accepted criteria of objectivity in interexperimenter agreement, and so forth [p. 287].

Rigorous Methodology

We believe that further research should also remedy several methodological inadequacies that have characterized this area of inquiry. These include failure to determine the reliability of the criterion instrument, failure to check for the effectiveness of the independent variable manipulation, and failure to use control groups.

Reliability of instrument. To the best of our knowledge, the reliability of the instrument used in the great majority of studies in this area (the person-perception task) has not been determined. Although the question of reliability is quite complex (Barber, 1965, pp. 813–814; Cattell, 1964), the basic issue here can be stated simply: When subjects are tested in the same way twice on the person-perception task, do the test-retest correlations differ significantly from zero? Ascertaining the reliability of this instrument is especially important because reliability may be regarded as an independent variable—it is important to know whether the experimenter bias effect operates on reliable measures as well as on unreliable ones.

Presence of independent variables. The great majority of studies in this area failed to check the effectiveness of the independent variable manipulation. Some minutes or hours prior to conducting the experiment, the student experimenters were told that they should expect high or low ratings from their subjects. When the experimenters were told what to expect, they may not have paid close attention. Furthermore, by the time the experimenters ran their subjects, they may have forgotten what they had been told to expect. In further studies we should ascertain that experimenters told to expect high or low ratings actually expect high or low ratings when they are running their subjects.

Control group. With very few exceptions, studies in this area did not include a no-expectancy control group of experimenters. However, in those few studies which included a control group, the no-expectancy controls typically elicited either higher ratings than the high-expectancy group or lower ratings than the low-expectancy group (Barber *et al.*, 1966; Friedman, 1964; Pflugrath, 1962). We believe that this area of inquiry will advance more rapidly if further studies consistently include a control group.

Delineation of Mediating Variables

The evidence at present indicates that the variables which mediate the experimenter bias effect include the following:

1. At times, experimenters appear to bring the outcome of their experiment in line with their biases by intentionally or unintentionally misjudging, misrecording, or misreporting the results.

2. At times, the biases of the experimenter appear to affect the subjects' responses. The effect upon the responses of the subject may be mediated in several ways: (*a*) the experimenter may intentionally or unintentionally reward his subjects verbally or nonverbally for expected or desired responses; (*b*) he may wittingly or unwittingly transmit his biases by paralinguistic cues, such as variations in his tone of voice (Barber & Calverley, 1964); or (*c*) he may intentionally or unintentionally communicate his biases by bodily movements or by facial movements, such as smiling or frowning (kinesic cues).

Further studies are needed to determine which of these modes of mediation play the most important role in producing the experimenter bias effect. It appears likely that different modes of mediation will be found to be the most prominent in different experimental situations. For instance, when an experimenter bias effect is found in a situation in which student experimenters test student subjects on relatively well-structured tasks, the most prominent mode of mediation may consist of intentional misreporting of data by the experimenters; and, when the effect is obtained in a situation in which teacher experimenters test student subjects on relatively ambiguous tasks, the most prominent mode of mediation may consist of the unintentional transmission of paralinguistic or kinesic cues.

Further research concerned with the mechanisms underlying the experimenter bias effect should note that: (*a*) the various possible modes of mediation can be subdivided into those comprised of unintentional behaviors on the part of the experimenter and those which are comprised of intentional behaviors; and (*b*) when the experimenter brings his results in line with his expectancies or desires by intentionally misjudging, misrecording, or misreporting his results, or by intentionally administering verbal or nonverbal reinforcement, or by intentionally transmitting paralinguistic or kinesic cues, the mediating behaviors are very difficult to differentiate from those that are commonly termed cheating. Consequently, further studies in this area should make special efforts to ascertain how often and under what conditions the experimenter bias effect is due to cheating on the part of the student experimenters and how often and under what circumstances it is due to nonintentional, noncheating behavior.

A further consideration is relevant here. In studies which showed the experimenter bias effect, expectancies were apparently transmitted from the principal investigator to the student experimenter, and from the experimenter to the subject. In fact, an eight-step transmission process was apparently involved (cf., McGuire, 1967): (*a*) The student experimenter attended to the expectancy communication from the principal investigator. (*b*) The experimenter comprehended the expectancy communication. (*c*) The experimenter retained the communication. (*d*) The experimenter (intentionally or unintentionally) attempted to transmit the expectancy to the subject. (*e*) The subject (consciously or unconsciously) attended to the expectancy communication from the experimenter. (*f*) The subject (consciously or unconsciously) comprehended the experimenter's expectancy. (*g*) The subject (consciously or unconsciously) retained the experimenter's expectancy. (*h*) The subject (wittingly or unwittingly) acted upon (gave responses in harmony with) the experimenter's expectancy.

In studies which failed to show an experimenter bias effect, the transmission process could have broken down at any one of these eight links in the chain. There are a large number of possibilities here. The principal investigator may fail to transmit the expectancy communication to the experimenter; the experimenter may comprehend the expectancy communication but may not retain it; the experimenter may retain it but may fail to transmit it to the subject, etc. It is apparent that a sophisticated methodology, commensurate with the complexities of the problem, is needed to determine under what circumstances the transmission of expectancies is most likely to break down at each of the eight steps.

Variables Maximizing the Effect

Further research is needed to determine under what circumstances we are most likely and also least likely to obtain an experimenter bias effect. The parameters to be considered include the characteristics of the participating individuals (principal investigators, experimenters, and subjects), the relationship between these individuals, the methods used to induce expectancy biases, and the nature of the experimental tasks.

Participating individuals. In most of the studies in this area, the principal investigators were college teachers and the experimenters were college students (graduates or undergraduates). Friedman (1964) has asked a pointed question here: Is the experimenter bias effect dependent upon the experimenters being in a subordinate-superordinate (student-teacher) relationship with their principal investigators? Also, in almost all of the studies, the subjects were college freshmen or sophomores. Is the effect also dependent upon the subjects being lower level students and the experimenters being upper level undergraduates or graduates? Stated more broadly, what type of role relationships between principal investigator and experimenter, and between experimenter and subject, maximizes the effect? There are many other questions that can be asked. Is the effect limited to student subjects or can it also be obtained with nonstudents, say, working-class adults? Are we more likely to obtain the effect when student experimenters volunteer to conduct the study, or when they are required to carry out the study as part of a laboratory course?

Methods of inducing bias. In most of the experiments in this area, expectancies were confounded with desires; that is, the student experimenters were told explicitly or implicitly that it was desirable to obtain the expected results. Is the experimenter bias effect dependent upon the experimenters both expecting and wanting a specified outcome? Is the effect obtained when experimenters expect but do not desire certain results or when they desire but do not expect the results?

Expectancies and desires can be induced in a large variety of ways. For instance, in some studies the student experimenters were told they would be given practice in duplicating (expected) results which had been well established in previous research. In other studies the experimenters were told that the results were expected on the basis of personality tests which had been previously administered to the subjects. Also, in some studies the experimenters were told that all of the subjects would give one type of (expected) rating, whereas in other studies the experimenters were told that some subjects would give one type of rating and other subjects would give another type. Furthermore, in many studies the student experimenters were offered a higher rate of pay ("bribed"?) to obtain the expected-desired results. It is apparent that additional work is needed to clarify the role played by these and various other possible methods of inducing bias.

Nature of experimental task. Several studies in this area used relatively structured or factual tasks, such as the Wechsler Adult Intelligence Scale, the Taylor Manifest Anxiety scale, and a number-estimation task; none of these studies showed an experimenter bias effect. Some of the studies which used more ambiguous or less structured tasks, for example, the person-perception task, showed the effect. The hypothesis suggested by these general findings and by a recent experiment (Shames & Adair, 1967) is that the effects of the experimenter's expectancies on the results of his research vary directly with the ambiguity, lack of structure, or nonfactualness of the experimental task. Further research is needed to test this hypothesis. Although several of the studies which we criticized earlier in this paper included data pertaining to some of the questions we have raised in this section, it is our opinion that these studies do not permit clear-cut conclusions and that further research is needed to provide definite answers. Rigorous research is needed which varies the characteristics of the participating individuals (principal investigators, experimenters, and subjects), the relationships between these individuals, the methods for inducing biases, and the types of experimental tasks. Studies of this type may find that the strength of the experimenter bias effect depends upon these variables and also upon many other interacting variables that remain to be specified.

General Conclusions and a Recommendation

This review indicates that (*a*) experimenters' biases may at times influence their results, and (*b*) investigators may at times draw misleading conclusions from inadequate data analysis. Also, studies which we have not reviewed in this paper suggest that, irrespective of biases or faulty data analysis, (c) experimenters differing in personal attributes (traits of personality, sex, age, status, and ethnic characteristics) may at times obtain different responses from comparable groups of subjects (Masling, 1960, 1966; Rosenthal, 1966, Chs. 4 and 5), and (*d*) investigators may at times obtain misleading data as a result of conditions that are unique to their own milieu, such as the types of subjects, staff, and other research facilities that are available to them (Neher, 1967). These considerations indicate a general conclusion that has been previously emphasized by Rosenthal (1966, Ch. 18), Neher (1967), and others: The behavioral sciences should adopt a rule that has long been prevalent in the physical and biological sciences, namely, research results should not be accepted until they have been replicated in independent laboratories.

NOTES

1. Writing this paper was made possible by a research grant (MH-11521) to the senior author from the National Institute of Mental Health, United States Public Health Service. The authors are indebted to Robert Rosenthal, Ralph L. Rosnow, Herbert J. Greenwald, Maressa Orzack, Dick Murray, Ambellur N. D. Frederick, Gerald Borofsky, Daniel E. Daum, and Dennis G. Canali for their helpful comments on a preliminary draft of the manuscript, though the ideas presented here are, of course, solely the responsibility of the writers.

2. The following passage, which presents data that appear to imply a fourth-order interaction, will convey to the reader the type of complex comparisons that were made in this study: "In the present study there was no difference between male and female *S*s run by either *E*s or *A*s [assistants] in susceptibility to *E*s' or *A*s' biasing ... Among male *S*s run by both *E*s and *A*s there was no difference in susceptibility to *E* or *A* bias between first- and later-borns. Considering only *A*s' Ss, however, there was a slight tendency for later-born males to be more

susceptible to biasing, two-tailed $p = .20$. Among female Ss run by both Es and As, there was a tendency (two-tailed $p = .18$) for first-borns to be more susceptible to biasing than later-borns. . . . Considering only male As, those who were first-born did not differentially bias either their male or female Ss as a function of their Ss' birth-order. Later-born As also did not differentially bias their female Ss as a function of their birth-order. Later-born As did, however, bias their later-born male Ss significantly more than their first-born male Ss, two-tailed $p = .05$" [Rosenthal, Persinger, Vikan-Kline, & Mulry, 1963, pp. 327–328].

3. The series of criticisms that we have delineated in detail with respect to this study (Study 6) also apply to other studies in this area. For instance, similar criticisms can be made of Study 1, by Persinger (1963), which we briefly described earlier in this paper. Although Persinger did not show that bias was present in his study, he computed many statistics which purported to relate "bias scores" (which could be interpreted as chance fluctuations) to experimenters' sex, subjects' sex, experimenters' level of anxiety, subjects' level of anxiety, degree of prior acquaintanceship between experimenter and subject, experimenters' need for social approval and other variables.

4. All F tables assign a probability of .15 to an F of 3.60 with $1/4$ df. However, the authors of the paper reported that the p for an F of 3.60 with $1/4$ df was .07. Apparently, the .07 value presented by the authors was derived not from an F test but from a one-tailed t test. In many of the other experiments in this area, one-tailed tests were also used to test the significance of "expectancy" data. It appears to us that the use of one-tailed tests is difficult to justify in this context for two interrelated reasons: (a) In at least five experiments the means are in the opposite direction from those expected (e.g., Friedman, 1964; Marcia, 1961; Persinger, 1963; Rosenthal, Friedman, Johnson, Fode, Schill, White, & Vikan-Kline, 1964; White, 1962) and in a sixth experiment (Pflugrath, 1962) the neutral (control) group obtained higher ratings than the high-expectancy group. (b) If researchers consistently apply one-tailed tests to "expectancy" data they cannot determine the significance of data in the opposite direction and they do not allow for the possibility of a result that contradicts the expectancy hypothesis (Cohen, 1965).

5. Another study (Rosenthal, Persinger, Vikan-Kline, & Fode, 1963a) which was interpreted as supporting the early data returns hypothesis also appears to involve a misleading statistical procedure. In this study the analysis of variance yielded an F of 2.74 with $2/9$ df for the early data returns effect. Although all F tables give an associated probability of .13 for this F, the authors stated that they had performed a "one-tailed F test" and they halved the p value to .07. As we have stated previously in this paper, it does not appear legitimate to convert a p value of .13, as given in an F table, to a p value of .07 by referring to a "one-tailed F test" because the F ratio in an analysis of variance always provides a one-tailed test of the null hypothesis in terms of the sampling distribution of F (Hays, 1963, pp. 349–351, p. 369).

In brief, it is our opinion that the data presented in support of the early data returns hypothesis are open to criticism and that the hypothesis needs to be tested again in further research.

6. At the University of Manitoba, Winnipeg, Canada, John G. Adair also failed to obtain the experimenter bias effect in three unpublished studies which used the person-perception task (personal communication to T. X. Barber, May 25, 1967).

7. Several additional investigations that may have demonstrated an experimenter bias effect have been briefly described in a recent text (Rosenthal, 1966). These include studies by Suzanne Haley, by Karl Weick, by C. Knutson and G. Persinger (in which mental patients administered the person-perception task to other mental patients), and one carried out by K. Fode during 1961 that was to be submitted as a doctoral dissertation to the University of North Dakota (but which as of early 1967 had not yet been submitted). Since copies of these reports were not available when we reviewed the literature, we were not able to evaluate them.

We will also not review another study (Rosenthal, Kohn, Greenfield, & Carota, 1966) in which variables were intentionally confounded—the experimenters were "explicitly taught how such [verbal] behavior could be intentionally manipulated thereby confounding the unintentional biasing process with the intentional reinforcement process" [p. 26].

REFERENCES

Adair, J. G., & Epstein, J. Verbal cues in the mediation of experimenter bias. Paper presented at the meeting of the Midwestern Psychological Association, Chicago, May 1967.

AZRIN, N. H., Holz, W., Ulrich, R., & Goldiamond, I. The control of the content of conversation through reinforcement. *Journal of the Experimental Analysis of Behavior*, 1961, **4**: 25–30.

BARBER, T. X. Measuring "hypnotic-like" suggestibility with and without "hypnotic induction"; psychometric properties, norms, and variables influencing response to the Barber Suggestibility Scale (BSS). *Psychological Reports*, 1965, **16**: 809–844.

BARBER, T. X., & Calverley, D. S. Effects of *E*'s tone of voice on "hypnotic-like" suggestibility. *Psychological Reports*, 1964, **15**: 139–144.

BARBER, T. X., Calverley, D. S., Forgione, A., McPeake, J. D., Chaves, J. F., & Bowen, B. Five attempts to replicate the experimenter bias effect. Harding, Mass.: Medfield Foundation, 1966. (Mimeo.)

BINDER, A. Statistical theory. *Annual Review of Psychology*, 1964, **15**: 277–310.

CATTELL, R. B. Validity and reliability: A proposed more basic set of concepts. *Journal of Educational Psychology*, 1964, **55**: 1–22.

CATTELL, R. B. (Ed.) *Handbook of multivariate experimental psychology.* Chicago: Rand McNally, 1966.

CHAPANIS, N. P., & Chapanis, A. Cognitive dissonance: Five years later. *Psychological Bulletin*, 1964, **61**: 1–22.

COHEN, J. Some statistical issues in psychological research. In B. B. Wolman (Ed.), *Handbook of clinical psychology.* New York: McGraw-Hill, 1965.

CORDARO, L., & Ison, J. R. Observer bias in classical conditioning of the planarian. *Psychological Reports*, 1963, **13**: 787–789.

CRESPI, L. P. The cheater problem in polling. *Public Opinion Quarterly*, 1946, **9**: 431–445.

FRIEDMAN, N. The psychological experiment as a social interaction. Unpublished doctoral dissertation, Harvard University, 1964.

FRIEDMAN, N. *The social nature of psychological research.* New York: Basic Books, 1967.

FRIEDMAN, N., Kurland, D., & Rosenthal, R. Experimenter behavior as an unintended determinant of experimental results. *Journal of Projective Techniques and Personality Assessment*, 1965, **29**: 479–490.

GOLDSTEIN, A. P. *Therapist-patient expectancies in psychotherapy.* New York: Macmillan, 1962.

GUEST, L. A study of interviewer competence. *International Journal of Opinion and Attitude Research*, 1947, **1**: 17–30.

GUILFORD, J. P. *Psychometric methods.* (2nd ed.) New York: McGraw-Hill, 1954.

HANSEL, C. E. M. *ESP: A scientific evaluation.* New York: Charles Scribner's Sons, 1966.

HAYS, W. L. *Statistics for psychologists.* New York: Holt, Rinehart & Winston, 1963.

HYMAN, H. H. *Interviewing in social research.* Chicago: University of Chicago Press, 1954.

INGRAHAM, L. H., & Harrington, G. M. Experience of *E* as a variable in reducing experimenter bias. *Psychological Reports*, 1966, **19**: 455–461.

KERLINGER, F. N. *Foundations of behavioral research.* New York: Holt, Rinehart & Winston, 1964.

KINTZ, B. L., Delprato, D. J., Mettee, D. R., Persons, C. E., & Schappe, R. H. The experimenter effect. *Psychological Bulletin*, 1965, **63**: 223–232.

LASZLO, J. P., & Rosenthal, R. Subject dogmatism, experimenter status and experimenter expectancy effects. Cambridge, Mass.: Harvard University, Department of Social Relations, 1967. (Mimeo.)

LYONS, J. *A primer of experimental psychology.* New York: Harper & Row, 1965.

MARCIA, J. E. The need for social approval, the condition of hypothesis-making, and their effects on unconscious experimenter bias. Unpublished master's thesis, Ohio State University, 1961.

MARWIT, S. J., & Marcia, J. E. Tester bias and response to projective instruments. *Journal of Consulting Psychology,* 1967, **31**: 253-258.

MASLING, J. The influence of situational and interpersonal variables in projective testing. *Psychological Bulletin,* 1960, **57**: 65-85.

MASLING, J. Differential indoctrination of examiners and Rorschach responses. *Journal of Consulting Psychology,* 1965, **29**: 198-201.

MASLING, J. Role-related behavior of the subject and psychologist and its effects upon psychological data. *Nebraska Symposium on Motivation,* 1966, **14**: 67-103.

McFALL, R. M. "Unintentional communication": The effect of congruence and incongruence between subject and experimenter constructions. Unpublished doctoral dissertation. Ohio State University, 1965.

McGUIRE, W. J. Personality and susceptibility to social influence. In E. F. Borgatta & W. W. Lambert (Eds.), *Handbook of personality theory and research.* Chicago: Rand McNally, 1967.

MORGAN, C. T., & King, R. A. *Introduction to psychology.* (3rd ed.) New York: McGraw-Hill, 1966.

NEHER, A. Probability pyramiding, research error and the need for independent replication. *Psychological Record,* 1967, **17**: 257-262.

PERSINGER, G. W. The effect of acquaintanceship on the mediation of experimenter bias. Unpublished master's thesis, University of North Dakota, 1963.

PFLUGRATH, J. Examiner influence in a group testing situation with particular reference to examiner bias. Unpublished master's thesis, University of North Dakota, 1962.

ROSENTHAL, R. On the social psychology of the psychological experiment: The experimenter's hypothesis as unintended determinant of experimental results. *American Scientist,* 1963, **51**: 268-283.

ROSENTHAL, R. The effect of the experimenter on the results of psychological research. In B. A. Maher (Ed.), *Progress in experimental personality research.* Vol. 1. New York: Academic Press, 1964. (a)

ROSENTHAL, R. Experimental outcome-orientation and the results of the psychological experiment. *Psychological Bulletin,* 1964, **61**: 405-412. (b)

ROSENTHAL, R. *Experimenter effects in behavioral research.* New York; Appleton-Century-Crofts, 1966.

ROSENTHAL, R. Covert communication in the psychological experiment. *Psychological Bulletin,* 1967, **67**: 346-367.

ROSENTHAL, R., & Fode, K. L. The effect of experimenter bias on the performance of the albino rat. *Behavioral Science,* 1963, **8**: 183-189. (a)

ROSENTHAL, R., & Fode, K. L. Three experiments in experimenter bias. *Psychological Reports,* 1963, **12**: 491-511. (b)

ROSENTHAL, R., Friedman, C. J., Johnson, C. A., Fode, K., Schill, T., White, R. C., & Vikan, L. L. Variables affecting experimenter bias in a group situation. *Genetic Psychology Monographs,* 1964, **70**: 271-296.

ROSENTHAL, R., Friedman, N., & Kurland, D. Instruction-reading behavior of the experimenter as an unintended determinant of experimental results. *Journal of Experimental Research in Personality*, 1966, 1: 221–226.

ROSENTHAL, R., & Jacobson, L. Teachers' expectancies: Determinants of pupils' IQ gains. *Psychological Reports*, 1966, 19: 115–118.

ROSENTHAL, R., Kohn, P., Greenfield, P. M., & Carota, N. Experimenters' hypothesis-confirmation and mood as determinants of experimental results. *Perceptual and Motor Skills*, 1965, 20: 1237–1252.

ROSENTHAL, R., Kohn, P., Greenfield, P. M., & Carota, N. Data desirability, experimenter expectancy, and the results of psychological research. *Journal of Personality and Social Psychology*, 1966, 3: 20–27.

ROSENTHAL, R., & Lawson, R. A longitudinal study of the effects of experimenter bias on the operant learning of laboratory rats. *Journal of Psychiatric Research*, 1964, 2: 61–72.

ROSENTHAL, R., Persinger, G. W., Mulry, R. C., Vikan-Kline, L., & Grothe, M. Changes in experimental hypotheses as determinants of experimental results. *Journal of Projective Techniques and Personality Assessment*, 1964, 28: 465–469. (a)

ROSENTHAL, R., Persinger, G. W., Mulry, R. C., Vikan-Kline, L. & Grothe, M. Emphasis on experimental procedure, sex of subjects, and the biasing effects of experimental hypotheses. *Journal of Projective Techniques and Personality Assessment*, 1964, 28: 470–473. (b)

ROSENTHAL, R., Persinger, G. W., Vikan-Kline, L., & Fode, K. L. The effect of early data returns on data subsequently obtained by outcome-biased experimenters. *Sociometry*, 1963, 26: 487–498. (a)

ROSENTHAL, R., Persinger, G. W., Vikan-Kline, L., & Fode, K. L. The effect of experimenter outcome-bias and subject set on awareness in verbal conditioning experiments. *Journal of Verbal Learning and Verbal Behavior*, 1963, 2: 275–283. (b)

ROSENTHAL, R., Persinger, G. W., Vikan-Kline, L., & Mulry, R. C. The role of the research assistant in the mediation of experimenter bias. *Journal of Personality*, 1963, 31: 313–335.

RYAN, T. A. Multiple comparisons in psychological research. *Psychological Bulletin*, 1959, 56: 26–47.

SHAMES, M. L., & Adair, J. G. Experimenter-bias as a function of the type and structure of the task. Paper presented at the meeting of the Canadian Psychological Association, Ottawa, May 1967.

SILVER, M. J. A critical note on the experimenter modeling effect. Harding, Mass.: Medfield Foundation, 1967. (Mimeo.)

SILVERMAN, I. The effects of experimenter outcome expectancy on latency of word association. Paper presented at the meeting of the Eastern Psychological Association, New York, April 1966.

STEVENSON, H. W., & Allen, S. Adult performance as a function of sex of experimenter and sex of subject. *Journal of Abnormal and Social Psychology*, 1964, 68: 214–216.

SYMPOSIUM. Survey on problems of interviewer cheating. *International Journal of Opinion and Attitude Research*, 1947, 1: 93–106.

WARTENBERG-EKREN, U. The effect of experimenter knowledge of a subject's scholastic standing on the performance of a reasoning task. Unpublished master's thesis, Marquette University, 1962.

WHITE, C. R. The effect of induced subject expectations on the experimenter bias situation. Unpublished doctoral dissertation, University of North Dakota, 1962.

Robert Rosenthal

Experimenter Expectancy and the Reassuring Nature of the Null Hypothesis Decision Procedure[1]

On the basis of their recent review, Barber and Silver (1968) questioned the generality and robustness of the effects of experimenters' expectancies on the results of their research. They correctly imply that to the extent that such experimenter effects are not general and not robust there is a correspondingly lessened need to employ the procedures (Rosenthal, 1966) designed specifically to permit the reduction and/or assessment of the effects on their research results of the experimenters' expectancies.

For their analysis, Barber and Silver selected 31 studies for discussion in the body of their paper and a 32nd for discussion in a footnote.[2] They concluded that 12 of the studies "apparently showed an experimenter bias effect" [p. 2] and that 20 studies (including one they described in a footnote) "did not clearly demonstrate an experimenter bias effect" [p. 2]. The statistical procedures employed in many of the studies reviewed were criticized by Barber and Silver. Recommendations were made which are derived from a null hypothesis decision procedure model, for example, "The probability value (p) required for rejection of the null hypothesis will be specified in advance" [Barber & Silver, 1968, p. 24].

One purpose of the present paper is to consider the overall implications of the results of the 32 studies analyzed by Barber and Silver by formulating a single statement about a single hypothesis tested 32 times, rather than formulating 32 statements about 32 hypotheses each tested once. Such a more general formulation would appear to be more

From *Psychological Bulletin*, 1968, **70** (6, Pt. 2): 30–47. Copyright © 1968 by The American Psychological Association and reprinted with permission of author and The American Psychological Association.

consistent with the frequently sounded clarion call for "further replica-tion," a call that has been sounded by Barber and Silver (1968), by the present writer (Rosenthal, 1966), and probably by every other behavioral researcher who has touched pen to paper. The model of statistical analysis advocated by Barber and Silver, however, appears to be quite irrelevant to such questions as whether an experiment has been replicated, how many times, and with what results. If replications are really helpful, then there must be some way in which the results of replications have some cumulative bearing on what we think we should believe about the nature of some relationship. Another purpose of the present paper is to provide a commentary on the critical analyses performed by Barber and Silver in the hope that some substantive and some methodological issues may thereby be clarified.

THE ANALYSIS OF EXPERIMENTAL SERIES

Table 5–2 shows the studies judged by Barber and Silver to "appar-ently" show the effect of experimenter expectancy. Although there were 12 studies, 17 samples have been listed. A sample within a paper was given independent status if, and only if, the second sample involved different subjects *and* a substantial difference in procedure. Thus, in the studies by Cordaro and Ison (1963) and Ingraham and Harrington (1966) there were (*a*) samples of experimenters who expected either good or poor performance from their animals and (*b*) samples of experimenters who expected both good and poor performance but from different subsets of their animal subjects. In one of the samples in the study by Adair and Epstein (1967), subjects were contacted by "real" experimenters, but in the other sample, subjects were contacted only by tape-recorded voices of biased experimenters. In the study by Shames and Adair (1967), three different samples were employed, two of which showed little effect of experimenter expectancy. If, tempor arily, a z of 1.48 is considered necessary to suggest expectancy effect, only 88 percent of the samples meet that criterion among the 12 studies summarized by Barber and Silver.

What do these results mean? Mosteller and Bush (1954) described a number of methods for combining the probabilities from a run of experiments. One of the simplest (Stouffer's method) gives an overall z by cumulating the sum of the successive standard normal deviates associated with the successive probability (p) values and then dividing by the square root of the number of samples over which the standard normal deviates (zs) have been cumulated. In addition to its simplicity this method seems to be more powerful than some others and has the nice property of permitting a kind of forecasting of the number of additional samples with any type of results that will be required to bring the obtained z to any particular level of p. Thus, for the z values shown in Table 5-2, all of which were in the predicted direction, we can state the number of additional studies required to have a mean directional z of o before the obtained combined z is lowered to any

Table 5-2   *Standard Normal Deviates* (z) *Associated with Two-Tailed ps of Studies Judged by Barber and Silver to Suggest Experimenter Expectancy Effects*

Barber and Silver Review No.	Study	Sample No.	Sample	z
1.	Rosenthal and Fode (1963a)	1.	Rats	2.33
2.	Rosenthal and Lawson (1964)	2.	Rats	2.17
3.	Cordaro and Ison (1963)	3.	Planaria	3.96
		4.	Planaria	3.25
4.	Ingraham and Harrington (1966) (Rosenthal, 1967b)	5.	Rats	1.48*
		6.	Rats	2.10
5.	Rosenthal and Fode (1963b)	7.	Person perception	2.46
6.	Rosenthal and Fode (1963b)	8.	Person perception	3.44
7.	Laszlo and Rosenthal (1967)	9.	Person perception	1.75
8.	Masling (1965, 1966)	10.	Rorschach	1.75
9.	Silverman (1966)	11.	Reaction time	1.88*
10.	Adair and Epstein (1967)	12.	Person perception	1.65
		13.	Taped instructions	1.64
11.	Shames and Adair (1967)	14.	Person perception	1.70
		15.	Number estimation	0.37
		16.	Number estimation	0.28
12.	Marwit and Marcia (1967)	17.	Rorschach	3.25

Sum z 35.46

$z = $ sum $z/\sqrt{17} = $ 8.60
two-tailed $p < 1/$
$(1,000,000)^2$

* Median of several alternative zs.

particular level. If the next 115 samples show a mean directional z of o, the combined p will drop to .002, two-tailed. If the next 448 samples show a mean z of exactly o, the overall two-tailed p will go to .10.

Of course the combined directional z could be brought to o very quickly if the next 17 samples showed an equal but opposite effect of experimenter expectancy. In that case we could no longer believe (that is, and be considered reasonable) that experimenters too often obtain the results they expect. Equally unreasonable, however, would be the belief that experimenter expectancies bear no relationship to the results of their research. A run of 17 results strongly in one direction followed by a run of 17 results strongly in the opposite direction has an extraordinarily low p under the hypothesis that the variable under investigation makes no difference.

So far we have considered only those studies regarded by Barber and Silver as suggesting some effect of experimenter expectancy, while disregarding the studies judged by them as equivocal. Let us now consider this "equivocal" set of results, while disregarding those we have already summarized. Table 5–3 shows these 20 studies as 18 samples. Once again we regard as separate studies those within a single article that employ an independent sample and some consequentially different experimental procedure. Of the 18 samples listed, 14 involved the assessment of one or more interactions of experimenter expectancy and some other variable. To simplify our bookkeeping only the primary two-way interaction assessed in each sample is listed with the main effect of experimenter expectancy.[3] As in Table 5–2, where more than one statistic was computed to test the same hypothesis, the median p value was the one recorded. Whenever a two-tailed p was greater than .20 it was arbitrarily assigned a z value of 0, a practice which increases the likelihood of Type II errors, a type of error unlikely to be committed, however, when the cumulated results of Table 5–3 are inspected. The combined likelihoods of obtaining interactions or main effects of the magnitude shown in Table 5–3 are very small and it seems implausible to conclude that the effects of experimenter expectancy as a main effect or in interaction with another variable are trivial.

Tables 5–2 and 5–3 together show that there were 10 studies showing main effects with associated ps greater than .20. Of these 10 studies, 7 also tested a primary two-way interaction of experimenter expectancy and some other variable, and 5 of these interactions were "significant" at $p < .20$, two-tailed. All 5 interactions were replicated at least once. Nevertheless, considering only main effects, we may summarize by saying that at $p < .20$, two-tailed, we find 25 studies rather than the expected 7, and 22 of the 25 show the predicted directionality ($p = .0002$, one-tailed). At $p \leq .10$, two-tailed, we find 20 of the 35 studies instead of the expected 3.5, and 18 of the 20 are in the predicted direction ($p < .0005$, one-tailed). At $p \leq .05$, two-tailed, we find 12 of the 35 studies instead of the expected 2, and 11 of the 12 are in the predicted direction ($p < .003$, one-tailed). The one really large reversal (White, 1962) was a main effect ($df = 5/72$) in which the interaction ($df = 25/72$) was more significant than the main effect. To say that the results of *that* experiment were unpredicted is to put it mildly (Rosenthal, 1966). The interaction obtained in that study has not been replicated, but inspection of Table 5–3 shows that the

Table 5-3   *Standard Normal Deviates* (z) *Associated with Two-Tailed ps of Studies Judged by Barber and Silver Not to Show Clearly the Effects of Experimenter Expectancy*

Barber and Silver Review No.	Study	Sample No.	Interacting variable	Inter-action z	Main effect z
1.	Persinger (1962)	1.	Acquaintanceship	2.02*	.00
2.	Marcia (1961)	2.	Approval need	2.58*	.00
3.	Pflugrath (1962)	3.	None	None	1.75†
4.	Wartenberg-Ekren (1962)	4.	None	None	.00
5.	White (1962)	5.	Subject set	3.29	2.81
6.	Rosenthal, Persinger, Vikan-Kline, and Mulry (1963)	6.	Own expectancy	.00	.00
		7.	Principal investiga-tor expectancy	1.56	1.96†
7.	Rosenthal and Fode (1963b III)	8.	Excess reward	1.88*	1.64
8.	Rosenthal, Persinger, Vikan-Kline, and Fode (1963b)	9.	Subject set	.00	1.48
9.	Rosenthal, Persinger, Mulry, Vikan-Kline, and Grothe (1964b)	10.	None	None	3.09‡
10.	Rosenthal, Persinger, Mulry, Vikan-Kline, and Grothe (1964a I)	11.	Sex of E and S	1.64*	1.44
11.	Rosenthal, Persinger, Mulry, Vikan-Kline, and Grothe (1964a II)	12.	Sex of E and S	2.17*†	.00
12.	Rosenthal, Friedman, Johnson, Fode, Schill, White, and Vikan-Kline (1964)	13.	Excess reward	.00	1.52
13.	Rosenthal, Kohn, Greenfield, and Carota (1965)	14.	Disconfirmation	1.40*	.00
14.	McFall (1965)	15.	Disconfirmation	1.64*	.00
		16.	Disconfirmation	.00	.00
15-19	Barber, Calverly, Forgione, McPeake, Chaves, and Bowen (1967); Rosenthal (1967c)	17.	Sex of E and S	1.51*‡	1.40†‡
20.	Rosenthal, Persinger, Vikan-Kline, and Fode (1963a)	18.	None	None	2.17†

$$\text{Sum } z \quad 19.69 \quad 19.26$$
$$z = \text{sum } z/\sqrt{N} = \quad 5.26 \quad 4.54$$
$$\text{two-tailed } p< \quad .000006$$
$$.0000002$$

---

* Replicated.   † Median z.   ‡ Pooled samples.

majority of interactions have been replicated, many of them in more than one additional study.

When we consider now the results of all 35 studies, disregarding how they were classified by Barber and Silver, we arrive at a combined p of less than one in a million-raised-to-some-power-greater-than-two ($z = 9.25$ for 35 main effects). The two-tailed p of this result can be changed to an overall two-tailed p of .01 by adding 416 studies with perfectly null results. With the addition of 1,072 studies of perfectly null results, we can change the overall p to a two-tailed p of .10.

For reasons spelled out elsewhere (Rosenthal, 1966), it seems desirable to assess the effects of experimenter expectancy separately for all those studies in which the present writer had no direct contact whatever with the principal investigators prior to their conduct of their experiments. There were 15 such studies with a Σ z of 21.46, $z = 5.54$, two-tailed $p < .0000001$.[4] The median p of .10, two-tailed, was the same as that obtained when all 35 studies were considered.

All in all, the results of the series of studies reviewed by Barber and Silver provide us with little reassurance that the results of behavioral research are unaffected by our hypotheses or expectations. It is true that in 29 percent of the studies the p for the main effect was .20 or greater, but in half of those studies the primary interaction of experimenter expectancy and another variable was significant at $p \leq .10$ (median $p < .05$, two-tailed). Barber and Silver preferred to regard such significant interactions as evidence unfavorable to the hypothesis of experimenter expectancy effects, and each reader will have to decide for himself whether or not to agree with such a reassuring interpretation.

The implications for research methods in the behavioral sciences of the findings summarized have been given elsewhere and need not be discussed here (Rosenthal, 1964a, 1966, 1967a). Some mention should, however, be made of the problem of magnitude of effect aside from the question of statistical significance. As we might expect, the absolute magnitudes of effect varied considerably from study to study, but in only a relatively small number of studies was most of the total variance attributable to the effects of the experimenter's expectancy. Two considerations are relevant here. First is the fact that a great deal of behavioral research takes the form "$N = 50, p = .01$," which is to say that we account for 13 percent of the variance and reduce our predictive errors by about 6 percent (Rosenthal, 1966, p. 110). Relative to the proportion of total variance accounted for by most of the variables studied by behavioral researchers, the proportion of total variance attributable to the effects of experimenter expectancy is large. Exactly how large we cannot say, but the techniques suggested for assessing this seem worth employing (Rosenthal, 1966).

A second consideration has to do with the number of subjects contacted by "real" experimenters in behavioral research relative to the number of subjects seen by each experimenter in studies of expectancy effects. Almost without exception, experimenters in studies of expectancy effects contacted only a small fraction of the number of subjects contacted by "real" experimenters. There are few studies of expectancy effects in which experimenters contacted more than 10 subjects each and in most studies the average is closer to a half dozen. Even when the effects of experimenter expectancy are small per subject, they can be large (in terms of a low p) when distributed over the larger number of subjects usually contacted in "real" experiments. Studies of the effects of experimenter expectancy, then, tend to be biased in the direction of Type II errors. They tend to underestimate the effects of the expectancy of a single experimenter to the extent that the number of subjects employed per experimenter is substantially lower than the number of subjects ordinarily employed by an experimenter conducting behavioral research.

It is instructive to compare the overall results of studies of experimenter expectancy with the overall results of one of the most carefully and systematically investigated areas of behavioral research: the relationship between anxiety level and eyelid conditioning (Spence, 1964). The proportion of studies reaching the .05 level is greater in the conditioning series, while the proportion reaching the .01 level is greater in the expectancy series. In the 25 studies of the conditioning series the median effects were appreciably different when the studies were carried out in other than the primary laboratories, while in the expectancy series the median effects were identical for studies including or excluding the primary locales of the conducted research. If now one wants to judge that the effects of experimenter expectancy are not general and not robust one wonders what, if any, effect investigated by behavioral researchers can be considered general and robust.

ON THE ANALYSIS AND INTERPRETATION OF DATA

Early in their paper, Barber and Silver stated that if the effects of experimenters' expectancies occurred often there would be important implications for research methods in the behavioral sciences. These implications have been spelled out elsewhere (Rosenthal, 1966), but here we note that Barber and Silver never seem to return to this fundamental point of their paper. They do not define what they mean by "often." Can main effects occurring 57 percent of the time at the .10 level, two-tailed, be regarded as "often"? Each reader must probably decide for himself what he shall mean by "often," but by not returning to this important question Barber and Silver imply that perhaps the effects of experimenter expectancy occur with insufficient frequency (say, only half the time, depending on one's choice of p level) to warrant much concern on the part of the behavioral researcher. That is a cheerful and reassuring assessment of the situation and perhaps we can all use a bit of cheering up and a bit of reassurance. (One intuits here a potentially interesting dissertation topic on the personal and methodological correlates of high versus low reassurance thresholds.) Those with higher thresholds of reassurance may want to judge for themselves whether the control procedures required only if the experimenter's expectancy "often" makes a difference are really expensive as Barber and Silver state (Rosenthal, 1966, Chs. 17–23). The present writer, who claims no lack of bias about the ratio of costs to utilities involved, tends to find them relatively quite inexpensive.

In their paper, Barber and Silver formulate a set of studies characterized by one or more "inadequacies" in the statistical analyses. These "inadequacies" are now listed, together with some comments that may serve to clarify the issues and facts involved.

1. "An overall statistical analysis was not performed to exclude chance findings" [p. 3].

The present writer has, in fact, never performed any overall tests that "exclude chance findings" and is not optimistic that such tests will be developed even given the rapid advances in mathematical statistics. In fairness, it should be reported that in the case of one study (to be described later) the results of an overall test were not clearly reported. The results of such overall analyses, however, were reported to Barber and Silver and are reported later in the present paper. These results, which any interested reader may compute from the data provided in the study in question, amply supported the results of the readers' interocular traumatic test with $ps < .01$.

2. "The authors performed a large number of post hoc statistical tests after the overall analysis had failed to reject the null hypothesis at a conventional level of significance. The authors failed to make clear that the results of such postmortem analyses are far from definitive and can, at best, only suggest new hypotheses to be validated in further research" [p. 3].

It should first be pointed out that there are no statistical tests that reject or fail to reject hypotheses; only people do that and they differ in how they do it, and in whether they feel it wise to do it at all. Rozeboom's (1960) discussion of some of the issues is well known and relevant. Less well known to most psychologists is the fact that R. A. Fisher, although more identified with problems of experimental tactics (e.g., the single experiment) than with problems of experimental strategy (e.g., runs of experiments; Neyman, 1967), nevertheless, showed little patience with handy hints as to how and when to "accept" or "reject" hypotheses (Cochran, 1967). He preferred to keep track of whatever p value was obtained and to wait and see what happened in subsequent observations.

Then there is the matter of "a conventional level of significance," its choice being a reflection of the chooser's preference for the rate of miracles. Fermi, for example, thought $p = .10$ to be the wise operational definition of a miracle (Polanyi, 1961) while research on psychologists' beliefs shows that $p = .05$ is the preferred (and statistically discontinuous) definition of a miracle (Rosenthal & Gaito, 1963, 1964). If an accept-reject model can ever be defended it is in the case of the single experiment that, for some reason, cannot be replicated and on the basis of which some dichotomous choice of action must be taken. In those rare instances the scientist-action taker can most reasonably set some a priori alpha level. But what level? Some "conventional" level, for example, .05 or .01? Yes, sometimes, but sometimes it should be .50, asymptotically. Suppose two equally expensive drugs with equal side effects are being tested for efficacy. The most sensible decision is to use the better drug no matter what the p value associated with the difference in magnitude of efficacy. As Kaplan (1964) pointed out in agreement with Churchman, correct inference is not basically a statistical matter at all, though statistics can be useful tools to guide judgment. Good judgment involves probably some calculation of the risks of errors of the first and second kind. It seems not unreasonable to argue, and the present writer quickly admits his biased view of the matter, that when the question has serious implications for action, the uniform minimization of errors of the first kind has little to recommend it when the consequences of an error of the second kind can be so serious. If only a single experiment were conducted and its results showed, say, one chance in two, or one in three, or one in four, that the hypothesis of the experimenter might determine his results, one might be given pause for reflection.

The discussion seems worthwhile, but there is a sense in which it is only tangentially relevant to the criticism by Barber and Silver. The fact, of course, is that we are dealing not with a single experiment but with many more—32 when we restrict the discussion to just those studies selected by Barber and Silver. The post hoc tests to which they refer were post only relative to the overall test. With the possible exception of the first time a given relationship was examined, the so-called post hoc tests in study after study were planned comparisons, replications of particular relationships that were carried out from two to two dozen times.

Such analyses Barber and Silver seem to feel are "far from definitive and can, at best, only suggest new hypotheses to be validated in further research" [p. 3]. The present writer agrees that almost nothing is definitive but feels it would be helpful to the reader to note that almost all the studies discussed *were* part of just that further research for which Barber and Silver issued their call. The progress of behavioral science is slow enough; it will be slower still if the results of every experiment are evaluated in the empirical vacuum created by a disregard of the history of prior research in a given area.

3. "Problems of 'probability pyramiding' were not avoided; for instance, there was a failure to take account of changing levels of significance when many statistical tests were performed on a single set of data" [p. 3].

This criticism is related to the former criticism of post hoc testing. What Barber and Silver fail to mention is that most of the tests made were of a variety of subsidiary hypotheses, almost all of which had been made several times in several studies. The generally accepted treatment for the ailment of probability pyramiding, as for related ailments, is replication. Barber and Silver named the ailment but failed to note that the cure had set in several dozen studies earlier.

There is in their criticism an implicit disapproval of the use of one set of data for more than one purpose. Here, then, is another way to decelerate the accumulation of behavioral science knowledge; it requires only following the dictum "one hypothesis, one experiment, one overall test."

There is, of course, a very real and very sophisticated statistical issue involved when nonorthogonal hypotheses are tested in a variety of ways in a nonreplicated experiment. It is well known that when highly related hypotheses are tested sequentially, the p values change in meaning over testing. The basic cure, again, is replication but there are interesting possibilities to be developed in the statistical analysis of an unreplicated experiment and they seem worthy of brief mention. Suppose an original experiment that for some reason cannot be replicated. Suppose further, a nonsignificant overall test but a particular interocular traumatic test that is very significant. Two classes of cases of this sort predominate.

In the first class of cases, the investigator simply chose his overall test unwisely. Perhaps he had five treatment conditions varying in some linear way in magnitude of treatment applied. The overall randomized-groups F is trivial, the investigator cannot reject the null hypothesis, and he sheds a tear as he observes the lovely linear, predicted arrangement of the five means. Had the investigator employed his prior information, he could have partitioned his treatment variance into a linear regression component and a deviation component and had an F more in keeping with what his eyes told him. Sometimes, then, when eye test and overall test disagree radically, it is only because an insufficiently powerful overall test was employed.

The other class of cases of the nonsignificant overall test, but with a dramatic effect tucked somewhere into the data, will be of greater interest to statisticians. For many reasons omnibus tests are often not very powerful for specific purposes. If an investigator finds the p associated with an overall test very high but sees a strong relationship in some subset of his data, it is not accurate to say that the subset comparison is invalid or unwarranted. The subset comparison may be capitalizing on chance but the interesting possibility is that it may be possible to assign a meaningful p to just such a singled-out comparison. The mathematics for working out the problem seem to be known but the application may be somewhat less than routine.[5] Hopefully, the p associated with such a comparison would be used in the service of someone's judgment of what to conclude from it all, but without the make it or break it binary decision process associated with the null hypothesis decision procedure.

In addition to the intrinsic value of having a means of assessing the p of an unpredicted subset comparison, there would be psychological benefits as well. Graduate students could feel less guilty about really looking at their data no matter what an omnibus test showed. Discovering something new might then be as legitimate an enterprise as testing an hypothesis. Psychologists too often (but statisticians only rarely) have prized the latter over the former as a way of making science. The data themselves have always been impartial in the matter, not knowing, in fact, for which purpose they were collected.

4. "The authors 'strained for significance' by accepting questionable p values (e.g., p values $> .10$) as substantiating the experimental hypothesis" [p. 3].

Barber and Silver seem to mean by this that $ps > .10$ were reported. Tables 5-2 and 5-3 show that this is indeed the case. What seems debatable is whether these p values were "accepted." The language of the null hypothesis decision procedure has the vocational analogue of the judge in court. The judge, like the investigator of an unreplicable experiment on the basis of which action must be taken, must make some decision and, in most cases, it has an either-or quality about it. The present writer prefers the vocational analogue of a reporter. The reporter, like the investigator who can replicate and defer action, can afford to tell it as it seems to be for the time being, revising his assessment of the situation pretty much continually as the news or data continue to come in.

5. " 'Negative' data (data which were significantly opposite to the experimental hypothesis) were not used in the statistical analysis which ostensibly showed the experimenter bias effect. The decision not to use the negative data was made after inspection of the results and on the basis of the dependent variable criterion alone" [p. 3].

So-called "negative" data have never been excluded from our analysis. In several studies where overall analysis suggested bimodality at a low p value, both subdistributions were examined but only after bimodality was clearly established.

6. "The authors failed to perform a multivariate statistical analysis, such as multiple-discriminant analysis or canonical correlation, in studies which included many independent and many dependent variables. Instead a multitude of comparisons was made on overlapping data by individual t tests and Spearman rho correlation coefficients" [p. 3].

Barber and Silver are quite right. We have often looked at many relationships within a given experiment. What Barber and Silver did not note was that in most studies most of the relationships tested by ts and rhos were replications. We appreciate the value of multivariate statistical analysis under certain conditions but wonder whether factor analysis (as they suggest) is really very helpful for an N of 13 sampling units!

After summarizing the selected studies in considerable detail, Barber and Silver drew a number of conclusions and made a number of recommendations. Their prime conclusion was that "most of the studies" did not clearly demonstrate the effects of experimenter expectancy. The conclusions one wants to draw from an array of data are a matter of taste and judgment. Considering only the main effects of expectancy, 20 of the 35 reached a two-tailed p of .10 and 5 of the 15 "negative" results ($p > .10$) showed the primary interaction to be significant at the .10 level (two-tailed). Barber and Silver feel that these results indicate that expectancy effects are difficult to demonstrate. The present writer feels, on the other hand, that these are strikingly consistent results when compared to the results of sets of experiments in other areas of behavioral research. Each reader will, of course, have to make his own judgment of what is to be regarded as a strong or a weak overall finding.

Barber and Silver go on to make some fairly standard remarks on the process of data analysis, some of which are repetitions of points made earlier. They have to do with the value of overall tests, not dropping data, and replicating subset comparisons. With all this we can agree and a careful reading of the studies summarized will show that just those procedures were followed. In defense of Barber and Silver it must be said that with so many studies to review, and with so many of them replicating specific relationships, it is not always easy to trust to memory the task of keeping track of what tests were replications. It was because there were so many replications that it was felt desirable to summarize them more conveniently in a single source (Rosenthal, 1966).

The only standard comment on data analysis made by Barber and

Silver that we may question is their stricture that, "The probability value (p) required for rejection of the null hypothesis will be specified in advance" [p. 24]. For reasons given earlier in some detail, the present writer does not feel this a particularly valuable method in the making of science.

(One other statistical reference by Barber and Silver is to the "Bayesian approach to statistical inference" but the present writer does not understand what they mean to say.)

Barber and Silver enter a plea for "rigorous methodology." The present writer earnestly wishes to be counted as one of those in favor. With respect to the experiments discussed in their paper, Barber and Silver raise several questions of "rigor." First, they wonder why the reliability of the photo-rating task was not determined. It is to be found on page 42 of Friedman's (1967) book listed in their references. The mean weighted reliability of four samples was $+.60$, combined $p < .0000025$, with subsample reliabilities of $+.45$, $+.62$, $+.62$, and $+.76$ ($N = 62$). What Barber and Silver do not make clear is why they want to know the reliability. They imply that expectancy effects are easier to obtain if the reliability does not differ from 0. But one wonders how it is possible to influence a perfectly unreliable task in a fairly reliable manner.

An excellent point is made by Barber and Silver when they note that in many studies no checks have been imposed to be sure that experimenters ever heard, read, or remembered the hypothesis they were given. What Barber and Silver did not add is that this should in many cases have drastically reduced the effects of experimenter expectancy. (When Barber & Silver, citing McGuire, 1967, describe eight steps at which the transmission of experimenters' expectancies may break down, they do seem to be aware of the implications for Type II errors.)

Barber and Silver make another good point when they mention that no-expectancy controls have not always been used. They have been employed in over 10 samples and always they yielded the most extreme results. Apparently the simple giving of an expectancy (or the deprivation of an hypothesis) has some effect independent of the specific nature of the expectancy.

Barber and Silver present a delineation of mediating variables. Their prime conclusion is that experimenters at times bring their experimental results "in line with their biases" by intentional or unintentional misjudging, misrecording, or misreporting of the results. That seems a strange conclusion following their discussion of methodological rigor. They present not a single p value that such mechanisms accounted for the results of even a single experiment. Several studies have shown that such "errors" occur but none have shown that they account for the results of studies of the effects of experimenter expectancy. On the other hand, Barber and Silver do not point out that the experiment by Adair and Epstein (1967), by having only tape recordings instruct the subjects, effectively eliminated intentional and unintentional errors of the sort described. Barber and Silver also fail to note that where an exact tally of the *sum* of misjudging, misrecording, and misreporting errors was possible, the total error rate was .67 percent (Rosenthal, 1966, p. 12), a rate that had no measurable effect on the means. (A recent replication gives a value of .72 percent with similarly trivial effects on means.)

Another major mediating mechanism of the expectancy effect was suggested by Barber and Silver to be a process of reinforcement. In this connection they again fail to mention that not a single p (specified in advance or not) exists to support the contention. On the other hand, Adair and Epstein (1967), Masling (1965, 1966), and four additional studies (Rosenthal, 1966, pp. 290–292) provide evidence effectively ruling out the operation of a reinforcement process.

Barber and Silver suggest, again on the basis of no research known to the present writer, that student experimenters are more likely to cheat to get the desired results, while teacher experimenters are more likely to influence their outcomes unintentionally. That is a comforting hypothesis but the history of science provides us with little reassurance (and certainly with no p values) to enable us to hold that view with confidence (e.g., Rosenhan, 1967; Rosenthal, 1966).

Barber and Silver raise a number of interesting questions to be answered by future research. A number of studies have been reported which do provide some information on the questions raised. Readers may wish to know that subjects in expectancy research have not always been undergraduates but rats, planaria, schoolchildren, and mental patients as well. Experimenters have included not only graduate and undergraduate students but also classroom teachers, hospital staff members, and neuropsychiatric patients. Experimenters' expectancies have been varied orthogonally to their desires. The results of most of these studies are available elsewhere (Rosenthal, 1966) and they are alluded to here only to correct the impression given by Barber and Silver that nothing was yet known about such questions.

APPENDIX: A COMMENTARY ON SIGNIFICANT OMISSIONS

In their paper, Barber and Silver undertake a detailed analysis of some 32 studies and present some substantive and methodological conclusions based on their analyses. Since it must be assumed that most readers will not be familiar with the details of the studies discussed, it is necessary to supply a more detailed commentary on those facts selected by

Barber and Silver for their presentation. There were many serious omissions of fact in the analyses presented by Barber and Silver, and, as will be shown, many of these omissions appeared to be nonrandom. In general, the same sequence will be followed here as was followed by Barber and Silver.

Persinger (1962)

Barber and Silver correctly point out that there was no significant main effect of experimenter expectancy. They are incorrect in saying that no overall analysis was performed and they seem particularly selective in failing to mention that an interaction F of 5.03, $p = .04$, two-tailed, was obtained showing male experimenters to bias their acquainted subjects more than their unacquainted subjects. That exactly was Persinger's prediction, and in view of Barber and Silver's constant reference to the importance of replication, they should have felt obligated to mention that this study was itself a replication of an earlier finding. Barber and Silver felt that because of the very small main effect that the association between magnitude of expectancy effect and acquaintanceship was an association involving a set of random numbers. They fail to mention (a) that the p gives the likelihood that the array is based on random numbers, and (b) the fact that the relationship was replicated in another study (also one with a small main effect, Table 5–3, Barber & Silver No. 6). It is a rather interesting occurrence for an array of random numbers to yield significant, replicable findings.

Marcia (1961)

No significant main effect was found but the "overall" test of Marcia's primary hypothesis supported it at the .01 level. Barber and Silver give the impression that this result could not be replicated but fail to mention that for comparable experimenters, significantly similar results (median rho = .62) were found in a set of eight replicates, many of them also based on studies showing "nonsignificant" main effects (Rosenthal, 1966). For predictably different experimenters (extreme scorers on anxiety scales), the relationship was reversed (median rho = −.40).

Pflugrath (1962)

Barber and Silver mentioned that no main effect was found for experimenter expectancy in the analysis of variance. They did not report, however, that the overall chi-square had an associated two-tailed $p < .08$. (The situation is analogous to that in the study by Barber, Calverley, Forgione, McPeake, Chaves, & Bowen, 1967, cited by Barber and Silver, in which it was reported that F was small but not that chi-square was large, $p < .10$, two-tailed.) Barber and Silver also neglected to mention the effect ($p < .05$) of the experimental treatments on the reliability of the anxiety measures. In summary, Barber and Silver selected for report the one analysis with $p > .10$ and failed to report the two analyses with $ps < .10$.

Wartenberg-Ekren (1962)

By any criterion, this study showed no effects of examiner expectancy. It might have been of interest to readers of this journal, however, if Barber and Silver had reported that two of the eight examiners contacted all or some of their subjects under double-blind conditions! When expectancy effects appear to occur, Barber and Silver carefully point out all possible alternatives to account for the effect; when the effect is equivocal or not present, no explanation seems called for. Such differential attention reflects a firm if implicit commitment to the null hypothesis.

White (1962)

Barber and Silver state that "overall, the results were not significant...." leaving the impression of solid support of the null hypothesis. They fail to mention that the main effect of expectancy was significant at the .005 level, two-tailed, and that the interaction testing the major hypothesis of the study was significant at the .001 level! The results were complex and not as predicted, but it hardly seems warranted to leave readers with the impression that the experimenters' expectancies had no effect on their subjects' responses.

Rosenthal, Persinger, Vikan-Kline, and Mulry (1963)

In their discussion of this experiment, Barber and Silver correctly state the hypothesis under investigation, then choose their own test of this hypothesis and decide not to reject the null hypothesis. Two sets of experimenters were employed and the results of the experiments conducted by the first set did not show a "significant" degree of expectancy bias. These experimenters then trained a set of research assistants and two overall tests were performed to see whether "a biased E might communicate his bias to his As without his telling them the nature and magnitude of his bias" [Rosenthal, Persinger, Vikan-Kline, & Mulry, 1963, p. 313; Barber & Silver, 1968). In the first test, data obtained by "assistants" whose trainers had been given expectancies for high photo ratings and who initially actually expected to obtain high photo ratings were compared to data obtained by assistants trained by experimenters who either had not been led to expect high photo ratings or did not initially believe they would obtain high photo ratings. The resulting t of 2.09 had an associated one-tailed p of .04. The other analysis ranked the degree of bias shown by each experimenter alongside the degree of bias later shown by his research assistants. The rho of .67 had an associated p of .01, one-tailed. These two tests of the major hypothesis are referred to by Barber and Silver as "one of its isolated findings," presumably embedded in the context of such other crucial correlations as that between anxiety and need for social approval. The "nonsignificant" (i.e., $p = .12$, two-tailed) interaction referred to by Barber and Silver was due to the fact that the research assistants trained by experimenters told to expect high photo ratings, and initially believing that they would obtain high photo ratings, obtained higher photo ratings than assistants trained by experimenters led to expect low photo ratings and experimenters led to expect high photo ratings but initially expecting low photo ratings. That set of results paralleled closely the pattern of results obtained by the experimenters themselves. All the data necessary for Barber and Silver to convince themselves of this fact were presented in the original article (one two-by-two table of means for each sample of data collectors). The $2 \times 2 \times 2$ analysis of variance would have shown an interaction effect at $p = .10$ between induced and idiosyncratic expectation even with only a single df for the error term. The 2×2 analysis of variance employing the means of each sample of data collectors as the replicates within cells would have shown the interaction significant at $p < .05$, two-tailed.

Barber and Silver were concerned about the use of a number of independent and dependent variables. All this, they felt, indicated a great need for replication. What Barber and Silver fail to mention is that many of these variables were included precisely in order that earlier obtained relationships could be replicated. Barber and Silver also fail to mention, though they could not fail to notice (Rosenthal, 1966), that many of the relationships being replicated in this study were still further replicated subsequently.

Barber and Silver suggest that we erred in not employing such multivariate statistics as multiple-discriminant analysis, factor analysis, etc. Most of the relationships investigated in this study were quite specific replications, and the use of such elegant techniques did not seem especially indicated. Furthermore, we know of few statistical consultants who would in all seriousness suggest, for example, a factor analysis based on an N of 13 sampling units!

Barber and Silver point out that because so many statistical tests were made, replication is essential. They fail to mention that most of the tests were in fact replicated, some before this experiment, some afterward (reported in Rosenthal, 1966). In their analysis of "how many of our results could have been due to chance," Barber and Silver computed a figure based on certain constraints that 9,107 F tests could have been computed and suggested that all our "significant" relationships might have come out of that 5 percent subsample of the 9,107 F tests that could have occurred by chance. One wonders why only 9,107 F tests were possible. As one of the replications in our study we employed dozens and dozens of items of personality tests (anxiety and need for approval measures) each of which could have served as a variable. One wonders about the rate of Type II errors when the number of "significant" relationships obtained in an experiment must exceed 5 percent of the possible relationships to be examined in the world. Their conceptualization of an experiment with 22 independent variables as a 2^{22} factorial is interesting in any case. Even the United States Census Bureau, which might employ 22 independent variables in a small pilot study, might have trouble obtaining the 8,388,608 subjects required to have only 2 subjects per cubicle. Researchers employing the MMPI and following Barber and Silver's analysis might have similar difficulties trying to fill the cells of a 2^{566+} factorial.

Finally, Barber and Silver quote a paragraph from this study that implies to them a four-way interaction. Careful reading of the original shows that the "four ways" are two ways replicated over two different sets of data collectors.

Rosenthal and Fode (1963b, Experiment 3)

Barber and Silver report that for male and female subjects the correlations between experimenters' predicted and obtained data were +.32 and +.30, respectively ("significant" at $p < .05$ only when corrected for restriction of range). Barber and Silver object to the correlation for all subjects based on equal weighting for male and female subjects and recommend collapsing over subject sex to obtain an overall correlation. They neglect to mention that photo ratings obtained from male and female subjects by the experimenters were negatively correlated and that experimenters contacted unequal and disproportional numbers of male and female subjects. The method of average tables seemed to be a reasonable way of dealing with the problem but we should note that (a) other methods, (e.g., combined p of the two correlations) are possible, and (b) the correlation based on some equal weighting of male and female subjects, while pleasant to have, is in no sense crucial to the argument developed. As Barber and Silver state again and again, the test of an equivocal result is whether it is replicable. In their survey Barber and Silver encountered many such replications, all of which remain unmentioned by them. The analogous correlations obtained by Ingraham and Harrington (1966) were .41 and .39, those obtained by Rosenthal and Fode (1963a) were +.43 and +.41, all four of the foregoing replicates having been based on rat subjects! Barber and Silver noted that for four experimental conditions the correlations between predicted and obtained ratings were given. Barber and Silver averaged these correlations and found a mean correlation of −.04. What they failed to mention was that this averaging process lumped rhos ranging from +.84 to −.60. The laws of averaging are such that anyone can take the mean of any numbers at all, but the question may fairly be asked whether such averaging serves to enlighten or to obscure our understanding. Once again, for all the expressed concern over the importance of replication Barber and Silver fail to mention that the admittedly complex pattern of relationships was considerably clarified by replication (Rosenthal, 1966, p.217).

Rosenthal, Persinger, Vikan-Kline, and Fode (1963b)

Barber and Silver erroneously quote the authors as having performed a "one-tailed *F* test." Barber and Silver at this point in their paper seem unaware of the relation between *t* and *F* for two treatment conditions and the fact that, for such situations, one-tailed tests are quite possible. Yet, in their Footnote 4, Barber and Silver do seem to recognize the relationship between *t* and *F*, though there the complaint is not over whether the null distribution has been worked out but whether one-tailed tests should be employed.

In their analysis of this experiment, Barber and Silver give the results of two of the three critical analyses. The one not mentioned was the one with the lowest associated *p* value. Also omitted was mention of the three *p* values associated with the test of the effects of consistency of experimenter expectancy and subject set (*p*s of .05, .05, and .02, one-tailed). Each reader may or may not regard such *p* values as suggestive, but it would seem that the reader should have access to the information required for him to reach his own decision. One wonders whether readers really require the kind of protection from exposure to the full results of experiments as has been provided by Barber and Silver.

Rosenthal, Persinger, Mulry, Vikan-Kline, and Grothe (1964b)

In this experiment, Barber and Silver claim that the data of 3 of the 20 experimenters were discarded from the analysis, a claim not substantiated in fact. No experimenters were "discarded" though each of the modes of the bimodal distribution were discussed separately. That is not the same as "discarding" data. For those not satisfied with the interocular traumatic test of overall asymmetry of distribution, all the data are provided to make any desired tests. Had Barber and Silver not agreed with the results of our interocular traumatic test they could have found the pooled *p* from three Kolmogorov-Smirnov tests to be less than .001 (there were three subsamples) of the single p from an overall analysis to be a great deal lower than .01. Similar results would be obtained if a chi-square for symmetry were calculated. (The present writer now feels that these results should have been included in our original report.)

In view of the enthusiasm for replication shared by Barber and Silver and the present writer, we might have hoped that Barber and Silver would have reported the replication in a fourth sample (Ingraham & Harrington, 1966; Rosenthal, 1967b) of just the same degree of bimodality and assymetry for a population of animal subjects.

It strikes one as strange that Barber and Silver, after suggesting our analyses to be inappropriate, computed means on data so highly skewed that a statistical test is hardly necessary to detect the skew. The grand mean they obtained was in the negative direction primarily because of the three significant outliers. Had they calculated the median, they would have known that it was considerably larger in magnitude than the mean and in the predicted direction.

A subsample of the experimenter-subject interactions had been filmed, and Barber and Silver wondered how it was possible that the filmed behavior of the experimenter could significantly predict the magnitude of the subsequent biasing effect on subjects (Friedman, Kurland, & Rosenthal, 1965) when the mean bias score was negative. The reason for the mean bias score being negative was of course the fact that 15 percent of the experimenters went in a significantly oppo-site direction—a phenomenon found in four samples.

Barber and Silver further calculate the basis for chance results at the .05 level by taking 5 percent of the correlations printed out by the computer, the vast majority of which are of no interest whatever. It just happens to be cheaper to get square correlation matrices. Barber and Silver are correct in thinking that the "normal" p values are difficult to determine even for the small subsection of the correlation matrix examined. It was for that reason that the research was replicated a fact which Barber and Silver do not mention when discussing this research.

Rosenthal, Persinger, Mulry, Vikan-Kline, and Grothe (1964a, Experiment 1)

Barber and Silver are correct in giving the overall one-tailed p of .07 as the p associated with the overall effects of experimenter expectancy and the overall two-tailed p of .10 associated with the interaction of experimenters' and subjects' sex as determinants of magnitude of expectancy effect. Subsequent to this overall test for interaction, we wanted to know where the effect was occurring. The subsequent tests performed were interpreted by Barber and Silver as involving the discarding of data which is a strange interpretation of *t* tests subsequent to overall *F* tests. Once again, in their discussion of this experiment with the implication of capitalizing on chance findings, Barber and Silver fail to note that the results were replicated—on the following page!

Rosenthal, Persinger, Mulry, Vikan-Kline, and Grothe (1964a, Experiment 2)

Barber and Silver correctly point out that the overall test for expectancy effect was not significant. They fail to mention, however, that this was due to the significant ($p < .01$) reversal of expectancy effect of female experimenters contacting male subjects. This reversal was itself a replication of a study reported on the preceding page of the published report, a fact not reported by Barber and Silver. The combined *p* (Stouffer's method) of both studies obtaining the individual *p* values associated with the four combinations of experimenters' and subjects' sex (Rosenthal, 1966, p. 299) is $< .00000025$, one-tailed ($z = 5.05$). An interesting replication of these findings is to be found in a study by Barber *et al.* (1967). Although these workers were not interested in checking our earlier results, they kindly made their data available for the analysis (Rosenthal, 1967c). In two analyses it turned out that despite the small magnitude of overall expectancy effect (median two-tailed *p* of .16), male experimenters contacting male or female subjects and female experimenters contacting female subjects all showed small positive expectancy effects. Female experimenters contacting male subjects, just as we had found twice before, obtained substantially negative expectancy effects.

Barber and Silver also discuss the analysis of films made of some of the experimenter-subject interactions of the study under discussion. In view of the *p* values given above, it does not seem necessary to comment on their evaluation that subjects' responses were only randomly related to their experimenters' expectancies. It would take the most incredible series of coincidences to make the results of this analysis and its replication "significant by chance," but we do agree with Barber and Silver that further research is needed in view of the fact that, although some of the relationships were quite significant in both replicates, at least one of these relationships was significantly opposite in direction in the two studies (Rosenthal, Friedman, & Kurland, 1966)!

Rosenthal, Friedman, Johnson, Fode, Schill, White, and Vikan-Kline (1964)

Barber and Silver report the results of an analysis of variance in which all *F*s were small. Barber and Silver do not report the results of the analysis yielding *F*s large and *p*s low that are given in the same table. Another analysis of variance with two-tailed *p* of .07 was also not mentioned by Barber and Silver. Also not mentioned by Barber and Silver was the fact that the major results of this study were replicated (Rosenthal, 1966, Ch. 13).

Rosenthal, Kohn, Greenfield, and Carota (1965)

Barber and Silver state correctly that the main effects of experimenter expectancy were not "significant," but they fail to mention that the predicted interaction t was "significant" at the .08 level, one-tailed. They also fail to mention the triple interaction significant at the .10 level, two-tailed. None of these p values are regarded by Barber and Silver as significant but it does not seem helpful to the readers of their paper that they not be given the facts and allowed to judge for themselves. In their discussion of this study Barber and Silver fail to mention its replicational nature and also the fact that its major hypothesis was tested again a third time.

In a footnote to this study, Barber and Silver report selected results of the original study of the effects of early data returns (Rosenthal, Persinger, Vikan-Kline, & Fode, 1963a—Study 20 in Table 2). They report that a "one-tailed F" test was performed yielding a p of .07. The F was computed and the associated one-tailed p of .07 is conservative since the ordering of three means was predicted. All the data are presented in the original paper so that if Barber and Silver had been interested in another value of the one-tailed p, they could have found it at $p = .05$ by Page's (1963) L test. While on the question of overall tests Barber and Silver might also have reported that the test for linear regression of treatment means was significant at $p < .03$, one-tailed (Rosenthal, 1966, p. 199). Finally, Barber and Silver might have reported to the reader that the difference between the two experimental groups was significant at $p = .01$, one-tailed, an obviously planned comparison. Another interesting result not reported by Barber and Silver was the correlation of .69 between data obtained from pretest subjects and data obtained from "real" subjects, $p < .01$, one-tailed.

McFall (1965)

Barber and Silver claim that the significant results of McFall's analysis were *post hoc* because it was based on only half the data. Barber and Silver fail to mention that the allegedly *post hoc* analysis was itself a replication of results obtained earlier, actually the third replicate of the effects of early data returns (Rosenthal, 1966, Ch. 12).

Barber *et al.* (1967)

In this study with five subsamples, Barber *et al.* claimed that "The procedure . . . was patterned as closely as possible after that used in an earlier study. . . ." In a subsequent paper (Rosenthal, 1967c), it was shown that in a number of very important ways the research by Barber *et al.* was nothing like the research after which it was supposedly patterned. Equally important, Barber and Silver report the results only from those analyses showing little effect of experimenter expectancy. Other analyses of which Barber *et al.* were informed showed ps of borderline "significance" ($p = .16$) and ps about which there could be little question ($p = .008$). This research was also the third replication of the finding of a reversal of expectancy effect by female experimenters contacting male subjects (Rosenthal, 1967c).

Variables Maximizing Expectancy Effects

In many of the studies reviewed, an effort was made to relate the magnitude of expectancy effect to various characteristics of experimenters and subjects. Barber and Silver feel that the results of these findings may be due to chance because the main effect of expectancy did not always reach the level of p they would regard as necessary. One example of such "possibly chance" findings deals with the effects of experimenter and subject sex on magnitude of expectancy effect. Barber and Silver make no effort to assess the p that these results, or others to be discussed, were likely to reflect only random fluctuations. In the case of experimenters' and subjects' sex we have already seen that the combined p is less than one in a million.

Barber and Silver refer to six studies of the effects of experimenter anxiety on the magnitude of expectancy effect. They do not give the overall likelihood that anxiety of the experimenter is unrelated to magnitude of expectancy effect. We give it now: $p = 7$ in 10 million, two-tailed, $z = 4.99$. It should be added that we have great need of a two-tailed test here because, while the relationships between experimenter anxiety and expectancy effect are much too often large, they are also largely unpredictable as to direction.

Barber and Silver refer to six studies of the effects of subjects' level of anxiety on magnitude of expectancy effect and again imply their underlying random nature without giving the p. That p is .00001, two-tailed, $z = 4.45$, and again the results, while providing little comfort for those who would prefer to uphold the null hypothesis, are not consistent in direction.

Barber and Silver also refer to studies of the relationship between experimenters' need for approval and expectancy effect as a function of experimenters' level of anxiety. At medium levels of anxiety, the relationship is positive in 7 out of 8 samples and, at high and low levels of anxiety, the relationship is negative 6 times out of 10. For many of the samples N is so low that Stouffer's method of calculating the combined p is difficult to apply, but all the data required for other analyses have been presented (Rosenthal, 1966, p. 238). A one-way analysis of variance of the ranks yields an overall $p < .03$, two-tailed ($\chi^2 = 7.59$, $df = 2$), to suggest the nonrandom nature of the pattern of results. The median test shows .875 of the correlations among medium-anxious experimenters to be above the median compared to .20 of the correlations among the high- and low-anxious experimenters (Fisher's exact test $p < .02$, two-tailed). The reader may also wish to know that of the individual correlations based on 12 or more cases, three out of three are significant at the .05 level, two-tailed; for $N \geq 10$, three out of four reach that level and for $N \geq 8$, four out of six reach the .05 level.

Rosenthal and Fode (1963a)

Barber and Silver agree that expectancy effects occur, mention that there was evidence of prodding of the animals, but fail to mention that the net effect of these procedural deviations was more likely to decrease than to increase the effects of experimenter expectancy.

Rosenthal and Lawson (1964)

Barber and Silver correctly mention that two of the eight rats labeled as "dull" died early during the course of the experiment. They also state that the "dull" rats were all housed together so that the illness which killed two of them may have led to the poorer performance of those "dull" rats who did not die. It is unclear how Barber and Silver came to the conclusion that all animals in one condition were housed together since the original report clearly uses the plural in referring to the home cages of each group of animals.

Cordaro and Ison (1963)

Barber and Silver state that a "trial-by-trial analysis" had "indicated that the results were due to use of different criteria for judging the responses" [p. 20] by the two groups of experimenters. Barber and Silver fail to explain how any "trial-by-trial" analysis can "indicate" the criteria in the minds of the observers.

Ingraham and Harrington (1966)

Barber and Silver again conclude that it is the judgment of the experimenter that is affected by his expectation, but again no research evidence is presented in support of this conclusion.

Rosenthal and Fode (1963b, Experiments 1 and 2)

Once again, Barber and Silver imply that procedural deviations, recording errors, or intentional errors might have accounted for the results but, once again, no evidence is presented to suggest such an interpretation. The evidence that such an interpretation cannot very reasonably account for the results, evidence presented earlier in this paper, is not referred to.

A general tendency to asymmetry of interpretation must be pointed out. Thus, in studies suggesting to Barber and Silver the operation of expectancy effects, recording errors and intentional errors are invoked as mechanisms accounting for the "positive" results. In studies suggesting to Barber and Silver no operation of expectancy effects, the question of recording errors and intentional errors is never raised. In the absence of research evidence, it seems no more warranted to infer that obtained expectancy effects were due to errors of judgment or to cheating than to infer that the "absence" of expectancy effects was not due to the operation of these same errors. We sound once more the clarion call for further research.

Laszlo and Rosenthal (1967)

Barber and Silver note correctly that the experimenters of this study made computational errors and that more than half the errors were "biased" in one direction. No mention is made of the fact that in a related paper (Barber *et al.*, 1967) one of the *principal investigators* made more computational errors than the average experimenter of the Laszlo and Rosenthal study, and that more than half these errors were "biased" in one direction. In neither study, however, was the "bias" in error making "significant" statistically. For the study in which expectancy effects were judged significant, Barber and Silver imply that the computational errors may in some way have accounted for the positive results. For the study in which expectancy effects were not judged significant, Barber and Silver make no mention of the computational errors that occurred. As was mentioned earlier in this paper, on the basis of the research available, it seems unlikely that the results of these studies were nontrivially affected by recording or intentional errors.

Barber and Silver suggest that the presence of computational errors implies errors of observation in the collection of data. Careful reading of the research they reviewed would have provided evidence in support of that suggestion. A correlation (phi) of .48 was reported between recording error and computational error (Rosenthal, Friedman, Johnson, Fode, Schill, White, & Vikan-Kline, 1964). Further careful reading, however, would have shown that directionality of error in recording data was not especially related to directionality of error in making computations (rho = .05).

Masling (1965, 1966)

There appear to be no salient omissions in Barber and Silver's account of this study.

Silverman (1966)

Barber and Silver correctly point out that scoring errors were made by the experimenters of this study. However, Barber and Silver do not present the evidence given by Silverman that would weaken Barber and Silver's inference that such scoring errors could have accounted for the overall findings.

Adair and Epstein (1967)

There appear to be no salient omissions in Barber and Silver's account of this study.

Shames and Adair (1967)

Barber and Silver's description of this study is of interest because it represents the only one in which the salient material omitted would have strengthened their position. The omission is of a replication of the study requiring numerosity estimation in which effects of expectancy again were not found. (Both "negative" findings are listed in Table 5-2 along with the small normal deviates associated with the p values obtained.)

Marwit and Marcia (1967)

Barber and Silver correctly point out the possibility that verbal conditioning may have occurred in this study but again do not refer to those experiments (cited earlier) showing verbal conditioning to be insufficient to account for the operation of expectancy effects.

NOTES

1. Preparation of this paper and much of the research summarized were facilitated by research grants (G-17685, G-24826, GS-177, GS-714, and GS-1741) from the Division of Social Sciences of the National Science Foundation. The author wishes to thank Theodore X. Barber for making earlier drafts of the paper by Barber and Silver (1968) available for comment.

2. In order to simplify our discussion it is best to regard as the relevant population of studies only those selected by Barber and Silver. That omits the results of three studies in a readily available source (Rosenthal, 1966, pp. 149, 153, 405) that have associated one-tailed p values of .005, .01, and .002, respectively; combined $p < .000004$, $z = 4.49$. It also omits the results of the older relevant experiments and the rather well-documented literature of case studies (e.g., Rosenhan, 1967; Rosenthal, 1964b, 1966; Shor & Schatz, 1960). The studies reviewed include considerably less than half the studies conducted in over 30 different laboratories.

3. The zs listed in the interaction column are based sometimes on Fs and sometimes on other statistics. In Sample 2 for instance, interaction was tested by a correlation between the experimenter's need for approval and the degree to which he obtained data in the predicted direction. Barber and Silver claim that in the absence of a large main effect such interactions are meaningless, amounting to correlations between arrays of random numbers. They do not explain why such correlations between arrays of random numbers should achieve low levels of p and, more importantly, why such correlations between arrays of random numbers should be routinely replicable. In Table 5-3, interaction effects not based on Fs are given only when the same statistic has been applied in at least one replicate.

4. These samples include Samples 3–6 and 10–16 from Table 5.2 and Samples 4 and 15–17 from Table 5.3.

5. For some situations, the null distributions have already been worked out and Winer (1962) summarizes some of these. The author thanks Fred Mosteller and Paul Holland for their helpful discussions of some of the general issues involved.

REFERENCES

ADAIR, J. G., & Epstein, J. Verbal cues in the mediation of experimenter bias. Paper presented at the meeting of the Midwestern Psychological Association, Chicago, May 1967.

BARBER, T. X., Calverley, D. S., Forgione, A., McPeake, J. D., Chaves, J. F., & Bowen, B. Five attempts to replicate the experimenter bias effect. Harding, Mass.: Medfield Foundation, 1967. (Mimeo.)

BARBER, T. X., & Silver, M. J. Fact, fiction, and the experimenter bias effect. *Psychological Bulletin*, 1968, **70** (6, Pt. 2): 1–29.

COCHRAN, W. G. Footnote to an appreciation of R. A. Fisher. *Science*, 1967, **156**: 1460–1462.

CORDARO, L., & Ison, J. R. Observer bias in classical conditioning of the planarian. *Psychological Reports*, 1963, **13**: 787–789.

FRIEDMAN, N. *The social nature of psychological research*. New York: Basic Books, 1967.

FRIEDMAN, N., Kurland, D., & Rosenthal, R. Experimenter behavior as an unintended determinant of experimental results. *Journal of Projective Techniques and Personality Assessment*, 1965, **29**: 479–490.

INGRAHAM, L. H., & Harrington, G. M. Experience of E as a variable in reducing experimenter bias. *Psychological Reports*, 1966, **19**: 455–461.

KAPLAN, A. *The conduct of inquiry*. San Francisco: Chandler, 1964.

LASZLO, J. P., & Rosenthal, R. Subject dogmatism, experimenter status and experimenter expectancy effects. Cambridge, Mass.: Harvard University, Department of Social Relations, 1967. (Mimeo.)

MARCIA, J. E. Hypothesis-making, need for social approval, and their effects on unconscious experimenter bias. Unpublished master's thesis, Ohio State University, 1961.

MARWIT, S. J., & Marcia, J. E. Tester bias and response to projective instruments. *Journal of Consulting Psychology*, 1967, **31**: 253–258.

MASLING, J. Differential indoctrination of examiners and Rorschach responses. *Journal of Consulting Psychology*, 1965, **29**: 198–201.

MASLING, J. Role-related behavior of the subject and psychologist and its effects upon psychological data. *Nebraska Symposium on Motivation*, 1966, **14**: 67–103.

McFALL, R. M. "Unintentional communication": The effect of congruence and incongruence between subject and experimenter constructions. Unpublished doctoral dissertation, Ohio State University, 1965.

McGUIRE, W. J. Personality and susceptibility to social influence. In E. F. Borgatta & W. W. Lambert (Eds.), *Handbook of personality theory and research*. Chicago: Rand McNally, 1967.

MOSTELLER, F., & Bush, R. R. Selected quantitative techniques. In G. Lindzey (Ed.), *Handbook of social psychology*. Vol. I. Cambridge, Mass.: Addison-Wesley, 1954.

NEYMAN, J. R. A. Fisher (1890–1962): An appreciation. *Science*, 1967, **156**: 1456–1460.

PAGE, E. B. Ordered hypotheses for multiple treatments: A significance test for linear ranks. *Journal of the American Statistical Association*, 1963, **58**: 216–230.

PERSINGER, G. W. The effect of acquaintanceship on the mediation of experimenter bias. Unpublished master's thesis, University of North Dakota, 1962.

PFLUGRATH, J. Examiner influence in a group testing situation with particular reference to examiner bias. Unpublished master's thesis, University of North Dakota, 1962.

POLANYI, M. The unaccountable element in science. *Transactions of the Bose Research Institute*, 1961, **24**: 175–184.

ROSENHAN, D. On the social psychology of hypnosis research. In J. E. Gordon (Ed.), *Handbook of clinical and experimental hypnosis*. New York: Macmillan, 1967.

ROSENTHAL, R. The effect of the experimenter on the results of psychological research. In B. A. Maher (Ed.), *Progress in experimental personality research*. Vol. 1. New York: Academic Press, 1964. (a)

ROSENTHAL, R. Experimenter outcome-orientation and the results of the psychological experiment. *Psychological Bulletin*, 1964, **61**: 405–412. (b)

ROSENTHAL, R. *Experimenter effects in behavioral research*. New York: Appleton-Century-Crofts, 1966.

ROSENTHAL, R. Covert communication in the psychological experiment. *Psychological Bulletin*, 1967, **67**: 356–367. (a)

ROSENTHAL, R. Experimenter expectancy, experimenter experience, and Pascal's Wager. *Psychological Reports*, 1967, **20**: 619–622. (b)

ROSENTHAL, R. The eternal triangle: Investigators, data, and the hypotheses called null. Cambridge, Mass.: Harvard University, Department of Social Relations, 1967. (Mimeo.) (c)

ROSENTHAL, R., & Fode, K. L. The effect of experimenter bias on the performance of the albino rat. *Behavioral Science*, 1963, **8**: 183–189. (a)

ROSENTHAL, R., & Fode, K. L. Three experiments in experimenter bias. *Psychological Reports*, 1963, **12**: 491–511. (b)

ROSENTHAL, R., Friedman, C. J., Johnson, C. A., Fode, K. L., Schill, T. R., White, C. R., & Vikan-Kline L. L. Variables affecting experimenter bias in a group situation. *Genetic Psychology Monographs*, 1964, **70**: 271–296.

ROSENTHAL, R. Friedman, N., & Kurland, D. Instruction-reading behavior of the experimenter as an unintended determinant of experimental results. *Journal of Experimental Research in Personality*, 1966, **1**: 221–226.

ROSENTHAL, R., & Gaito, J. The interpretation of levels of significance by psychological researchers. *Journal of Psychology*, 1963, **55**: 33–38.

ROSENTHAL, R., & Gaito, J. Further evidence for the cliff effect in the interpretation of levels of significance. *Psychological Reports*, 1964, **15**: 570.

ROSENTHAL, R., Kohn, P., Greenfield, P. M., & Carota, N. Experimenters' hypothesis-confirmation and mood as determinants of experimental results. *Perceptual and Motor Skills*, 1965, **20**: 1237–1252.

ROSENTHAL, R., & Lawson, R. A longitudinal study of the effects of experimenter bias on the operant learning of laboratory rats. *Journal of Psychiatric Research*, 1964, **2**: 61–72.

ROSENTHAL, R., Persinger, G. W., Mulry, R. C., Vikan-Kline, L., & Grothe, M. Changes in experimental hypotheses as determinants of experimental results. *Journal of Projective Techniques and Personality Assessment*, 1964, **28**: 465–469. (a)

ROSENTHAL, R., Persinger, G. W., Mulry, R. C., Vikan-Kline, L., & Grothe, M. Emphasis on experimental procedure, sex of subjects, and the biasing effects of experimental hypotheses. *Journal of Projective Techniques and Personality Assessment,* 1964, **28**: 470–473. (b)

ROSENTHAL, R., Persinger, G. W., Vikan-Kline, L., & Fode, K. L. The effect of early data returns on data subsequently obtained by outcome-biased experimenters. *Sociometry,* 1963, **26**: 487–498. (a)

ROSENTHAL, R., Persinger, G. W., Vikan-Kline, L., & Fode, K. L. The effect of experimenter outcome-bias and subject set on awareness in verbal conditioning experiments. *Journal of Verbal Learning and Verbal Behavior,* 1963, **2**: 275–283. (b)

ROSENTHAL, R., Persinger, G. W., Vikan-Kline, L., & Mulry, R. C. The role of the research assistant in the mediation of experimenter bias. *Journal of Personality,* 1963, **31**: 313–335.

ROZEBOOM, W. W. The fallacy of the null-hypothesis significance test. *Psychological Bulletin,* 1960, **57**: 416–428.

SHAMES, M. L., & Adair, J. G. Experimenter bias as a function of the type and structure of the task. Paper presented at the meeting of the Canadian Psychological Association, Ottawa, May 1967.

SHOR, R. E., & Schatz, J. A critical note on Barber's case-study on "Subject J." *Journal of Psychology,* 1960, **50**: 253–256.

SILVERMAN, I. The effects of experimenter outcome expectancy on latency of word association. Paper presented at the meeting of the Eastern Psychological Association, New York, April 1966.

SPENCE, K. W. Anxiety (drive) level and performance in eyelid conditioning. *Psychological Bulletin,* 1964, **61**: 129–139.

WARTENBERG-EKREN, U. The effect of experimenter knowledge of a subject's scholastic standing on the performance of a reasoning task. Unpublished master's thesis, Marquette University, 1962.

WHITE, C. R. The effect of induced subject expectations on the experimenter bias situation. Unpublished doctoral dissertation, University of North Dakota, 1962.

WINER, B. J. *Statistical principles in experimental design.* New York: McGraw-Hill, 1962.

Robert Rosenthal and Lenore Jacobson

Self-fulfilling Prophecies in the Classroom:

Teachers' Expectations as Unintended
Determinants of Pupils' Intellectual
Competence

SOME FURTHER EVIDENCE[1]

A recent experiment was designed to test the hypothesis that, within
a given classroom, those children from whom the teacher expected
greater growth in intellectual competence would show such greater
growth (Rosenthal & Jacobson, 1966). The Harvard Test of Inflected
Acquisition was administered to all the children in an elementary school
in the spring of 1964. This test was purported to predict academic
"blooming" or intellectual growth. The reason for administering the
test in the particular school was ostensibly to perform a final check on
the validity of the test, a validity which was presented as already well
established. Actually, the Harvard Test of Inflected Acquisition was a
standardized relatively nonverbal test of intelligence, Flanagan's (1960)
Tests of General Ability.

Within each of the six grades of the elementary school, there were
three classrooms, one each for children performing at above-average,
average, and below-average levels of scholastic achievement. In each
of the eighteen classrooms of the school about 20 percent of the children
were designated as academic "spurters." The names of these children
were reported to their new teachers in the fall of 1964 as those who,
during the academic year ahead, would show unusual intellectual gains.

From Chapter 6, Self-Fulfilling Prophecies in the Classroom:
Teachers' Expectations as Unintended Determinants of Pupils'
Intellectual Competence by Robert Rosenthal and Lenore Jacobson,
from Social Class, Race, and Psychological Development edited by M.
Deutsch, I. Katz, and A. R. Jensen. Copyright © 1968 by Holt,
Rinehart and Winston, Inc. Reprinted by permission of Holt,
Rinehart and Winston, Inc.

415

The "fact" of their intellectual potential was established from their scores on the test for "intellectual blooming."

Teachers were cautioned not to discuss the test findings with either their pupils or the children's parents. Actually the names of the 20 percent of the children assigned to the "spurting" condition had been selected by means of a table of random numbers. The difference, then, between these children earmarked for intellectual growth and the undesignated control children was in the mind of the teacher.

The school as a whole. Four months after the teachers had been given the names of the "special" children, all the children once again took the

Table 5-4   *Means and Standard Deviations of Gains in Intellectual Performance*

	CONTROL			EXPERIMENTAL			Difference between Means	p†
	N	Mean	SD*	N	Mean	SD*		
Verbal IQ	269	7.8	17.7	68	9.9	21.9	2.1	
Reasoning IQ	255	15.7	28.6	65	22.9	31.3	7.2	0.03
Total IQ	255	8.4	13.5	65	12.2	15.0	3.8	0.02
Verbal MA	269	1.8	1.8	68	2.0	2.2	0.2	
Reasoning MA	255	2.3	2.4	65	3.0	2.8	0.7	0.02
Total MA	255	1.8	1.3	65	2.1	1.4	0.3	0.02

* SD, standard deviation.
† Error term for all tests of significance is mean square within treatments in classrooms.

same form of the nonverbal test of intelligence. Four months after this retest, the children took the same test once again. This final retest was at the end of the school year, some eight months after the teachers had been given the expectation for intellectual growth of the special children. These retests were not, of course, explained as "retests" to the teachers but rather as further efforts to predict intellectual growth.

The intelligence test employed, while relatively nonverbal in the sense of requiring no speaking, reading, or writing, was not entirely nonverbal. Actually there were two subtests, one requiring a greater comprehension of English—a kind of picture vocabulary. The other subtest required less ability to understand any spoken language, but more ability to reason abstractly. For shorthand purposes, we refer to the former as a *verbal* subtest and to the latter as a *reasoning* subtest. The pretest correlation between these subtests was +0.42.

Table 5-4 shows the means and standard deviations of gains in IQ and mental age (MA) by the children of the control group and the experimental group after eight months. For the school as a whole, the children of the experimental groups did not show a significantly greater gain in verbal IQ and mental age than did the control-group children. However, in total IQ and mental age, and especially in the reasoning IQ and mental age, the experimental children gained more than did the control children. Even after the fourth-month retest this trend was already in evidence though the effects were smaller.

Table 5-5   *Mean Ratings by Teachers of Children in Experimental and Control Groups*

Characteristics	Control	Experimental	Difference	p
Future success	5.53	6.48	0.95	0.0006
Interesting	5.46	6.43	0.97	0.0008
Curious	5.50	6.25	0.75	0.01
Happy	5.77	6.33	0.56	0.05
Appealing	5.78	6.23	0.45	0.14
Adjusted	5.67	6.04	0.37	0.22
Affectionate	5.72	6.01	0.29	0.28
Hostile	3.84	3.97	0.13	
Needs approval	5.35	4.97	--0.38	0.20

Toward the end of the school year of this study, all teachers were asked to rate each of their pupils on the following variables: the extent to which they would be successful in the future, and the degree to which they could be described as interesting, curious, happy, appealing, adjusted, affectionate, hostile, and motivated by a need for social approval. A comparison of the experimental and control children on each of these variables was thought to be valuable to obtain some idea of the effect of the experimental treatment on behavior other than intellectual-test performance. In addition, it was thought that differences in teachers' perceptions of the experimental and control children might be suggestive of the mechanism whereby a teacher communicates her expectation to her pupils. There is, of course, no way to be sure that the children's behavior was accurately described by the teachers. If it were, and if the experimental- and control-group children differed in their classroom behavior, we would know at least that changes in intellectual ability were accompanied by changes in other classroom behavior. If the teachers' descriptions of the children's behavior were not accurate, any differences in the descriptions of the experimental and control children could be ascribed to a kind of halo effect. Such a halo effect might suggest the possibility that altered perceptions of children's behavior might be associated with differences in teachers' treatment of the children, such treatment differences leading to differences in intellectual performance and remaining to be discovered. In Table 5-5 are found the mean ratings of the children of each experimental condition on each of the nine characteristics described earlier.

The children from whom intellectual growth was expected were described as having a significantly better chance of becoming successful in the future, as significantly more interesting, curious, and happy. There was a tendency, too, for these children to be seen as more appealing, adjusted, and affectionate and as lower in the need for social approval. In short, the children from whom intellectual growth was expected became more intellectually alive and autonomous, or at least were so perceived by their teachers.

Table 5-6   *Means and Standard Deviations of Gains in Total IQ for Six Grades*

Grade	N	CONTROL Mean	SD	N	EXPERIMENTAL Mean	SD	Difference between means	p*
1	48	12.0	16.6	7	27.4	12.5	15.4	0.002
2	47	7.0	10.0	12	16.5	18.6	9.5	0.02
3	40	5.0	11.9	14	5.0	9.3	0.0	
4	49	2.2	13.4	12	5.6	11.0	3.4	
5	26	17.5	13.1	9	17.4	17.8	−0.1	
6	45	10.7	10.0	11	10.0	6.5	−0.7	

* Error term for all tests of significance is mean square within treatments in classrooms.

We have already seen that the children of the experimental group gained more intellectually so that the possibility exists that it was the fact of such gaining that accounted for the more favorable ratings of these children's behavior and aptitude. But a great many of the control-group children also gained in IQ during the course of the year. Perhaps those who gained more intellectually among these undesignated children would also be rated more favorably by their teachers. Such was not the case however. The more the control-group children gained in verbal IQ the more they were regarded as less well-adjusted ($r = -0.13$, $p < 0.05$). Among the experimental-group children the greater their gains in verbal IQ the more they were regarded as more likely to be successful in the future ($r = +0.22$, $p < 0.10$), as happier ($r = +0.21$, $p < 0.10$), and as less affectionate ($r = -0.22$, $p < 0.10$).

Those children of the control group who gained more in reasoning IQ came to be regarded as less interesting ($r = -0.14$, $p < 0.05$) and less affectionate ($r = -0.13$, $p < 0.05$). The children of the experimental group who gained more in reasoning IQ came to be regarded as more likely to succeed ($r = +0.22$, $p < .10$), better adjusted ($r = +0.36$, $p < 0.01$), more affectionate ($r = +0.25$, $p < 0.05$), and as lower in their need for social approval ($r = -0.24$, $p < 0.10$). Relative to the control-group children who gained more in reasoning IQ, the experimental-group children who gained more in reasoning IQ were seen as significantly more interesting, more happy, better adjusted, and more affectionate. From these results and from the similar results based on total-IQ gains it would seem that when children who are expected to grow intellectually do so, they are considerably benefited in other ways as well. When children who are not especially expected to develop intellectually do so, they seem either to show accompanying undesirable behavior, or at least are perceived by their teachers as showing such undesirable behavior. If a child is to show intellectual gains it seems to be better for his real or perceived intellectual vitality and for his real or perceived mental health if his teacher has been expecting him to gain intellectually. It appears that there may be hazards to unpredicted intellectual growth.

The six grades. So far we have examined the effects of teachers' expectations only for the school as a whole. Table 5–6 shows the mean gains in total-IQ points from the pretest to the final posttest among experimental- and control-group children for each of the six grades. As we go from the higher grades to the lower grades we find the effects of teacher expectations increasing almost monotonically (*rho* = 0.94, *p* = 0.02) and only in the first and second grades do we find the total IQ changes to be affected to a statistically significant degree. In one of the three classrooms comprising the first grade, the control-group children gained an average of 16.2 IQ points, whereas the experimentals gained an average of 41.0 points, a difference of nearly 25 points (*p* < 0.006). The largest effect of teachers' expectations to occur in the second grade was in a classroom which found the control-group children gaining 4.3 IQ points while the experimental-group children gained 22.5 points, a difference of over 18 points (*p* < 0.002).

Another useful way to show the effects of teachers' expectations on their pupils' total-IQ gains is to show the percentage of experimental and control-group children who achieve various amounts of gain. In Table 5–7 such percentages are shown for the first and second grades only. Less than half the control-group children gained 10 or more total IQ points, but about four out of five experimental-group children did. Every fifth control-group child gained 20 or more total-IQ points, but nearly every second experimental-group child did. While only one out of twenty control-group children gained 20 or more total-IQ points, one out of five experimental-group children did.

Earlier it was noted that for the school as a whole the effects of teachers' expectations on children's gains in reasoning IQ were greater than they were on children's gains in verbal IQ. The results for grades and for classrooms were consistent with the overall finding. On the whole, verbal IQ was not much affected by teachers' expectations. In only twelve of the eighteen classrooms was there a greater gain in verbal IQ among children from whom intellectual gains were expected ($p = 0.12$) and the bulk of the verbal-IQ gain favoring the experimental-group children occurred in the first two grades.

Table 5–7   *Percentages of First- and Second-Grade Children Gaining 10 or more, 20 or more, 30 or more, Total IQ Points*

IQ Gain at Least	Control N = 95	Experimental N = 19	p of difference
10 points*	49	79	0.02
20 points†	19	47	0.01
30 points	5	21	0.04

* Includes children gaining 20 and 30 points or more.
† Includes children gaining 30 points or more.

It was in the gains in reasoning IQ that the effect of teachers' expectations showed itself more clearly. Of the seventeen classrooms in which the posttest reasoning-IQ tests had been administered (one class was inadvertently not retested for reasoning IQ) fifteen showed greater gains among the children from whom intellectual growth had been expected ($p < 0.001$). Although the advantage in terms of gain in reasoning IQ of having been predicted to "spurt" was significant statistically only in the second grade, the absolute magnitude of advantage was not trivial in any of the first five grades. In fourteen of the seventeen classrooms in which the comparison was possible, the excess of reasoning-IQ gain of the experimental- compared to the control-group children was greater than the excess of verbal-IQ gain ($p = 0.006$).

For each of the six grade levels, the mean rating made by teachers of the control-group children's classroom behavior was subtracted from the mean rating assigned the children of the experimental group. Table 5–8 shows the mean differences in ratings for each of the six grades and their statistical significance. It was in the first-grade classrooms that teachers saw the greatest differences in the classroom behavior of the experimental- and control-group children. Children who had been expected to show greater intellectual growth (and these were the children who *had* shown the greater intellectual growth) were seen as significantly more likely to succeed, more interesting, curious, happy, appealing, and better adjusted than were the children from whom no intellectual growth had been expected. First-graders were also seen as significantly lower in the need for social approval when intellectual growth had been predicted for them.

Among the children of the second grade, those who had been singled out for growth were judged more intellectually curious and more likely to succeed than the rest of the children.

Table 5–8   *Differences in Mean Ratings by Teachers of Children in Experimental and Control Groups in Six Grade Levels*

CHARACTERISTICS	GRADE LEVEL					
	1	2	3	4	5	6
Future success	+2.4§	+1.7‡	−0.0	+0.4	+0.6	+1.2*
Interesting	+3.0¶	+0.9	+0.2	+0.3	+0.1	+1.8‡
Curious	+2.4‡	+1.1*	−0.5	+0.7	−0.8	+1.9‡
Happy	+1.6*	+1.0	−0.5	+0.1	+0.5	+1.1
Appealing	+1.6*	+0.7	−1.3†	−0.1	−0.2	+2.2§
Adjusted	+2.2†	+0.9	−0.7	−0.2	+0.3	+0.7
Affectionate	+1.1	−0.1	−0.7	+0.8	−0.4	+1.2*
Hostile	+0.4	−0.2	+1.3*	−0.1	−0.4	−0.4
Needs approval	−2.2†	−1.0	−0.1	+0.6	−0.4	+0.3

* $p < .10.$ † $p < .05.$ ‡ $p < .01.$ § $p < .005.$ ¶ $p < .0005.$

Among the children of the third grade, those who had been predicted to show greater intellectual growth were perceived as less appealing and as more hostile than the rest of the children. It was in the third grade, too, that the children of the experimental group tended to show less gain in verbal IQ than did the control children.

In the fourth and fifth grades, the children of the experimental group were not judged to differ in their classroom behavior from the children of the control group. However, in the sixth grade, children who were expected to show intellectual gain were seen in much the same way as the experimental-group children in the first grade were seen, except that they did not differ from the control children in their need for social approval. It was surprising to find the sixth-graders of the experimental group as well-differentiated in their teachers' eyes from the control children as in the first grade, when in the sixth grade, unlike the first grade, there seemed to be no effect of teachers' expectations on their pupils' intellectual growth.

Within each grade separately, the correlations were computed between the gain in verbal, reasoning, and total IQ and the teachers' ratings of the children of the experimental and control groups. Since these computations resulted in 324 correlations, the tables are not shown, but the significant trends will be summarized. In the first grade, none of the teachers' ratings of the control children were correlated with their gain in verbal IQ. Among the children of the experimental group, however, those first-graders who showed greater gains in verbal IQ were rated as less interesting ($r = −0.93, p < 0.005$), less curious ($r = −0.89, p < 0.01$), and less affectionate ($r = −0.90, p < 0.01$) than the children who gained less in verbal IQ.

Still considering only the first-grade level, there was no relationship between the amount of gain in reasoning IQ and teachers' ratings of the children of the experimental group. Among the control-group children, however, those who showed a greater gain in reasoning IQ were rated as less interesting $(r = -0.32, p < 0.05)$, less curious $(r = -0.38, p < 0.01)$, and less affectionate $(r = -0.43, p < 0.005)$ than the children who gained less in reasoning IQ.

At least among first-graders, those who are expected to show intellectual growth are rated relatively more favorably when the gains they do show are in reasoning rather than in verbal intellectual performance. First-graders from whom no particular intellectual growth is expected, on the other hand, are regarded relatively more favorably by their teachers when the growth that occurs is found more in the verbal than in the reasoning areas of intellectual functioning. No such clear-cut patterns of correlations were found in the higher grades between amount of gain in verbal or reasoning IQ and teachers' ratings.

The three tracks. Within each of the six grades of the elementary school there were three classrooms arranged such that one was on a "fast" track, one on a "medium" track, and one on a "slow" track. (The mean pretest total IQ of the fast-track children was about 23 IQ points higher than the mean-pretest total IQ of the slow-track children.) After eight months, gains in IQ favored the experimental-group children in all tracks, with none of the tracks showing a significantly greater effect of the teachers' expectations than the other tracks, except that for total IQ, verbal IQ, and for reasoning IQ, it was the children of the medium track who showed the greatest effect numerically of their teachers' expectations. That was a surprising finding, for it had seemed most likely that the slowest-track children would have shown the greatest advantage attributable to a change in their teachers' expectations. It was they who had the furthest to go, and, in general, it is the children thought to be "slowest" academically who have been most often discussed by educational theorists as most affected by the teachers' expectations. The finding that it was the educationally most-average children who gained the most intellectually when their teachers expected such gains does not, of course, show that the "slower" children had not been affected in the past by negative expectations in the course of their having been labeled "slow."

For each of the three tracks, the mean rating made by teachers of the control-group children's classroom behavior was subtracted from the mean rating assigned the children of the experimental group. Table 5-9 shows the mean differences for each of the three tracks and the statistical significance of these mean differences. In the fast track, those children who had been expected to show intellectual gains were judged as more likely to succeed in the future and as more interesting. In the medium-track group, those children who had been expected to show intellectual gains were judged as more likely to succeed, more interesting, more curious, more appealing, better adjusted, and lower in the need for social approval. In the slow-track group, those children who had been expected to show intellectual gains were not judged to differ in their classroom behavior from those children for whom no intellectual gains had been expected.

Table 5-9 *Differences in Mean Ratings by Teachers of Children in Experimental and Control Groups in Three Tracks*

		TRACKS	
CHARACTERISTICS	Fast	Medium	Slow
Future success	+0.8*	+1.7§	+0.3
Interesting	+1.0†	+1.5‡	+0.4
Curious	+0.4	+1.6§	+0.4
Happy	+0.6	+0.8	+0.2
Appealing	+0.1	+1.1*	+0.2
Adjusted	−0.0	+1.0*	+0.3
Affectionate	+0.3	+0.5	+0.2
Hostile	+0.5	−0.6	+0.3
Needs approval	+0.2	−1.4†	−0.2

* $p < .10$. † $p < .05$. ‡ $p < .01$. § $p < .005$.

Within each of the three tracks, the correlations were computed between the gain in verbal, reasoning, and total IQ and the teachers' ratings of the children of the experimental and control groups. The resulting correlations, 162 of them are too many to present here, but some of the significant trends can be described. We shall consider first the correlations between teachers' ratings and gains in verbal IQ over the eight-month period of the experiment.

Among the children of the experimental group, those who gained more in verbal IQ were judged as significantly more likely to succeed, but only if they were in the fast or medium tracks (combined $r = +0.30$, $p = 0.05$) and not if they were in the slow track ($r = +0.03$). This was the case despite the fact that the slow-track children showed as great an average gain in verbal IQ as did the children of the fast track. There is, of course, no way to decide whether this finding was due to the slow-track children's acting less "successful" in class in spite of their intellectual growth, or whether it becomes difficult for a teacher even to see the "blooming" slow-track children as potentially successful intellectually.

Among the children of the medium track, those who gained more in verbal IQ were judged to be more appealing by their teachers, but only if they were the children who had been expected to show intellectual gains ($r = +0.48$, $p < 0.05$). The greater the gain in verbal IQ of children from whom no such growth had been expected, the less appealing they tended to be judged by their teachers ($r = -0.18$, NS, p of difference < 0.01).

Among the children of the experimental group, those who showed greater gains in reasoning IQ were judged as more interesting by their teachers, but only if they were in the fast or medium tracks (combined $r = +0.30$, $p = 0.06$), and not if they were in the slow track ($r = -0.05$), although the slow-track children had shown as great a gain in reasoning IQ as had the children of the fast track. Again, there is no way to decide whether the children of the slow track who gained more in reasoning IQ were actually relatively less interesting in their classroom behavior, or whether it is relatively more difficult to view a child known to be "slow-track" as more interesting when he has gained in intellectual abilities, particularly when these gains may not have been reflected in his verbal behavior.

Among the children of the control group, those who showed greater gains in reasoning IQ were seen as less happy ($r = -0.29$, $p < 0.01$), less appealing ($r = -0.19$, $p < 0.10$), less well-adjusted ($r = -0.20$, $p < 0.10$), and less affectionate ($r = -0.28$, $p = 0.02$), if they were in the slow track. In addition, these slow-track children were seen as less intellectually curious ($r = -0.21$, $p = 0.07$) and as less interesting ($r = -0.32$, $p < 0.01$), when they showed greater gains in reasoning IQ. Earlier, when the discussion was of results for the school as a whole, it was suggested that there may be hazards to unpredicted, unexpected intellectual growth. The data just presented suggest that this appears to be true primarily of those children placed in a slow track; none of the correlations between gains in reasoning IQ and teachers' judgments approached significance for the children of the fast or medium tracks. Again, it should be pointed out that we cannot say whether the teachers' ratings reflected the children's classroom behavior as an external paradigm observer might perceive it, or whether the teachers' ratings reflected only a more idiosyncratic halo effect. In either case, the finding may have some importance because it seems relevant to a child's course in school not only how he behaves "really," but also how his behavior is viewed by his teacher.

Among the children of the experimental group, those who showed greater gains in total IQ were judged as more interesting if they were in the fast or medium tracks (combined $r = +0.38$, $p < 0.02$) but not if they were in the slow track ($r = -0.21$, NS). Similarly those children of the fast and medium tracks who gained more in total IQ were judged as more appealing ($r = +0.33$, $p < 0.05$), better adjusted ($r = +0.37$, $p < 0.02$), and more affectionate ($r = +0.30$, $p < 0.07$); whereas, among children of the slow track, those who gained more in total IQ were not seen as more appealing ($r = -0.05$), or as better adjusted ($r = +0.02$), and were seen actually as *less* affectionate ($r = -0.47$, $p = 0.04$) and as lower in the need for social approval ($r = -0.59$, $p < 0.01$).

Reliabilities and Initial-IQ Values

To help in the interpretation of the results of this experiment, it was necessary to know the retest reliabilities of the verbal, reasoning, and total-IQ scores from the pretest to the posttest, one year later. These

Table 5-10   *Retest Reliabilities after One Year*

Grades	VERBAL IQ Control	VERBAL IQ Experimental	REASONING IQ Control	REASONING IQ Experimental	TOTAL IQ Control	TOTAL IQ Experimental
1	+0.74	+0.77	+0.46	+0.26	+0.59	+0.75
2	0.71	0.83	0.58	0.62	0.79	0.82
3	0.68	0.60	0.41	0.67	0.70	0.72
4	0.83	0.77	0.63	0.73	0.80	0.90
5	0.78	0.81	0.46	0.31	0.79	0.75
6	0.89	0.88	0.74	0.87	0.88	0.97
Tracks						
Fast	0.67	0.71	0.46	0.51	0.66	0.73
Medium	0.77	0.87	0.36	0.24	0.58	0.80
Slow	0.72	0.49	0.25	0.37	0.61	0.25
Total	0.75	0.76	0.50	0.47	0.74	0.78
N	269	68	255	65	255	65

reliabilities were computed separately for the experimental and control groups, for each grade level, for each track, and for the entire school. Table 5-10 shows these reliabilities. The overall mean reliability of the verbal and total IQs was +0.75, while the overall reliability of the reasoning IQ was +0.49. The average reliability of the IQ scores was not different among the experimental and the control groups, suggesting that among the children of the experimental group, where intellectual gains did occur, the gains did not disturb the ranking of the children within their own experimental condition.

In spite of random allocation of pupils to the experimental condition, the children of the experimental group scored slightly higher in pretest IQ than did the children of the control group. This fact suggested that those children who were brighter to begin with might have been the ones who would in any case have shown the greater gains in intellectual performance. To check this hypothesis, the correlations were computed between children's initial pretest IQ scores and the magnitude of their gains in IQ after eight months. If those who were brighter to begin with showed greater gains in IQ the correlations would be positive. Table 5–11 shows that such was not the case. In general, the overall correlations were negative: for total IQ, $r = -0.23$ ($p < 0.001$); for verbal IQ, $r = -0.04$ (NS); and for reasoning IQ, $r = -0.48$ ($p <$

Table 5–11　　　*Intellectual Performance Gain as a Function of Initial IQ*

	VERBAL IQ		REASONING IQ		TOTAL IQ	
Grades	Control	Experi-mental	Control	Experi-mental	Control	Experi-mental
1	−0.36*	−0.78*	−0.80‡	−0.93†	−0.65‡	−0.73*
2	−0.37†	+0.52*	−0.28*	+0.17	−0.37†	+0.39
3	+0.26*	−0.41	−0.37*	−0.08	−0.07	−0.09
4	−0.19	+0.17	+0.04	−0.18	−0.14	−0.01
5	−0.01	+0.03	−0.40*	−0.18	−0.02	+0.07
6	+0.11	+0.34	+0.01	+0.35	+0.05	+0.49
Tracks						
Fast	−0.01	+0.09	−0.29†	−0.10	−0.29†	+0.05
Medium	−0.27*	+0.46*	−0.77‡	−0.62*	−0.57‡	+0.11
Slow	−0.39‡	−0.70‡	−0.74‡	−0.06	−0.48‡	−0.76‡
Total	−0.08	+0.04	−0.54‡	−0.28*	−0.30‡	−0.05
N	269	68	255	65	255	65

* $p < .10$, two tail.　　† $p < .01$, two tail.　　‡ $p < .001$, two tail.

0.001). Although for the school as a whole the correlations between initial IQ and gain in IQ were somewhat less negative among the children of the experimental group than among the children of the control group, this seemed to be no simple effect. Instead there appeared to be an interaction effect of the experimental group's difference from the control group as a function of the type of IQ considered and the track position of the children. Thus, among the children of the medium track, those who started at a higher pretest level of verbal IQ gained less in verbal IQ if they were in the control group, but gained more in verbal IQ if they were in the experimental group. No such difference was observed in the children of the medium track when the pretest level and gains in reasoning IQ were considered. Among the children of the slow track, those who started at a higher pretest level of verbal IQ gained relatively less in verbal IQ if they were in the experimental rather than the control group. In this same track, there was no relationship for the children of the experimental group between their pretest level of reasoning IQ and their subsequent gain in reasoning IQ; whereas, for the children of the control group, the relationship was very large and negative ($r = -0.74$). More detailed examination of Table 5–11 shows only more such hard-to-explain interactions when individual grade levels are considered. To summarize, there appears to be no way in which the relatively greater gains of the experimental children can be accounted for on the basis of the correlations between initial level of IQ and magnitude of gain in IQ.

The Question of Mediation

How did the teachers' expectations come to serve as determinants of gains in intellectual performance? The most plausible hypothesis seemed to be that the children for whom unusual intellectual growth had been predicted would be more attended to by their teachers. If teachers were more attentive to the children earmarked for growth, we might expect that teachers might be robbing Peter to see Paul grow. With a finite amount of time to spend with each child, if a teacher gave more time to the children of the experimental group, she would have less time to spend with the children of the control group. If the teacher's spending more time with a child led to greater gains, we could test the "robbing-Peter" hypothesis by comparing the gains made by children of the experimental group with gains made by children of the control group in each class. The "robbing-Peter" hypothesis predicts a negative correlation. The greater the gains made by the children of the experimental group (with the implication of more time spent on them), the less should be the gains made by the children of the control group (with the implication of less time spent on them). In fact, however, the correlation was positive, large and statistically significant (*rho* = +0.57, *p* = 0.02, two tail). The greater the gain made by the children of whom gain was expected, the greater the gain made in the same classroom by the children from whom no special gain was expected. The evidence presented that teachers did not take time from control-group children to spend with the experimental-group children is indirect. More direct evidence was available.

Some ten months after the posttest had been administered, each of the teachers was asked to estimate how much time, relatively, she had devoted to each of four children. All four of these children had been in her classroom the preceding academic year; two had been in the control group and two had been in the experimental group. There was one boy and one girl in each of these two subgroups. The boys of each group were matched on their pretest IQ, as were the girls. The mean difference in IQ was less than one-half point in favor of the children of the experimental group (*t* <0.71). The specific question asked of the teacher was: Given a unit of time available to spend on these four children (100 percent), how much of that unit was spent with each child? For each matched pair of boys and girls, the percentage of time allocated to the control-group child was subtracted from the percentage of time allocated to the experimental-group child. A positive difference score, then, meant that the experimental-group child was given more time by the teacher according to her own assessment. Table 5–12 shows the mean and median difference scores for the entire school, for boys and girls, for each of the three tracks, and for each of the six grades. None of the obtained mean differences was significantly different from zero. In fact, there was a slight tendency for the children of the experimental group to be given less time than the children of the control group ($t < 0.66$).

Table 5–12   *Differences in Time Spent with Children of the Experimental and Control Groups*

	Mean Difference, %	Median Difference, %	N of Pairs*
All children	−2.6	0.0	31
Boys	+0.3	+5.0	15
Girls	−5.3	0.0	16
Fast track	−2.4	0.0	12
Medium track	−5.0	0.0	8
Slow track	−1.1	0.0	11
Grade 1	+5.0	0.0	6
Grade 2	−8.8	0.0	5
Grade 3	+10.0	+10.0	4
Grade 4	−3.3	0.0	6
Grade 5	−2.5	−2.5	4
Grade 6	−12.8	0.0	6

* No data were available from the two teachers who had left the school.

That the children of the experimental group were not favored with a greater investment of time seems less surprising in view of the pattern of their greater intellectual gains. If, for example, teachers had talked to them more we might have expected greater gains in verbal IQ but, we recall, the greater gains were found not in verbal but in reasoning IQ. It may be, of course, that the teachers were inaccurate in their estimates of time spent with each of the four children. Possibly direct observation of the teacher-pupil interactions would have given different results, but that method was not possible in the present study. Even direct observation by judges who could agree with one another might not have revealed a difference in the amounts of teacher time invested in each of the two groups of children. It seems plausible to think that it was not a difference in amount of time spent with the children of the two groups which led to the difference in their rates of intellectual development. It may have been more a matter of the type of interaction which took place between the teachers and their pupils which served as the determinant of the expected intellectual development.

By what she said, by how she said it, by her facial expressions, postures, and perhaps, by her touch, the teacher may have communicated to the children of the experimental group that she expected improved intellectual performance. Such communications together with possible changes in teaching techniques may have helped the child learn by changing his self-concept, his expectations of his own behavior, his motivation, as well as his cognitive skills. It is self-evident that further research is needed to narrow the range of possible mechanisms whereby a teacher's expectations become translated into a pupil's intellectual growth. It would be valuable, for example, to have sound films of teachers interacting with their pupils. We might then look for differences in the way teachers interact with those children from whom they expect more intellectual growth compared to those from whom they expect less. On the basis of films of psychological experimenters interacting with subjects from whom different responses are expected, we know that even in such highly standardized situations unintentional communications can be incredibly subtle and complex (Rosenthal, 1966). How much more subtle and complex may be the communications between children and their teachers who are not constrained by the demands of the experimental laboratory.

Before leaving the topic of the mediation of the teacher's expectation we must raise the question of whether these effects of her expectation were gradual and cumulative over the course of the year, or whether they acted primarily on the children's test-taking behavior. Because that is the way standardized tests are administered in schools, we had the teachers themselves administer the posttests to their classes in a group administration. This posttest was administered some eight months after the teacher had been given the names of the "special" children. Perhaps during the posttest she treated these children differently from the way she treated the other children, A number of considerations weaken the plausibility of this interpretation. First, while from our point of view the retest was a posttest from which to measure differential gains in IQ, from the teachers' point of view the retest was more like a pretest from which we would again, as we had the year before, make predictions as to which children would in the future show spurts of intellectual growth. Second, postexperimental interviews with the teachers one year later suggested that they could neither accurately recall the names of the children destined for intellectual growth, nor even select their names out of a larger list of children which included the names of an equal number of experimental and control children. The worst recall occurred among teachers of the second-grade children. Of the twelve children originally alleged to be potential spurters who remained in the school for the entire year of the experiment, not a single one was recalled as a potential spurter by any second-grade teacher. Yet, it will be recalled, effects of teachers' expectations were prominent in the second grade. It was of special interest, too, to learn that most of the teachers had merely "glanced at the names" of the "special" children when these were first given them and then "forgot about them." If the ordinary laws of forgetting apply, this suggests that whatever mediated the effects of teachers' expectations operated early in the academic year.

A third consideration weakening the plausibility of the hypothesis of differential treatment of children during the retest has to do with the nature of the test itself. The verbal subtest is administered by the teacher while the reasoning subtest is self-administered. During the administration of the verbal subtest the teacher contacts children individually to see whether they are following the instructions properly. During the administration of the reasoning subtest the teacher does not contact children individually. We would expect, therefore, that differential treatment of the children might occur during the administration of the verbal, but not the reasoning, subtest. Yet it was on the reasoning subtest that we found the major effect of the teachers' expectations to occur.

Though it seemed unlikely that differential treatment of the experimental-group children during retesting could account for our results we wanted to know whether someone who did not know the children's experimental- or control-group membership would obtain similar posttest results. Therefore, three classrooms were retested by a school administrator not attached to the particular school. She did not know which of the children were in the experimental group, and the results of her retesting were no different from the results of the classroom teachers' retesting. In fact, there was a tendency for the results of her retesting to show even greater effects of teachers' expectations.

SOME IMPLICATIONS

The results of the experiment just now described provide further evidence that one person's expectations of another's behavior may serve as a self-fulfilling prophecy. When teachers expected that certain children would show greater intellectual development, those children did show greater intellectual development. The effect was in evidence, however, primarily at the lower-grade levels, and it is difficult to be certain why that was the case. A number of interpretations suggest themselves, and these are not mutually exclusive.

First, younger children are generally regarded as more malleable, less fixed, more capable of change. It may be, then, that the experimental conditions of this experiment were more effective with younger children simply because younger children are easier to change than older ones. (It should be recalled that when we speak here of change we mean it as change relative to control-group change. Table 5-6 shows that even fifth-graders can change dramatically in IQ, but there the change of the experimental-group children is not greater than the change of the control-group children.)

A second interpretation is that younger children within a given school have less well-established reputations within the school. It then becomes more credible to a teacher to be told that a younger child will show intellectual growth. A teacher may "know" an older child much better by reputation and be less inclined to believe him capable of intellectual growth simply on someone else's say-so.

A third interpretation is a combination, in a sense, of the first two. It suggests that younger children show greater gains associated with teachers' expectancies not because they necessarily *are* more malleable but rather because they are believed by teachers to be more malleable.

A fourth interpretation suggests that younger children are more sensitive to, and more affected by, the particular processes whereby teachers communicate their expectations to children. Within this interpretation, it is possible that teachers react to children of all grade levels in the same way if they believe them to be capable of intellectual gain. But perhaps it is only the younger children whose performance is affected by the special things the teacher says to them, the special ways in which she says them, the way she looks, postures, and touches the children from whom she expects greater intellectual growth.

A fifth interpretation suggests that the effects of teachers' expectations were more effective in the lower-grade levels not because of any difference associated with the children's age but rather with some correlated sampling errors. Thus it is possible that the children of the lower grades are the children of families which differ systematically from the families of the children of the higher-grade levels.

A sixth interpretation also suggests that the greater IQ gain in younger children attributable to teacher expectation is a result of sampling error, not in the sampling of children this time but in the sampling of teachers. It may be that in a variety of demographic, intellectual, and personality variables the teachers of the younger children differed from the teachers of the older children such that they may have (1) believed the communications about their "special" children more, or (2) been more effective communicators to their children of their expectations for the children's performance.

Those children from whom greater intellectual gains were expected showed advantages over their classmates other than greater gain in intellectual performance. They were also judged by their teachers to be more likely to succeed, to be more intellectually alive and to be more superior in their socioemotional functioning and mental health. These effects on teachers' perceptions of the children might have been reflective of either actual behavior differences in the children or of the operation of a halo effect. Even if these ratings reflected only halo effects, however, they may not be trivial in implications. Halo effects may determine not only teachers' perceptions of children but, as the results of this experiment suggest, the subsequent behavior of children as well.

The more the children who were expected to gain intellectually did so, the more favorably they were evaluated by their teachers. Not so, however, for the children who were not expected to show any particular growth in intellectual functioning. The trend, in fact, was for these children to be regarded less favorably the more they gained intellectually. That finding suggests the hypothesis that there may be hazards to unexpected intellectual growth. Classroom teachers may not be prepared to assimilate the unexpected classroom behavior of the intellectually upwardly mobile child.

If the hypothesis were tenable that there are hazards to unexpected intellectual development, we would expect to find that among the children of the slow track there is the greatest negative relationship between intellectual growth and favorable evaluation by the classroom teacher. It is from the slow-track children, almost by definition, that the least intellectual gain is expected. The results of this experiment support the tenability of the hypothesis. It was among the slow-track children of the control group from whom no particular intellectual growth had been expected by virtue of both their experimental condition and their slow-track status that the effects of intellectual gains were most adverse in terms of teachers' perceptions of their behavior. Even within the experimental group, the children of the slow track did not show the advantages of more favorable perceptions by their teachers which had been shown by those children of the fast and medium track from whom intellectual growth had been expected. This result was obtained despite the fact that the experimental-group children of the slow track showed as great a gain in IQ relative to the control-group children as did the experimental-group children of the fast track.

The substantive implications of the evidence presented in this chapter have been primarily short-range implications. There is also a longer-range implication which suggests that as teacher-training institutions acquaint teachers-to-be with the possibility that their expectations of their pupils' performance may serve as self-fulfilling prophecies, these teacher-trainees may be given a new expectancy—that children can learn more than they had believed possible (as Bruner [1960] has suggested, though for different reasons).

In addition to the substantive implications discussed up to now, there are methodological implications of the evidence presented in this chapter. These are best introduced by citing the results of a "total-push" educational program, which after three years led to a 10-point IQ gain by 38 percent of the children and a 20-point IQ gain by 12 percent of the children (Clark, 1963). Table 5 7 of the present chapter shows that such gains were smaller than the gains found among the first- and second-grade children of our control group and very much smaller than the gains found among the children of our experimental group.

It is not possible to be sure about the matter but it may be that the large gains shown by the children of our control group were attributable to a Hawthorne effect. The fact that university researchers, supported by federal funds, were interested in the school in which the research was conducted may have led to a general improvement of morale and teaching technique on the part of all the teachers. Such improvements may have led to the substantial gains in IQ shown by the children of the control group. (In part, of course, such gains may simply have reflected a practice effect in the taking of the specific IQ test or even a tendency for teachers to "teach the test" though the nature of the test makes that unlikely.) In any case, the possibility of a Hawthorne effect cannot be ruled out either in the present experiment or in other studies of educational practices. Any educational practice which is assessed for effectiveness must be able to show some excess of gain over what Hawthorne effects alone would yield. Some investigators have been well aware of this problem (Bruner, 1965), but others seem not to have been.

When the efficacy of an educational practice is investigated we want to know its efficacy relative to the Hawthorne effect of "something new and important" but the present chapter suggests that another base line must be introduced. We will want to know, too, whether the efficacy of an educational practice is greater than that of the easily and inexpensively manipulable expectation of the teacher. Most educational practices are more expensive in time and money than giving teachers names of children "who will show unusual intellectual development."

When educational innovations are introduced into ongoing educational systems, it seems very likely that the administrators whose permission is required and the teachers whose cooperation is required will expect the innovation to be effective. If they did not, they would be unlikely to give the required permission and cooperation. The experimental innovation, then, will likely be confounded with favorable expectations regarding their efficacy.

When educational innovations are introduced into newly created educational systems with specially selected and specially trained teachers and administrators, the problems are similar. Those teachers and those administrators who elect to go, and are selected to go, into newly created educational systems are likely to have expectations favorable to the efficacy of the new program. In this situation, as in that in which changes are introduced into preexisting systems, teachers' and administrators' expectations are likely to be confounded with the educational innovations. All this argues for the systematic employment of the "Expectancy-Control Group" (Rosenthal, 1966).

In expectancy-control designs applied to a simple experiment in educational innovation in which only an experimental and control group are employed, the experiment is subdivided into a total of four conditions, two of them involving the experimental treatment and two of them involving the control "treatment." In one experimental treatment subcondition, teachers are given reason to believe that the experimental innovation will be successful. In the other experimental subcondition teachers are led to believe that the treatment is "only a control condition." In one of the control group subconditions, teachers are led to believe that their condition is "only a control condition" which, in fact, it is. In the other control-group subcondition, teachers are given reason to believe that the "treatment" is actually an experimental innovation which should give good results.

The data from such an expectancy-controlled experiment can be analyzed by a simple two-way analysis of variance. Such an analysis permits us to make inferences about the magnitudes of the effects of the educational innovation, the teachers' expectations, and the interaction between these two sources of variance. There may be experiments in which the magnitude of the effects of the innovation will be large relative to the effects of the teachers' expectations. But there may also be experiments in which the effects of teachers' expectations turn out to be more important sources of variation than the educational innovation under investigation. Without the use of expectancy-control groups, however, it is impossible to tell whether the results of experiments in educational practices are due to the practices themselves or to the correlated expectations of the teachers who are to try out the educational reforms.

Perhaps the most suitable summary of the hypothesis discussed in this chapter and tested by the described experiment has already been written. The writer is G. B. Shaw, the play is *Pygmalion*, and the speaker is Eliza Doolittle:

> You see, really and truly, apart from the things anyone can pick up (the dressing and the proper way of speaking, and so on), the difference between a lady and a flower girl is not how she behaves, but how she's treated. I shall always be a flower girl to Professor Higgins, because he always treats me as a flower girl, and always will; but I know I can be a lady to you, because you always treat me as a lady, and always will.

ADDENDUM

Some time after the preparation of this chapter a number of questions about our school experiment were raised by a helpful reader. These questions seem to be of sufficient general interest that they may be usefully discussed here, though it will be necessary to be brief. One question deals with the small number of first- and second-grade children (nineteen) of the experimental group for whom the gains in total IQ as a function of teacher expectation were large. That is not a serious statistical problem since a wise statistic always knows its own N. More importantly, this question should remind us that for the school as a whole, and not only for the lower grades, experimental-group children gained more than control-group children in both total IQ and in reasoning IQ. In verbal IQ, we recall, the "special" children were benefited more than "ordinary children" in only 67 percent of the classrooms ($p = 0.12$), while in reasoning IQ the "special" children benefited more in 88 percent of the classrooms ($p < 0.001$). Just exactly why expectancy advantages occurred for reasoning IQ, but not verbal IQ, is a question for which we have no answer.

Another question deals with the relative statistical unreliability of the intelligence test employed. The reasoning subtest is less reliable than the verbal subtest, which itself is less reliable than an individually administered test of intelligence. In point of statistical fact, however, the unreliability of the instrument makes the results the more dramatic. The reason is that as test reliability decreases a more robust relationship must exist between the instrument and other variables for these relationships to become significant statistically.

Another question deals with the fact that in several places we report several correlation coefficients that have been chosen for mention because they were "significant" statistically. Such a procedure, though a great space-saver, can lead to difficulties. In an array of correlation coefficients made up of variables that are in fact unrelated to one another, one will by chance find a few significant correlations. In such an array of correlation coefficients, however, the laws of probability lead us to expect half these significant correlations to speak for any given interpretation and half to speak against that interpretation. Whether a given pattern of correlations fits a given interpretation is a matter to be judged first by the investigator, then by the reader. What should be pointed out most explicitly is the fact that *all* rs reaching a $p < 0.10$ were reported, not simply those favoring any given position or interpretation.

The final question deals with the generality and persistence of the expectancy advantages reported. No information was available on these questions at the time the chapter was prepared. Additional data, now being analyzed, will become available and will be reported in due course. A preliminary analysis suggests that gains in reading achievement were significantly greater among children from whom greater intellectual gains were expected. Preliminary data from a one-year follow-up shows very little overall loss in the IQ advantage of children who had been expected to "bloom" by different teachers the year before.

Since preparing this chapter and its addendum, the authors have had a much fuller report of their research published in *Pygmalion in the classroom: Teacher expectation and pupils' intellectual development,* New York: Holt, Rinehart and Winston, 1968.

NOTE

1. The research to be described was supported by the Division of Social Sciences of the National Science Foundation (GS-177 and GS-714). We are grateful to Dr. Paul Nielsen, Superintendent, South San Francisco Unified School District, for making this study possible. We also thank Dr. Jerome Kagan and Dr. David Marlowe for their valuable advice, and Mae Evans, Nancy Johnson, John Laszlo, Susan Novick, and especially George Smiltens for their assistance.

REFERENCES

ALLPORT, G. W. The role of expectancy. In H. Cantril (ed.), *Tensions that cause wars.* Urbana, Ill.: University of Illinois, 1950, Pp. 43–78.

ASBELL, B. Not like other children. *Redbook,* October, 1963.

BECKER, H. S. Social class variations in the teacher-pupil relationship. *Journal of Educational Sociology,* 1952, **25:** 451–465.

BRUNER, J. S. *The process of education.* Cambridge, Mass.: Harvard University Press, 1960.

BRUNER, J. S. The growth of mind. *American Psychologist,* 1965, **20:** 1007–1017.

CLARK, K. B. Educational stimulation of racially disadvantaged children. In A. H. Passow (Ed.), *Education in depressed areas.* New York: Teachers College, Columbia University, 1963. Pp. 142–162.

FLANAGAN, J. C. *Tests of general ability: Technical report.* Chicago: Science Research Associates, 1960.

FLOWERS, C. E. Effects of an arbitrary accelerated group placement on the tested academic achievement of educationally disadvantaged students. Unpublished doctoral dissertation, Teachers College, Columbia University, 1966.

GIBSON, G. Aptitude tests. *Science,* 1965, **149:** 583.

GRUENBERG, B. C. *The story of evolution.* Princeton, N.J.: Van Nostrand, 1929.

HARLEM YOUTH OPPORTUNITIES UNLIMITED, INC. *Youth in the ghetto.* New York: HARYOU, 1964.

HURWITZ, S., & Jenkins, V. Effects of experimenter expectancy on performance of simple learning tasks. Unpublished paper, Harvard University, 1966.

JASTROW, J. *Fact and fable in psychology.* Boston: Houghton Mifflin, 1900.

KATZ, I. Review of evidence relating to effects of desegregation on the intellectual performance of Negroes. *American Psychologist,* 1964, **19:** 381–399.

KVARACEUS, W. C. Disadvantaged children and youth: Programs of promise or pretense? *Proceedings of the 17th annual state conference on educational research.* California Advisory Council on Educational Research, Burlingame: California Teachers' Association, 1965.

MacKinnon, D. W. The nature and nurture of creative talent. *American Psychologist,* 1962, **17**: 484-495.

Marwit, S., & Marcia, J. Tester-bias and response to projective instruments. Unpublished paper, State University of New York at Buffalo, 1966.

Masling, J. Differential indoctrination of examiners and Rorschach responses. *Journal of Consulting Psychology,* 1965, **29**: 198-201.

Merton, R. K. The self-fulfilling prophecy. *Antioch Review,* 1948, **8**: 193-210.

Moll, A. *Hypnotism.* (4th ed.) New York: Scribner's, 1898.

Orne, M. T. The nature of hypnosis: Artifact and essence. *Journal of Abnormal and Social Psychology,* 1959, **58**: 277-299.

Orne, M. T. On the social psychology of the psychological experiment: With particular reference to demand characteristics and their implications. *American Psychologist,* 1962, **17**: 776-783.

Pfungst, O. *Clever Hans (the horse of Mr. von Osten): A contribution to experimental, animal, and human psychology.* (Translated by C. L. Rahn.) New York: Holt, Rinehart and Winston, 1911.

Rice, S. A. Contagious bias in the interview: A methodological note. *American Journal of Sociology,* 1929, **35**: 420-423.

Riessman, F. *The culturally deprived child.* New York: Harper & Row, 1962.

Riessman, F. Teachers of the poor: a five point plan. *Proceedings of the 17th annual state conference on educational research.* California Advisory Council on Educational Research. Burlingame: California Teachers' Association, 1965.

Rose, A. *The Negro in America.* Boston: Beacon Press, 1956.

Rosenthal, R. The effect of the experimenter on the results of psychological research. In B. A. Maher (Ed.), *Progress in experimental personality research.* (Vol. I.) New York: Academic Press, 1964. Pp. 79-114.

Rosenthal, R. Clever Hans: A case study of scientific method. Introduction to O. Pfungst, *Clever Hans.* New York: Holt, Rinehart and Winston, 1965. Pp. ix-xlii.

Rosenthal, R. *Experimenter effects in behavioral research.* New York: Appleton-Century-Crofts, 1966.

Rosenthal, R. & Fode, K. L. The effect of experimenter bias on the performance of the albino rat. *Behavioral Science,* 1963, **8**: 183-189.

Rosenthal, R. & Jacobson, L. Teachers' expectancies: Determinants of pupils' IQ gains. *Psychological Reports,* 1966, **19**: 115-118.

Rosenthal, R. & Lawson, R. A longitudinal study of the effects of experimenter bias on the operant learning of laboratory rats. *Journal of Psychiatric Research,* 1964, **2**: 61-72.

Sommer, R. Rorschach M responses and intelligence. *Journal of Clinical Psychology,* 1958, **14**: 58-61.

Wartenberg-Ekren, U. The effect of experimenter knowledge of a subject's scholastic standing on the performance of a reasoning task. Unpublished master's thesis, Marquette University, 1962.

Whyte, W. F. *Street corner society.* Chicago: University of Chicago Press, 1943.

Wilson, A. B. Social stratification and academic achievement. In A. H. Passow (Ed.), *Education in depressed areas.* New York: Teachers College, Columbia University, 1963. Pp. 217-235.

Wysocki, B. A. Assessment of intelligence level by the Rorschach Test as compared with objective tests. *Journal of Educational Psychology,* 1957, **48**: 113-117.

Index

Index